Real World Research

B

Real World Research

*A Resource for Social Scientists
and Practitioner–Researchers*

COLIN ROBSON

BLACKWELL
Oxford UK & Cambridge USA

First published 1993
Reprinted 1994 (twice), 1995 (twice)

Blackwell Publishers Ltd
108 Cowley Road
Oxford OX4 1JF, UK

Blackwell Publishers Inc.
238 Main Street
Cambridge, Massachusetts 02142
USA

British Library Cataloguing in Publication Data

A CIP catalogue record for this book is available from the British Library.

Library of Congress Cataloging in Publication Data

Robson, Colin.
    Real world research : a resource for social scientists and
practitioner-researchers / Colin Robson.
        p.   cm.
    Includes bibliographical references and indexes.
    ISBN 0–631–17689–6 (pbk)
        1. Social sciences—Research—Methodology.   2. Psychology—
Research—Methodology.   I. Title.
    H62.R627   1993
    300'.72—dc20   91–21782
                                                        CIP

Typeset in 10½ on 12 pt Sabon
by Graphicraft Typesetters Ltd, Hong Kong
Printed in Great Britain by T.J. Press Ltd, Padstow

This book is printed on acid-free paper

Contents

Preface

This book is about doing your own research, and about assisting others to do research. (I have found that 'research' tends to put some people off. They see it as some esoteric enterprise necessarily done by outside experts. In fact it is simply another word for 'enquiry', and the two terms are used interchangeably here.) It is for those who want to carry out 'real world enquiry': research on and with people, outside the safe confines of the laboratory. The focus is on the relatively small-scale study carried out by an individual or by a group of colleagues, rather than on the big project. It is about 'human' research not only in the sense of covering studies about people, but also in trying to take account of the advantages accruing from the enquirers themselves being people. The experience and understanding that we bring to the research, and which we develop during it, are an important ingredient of the research.

I have tried to walk the tightrope between stressing how easy the enquiry task is – because much of what you have to do is common sense – and how difficult it is for exactly the same reason. The core skills are watching people and talking to them. These are based on very common human activities and any reader will have had extensive experience of them. The trick is to avoid 'de-skilling' yourself by devaluing this experience, while appreciating the need to do these things with an uncommon degree of both system and sensitivity.

As an experimental psychologist I started with a virtually unquestioned assumption that rigorous and worthwhile enquiry entailed a laboratory, and the statistical analysis of quantitative data obtained from carefully controlled experiments. More recently I have developed doubts – in part planted by working in a department alongside social psychologists and sociologists who seemed to go about things in very different ways; and not without their own very different dogmatisms. Also, my developing interests in more 'applied' fields, in particular working with practitioners in schools and hospitals, precipitated a fundamental reconsideration of the style and approach to enquiry which are appropriate if one wants to say something sensible about such complex, messy, poorly controlled 'field' settings.

The book is for the person wanting to say something sensible and helpful about such settings. There are many methods of enquiry which can be used in this task, and I have attempted to give a fair run to several of them, with a nod in the direction of others that might be considered. All methods have their strengths and weaknesses. Recognizing this leads to a preference for multi-method approaches. A theme of the book is that several methods of enquiry are likely to be better than any single one in shedding light on an issue. Another theme is that very often the real-world enquirer has a direct research interest in and concern for the particular setting or situation under investigation (rather than seeing it simply as a sample from which generalizations about a wider population are made). These two themes are brought together in an advocacy of multi-method case studies as a serious and respectable research strategy for real world investigations.

'Wanting to say something helpful' raises the issue that we are often seeking not simply to understand something, but also to try to change it. Effectively, many real world studies are evaluations. They try to provide information about how some intervention, procedure, system, or whatever, is functioning; and how it might be improved. This kind of involved, 'action', agenda brings to the fore many difficult practical and ethical issues, which form a third theme.

The book tries to meet the needs of that large proportion of those trained in psychology and the social sciences who do not go on to profess their discipline directly, but who are called upon to carry out some empirical enquiries as part of their job. It is highly unlikely that this will involve laboratory experimentation. The book also addresses the needs of the specialist acting in a consultancy role for 'real world' studies. Practitioners and professionals in 'people' jobs in industry and commerce as well as education and the helping and caring professions, are increasingly being called upon to carry out evaluative and other enquiry projects. My experience has been that with advice and support, which can at least in part be provided by the type of material here, they are often in a position to do very effective studies.

As a course text it is targetted at those higher education courses which seek to prepare students to carry out empirical investigations. While initially developed for undergraduate use, I have found that it provides a useful framework for the formal research training increasingly called for in preparation for research degrees and postgraduate courses. It links with the growing number of more 'applied' courses in psychology and the social sciences, and at professional courses for teachers, health and social services related fields, and in business and management. Although it is written from the perspective of a psychologist, I have made particular efforts to incorporate approaches and methods traditionally seen as falling within other disciplines (e.g. in the coverage of participant observation and other approaches which generate qualitative data). This is a deliberate attempt to break down a form of apartheid which in my view serves little useful purpose.

Other features include an attempt to come to terms with the micro-computer revolution as far as the analysis of data (both qualitative and quantitative) is concerned. The treatment of quantitative analysis is influenced by 'exploratory data analysis' approaches, which appear to be particularly apposite for 'real world' studies; that of qualitative analysis by a wish to see it achieve a corresponding degree of rigour to that conventionally expected of quantitative analysis. The hegemony of the journal article as *the* preferred style of reporting is also put into question by giving serious attention to the notion of 'audience'; i.e. by considering who the report is for, and what one is seeking to achieve by writing it. Both the language of the book, and the general approach to enquiry which is advocated within it, are intended to be non-sexist and take note of recent feminist critiques of social science methodology. Wherever possible, results of research on research (on the presentation of graphical information, the effects of experimenters on experimental results, etc.) have been incorporated and referenced.

Finally, I do appreciate that the 'real world' is something of a questionable concept. Attempts have been made to wean me off it, but it is the best metaphor I can come up with to express my intentions. As the text suggests, it is more of a state of mind than a real 'real world'.

Acknowledgements

I am grateful to many colleagues and students who, over the years, have contributed much to my education. One important influence has undoubtedly been the series of research projects, carried out in collaboration between Huddersfield Polytechnic and the Hester Adrian Research Centre of the University of Manchester, with which I have been involved. The difficult challenges set up in trying to do something both for, and with, practitioners greatly modified my views about research. I would wish, in particular, to acknowledge the help and support of James Hogg, Alan Jones, Chris Kiernan, Peter Mittler, Mike Storey, Sue Tatum and, by no means least, Judy Sebba.

I have been fortunate in working at Huddersfield with a group of extraordinarily committed psychologists and sociologists. The latter in particular have encouraged me to look beyond the traditional confines of psychological experimentation constituting another clear influence. It would, in that connection, be invidious to name names – as it would in the case of the group of enriching and invigorating research students which it has been my privilege to supervise.

I am very grateful for the stylistic advice generously provided by my wife, Pat. I am sure that readers will be too. I would also like to thank Bob Burgess, Tony Gale, Jim Hartley and Steve Newstead for their perceptive, constructive and complementary comments on an earlier draft. I would also like to thank Caroline Callaghan for her helpful comments on chapter 8, and Dallas Cliff for his very generous loan of a substitute computer system at a crucial late stage when an intermittent fault in my own system was wreaking havoc.

I would also wish to give formal acknowledgement of permissions given to reprint the following material. To the British Psychological Society (Appendix B: 'Ethical Principles for Conducting Research with Human Participants'). To the British Sociological Association (Appendix C: 'BSA Guidelines on Anti-sexist Language'). To Deakin University Press (box 2.4, from Kemmis and McTaggart, 1981, pp. 43–4, © Deakin University). To Sage Publications Inc. (figure 4.5, from Thyer and Geller, 1987, *Environment and Behavior*, 19, figure 2, p. 490, © Sage Publications Inc., and figure 12.1, from Miles and Huberman, 1984, *Oualitative Data Analysis*, p. 84, © Sage Publications Inc.). To Professor Ned Flanders (box 8.6, from Flanders, 1970, *Analyzing Teaching Behavior*, p. 34. To the *Journal of Applied Behavior Analysis* (figure 4.7, from Lancioni, 1982, *Journal of Applied Behavior Analysis*, 15, figure 1, p. 23, © *Journal of Applied Behavior Analysis*). To the Open University Press (box 13.3, from Hartley 1989, *The Applied Psychologist*, figure 7.2, p. 90). To the Controller of Her Majesty's Stationery Office (figure 12.3, from Evans et al., 1989, *Developing Services for Children with Special Educational Needs*, pp. 131–2). To the American Psychological Association (box 9.8, from Fibel and Hale, 1978, *Journal of Consulting and Clinical Psychology*, 46, p. 931, © 1978 American Psychological Association). To University Associates, Inc. (box 15.3, from Lippitt and Lippitt, 1978, *The Consulting Process in Action*, p. 31, © University Associates, Inc.). To Dallas Cliff (box 9.3, interview schedule, *Looking for Work in Kirklees*). To Graham Gibbs (figure 9.1, questionnaire on 'Consumer behaviour and green attitudes').

Ways of Using the Book

Recommendations

• If you are following a course of some kind, then the needs of the course will shape your use. Broadly speaking, however, it is likely that the course will be about methods and methodology of investigation. To get an appreciation of the issues involved, my view is that it is best to start at the beginning and work through to the end. My own preference is to go through initially at some speed so that your momentum keeps you going through any bits that you don't take in fully. From this you get a feeling for the general lie of the land, and can then return at more leisure to sections which are important for your needs or which you found difficult.

• If you want to use the book to help carry out an enquiry, then I think you have two main choices. You could do the same as suggested above and effectively use the book as a self-study course guide – then home into the bits you need . . .

• . . . alternatively, you could jump straight in and use it more as a 'how to' cook book. (As an enthusiastic cook, I have never understood the denigration of 'methods' cook books by some psychologists. Obviously some are mere recipe books but I would be proud to have produced the equivalent of a Jane Grigson or Elizabeth David cookery book!) To do this, use the marked pages, which are intended to provide an overview of the main stages of the enquiry process and appear at intervals throughout the book. They can be picked out from the contents list where their headings are given in italic type.

• If you want to use this book to help others to carry out enquiries, then the main explicit material for you is in the final chapter. You are likely to be familiar with much of the material in the preceding chapters and a quick glance should locate aspects to recommend to those working with you. Some of the material differs from the traditional, however (e.g. in the treatment of case studies – see chapter 6 and parts of chapter 3) and you are recommended to review this to key you in to the line taken.

Disclaimers

•   No single text could hope to cover all you need to carry out 'real world enquiry'. Each chapter contains annotated suggestions for further reading. This is particularly important in the case of specific methods and techniques of investigation and analysis, where it is highly likely you will have to go beyond what is provided here.

•   All the reading in the world won't make you into a skilled enquirer. There is the danger of the centipede problem (it never moved again after trying to work out which leg it moved first) and much to be said for jumping in, carrying out enquiries and developing skills through experience – using this text as a reference along the way. The book will make more sense when you have faced up to practicalities than it will if you regard carrying out an enquiry as a complex intellectual exercise where everything has to be thought through in advance before you make a move.

Carrying Out an Enquiry

To carry out an enquiry you need to give attention to a wide range of things. These are some of the main ones:

- deciding on the focus;
- developing the research question(s);
- choosing a research strategy;
- selecting the method(s);
- arranging the practicalities;
- collecting the data;
- preparing for, and carrying out, analysis;
- reporting what you have found; and, possibly;
- acting on the findings.

The book is concerned with giving advice and suggestions on these activities. Some of them are relatively straightforward and can be dealt with in a page or so. Others need more detailed consideration. For example, before deciding on a research strategy, you need to know something about the possibilities open to you; the reasons why you might go for, say, a case study rather than an experiment; and the implications of this choice. A full chapter is devoted to each of the strategies. Similarly, there is a wide variety of different methods or techniques (interviews of various types; structured or participant observation; documentary analysis, etc.) for collecting and analysing data, which take up further chapters.

You will find *general* discussion on these issues at various points in the book, as indicated below. These general discussion pages are marked in the same way that this section is.

- deciding on the focus   page 20
- developing the research question(s)   page 27
- choosing a research strategy   pages 39 & 167
- selecting the methods   page 188
- arranging the practicalities   page 294
- collecting the data   page 304
- preparing for, and carrying out,
  analysis   page 306
- reporting what you have found   page 411
- acting on the findings   page 429

Where two page numbers are given, the first provides an *overview* and the second a *summary*.

Part I

Before You Start

Before leaping into an enquiry, you need to have an idea about what you are letting yourself in for. Real world studies tend to be 'away fixtures' and hence more visible to others than those on the home territory of the laboratory. False moves can inoculate a firm, school or whatever against future involvements, not only with you, but with other potential researchers – and, possibly, against the whole idea of systematic enquiry as a possible approach to dealing with problems or understanding situations.

This is not to argue for everything being cut and dried before starting. Any proposals you make for carrying out the enquiry will benefit from some real world exposure, and there is much to be said in favour of collaborative ventures, with the 'client' or whoever you are dealing with having a substantial say in the enterprise.

1

Real World Enquiry

This chapter discusses some of the implications of venturing outside the laboratory to carry out the enquiry.

It introduces possible approaches to enquiry and makes the case for your knowing something about methodology (the 'science of finding out').

Finally, it reveals the author's assumptions about what you are after, and attempts to give the flavour of real world enquiry.

Focusing on the Real World

The purpose of this book is to give assistance, ideas and confidence to those who, for good and honourable reasons, wish to carry out some kind of investigation involving people in 'real life' situations; to draw attention to some of the issues and complexities involved; and to generate a degree of informed enthusiasm for a particularly challenging and important area of work.

The 'real life' situation refers in part to the actual context where whatever we are interested in occurs, whether it be an office, school, hospital, home, street or football ground. This book is not primarily about studies carried out in purpose-built laboratories. Not that there is anything particularly unreal about a laboratory. Indeed, a study of the 'real life' in a laboratory could make a fascinating topic almost worthy of a soap opera – see for example Lynch (1985), a study of '... shop work and shop talk in a research laboratory'. The point about the laboratory is that it permits a large degree of control over conditions; what is done to people can be very carefully determined and standardized. The slightly sinister undertone which 'experiment' tends to have, particularly when one hears about 'experiments with human beings', is a reflection of the fact that deliberate and active control over what is done to people is central to the psychological experiment.

In the 'real world' – or 'the field', as the world outside the laboratory is often referred to by psychologists and other behavioural or social scientists (conjuring up visions of intrepid investigators in pith helmets) – that kind of control is often not feasible, even if it were ethically justifiable. Hence, one of the challenges about carrying out investigations in the 'real world' is in seeking to say something sensible about a complex, relatively poorly controlled and generally 'messy' situation.

There is a more specific difference between what is usually possible in laboratory and 'real life' situations. Whereas in general usage, the term 'experiment' is virtually synonymous with investigation or enquiry, it has tended in psychology to have a more restricted technical usage. The difference is commonly signalled by referring in the latter context to 'true' experiments. Technically there are two main hallmarks of the true experiment. The first involves choosing the persons who are to take part ('subjects' in experiment-speak) so that they are representative of a known group – say, junior schoolchildren in the United Kingdom, or old age pensioners in Liverpool. This is usually referred to in terms of 'samples' and 'populations'. The theory is that a random sample of subjects is chosen from a known population. It then becomes possible, by using well established statistical principles, to make generalizations from what is found out about the sample to the state of affairs in the whole population.

The second requirement is for the random allocation of the subjects to different experimental conditions. Thus a study of some aspect of memory in old age pensioners might involve selecting a given number of them from an existing pool of volunteers in such a way that all members of the pool had equal chances of being selected. (Whether this pool is representative of pensioners in general is another matter – volunteers are to some extent self-selected and may well be more physically active and mentally alert than the pensioner population as a whole.) Then, perhaps, half would be allocated to one experimental condition where material is presented in a particular way; the other half to a second condition where material is presented in a different way. The principle of selection for the two conditions should be such that there is an equal chance of an individual appearing in either – most simply by tossing a coin to decide this.

Random allocation to the different experimental conditions enables one to capitalize on what is seen by many as the main advantage of the experimental approach – its ability to provide clear evidence about causal relationships. However, unfortunately, it is very difficult to achieve either representative sampling from a known population or random allocation to different experimental conditions in real world experiments. There may well be virtually insurmountable practical or ethical problems. Consider, for example, an experiment on the effect of smoking on cancer – can you imagine allocating persons randomly to 'smoking' and 'non-smoking' groups?

Alternative experimental approaches, with less stringent requirements as to allocation and sampling, are, however, possible. These are usually referred to as 'quasi-experiments', deriving from the work of Campbell and Stanley (1963), and are discussed in some detail in chapter 4. An example of this approach would be the use of already existing groups such as school classes for the different conditions of the experimental study, rather than pupils being randomly allocated to new classes from within a year group for the purpose of the study.

There is a tradition of empirical work outside the laboratory which aspires to quantitative rigour comparable to that of experimentation. This is the *survey* strategy, which has been extensively developed by social researchers, particularly certain types of sociologist and social psychologist, and also of course by market researchers and political pollsters. Central to surveys is the putting of carefully standardized questions to a carefully chosen set of people. Interviews or questionnaires are used in most surveys. Except in rare occasions, such as a general census, it is not possible to survey the whole of a population. It is therefore necessary to select a sample. Again, then, there is a concern for representative sampling, so that generalization can be made to a known population.

Sampling for surveys can cause problems, and is a major concern of political pollsters seeking to ensure that they 'get it right'. However, it presents less formidable practical and ethical difficulties than sampling for 'real world' experiments, in part because the 'demand' made on a respondent is typically very small in terms of time and effort, certainly so by comparison with participation in virtually any experiment. Although convenient in this respect, the low demands that surveys make on respondents constitute one of their weaknesses. How much trust can be put on the 'chance encounter' comments made to a stranger, or to a piece of paper?

Surveys differ fundamentally from experiments in that they do not normally involve manipulation or control of variables (although they could do). Hence the logic of causal inference as used in experimentation is not available. There are, however, other approaches to teasing out possible causal relationships which are feasible with survey data, though often the reasoning is less compelling than that derived from experimentation. Enquiry, however, is not solely concerned with establishing causation. Carefully designed and and administered surveys are the method of choice for answering certain types of descriptive research questions – particularly of the 'how many' and 'how much' variety. Kinsey's study of the sexual behaviour and attitudes of American females (Kinsey et al., 1953) is a classic example of the value of the survey in obtaining this kind of information.

For most purposes, a good survey is a large-scale survey involving a substantial band of trained interviewers, or the resources to command a high response rate on a postal questionnaire. There is, however, an important place for surveys in the type of small-scale study covered in this book; not least because this type of approach is readily understood by the 'consumer' – the person who has asked you to carry out the work, or whom you hope to influence. See, for example, Lindblom and Cohen (1979), who argue convincingly that the survey is probably the best tool that social scientists possess for generating usable knowledge.

Studying Cases

For many of the purposes and situations in which enquiry in the real world takes place, a different strategy which concentrates on studying 'cases' is worth serious consideration. Rather than seeking to carry out weak versions of laboratory experiments, paying lip-service to canons of procedure which it is virtually impossible to replicate, or assuming that the alternative is necessarily a survey, it may be preferable to follow this different approach.

I will explain later in some detail what the term case study means; or rather, what I am going to take it to mean, as the term has been used very variously. For the moment the following, I hope, gives the flavour:

> *Case study is a strategy for doing research which involves an empirical investigation of a particular contemporary phenomenon within its real life context using multiple sources of evidence.*

This is a view of case study as a quite eclectic approach similar to that developed by Robert Yin (1981, 1989) who has done much to resuscitate case study as a serious research strategy. At the heart of it is the idea that *the case is studied in its own right, not as a sample from a population.* The 'multiple sources of evidence' commonly produce not only quantitative data, as is usual in experiments and surveys, but copious amounts of qualitative data as well. These very different features call for a fundamental review of what one is doing when carrying out an enquiry. Essentially it requires discussion and analysis of what we mean by 'science' – a necessary and enjoyable exercise if only because inaccurate stereotypes about the nature of science in general and of the natural sciences in particular, and of the so-called 'scientific method' (or methods?) are rife among those studying and working in psychology and the social sciences.

Can All This Be Safely Skipped?

I sense that those approaching this text in an instrumental vein – perhaps attracted by the notion that they are in fact going to get the advice, support and assistance in carrying out investigations in the real world which was promised – may be somewhat dismayed to find that they are letting themselves in for even a brief detour into methodology and the philosophy of science. Obviously, one of the beauties and enduring strengths of books is that they are 'random access devices'. It is up to readers what they select or skip. The marked pages, chapter headings and index are all ways of giving rapid and direct access to the more 'nuts and bolts' aspects, such as the choice and use of different methods of gathering evidence, of analysing different kinds of data, of writing a report appropriate to a particular audience, and so on.

Far be it from me to seek to constrain your freedom of access. However, entering into any kind of investigation involving other people is necessarily a complex and sensitive undertaking and to do this effectively you need to know what you are doing. It is not possible to pre-specify with any confidence exactly what you will need to do to capture what is important in these complex real life situations. For example, while there are things that you should know about the design of case studies which are covered in later chapters, case study research design is necessarily flexible and interactive, enabling the sensitive enquirer to capitalize on unexpected eventualities. My faith is that this process is facilitated by your acquiring some knowledge and understanding of these more general matters covered in the early chapters.

There is a secondary reason for their inclusion which I should make explicit. Advocating case study as a serious strategy for enquiry in the real world is likely to be viewed as a radical departure by many psychologists, especially those steeped in the statistical sampling paradigm dominant in experimental psychology. Justification is called for.

Taking a multi-method stance involving the collection of both qualitative and quantitative data, and claiming that the whole is, or should be, regarded as a scientific enterprise is also likely to antagonize those of both scientistic and humanistic persuasion. There are strongly held views that the divide between qualitative and quantitative represents an ideological divide and that that particular twain should never meet. Following Bryman (1988a), my view is that many of these differences are more apparent than real and that there is in practice a considerable underlying unity of purpose.

Evaluation and Change

Much enquiry in the real world is essentially some form of evaluation. Is the organization of educational provision for children with special needs such as learning difficulties, or problems with sight or hearing, working effectively in a particular local authority area? Does a child abuse service actually serve the interests of the children concerned? Can a business improve its interviewing procedures for new sales staff? Evaluation brings to the fore a very different agenda of issues from those usually associated with 'pure' research. For example, the need to understand the phenomenon may still be there, but issues to do with change (How can it be implemented? What are the barriers to implementation and how might they be overcome?) often loom large.

There is the fundamental issue as to whether or not the researcher should get involved in these aspects at all. A possible stance is to say that their responsibility stops with understanding what is going on and getting that information over to those directly concerned. An alternative is to say that it is part of the researcher's job to use this understanding to suggest ways in which desirable change might take place; and perhaps to monitor the effectiveness of these attempts. There are no general solutions to these issues. The answers in each case depend to a considerable extent on the situation in which you find yourself. Certainly someone attempting to carry out a form of enquiry into the situation in which they themselves are working or living will find that the change aspects become virtually impossible to separate out from the enquiry itself.

This mention of what amounts to 'self-evaluation' opens up a further Pandora's Box. At one extreme, some would doubt the feasibility of the insider carrying out any worthwhile, credible or objective enquiry into a situation in which she or he is centrally involved. At the other extreme, those associated with movements such as the 'professional-as-scientist' (e.g. Barlow et al., 1984) or the 'teacher-as-researcher' (e.g. Carr and Kemmis, 1986) maintain essentially that outsider research is ineffective research, at least as far as change and development is concerned. My sympathies tend to lie in the latter camp, while recognizing both the problems and stresses of doing 'insider' research, and the need for specialists in research and methodology. The role that such specialists should take on then becomes an important issue. One thing they need to be able to do is to 'give away' skills, an important skill in its own right, which is covered in the final chapter.

All of this carries with it the implication that the 'real world enquirer' needs to have knowledge, skills and expertise in areas outside the likely competence of most laboratory – oriented researchers. How change comes about in individuals and groups is itself an immense research area about which many real world enquirers need to have a working knowledge if they are going to do the job properly. At a more down-to-earth level, a very strong sense of audience is needed to guide the style, content and length of any report or other communication arising from the enquiry. If an important objective is concerned with change, then a report which does not communicate to the decision-makers in that situation is a waste of time.

The Audience for this Book

Having just stressed the need for a sense of audience when writing, I need to make clear for whom this book is written. In one sense it is written for myself. I have carried out various kinds of 'enquiry in the real world' for the past two decades with various colleagues, often under severe pressure of time and resources so that there wasn't much opportunity to reflect on what was going on. It has been very instructive to stand back and try to work out what, in fact, we were doing, and what skills and knowledge were needed to do it properly.

I have been increasingly involved in recent years in teaching courses at both undergraduate and postgraduate level which try to deliver real world enquiry skills; also in assisting, through supervision and consultancy, individuals or small groups wishing to carry out some study, often one directly relevant to the setting in which they work. These have included both professional psychologists and other social scientists responsible for providing advice and support to others in both private and public sectors, as well as teachers, social workers, health service professionals and others working directly with particular client groups. In carrying out these studies, they are usually seeking to meet some perceived, often pressing, need.

Such groups form the main target audience. That is, *the main focus is on those wanting to carry out, or advise on the carrying out of, small-scale projects about individuals and groups and their problems and concerns; and about the services, systems and organizations in which they find themselves.*

In part, this is an attempt to arm the overwhelmingly large proportion of psychologists who do not go on to be laboratory-based experimentalists with tools and expertise that they can both use for themselves and 'give away' to others to use. I also have the hope, based on experience, that *practitioners* in the helping and caring professions, and others working with people, can usefully enquire into their own practice, with a view to developing and changing it.

A Word to Psychologists – Aspiring and Actual

In the United Kingdom, approximately three-quarters of those graduating in psychology go on to jobs not directly related to psychology. This large and growing pool of people need tools with which they can carry over their psychological, particularly methodological, expertise into their work. The minority going into jobs directly related to psychology are increasingly being asked to take on a consultancy role *vis-à-vis* their professional setting – whether in industry, commerce, education, health or another government agency – where they are expected to assist in answering other people's questions. This is not to argue for a supine acceptance of the terms in which their questions are posed, or the time-scale set for getting answers. Confidence and experience are needed so that you can negotiate on such matters. It is more an acknowledgement of the realities of the 'real world'; unless psychologists are seen to be useful, they won't be used.

There are also reservations about the applicability and relevance of much that has come out of the laboratory. Bronfenbrenner's criticism of much of contemporary developmental psychology as the 'science of the strange behaviour of children in strange situations with strange adults for the briefest possible period of time' (Bronfenbrenner, 1977) is paralleled by Tajfel's view of the typical laboratory experiment as 'a temporary collection of late adolescent strangers given a puzzle to solve under bizarre conditions in a limited time during their first meeting while being peered at from behind a mirror' (Tajfel, 1984, p. 474). A corpus and tradition of field research, of a rigour equivalent to that obtained in laboratory experimentation, gives at least a prima facie case for being the avenue to the development of a more applicable psychology.

A Word to Others with a Social Science Background

It is my strong impression that, for carrying out real world enquiry, the exact social science discipline background of the potential researcher is not all that important. A psychology graduate is likely to have been well steeped in experimental design and to know little about qualitative approaches, whereas a sociology graduate will be likely to have had the reverse experience.

The approach taken in this book is deliberately promiscuous. Strategies and techniques which have tended to be linked to different disciplines have been brought together in the attempt to give enquirers a range of options appropriate to the research questions they are asking. Hence it is hoped that those from other social science disciplines will find material which is both useful and accessible.

A Word to Those without a Social Science Background

My experience is that the approaches advocated here, particularly the eclectic case study approach, can be accessible to those without a background or training in psychology or the social sciences. It remains a matter of controversy how far psychology is 'common sense' (see, for example, the debate between Lamal, 1991, and Locke and Latham, 1991). A problem is that you 'know not what it is that you know not' and may rush in blindly or blithely without realizing the complexity of the situation. My advice is that you seek to appreciate the implications of carrying out a *scientific* study. If you are not from a scientific background, or are 'anti-science', please try to keep your prejudices in check. The next chapter aims, among other things, to clear away some common misconceptions about the scientific approach. You won't be expected to wear a white coat, nor, necessarily, to wear out a calculator or computer by crunching numbers.

Associated with the scientific approach is the need for rigour and for principles – both in the sense of following agreed practices and in that of having sensitivity to ethical implications. However, many real world studies both permit and require a flexibility in design and prosecution which may well appeal to those with a background in the arts or humanities. Well written up, they can provide a compelling account. A major theme of this book is how to introduce rigour into all aspects of enquiry so that we achieve a justified believability and trustworthiness in what we find and write up.

You will be at a disadvantage compared to those with a psychology or social science background in two main ways. First, the carrying out of a systematic enquiry calls for a set of skills – for example, in observing and interviewing, designing, analysing, interpreting and reporting. The development of these skills requires practice, which takes time. This can and should have taken place during a training in psychology but in the absence of this, you will have to learn 'on the job'. Second, and more difficult to remedy, psychology and the related social sciences have a substantive content of theories, models and findings which in general you will wot not of. I am genuinely unsure as to how much of a disadvantage this puts you under. One obvious solution is to work in partnership, or on some kind of consultancy basis, with a professional, chartered psychologist. However, when, as will often be the case, the intention is to assist individuals, groups or organizations to understand, and possibly develop or change, some aspect of themselves and the situation in which they find themselves, there is virtue in staying close to the concepts and language they themselves use. Certainly, unassimilated jargon often accentuates the commonly acknowledged theory/practice divide.

The basic claim is that principled enquiry can be of help in gaining an understanding of the human situation and its manifestations in office, factory, school, hospital or wherever, and in initiating sensible change and development. It is important not to claim too much, however. Common sense, management fiat, hunches, committee meetings and the like are going to continue to form the main precursors to action. But getting enquiry on the agenda as something likely to be of assistance if there is an important decision to be made or problem to be dealt with, would be a step forward. And if you can consult a sympathetic psychologist for advice and support, you may well find that your efforts are more effective.

Returning to the Real World

The proposal for a real world emphasis is as much about an attitude of mind as an invitation to come out of the laboratory closet. It is reflected in several dichotomies – suggesting applied research rather than pure or basic research; policy research, not theoretical research. These dichotomies are probably not very helpful as they suggest absolute distinctions. Hakim (1987) sees these differences more in terms of emphasis. For her the main features that distinguish policy research from theoretical research are

> an emphasis on the substantive or practical importance of research results rather than on merely 'statistically significant' findings, and second, a multi-disciplinary approach which in turn leads to the eclectic and catholic use of any and all research designs which might prove helpful in answering the questions posed. (p. 172)

As Rossi (1980) has pointed out, well designed policy research can not only be of value to those concerned with determining policy, but may also be of interest to one or more academic disciplines. Trist (1976) goes further and claims that while the natural sciences first generate pure research findings and then apply them, social sciences only make theoretical progress through application. The argument is that it is only feasible to get the proper access needed to study people in real life settings through proving your 'competence in supplying some kind of service' (p. 46). Hence practice helps to improve theory, which in turn helps to improve practice. This is the 'action research' perspective, discussed in chapter 14. It is an overstatement to claim that all real world research must follow this pattern, but an active symbiotic link between researcher and researched is a very common feature.

The emphases flagged by adopting the metaphor of the real world are very different from those of laboratory-based experimentalists. Box 1.1 suggests some of the dimensions involved. Box 1.2 points up the distinction in a more concrete fashion by contrasting examples of relatively 'artificial' and relatively 'real' approaches to investigating a range of issues. In crude terms, while you might, say, be better able to vary anticipatory stress experimentally and control other factors in a laboratory study, there is much to be gained by transferring the enquiry to the dentist's chair (cf. Anderson et al., 1991).

Box 1.1 Characterizing real world enquiry

In real world enquiry the emphasis tends to be on:

solving problems	rather than	*just gaining knowledge*
predicting effects	rather than	*finding causes*
getting large effects (looking for robust results)	rather than	*relationships between variables* (and assessing statistical significance)
and		
concern for actionable factors (where changes are feasible)		
developing and testing programmes, interventions, services, etc.	rather than	*developing and testing theories*

---

field	rather than	*laboratory*
outside organization (industry, business, school, etc.)	rather than	*research institution*
strict time constraints	rather than	*as long as the problem needs*
strict cost constraints	rather than	*as much finance as the problem needs* (or the work isn't attempted)
little consistency of topic from one study to the next	rather than	*high consistency of topic from one study to the next*
topic initiated by sponsor	rather than	*topic initiated by researcher*
often generalist researchers (need for familiarity with range of methods)	rather than	*typically highly specialist researchers* (need to be at forefront of their discipline)
little use of 'true' experiments	rather than	*much use of 'true' experiments*
multiple methods	rather than	*single methods*
oriented to the client (generally, and particularly in reporting)	rather than	*oriented to academic peers*
currently viewed as dubious by many academics	rather than	*high academic prestige*
need for well developed social skills	rather than	*some need of social skills*

Box 1.2   Examples of 'artificial' and 'real world' approaches

	artificial	*real world*
giving bad news	subject has to inform lab partner he is going to receive a shock (Tesser and Rosen, 1972)	coroner announcing death next of kin (Charmaz, 1975)
inter-personal attraction	anticipating interaction with a stranger whose traits are listed as more or less similar to one's own (Byrne, 1961)	'fear and loathing' at a college social function (Schwartz and Lever, 1976)
behaviour on a train	response to an 'implanted' crisis (Piliavin et al., 1969)	defence of common territory (Fried and DeFazio, 1974)
reactions to fear	anticipating electric shock (Folkins, 1970)	learning first hand how to work on high steel in a 21-storey building (Haas, 1977)
superstition	predicting sequence in which bulbs will light up (Wright, 1960)	'poker parlors' in California (Hayano, 1980)
loosening of internal controls in response to anonymity	students delivering shock when clothed in lab gowns and hoods (Zimbardo, 1969)	tenants in high-rise housing exposed to danger (Zito, 1974)
impression formation	students reading lists of adjectives (Anderson, 1965)	folk-singers trying to 'psych out' an audience (Sanders, 1974)
response vs. place learning	infants in lab study (Acredolo, 1978)	waiters and 'switching' diners (Bennett, 1983)

(Several of these examples are adapted from Weick, 1985 who provides further details.)

Bickman (1980) presents an extended analysis of these differing emphases in the context of approaches to social psychology research. Not all of the aspects shown in box 1.1 will occur in any particular enquiry, but together they go some way to capturing the kind of enterprise that this book is seeking to foster. Academic researchers may not feel that the suggestions about open-ended availability of time and money chime in too well with their experience but, to take a strict line, there is little point in their carrying out studies intended to advance their discipline if the resources available are inadequate. In the real world context, the game is different – in its crudest form, you tell the sponsors what they will get for their money, and either they buy it or they don't!

Entering into this kind of real world enquiry could, with some justice, be viewed as capitulation to the values of an enterprise culture. There are obvious dangers in being a 'hired hand', and in being hired to seek sticking-plaster solutions to complex and intractable problems. However, there is the advantage that letting society, in the guise of the client or sponsor, have some role in determining the focus of an enquiry makes it more likely that findings are both usable and likely to be used. Some support for this assertion comes from a study by Weiss and Bucuvalas (1980a). They analysed fifty studies in the field of mental health. Thirteen were commissioned to answer specific questions, the rest were initiated by researchers. At least six decision-makers rated each study. Although differences were small, the commissioned research studies tended to get higher ratings on usefulness than the others. It is important to note, though, that the quality of the research was seen as a more important factor than this. Studies rated higher on methodological quality were judged significantly more useful. The need, then, is for high-quality, methodologically sophisticated, research – both where researchers follow their own noses, and also where they work on others' questions.

Enquiry may be thought of as a way of solving problems – which may range from the purely theoretical to the totally practical. Box 1.3 presents a list of different possible approaches to problem-solving (based on Heller, 1986). It describes a dimension from pure to applied, and of increasing contribution from the client. The main thrust of this book is towards the mid-range of these approaches, say from 3 through to 9. Where a particular study will lie on this continuum depends crucially on your individual circumstances. The more client–dominated approaches (from 10 to 12) do not concern us here, irrespective of any views one might have about them, as they involve little or no empirical data collection. There is no intention to make a value judgment suggesting that any one of the mid-range methods is intrinsically superior or inferior to any other. Heller (1986) claims that, in terms of utilization of research outcomes, there is evidence in favour of the approaches within section B ('Building Bridges between Researcher and User') and section C ('Researcher–Client Equality'). He goes on to point out, however, that the limitation of depending on these approaches is their emphasis on current issues.

Box 1.3 Approaches to problem-solving

A The traditional approach: 'science only'

1 Basic research. Application to problem-solving in the real world not usually seen as an objective.

2 Less basic, but still 'pure' or 'theoretical'. Application not a high priority and usually left to others.

3 Research on practical problems. Application seen as a possible but not a necessary outcome, and is often left to others.

B Building bridges between researcher and user

4 Researcher believes work has practical implications and should be used. Seeks to disseminate results widely and in accessible language.

5 Researcher obtains client collaboration on researcher-designed project. Researcher would like client to be influenced by research outcome.

6 As (5), but in addition researcher takes steps to give client regular feedback on progress, problems and outcomes. During feedback, client has an opportunity to check on interim findings and contribute own analysis and interpretation. Researcher attempts to help in implementation.

C Researcher–client equality

7 Researcher and client together discuss problem area(s) and jointly formulate research design. Research involves active collaboration and some measure of control on part of client. Implementation is part of the collaborative design. May be termed 'research action' as fact-finding takes precedence over implementation.

8 As (7), but initiative taken by client who identifies the problem. This is taken by researcher as the 'presenting problem'. Early stages of the research consider whether there are other issues which should receive primary attention. 'Research action' or 'action research' depending on relative attention to research and implementation.

9 As (8), but the problem identified by the client is not questioned and research proceeds on that basis. Likely to be 'action research' with the researcher paying most attention to implementation.

D Client–professional exploration

10 A client with a problem requests help from a researcher/academic. Collection of new data (if any) is minimal. Advice or recommendation is based on researcher's past experience and knowledge of the field. If this takes place in an organization, then training or organization development is a frequent outcome.

E Client–dominated quest

11 Client requests help from a specialist or colleague with social science background. Specialist examines problem, interprets 'best current knowledge', makes a diagnosis and suggests a line of action.

12 As (11), but help is requested from non-specialist without social science background (may be familiar with more popular literature). 'Best current knowledge' will be interpreted at second or third hand, heavily influenced by personal experience and 'common sense'.

(Adapted and abridged from Heller, 1986, pp. 4–6.)

Research on the effect of the media on imitative behaviour should not wait for an increase in violence or political misgivings. Research on trade-union decision-making practices should not wait until there is a political demand for change: social cost research should precede redundancy crises. (p. 10)

This argues for a broad spread of approaches with researchers choosing the one most suitable to the research questions that interest them. The next chapter starts on this quest.

Further Reading

Burgess, R. G. (1984) *In the Field: an introduction to field research*. London: Allen & Unwin. Covers the main issues and problems involved in the 'field' research approach which originated in anthropology but is now widely used in the social sciences.

Burgess, R. G. (ed.) (1982) *Field Research: a sourcebook and field manual*. London: Allen & Unwin. Companion volume to above text consisting of wide-ranging set of readings which cover all phases of the research activity.

Gale, A. and Chapman, A. J. (eds) (1984) *Psychology and Social Problems: an introduction to applied psychology*. New York: Wiley. An integrated approach covering major 'problems of living' such as unemployment, drug abuse and accidents. Incorporates discussion of research methodology as well as problems of practical implementation.

Gross, R. (1982) *The Independent Scholar's Handbook*. Reading, Mass.: Addison-Wesley. Very useful resource for those working by themselves. A lot of practical advice. Examples of how others have done it.

Hakim, C. (1987) *Research Design: strategies and choices in the design of social research*. London: Allen & Unwin. Valuable not only for its emphasis on design, particularly in multidisciplinary studies, but for its relatively non-technical manner aiming to bridge the gaps between those who do research, those who pay for it, and those who will use the results.

Hartley, J. and Branthwaite, A. (eds) (1989) *The Applied Psychologist*. Milton Keynes: Open University. Argues the case for applied psychologists as professionals who have many skills, deployable in different ways in different circumstances. Organized around fourteen applied roles (tool maker, agent for change, etc.) in very varied content areas including marriage, depression and nuclear warfare.

Kaplan, A. (1964) *The Conduct of Inquiry: methodology for behavioral science*. San Francisco: Chandler. Classic book on methodology by friendly but critical philosopher. Emphasizes the common concerns of the different disciplines and the community of scholarship between the humanities and the social sciences. Wise, readable and challenging.

Kerlinger, F. N. (1986) *Foundations of Behavioural Research*, 3rd edn. New York: Holt, Rinehart and Winston. One of the best standard texts. Not specifically 'real world', but covers wide range with extensive examples.

Oskamp, S. (1984) *Applied Social Psychology*. Englewood Cliffs, NJ: Prentice-Hall. Emphasizes real world problems and social issues including health care, environmental problems, legal issues, educational questions, the mass media and life in organizations. Multidisciplinary; covers work by sociologists, communication researchers and economists as well as social psychologists. Discusses applicability and the applied versus theoretical conflict (chapter 1).

Walker, Robert (ed.) (1985) *Applied Qualitative Research*. Aldershot: Gower. Set of reading limited to qualitative research methods but valuable because of the strong emphasis on the useful and the practical.

Walker, Rob. (1985) *Doing Research: a handbook for teachers*. London: Methuen. Discusses applied research in the context of teachers enquiring into their own, or others', practice. Does not assume a social science background, but neither does it deny its value.

2

Developing a Proposal

This chapter reviews traditional models of research and finds some problems in applying them to real world enquiry.

It seeks to help you decide on the focus of your enquiry.

Then it discusses how this focus can be refined into research questions.

Finally, ethical issues are emphasized.

Models of the Research Process

The task of carrying out an enquiry is complicated by the fact that there is no overall consensus about how to conceptualize the doing of research. This shows in various ways. There are, for example, different views about the place and role of theory; also about the sequence and relationship of the activities involved. One model says that you collect all the data before starting to analyse it. A different one has data collection and analysis intertwined.

These differences fall within two main traditions which continue to engage in sporadic warfare. One is variously labelled as positivistic, natural-science based, hypothetico-deductive, quantitative or even simply 'scientific'; the other as interpretive, ethnographic or qualitative – among several other labels.

The 'scientific' approach is usually regarded as starting with theory. A theory is a general statement that summarizes and organizes knowledge by proposing a general relationship between events – if it is a good one, it will cover a large number of events and predict events that have not yet occurred or been observed. The scare quotes around 'scientific' are there to give warning that this is only one, relatively rigid and narrow, view about science and the scientific method – see p. 57.

The 'scientific' approach is commonly regarded as involving five sequential steps: –

1 Deducing a hypothesis (a testable proposition about the relationship between two or more events or concepts) from the theory.
2 Expressing the hypothesis in operational terms (i.e. ones indicating exactly how the variables are to be measured) which propose a relationship between two specific variables.
3 Testing this operational hypothesis. This will involve an experiment or some other form of empirical enquiry.
4 Examining the specific outcome of the enquiry. It will either tend to confirm the theory or indicate the need for its modification.
5 If necessary, modifying the theory in the light of the findings. An attempt is then made to verify the revised theory by going back to the first step and repeating the whole cycle.

However, this kind of model with its orderliness and separation into a clear linear sequence is more of a reconstruction enshrined in methods textbooks and conventional journal formats than an account of the scientific research process in practice. As the distinguished biologist Sir Peter Medawar put it when urging that what scientists actually *do* should be studied, '. . . It is no use looking to scientific "papers" for they not only merely conceal but actively misrepresent the reasoning that goes into the work they describe' (Medawar, 1969, p. 169). Real life science does not escape the messiness of other aspects of real life.

A major difference in the interpretive approach is that theories and concepts tend to arise from the enquiry. They come after data collection rather than before it. Because of this, it is often referred to as 'hypothesis generating' (as against 'hypothesis testing') research. Also, in the interpretive approach, data collection and analysis are not rigidly separated. An initial bout of data collection is followed by analysis, the results of which are then used to decide what data should next be collected. The cycle is then repeated several times. Initial theory formulation also goes on at an early stage, and is successively elaborated and checked as the process continues.

Spradley (1980) compares positivistic and interpretive researchers to petroleum engineers and explorers respectively.

> The [petroleum] engineer has a specific goal in mind; to find oil or gas buried far below the surface. Before the engineer even begins an investigation, a careful study will be made of the maps which show geological features of the area. Then, knowing ahead of the time the kinds of features that suggest oil or gas beneath the surface, the engineer will go out to 'find' something quite specific. (p. 26)

Theory and previous research similarly put scientific researchers into the position of knowing what they are looking for; they have specific hypotheses to be tested. However, those following an interpretive approach begin much more generally. They explore, gathering information, going first in one direction then perhaps retracing that route, then starting out in a new direction. On discovering a lake in the middle of a large wooded area, the explorer would take frequent compass readings, check the angle of the sun, take notes about prominent landmarks, and use feedback from each observation to modify earlier information. (p. 26)

For those interested in carrying out relatively small-scale real world investigations, each of these traditional models presents difficulties. A problem in following hypothetico-deductive scientific approaches is that one is often forced to work without maps, or with very sketchy ones; in other words, the firm theoretical base that is called for is just not there. And, anyhow, as emphasized in box 1.1 (p. 11), the primary concern is not in developing theory. Similarly, free-range exploring is seldom on the cards. For one thing there isn't the time, and the reality is often that the real world enquirer has a good idea of the 'lie of the land', and is looking for something quite specific while still being open to unexpected discoveries.

This suggests the need for some rethinking of the approach to be taken to real world enquiry. Fortunately, that task has been made easier by Alan Bryman in a recent text on *Quality and Quantity in Social Research* (Bryman, 1988a). He makes out a strong case that many of the differences between the two traditions are in the minds of philosophers and theorists, rather than in the practices of researchers. For example, he concludes that

> the suggestion that quantitative research is associated with the testing of theories, whilst qualitative research is associated with the generation of theories, can . . . be viewed as a convention that has little to do with either the practices of many researchers within the two traditions or the potential of the methods of data collection themselves. (p. 172)

Undoubtedly there are situations and topics where a 'scientific' quantitative approach is called for, and others where a qualitative naturalistic study is appropriate. But there are '. . . still others [which] will be even better served by a marriage of the two traditions' (p. 173). This view that the differences between the two traditions can be best viewed as technical rather than epistemological, enabling the enquirer to 'mix and match' methods according to what best fits a particular study, is central to the approach taken in later chapters of this book.

Deciding on the Focus

A The Need for a Focus

Before you can start, you obviously need to have some idea of what area you are going to deal with. This amounts to deciding on your focus. My experience is that this tends either to be quite straightforward, almost self-evident (especially when you are told what to do); or pretty problematic (when you have an open field).

Finding the focus involves identifying what it is that you want to gather information about. Until you have done this, further planning is impossible. If you are deciding for yourself, with few or no external constraints, the decision will be driven by what you are interested in and concerned about. Any research or enquiry experience that you already have can be a legitimate influence on this decision, but you should beware of this having a straitjacket effect (e.g. simply looking for topics where you might use your survey experience). Conversely, it is also legitimate to select a focus which leads you to branch out and gain experience of a strategy or technique not already within your 'toolbag'. Glueck and Jauch (1975) provide an analysis of the sources of research ideas among 'productive' scholars.

It is helpful to try to write down the research focus at this stage, even if you can only do this in a vague and tentative form. Later stages in the process will help to refine it and get it more clearly focused. Box 2.1 gives a varied set of examples.

Box 2.1   Examples of initial proposals for research foci

The 'quality of life' in the community for ex-patients of a closed-down psychiatric hospital

A successful 'job club'

The effectiveness of 'Work-Link' in providing jobs for the young disabled

Helping carers of geriatric relatives

Evaluating a short course in Rogerian counselling

Dramatherapy and the thought-disordered

Approaches to curriculum in 16–19-year-old pupils with severe learning difficulties

Facilitating change in small organizations through a microcomputer version of the Delphi Nominal Group approach

The 'Young Terriers': youth section of a football supporters club

Failing the first year of an engineering degree: how not to do it

The social function of a hairdressing salon

Introducing a student-led assessment into a course

B   Making a Group Decision

If you are proposing to carry out a group project with colleagues or friends, it is valuable for each member to independently think about, and write down, her or his proposals for the research focus. The group then comes together to decide on an agreed focus. In this way all members of the group have some input into the process, and ideas of combining individual input with group collaboration and negotiation get built in at an early stage.

C   Having the Decision Made for You

In many cases the focus of a real world enquiry is given to the investigator(s) as a part of the job, or as a commission or tender. That is not to say that the people giving the task to the investigators necessarily know what they want, or that the investigators agree that this is what they should be wanting. The main task in this situation is clarificatory: translating the presenting problem into something researchable, and moreover 'do-able' within the parameters of time, resources and finance that can be made available.

D   Starting Where You Are

If you do have some say in the choice of topic, there are several factors which might be taken into account. *Interest* is probably the most important. *All enquiry involves drudgery and frustration and you need to have a strong interest in the topic to keep you going through the bad times.* Such interest in the focus of the research is not the same thing as having a closed and prejudged view of the nature of the phenomenon to be researched or the kind of outcomes that will be found, which is likely to affect the objectivity and trustworthiness of the research. All of these aspects however are a part of what Lofland and Lofland (1984) call 'starting where you are'. As Kirby and McKenna (1989) put it:

> Remember that who you are has a central place in the research process because you bring your own thoughts, aspirations and feelings, and your own ethnicity, race, class, gender, sexual orientation, occupation, family background, schooling, etc. to your research. (p. 46)

This kind of open acknowledgement of what the enquirer brings to the enquiry is more common in some research traditions than others. However, even in traditional laboratory experimentation, the work of Robert Rosenthal and colleagues (e.g. Rosenthal, 1966) has led to a recognition of 'experimenter effects' of various kinds, although they tend to be viewed solely in terms of the difficulties they produce.

Enquirers selecting their own foci, make the choice for a variety of reasons. It may be, for example, to address a problem of 'practice'. That is, as professionals (psychologists, social workers, health service workers, teachers, managers, personnel officers, etc.) they wish to look at, perhaps evaluate or change, some aspect of practice that interests or concerns them. It may be their own, or colleagues', practice or professional situations, or those of others whom they have a responsibility to advise or support. Frequently encountered problems are obviously a sensible choice for a research focus as anything useful that you find out has a direct spin-off; and, importantly, there will be no shortage of instances to study.

E Researching the Background

The kind of approach to deciding on the research focus suggested here is very different from traditional views of the origins of research tasks. These see them as rooted in the academic discipline, revealed through the research literature and theoretical or methodological concerns. This places a considerable onus on researchers. They must have a thorough and up-to-date understanding of the 'literature'; detailed background knowledge of the relevant discipline; technical proficiency; and substantial time and resources.

In many 'real world' studies, it can be argued that the research literature, and the discipline, provide a *background resource* rather than the essential starting point for research designs (Walker, 1985, p. 13). This change of view is important because of the change in power relationship between investigator and practitioner that it suggests. Crudely, the psychologist or other social scientist does not set the agenda, but acts in partnership with a variety of client groups. One way in which this can be implemented is for those who have been, in the past, the *subjects* of research now to play a role in carrying out the research. This applies with particular force to the part of the enquiry that is concerned with conceptualizing the task and deciding on the research questions. The final chapter of the book returns to these issues.

A good understanding about what is already known, or established, does not then have the absolutely central role in applied real world enquiry that it does in fundamental, discipline-developing research. However, it is still very important. It may be possible to get background information from persons who have done related work, either directly or through the 'literature'. Unfortunately, for many real world topics, that literature tends to be somewhat inaccessible and fragmentary.

A general strategy would start with 'abstracting' journals such as *Psychological Abstracts* and equivalent computerized sources (including those available on 'CD-ROM', i.e. on compact discs which can be 'played' on a monitor screen). Any good library should be able to help you. Cooper (1989) provides a useful guide. 'Key word' searches can be an efficient way of pinpointing relevant material – although my experience has been that quite often when key words have indicated a specific journal article, adjacent articles in the same journal have been of greater interest or relevance (perhaps a variant of the dictionary phenomenon, where words next to the one you are looking up are always more interesting!). 'Citation indices' are valuable as they enable you to travel forward in time from a particular reference via later authors who have cited the initial work. Howard and Sharp (1983, ch. 4) provide a good detailed introduction to literature searching. Gash (1989) covers computer sources and on-line searching in some detail.

It is not too difficult to use these suggestions for the starting point of a hunt through what is currently in print which is relevant to your study. From this, you then find out what is known about the topic; what is seen as problematic; the approaches that have been taken; etc. While it is important to get a good feel for this, it is however all too easy to be imprisoned by what others have done into a particular way of looking at and of investigating the topic. Beware.

F Acknowledging the Constraints

Any real world study must obviously take serious note of real world constraints. Your choice of research focus must be realistic in terms of the time and resources that you have available. If you have a maximum of three weeks you can devote to the project, you choose something where you have a good chance of 'getting it out' in that time. Access and co-operation are similarly important, as well as having a nose for situations where any enquiry is likely to be counter-productive (getting into a sensitive situation involving, say, the siting of a hostel for mentally handicapped adults when your prime aim is to develop community provision is not very sensible if a likely outcome is the stirring up of a hornet's nest). These are themes which will recur throughout our discussions and are particularly important when deciding on the kind of research strategy to be used and the practicalities of actually carrying out the study, but they need to be at least in the background when considering the research focus.

Deciding on the Research Question(s)

There is no foolproof, automatic way of generating research questions. While the sequence envisaged here, of first deciding on a general research focus and then refining that down into one or more relatively specific research questions, has an intuitive reasonableness, things may not work out like this. The question may come first – perhaps stimulated by theoretical concerns. You then seek an appropriate context, a research focus, in which to ask the question.

There is evidence, however, that some ways of approaching the generation of research questions are more likely to result in successful and productive enquiries than others. Campbell et al. (1982) have looked at these issues by using a range of empirical techniques, including contrasts between studies judged by their originators as being either successful or unsuccessful. Their remit was limited to research in industrial and organizational psychology, but many of their conclusions seem to have general relevance to studies in the behavioural sciences.

An idea that emerges strongly from their work is that

> the selection of innovative research questions is not a single act or decision. Significant research is a process, an attitude, a way of thinking. Significant research is accomplished by people who are motivated to do significant research, who are willing to pay the cost in terms of time or effort. (p. 109)

Box 2.2 lists features considered by researchers to be associated with their successful and unsuccessful projects. Campbell et al. view the choice process for selecting the research questions as being often non-linear and involving considerable uncertainty and intuition. Research starting with mechanistic linear thinking, closely tied to the known and understood, may be clean and tidy but is unlikely to be of any significance. However, something that starts out as poorly understood, given considerable theoretical effort to convert it into something which is clearly defined, logical and rational, could well be of value.

Campbell et al. also conducted a relatively informal interview study with investigators responsible for what are considered important 'milestone' studies in the study of organizations and reached conclusions which supported their previous ones. Specifically, it did not appear that these milestone studies had arisen simply from seeking to test, or extend, an existing theory previously used in that field of research. In fact, in virtually all cases the relevant theory or knowledge was imported from some other field. What was clear was that these important studies were driven by some specific problem to be solved; that they were characterized by a problem in search of a technique, rather than the reverse. Each of the researchers was deeply involved in the substantive area of study, and it was interesting to note that many of them reported

---

Box 2.2   Features considered by researchers to characterize the antecedents of their successful and unsuccessful research

Successful research develops from:

a *Activity and involvement* Good and frequent contacts both out in the field and with colleagues.

b *Convergence* Coming together of two or more activities or interests (e.g. of an idea and a method; interest of colleague with a problem or technique).

c *Intuition* Feeling that the work is important, timely, 'right' (rather than logical analysis).

d *Theory* Concern for theoretical understanding.

e *Real world value* Problem arising from the field and leading to tangible and useful ideas.

Unsuccessful research starts with:

a *Expedience* Undertaken because it is easy, cheap, quick or convenient.

b *Method or technique* Using it as a vehicle to carry out a specific method of investigation or statistical technique.

c *Motivation by publication, money or funding* Research done primarily for publication purposes rather than interest in the issue.

d *Lack of theory* Without theory the research may be easier and quicker, but the outcome will often be of little value.

(Adapted from Campbell et al., 1982, pp. 97–103.)

---

an element of luck in either the creation or the development of the research problem. However, it is well known in scientific creativity that Lady Luck is more willing to bestow her favours on the keenly involved and well prepared (see e.g. Medawar, 1979, p. 89).

The information from Campbell et al. (1982) and some related studies provides suggestions for the strategies one might adopt in generating research questions which are developed in the marked pages which follow.

Developing the Research Question(s)

A *Know the Area*

It obviously helps to be really familiar with the area on which your research focuses. A good strategy to force yourself into this position is to 'go public' in some way – produce a review paper, do a seminar or other presentation with colleagues whose comments you respect (or fear!).

B *Widen the Base of Your Experience*

You should not be limited by the research (and research questions) current in the specific field you are researching. Researchers in other fields and from other disciplines may well be wrestling with problems similar to yours, or from which useful parallels can be drawn. An afternoon's trawling through journals in cognate disciplines is one way. Contact and discussion with practitioners may give a different perspective on what the questions are.

C *Consider Using Techniques for Enhancing Creativity*

There is a substantial literature on creativity and on methods of promoting innovation which is relevant to the process of generating research questions. The methods include *brainstorming* (e.g. Osborn, 1963), the *nominal group technique* (e.g. DelBecq et al., 1975), the *delphi technique* (e.g. DelBecq et al., 1975), *synectics* (e.g. Prince, 1970), and *creative confrontation* (e.g. Schaude, 1979).

Note that the techniques for enhancing creativity are primarily concerned with groups. Even if you are going to carry out the project on an individual basis, there is much to be said for regarding this initial stage of research as a group process and enlisting the help of others.

Consider, for example, the Delphi technique. In this context it might mean getting together a group of persons, either those who are involved directly in the project or a range of colleagues with interests in the focus of the research. (Bear in mind the point made in section B, that there is advantage in including in the group colleagues from other disciplines and practitioners. Each individual is then asked, to generate *independently*, i.e. not in a group situation, say, up to three specific research questions in the chosen area. They may be asked also to provide additional information, perhaps giving a justification for the questions chosen. The responses from each individual are collected, and all responses are passed on in an unedited and unattributed form to all members of the group. A second cycle then takes place. This might involve individuals commenting on other responses, and/or revising their own contribution in the light of what others have produced. Third and fourth cycles might take place, either of similar form or seeking resolution or consensus through voting, or ranking, or categorizing responses.

D *Avoid the Pitfalls of:*

* Allowing a pre-decision on method or technique to decide the questions to be asked. A variant of this concerning the use of computerized packages for statistical analysis is also worth flagging. Developing research questions *simply* on the basis that they allow the use of a particular package that you have available is almost as big a research sin as designing and carrying out a study that you don't know how to analyse.
* Posing research questions that can't be answered (either in general or by the methods that it is feasible for you to use).
* Asking questions that have already been answered satisfactorily (deliberate replication resulting from a concern about the status of a finding is different from ignorance of the literature).

Research Questions and Hypotheses

As already pointed out, there is a tradition within experimental methodology of presenting formal hypotheses which are tested by the experiment, usually by means of statistical inference. However, there is a sense in which hypotheses form part of all forms of enquiry. This is the hypothesis as tentative guess, or intuitive hunch, as to what is going on in a situation.

Such tentative hypotheses can provide a very useful bridge between the research question and the design of the enquiry. Suppose that we are interested in the research question:

> *How is educational achievement in a primary school affected by the introduction of standard attainment testing at age seven?*

At the time of writing this is one of a number of questions of interest arising from the introduction of the National Curriculum into schools in the United Kingdom. Issues like this are obviously of concern to society at large, and parents in particular, as well as to the education profession and government policy-makers. Enquirers coming to this topic will, through some amalgam of personal experience, ideological conviction, involvement in schools, and knowledge of the educational research literature relating both to this country and others, develop tentative hypotheses relating to the question. Perhaps:

> *A primary school in which standard attainment testing has been introduced gives greater emphasis to preparing its pupils for formal tests.*

and

> *Pupils in a primary school which gives greater emphasis to formal testing show greater educational achievement as measured by formal tests.*

Such hypotheses are interim guesses about what lies behind the 'how' in the question. They help in developing the framework for the enquiry and assist in guiding the choice of research strategy and methods. The following chapters take up these design issues.

Ethical Considerations

Participants in real world studies may sometimes be involved without their knowledge. Sometimes they may be misled about the true nature of the study. Or they may be faced with situations that cause stress or anxiety. Should they be? In other words, is the investigator acting ethically? Put baldly like this, the answer seems to be clearly, no. However, there is another side. These considerations might be put alongside your time and effort as 'costs' of carrying out the enquiry. 'Benefits' include the knowledge gained from the study, and possible changes and improvements to situations or services.

These questionable practices arise from the kind of research questions we are asking, and the methods used to seek answers, particularly the procedures used to avoid misleading results. It may be that we can go about things differently and avoid deception, stress and the like. If this is not possible then there is a conflict. How is our 'right to know' balanced against the participants' right to privacy, dignity and self-determination? And should the investigator act as both judge and jury?

It is vital that, at a very early stage of your preparations to carry out an enquiry you give serious thought to these ethical aspects of what you are proposing. Ethics refers to rules of conduct; typically to conformity to a code or set of principles (Reynolds, 1979). Many professions working with people have such codes. Appendix B presents the code developed by the British Psychological Society (1991). The American Psychological Association (APA) has produced a very useful case-book on ethical principles (1987).

A distinction is sometimes made between *ethics* and *morals*. While both are concerned with what is good or bad, right or wrong, ethics are usually taken as referring to general principles of what one ought to do. Morals are usually taken as concerned with whether or not a *specific* act is consistent with accepted notions of right or wrong. For example, a psychologist might punctiliously follow the profession's ethical guidelines but still be accused of behaving immorally. Controversial research on perception in kittens, involving the sewing together of their eyelids, is a case which illustrates this divide sharply. Views about the morality or otherwise of this work depend crucially, of course, on what constitute 'accepted' notions of right and wrong. One position would be that it is simply and absolutely wrong to do this to an animal. An opposing view would seek to balance the costs (to the animal, and possibly to the researcher through adverse publicity) and the benefits (to science, with possible medical or other 'spin-offs').

The terms 'ethical' and 'moral' are subsequently used interchangeably in this text to refer to 'proper' conduct, except where the context makes codified principles relevant. Ethical and moral concerns in scientific studies have come to the fore alongside the changing views of the nature of science discussed in chapter 3. A traditional view was that science was 'value-free' or 'value-neutral' and the task of the scientist was simply to describe what *is* in an objective manner. This is a different task from determining what *ought* to be done to behave ethically. If, however, objectivity can not be guaranteed when doing science, and the values of the researcher are inevitably involved in the research, the worlds of 'is' and 'ought' become much more difficult to disentangle.

Experimental research with people poses ethical problems in sharp forms. Science viewed as leading to *prediction* gives the possibility of *control* over what people do, which obviously has a moral dimension. While this is most obvious in experimental situations where subjects are explicitly manipulated, ethical dilemmas lurk in *any* research involving people. In 'real world' research we may not be able to, or wish to, control the situation but there is almost always the intention or possibility of change associated with the study. This forces the researcher, wittingly or not, into value judgements and moral dilemmas. Suppose we are looking at a new approach to the teaching of reading. It is highly likely that we start with the premise that this looks like being a 'good thing'; probably an improvement on what is currently on offer. Life – your own and the participants – is too short to waste it on something which does not appear to have this 'prima facie' value.

A possible exception would be where the latest educational fad was sweeping the schools and a demonstration of its drawbacks might be a useful inoculation for the system – although even in this case, my experience has been that the conclusion ends up something like 'if you want to take on this new approach, these are the conditions under which it seems to be most effective'.

Reverting to consideration of the likely 'good' intervention, an immediate issue becomes 'which schools are to be involved?' Do you choose the fertile soil of a friendly, innovative school? Or the stony ground of a setting where there is probably a greater, though unacknowledged, need for something new? These are partly research issues but they have a clear ethical dimension.

Ethical problems start at the very beginning of a study. It may appear unethical to select certain foci for research because of the likely exacerbation of an explosive situation simply by carrying out research in that area. Problems continue through into the choice of a venue and indeed can permeate the whole of a study. For example:

- Is the giving of necessary additional resources of staff, equipment or whatever to the places where the research takes place, simply part of the deal; the investigator showing good faith by giving as well as taking? Or is it unfair coercion to take part, reminiscent of prisoners gaining food or an early release for taking part in trials of potentially dangerous drugs?
- Do individuals have the right not to take part? And even if they do, are there any overt or covert penalties for non-participation ('it will look good on your reference if you have taken part in this study')?
- Do they know what they are letting themselves in for? Is their consent 'fully informed'?
- Will individuals participating be protected, not only from any direct effects of the intervention, but also by the investigator ensuring that the reporting of the study maintains confidentiality?
- Is, on the other hand, confidentiality always appropriate? If people have done something good and worthwhile, and probably put in extra effort and time, why shouldn't they get credit for it? Conversely, if inefficiency or malpractice is uncovered in the study, should the investigator let the guilty ones hide?
- What responsibility do investigators have for the knowledge that they have acquired? Are they simply the 'hired hand' doing the bidding of the paymaster? Or – changing the metaphor to one used by Carl Rogers – are they simply ammunition wagons, loaded with powerful knowledge just waiting to be used, whether the users are the 'good guys' or the 'bad guys'? Incidentally, Rogers' (1961) view is 'don't be a damn ammunition wagon, be a rifle'. That is, those doing applied studies have to target their knowledge and take responsibility for what they 'hit'.

Each of these issues is complex. Although general guidelines can be given as indicated in appendix B, they must be carefully thought through in each specific situation.

Consider, for example, whether or not people should always be asked in advance whether they are prepared to take part. It may not be possible or practicable to do this. You may have good grounds for believing that telling them would alter the behaviour you are interested in. But not telling them means that you have taken away their right not to participate.

There are several questions you can ask to help decide. Will the study involve them doing things they would not otherwise do? If not, it is less of an infringement. So, an observational study of naturally occurring behaviour is less questionable than a field experiment where you contrive something which would not otherwise happen. Not that all experiments are equivalent. One which involved you stalling a car when the traffic lights turn green to study the effects on driver behaviour, while questionable in its own right, is probably less so than a simulated mugging on a tube train to study by-stander behaviour. Reasonable things to take into account are the degree of inconvenience, and of likely emotional involvement, to participants. In studies where the judgement is made that prior permisssion must be sought, it is increasingly the practice to present all potential participants with an 'in-formed consent' form (see chapter 10, p. 283).

However, even this apparently highly ethical procedure can have its pit-falls. In research on socially sensitive topics such as drug abuse or AIDS, it is possible that the investigator would be under legal pressure to disclose all research information including such signed forms. American investigators have been subpoena'd to appear in court, and in a similar situation two journalists have faced prison rather than reveal their sources. Hence in such situations it might be preferable to proceed informally, and not use a form as such.

Box 2.3 presents a list of questionable practices which you might be tempted to indulge in. The presumption is that you do not do so, unless in a particular study you can convince yourself, and an appropriate 'ethical committee', that the benefits accruing outweigh the costs. Ethical commit-tees are now commonplace in many settings. They are not necessarily separ-ate committees; for example ethical considerations may be one of the responsibilities for a more general approving committee whose agreement must be sought before a study is started.

There are particular ethical problems associated with working with some groups such as children, persons with mental handicap or mental distur-bance, prisoners and other 'captive' populations (e.g. persons in homes for the aged, or students on a course). The issues are whether they can ration-ally, knowingly and freely give informed consent. For legally under-age children, and others who may not be in a position to appreciate what is involved, the parents or guardians should be asked for their consent. In many cases the child will be able to appreciate at least something of what is involved and should be asked directly in addition to the parent. Ethical committees or review boards, including lay persons and legal experts as well as experienced researchers, can play a key role. They may be particularly important in studies of relatively powerless groups such as the elderly or homeless.

Whenever anyone takes part in a study for a 'consideration' of some kind, whether financial or as an explicit or implicit part of their duties or position, there are ethical implications. The situation can lead to researchers and participants taking on employer and employee roles respectively. The 'em-ployer' has to guard against the notion that payment justifies placing the

Box 2.3 Ten questionable practices in social research

1 Involving people without their knowledge or consent

2 Coercing them to participate

3 Withholding information about the true nature of the research.

4 Otherwise deceiving the participant.

5 Inducing them to commit acts diminishing their self-esteem.

6 Violating rights of self-determination (e.g. in studies seeking to promote individual change).

7 Exposing participants to physical or mental stress.

8 Invading their privacy.

9 Withholding benefits from some participants (e.g. in comparison groups).

10 Not treating participants fairly, or with consideration, or with respect.

(Kimmel, 1988 provides further discussion on these issues, together with useful exercises on ethical issues.)

participant at risk. On the 'employee's' side there is the likely tendency to 'give them whatever I think that I am being paid for'.

Certain styles of real world research carry with them additional ethical implications. For example, 'action research' (discussed in chapter 14, p. 437) goes beyond the usual concerns for consent, confidentiality and respect for the participants' interests covered in the preceding discussion. There is a commitment to genuine participation in the research to the extent that this is seen as a collaborative effort between researcher and 'researched'. The ethical guidelines for this type of research, given in box 2.4 bring the need for negotiation to the fore.

Box 2.4 Ethical principles in 'action research'

1 *Observe protocol.* Take care to ensure that the relevant persons, committees and authorities have been consulted and informed and that the necessary permission and approval has been obtained.

2 *Involve participants.* Encourage others, who have a stake in the improvement you envisage, to shape the form of the work.

3 *Negotiate with those affected.* Not everyone will want to be directly involved. Your work should take account of the responsibilities and wishes of others.

4 *Report progress.* Keep the work visible and remain open to suggestions so that unforeseen and unseen ramifications can be taken account of. All involved must have the opportunity to lodge a protest to you.

5 *Obtain explicit authorization before you observe.*

6 *Obtain explicit authorization before you examine files, correspondence or other documentation.* Take copies only if specific authority to do this is obtained.

7 *Negotiate descriptions of people's work.* Always allow those described to challenge your accounts on the grounds of fairness, relevance and accuracy.

8 *Negotiate accounts of other points of view* (e.g. in accounts of communication). Always allow those involved in interviews, meetings and written exchanges to require amendments which enhance fairness, relevance and accuracy.

9 *Obtain explicit authorization before using quotations.* This applies to verbatim transcripts, attributed observations, excerpts of audio and video recordings, judgements, conclusions or recommendations in reports (written or to meetings).

10 *Negotiate reports for various levels of release.* Different audiences demand different levels of reports.

11 *Accept responsibility for maintaining confidentiality.*

12 *Retain the right to report your work.* Provided that those involved are satisfied with the fairness, accuracy and relevance of accounts which pertain to them, and that the accounts do not unnecessarily expose or embarrass those involved, then accounts should not be subject to veto or be sheltered by prohibitions of confidentiality.

13 *Make your principles of procedure binding and known.* All of the people involved in your project must agree to the principles before the work begins. Others must be aware of their rights in the process.

(Adapted from Kemmis and McTaggart, 1981, pp. 43–4.)

Further Reading

Agnew, N. M. and Pyke, S. W. (1982) *The Science Game: An introduction to research in the behavioral sciences*, 3rd edn. Englewood Cliffs, NJ: Prentice-Hall. Entertaining, idiosyncratic and provocative introductory text. Particularly strong on the charms and the power of science.

Bell, J. (1987) *Doing Your Research Project: a guide for first-time researchers in education and social science*. Milton Keynes: Open University Press. Short down-to-earth guide, emanating from education management, but more generally relevant.

Bryman, A. (1988) *Quantity and Quality in Social Research*. London: Unwin Hyman. Discusses the nature of qualitative and quantitative research, and how they can be combined and compared.

Bulmer, M. (ed.) (1982) *Social Research Ethics*. London: Macmillan. Collection of papers covering wide range of ethical issues.

Campbell, J. T., Daft, R. L. and Hulin, C. L. (1982) *What to Study: generating and developing research questions*. Newbury Park and London: Sage. Delivers what it promises in a clear and down-to-earth manner.

Judd, C. M., Smith, E. R. and Kidder, L. H. (1991) *Research Methods in Social Relations*, 6th edn. New York: Holt, Rinehart and Winston. Hardy perennial. Very thorough and valuable general social science methodology text. Advocates multiple research strategies, multiple methods of measurement and multiple techniques of data analysis. Excellent discussion of ethical issues.

Kimmel, A. J. (1988) *Ethics and Values in Applied Social Research*. Newbury Park and London: Sage. Essential reading for the serious real world researcher.

Lincoln, Y. S. and Guba, E. G. (1985) *Naturalistic Inquiry*. Newbury Park and London: Sage. A challenging and coherent exposition of the 'alternative' paradigm of scientific research – here termed 'naturalistic' but otherwise referred to as post-positivistic, ethnographic, phenomenological, hermeneutic or humanistic.

Miller, E. (1989) Preparing a Research Project. In G. Parry and F. N. Watts (eds), *Behavioural and Mental Health Research: a handbook of Skills and Methods*. Hove: Laurence Erlbaum Associates. Clinically oriented discussion of what is involved in selecting a problem area, formulating questions, etc.

Smith, H.W. (1975) *Strategies of Social Research: the methodological imagination*. London: Prentice-Hall. Stimulating general text from a sociological social science perspective. A more theory-derived section on 'Formulating a Research Problem'.

Part II

Designing the Enquiry

It is useful to distinguish between the *strategy* and the *tactics* you adopt when carrying out an enquiry. Strategy refers to the general broad orientation taken in addressing research questions – the style, if you like. These strategic considerations are the major concern of this second part of the book. Tactics, the specific methods of investigation, are dealt with in part III.

3

General Design Issues

This chapter considers the traditional strategies of experimentation, surveys and case studies in relation to the purposes of enquiry.

It also considers alternative hybrid and combined strategies.

It explores the implications of taking case study seriously, leading to a discussion of post-positivistic science.

Finally, the chapter addresses the issue of what it takes to produce trustworthy findings.

Design is concerned with turning research questions into projects. This is a crucial part of any enquiry, but it is often slid over quickly without any real consideration of the issues and possibilities. There is a strong tendency for both those carrying out projects, and those who want them carried out, to assume that there is no alternative to their favoured approach. Comments have already been made on the assumption by many psychologists that an experimental design is inevitably called for. For other social scientists, and for quite a few clients when commissioning studies, designs involving the statistical analysis of sample survey data are seen as the only possible approach.

Manstead and Semin (1988) make the obvious but often neglected point that the strategies and tactics you select in carrying out a piece of research depend very much on the type of research question you are trying to answer. They adopt a river-crossing analogy. The task of crossing the river corresponds to the general *research focus*. Specific *research questions* are analogous to asking how many people want to cross the river; the frequency with which they want to cross; the current of the river, etc. The choice of *research strategy* is akin to a choice between swimming, walking, flying or sailing across. The *research tactics* (or methods of investigation) concern the particular type of boat, bridge, aircraft, etc.

> The general principle is that the research strategy or strategies, and the methods or techniques employed, must be appropriate for the questions you want to answer.

Hakim (1987), in one of the few books which focuses on design issues across a range of social science disciplines, makes a comparison between designers of research projects and architects, and then goes on to extend this to suggest that those who actually carry out projects are like builders. For her,

> design deals primarily with aims, purposes, intentions and plans within the practical constraints of location, time, money and availability of staff. It is also very much about *style*, the architect's own preferences and ideas (whether innovative or solidly traditional) and the stylistic preferences of those who pay for the work and have to live with the finished result. (p. 1)

In small-scale research the architect–designer and builder–enquirer are typically one and the same person. Hence the need for sensitivity to design issues, to avoid the research equivalent of the many awful houses put up by speculative builders without benefit of architectural expertise.

Such muddling through should be distinguished from the opportunity to develop and revise the original plan, which is easier in a small-scale project than in one requiring the co-ordination of many persons' efforts. Design modification is more feasible with some research strategies than with others – it is in fact an integral part of the case study approach. However, that kind of flexibility calls for a concern for design *throughout* the project, rather than providing an excuse for not considering design at all.

Getting a Feel for Design Issues

After an overview in the marked pages of what is involved in choosing a research strategy, the immediately following part of this chapter gives a short review of the traditional strategies of experimentation, surveys and case studies. This is followed by a separate chapter on each giving a more detailed discussion, concentrating on design issues specific to each strategy. The rationale for this presentation is that you need to have some understanding of these issues for each strategy before you are in a position to make an informed choice of strategy.

Do not feel straitjacketed into simply choosing one of these three approaches 'off the shelf'. It may well be appropriate to have a rather different style – perhaps a hybrid which combines aspects of two or three of the traditional strategies. Or a study might combine them, including, say, both a survey and one or more case studies. There is discussion of such hybrid and combined strategies at the end of part II of the book.

Choosing a Research Strategy – Overview

This section seeks to sensitize you to the issues involved in choosing a research strategy.

A   Is One of the Traditional Strategies Appropriate?

The general approach taken in an enquiry is commonly referred to as the RESEARCH STRATEGY. Research strategies have been classified in many different ways. One simple approach which is widely used distinguishes between three main strategies; EXPERIMENTS, SURVEYS and CASE STUDIES. Box 3.1 summarizes their characteristics.

Box 3.1   Three traditional research strategies

1 *Experiment*: measuring the effects of manipulating one variable on another variable.

Typical features: selection of samples of individuals from known populations; allocation of samples to different experimental conditions; introduction of planned change on one or more variables; measurement on small number of variables; control of other variables; usually involves hypothesis testing.

2 *Survey*: collection of information in standardized form from groups of people.

Typical features: selection of samples of individuals from known populations; collection of relatively small amount of data in standardized form from each individual; usually employs questionnaire or structured interview.

3 *Case study*: development of detailed, intensive knowledge about a single 'case', or of a small number of related 'cases'.

Typical features: selection of a single case (or a small number of related cases) of a situation, individual or group of interest or concern; study of the case in its context; collection of information via a range of data collection techniques including observation, interview and documentary analysis.

A note on 'field research'

You may come across the term FIELD STUDIES, or FIELD RESEARCH. This is sometimes used not simply to refer to location (i.e. outside the laboratory) but also to signify a particular research approach. For social anthropologists, for example, FIELDWORK is synonymous with the collection of data using observational methods. Some social scientists also use the term to refer to the collection of data using a social survey (Moser and Kalton, 1971), although for others it is much closer to case study as used in this book:

> the term *field research* will be used . . . to incorporate different theoretical perspectives and to explore the relationship between a variety of different methods. It covers what is colloquially known as participant observation, unstructured interviews and documentary methods: although depending on the problem at hand other approaches can be used. (Burgess, 1984a, p. 4)

B Don't Rule Out other Possible Strategies at this Stage

It is important to note that the *three traditional research strategies do not provide a logical partitioning covering all possible forms of enquiry*. They are more of a recognition of the camps into which enquirers or researchers have tended to put themselves, signalling their preferences for certain ways of working. Such camps have the virtue of providing secure bases within which fledgling researchers can be inculcated in the ways of the tribe, and, more generally, high professional standards can be maintained. However, they carry the danger of enquiry being 'strategy driven' in the sense that someone skilled in, say, the ways of surveys assumes automatically that every problem has to be attacked through the survey strategy.

It may well be that some *hybrid strategy* falling somewhere between these 'ideal types' is appropriate for the study with which you are involved. For example, there is nothing to stop you collecting a substantial amount of largely standardized survey-type data from a relatively small number of cases. Or doing an experiment for which the data are obtained by a survey.

It can also make a lot of sense to *combine strategies* in an investigation. One or more case studies might be linked to a survey or an experiment. Alternatively, a small experiment or small-scale survey might be incorporated actually within a case study. Issues involved in the carrying out of hybrid and combined studies are discussed in the marked pages at the end of chapter 6 (pp. 167–169) after separate description of the traditional strategies.

C Consider the Purpose(s) of Your Enquiry

Enquiries can be classified in terms of their purpose as well as by the research strategy used. A tripartite classification is again commonly used, distinguishing between EXPLORATORY, DESCRIPTIVE and EXPLANATORY purposes. These are summarized in box 3.2. A 'predictive' category is also sometimes (see Marshall and Rossman, 1989, p. 78) but is regarded here as a variant of the explanatory purpose. *A particular study may be concerned with more than one purpose,* possibly all three, but often one will predominate. *The purpose may also change as the study proceeds.*

Box 3.2   Classification of the purposes of enquiry

1   *Exploratory*
   • To find out what is happening.
   • To seek new insights.
   • To ask questions.
   • To assess phenomena in a new light.
   • Usually, but not necessarily, qualitative.

2   *Descriptive*
   • To portray an accurate profile of persons, events or situations.
   • Requires extensive previous knowledge of the situation etc. to be researched or described, so that you know appropriate aspects on which to gather information.
   • May be qualitative and/or quantitative.

3   *Explanatory*
   • Seeks an explanation of a situation or problem, usually in the form of causal relationships.
   • May be qualitative and/or quantitative.

It is taken as given that all enquiry is concerned with *contributing to knowledge*. Real world enquiry also commonly seeks a potential usefulness in relation to policy and practice.

D   *The Purpose(s) May Help in Selecting the Strategy*

The three traditional strategies represent different ways of collecting and analysing empirical evidence. Each has its particular strengths and weaknesses. It is also commonly suggested that there is a hierarchical relationship between the three strategies, related to the purpose of the research; that

- case studies are appropriate for exploratory work;
- surveys are appropriate for descriptive studies; and
- experiments are appropriate for explanatory studies.

There is some truth in this assertion – certainly as a description of how the strategies have tended to be used in the past. There is a further sense in which the flexibility of the case study strategy lends itself particularly well to exploration; a sense in which certain kinds of description can be readily achieved using surveys; and a sense in which the experiment is a particularly appropriate tool for getting at cause and effect relationships. However this is not a necessary or immutable linkage. *Each strategy can be used for any or all of the three purposes.* For example, there can be, and have been, exploratory, descriptive and explanatory case studies (Yin, 1981).

E The Research Question Does Have a Strong Influence on the Strategy Chosen

While purpose is of some help in selecting the research strategy, the type of research questions you are asking is of greater assistance. There are other factors, for example

- the degree of control that the investigator has, or wishes to have, over events; and
- whether the focus is on current or past events.

Box 3.3 relates each of these to the different strategies.

Box 3.3 Appropriate uses of different research strategies

Strategy	Type of research question	Requires control over events?	Focus on current events?
experiment	how why	yes	yes
survey	who what[1]	no	yes

	where how many how much		
case study	how why	no	usually but not necessarily

[1] some 'what' questions are exploratory; any of the strategies could be used.

(Adapted from Yin, 1989, p. 17; note that Yin also considers archival analysis and 'histories' which are not covered in this text.)

Examples

what (exploratory)   What are the ways in which an effective support service for elderly confused persons is operated?

Comment: the intention here would be to develop an appreciation of issues and questions for further study. Any strategy could be used but if little is known then a case study may well be preferable.

what (as how many/much) What have been the outcomes of reorganizing a support service?

who   Who does the service provide support for?

where   Where is the service located?

Comment: suited to the survey strategy.

how   How do persons get support?

why   Why do particular persons go into residential care?

Comment: probably best dealt with by a case study strategy. An experiment is not feasible unless the investigator has control over events, or there are changes occurring (e.g. of provision or of policy) which can form the basis of a natural or quasi-experiment.

F   Specific Methods of Investigation Need Not be Tied to Particular Research Strategies

The methods or techniques used to collect information, what might be called the *tactics of enquiry*, such as questionnaires or various kinds of observation, are sometimes regarded as necessarily linked to particular research strategies. Thus surveys may be seen as being carried out by structured questionnaire; case studies by less structured interview; and experiments through specialized forms of observation, often requiring the use of measuring instruments of some sophistication.

However, this is not a tight or necessary linkage. For example, case studies have already been presented as essentially multi-method. While interviews are likely to be involved, a range of observational techniques, analysis of the content of documents, and the application of various tests or scales, among other techniques, could also play a part. Similarly, there is no reason in principle for either experiments or surveys to be linked to specific data collection techniques. Surveys could well be carried out using observation; the effect of an experiment assessed through questionnaire responses.

Just as each research strategy can be used for any or all of descriptive, exploratory or explanatory purposes, so any method or technique, or combination of methods, can be used with any of the three traditional research strategies.

You should now some appreciation of what is involved in selecting an appropriate research strategy. Before plunging in and making a decision you need to know more about the isssues involved in working within each of the traditional strategies (this is necessary even if you decide to 'pick and mix' and depart from the traditional – the same kind of issues will surface). The rest of this chapter reviews methodological issues central to each strategy.The following three chapters examine design issues raised in experiments, surveys and case studies respectively.

General issues in 'choosing a research strategy' are then summarized (pp. 47–50).

Experimental Methodology

The so-called 'psycho-statistical' paradigm (Fienberg, 1977) dominates the mainstream view of how empirical studies in psychology should be carried out. Certainly this is the impression gained from the content and approach of the multitude of methodology texts on experimental psychology. The work of Sir Ronald Fisher, particularly his *The Design of Experiments* (1935) is usually cited as the major influence in this development. Fisher, working in agricultural research, saw that random sampling from known populations allows the use of probability theory to estimate error, and through this the development and use of statistical tests of significance. His approach provides a solution to two very important issues that permeate scientific enquiry. These are the problems of INTERNAL VALIDITY (concerned with the extent to which a study establishes that a factor or variable has actually caused the effect that is found) and EXTERNAL VALIDITY (the degree to which findings can be generalized from the specific sample in the study to some target population).

The elegance of Fisher's solution to these problems and, one suspects, the access which his approach gave to a satisfyingly complex application of mathematics, may well have played a part in its wholesale adoption. This is notwithstanding strong attacks made on the use of his central concept of statistical significance (discussed in chapter 11, p. 351). It is also worth noting that there were earlier experimentalists, such as Pavlov, who made a strong contribution without the use of statistics; and that later highly influential figures in the development of psychology, such as Skinner and Piaget, and their adherents and followers, appeared immune to these statistical blandishments.

In moving from the laboratory to the 'real world' there is an immediate difficulty in using Fisherian methodology. Random sampling from known populations, although in principle still feasible, appears to present extremely difficult practical and ethical problems. Certainly, real world studies which play the game strictly according to Fisher's rules appear rarer than politicians applauding their opponents' actions or policies.

What to do? A common device, surely only defensible for the psychological comfort derived from conformity, is to pretend that all is well; to quote statistical significance levels which have meaning only within the Fisherian model, without making it explicit that the required assumptions were not met. In fact, the extent to which one can stay within this paradigm and make sensible statements about populations from non-random samples is a complex and murky area (see Smith, 1983 and discussion in chapter 5, p. 136).

An alternative and more honest approach has been pioneered by Campbell and his colleagues, starting with the influential Campbell and Stanley (1963) monograph, which was further developed by Cook and Campbell (1979). They advocate 'QUASI-EXPERIMENTATION' as a valuable approach to the development and analysis of studies in field settings. A wide range of designs is covered which are more easily realizable outside the laboratory than 'true' experiments. This includes, for example, the comparison of 'intact groups' (e.g. existing classes in schools) rather than samples randomly selected and allocated for the purposes of the study. The concern is to tease out the threats to valid inference about causation present in a particular design, and to evaluate how far these threats can be discounted in a particular study, taking into account the specific features of the study and the pattern of results obtained.

The quasi-experimental approach attempts to liberalize the experiment to cope more realistically with conditions outside the laboratory. It shares the same notions about the nature of scientific activity as true experimentation. Hypotheses are tested; cause and effect are investigated; validity is assessed; and generalizations to the population and different settings and times is attempted. There are differences of course. The logic of the Fisherian 'randomized assignment to conditions model' is that randomization attempts to control an infinite and *unspecified* number of 'rival hypotheses'. Strictly speaking, randomization can never totally control for these hypotheses, but renders them implausible to a specified probability. In quasi-experimentation each rival hypothesis must be specified and specifically controlled for.

This latter approach has strong similarity to an earlier tradition of experimental work, most clearly seen in physics, but also central to Pavlov's work in the laboratory. This might be termed the 'experimental isolation' or 'laboratory control' model. Pavlov made use of heavy sound insulation by means of thick walls. There was close control also of temperature and, generally, of all extraneous stimulation. In this tradition the control is for a relatively few, well specified, alternative hypotheses. The specific alternatives controlled for (never perfectly, but sufficiently well to render them implausible) depend on what seems to be important at the time – essentially, that is, on the current theories and models. Moving out of the laboratory does not negate this approach, but does make it much more difficult to achieve the required degree of 'plausibility-reduction' of specific hypotheses, simply because we cannot have comparable isolation or control (Campbell, 1989).

The next chapter covers the design of both true and quasi-experiments in field settings. The special case of single-subject experimental designs, deriving from Skinner's approach to the experimental analysis of behaviour, is also covered.

Box 3.4 Example of the use of an experimental strategy

Diaper (1990) describes a study which compares the relative effectiveness of three approaches to the teaching of reading to children in a junior school. The approaches were variants of 'paired reading' (Topping, 1988) – a technique involving the use of parents as teachers.

One approach was 'classical' paired reading. This involves the child and parent initially reading the book out loud together in close synchrony ('simultaneous reading'). When children have gained confidence they read alone to the parent ('independent reading'), with the parent asked to refrain from any criticism. At the first error children are given 5–6 seconds to correct; if they don't the parent returns to simultaneous reading.

'Classical' paired reading was contrasted in the study with two other approaches where either the 'simultaneous' or the 'independent' technique was used by itself. There are advocates of these simplified versions of paired reading, which are known as 'shared reading' and 'relaxed reading' respectively.

Three groups of fifteen children with parents selected from those who agreed to participate were randomly assigned to the three conditions of 'classical', 'shared' or 'relaxed' reading. A control group, randomly selected from children who, so far as it was possible to ascertain, were not being read to by their parents, continued (as did other groups) to receive normal reading tuition in the classroom.

During a nine-week intervention period experimental group children had fifteen-minute sessions six times a week with their parents. A standard reading test (the 'Edinburgh' test) was administered to the whole of the year group immediately before the intervention, and immediately afterwards.

Means and standard deviations of the change in reading were:

	Mean change	Standard deviation
Classical	9.13	4.44
Shared	5.53	6.29
Relaxed	5.20	5.71
Control	5.93	5.48

Diaper's hypothesis of significantly greater progress being made in the 'classical' conditions, as against the other two experimental conditions and the control condition, was supported by statistical analysis.

Comments

An experiment was *feasible* here because substantial previous work of a less formal nature had established the conditions likely to be of interest and appropriate measures of the dependent variable.

It was also *desirable* as methodological weaknesses of some earlier studies by 'enthusiastic teachers with varying degrees of acquaintance with research methods' had lead to critical comments such as those of Hannon and Tizard (1987) to the effect that the claims of paired reading were overstated and its findings dubious.

The 'classical' condition differed from the 'shared' and 'relaxed' reading conditions, not only in the reading conditions but also in that while the former involved a series of fortnightly visits from the author, the other two involved a similar number of telephone calls from him. While this is appropriate, in that it mimics the conditions under which they are typically used, it leaves open the possibility that it is 'home visits' which are the active ingredient in the difference between the conditions.

Whereas the three experimental groups were randomly assigned, the control group was simply selected (on a random basis) from those not otherwise participating in the study. These later parents were, apparently, ones who had not volunteered. There are understandable difficulties in choosing a control group from among the volunteers (volunteering to do nothing with their children!) but it leaves open the possibility that there are systematic differences between parents in the experimental and control groups.

(*Source*: Diaper, G., 1990.)

Survey Methodology

The term 'survey' is used in a variety of ways, but commonly refers to the collection of standardized information from a specific population, or some sample from one, usually but not necessarily by means of questionnaire or interview. Generally, a relatively small amount of information is collected from any one individual, contrasting with a case study, where a great deal of information might be obtained from a 'key informant'. There is normally no attempt to manipulate variables, or control conditions, as would be the case in experimentation. Surveys are well suited to descriptive studies where the interest is, say, in how many people in a given population possess a particular attribute, opinion or whatever. However, survey data can also be used to explore aspects of a situation, or to seek explanation and provide data for testing hypotheses.

Samples tend to be large in surveys and the questions asked are usually of a type that requires careful attention to how samples are drawn, typically on a representative and/or random basis. The interest is not normally on individuals per se, but on profiles and generalized statistics drawn from the total sample and generalized to the population.

Surveys are often CROSS-SECTIONAL STUDIES. That is, the focus is on the make-up of the sample, and the state of affairs in the population at just one point in time. The value of this kind of 'snap-shot' approach depends crucially on choosing a representative, non-biased sample. This is usually large in size to ensure that, through statistical means, we have a high degree of confidence as to the state of affairs in the population. However, in a psychological rather than statistical sense, confidence in the overall picture is dependent on the quality of the individual responses and there is legitimate scepticism about whether or not the often perfunctory survey responses carry real meaning. Try observing yourself the next time you are asked to fill in a market research or other survey form, and see how far you feel that similar responses, aggregated, are likely to be trustworthy!

When the main interest is in describing or assessing change or development over time, some form of LONGITUDINAL RESEARCH is the method of choice. The same set of people, and/or the same issue or situation, is studied over a period of time. This form of research tends to be difficult to carry out and is demanding on the time and resources of the investigator. 'Mortality' within the sample can be a problem, not so much in terms of the actual death of people, but more their inaccessibility or non-availability through geographical moves or an unwillingness to continue co-operating with the study. A survey is often the main approach in this kind of research, but there is no reason in principle why experiments or case studies could not be chosen.

Box 3.5   Example of the use of a survey strategy

Newcombe et al. (1991) surveyed 388 American university students through a 'drinking and driving' questionnaire. Those students answering positively to the question 'Have you been in the situation where you saw someone who you thought was too drunk to drive within the past year?' (303 students) were used in the analysis. Sixty-three per cent of this sample were women, 66 per cent of whom reported having intervened to present the person from driving while drunk; 63 per cent of the men had done so.

Thirty-eight items and scales in the questionnaire related to the individual's background and her or his responses in the situation. Additional questions were asked about the persons involved, the driver, prior 'driving under the influence' experiences, and the context of the intervention.

The paper includes a review of the very extensive experimental research on 'helping', which has primarily taken place in controlled laboratory settings. This has led to the development of several conceptual models of helping behaviour. However, little is known about the prevalence or the processes of helping behaviour in real world settings. This laboratory research, and the relatively small specific literature on drunk driving intervention, provided the hypotheses for the study.

Partial support was found for these hypotheses. The most important variables relating to intervention were: –

a how well the respondent knew the driver;
b having a conversation that encouraged her/him to intervene;
c whether the driver was in need of help; and
d the respondent's perceived ability to intervene.

Overall there are puzzling discrepancies between the laboratory findings on helping and the results of the survey. The authors recommend supplementing surveys with participant observation and in-depth interviews. They conclude that 'the flexibility, complexity and interplay between the person, their relationship to the potential drunk driver and to others in the situation, and to the situation itself suggests a complexity that implies that laboratory studies may no longer be useful in understanding this type of helping behaviour' (p. 203).

(*Source*: Newcomb et al., 1991.)

Case Study Methodology

In case study, the CASE is the situation, individual, group, organization or whatever it is that we are interested in. Case study has been around for a long time and to some it will suggest the legal system, to others the medical one. Bromley (1986) points out that case study can be found in areas as disparate as administration, anatomy, anthropology, artificial intelligence, biochemistry, business studies, clinical medicine, counselling, crimimology, education, gerontology, history, industrial relations, jurisprudence, management, military studies, personality, politics, psychiatry, social work and sociology. We will in fact find that the strategies developed for dealing with cases in other disciplines have useful lessons for us, suggesting solutions to problems with case study methodology, including the thorny one of generalizing from the individual case.

There is some danger in using a well worn term like case study. Paradoxically, all such terms carry 'excess baggage' around with them; surplus meanings and resonances from these previous usages. Miles and Huberman (1984) prefer to use the term 'site' rather than case, but this carries a strong geographical flavour rather than the desired human one. So let us stick with case study.

The intention is to provide guidance in carrying out *rigorous* case studies. This involves attention to matters of design, data collection, analysis, interpretation and reporting which form a major part of later chapters. Before getting on with this, however, let us be clear as to what we mean by case study. The definition given in the first chapter was:

Case study is a strategy for doing research which involves an empirical investigation of a particular contemporary phenomenon within its real life context using multiple sources of evidence.

The important points are that it is:

- a *strategy*, i.e. a stance or approach, rather than a method, such as observation or interview;
- concerned with *research*, taken in a broad sense and including, for example, evaluation;
- *empirical* in the sense of relying on the collection of evidence about what is going on;
- about the *particular*; a study of that specific case (the issue of what kind of generalization is possible from the case, and of how this might be done, will concern us greatly);
- focused on a *phenomenon in context*, typically in situations where the boundary between the phenomenon and its context is not clear; and
- using *multiple methods* of evidence or data collection.

Box 3.6   Example of the use of a case study strategy

Barrett and Cooperrider (1990) describe a case study based on their involvement as consultants with the 'Medic Inn': a hotel, originally privately owned, which was bought by the Midwest Clinic Foundation in conjunction with a local hospital and clinic, so that they could provide lodging and food to patients and their families.

The foundation wished to move the hotel up-market to become a 'four-star' facility. The consultants were brought in because interpersonal and interdepartmental conflicts were impeding the change.

Their involvement included an attitude survey of all 260 employees, participant observation of meetings of the four top managers of the hotel, and private interviews with them. Similar data were collected from thirteen middle managers.

This initial involvement over a period of more than a year fully documented the conflicts, tensions and competition within the organization. A traditional 'action research' approach at this stage would have involved a sequence of analyzing the causes of the problems; feeding back the themes; and asking group members to face up to the issues and generate collaborative action plans.

In this case that approach was judged to be likely to be counterproductive in that members knew all too well what their problems and tensions were. The consultants sought to break through this existing framework by organizing a five-day visit with thirty of the managers to a very successful four-star hotel in another part of the country. They asked for interpersonal and intergroup difficulties in the Medic Inn to be put on one side, so that the group could become a 'learning system' free of day-to-day responsibilities.

Using a technique known as 'appreciative inquiry' (Cooperrider and Srivastva, 1987), the visiting managers were asked to be field researchers, establishing through observation and interviews the ways in which the successful hotel worker – and might work even better. The intention was to help the managers learn about themselves indirectly through immersing themselves in the life and detail of another organization.

The study concludes with a discussion of the (apparently very successful) consequences of this intervention on the functioning of the Medic Inn. It concentrates specifically on the changes in the discourse of various staff groups in the months immediately after the visit.

The case study is essentially exploratory. It seeks to document a particular approach to facilitating organizational development. In addition to being a piece of practical consultancy, it also seeks to provide support for the utility of a particular theoretical framework – the 'generative metaphor' (Schon, 1979).

Note: See also Krantz (1990), who provides a commentary which, while fully accepting the interest and value of the intervention, queries the value of the theoretical framework used.

(*Source*: Barrett and Cooperrider, 1990.)

Treating Other Enquiries as Case Studies

An experiment or a survey necessarily takes place in a specific context or contexts, at a particular time. It constitutes for you, as an enquirer, an episode in your life and career. It will often be possible to buttress the main method of data collection by additional ones; perhaps interviews or questionnaires in an experiment, some form of observation in a survey. Hence such studies can, not unreasonably, be viewed as case studies.

To qualify as experiments or surveys they must, of course, also fulfil canons of experimental or survey design such as random allocation of subjects to conditions, or whatever. Looking at them in case study terms encourages the use of multiple methods of investigation. It also licenses the enquirer to adopt the more flexible and overtly involved stance which characterizes case study. For example, your own impressions and perceptions about the processes you are studying can be brought out into the open (rather than being smuggled in or left unacknowledged). An alternative way of viewing this is to see such studies as using rather different, hybrid, strategies (see below); or to say that there is likely advantage if case study thinking were to permeate the other strategies.

Box 3.7   Example of the use of a multiple strategy

Kiely and Hodgson (1990) examined the place of stress in the job and role of prison officers, to assess the value and benefits of exercise programmes. Their study involved a substantial review of the research literature and theoretical conceptualizations of occupational stress; and of existing research on the value of exercise to offset that stress.

The empirical study was multi-method and included three data collection exercises, two of these being case studies and the third a small survey.

First, a visit was made to a young offender prison establishment in the north-east of England, which had been operating an exercise programme for its staff for three years. This in itself effectively constituted an abbreviated case study, conducted by means of informal semi-structured interviews with the governor and fourteen other officers. The latter represented about a quarter of the staff on duty, and were selected by the interviewer to cover a range of grades and specialisms.

Second, the governors of each of the closed young offender prisons in a geographical region (the midlands) were surveyed by means of a postal questionnaire. The questionnaire asked for statistical information on both staff and inmate populations, including details of staff sick leave, overtime and staff voluntary physical education hours. A second section covered open-ended questions on governors' beliefs about the main causes of occupational stress in their prison officers' work.

Third, in-depth interviews were carried out with a selection of staff who had experienced an illness which had been attributed to stress. Three case reports were presented 'in order to provide a richer picture of some of the effects of stress on prison officers' lives'.

The combination of survey and case studies (both institutional and individual) provides useful complementary information giving valuable insights into the issues.

The study is primarily exploratory and makes suggestions about ways in which physical exercise programmes might be evaluated and, more generally, how occupational stress in this context might be combatted.

(*Source*: Kiely and Hodgson, 1990.)

Implications of Taking Case Study Seriously

Box 3.8 Example of the use of a hybrid strategy

Littlewood et al. (1990) carried out a study based on a sample of twenty home kidney dialysis patients. Half (five males and five females) were undergoing hemodialysis, involving the removal by machine of toxic substances. The other half (also five males and five females) were undergoing peritoneal dialysis which involves fluid circling through the peritoneum either from bags or via a machine. One person of each sex from both treatment groups was taken from each decade between 20 and 60 years of age.

The data were collected by means of a semi-structured interview designed to explore relevant issues, tasks and coping strategies.

The data were analysed qualitatively and revealed three types of strategy used by people to cope with their condition. These were typified as *cognitions* (thinking about people in a worse situation and thinking of pleasant past experiences); *social relations* (e.g. descriptions of support received from others including family, friends and hospital staff); and *leisure activities* (a wide range of strategies engaged in, either during or between dialysis sessions).

All respondents used all of these coping strategies and there was no evidence that some used particular strategies more than others.

However, they did appear to have different coping *styles*. Four viewed dialysis as a temporary phase – even though for two of them this phase had already been going on for several years. Seven coped by adjusting their lifestyle. Four were resigned and coped by giving up activities. The remaining five actively resisted the implications of dialysis.

The study is exploratory and could, for example, form the basis for a larger-scale survey where tentative suggestions made here about possible relationships between coping style, age, sex, type of treatment and length of time on dialysis could be investigated.

Comment: The study has some features of a survey. Careful attention has been given to the construction of a representative sample. However, semi-structured interviews are employed yielding qualitative data. It also has some features reminiscent of a case study. Attempts were made to understand the lifestyle of each individual in his or her particular context. However, only one data collection method is used.

(*Source*: Littlewood et al., 1990.)

Valsiner (1986) claims that 'the study of individual cases has always been the major (albeit often unrecognized) strategy in the advancement of knowledge about human beings' (p. 11). In similar vein, Bromley (1986) maintains that 'the individual case study or situation analysis is the bed-rock of scientific investigation' (p. ix). But he also notes, in an unattributed quotation, the common view that 'science is not concerned with the individual case' (p. xi). These widely divergent claims betray a deep-rooted uncertainty about the place and value of studying cases.

Case study is commonly considered in methodology texts as a kind of 'soft option', possibly admissible as an exploratory precursor to some more 'hard-nosed' experiment or survey, or as a complement to such approaches, but of dubious value by itself. Campbell and Stanley (1963) present an extreme version of this view:

> Such studies often involve tedious collection of specific detail, careful observation, testing and the like, and in such instances involve the error of misplaced precision. How much more valuable the study would be if the one set of observations were reduced by half and the saved effort directed to the study in equal detail of an appropriate comparison instance. It seems well-nigh unethical at present to allow, as theses or dissertations in education, case studies of this nature. (p. 177)

However, Campbell has subsequently recanted to some extent. Cook and Campbell (1979), for example, see case study as a fully legitimate alternative to experimentation in appropriate circumstances, and make the point that 'case study as normally practiced should not be demeaned by identification with the one-group post-test-only design' (p. 96). The central point that they have conceded is that *case study is not a flawed experimental design; it is a fundamentally different research strategy with its own designs.*

It is useful to separate out criticisms of the practice of particular case studies from what some have seen as inescapable deficiencies of the strategy itself. As Bromley (1986) points out, 'case studies are sometimes carried out in a sloppy, perfunctory, and incompetent manner and sometimes even in a corrupt, dishonest way' (p. xiii). Even with good faith and intentions, biased and selective accounts are undoubtedly possible. Similar criticisms could be made about any research strategy, of course. The issue is whether or not it is possible to devise appropriate checks to demonstrate what in experimental design terms is referred to as the reliability and validity of the findings (see p. 67).

Nisbet and Watt (1980) make the rather different point that case study is not considered by some as research in that it is 'thought to require artistic or literary skills, in contrast to 'true research' which was thought to depend on skills of numeracy and statistical analysis' (p. 8). This is a strange criterion for deciding what constitutes research, and seems difficult to justify. Admittedly, there is truth in the claim that case study reports call on artistic and literary skills and that some of the potential advantages of case study, such as giving what Nisbet calls the 'three-dimensional reality of a good documentary', depend crucially on well developed literary skills. It has to be said, though, that the account of even the most quantitative laboratory study benefits from writing skills – with an unfortunately not uncommon lack of communication to the reader when they are absent.

The notion that 'true research' depends on skills of numeracy and statistical analysis requires careful unpacking. The view of case study presented here in no sense excludes the use of quantitative methods – though, admittedly, many case studies rely exclusively on a set of qualitative techniques. Numeracy, then, may well be called on for case study research. Admittedly, the type of quantitative analysis appropriate for case study can differ radically from that called for in experimental research, and is currently poorly developed.

In what sense would a case study which relied solely on qualitative techniques not be 'true research'? This perhaps turns on whether or not it is possible to attain a corresponding degree of rigour in dealing with qualitative data to that achievable with quantitative data. This is an issue which will greatly exercise us in chapter 12. It may however be that the hidden concern is that this is not 'true' research in the sense that it is not scientific. This returns us to the fundamental issue. Can case study, quintessentially the study of the particular, be scientific?

Is Case Study Scientific?

Contrary to common preconceptions, including those of many who regard themselves as scientists, and not a few of those who would be disturbed to be so labelled, it is not obvious what is meant by science or the scientific method. Chalmers (1982), for example, spends nearly two hundred pages trying to answer his own question: 'What is this thing called science?'

The *achievements* of natural science (prototypically physics and chemistry) in Western society are undoubtedly spectacular, even though not universally regarded as beneficial. Following this success, rational enquiry and the scientific method are, in many quarters, regarded as the primary means whereby problems in society can be solved (Ehrenfeld, 1978).

Why? What is it about science that has produced these effects? A major breakthrough is usually attributed to Francis Bacon and his seventeenth-century contemporaries who insisted that 'to understand nature we must consult nature' rather than seek to interpret received knowledge from Aristotle or other ancient philosophers. This empiricist view of experience as the source of knowledge remains central to mainstream views of science.

The common popular view of science derives from this. Chalmers (1982) presents the following as a widely held common-sense view of science:

> Scientific knowledge is proven knowledge. Scientific theories are derived in some rigorous way from the facts of experience acquired by observation and experiment. Science is based on what we can see and hear and touch, etc. Personal opinion or preferences and speculative imaginings have no place in

science. Science is objective. Scientific knowledge is reliable knowledge because it is objectively proven knowledge. (p. 1)

Chalmers, in his very readable account of recent developments in the philosophy of science, demolishes this 'naive inductivist' view of science. None of the above statements is defensible either as a view of science or as an account of how scientists (including 'hard-line' natural scientists) actually go about 'doing science'. He shows that:

- ultimately, there is no fully proven scientific knowledge;
- there is no foolproof or automatic method for deriving scientific theories from the 'facts' of experience;
- science is based on many other things as well as what we can see, hear, etc.;
- the person of the scientist and her or his opinions, prejudices, etc. loom large in science;
- objectivity can not be guaranteed.

To take just one aspect: whereas the traditional, common-sense view is that 'facts are facts' – that is, they are 'objectively true' and independent of the theories we might have – it is now appreciated that observation is 'theory-laden'. All perception is to an extent shaped by the preconceptions and purposes of the observer. This comes as no surprise to psychologists who have studied perception and is central to the HERMENEUTIC VIEW which holds that our perceptions are actively created rather than passively received. This applies just as much to the specialized situations which scientists find themselves observing, as to the lay person in an everyday setting. The implication is that what we see depends upon more than what we are looking at. Hence, science cannot rest on observation alone; theory and observation are inextricably linked (Manicas and Secord, 1983).

This is not the place to detail modern attempts to improve on and replace naïve inductivism. Such an undertaking would cover Karl Popper's falsificationism and Imre Lakatos's elaboration and critique of Popper; Thomas Kuhn's views about theories and how science develops; and Paul Feyerabend's anarchistic dismissal of scientific method, to name but a few (e.g. Kuhn, 1970; Lakatos and Musgrave, 1970; Feyerabend, 1975; Toulmin, 1967).

It is clear that there is a large gap between the practices of scientists, and the philosophy of science which is commonly offered as a 'rational reconstruction' of these practices; and that there may be very little resemblance between the work-site practices of science and our widely shared understanding of science (Manicas, 1987, p. 242). For example, Becher (1990), talking to physicists on physics, is told by them that the notion of a 'value-free' scientific method is incorrect. The paradox is that while

the practices of physical scientists bear little resemblance to the dominant philosophy of science, it is no exaggeration to say that in consequence of their relatively late beginning as 'sciences' the *practices of mainstream social science have long since been constituted by it.* (Manicas, 1987, pp. 242–3)

It is heartening to note the philosopher Chalmers (1982) concluding that

> philosophers do not have resources that enable them to legislate on the criteria that must be satisfied if an area of knowledge is to be deemed acceptable or 'scientific'. Each area of knowledge can be analyzed for what it is. . . . From this point of view we do not need a general category 'science' with respect to which some area of knowledge can be acclaimed as science or denigrated as non-science. (p. 166)

While this appears to have a 'relativist' flavour, suggesting that 'anything goes', Chalmers tempers this by also stressing the 'realist' aspect that the whole point of the activity, why the theory is developed etc. is 'to attempt to come to grips with some aspect of the world'.

Given, then, that there are no universal conceptions of science and scientific method which will allow us to decide whether or not a particular area falls within the pale, how do we proceed? His suggestion is that if we wish to make decisions about X (which might be Marxism, astrology, or whatever) we need to concern ourselves with: –

- What are its aims?
- What are the methods used to achieve these aims?
- To what extent do the methods enable the aims to be achieved?
- What interests does it serve?

Case study does not appear to present any special difficulties on this view of science. The study of the particular, which is central to case study, is not excluded in principle; it is the aims and intentions of the study, and the specific methods used, that have to concern us. Carr and Kemmis (1986) reach very similar conclusions:

> what distinguishes scientific knowledge is not so much its logical status, as the fact that it is the outcome of a process of enquiry which is governed by critical norms and standards of rationality. (p. 121)

Post-positivist Science and Case Study

The undoubted deficiencies of the traditional view of science have stimulated the development of a very different paradigm, variously labelled as 'post-positivistic', 'ethnographic', 'phenomenological', 'subjective', 'hermeneutic', 'humanistic' and 'naturalistic' (this is not to suggest that their aficionados would accept the interchangeability of these labels). Some proponents of what is sometimes termed 'new paradigm research' are antagonistic to it being labelled as 'scientific', but many seek to reassure the reader that it is fully encompassable within science (e.g. Lincoln and Guba, 1985).

Most of the distinguishing features of the post-positivist paradigm have emerged from within 'hard' science (Hesse, 1980). Indeed, Garrison (1986) claims that 'all sciences are, to some degree, interpretive and hermeneutical, all observation participant observation' (p. 16). However, the new paradigm appears particularly compelling for studies involving human beings, where particular problems and opportunities arise from the fact that both the enquirer and the subjects of the enquiry are from the same species (Heron, 1981). Susman and Evered (1978) stress the difficulties of positivistic science when working with humans. Values necessarily intrude. Treating people as objects ignores their ability to reflect on problems and situations, and act upon this. Their solution is ACTION RESEARCH. As the name indicates, this is concerned both with action (solving concrete problems in real situations) and research (trying to further the goals of science) (Rapoport, 1970). Action research is further discussed in the final chapter as a possible solution to the problem of ensuring that research findings actually get used. It is at present unclear whether the post-positivist view can reach some kind of rapprochement with more traditional views of what constitutes experimental psychology, and in particular the kind of hypothesis-testing approach of Fisherian designs (see Campbell, 1989 for a positive view).

Lincoln and Guba (1985) list a range of characteristics of what they term as 'naturalistic enquiry', summarized in box 3.9. They make a strong point of the interdependence and coherence of this set of characteristics. For example:

- In doing research from a naturalistic perspective, the enquirer must work in the natural setting.
- If starting without a formal a priori theory or hypotheses then it is not possible to specify properly what should be controlled, or even exactly what should be studied.
- In advance of time and involvement in the setting, the focus can not be specified, except in very broad or general terms, nor can boundaries be put on the study. An experiment could not be designed because the experimenter would not know the relevant variables.
- To 'ground' theory in data, the data must be collected and then analysed (inductively).
- Not knowing the precise form of the data to be collected, the flexibility and adaptability of the human as instrument come into their own.
- The congeniality to humans of seeing, hearing and reading, facilitates their formalization into the qualitative methods of observation, interviewing and documentary analysis respectively.
- Idiographic interpretations arise from this, negotiated with respondents.
- These have only tentative applicability to other settings.
- The case study report is well suited to this exercise.
- It makes contact with the readers' own tacit knowledge of related or similar situations, and hence encourages generalization.
- The trustworthiness of this whole enterprise must be assessed through criteria appropriate to the nature of the enquiry.

The 'naturalistic enquiry' they advocate, as being particularly appropriate for real world research, shares many characteristics with case study as conceptualized here.

Box 3.9 Characteristics of 'naturalistic enquiry'

1 *Natural setting* Research is carried out in the natural setting or context of the entity studied.

2 *Human instrument* The enquirer(s), and other humans, are the primary data-gathering instruments.

3 *Use of tacit knowledge* Tacit (intuitive, felt) knowledge is a legitimate addition to other types of knowledge.

4 *Qualitative methods* Qualitative rather than quantitative methods tend to be used (though not exclusively) because of their sensitivity, flexibility and adaptability.

5 *Purposive sampling* Purposive sampling is likely to be preferred over representative or random sampling, as it increases the scope or range of data exposed and is more adaptable.

6 *Inductive data analysis* Inductive data analysis preferred over deductive as it makes it easier to give a fuller description of the setting and brings out interactions between enquirer and respondents.

7 *Grounded theory* Preference for theory to emerge from (be grounded in) the data.

8 *Emergent design* Research design emerges (unfolds) from the interaction with the study.

9 *Negotiated outcomes* Preference for negotiating meanings and interpretations with respondents.

10 *Case study reporting mode* Preferred because of its adaptability and flexibility.

11 *Idiographic interpretation* Tendency to interpret data idiographically (in terms of the particulars of the case) rather than nomothetically (in terms of law-like generalizations).

12 *Tentative application* Need for tentativeness (hesitancy) in making broad applications (generalizations) of the data.

13 *Focus-determined boundaries* Boudaries are set on the basis of the emergent focus of the enquiry.

14 *Special criteria for trustworthiness* Special criteria for trustworthiness (equivalent to reliability, validity and objectivity) devised which are appropriate to the form of the enquiry.

(Adapted from Lincoln and Guba, 1985, pp. 39–45.)

Experimenters and Case Study

Readers with a psychological background, steeped in traditional experimental design methodology, might, notwithstanding the earlier discussion of the inadequacies of the positivistic paradigm, be unwilling to take this naturalistic, case study approach seriously.

Without wishing to caricature such readers as the equivalent of the 'Paduan professors who refused to look through Galileo's telescope' (Harré, 1981), sceptical experimentalists might like to reflect on the relationship between the account given of an experimental study in the standardized journal format and the reality of the experiences and processes that the author went through in actually carrying out the experiment.

Bargar and Duncan (1982) consider that reporting practices lead scientists to 'inadvertently hide from the real inner drama of their work, with its intuitive base, its halting time-line and its extensive recycling of concepts and perspectives' (p. 2). Shipman (1988), in an analysis of discrepancies between scientific activity in practice and in theory, claims that 'the deception of science publicised as the impinging of facts on an open mind followed by induction to derive theories from this evidence is built into every scientific paper'. Medawar (1963) goes so far as to argue that the scientific paper is a fraud because it suggests that observation and experiment are followed by discussion of the results obtained, whereas the actual process in fact starts with the expectations, built into models, that guide the observations made and their interpretation.

It is, in fact, the first stage, the 'inspiration, creation, imagination and guesswork that finally leads to a hypothesis' (Shipman, 1988, p. 10) which might be thought of as the 'real' science. The confirmatory process, admittedly involving rigorous testing, is essentially run-of-the-mill. Psychological experimentation is a particular slave to this confirmatory aspect. Cronbach (1982) has suggested that confirmation has taken precedence over discovery within experimental psychology because Fisher, though personally conscious of, and indeed stressing in his writings, the heuristic, discovery aspect to experimental work, was only able to offer a theory covering the confirmatory aspects. Hence, because of the lack of systematization of the former part, there has been undue concentration on the formalized confirmatory aspect.

My own experience, particularly with quasi-experiments in field settings, suggests that in practice, they come much closer to the case study and the naturalistic paradigm, with greater reliance on emergent design, inductive analysis, human-as-observer, inclusion of qualitative data, etc., than would ever be guessed by the reader of the resulting publication (Robson, 1985). This might be taken as a reversion to the older view that case study is 'primarily a preliminary or adjunct research technique in the social sciences, rather than a workable method in its own right' (Neale and Lambert, 1986, p. 31). However, while experimental researchers might well conduct rigorous case studies as a precursor to work in the laboratory, or as an adjunct or subsequent to laboratory work, the argument is that case study methodology 'in the real world' can provide a rigorous approach to all aspects of the enquiry where you can 'tell it as it is', rather than disguise it in the formalized straitjacket of the experimental report.

This may seem too radical a departure, ensuring rejection of your cherished article by traditionally minded journal editors. A more modest proposal is to follow the earlier suggestion and conceptualize your immaculately designed experiments *also* as case studies. This may provide a means of formalizing and highlighting the 'discovery' aspect of what you are doing. In its turn, this may help in interpreting what the experiment is actually telling you.

Feminist Research and Sexism

Feminist commentators and researchers have, in the past twenty years, made a convincing case for the existence of sexist bias in research. This is seen in all areas of science, including the natural sciences (e.g. Harding and Hintikha, 1983) but is obviously of great concern in the social sciences where the human, in one or both genders, is the enquirer and the enquired-upon. There is now a substantial literature on this area (e.g. Harding, 1987; Roberts, 1981; Stanley and Wise, 1983; Smith, 1987; Hollway, 1989; Eichler, 1980).

Eichler (1988), in a clear and readable analysis applicable to all social science disciplines, suggests that sexism in research arises from four 'primary problems': androcentricity, overgeneralization, gender insensitivity and double standards. She also argues that there are three further problems, which while logically derived from and falling within the primary problems, occur so frequently as to merit separate identification – sex appropriateness, familism and sexual dichotomism. Box 3.10 gives an indication of the meaning of these terms.

This analysis covers a much wider range of issues than the use of sexist language. It is now generally accepted that such language should be avoided when reporting research and several sets of guidelines exist aiming to sensitize people to the forms that sexist language takes and suggesting nonsexist alternatives. For example, the BSA'S 'Guidelines on Anti-Sexist Language' (British Sociological Association, 1989a) include:

sexist	*anti-sexist*
man/mankind	person, people, human beings
man-made	synthetic, artificial, manufactured
manpower	workforce, staff, labourpower
manhours	workhours
forefathers	ancestors
master copy	top copy, original

Box 3.10   Sexism in research: sources of bias

1 *Androcentricity*   Viewing the world from a male perspective: e.g. when a test or other research instrument is developed and tested on males, and then assumed to be suitable for use with females. Note that *gynocentricity* (viewing the world from a female perspective) is, of course, also possible, though relatively rare.

2 *Overgeneralization*   When a study deals with only one sex but presents itself as generally applicable: e.g. a study dealing solely with mothers which makes statements about parents. *Overspecificity* can also occur when single-sex terms are used when both sexes are involved; e.g. many uses of 'man', either by itself or as in 'chairman'.

3 *Gender insensitivity*   Ignoring sex as a possible variable: e.g. when a study omits to report the sex of those involved.

4 *Double standards*   Evaluating, treating or measuring identical behaviours, traits or situations by different means for males and females: e.g. using female-derived categories of social status for males (or vice versa). This may well be not inappropriate in a particular study but nevertheless could lead to bias which should be acknowledged.

5 *Sex appropriateness*   A commonly used and accepted form of 'double standards': e.g. that child rearing is necessarily a female activity.

6 *Familism*   A particular instance of 'gender insensitivity'. Consists of treating the family as the smallest unit of analysis when it would be possible and appropriate to treat an individual as the unit.

7 *Sexual dichotomism*   Another instance of 'double standards': treating the sexes as two entirely distinct social groups rather than as groups with overlapping characteristics.

(Adapted from Eichler, 1988.)

The full guidelines are presented as appendix C. (There is a set of corresponding issues concerning racist language; see e.g. British Sociological Association, 1989b.)

Sexist language of this type is offensive to many as, in the language of the legal definition, the male term is simply assumed to 'embrace the female'. It can also be ambiguous, as in the use of 'businessman' (which can be generic in the sense of covering females as well as males), when only male managers are being referred to. Empirical studies have shown that the use of sexist language does make a difference in the inferences that readers draw (Adams and Ware, 1989; Pearson, 1985).

Problems arising from sexism can affect all aspects and stages of the research process, and both female and male readers and researchers are urged to be on their guard. Eichler (1988, pp. 170–5) provides a comprehensive 'Nonsexist Research Checklist' giving examples of how the various problems arise in the concepts employed in the research, its design, methods, data interpretation, etc.

Feminist Research Methodology

Some feminist researchers provide a more radical critique of science, and particularly of objectivity. Stanley and Wise (1983) maintain that objectivity is, in principle, impossible to achieve and that all research is effectively '... "fiction" in the sense that it views and so constructs "reality" through the eyes of one person' (p. 174). This stance casts serious doubts on the possibility of a science based on research generating cumulating knowledge. Others have suggested that it is possible to tease out some aspects of objectivity which are defensible from other indefensible aspects which have arisen from science having been to a large extent a male preserve. Keller (1985), for example, shows how objectivity has been equated with masculinity, leading to an assumed requirement that to be objective requires a distancing and detachment both emotionally and intellectually. Fee (1983) rejects this requirement, suggesting that emotional and social commitment is not inimical to scientific rationality. She also rejects the view that objectivity requires the separation of the production of knowledge through enquiry from its use, and the assumption that this knowledge is necessarily produced by experts who then pass it on to non-expert consumers in a one-way non-interactive manner.

Feminists have challenged not only the view of the way in which knowledge is produced but also whose view of the world it represents. For example: 'Research ... has been largely the instrument of dominance and legitimation of power elites' (Mies, 1983, p. 123). These reformulations of the nature of objectivity and of the enquiry process are very much in line with those developed earlier in this chapter in the discussion of postpositivistic science, and of the kinds of naturalistic enquiry which seem best fitted for carrying out 'real world' studies. Detachment in such studies is, as we have already seen, neither feasible nor desirable, especially not in those cases where there is a commitment to assist in change. As Chisholm (1990) puts it, 'the collision between theory and praxis [abstracted reflection on practice] is as emotionally significant as it is intellectually interesting' – there is a need to look coolly *and* passionately.

Nevertheless, we should strive to approach objectivity through:

1) a commitment to look at contrary evidence
2) a determination to aim at maximum replicability of any study (which implies accurate reporting of all processes employed and separation between simple reporting and interpretation ...)

3) a commitment to 'truth-finding' ... , and
4) a clarification and classification of values underlying the research ...
(Eichler, 1988, pp. 13–14)

Establishing Trustworthiness

How do you persuade your audiences, including most importantly yourself, that the findings of your enquiry are worth taking account of? What is it that makes the study believable and trustworthy? What are the kinds of argument that you can use? What questions should you ask? What criteria are involved?

Much of this is in the realms of common sense. Have you done a good, thorough and honest job? Have you tried to explore, describe or explain in an open and unbiased way, or are you more concerned with delivering the required answer or selecting the evidence to support a case? If you can't answer these questions with yes, yes and no respectively, then your findings are essentially worthless in enquiry terms. However, pure intentions do not guarantee findings that attract notice. You persuade others by clear, well written and presented, logically argued accounts which address the questions that concern them. These are all issues to which we will return in chapter 13 on reporting.

This is not simply a presentational matter, however. There are fundamental issues about the enquiry itself. Two key ones are VALIDITY and GENERALIZABILITY. Validity is concerned with whether the findings are 'really' about what they appear to be about. Are any relationships established in the findings 'true', or due to the effect of something else? (The scare quotes around 'really' and 'true' are intended to sensitize you to the problematic nature of these concepts.) Generalizability refers to the extent to which the findings of the enquiry are more generally applicable, for example in other contexts, situations or times, or to persons other than those directly involved.

Validity

Suppose that we have been asked to carry out some form of enquiry to address the research question

> *Is educational achievement in primary schools improved by the introduction of standard assessment tests at the age of seven?*

Leave aside, for the time being, issues about whether or not this is a sensible question and about the most appropriate way to approach it. Suppose that the findings of our enquiry indicated a 'yes' answer – possibly qualified in various ways. In other words, we measure educational achievement, and it appears to increase following the introduction of the tests. Is this relationship what it appears to be – is there a 'real', direct, link between the two things?

Central to the scientific approach is a degree of scepticism about our findings and their meaning (and even greater scepticism about other people's!). Can we have been fooled so that we are mistaken about them? Unfortunately, yes – there is a wide range of possibilities for confusion and error.

Reliability Some problems come under the heading of reliability. For example, consider how we are going to assess educational achievement. This is no easy task. Possible contenders, each with their own problems, might include:

- a formal 'achievement test' administered at the end of the primary stage of schooling;
- teachers' ratings, also at the end of the primary stage;
- the number, level and standard of qualifications gained throughout life.

Let's say we go for the first. It will not be difficult to devise something which will generate a score for each pupil. However, this might be unreliable in the sense that if a pupil had, say, taken it on Thursday rather than Wednesday, she would have got a quite different score. There are logical problems in assessing this, which can be attacked in various ways (e.g. by having parallel forms of the test which can be taken at different times, and their results compared). These are important considerations in test construction – see chapter 9, p. 266 for further details.

Unless a measure is reliable, it cannot be valid. However, while reliability is necessary, it is not sufficient. A test for which all pupils always got full marks would be totally reliable but would be useless as a way of discriminating between the achievements of different pupils (there could of course be good educational reasons for such a test if what was important was mastery of some material).

Unreliability may have various causes. One is usually termed SUBJECT ERROR. In our example the pupil's performance might fluctuate widely from occasion to occasion on a more or less random basis. Tiredness due to late nights could produce changes for different times of the day, pre-menstrual tension monthly effects or hay fever seasonal ones. There are tactics which can be used to ensure that these kinds of fluctuations do not bias the findings, particularly when specific sources of error can be anticipated (e.g. keep testing away from the hay fever season). More problematic from a validity point of view are sources of SUBJECT BIAS. It could be that pupils might seek to please or help their teacher, knowing the importance of 'good results', by making a particularly strong effort at the test. Here it would be very difficult to disentangle whether this was simply a short-term effect which had artificially boosted the test scores, or a desirable more long-lasting side-effect of a more testing-oriented primary school educational system. Consideration of potential errors of these kinds is part of the standard approach to experimental design – see chapter 4, p. 87 for details.

OBSERVER ERROR is another possible source of unreliability. This would be most obvious if the second approach, making use of teachers' ratings as the measure of pupil achievement, had been selected. These could also lead to more or less random errors if, for example, teachers made the ratings at a time when they were tired or overstretched and did the task in a cursory way. Again, there are pretty obvious remedies (perhaps involving the provision of additional resources). OBSERVER BIAS is also possible and, like subject bias, causes greater problems in interpretation. It could be that teachers in making the ratings were, consciously or unconsciously, biasing the ratings they gave in line with their ideological commitment either in favour of or against the use of standard assessment tests. This is also a well worked area methodologically, with procedures including 'blind' assessment (the ratings being made by someone in ignorance of whether the pupil had been involved in standard assessment tests) and the use of two independent assessers (so that inter-observer agreements could be computed). Further details are given in chapter 8, p. 221.

Construct validity   If you have made a serious attempt to get rid of subject and observer biases and have demonstrated the reliability of whatever measure you have decided on you will be making a pretty good job of measuring something. The issue then becomes – does it measure what you think it measures? In the jargon – does it have construct validity?

I have a vivid recollection of my first conscious involvement with research. This was at the age of ten when we were told at school one morning, without warning, that we were to be doing a research test. The test in question, emanating from a local university, involved the translation of passages from Latin into English. As we had had no previous language instruction in anything other than English, this caused some consternation, but being docile creatures, we got on and did as we were told. And had a repeat dose a few weeks later. I have never been able to discover the purpose of this exercise, though I am willing to believe that it had some influence on my later interest in both Latin and then research. However, suppose that this test were presented as a way of assessing educational achievement. The reliability of the test could well be unimpeachable. But is performance at this task a valid measure of educational achievement?

There is no easy, single, way of determining construct validity. At its simplest, one might look for what seems reasonable, sometimes referred to as FACE VALIDITY. On this, the Latin test would seem very dubious. The other extreme of effort might look at possible links between scores on the Latin test and the third suggested measure – the pupils' actual educational achievement in their later life (i.e. how well does it predict performance on the criterion in question, or PREDICTIVE CRITERION VALIDITY). These and other aspects of construct validity are central to the methodology of testing, which is discussed in detail in chapter 9, p. 255).

The methodological complexities of determining construct validity can lead to an unhealthy concentration on this aspect of carrying out an enquiry. For many studies there is an intuitive reasonableness to assertions that a certain approach provides an appropriate measure. One solution is to stay at the level of what is measured or observed, and not to attempt to go beyond this to some theoretical construct. This is central to the approach taken by Skinner and his colleagues (Sidman, 1960) which is discussed in more detail in the section of chapter 4 dealing with single-subject experimentation (p. 109).

Another tactic is to acknowledge that any one way of measuring or gathering data is likely to have its shortcomings and hence to take the *multi-method approach* which has already been advocated. One could use all three of the approaches to assessing educational achievement discussed above (achievement tests, teachers' ratings, and 'certificate counting') rather than relying on any one measure. Similar patterns of findings from very different methods of gathering data increase confidence in their validity. Discrepancies between them can be revealing in their own right. These issues are revisited in chapter 10, p. 289. It is important to realize, however, that multiple methods do not constitute a panacea for all methodological ills. They raise their own theoretical problems; and they may in many cases be so resource-hungry as to be impracticable.

Internal validity   Let us say that we have jumped the preceding hurdle and have demonstrated satisfactorily that we have a valid measure of educational achievement. However, that achievement increases *after* the introduction of the tests does not necessarily mean that increased *because* of the tests.

What we would like to do is to find out whether the treatment (introduction of the tests) actually caused the outcome (the increase in achievement). If a study can plausibly demonstrate this causal relationship between treatment and outcome, it is referred to as having INTERNAL VALIDITY. This term was introduced by Campbell and Stanley (1963), who provided an influential and widely used analysis of possible 'threats' to internal validity.

These threats are other things that might happen which confuse the issue and make us mistakenly conclude that the treatment caused the outcome (or obscure possible relationships between them). Suppose, for example, that the teachers of the primary school children involved in the study are in an industrial dispute with their employers at the same time that testing is introduced. One might well find, in those circumstances, a decrease in achievement related to the disaffection and disruption caused by the dispute, which might be mistakenly ascribed to the introduction of tests per se. This particular threat is labelled as 'history' by Campbell and Stanley – something which happens at the same time as the treatment. (There is the complicating factor here that a case might be made for negative effects on teaching being an integral part of the introduction of formal testing into a child-centred primary school culture, i.e. that they are part of the treatment rather than an extraneous factor. However, for simplicity's sake, let's say that the industrial dispute was an entirely separate matter.)

Campbell and Stanley (1963) suggested eight possible 'threats' to internal validity which might be posed by other, extraneous variables. Cook and Campbell (1979) have developed and extended this analysis, adding a further four threats. All twelve are listed in box 3.11.

Box 3.11   Threats to internal validity

1 *History* Things that have changed in the participants' environments other than those forming a direct part of the enquiry (e.g. occurrence of major air disaster during study of effectiveness of desensitization programme on persons with fear of air travel).

2 *Testing* Changes occurring as a result of practice and experience gained by participants on any pre-tests (e.g. asking opinions about factory farming of animals pre some intervention may lead respondents to think about the issues and develop more negative attitudes).

3 *Instrumentation* Some aspect(s) of the way participants were measured changed between pre-test and post-test (e.g. raters in observational study using a wider or narrower definition of a particular behaviour as they get more familiar with the situation).

4 *Regression* If participants are chosen because they are unusual or atypical (e.g. high scorers), later testing will tend to give less unusual scores ('regression to the mean'); e.g. an intervention programme with pupils with learning difficulties where ten highest-scoring pupils in a special unit are matched with ten of the lowest-scoring pupils in a mainstream school – regression effects will tend to show the former performing relatively worse on a subsequent test; see further details on p. 103.

5 *Mortality* Participants dropping out of the study (e.g. in study of adult literacy programme – selective drop-out of those who are making little progress).

6 *Maturation* Growth, change or development in participants unrelated to the treatment in the enquiry (e.g. evaluating extended athletics training programme with teenagers – intervening changes in height, weight and general maturity).

7 *Selection* Initial differences between groups prior to involvement in the enquiry (e.g. through use of arbitrary non-random rule to produce two groups: ensures they differ in one respect which may correlate with others).

8 *Selection by maturation interaction* Predisposition of groups to grow apart (or together if initially different); e.g. use of groups of boys and girls initially matched on physical strength in a study of a fitness programme.

9 *Ambiguity about causal direction* Does A cause B, or B cause A? (e.g. in any correlational study, unless it is known that A precedes B, or vice versa – or some other logical analysis is possible).

10 *Diffusion of treatments* When one group learns information or otherwise inadvertently receives aspects of a treatment intended only for a second group (e.g. in a quasi-experimental study of two classes in the same school).

11 *Compensatory equalization of treatments* If one group receives 'special' treatment there will be organizational and other pressures for a control group to receive it (e.g. nurses in a hospital study may improve the treatment of a control group on grounds of fairness).

12 *Compensatory rivalry* As above but an effect on the participants themselves (referred to as the 'John Henry' effect after the steel worker who killed himself through over-exertion to prove his superiority to the new steam drill); e.g. when a group in an organization sees itself under threat from a planned change in another part of the organization and improves performance).

(After Cook and Campbell, 1979, pp. 51–5.)

The labels used for the threats are not to be interpreted too literally – mortality doesn't necessarily refer to the death of a participant during the study (though it might!). Not all threats are present for all designs. For example, the 'testing' threat is only there if a pre-test is given, and in some cases, its likelihood, or perhaps evidence that you had gained from pilot work that a 'testing' effect was present, would cause you to avoid a design involving this feature.

In general design terms, there are two strategies to deal with these threats. If you know what the threat is, you can take specific steps to deal with it. For example, the use of comparison groups who have the treatment at different times or places will help to neutralize the 'history' threat. This approach of designing to deal with specific threats calls for a lot of forethought and is helped by knowledge and experience of the situation that you are dealing with. Moreover, you can only hope to deal with a fairly small number of predefined and articulated threats in this way. The alternative strategy, central to design philosophy in true experiments, is to use randomization, which helps offset the effect of a myriad of unforeseen factors.

True experiments are therefore very effective at dealing with these threats, though by no means totally immune to them. The threats have to be taken very seriously with quasi-experimental designs, surveys and case studies, and a study of the plausibility of the existence of various threats provides a very useful tool in interpretation. The interpretability of designs in the face of these threats depends not only on the design itself but on the specific pattern of results obtained (see chapter 4, p. 103 for an example).

If you rule out these threats, you have established internal validity. You will have shown (or, more strictly, demonstrated the plausibility) that a particular treatment caused a certain outcome. This might be what you are primarily interested in. You may have shown, say, that a new group work-shop approach leads to increases in self-esteem and subsequent maintained weight loss in obese teenagers at a residential unit. This may be the main thing that you are after if you are only concerned with whether or not the approach works with that specific group of individuals at the unit.

Generalizability

If, however, you are interested in what would happen with other client groups or in other settings, or with these teenagers when they return home, then you need to concern yourself with the generalizability of the study. Campbell and Stanley (1963) use the alternative term 'external validity'. Both this and generalizability are in common use. Internal and external validity tend to be inversely related in the sense that the various controls imposed in order to bolster internal validity often fight against generalizability. In particular, the fact that the laboratory is the controlled environment *par excellence* makes results obtained there very difficult to generalize to any settings other than close approximations to laboratory conditions.

If your teenagers are a representative sample from a known population, then the generalization to that population can be done according to the usual rules of statistical inference. Generalizability to other settings or to other client groups has to be done on other, non-statistical, bases. LeCompte and Goetz (1982) have provided a classification of threats to external validity similar to that given for internal validity, which is listed in box 3.12.

There are two general strategies for showing that these potential threats are discountable: direct demonstration and making a case. Direct demonstration involves you, or someone else who wishes to apply or extend your results, carrying out a further study involving some other type of participant, or in a different setting, etc. Making a case is more concerned with persuading that it is reasonable for the results to generalize, with arguments that the group studied, or setting, or period is representative in that it shares certain essential characteristics with other groups, settings or periods. This sorting out of the wheat of what is central to your findings from the chaff of specific irrelevancies can be otherwise expressed as having a theory or theoretical framework to explain what is going on.

Such a theory may be expressed in formal and explicit terms by the

---

Box 3.12 Threats to external validity

1 *Selection* Findings being specific to the group studied.

2 *Setting* Findings being specific to, or dependent on, the particular context in which the study took place.

3 *History* Specific and unique historical experiences may determine or affect the findings.

4 *Construct effects* The particular constructs studied may be specific to the group studied.

(After LeCompte and Goetz, 1982.)

---

presenter of the findings. Alternatively, the kind of rich or 'thick' description provided in a well written case study report can make contact with the more implicit and informal understandings held by readers who are able to see parallels with the situation in which they work or otherwise have knowledge about.

A study may be repeated with a different target group or in a deliberately different setting to assess the generalizability of its findings. There is also a case, particularly with important or controversial findings, for attempting a direct repetition of the original study. This is to try to assess the reliability of the findings (see p. 67). If a study were to be repeated with everything the same as the first time (known as an 'exact replication') and exactly the same results were obtained, then we would have total reliability. Such an enterprise is not at all straightforward. You couldn't use the same participants as they are not the same! They have been through the first study and will almost inevitably have been in some way affected or influenced by it. If you are in a position to use random samples from a defined population, then a solution is available which gives you similar participants. There are corresponding problems in dealing with the setting and just about every other feature of the study.

So, while in practice no replication is ever exact, an attempt to repeat the study as closely as possible which reproduces the main findings of the first study is the practical test of the reliability of your findings. Whether it is worthwhile to devote scarce resources to replication depends on circumstances. It is probably fair to say that it is nowhere near as common as it should be, and that in consequence we may well be seeking to build on very shaky foundations. The argument is sometimes put that as validity depends on reliability then we should simply worry about the validity; if we can show that validity is acceptable then, necessarily, so is reliability. The difficulty here is that it becomes more difficult to disentangle what lies behind poor validity. It might have been that the findings were not reliable in the first place.

It is easy to guarantee unreliability. Carelessness, casualness and lack of commitment on the part of the enquirer help, as does a corresponding lack of involvement by participants. Reliability is essentially a quality control issue. Punctilious attention to detail, perseverance and pride in doing a good job are all very important, but organization is the key. While validity and generalizability are probably the central elements in establishing the value and trustworthiness of an enquiry, there are many other aspects to which attention should be given. They include in particular objectivity and credibility.

Objectivity

The traditional, scientific approach to the problem of establishing objectivity is exemplified by the experimental approach, where, as Campbell (1969) puts it, 'The experiment is meticulously designed to put questions to "Nature Itself" in such a way that neither the questions, nor their colleagues, nor their superiors can affect the answer'. The solution here is seen to be to distance the experimenter from the experimental subject, so that any interaction that takes place between the two is formalized – indeed, some experimenters go so far as to not only have a standardized verbatim script but even to have it delivered via a tape-recorder.

To some, this artificiality is lethal for any real understanding of phenomena involving people in social settings. An alternative is to erect an objective/subjective contrast. 'Objective' is taken to refer to what multiple observers agree to as a phenomenon, in contrast to the subjective experience of the single individual. In other words, the criterion for objectivity is intersubjective agreement. This stance tends to go along with an involved rather than a detached investigator, and notions of 'triangulation' (see chapter 10, p. 290) where the various accounts of participants with different roles in the situation are obtained by investigators who, by combining them with their own perceptions and understandings, reach an agreed and negotiated account.

Formulated in terms of threats, objectivity can be seen to be at risk from a methodology where the values, interests and prejudices of the enquirer distort the response (experiment being for some the answer, and for others an extreme version of the problem). Relying exclusively on data from a single individual can similarly threaten objectivity. And again, enquiry carried out for an ideological purpose other than that of enquiry itself clearly threatens objectivity.

Credibility

Shipman (1988) has suggested that we should go beyond the traditional concerns for reliability, validity and generalizability when considering the trustworthiness of research and also ask the question: 'Is there sufficient detail on the way the evidence is produced for the credibility of the research to be assessed?' (p. x) We cannot satisfy ourselves about the other concerns unless the researcher provides sufficient information on the methods used and the justification for their use. This is a responsibility which has always been accepted by those using experimentation. The report of an experiment in a journal article carries an explicit requirement that sufficient detail must be given about procedures, equipment, etc. for the reader to carry out an exact replication of the study.

This kind of requirement may be rejected as scientist by some practitioners working within 'softer' interpretive or ethnographic traditions and relying virtually exclusively on qualitative data. However, there is a strong case for such research calling for an even greater emphasis on the methods used and the warrant for the conclusions reached, because of the lack of codification of the methods of data collection or of approaches to analysis. This need is increasingly recognized by methodologists sympathetic to qualitative approaches (e.g. Miles and Huberman, 1984; Strauss, 1987; Marshall and Rossman, 1989). Chapter 12 pays considerable attention to this issue.

Further Reading

Bromley, D. (1986) *The Case-study Method in Psychology and Related Disciplines.* Chichester: Wiley. Fundamental reappraisal of the place of case study. Repays serious study.

Campbell, D. T. and Stanley, J. C. (1963) Experimental and Quasi-experimental Designs for Research on Teaching. In N. L. Gage (ed.), *Handbook of Reseach on Teaching.* Chicago: Rard McNally. Also published separately as *Experimental and Quasi-experimental Designs for Research.* Chicago: Rand McNally. Slim monograph with classic exposition of the 'threats to validity' approach. To some extent superseded by Cook and Campbell (1979) but still worth reading as an easy introduction.

Chalmers, A. F. (1982) *What is This Thing Called Science?*, 2nd edn. Milton Keynes: Open University Press. Very accessible introduction to the 'new' philosophy of science.

Cook, T. D. and Campbell, D. T. (1979) *Quasi-Experimentation: design and analysis issues for field settings.* Chicago: Rand McNally. Invaluable aid to the design of field experiments. Chapter two provides essential reading on validity in field settings.

Hakim, C. (1987) *Research Design: Strategies and choices in the design of social research.* London: Allen & Unwin. Systematic coverage of all aspects of design. Includes both pure and applied (policy) research.

Harding, S. (ed.) (1987) *Feminism and Methodology.* Milton Keynes: Open University Press. Wide range of papers covering several disciplines.

Hollway, W. (1989) *Subjectivity and Method in Psychology: gender, meaning and science.* Newbury Park and London: Sage. Feminist re-creation of methodology from viewpoint that knowledge is produced and reproduced within specific historical conditions and power relations.

Kidder, L. H. (1981) Qualitative Research and Quasi-Experimental Frameworks. In M. B. Brewer and B. E. Collins (eds), *Scientific Inquiry and the Social Sciences*. San Francisco: Jossey-Bass. Applies the quantitative researcher's criteria for reliability and validity to qualitative studies.

Kirk, J. and Miller, M. L. (1986) *Reliability and Validity in Qualitative Research*. Newbury Park and London: Sage. Considered within an essentially traditional scientific perspective.

Marshall, C. and Rossman, G. B. (1989) *Designing Qualitative Research*. Newbury Park and London: Sage. Very accessible little book on issues involved in the design of case study type studies. Extensive use of illustrative vignettes.

Shipman, M. (1988) *The Limitations of Social Research*, 3rd edn. London: Longman. Critical examination of a range of social research in terms of reliability, validity, generalizability and credibility. Very readable.

Valsiner, J. (ed.) (1986) *The Individual Subject and Scientific Psychology*. New York: Plenum. Collection of papers advocating case and individual studies in different areas of psychology.

4

Experimental Design Outside the Laboratory

This chapter rehearses some advantages and disadvantages of the experimental strategy.

It explores the implications of taking the experiment outside the laboratory.

It presents some simple true experimental designs.

It also explains the attractions of quasi-experimental and single-subject approaches.

Finally, there is discussion of the use of the experimental style in situations where the enquirer cannot manipulate variables.

Introduction

Many texts cover the design and analysis of simple laboratory experiments in psychology. Many more cover complex laboratory experiments, typically concentrating on the use of the statistical technique known as Analysis of Variance (ANOVA). Miller (1989) has commented, with some justice, that psychologists are often lead to believe that 'the design of investigations is little more than the problem of selecting a suitable statistical model with the best experiments using a sophisticated form of analysis of variance' (p. 21). However, the problem of experimental design is much more a question of logic than one of statistics.

Surprisingly few texts give anything more than cursory attention to the issues involved in carrying out experiments outside the laboratory – with the shining exception of Cook and Campbell (1979), whose book *Quasi-Experimentation: design and analysis issues for field settings* (which as the title suggests concentrates on a particular variant of experimentation), devotes a chapter to the conduct of traditional randomized experiments.

It is, of course, true that the *principles* of experimental design apply wherever the experiment takes place. They do not alter simply by moving outside the laboratory door into the world outside. What does change is the difficulty of putting these principles into practice, which increases dramatically. However, there are corresponding gains. The following discussion tries to illustrate some of the main issues. Before getting down to this it will be helpful to clarify what we mean by an experiment.

At one level of generality, to be *experimental* is simply to be concerned with trying new things – and seeing what happens, what the reception is. Think of 'experimental' theatre, or an 'experimental' car, or an 'experimental' introduction of a mini-roundabout at a road junction. There is a change in something, and a concern for the effects that this change might have on something else. Looked at in this light, and bearing in mind that the experimental approach is applied both to situations where there is an active manipulation of the situation by the experimenter, and also to other situations (sometimes known as 'natural experiments') where the change investigated is outwith the control of the experimenter, there are strong similarities to other approaches to doing research. Both case studies and surveys *may* be concerned with the same set of issues.

However, when experimentation is contrasted with the other research strategies, a stricter definition is employed, usually involving the control and active manipulation of variables by the experimenter. For example:

> *Experimentation is a research strategy involving*
> - *the assignment of subjects to different conditions;*
> - *manipulation of one or more variables (called 'independent variables') by the experimenter;*
> - *the measurement of the effects of this manipulation on one or more other variables (called 'dependent variables'); and*
> - *the control of all other variables.*

Experimentation in this sense within the social sciences is in the United Kingdom to a large extent restricted to psychologists – whether working within their own discipline or using the strategy in some more applied field. The experimental approach appears to have wider currency in the United States; Luce et al. (1990) provide a good range of examples.

A central feature of the experiment is that you need to know what you are doing before you do it. It is a precise tool that can only map a very restricted range. A great deal of preparatory work is needed (either by you or someone else) if it is going to be useful. In other words, an experiment is an extremely *focused* study – you can only handle a very few variables, often only a single independent variable and a single dependent variable. These variables have to be selected with extreme care; perhaps on the basis of previous work that you, or some other workers, have carried out, or because of a prediction from a theory. The major problem in doing experiments in the real world is that you often don't know enough about the thing you are studying for this selectivity of focus to be a sensible strategy. Both surveys and case studies are much more forgiving in this respect. In surveys, variables tend to be numerous. In case studies, there is flexibility to develop and change the focus during the study.

Experimentation and Causality

While all the research strategies may share the goal of providing evidence about causal relationships (that is, about what leads to what) the experiment, defined in this narrower sense, is commonly cited as being *the* approach of choice for getting at causal relationships. This is an overstatement and an oversimplification, but it is probably fair to say that both the logic and the practicalities of establishing causal relationships are more straightforward in experimental research than with other research strategies (Blalock, 1964, provides an analysis of causal inferences in non-experimental research).

To see why this is the case requires a little delving into history. The version of experimental design dominant in experimental psychology was developed in the nineteenth century, and largely systematized by Sir Ronald Fisher, in the service of agricultural research. Here, the interest was whether a new practice, technique, fertiliser or whatever, would affect the yield of a crop. The implication is that there is a particular, single, cause. The experimenter measures the effect of this by creating different plots of soil, and deliberately assigns to each plot one of the kinds of seed or fertilizer which is on trial. The type of seed, fertilizer or whatever is known as the TREATMENT (or, as has been pointed out, more usually in psychological research, the INDEPENDENT VARIABLE – the variable which is manipulated by the experimenter). The possible effects of the treatment are known as OUTCOMES (or DEPENDENT VARIABLES). The measurement of outcomes, and the timing or phasing of such measurements (e.g. immediately before, during, and after treatment) is an important tool in detecting effects, and in relating them causally to the treatment.

Other comparisons are of course possible (e.g. between plots which have received different treatments). However, a major problem in interpretation, and in getting at cause and effect relationships, is that there are many other circumstances potentially functioning as variables (e.g. differences in rainfall, type of ground, amount of sunshine, temperature, etc.) which can effect the outcome as well as the treatment itself. Fisher's major breakthrough was his realization that *random assignment* of plots to different treatments enabled one to rule out most of these alternative explanations – in effect to control for a myriad of other variables without necessarily having to know or specify them.

The 'experimental unit' need not necessarily be a plot of land, of course. Experiments based on this principle, typically with the unit being an individual person, are the mainstay of laboratory experimental psychology and are referred to as TRUE EXPERIMENTS (or RANDOMIZED EXPERIMENTS).

When the experimental units, be they persons, plots or whatever, form a random sample from a known population (e.g. a sample of twenty children selected at random from the population of 600 attending a particular school) then it is also possible to GENERALIZE the effects from the sample involved in the experiment to the population from which they were drawn. Many tests of statistical inference, including *t*-tests and analyses of variance, are based on this type of sampling methodology.

Why Emphasize Causality?

Getting at causal relationships, finding out the effect that one thing has on another, is seen by many scientists as their central task. So if we want to join in the 'science game' (Agnew and Pyke (1982), in a book of that title, provide a clear and entertaining introduction to what is involved in joining in this game), and to be associated with a scientific approach, this provides a strong motivation for carrying out experiments. A related and powerful reason is that many potential consumers of our enquiries give high value to what they see as scientifically validated findings, about cause and effect, perceiving them as leading to practical, relevant knowledge. Bryman (1989) develops this argument in the context of studies of research on organizations. He takes the example of the effects of a participative approach to organizing work, claiming that if this is shown to lead causally to greater job satisfaction and individual performance than a non-participative approach, then 'the resulting evidence may be deemed to have considerable practical importance, since the evidence contains an implicit prescription about the appropriate distribution of influence within work organisations' (p. 71).

The larger question as to how far it is appropriate to follow such essentially natural science approaches when studying people, as considered in chapter 3, is obviously of central relevance here. Bhaskar (1978) considers that the key assumption in experimentation is that factors operating under the 'closed system' of the experiment operate in the 'open systems' of nature. Do they retain their identities and properties outside the controlled experimental situation? In simple terms, is what people do in experimental situations relatable to what they do in other situations?

Laboratory Experiments and the Real World

This book is primarily concerned with enquiry outside the laboratory. It is based on the premise that psychologists and others, whose interests are primarily applied and concerned with understanding and possibly influencing what is taking place in the real world, should take part in what Skinner (1963) refers to disapprovingly as the 'flight from the laboratory'. However, the notion that real world phenomena are best studied outside the laboratory needs justification. Leaving aside the trite point that laboratories are in themselves part of the real world (if you are interested in laboratories per se then by all means stick to that particular corner of the world), an important issue is whether particular features of laboratory experimentation tend to vitiate its value in understanding the real world.

Aronson and Carlsmith (1986) have distinguished two senses in which laboratory experimentation may lack realism. One is EXPERIMENTAL REALISM. In this sense an experiment is realistic if the situation which it presents to the subject is realistic, if it really involves the subjects, and has impact upon them. In the well known Asch (1956) experiment on conformity, subjects made what seemed to them to be straightforward judgements about the relative length of lines. These judgements were contradicted by others in the room whom they took also to be subjects in the experiment. This study showed experimental realism in the sense that subjects were undergoing an experience which caused them to show strong signs of tension and anxiety. They appeared to be reacting to the situation in the same realistic kind of way that they would outside the laboratory.

However, it might be argued that the Asch study lacks what Aronson and Carlsmith term MUNDANE REALISM. That is, the subjects were encountering events in the laboratory setting which were very unlikely to occur in the real world. Asch, following a common strategy in laboratory experimentation, had set up a very clearly and simply structured situation to observe the effects of group pressure on individuals. The real life counterpart, if one could be found, would be more complex and ambiguous, and in all probability would result in findings which were inconclusive. (The ethics of Asch's study are a different matter – see p. 29.)

Simplification of the situation, which is central to the experimental approach, may lead to clear results, but it does not protect against bias in them. The effects of two types of bias have been investigated in some detail. These are the DEMAND CHARACTERISTICS of the experimental situation, and EXPERIMENTER EXPECTANCY effects. In a very general sense, these are the consequences of the 'experimental units' (the subjects) and the experimenters, respectively, being human beings (see Barber, 1976, for a thorough analysis of such 'pitfalls' in experimentation with humans).

Bias due to demand characteristics occurs because subjects know that they are in an experimental situation; know that they are being observed; know that certain things are expected or demanded of them (Orne, 1962). Hence the way in which they respond is some complex amalgam of the experimental manipulation and their interpretation of what effect the manipulation is supposed to have on them. Their action based on that interpretation is likely to be co-operative but could well be obstructive. Even in situations where subjects are explicitly told that there are no right or wrong answers, that one response is as valued as another, subjects are likely to feel that certain responses show themselves in a better light than others. There is evidence that persons who volunteer for experiments are more sensitive to these effects than those who are required to be involved (Rosenthal and Rosnow, 1975).

The classic ploy to counteract this type of bias is deception by the experimenter. Subjects are told that the experiment is about X when it is really about Y. X is made to appear plausible and is such that if the subjects modify their responses in line with, or antagonistically to, what the experimenter appears to be after, there is no systematic effect on the experimenter's real area of interest. Increasing sensitivity to the ethical issues raised by deceiving subjects means that this ploy, previously common in some areas of social psychology, is now looked on with increasing suspicion.

Experimenter expectancy effects are reactive effects produced by the experimenters who have been shown, in a wide variety of studies, to bias findings (usually unwittingly) to provide support for the experimental hypothesis. Rosenthal and Rubin (1978) discuss the first 345 such studies! The effects can be minimized by decreasing the amount of interaction between subject and experimenter: using taped instructions, automated presentation of materials, etc. However, for many topics (apart from things like studies of human-computer interaction) this further attenuates any real world links that the laboratory experiment might possess. Double-blind procedures can also be used, where data collection is subcontracted so that neither the person working directly with the subjects, nor the subjects themselves, are aware of the hypothesis being tested.

Knowledge about determinants of laboratory behaviour (demand characteristics, etc) can be of value in real life settings. Wells and Luus (1990), for example, conceptualize police identity parades as experiments, and make suggestions for improving them based on this knowledge and on general principles of experimental design (use of control groups, etc.).

In Defence of Laboratories

It would be foolish to deny, however, that the experimental laboratory has its advantages and attractions. It may be strange and artificial to the incoming subjects, but for experimenters it is a home territory in which 'cub' researchers can disport themselves and develop their skills. What is a laboratory anyhow? Originally the term referred to a chemist's workroom, but now it is simply any space dedicated to experimental work, or even to research in general. For many studies, the degree of control of the environment, and of what happens to the subjects involved, is crucial in obtaining reliable data about the phenomenon of interest, and the contrivance and artificiality of laboratory conditions relatively unimportant. Locke (1986) argues that the generalizability of findings from laboratory to real world settings is, in fact, considerable. At the expense of some deception it may be possible for people to be subjects in a laboratory experiment without them knowing that they are. Zeisel (1984) cites a study by Mintz (1956) in which he had assistants administer a range of tests to randomly assigned subjects in rooms which were decorated differently – one 'beautiful' and one 'ugly', this constituting the experimental variable.

Field Experiments

The last example blurs the distinction between laboratories and the real world. A particular 'purpose-built' laboratory could well be a realistic simulation of some real life setting – an office, workshop or classroom. Or a 'real' office, workshop or classroom might be used as a laboratory for the purposes of the experiment. There may still be artificiality, though, in the way that strangers come together for short periods of time, as compared with the real life situation of established groups with past and continuing experience in the situation. Even with established groups working in familiar settings, there remains an almost inevitable artificiality when the studies are carried out for research purposes.

Things do happen, though, for many other purposes; sometimes they just happen. Such 'real' happenings can, in some cases and with some ingenuity, be made the basis of field experiments. They are sometimes called 'natural experiments'. They may permit study of phenomena which ethical or practical considerations would normally rule out. A true experiment on the effect of smoking on health in humans is a no-go area (random assignment of teenagers to smoking and non-smoking conditions?). But people do smoke, and some stop smoking, and others never start – so there are the makings of some kind of experimental study (see the following section on quasi-experimental designs, p. 95). The occurrence of identical twins, and the fact that some of them get reared apart from each other has been used as the basis for numerous nature/nurture studies. Studying the support systems which were set up to help those involved in the disasters at the Bradford and Hillsborough soccer clubs can tell us much about the effects of such tragedies (Kasl et al., 1981, give an experimental study of the impact of a nuclear accident on the workers involved).

However, planned interventions and innovations provide the most important focus for natural experiments, largely because their planned nature gives the opportunity of using relatively strong experimental designs, using for example, data obtained pre-intervention. Studies can be based on changes planned for some business, social, educational or other non-research purpose. Perhaps the introduction of new legislation on the wearing of seatbelts; or an incentive scheme in a business; or a new approach to teaching in a school or college. Such studies are sometimes referred to as 'reforms as experiments' (Campbell, 1969). They constitute one form of evaluation research (Bulmer, 1986; see also chapter 7).

The line between the natural and the artificial is again blurred with this type of study; particularly so when some aspect of the intervention or change is modified to suit the needs of a research design, or the experience of participants is modified by the presence of researchers or by the demands that they make.

True Experiments Outside the Laboratory

Given that the chief strength of true experiments lies in their ability to get at causal relationships – or, in other words, their high *internal validity* – it is unsurprising that experimentalists worry about control over variables. The greater such control, the higher the internal validity. And this applies not only to the independent variables, but also to a whole host of possible extraneous additional variables. The laboratory, as well as being a safe haven for the experimenter, is essentially a place for maximizing control over extraneous variables.

Move outside the laboratory door and such tight and comprehensive control becomes impossible. And problems of experimentation remain. Any special conditions marking out what is happening as 'an experiment' can lead to reactive effects. The classic demonstration of such effects comes from the well known series of experiments carried out at the Hawthorne works of the Western Electric Company in the USA in the 1920s and 1930s (Roethlisberger and Dickson, 1939), and hence called the 'Hawthorne effect'. Their studies investigating changes in length of working day, heating, lighting and other variables, found increases in productivity during the study which were virtually irrespective of the specific changes; the workers were in effect reacting positively to the attention and special treatment given by the experimenters. Problems in carrying out field experiments are listed in box 4.1.

Box 4.1   Problems of randomized experiments in the real world

Moving outside the safe confines of the laboratory may well be traumatic. Particular practical difficulties include:

1   Random assignment

There are practical and ethical problems of achieving random assignment to different experimental treatments or conditions (e.g. in withholding the treatment from a no-treatment control group). Random assignment is also often only feasible in atypical circumstances or with selected respondents, leading to questionable generalizability. Faulty randomization procedures are not uncommon (e.g. when procedures are subverted through ignorance, kindness, etc.). For small samples of the units being randomly assigned, sampling variability is a problem. Treatment-related refusal to participate or continue can bias sampling.

2 Validity

The actual treatment may be an imperfect realization of the variable(s) of interest, or interest, or a restricted range of outcomes may be insensitively or imperfectly measured, resulting in questionable validity. A supposed no-treatment control group may receive some form of compensatory treatment, or be otherwise influenced (e.g. through deprivation effects).

3 Ethical issues

There are grey areas in relation to restricting the involvement to volunteers, the need for informed consent and the debriefing of subjects after the experiment. Strict adherence to ethical guidelines is advocated, but this may lead to losing some of the advantages of moving outside the laboratory (e.g. leading to unnecessary 'obtrusiveness', and hence reactivity, of the treatment). Common sense is needed. If you are studying a natural experiment where some innovation would have taken place whether or not you were involved, then it may simply be the ethical considerations relating to the innovation which apply (fluoridation of water supplies raises more ethical implications for users than an altered design of a road junction).

4 Control

Lack of control over extraneous variables may mask the effects of treatment variables, or bias their assessment. Interaction between subjects may vitiate random assignment and violate their assumed independence.

There are gains, of course. Notwithstanding some degree of artificiality, and related reactivity, *external validity* – generalizability to the 'real world' – is almost self-evidently easier to achieve when the study takes place outside the laboratory in a setting which is almost real 'real life'. (Note, however, that there are claims of good generalization of some findings from laboratory to field settings.) Other advantages are covered in box 4.2.

Experimental designs as such are equally applicable both inside and outside laboratories. The crucial feature is RANDOM ALLOCATION TO EXPERIMENTAL

Box 4.2   Advantages in carrying out experiments in natural settings

Compared to a laboratory, natural settings have several advantages:

1   *Generalizability*

The laboratory is necessarily and deliberately an artificial setting where the degree of control and isolation sets it apart from real life. If we are concerned with generalizing results to the real world the task is easier if experimentation is in a natural setting. Much laboratory experimentation is based on student subjects, making generalization to the wider population hazardous. Although this is not a necessary feature of laboratory work, there is less temptation to stick to student groups when experiments take place in natural settings.

2   *Validity*

The *demand characteristics* of laboratory experiments, where subjects tend to do what they think you want them to do, are heightened by the artificiality and isolation of the laboratory situation. Real tasks in a real world setting are less prone to this kind of game playing. So you are more likely to be measuring what you think you are measuring.

3   *Subject availability*

It is no easy task to get subjects to come into the laboratory. You have to rely on them turning up. Although it depends on the type of study, many real life experiments have subjects in abundance, limited only by your energy and staying power; and possibly your charm.

CONDITIONS. If you can find a feasible and ethical means of doing this when planning a field experiment, then you should seriously consider carrying out a true experiment. An all too rare example is provided in a series of studies by Ian Berg and colleagues (e.g. Brown et al., 1990), which involved a juvenile court randomly allocating school truants to different treatments. Truancy cases often arose where the magistrates felt that there was no good reason to favour either adjournment or the use of a supervision order. In these cases, magistrates were provided with a series of sticky labels which covered a random sequence of the alternatives to be chosen. This particular study provided very clear evidence that adjournment was a much more effective procedure in terms of children returning to school. Random allocation ensures that there is no systematic bias on factors such as age, ethnic or home background, or behaviour in the court, giving strong evidence that the different outcomes are causally related to the different treatments.

The advantage of random allocation or assignment is that it allows you to proceed on the assumption that you have equivalent groups under the two (or more) experimental conditions. This is a probabilistic truth, which allows you among other things to employ a wide battery of statistical tests of inference legitimately. It does not guarantee that in any particular experiment the two groups will in fact be equivalent. No such guarantee is ever possible, although the greater the number of persons being allocated the more confidence you can have that the groups do not differ widely.

An alternative way of expressing this advantage is to say that randomization gets rid (probabilistically at least) of the *selection* threat to internal validity discussed in the previous chapter, (p. 71). That is, it provides a defence against the possibility that any change in a dependent variable is caused not by the independent variable but by differences in the characteristics of the two groups. The other potential threats to internal validity remain, of course, and the discussion of some of the designs that follows is largely couched in terms of their adequacy, or otherwise, in dealing with these threats.

True Experimental Designs

A small number of simple designs are presented here. Texts on experimental design give a range of alternatives, and of more complex designs (see the 'Further Reading' section at the end of the chapter).

> *Often those involved in real world experimentation restrict themselves to the very simplest designs, commonly the 'two group' design given below. However, the main hurdle in carrying out true experiments outside the laboratory is in achieving the principle of random allocation, and once this is achieved there may be merit in considering a somewhat more complex design.*

The Simple Two Group Design

Subjects are randomly assigned to the experimental treatment group or to a comparison group as explained in box 4.3. The effect of the treatment is assessed by comparing the results of the two post-tests. Statistical analysis enables one to determine the probability that the observed difference

---

Box 4.3   The post-test only, two-group design

1 Set up an 'experimental group' and a 'comparison group' using random assignment.

2 The experimental group gets the 'treatment'; the comparison group gets no special treatment.

3 Give 'post-tests' (i.e. after the experimental group's 'treatment') to both groups.

---

occurred purely by chance. If that probability is sufficiently low, then the decision is made that it was the experimental treatment that had the effect.

This is probably the simplest true experimental design. Several possible threats to internal validity can be ruled out, as well as the *selection* threat covered by random allocation. *Maturation* (e.g. effects of development, ageing, fatigue) can be ruled out if both groups are tested at the same time after random allocation. Similarly, *history* can be eliminated if both groups are involved with the experiment over the same period, as can *instrumentation* if both groups were tested or observed using the same instrument.

Minor variants of the design are possible involving two or more treatment groups, as shown in box 4.4. Here the difference between the two post-tests provides an assessment of the differential effects of the two treatments. It could in fact be argued that the single treatment design is better represented in this way as any comparison group will have something happening to it in the period between allocation and observation. A slightly more complicated design could involve two treatment conditions as well as a comparison group.

Box 4.4   The post-test only, two-group design, used to compare two treatments

1 Set up 'experimental group 1' and 'experimental group 2' using random assignment.

2 Experimental group 1 gets 'treatment 1'; experimental group 2 gets 'treatment 2'.

3 Give 'post-tests' (i.e. after the 'treatment') to both groups.

The Before and After Two Group Design

This design incorporates an additional set of observations (pre-tests) before the experimental treatment, as shown in box 4.5. While there are several advantages of the pre-tests, there are also disadvantages. The advantages are fairly obvious. There is a direct check on the effectiveness of random allocation in producing equivalent groups. If the groups prove not to be equivalent, it is possible to provide a statistical adjustment to the post-treatment observations which may give a fairer assessment of the effect of the treatment. The design also gives the opportunity of using the pre-post differences in individual subjects as a basis for assessing the effect of the treatment. This provides a means of taking into account individual differences and hence can provide a more sensitive measure of treatment effects.

Box 4.5　The pre-test post-test, two-group design

1　Set up an 'experimental group' and a 'comparison group' using random assignment.

2　Give 'pre-tests' (i.e. before the experimental group's 'treatment') to both groups.

3　The experimental group gets the 'treatment'; the comparison group gets no special treatment.

4　Give 'post-tests' (i.e. after the experimental group's 'treatment') to both groups.

The main disadvantage, apart from the additional work in carrying out the pre-tests, is that they may in some way sensitize those taking part, so that their subsequent post-tests are affected (the 'testing' threat to internal validity). This is of particular concern if there is a differential effect between treatment and comparison groups, as this may well be mistaken for an effect of the treatment itself. There is no easy way of determining whether or not this has taken place beyond assessing its plausibility in each individual study.

As with the first design, variants are possible, for example using two treatment groups, or two treatment groups and a comparison group.

The Solomon Four Group Design

This is essentially a combination of the two previous designs. Two groups form an experimental treatment and comparison group pair without pre-tests; two other groups include the pre-tests. Box 4.6 provides details. To the methodological purist, this is a satisfying design. It combines the advantages of the two previous designs – no possible interference from pre-testing effects in the third and fourth groups, and the possibility of achieving greater precision by measuring the treatment effect on a within-subject basis in the first two groups. It also enables a comparison to be made of the effects of pre-testing plus treatment (first group) and the added effects of pre-testing (second group) and treatment only (third group).

Box 4.6   The Solomon four-group design

1 Set up four groups using random assignment. First experimental group has post-tests only; second experimental group has both pre-tests and post-tests; first comparison group has post-tests only; second comparison group has both pre-tests and post-tests.

2 Give pre-tests to the second experimental group and the second comparison group.

3 The experimental groups get the treatment; the comparison groups get no special treatment.

4 Give post-tests to all four groups.

In practical terms, however, this is a rather expensive design. Four separate, randomly allocated groups are required to test the effects of a single treatment, or to assess the comparative effects of two treatments. (This latter requires a slight modification to the design, of course.) The 'expense' may well account for the relative rarity with which this design is used. For the same cost in terms of time and effort it would be possible to include additional experimental groups, or to move to the kind of factorial design considered next. However, Wilson and Putnam (1982), and others who have analysed studies assessing the effects of pre-testing, conclude that these are serious and virtually all-pervasive.

These problems no doubt account for the popularity of designs using post-tests only (e.g. the simple two groups design, and its variants) – and corresponding factorial designs, which are discussed below.

Factorial Designs

Factorial designs involve more than one independent variable. Such variables necessarily have more than one value or level (in the simplest form this would be the presence or absence of the variable – perhaps a certain level of noise, or no noise at all). The factorial design involves all possible combinations of the levels of the different independent variables. Thus a relatively simple factorial experiment with, say, three independent variables, one having two levels, one with three, and one with five, would have thirty (two, times three, times five) combinations of treatment levels.

As things can easily get out of control with this number of combinations let us restrict ourselves to the simple, and common, two by two design. This is represented in box 4.7.

Box 4.7   A post-test only factorial design

1   Set up four experimental groups using random assignment.

2   Experimental group 1 gets the treatment with both independent variables at level 1;
   Experimental group 2 gets the treatment with independent variable A at level 1 and independent variable B at level 2;
   Experimental group 3 gets the treatment with independent variable A at level 2 and independent variable B at level 1;
   Experimental group 4 gets the treatment with independent variable A at level 2 and independent variable B at level 2.

3   Give post-tests to all four groups.

This is 'two by two' in the sense that there are two independent variables, each of which has two levels. The four resulting treatments represent all possible combinations of levels of the independent variables.

This design enables one to assess the effect, separately, of each of the independent variables (known as its 'main effect') and also whether the effect of one variable differs from one level to another of the second variable. If there is such a change of effect, this is known as an 'interaction' between the variables, as exemplified in figure 4.1.

The simple factorial design is effectively an extension of the first, simple two-group design. It would be possible to incorporate pre-testing into the design as in the pre-test post-test design.

Note that both the two by two factorial design and the preceding Solomon design involve a total of four groups. The factorial design enables you, as it were, to cover more ground – there is an assessment of the effects of two variables, and also of whether they interact. The penalty is that you have less purchase on whether these effects are actually caused by the treatment.

Parametric Designs

A parametric design involves incorporating a range of several levels or values of an independent variable into the experiment so that a fuller picture of its effect can be obtained. A simple parametric design is shown as Box 4.8. It is, of course, possible to include a 'no treatment' comparison, and/or pre-tests, into the design.

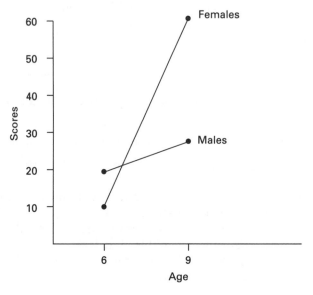

Figure 4.1 Example of an interaction
The difference between male and female scales is not constant: it depends on age, i.e. the effect of one variable (gender) depends on the level of the second variable (age).

Box 4.8 A single-variable, post-test only, parametric design

1 Set up a number (say five) of experimental groups using random assignment.

2 Experimental group 1 gets the treatment at level 1 of the independent variable;
   Experimental group 2 gets the treatment at level 2 of the independent variable;
   Experimental group 3 gets the treatment at level 3 of the independent variable;
   Experimental group 4 gets the treatment at level 4 of the independent variable;
   Experimental group 5 gets the treatment at level 5 of the independent variable.

3 Give post-tests to all five groups.

Designs Involving Matching

In its simplest form, the MATCHED PAIRS DESIGN, matching involves testing subjects on some variable which is known to be related to the dependent variable on which observations are being collected in the experiment. The results of this test are then used to create 'matched pairs' of subjects, that is, subjects giving identical or very similar scores on the related variable.

Random assignment is then used to allocate one member of each pair to the treatment group and one to the comparison group. In this simplest form, the design can be considered as an extension to the simple two group design, but with randomization being carried out on a pair basis rather than on a group basis. The principle can be easily extended to other designs, although of course if there are, say, four groups in the design then 'matched fours' have to be created and individuals randomly assigned from them to the four groups.

While the selection and choice of a good matching variable may pose difficult problems in a field experiment, it is an attractive strategy because it helps to reduce the problem of differences between individuals obscuring the effects of the treatment in which you are interested. Generally we need all the help we can get to detect treatment effects in the poorly controlled field situation, and matching can help without setting strong restrictions on important variables (which could have the effect of limiting the generalizability of your findings). To take a simple example, suppose that age is a variable known to be strongly related to the dependent variable in which you are interested. It would be possible to control for age as a variable by, say, only working with people between 25 and 30 years old. However, creating matched age pairs allows us to carry out a relatively sensitive test without the conclusions being restricted to a particular and narrow age range.

In practice it is often difficult to come up with a good matching variable. In this aspect, as in so much of experimental design, the need for careful pre-planning and thought and, in particular, exploration of the field through other approaches, is crucial.

There are other possible disadvantages of matching beyond the purely practical one of finding a good matching variable. The observation or measurement necessary to establish someone's position on a matching variable may be very similar to pre-testing. Hence there are the issues about whether or not the testing affects the person's subsequent performance in the experiment itself. When deciding whether the 'testing for matching' is likely to make someone approach the experiment in a different way – and in particular whether 'treatment' subjects are differentially affected from 'control' subjects – each situation has to be considered carefully and individually. Finding out a person's age and using that for matching purposes, particularly if it is collected among other demographic information, is unlikely to have this kind of effect. Having, say, some form of 'anxiety' test prior to a relatively stressful experimental treatment could well sensitize subjects and affect their subsequent performance.

Designs Involving Repeated Measures

The ultimate in matching is achieved when an individual's performance is compared under two or more conditions. Designs with this feature are known as REPEATED MEASURES or WITHIN-SUBJECTS designs. We have come across this already in one sense in the 'before and after' design – although the emphasis there is not on the before and after scores per se, but on the relative difference between them in the treatment and comparison groups as a measure of the treatment effect.

These are very seductive designs, but they do suffer from severe problems. Their attraction lies not only in the near perfection of the matching – the person undergoing the two or more treatments or whatever in the experiment has the same heredity, environment, age, personality, gender, etc., etc.; but also in your getting more data from fewer subjects. The problems stem from the central fact that the individual has more than one involvement in the experiment. Almost inevitably, this introduces a possible ORDER EFFECT. One treatment is undergone first, the other second. It may be that whatever is first results in a tendency to a superior performance to that which comes after – perhaps some kind of 'fatigue' effect. Or there can be the reverse tendency – some kind of 'practice' effect.

Additionally, there may be some specific effect on the effect of the second treatment, resulting from the particular nature of whatever is done first – usually referred to as a 'carry-over' effect. This may be a short-term effect, say resulting from some drug treatment, or longer-term, such as being led to approach a problem in a different way.

Order effects can be minimized by careful attention to detail. Practice effects can be reduced by incorporating substantial pre-experimental practice; fatigue effects by ensuring that the demands within the experiment are unlikely to tax the subjects. Likely carry-over affects will be highly specific to the types of treatment used, as will the approach to minimizing them; although in general this calls for increasing the time interval between treatments. Notwithstanding your best efforts, it is impossible to ensure that order effects are not present. An obvious strategy is to ensure that different subjects carry out the treatments in different orders. One approach is to determine randomly, for each subject, which treatment they undergo first, which second, and so on if there are more than two treatments. In its pure form, randomization will not ensure that the order effect is balanced, in the sense that equal numbers of subjects follow the different orderings. Any particular randomization exercise may have different numbers in the groups, although if the exercise were carried out repeatedly they would tend to equality.

The solution more usually advocated for dealing with order effects is COUNTER-BALANCING. This means adopting some system whereby subjects are randomly assigned to different orders of carrying out the treatments so that the order effect is balanced out. This is illustrated, for the simple two group design, in box 4.9. The change from a pure randomization approach to a counter-balancing one may seem minimal but has substantial implications for the type of analyses which are possible and appropriate. Technically, this type of factorial design is called a MIXED DESIGN. That is, it includes both a 'between subjects' independent variable (i.e. one where there are different groups of subjects for the different treatments), as well as a 'within subjects' (repeated measures) independent variable. More complex designs involve more than one of each type of variable.

Box 4.9   A simple repeated measures design, using counter-balancing

1   Set up two experimental groups using random assignment.

2   Group 1 gets treatment 1 followed by treatment 2. Group 2 gets treatment 2 followed by treatment 1.

3   Both groups are tested after they have received the first treatment (whichever that is), and after the second treatment.

Box 4.10 gives some suggestions for choosing among true and randomized experimental designs when working outside the laboratory.

Box 4.10   Considerations in choosing among true experimental designs

1   *To do any form of true experimental design you need to be able to carry out random assignment to the different treatments.* This is normally random assignment of *persons* to treatments (or of persons to the order in which they receive different treatments, in repeated measures designs). Note, however, that the unit which is randomly assigned need not be the person; it could be a group (e.g. a school class), in which case the experiment, and its analysis, is on classes, not individuals.

2   *Use a matched subjects design when:*
   a   you have a matching variable which correlates highly with the dependent variable;
   b   obtaining the scores on the matching variable is unlikely to influence the treatment effects;
   c   individual differences between subjects are likely to mask treatment effects.

3   *Use a repeated measures design when:*
   a   order effects appear unlikely;
   b   the independent variable(s) of interest lend themselves to repeated measurement (subject variables such as sex, ethnic background or class

don't – it is not easy to test the same person as a man and as a woman);
   c in real life, persons would be likely to be exposed to the different treatments;
   d individual differences between subjects are likely to mask treatment effects.

4 *Use a simple two-group design when*:
   a order effects are likely;
   b the independent variable(s) of interest don't lend themselves to repeated measurement;
   c in real life, persons would tend not to receive more than one treatment;
   d persons might be expected to be sensitized by pre-testing or being tested on a matching variable.

5 *Use a before–after design when*:
   a pre-testing appears to be unlikely to influence the effect of the treatment;
   b there are concerns about whether random assignment has produced equivalent groups (e.g. when there are small numbers in the groups);
   c individual differences between subjects are likely to mask treatment effects.

6 *Use a factorial design when*:
   a you are interested in more than one independent variable.
   b interactions between independent variables may be of concern.

7 *Use a parametric design when*:
   a the independent variable(s) have a range of values or levels of interest;
   b you wish to investigate the form or nature of the relationship between independent variable and dependent variable.

Cook and Campbell (1979) have discussed some of the real world situations which are conducive to carrying out randomized experiments. Box 4.11 is based on their suggestions.

Box 4.11 Real life situations conducive to randomized experiments

1 *When lotteries are expected*. Lotteries are sometimes, though not commonly, regarded as a socially acceptable way of deciding who gets scarce resources. When done for essentially ethical reasons it provides

a good opportunity to use this natural randomization for research purposes.

2 *When demand outstrips supply.* This sets up a situation where randomized allocation may be seen as a fair and equitable solution. There are practical problems. Do you set up waiting lists? Or allow reapplication? Cook and Campbell (1979) advocate using the initial randomization to create two equivalent no-treatment groups, as well as the treatment group. One no-treatment group is told that their application is unsuccessful, and that they cannot reapply. This group acts as the control group. The second no-treatment group is permitted to go on a waiting list, they are accepted for the treatment if a vacancy occurs, but data from them are not used.

3 *When an innovation cannot be introduced in units simultaneously.* Many innovations have to be introduced gradually, because of resource or other limitations. This provides the opportunity for randomization of the order of involvement. Substantial ingenuity may be called for procedurally to balance service and research needs, particularly when opportunities for involvement arise irregularly.

4 *When experimental units are isolated from each other.* Such isolation could be temporal or spatial – or simply because it is known that they do not communicate. Randomization principles can then be used to determine where or when particular treatments are scheduled.

5 *When it is agreed that change should take place but there is no consensus about solutions.* In these situations decision-makers may be more susceptible to arguments in favour of a system of planned variation associated with random allocation.

6 *When a tie can be broken.* In situations where access to a particular treatment is based upon performance on a task (e.g. for entry to a degree or other course) there will be a borderline. It may be that several persons are on that border (given the less than perfect reliability of any such task, this is more accurately a border region than a line). Randomization can be used to select from those at the border who then form the treatment and no treatment control groups.

7 *When persons express no preference among alternatives.* In situations where individuals indicate that they have no preference among alternative treatments, their random assignment to the alternatives is feasible. Note that you will be comparing the performance on the treatments of those without strong preferences, who may not be typical.

8 *When you are involved in setting up an organization, innovation, etc.* Many opportunities for randomization present themselves if you as researcher can get in on the early stages of a programme, organization

> or whatever. It would also help if guidelines for local and national initiatives were imbued with a research ethos, which would be likely to foster the use of randomization.
>
> (After Cook and Campbell, 1979, pp. 371–86.)

There are occasions when one starts out with a true experiment but along the way problems occur, perhaps in relation to assignment to conditions, or to mortality (loss of subjects) from one or other group, or where you don't have the time or resources to carry out what you originally intended. Such situations may be rescuable. As what frequently happens is that the true experiment thereby turns itself into a quasi-experiment, this issue is dealt with at the end of the next` section which is devoted to quasi-experimental design.

Quasi-experimentation

The term 'quasi-experiment' has been used in various ways, but its rise to prominence in social experimentation originates with a very influential chapter by Campbell and Stanley in Gage's *Handbook of Research on Teaching*. This was republished as a separate slim volume (Campbell and Stanley, 1963). For them, a quasi-experiment is

> *a research design involving an experimental approach but where random assignment to treatment and comparison groups has not been used.*

Campbell and Stanley's main contribution has been to show the value and usefulness of several such designs. More generally, they have encouraged a flexible approach to design and interpretation, where the particular pattern of results and circumstances under which the study took place interact with the design to determine what inferences can be made. Their concern is very much with the *threats to validity* present in such studies, and with the extent to which particular threats can be plausibly discounted in particular studies. Quasi-experimental approaches have considerable attraction for those seeking to maintain a basic experimental stance in work outside the laboratory.

The position taken by most writers on the topic (e.g. Judd et al., 1991) is that quasi-experiments are a second-best choice: a fall-back to consider when it is not possible to randomize allocation. Cook and Campbell (1979), however, prefer to stress the relative advantages and disadvantages of true and quasi-experiments, and are cautious about advocating randomized experiments even when they are feasible. They advocate considering all possible design options without necessarily assuming the superiority of a randomized design – and with the proviso that if a randomized design is chosen then it should be planned in such a way as to be interpretable as a quasi-experimental design, just in case something goes wrong with the randomized design, as it may well do in the real world.

Quasi-experimental Designs to Avoid – the 'Pre-experiments'

Quasi-experimental designs are essentially defined negatively – as not true experimental designs. They include several which are definitely to be avoided; although these so-called 'pre-experimental' designs continue to get used, and even published. Three of them are presented here (in boxes 4.12, 4.13 and 4.14) to enable you to recognize and avoid them, and also because the reasons why they are problematic present useful methodological points.

Box 4.12   Designs to avoid, no. 1: the one-group post-test only design

Scenario	A single experimental group is involved in the treatment and then given a post-test.
Disadvantages	As an *experiment*, where the only information that you have is about the outcome measure, this is a waste of time and effort. Without pre-treatment measures on this group or measures from a second no-treatment control group, it is virtually impossible to infer any kind of effect.
Improvements	Either improve the experimental design or adopt a case study methodology.

Note: This is not the same thing as a case study. Typically the case study has multiple sources of data (both qualitative and quantitative) extending over time, and there is also information about the context.

The third of these, what I have termed the 'pre-test post-test single group' design, is commonly found and it is important to stress that the deficiencies covered here concern its nature as an *experimental design*. If the concern is simply to determine whether there is an increase of performance after a treatment, or even to assess its statistical significance, there are no particular problems. The difficulty is in inferring causality. If the design is in effect a survey administered on two separate occasions with a large number of

Box 4.13 Designs to avoid, no. 2: the post-test only non-equivalent groups design

Scenario

As no. 1 but with the addition of a second non-equivalent (i.e. not determined by random assignment) group that does not receive the treatment, i.e.:

1 Set up an experimental and a comparison group on some basis other than random assignment.
2 The experimental group gets the treatment, the comparison group don't.
3 Do post-tests on both groups.

Disadvantages

It is not possible to determine whether any difference in outcome for the two groups is due to the treatment, or to other differences between the groups.

Improvements

Strengthen the experimental design by incorporating a pre-test, or by using random assignment to the two groups; or use case study methodology.

Box 4.14 Designs to avoid, no. 3: the pre-test post-test single group design

Scenario

As no. 1, but with the addition of measurement on the same variable before the treatment as well as after it; i.e.: the single experimental group is pre-tested, gets the treatment, and is tested again.

Disadvantages

Although widely used, it is subject to lots of problems. It is vulnerable to many threats to validity – including *history* (other events apart from T occurring between measures), *maturation* (developments in the group between measures), *statistical regression* (e.g. choice of a group 'in need' in the sense of performing poorly on the measure used, or some other measure which correlates with it, will tend to show an improvement for random statistical reasons unconnected with the treatment).

Improvements

Strengthen the experimental design, e.g. by adding a second pre-tested no-treatment control group, or use case study methodology.

> *Note*: It may be possible on particular occasions to show that this design *is* interpretable. This may be because the potential threats to validity have not occurred in practice: for example, if you can isolate the group so that other effects do not influence it; or if you have information that there are no pre-treatment trends in the measures you are taking – although strictly that type of information turns this into a kind of time series design (see p. 105).

variables, or a case study with multiple sources of evidence, buttressed by some quantitative pre- and post-intervention data on a small number of variables, it may also be perfectly adequate.

Quasi-experimental Designs to Consider

It is possible to get at a feasible quasi-experimental design by considering the main problems with the previous two designs – the 'post-test only non-equivalent groups' design, and the 'pre-test post-test single group' design. With the former, we do not know whether or not the two groups differ before the treatment. With the latter we do not know how much the group would have changed from pre-test to post-test in the absence of the treatment.

One tactic used to strengthen the design is, effectively, to combine the two designs into a 'pre-test post-test non-equivalent groups' design. A second tactic is to make additional observations,

a   over time with a particular group, leading to the 'interrupted time-series design, and/or

b   over groups at the same time, leading to the 'regression-discontinuity' design.

Pre-test Post-test Non-equivalent Groups Design

This design is represented in box 4.15. The pattern of pre-test and post-test results has to be investigated to assess the effectiveness of the treatment. It is a general rule of quasi-experimental designs that it is necessary to consider not only the DESIGN of a study, but also the CONTEXT in which it occurs, and the particular PATTERN OF RESULTS obtained, when trying to decide whether a treatment has been effective. Box 4.16 illustrates and discusses some possible patterns. Note that the issue is not simply a matter of statistical significance. It is more that, given there is statistical significance, we can reasonably conclude that it is the independent variable which is affecting the dependent variable.

Box 4.15   Pre-test post-test non-equivalent groups design

1   Set up an experimental group and a comparison group on some basis other than random assignment.

2   Give pre-tests to both groups.

3   The experimental group gets the 'treatment'; the comparison group gets no special treatment.

4   Give post-tests to both groups.

Box 4.16   Possible outcomes of a pre-test post-test non-equivalent groups design in relation to threats to validity

Outcome A

Situation: experimental group starts higher.
Outcome: increase in experimental group. No change in comparison group.
Issue: plausibility that causally irrelevant variables are affecting the experimental group but not the comparison group.

Outcome B

Situation: experimental group starts higher.
Outcome: increase in experimental group. Smaller increase in comparison group.
Issues: it appears that the comparison group may be changing – is the experimental group with the pre-test advantage changing (maturing) at a faster rate irrespective of the experimental treatment?

Outcome C

Situation: experimental group starts lower.
Outcome: increase in experimental group. No change in comparison group.

Issues: Regression may be a threat, depending on how the groups have been selected. It may be implausible that an experimental group with a pre-test disadvantage 'matures' more rapidly.

Outcome D

Situation: experimental group starts lower.
Outcome: increase in experimental group taking it above the comparison group at post-test. No change in comparison group.
Issue: a highly desirable pattern from point of view of making causal inferences. The switching of the two groups from pre- to post-test permits many threats to be ruled out.

Seeking equivalent groups through matching   A common design strategy is to use one or more matching variables to select a comparison or control group in this type of design. This is different from the matching strategy used in true or randomized experiments where the experimenter matches subjects and randomly assigns one member of the matched pair to either treatment or comparison group. Here the researcher tries to find subjects who match subjects who are receiving a treatment. This approach is unfortunately subject to a particular threat to internal validity which has not so far been highlighted; REGRESSION TO THE MEAN. While this threat is always present when matching is used without random assignment, it appears particularly clearly in situations where some treatment intended to assist those with difficulties or disadvantage is being assessed. Suppose that a comparison is being made of the achievements of a 'disadvantaged' with a 'non-disadvantaged' control group. The pre-treatment levels of the disadvantaged *population* will almost inevitably differ from those of the non-disadvantaged *population*, with the strong likelihood that those of the disadvantaged population tend to be lower. Hence in selecting matched pairs from the two populations, we will be pairing individuals who are pretty high in the disadvantaged group with individuals pretty low in the non-disadvantaged group. Figure 4.2 indicates what is likely to be going on.

Because pre-test scores are not 100 per cent reliable (no scores ever are) they will incorporate some random or error factors. Those scoring relatively high in their population (as in the selected disadvantaged group) will have some tendency to have positive error factors inflating their pre-test score; those scoring relatively low in their population (as in the selected non-disadvantaged group) will have some tendency to have negative error factors reducing their pre-test score. On post-test, however, such random factors (simply because they are random) will be just as likely to be positive as negative, leading to the 'regression to the mean' phenomenon – post-test

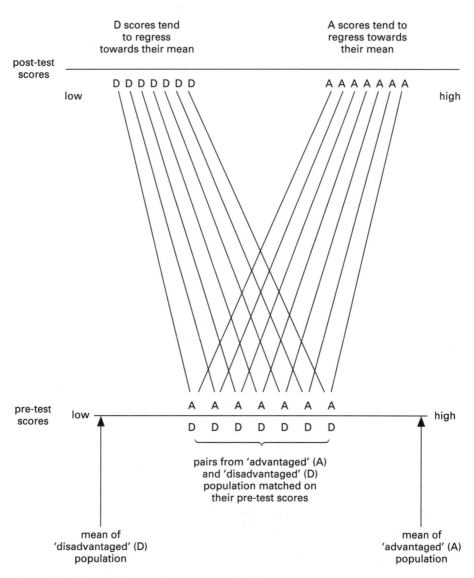

Figure 4.2 Effects of 'regression to the mean' when using extreme groups

scores of originally extreme groups tend to be closer to their population means.

As can be seen from the figure, the effect of this is to produce a tendency for the disadvantaged groups to score lower *in the absence of any treatment effects*. Depending on the relative size of this effect and any treatment effect, there will appear to be a reduced treatment effect, or zero, or even a negative one.

Interrupted Time Series Design

In the simplest form of this design, there is just one experimental group, and a series of observations or tests before and after an experimental treatment. The time series approach is widely used in some branches of the social sciences (e.g. in economics) and has a well developed and complex literature, particularly on the analysis of time series data (Skinner, 1991). Textbooks covering this field suggest rules of thumb for the number of data points needed in the before and after time series, typically coming up with figures of fifty or more.

This extent of data collection is likely to be outside the scope of the small-scale study targeted in this book. However, there are likely to be situations where, although fifty or so observations are not feasible, it is possible to carry out more than a single pre- and single post-test. Certainly, advantages accrue if even one additional pre- and/or post-test (preferably both) can be added. This is essentially because one is then gathering information about possible *trends* in the data, which help in countering several of the threats to the internal validity of the study.

With more data points, say five before and five after, the experimenter is in a much stronger position to assess the nature of the trend – does the series appear to be stationary (i.e. show no trend to increase or decrease)? Or does it appear to increase, or decrease? And is this a linear trend, or is the slope itself tending to increase, etc., etc.? Techniques for the analysis of such short time series are available, although not universally accepted (see chapter 11, p. 366). However, as with other quasi-experimental designs, their interpretation is based on a knowledge of the design itself in interaction with the particular pattern of results obtained, and contextual factors. Figure 4.3 illustrates a range of possible patterns of results.

Collecting data for a time series design can obviously become a difficult and time-consuming task. The observations must be ones that can be made repeatedly without practical or methodological problems. Simple, non-obtrusive measures (e.g. of play in a school playground) are more appropriate than, say, the repeated administration of a formal test of some kind.

If pre-existing archive material of some kind is available, then it may be feasible to set up a time series design, even with an extended time series, at relatively low cost of time and effort for the experimenter. Increasingly, such material is gathered in conjunction with management information systems (see p. 283). However, it will require very careful scrutiny to establish its reliability and validity, and general usefulness, for research purposes. Generally it will have been gathered for other purposes (although if, as is sometimes the case, you are in a position to influence what is gathered and how it is gathered, this can be very helpful), which may well mean that it is inaccessible to you, or is systematically biased, or is being collected according to different criteria at different times, or by different people, or is inflexible and won't allow you to answer your research questions.

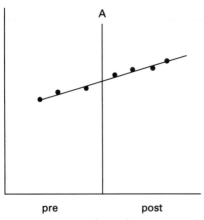

A   No effect. Note that making single pre- and post-tests (or taking pre- and post-test averages) would suggest a spurious effect.

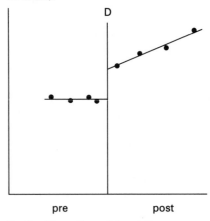

B   Clear effect. Stable pre and post – but at a different level. Several threats to validity still possible (e.g. history – something else may be happening at the same time as the treatment).

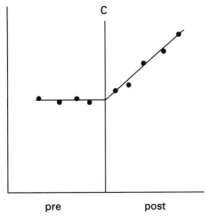

C Again, clear effect, but of a different kind (move from stability to steady increase). Similar threats still apply.

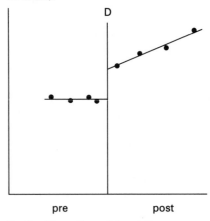

D   Combines effects of B and C.

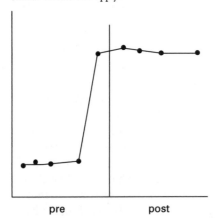

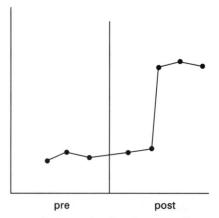

E   'Premature' and 'delayed' effects. Such patterns cast serious doubts on the effects being causally linked to the treatment. Explanations should be sought (e.g. may get a 'premature' effect of an intervention on knowledge or skill, if participants are in some way preparing themselves for the intervention).

Figure 4.3   Patterns of possible results in a simple time series experiment

More complex time series designs are possible. For example, a non-equivalent comparison group can be added with the same series of pre- and post-treatment tests or observations being made for both groups. The main advantage of adding the control group is its ability to test for the 'history' threat. A selection-history interaction is still possible, though: that is, that one of the two groups experiences a particular set of non-treatment related events that the other does not. In general the plausibility of such a threat will depend on how closely comparable in setting and experiences the two groups are.

One way of discounting history-related threats is to use the group as its own control, and to take measures on a second dependent variable which should not be affected by the treatment. Ross et al. (1970) used this design to analyse the effect of the introduction of the 'breathalyser' on traffic accidents. They argued that serious accidents should decrease following the introduction of new legislation in Britain which brought in the 'breathalyser' *during the hours that pubs were open* (the 'experimental' dependent variable), but should be less affected during commuting hours when the pubs were shut (the 'control' dependent variable). They were able to corroborate this view, both by visual inspection of the time series and by statistical analysis.

Other time series designs involving the removal of treatment, and multiple and switching replications, have been used. A lot of the interest in these designs has been in connection with so-called 'single-subject' research, particularly in the 'behaviour modification' field (e.g. Kratochwill, 1978). Although having their genesis in a very different area of the social sciences, time series designs show considerable similarities to *single-subject research designs*. These designs are taken up in the next but one section, following discussion of the regression discontinuity design.

Regression Discontinuity Design

This rather fearsomely named design is conceptually straightforward. As in the true experiment, a known assignment rule is used to separate out two groups. However, whereas with the true experiment this is done on a random basis, here some other principle is used. In probably its simplest form, all those scoring below a certain value on some criterion are allocated to, say, the experimental group; all those scoring above that value are allocated to the control group. Trochim (1984) gives details.

It might be, for example, that entry to some compensatory programme is restricted to those scoring below a particular cut-off point on some relevant test; or conversely that entrance scholarships are given to those scoring above some cut-off. Figure 4.4 illustrates a possible outcome for this type of design. As with other quasi-experimental designs, the pattern of outcome, design and context must be considered when seeking to interpret the results of a particular experiment.

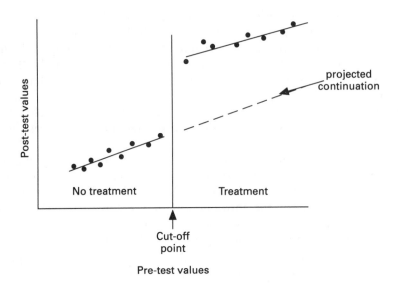

Figure 4.4 Illustrative outcome of a regression discontinuity design

There is a superficial similarity between the graphs obtained with this design and those for the time series design. Note, however, that, whereas the latter shows time on the horizontal axis of the graph, the regression discontinuity design has pre-test scores along this axis. The issues are in both cases about trends in the data; are they present, do they differ and so on. 'Eyeballing' the data, i.e. visual inspection to assess this, forms a valuable part of the analysis, although most would argue that this needs to be supplemented by more formal statistical analysis. Conceptually the analyses for the two designs are equivalent, although different statistical techniques have to be used.

Concluding Thoughts on Quasi-experimental Designs

Quasi-experimentation is more of a style of investigation than a slavish following of predetermined designs. The designs covered above should be seen simply as suggestions for starting points. If your prime concern is to get at cause and effect relationships, and you are not in a position to do true experiments, then with sufficient ingenuity you ought to be able to carry out a quasi-experiment to counter those threats to internal validity that are likely to be problematic. And if you are not solely concerned with cause and effect relationships, then some of the problems with real life experimentation, including generalizability difficulties (see p. 70) might reinforce your travelling down a quasi-experimental road.

Single-subject Experimental Designs

A distinctive approach to carrying out experiments originated in the work of B. F. Skinner (e.g. Skinner, 1938, 1953, 1974). It has subsequently been developed by his followers, variously known as Skinnerians, Radical Behaviourists, or Operant Conditioners – among other labels. Sidman (1960) has produced a very clear, though partisan, account of this approach concentrating on the methodological issues and strategies involved. The work of Skinner arouses strong passions and in consequence his approach to experimental design tends to be either uncritically adopted or cursorily rejected.

There is much of value here for the 'real world' investigator with a leaning to the experimental – mixed, as in Skinner's other work, with the unhelpfully polemical, the quirky and the rather silly. The approach is variously labelled, commonly as 'small-N' or 'single case' designs. This latter has the virtue, which would probably be resisted by Skinner (Robson, 1985), of making the point that the 'case' need not necessarily be the individual person – it could be the individual school class, or school itself, for example. It does, however, carry the possibility of confusion with 'case study', which as defined in this book is a multi-method enterprise (though this may incorporate a single-subject experiment within it). Barlow et al. (1984) have coined the term 'time series methodology' in an attempt to blur the distinction between case study and single-case experiments. It may be of considerable value to plan studies incorporating both of these traditionally divided approaches (see chapter 6, p. 149).

We will stick, then, to 'single-subject experimental designs', while acknowledging that Barlow et al.'s term does make it clear that such designs depend crucially on *repeated measures on the same individuals over time, typically before, during and after an intervention*. This concentration on the individual rather than the group is crucial for Skinner. His search was for a methodology and technology which produced meaningful, reliable data at the level of the individual – and which didn't require the 'monstrous engines' of statistical testing to decide whether or not an effect was present.

The approach is in essence very simple. Starting from the simplest, designs include the following.

A–B Design

Note that the terminology is different from that used in the previous designs, but is well established. This is essentially a *two-condition design*. The first condition (A) is referred to as the *base-line*; the second condition (B) corresponds to the treatment. Both conditions are 'phases' which extend over time, and a sequence of tests or observations will be taken in each phase.

The investigator looks for a clear difference in the pattern of performance in the two phases – this being an actual 'look' as typically the data are 'eyeballed' by Skinnerians who have a principled antipathy to statistical analysis. A distinctive feature of the Skinnerian approach is that the base-line phase is supposed to be continued until stability is reached; that is, so that there is no trend over time. In practice, this is not always achieved. The restriction to a stable base-line obviously assists in the interpretation of the data, but even so, the design is weak and subject to several validity threats (e.g. history–treatment interaction). *Because of this the design is probably best regarded as 'pre-experimental', with the same strictures on its use as with the other pre-experimental designs* considered in the preceding section on quasi-experiments (p. 99). The design can be strengthened in ways analogous to those employed in quasi-experimental design – effectively, extending the series of phases either over time, or cross-sectionally over different base-lines.

It is also a pragmatic point as to whether the necessary base-line stability can be achieved, although Skinnerians would consider it an essential feature of experimental control that conditions be found where there is stability. As with lengthy time series designs, this approach presupposes an observation or dependent variable where it is feasible to have an extended series of measures. Skinnerians would insist on the dependent variable being *rate of response* but this appears to be more of a historical quirk than an essential design feature.

A–B–A Design

This improves upon the previous design by adding a *reversal* phase – the second A phase. The central notion is that the investigator removes the treatment (B) and looks for a return to base-line performance. Given a stable pre-treatment base-line, a clear and consistent shift from this during the second phase, and a return to a stable base-line on the reversal, the investigator is on pretty strong ground for inferring a causal relationship.

The problems occur when this does not happen, particularly when there is not a return to base-line in the final phase. This leaves the experimenter seeking explanations for the changes that occurred during the second phase other than that it was caused by the treatment (B); or evaluating other possible explanations for the failure to return, such as carry-over effects from the treatment. The design is also open to ethical objections, particularly when used in an applied setting. Is it justifiable deliberately to remove a treatment when this appears to be effective? This is not too much of an issue when the goal of an enquiry is to establish or demonstrate some phenomenon, but when the intention is to help someone, many practitioners would have reservations about this design.

A–B–A–B Design

A simple, though not entirely adequate, answer to the ethical problems raised by the preceding design is to add a further treatment phase. In this way the person undergoing the study ends up with the – presumed beneficial – treatment. Figure 4.5 provides an example.

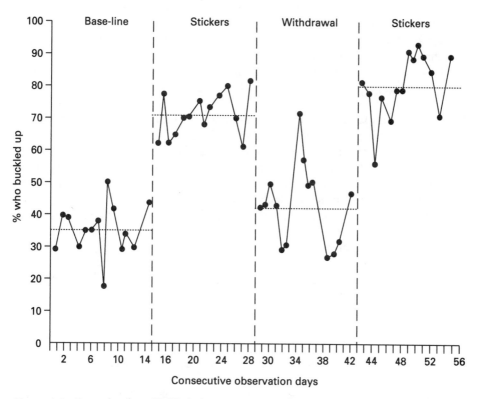

Figure 4.5 Example of an ABAB design: 'percentage of passengers who buckled up over 58 consecutive observation days, two weeks per consecutive base-line, intervention, withdrawal and intervention phase'

Note: group data are shown here rather than those for single subjects (which would not have been feasible in this study). This would be frowned upon by Skinnerian purists.

Source: Thyer and Geller, 1987.

All additions to the sequence of base-line and treatment phases, with regular and consistent changes observed to be associated with the phases, add to one's confidence about the causal relationship between treatment and outcome. There is no reason in principle why this AB alternation should not continue as ABABAB – or longer. However, it does involve extra time and effort which could probably be better spent in other directions. The design does also still call for the treatment to be withdrawn during the sequence, and there are more popular designs which avoid this.

Multiple Base-line Designs

The approach in this design involves the application of the treatment at different points in time to different base-line conditions. If there is a corresponding change in the condition to which the treatment is applied, and *no change in the other conditions* at that time, then there is a strong case that the change is causally related to the treatment.

Three versions of the design are commonly employed; multiple base-lines *across settings*, *across behaviours* and *across subjects*.

- In the across settings design, a particular dependent variable (behaviour) of a subject is monitored in a range of different settings or situations and the treatment is introduced at a different time in each of the settings.
- In the across behaviours design, data is collected on several dependent variables (behaviours) for a particular subject and the treatment is applied at different times to each of the behaviours.
- In the across subjects design, data is collected on a particular base-line condition for several subjects and the treatment is applied at different times to the different subjects.

The general approach is illustrated in figure 4.6 and a specific example in figure 4.7.

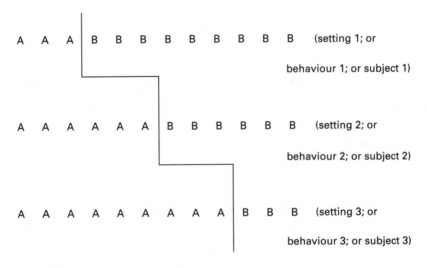

Figure 4.6   The multiple base-line design

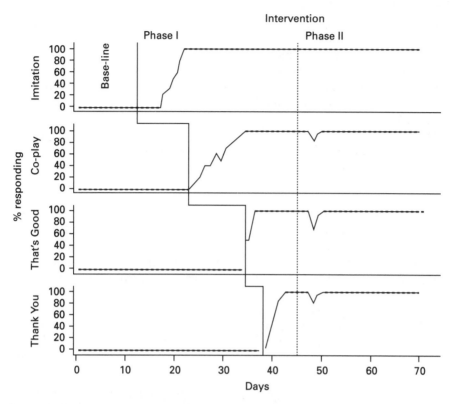

Figure 4.7   Example of a multiple base-line design
Source: Figure 1 in Lancioni, 1982.

Further Single-subject Designs

Other designs have been used and are briefly explained here.

Changing Criterion Designs   A criterion for performance is specified as a part of the intervention. That criterion is changed over time in a pre-specified manner, usually progressively in a particular direction. The effect of the intervention is demonstrated if the behaviour changes to match the changes in criterion.

This design has not been widely used but appears attractive in inter-ventions where the intention is to achieve a progressive reduction of some problem behaviour, or progressive increase in some desired behaviour. It is probably most useful for situations involving complex behaviours, or where the intention is to try to achieve some major shift from what the person involved is currently doing. Certainly the notion of 'successive approximations' which is built in to this design sits very naturally with the 'shaping of be-haviour' approach central to Skinnerian practice and applicable by others.

Multiple Treatment Designs   These involve the implementation of two or more treatments designed to affect a single behaviour. So, rather than a treatment being compared with its absence (which is effectively what base-line comparisons seek to achieve), there are at least two separate treatments whose effects are compared. In its simplest form this would be ABC – i.e. a base-line condition (A), followed in sequence by two treatment conditions (B and C). This could be extended in several ways: ABCA or ABACA or ABACABCA, etc.

The latter gives some kind of assessment of 'multiple treatment interference' – the extent to which there are sequence effects, where being exposed to one condition has a subsequent influence on the apparent effect of a subsequent condition.

There are several more complex variants. In one (known as a MULTIPLE SCHEDULE DESIGN), each treatment or intervention is associated in a consistent way, probably for a substantial number of times, with a particular 'stimulus' (e.g. a particular person, setting or time) so that it can be established whether or not the stimulus has consistent control over performance. An alternative (known variously as a SIMULTANEOUS TREATMENT or ALTERNATING TREATMENT DESIGN) is for each of the settings to be balanced across stimulus conditions (persons, settings or times) so that each of the settings has been associated equivalently with each of the stimuli. This then permits one to disentangle the effects of the settings from 'stimulus' effects. Kazdin (1982) gives details.

These designs have several advantages. As the main concern is for differential effects on the two conditions, the establishment of a stable base-line becomes less crucial. In the two latter variants, there is no need for treatment to be withdrawn or removed, and the relative effects of the different conditions can be determined without the need for lengthy successive involvement with different phases.

It is possible to generate what might be called 'combined designs' by putting together features from the individual designs considered above. For example an ABAB design could be combined with a multiple base-line approach. Barlow et al. (1984) present a very helpful approach in terms of 'design elements' which can be combined in a variety of ways to generate tailor-made designs.

The general approach taken to design in single-subject experimentation bears some similarities to that taken in quasi-experimentation. There is concern for specific threats to validity which might make the study difficult or impossible to interpret, particularly in relation to causality. These are taken into account in developing the design. However, there is often substantially greater flexibility and willingness to modify the design than is found in other types of experimentation. It is common to review and possibly alter the design in the light of the pattern of data which is emerging. Decisions such as when to move from one phase to another are made in this way. The attraction of a combined design is that additional or changed design features (which can counter particular threats to validity) can be introduced reactively to resolve specific ambiguities.

This approach is foreign to the general canons of design principles advocated by main-line psychological experimentalists, where a design is very carefully pre-planned and then rigidly adhered to. Interestingly, it is much closer to the stance adopted in case study design, which is discussed in chapter 6.

There are also similarities between single-subject experimentation and the way in which experiments are carried out in some branches of the natural sciences. Statistics play little part; the trick is so to set up the situation, through control of extraneous variables that would cloud the issue, so that the cause-effect relationship shines out for all to see. It may be necessary to 'fine-tune' your study so that unforeseen eventualities can be accounted for. With sufficient experimental skill and understanding you should be able to find out something of general importance about the specific focus of your study (whether this happens to be a person or a lump of iron). You will need to test it out on a few individuals just to assure yourself of typicality.

Passive Experimentation

Several types of study which appear to be cast as experiments, and which use the kind of language associated with experiments – referring for example to independent and dependent variables – do not have the *active manipulation of the situation by the experimenter* considered as a hallmark of the experimental approach. Risking a contradiction in terms, they will be referred to here as PASSIVE EXPERIMENTS, with concentration on two variants – RETROSPECTIVE STUDIES and NATURAL EXPERIMENTS.

Retrospective Studies

These studies investigate possible cause and effect relationships by observing an existing condition or state of affairs, and then searching back in time. Such studies have also been labelled as 'after the fact', or 'ex post facto'. That is, we are dealing with situations that have already happened and so cannot be controlled or manipulated by the experimenter. In more formal terms, the 'treatment' or operation of the independent variable has already occurred, or is inherently not amenable to manipulation by the researcher, who starts her study by observation of one or more dependent variables. The independent variable(s) are then looked at in retrospect for their possible relationship to the dependent variable(s).

A common situation where this occurs is when we are interested in the possible effect of some characteristic or attribute of a person on their performance in a situation or task. Suppose we are interested in why some youths become drug users. Variables such as home environment, personality and intelligence are attributes of the person that cannot be directly manipulated by the experimenter. We cannot randomly assign youths to different categories of these variables.

There are strong similarities between experimental and retrospective research. In both cases, the interest is in the discovery or confirmation of relationships among variables. Both can answer questions, test hypotheses, about the relationships between independent variables and dependent variables. The aim is to compare two groups, equivalent in all relevant characteristics but the one(s) under investigation, so as to measure the effect of that characteristic.

The differences between experimental and retrospective research are, however, frequently glossed over or even ignored. Retrospective research produces less convincing evidence about causal relationships between the variables. It is also common to find experimental studies with one or more actively manipulated variables which also incorporate 'attribute' variables (e.g. gender) – the strictures still apply about relationships involving these latter variables. The basic problem lies in the researcher not knowing about the antecedents of pre-existing differences in the independent variable. Suppose, for example, you are interested in the effect of anxiety on performance in examinations. A 'retrospective research' approach might involve measuring the anxiety levels of students at the time they are sitting the examination, and comparing the performance of, say, twenty who score as 'high anxiety' with a second group of twenty who score as 'low anxiety'. If a relationship is found between anxiety and performance, there are still substantial queries about whether this is a causal relationship. This turns on why the differences in anxiety have occurred. If the more intelligent candidates tend to be less anxious – and tend to score higher in the examination – then it could well be that general intelligence is the main cause both of level of anxiety and of examination performance.

Contrast this with an experimental approach. The researcher could set up two conditions, equivalent in all respects other than that one involves inducing a 'high anxiety' state (perhaps by emphasizing the difficulty or importance of the test), and the other represents a control or neutral condition. Given random assignment to the two conditions, any observed relationship between anxiety and performance in the test can be more confidently viewed as causal. There can still be problems, of course. Does the researcher's manipulation actually change or influence anxiety levels, or is something else being changed? Perhaps members of the experimental group just try somewhat harder than the control group in this somewhat artificial situation.

Few variables can be either viewed as a personal attribute, or actively manipulated in the way that anxiety was dealt with here. To the person interested in, say, gender differences, retrospective research provides an avenue into an experimental style of investigation notwithstanding the causality problem. It can of course tell you whether or not there is a relationship between variables. For some purposes, particularly in applied situations, this may well be sufficient. If we find that using scores on a particular test enables the personnel department to select successful salespersons, then this is clearly of value in its own right. In other situations the suggestive or exploratory nature of such findings could be used as a basis of further studies.

Box 4.17 provides an example of a study where the style is experimental but there is no active manipulation of variables. Box 4.18 lists advantages and disadvantages of retrospective experimentation.

Box 4.17   Example of 'retrospective' experimentation

Dhooper et al. (1990) tested the hypothesis that employees of the Kentucky Department for Social Services with a prior social work education qualification are better prepared for social work positions than are colleagues without such education.

In a retrospective study they used a range of instruments in what was effectively a post-test only non-equivalent groups design – comparing the performance of employees with social work degrees with those possessing other degrees.

They found that those with a Bachelor of Social Work degree scored significantly higher than other groups on quality assurance ratings (which had been routinely collected for other purposes).

Difficulties in interpretation of the results of the study are acknowledged, and attempts to strengthen it by checking whether workers with that qualification were in aspects of social work which tended to get higher ratings; whether there was an effect of prior work experience, etc.

(*Source*: Dhooper et al., 1990).

Box 4.18   Advantages and disadvantages of 'retrospective' experimentation

Advantages

1   It enables an experimental style of research to be carried out in situations where it is impossible or impracticable to have direct manipulation of the independent variable.

2   It is useful as an exploratory tool. It gives an indication of which variables are related or associated.

3   It can avoid some or all of the artificiality involved in experimentation (in connection with the manipulation of the independent variable).

4   It is valuable if establishing a relationship between variables is sufficient (i.e. irrespective of causality).

5   It can act as a useful precursor to true or quasi-experimental studies, particularly through suggesting hypotheses to be tested.

Disadvantages

1   There is a lack of control through the researcher being unable to manipulate the independent variable, or randomize allocation of subjects to the experimental conditions.

2   The causative factors of any relationships determined between independent variable and dependent variable may not have been directly incorporated into the study.

3   'Reverse causality' is a possibility – i.e. that the independent variable may be affecting the dependent variable, rather than the dependent variable affecting the independent variable.

4   A relationship between independent variable and dependent variable does not necessarily imply causation (in either direction).

5   There are possible problems in using personal attributes considered to be continuously distributed (e.g. personality traits) as a basis for classifying into dichotomous groups.

Correlational designs for retrospective studies   A common design concentrates on *correlational relationships* within a single group. At a simple level, we just have a treatment group with observations or tests made on a dependent variable. The treatment group is however split into a number of naturally occurring (i.e. not experimentally manipulated) comparison groups (e.g. based on introversion scores; or gender; or socio-economic status) which are regarded as the levels of the independent variable.

There are likely to be several such sub-groups. Sets of data corresponding to the independent variable and the dependent variable are collected. As the data on the independent variable are retrospective they may be prone to the various types of problem to which historical data are subject (see chapter 10, p. 272), though this will depend very much on the particular variable

– gender is unlikely to be problematic; prior involvement in a particular kind of experience may well be.

Typically, as well as there being several groupings on the independent variable, there are likely to be a range of actual independent variables. The analysis will look for correlations between these independent variables and the dependent variable (in fact the distinction between independent and dependent variables can become somewhat arbitrary in retrospective research). Jung (1990) provides an example of a single group correlational design using longitudinal measures, which aid in the interpretation of results.

Survey research is commonly retrospective in style and raises many of the issues sketched here. They are discussed in further detail in the following chapter.

Natural Experiments

Experiments carried out outside laboratories may be in the 'real world' but if carried out purely for research purposes there is a sense in which they are artificial. Practical and ethical issues preclude the carrying out of true experiments on a range of topics of considerable interest and social concern: for example, on the effects of cigarette smoking, or of parental divorce on children. Sometimes, however, naturally occurring situations can be capitalized upon to form the basis of an experimental investigation.

The classic case of this kind is probably the study of identical twins who have been reared apart from a very early stage in life, in studies of the relative effects of 'nature' and 'nurture'. Cataclysms and disasters have been used in studies on the effects of extreme stress and trauma. Green et al. (1990) provide an example of a quasi-experimental design comparing survivors from the 'Buffalo Creek' dam disaster with other non-equivalent groups. Verplanken (1989), in a study of attitude towards nuclear energy, was able to compare views of such groups both before and after the Chernobyl accident. Other major and sudden disruptions to a society or group (e.g. the effect of the discovery of oil on remote Shetland communities – Caetano et al., 1983) have been capitalized on.

A somewhat different situation is where there are deliberate, intended or engineered changes, carried out for purposes other than that of research but which can also be grist to the researcher's mill. Ross's (1973) analysis of the British 'Breathalyser' introduction, previously discussed in the context of quasi-experimentation, falls into this category. (See also Campbell, 1969, which provided an influential argument for the study of 'reforms as experiments'). As this example demonstrates, this kind of passive observation can, in appropriate circumstances, be used to form the basis of causal inference. Cook and Campbell (1979) show that for time series designs the main requirements are that the event being evaluated has to be abrupt in onset and precisely dated, and not a reaction to a prior change in level of the dependent variable.

Similarly, the 'treatment' being manipulated in a non-equivalent control group quasi-experimental design can be, for example, attendance at a particular training programme, even where the programme is a permanent institution and the researcher did not manipulate anything. However, as in the general approach to the interpretation of quasi-experimental designs, specific threats to validity such as selection-maturity interactions have to be rendered implausible, and the context should be so set up as to incorporate natural controls which reduce the equivocality of inference accompanying correlational data.

Cook and Campbell (1979) take further the problem of 'inferring cause from passive observation', and discusses a range of methods for getting at causal processes based on observations of sequences and concomitances as they occur in natural settings, without the advantage of deliberate manipulations and controls to rule out the effect of extraneous causal influences. These include path analysis, causal modelling, cross-lagged panel correlation and methods for comparing two time series.

Further Reading

Barlow, D. H., Hayes, S. C. and Nelson, R. O. (1984) *The Scientist Practitioner: research and accountability in clinical and educational settings*. Oxford: Pergamon. Good coverage of single-subject designs and the related methodology.

Cook, T. D. and Campbell, D. T. (1979) *Quasi-experimentation: Design and analysis issues for field settings*. Chicago: Rand McNally. Definitive presentation of issues to do with the design of quasi-experiments. Includes discussion on design of true experiments in the field.

Haimson, B. R. and Elfenbeim, M. H. (1985) *Experimental Methods in Psychology*. New York: McGraw-Hill. Standard text giving clear introductory treatment of experimental design. Includes quasi- and single-subject experiments.

Kazdin, A. E. (1982) *Single-case Research Designs: methods for clinical and applied settings*. Oxford: Oxford University Press. Very thorough and accessible treatment of all aspects of single subject experimentation.

Mitchell, J. and Jolley, J. (1985) *Research Design Explained*. New York: Holt, Rinehart and Winston. As Haimson and Elfenbeim but some treatment of field experiments.

Riecken, H. W. and Boruch, R. F. (eds) (1974) *Social Experimentation*. New York: Academic. Discusses the management of experiments conducted in everyday settings and their strengths and weaknesses.

Robson, C. (1983) *Experiment, Design and Statistics in Psychology*, 2nd edn. London: Penguin. Introductory treatment of the design and analysis of simple single-variable experiments.

Wright, G. and Fowler, C. (1986) *Investigative Design and Statistics*. London: Penguin. Follows on from Robson, with wide-ranging coverage of more complex experimental and correlational designs.

5

Designing Small Surveys

The chapter discusses the characteristics of surveys and their advantages and disadvantages.

It stresses the professionalism needed to carry out a high-quality survey.

It also outlines the simple descriptive survey and summarizes other possible designs.

The chapter concludes with a discussion on the why and how of sampling.

Introduction

Surveys are common. You will have to have led a very hermit-like existence not to have been asked to take part in some form of survey – which brand of washing powder or lager do you buy, and what other brands do you know? Who would you vote for if there were a General Election next week, do you think the Prime Minister is doing a good job? How do you rate the service in our hotel or restaurant? etc. etc. Similarly, the results of surveys of one form or another pepper the pages of newspapers and salt radio and television output. This week's top forty discs; 'Survey shows shortfall of 13,000 teachers'; '57 per cent of households now own a video-recorder compared with 4 per cent at the beginning of the decade' and half a dozen others in the paper I have in front of me.

Surveys have, however, been with us for a long time. The Domesday Book, and efforts to assess the effects of the plague in London in the seventeenth century, provide notable landmarks. Marsh (1982, ch. 1) gives a detailed and fascinating account as part of her defence of the strategy against critics of the use of surveys within sociology.

Much of their current use is highly instrumental and in the interests of better marketing and higher sales of some service or product. A substantial amount is academic in the sense of seeking to find out something about what is going on in society today. In either case there is a high premium on 'getting it right'; that is, on getting an accurate and unbiased assessment of whatever it is that is being measured. In some fields, most notably in political polling, error can be glaringly obvious – when the predicted winner loses, or there is wide discrepancy between polls purporting to measure the same thing. Often, however, there is no obvious reality test and judgments of reliability and validity have to fall back on an analysis of how the survey was carried out.

Large-scale surveys are big business and require substantial time and effort to carry out. Box 5.1 gives an estimate for a time budget for a survey involving about 1,000 interviews. Hoinville and Jowell (1977) and colleagues from the staff of 'Social and Community Planning Research' (a well regarded independent British institute for carrying out social survey research) have produced a detailed and very practical manual based on their experience. It is strongly recommended for anyone contemplating this scale of survey.

Box 5.1   Time budget for a survey of about 1,000 interviews

1 *Initial design work*, including sample design and selection, takes a minimum of six weeks.

2 *Questionnaire construction*, including pilot work and the design and printing of the final questionnaire, takes at least another six weeks.

3 *Briefing* the interviewers, followed by the *fieldwork phase* for, say, twenty interviewers, each covering fifty respondents, takes another six weeks.

4 *Editing and coding* can start at the same time as the fieldwork but, to allow for postage and sorting out problems, is likely to run on for a further six weeks.

5 *Computer entry and editing* takes about four more weeks. That is, a total of at least six months will be needed to get to the stage where analysis and interpretation can *begin*.

Analysis and interpretation will take at least another month, as will the production of a survey report. And as this timetable assumes that no problems will occur (and they will – you just don't know in advance what they are going to be – bad weather, school holidays, industrial disputes, flu or other epidemics, and computer breakdowns are not unknown) it is probably realistic to think in terms of a full year to complete the exercise.

A small-scale survey obviously requires fewer resources and can be completed in a shorter time. However, the same basic stages are involved – unless you are analysing manually rather than by computer at the final stage, which, while feasible with small samples, is not a time-saver. The initial design and questionnaire construction will, if anything, take up a greater proportion of the time in a small survey.

Survey Design and Experimental Design

This chapter is shorter than the preceding one on experimental design. This is because, in experimentation, design is a highly developed field. The selection of a design is often crucial in getting to a position where the research questions can be answered. Specific experimental methods, the tactics rather than the strategy of research, are idiosyncratic to the specific research field; they may well have to be designed specially for a particular study.

By contrast, much of the generalized knowledge about carrying out surveys is at the tactical level; i.e. how one goes about things to carry out a survey based on face-to-face interviewing, or the very different requirements of a postal questionnaire study. These issues to do with specific methods of investigation are taken up in detail in part III.

What is a Survey?

The time budget given in box 5.1 is couched in terms of a survey carried out by *interviewers*; those persons armed with clip-boards, and a structured questionnaire, who stop you in the street or knock on the front door and ask if you would mind answering a few questions. However, other forms of survey are possible, including the self-administered *postal questionnaire*, and (increasingly common in North America) the *telephone survey*. Indeed, surveys are not necessarily restricted to variants of interviewing or types of questionnaire. A traffic survey may be exclusively observational; a survey of the working life of lecturers in higher education may rely on a weekly diary (leaving on one side for the moment the likely trustworthiness of such information if it is to be used to seek to demonstrate to their paymasters how hard-working they are!).

Recall that, as discussed in chapter 2, the survey is a research *strategy* rather than a method or technique. Because of the ubiquity of surveys, it is likely that you will have a good common-sense appreciation of what the term means. It is however difficult to give a concise definition, precisely because of the wide range of studies that have been labelled as surveys. The central features of the survey strategy were presented in the earlier chapter as: –

- the collection of a small amount of data in standardized form from a relatively large number of individuals; and
- the selection of samples of individuals from known populations.

While this captures the large majority of surveys, there are examples where a considerable amount of data is collected from each individual; where the 'unit' involved is not an individual but some form of organization such as a school, firm or business; and, particularly in the latter case, where the number of 'units' sampled gets down to single figures.

Kerlinger (1964) suggests that survey research is typified by the collection of data from a population, or some sample drawn from it, to assess the relative incidence, distribution and interrelationships of naturally occurring phenomena. Bryman (1989) attempts a more formal definition:

> survey research entails the collection of data on a number of units and usually at a single juncture in time, with a view to collecting systematically a body of quantifiable data in respect of a number of variables which are then examined to discern patterns of association. (p. 104)

He warns against taking the 'single juncture in time' too literally. As our earlier example showed, practicalities will often dictate that data are collected over a period of weeks or even months; but they are treated as if collection were simultaneous. In other words, this is a cross-sectional design. There is, however, nothing in principle to stop the use of surveys in longitudinal designs.

There are surveys which make use of depth interviewing from which the systematization that Bryman refers to is difficult, and quantification likely to be inappropriate. Nevertheless, he is right to stress that survey research is almost always conducted in order to provide a *quantitative* picture of the individuals, or other units, concerned. The emphasis on *quantification*, on *variables* and on *sampling from known populations* shows how survey researchers share a basically similar scientific view of the nature of the research task to that adopted by researchers using experiments.

Surveys and the Other Research Strategies

The major divide between surveys and experiments lies in the presence of planned change in experiments, and its absence from almost all surveys. The typical survey is passive in that it seeks to describe and/or analyse, even in some cases to explore, some aspect of the world out there *as it is*. This often includes or even focuses totally on what the individuals surveyed think or feel about the topic. The experiment is active in that it asks: what happens if this is changed?

Surveys and case studies also have obvious fundamental differences from each other. Essentially, the survey studies the sample not in its own right but as a means of understanding the population from which it is drawn. Case studies have a prime concern for understanding that particular case per se.

These differences may be blurred in several ways. Surveys may be associated with the deliberate manipulation of one or more variables. For example, perhaps a sequence of surveys is carried out before, during and after an intervention (say to evaluate the effect of a local police force deciding to start a campaign of prosecuting kerb-crawling drivers soliciting prostitutes). A case study of a large organization might incorporate a survey of employees, using impeccable representative sampling of perhaps 10 per cent of them. These are examples of what I have called *hybrid* research strategies where the typical features of more than one strategy are combined within a single study.

This should be distinguished from the large project, or research programme incorporating more than one research strategy – which might be termed a *combined* strategy. A common pattern is to have a mainly survey-based study accompanied by a set of case studies. The surveys provide a general, representative, picture; the case studies, chosen often on the basis of the survey, illuminate, enrich and bring to life the survey findings. The work of Hegarty and his colleagues at the National Foundation for Educational Research on the integration of pupils with special needs into mainstream schools provides a good example (Moses et al., 1988; Hodgson et al., 1984).

Advantages and Disadvantages of the Survey

Researchers tend to have strong, frequently polarized, views about the place and importance of surveys. Some see the survey as *the* central 'real world' strategy. It may be that in non-laboratory situations where experiments are often neither feasible nor ethically defensible, surveys give that reassuring scientific ring of confidence. Associated with surveys is a satisfyingly complex set of technological concerns about sampling, question-wording, answer-coding, etc.

Others view surveys as generating large amounts of data of dubious value. Falsely prestigious because of their quantitative nature, the findings are seen as a product of largely uninvolved respondents whose answers owe more to some unknown mixture of politeness, boredom, desire to be seen in a good light, etc. than their true feelings, beliefs or behaviour.

As is often the case, such caricatures are not without foundation. The trustworthiness of the data depends to a considerable extent on the technical proficiency of those running the survey. If the questions are incomprehensible or ambiguous, the exercise is obviously a waste of time. This is a problem of *internal validity* where we are not obtaining valid information about the respondents and what they are thinking, feeling or whatever.

The problem of securing a high degree of involvement by respondents to a survey is more intractable. This is particularly so when it is carried out by post but is also still difficult when the survey is carried out face-to-face (remember that nearly all surveys carried out by interviewers involve fleeting interactions with total strangers – it is asking a great deal of the interviewer to establish a rapport with each and every respondent so that he or she is fully involved). Securing involvement is in part also a technical matter (a poorly designed and printed, lengthy questionnaire administered just before Christmas to workers in an organization who are currently trying to meet a seasonal deadline is unlikely to get a good response), but it has to be accepted as a likely hazard of the strategy per se.

If the sampling is faulty, this produces an *external validity* problem such that we can't generalize our findings. Another type of external validity problem occurs if we seek to generalize from what people say in a survey to what they actually do. The lack of relation between attitude and behaviour is notorious – see, for example, Hanson (1980), who in a review of forty-six studies found twenty which did not demonstrate a positive relationship between attitudes and behaviour.

Reliability is more straightforward. By presenting all respondents with the same standardized questions, carefully worded after piloting, it is possible to obtain high reliability of response.

None the less, a good, competently run survey is something which psychologists and others purporting to do research with humans should be able to offer. Surveys provide the sort of data which is not difficult for an intelligent lay audience to understand, particularly an audience which is scientifically literate. Lindblom and Cohen (1979) make a strong case that, of the various forms of 'usable knowledge' those carrying out professional social enquiry might provide, the humble survey may well be the most influential. Zeisel (1981) presents the somewhat back-handed, but realistic, compliment that

> the apparent exactness and rigorousness of statistical analysis [of survey data] is a useful device to win arguments with people who do not understand the value of qualitative knowing in scientific research. This is an important characteristic of the method when research results are to be used in a court of law, in a political setting, in applied design – in any competitive decision-making situation. (pp. 160–1)

Hakim (1987) makes a related point in referring to the main attractions of the sample survey as its *transparency* (or *accountability*): In other words, that

> the methods and procedures used can be made visible and accessible to other parties (be they professional colleagues, clients, or the public audience for the study report), so that the implementation as well as the overall research design can be assessed. (p. 48)

A standardized language is used to refer to the sampling procedures employed. Questionnaires, code-books, introductory letters, analyses of non-response, etc are expected to be included in the report. Increasingly, raw survey data are deposited in data archives (e.g. the ESRC Data Archive at Essex University), permitting both checking and further analysis by other workers. This standard of professionalism found in quality survey work mirrors that expected in experimental studies, and is an urgent requirement within the case study tradition and more generally in connection with qualitative data. This latter is, of course, a strong theme in chapters 6 and 12, dealing with case study and the analysis of qualitative data respectively.

Box 5.2 lists some of the advantages and disadvantages of the survey.

Why Carry Out a Survey?

As stressed in chapter 2, a survey can be carried out for *any* of the research purposes whether exploratory, descriptive or explanatory. In practice, however, surveys are not particularly well suited to carrying out exploratory work. While there is nothing to stop you asking a wide range of largely open-ended questions in an attempt to explore some area, this is likely to be an inefficient and ineffective procedure taking a great deal of time to analyse. Surveys work best with standardized questions where we have confidence that the questions mean the same thing to different respondents, a condition which is difficult to satisfy when the purpose is exploratory. The requirement is that you know what kind of information you want to collect.

Many, probably most, surveys are carried out for descriptive purposes. They can provide information about the distribution of a wide range of 'people characteristics', and of relationships between such characteristics. For example, a political party might be interested in voters' views about their policies, and on how such views are related to, say, age, gender, income, region of the country, etc. At a local level, there may be a need to find the relative degree of support or opposition to alternative development plans.

It is possible to go beyond the descriptive to the interpretive: that is, to use the survey to provide explanations of what is described, essentially to get at causal relationships. This is not an easy or a straightforward undertaking because the information is typically in the form of correlations. And as will no doubt be burned into the brain of anyone who has followed even an elementary course in statistics, correlation does not imply causation. What is required is a sophisticated analysis of the detailed pattern of correlations. The logic of such an analysis is similar to that employed in quasi-experimentation and involves consideration of the possible threats to internal validity.

For example, suppose that we are interested in the jobs that pupils from different ethnic backgrounds go into after leaving school; and that we want not only to see who goes to what kind of job, but also to interpret this.

Box 5.2   Advantages and disadvantages of the survey strategy

1   Disadvantages

General to all surveys using respondents

a   Data are affected by the characteristics of the respondents (e.g. their memory; knowledge; experience; motivation; and personality).

b   Respondents won't necessarily report their beliefs, attitudes, etc. accurately (e.g. there is likely to be a social desirability response bias – people responding in a way that shows them in a good light).

Postal and other self-administered surveys

c   Typically have a low response rate. As you don't usually know the characteristics of non-respondents you don't know whether the sample is representative.

d   Ambiguities in, and misunderstandings of, the survey questions may not be detected.

e   Respondents may not treat the exercise seriously; and you may not be able to detect this.

Interview surveys

f   Data may be affected by characteristics of the interviewers (e.g. their motivation; personality; skills; and experience). There may be interviewer bias, where the interviewer, probably unwittingly, influences the responses (e.g. through verbal or non-verbal cues indication 'correct' answers).

g   Data may be affected by interactions of interviewer/respondent characteristics (e.g. whether they are of the same or different class or ethnic background).

h   Respondents may feel their answers are not anonymous and be less forthcoming or open.

2   Advantages

General to all surveys using respondents

a   They provide a relatively simple and straightforward approach to the study of attitudes, values, beliefs and motives.

b They may be adapted to collect generalizable information from almost any human population.

c Highly structured surveys have high amounts of data standardization.

Postal and other self-administered surveys

d Often this is the only, or the easiest, way of retrieving information about the past history of a large set of people.

e They can be extremely efficient at providing large amounts of data, at relatively low cost, in a short period of time.

f They allow anonymity, which can encourage frankness when sensitive areas are involved.

Interview surveys

g The interviewer can clarify questions.

h The presence of the interviewer encourages participation and involvement (and the interviewer can judge the extent to which the exercise is treated seriously).

Notes
1 Advantages (d) and (e) may be disadvantages if they seduce the researcher into using a survey when it may not be the most appropriate strategy to answer the research question(s).
2 The telephone survey is a variation of the interview survey which does not involve face-to-face interaction and has rather different advantages and disadvantages (see chapter 9, p. 241).

When we try to explain why there is a differential involvement of, say, Pakistani, Afro-Caribbean and white youths in particular types of employment, we might find from a survey that there are differences in educational attainment in the groups from different ethnic backgrounds and, further, that this attainment is related to occupational type. It is not legitimate simply to make the connection that differences in educational attainment explain (cause) the differential pattern of occupation for the pupils from different educational backgrounds. Leaving aside practical problems such as how jobs can be classified, and the more intractable measurement problem of ensuring that tests of educational attainment are 'culture-free' (that is, that they do not introduce biases related to ethnic background – which itself constitutes a threat to the internal validity of the study), it is patently obvious that the different ethnic groups are likely to differ in a host of other ways apart from their educational attainment. Differential encouragement from the home; family income; parental and friends' occupations; careers advice (or the lack of it); attitudes of potential employers – these are just a few of the possibilities.

Explanation and interpretation depend on incorporating into the study information on a substantial number of such variables and then analysing the pattern of correlations, seeing where relationships are strong and where they are weak or non-existent. From this you seek to tell the most convincing story that you can. What goes into the pot, that is, which variables you seek information on, is determined by pilot work (perhaps involving unstructured or depth interviews) and by previous studies, as well as any theoretical framework you have developed. How to do such an analysis is covered in chapter 11, p. 344.

It is perhaps worth reiterating that causal analysis is much easier and more straightforward when you can do a true experiment. In the example quoted above, however, randomized assignment of individuals to different ethnic groups would pose a tricky problem! An alternative, which can assist when you want to go beyond mere description, is to use a somewhat more sophisticated survey design than the single, simple 'one-shot' survey, such as the 'panel' design discussed below.

Formal Designs for Surveys

There is not the wide range of formal design possibilities for small-scale surveys that is available to the designer of an experiment. Experimental design has been elaborated and formalized primarily in the service of getting at cause and effect relationships. If, as is the case for many surveys, the intention is purely descriptive and we wish simply to get at the distribution of, say, attitudes to 'green' issues, then it is not necessary to conceptualize a formal research design in this sense. We can similarly *describe* relationships between variables – between, say, 'green' attitudes and age or occupation; it is when we wish to go beyond this to seek explanations and make interpretations that formal design becomes important.

The Simple Survey

In its simplest form, the survey involves collecting the same standardized data from an undifferentiated group of respondents over a short period of time. The respondents are almost always selected as a representative sample from some larger population. Such a survey is sometimes referred to as an 'ad hoc sample survey'. Formally, it is equivalent to the simplest of the 'pre-experimental' designs: the 'one-group post-test only' design (see Box 4.12, p. 99) which was castigated in chapter 4 as a design to avoid if you are seeking causal relationships. However, it is perfectly adequate if all you are seeking to do is to find information about the incidence and distribution of particular characteristics, and of possible relationships among them.

As the group of respondents is likely to incorporate naturally occurring variables with several levels (e.g. sex as female/male; or age as 15–19/20–24/ 25–29 etc.), it is also possible to view this as a 'comparison group' survey. Thought of in this way it becomes formally equivalent to a second type of 'pre-experiment', the 'post-test only non-equivalent groups design' (see box 4.13, p. 100). Alternatively, comparison groups covering variables of particular interest can be built explicitly into the design, with appropriate sampling to ensure representativeness. In either case, moving from description to establishing causation is difficult with this design.

It is, in principle, perfectly feasible to repeat a survey at different points in time. The resources required to do this can be substantial, particularly if the move is made from an 'ad hoc' survey to a 'regular' survey where a continuing series of surveys is planned. This is the strategy adopted by government agencies and other large survey organizations – e.g. the Social Attitudes Survey, the British Crime Surveys, the General Household Surveys and the Family Expenditure Survey; Hakim (1987, ch. 7) gives references and further details. They are well outside the scope of this book, except in the sense of providing a resource base which can be used in designing surveys and a data base to which small-scale surveys might link.

A repeated survey can make use of a different sample of respondents for each repetition, in which case it remains a cross-sectional survey. We are simply getting more than one cross-section at different times. It is however possible to use the same sample and hence introduce a longitudinal element into the design. This then becomes a 'panel' survey.

The Panel Survey

In a 'panel' survey, design data are collected on the same set of respondents at two or more points in time. As with the simple survey, this can also be characterized as incorporating two or more comparison groups by virtue of the inclusion of naturally occurring variables. Such a survey is likely to demand considerable resources of both time and effort, particularly when the phenomena of interest require substantial time intervals between the bouts of data collection. For example, a panel survey of the effects of higher education would call for an involvement lasting over at least four or five years. Similar problems to those encountered in repeated measures experiments occur: a 'test' at one point in time may influence performance on a later 'test'; there may be 'mortality' in the group where members of the original panel are lost, move away or whatever.

The big advantage of the panel survey is the inclusion of a clear temporal sequence in the data obtained. If A precedes B in time we know that while A might have caused B, B can not have caused A. This provides a useful additional tool in interpreting relationships. However, a substantial number of threats to validity still lurk, as in the corresponding quasi-experimental design.

Most panel surveys are ruled out of court for the small-scale type of enquiry covered in this text, because of the amount of time and effort they require. It is, however, possible to use logic and common sense to produce a time sequence for the effects of a range of variables even when the data are collected cross-sectionally (i.e. at one point in time) rather than longitudinally (i.e. extending over time). Kidder and Judd (1986, p. 133) refer to this as a 'pseudo-panel' design, though it might perhaps be thought of as part of the analytic treatment of a simple survey design. For example, a study of occupational choice might erect a sequence of:

1st   father's educational level;
2nd   eldest brother's educational level;
3rd   respondent's educational level;
4th   respondent's first job;
5th   respondent's job at time of survey.

The father's formal education can reasonably be considered to have been completed before that of the eldest brother, and hence might be viewed as the causative factor in any relationship which is found; and so on.

Rotating Sample Survey

This is a hybrid somewhere between the repeated cross-sectional simple survey and the panel survey. On each repetition of the survey, the sample will include some members from the previous survey and some new members. Typically, the same fraction of new and repeating participants is involved with each repetition – e.g. there might be one-quarter new members each time with the total sample size kept constant. The attraction of this approach is that it provides both a series of overall snapshots and the tracking of individual changes over time.

Practicalities of Design

In practical design terms, the main issues are:

Who do you ask?
How do you ask?
What do you ask?
What resources do you need?

The 'who' refers to the *population* of interest (e.g. profoundly deaf young people aged between 16 and 19 years in West Yorkshire; or homeless persons in central London) and, unless the whole population is to be surveyed, the specific *sample* from that population which will be surveyed. The sample should be representative of the population, which in many cases is not an easy task to ensure.

The 'how' is typically interview or questionnaire; face- to-face or 'distant' (by post or telephone). Different parts of the survey may call for different approaches. The 'what' requires the most work. Typically the research issue or overall purpose of the survey indicates areas of questioning which require elaboration into specific questions, themselves needing refinement through piloting. Finally, if you don't ensure that you have adequate resources actually to mount the survey and carry it through to completion, then there is not much point to the whole exercise.

Mounting a Small-scale Survey

The various steps in designing a simple survey are as follows.

1 Sort out the general purpose and the specific information requirements

a *You are doing a survey because your preliminary analysis* (see 'Choosing a Research Strategy' p. 39) *has indicated that a survey is the most appropriate way of addressing your research question(s).* You are not, of course, doing a survey because you happen to be familiar with the process and it seems easier than doing an experiment or case study. In the real world, it is accepted that you might be doing a survey because your boss has told you to, or for some similar pragmatic reason. You might well be combining a survey with some other type of enquiry, such as one or more case studies.

b *The first step is to clarify the research question(s).* The preliminary analysis should have helped with this. Put in other terms, this involves the translation of your general purpose into one or more specific aims.

c *Next develop a range of sub-questions, or subsidiary topics, relating to the central question.*

d *Work out the specific information required in connection with each topic or sub-question.*

Box 5.3 gives an example of the working out of these successive steps. While it is not unknown for this to be carried out as a desk exercise, with the individual or team involved using their common sense, experience and knowledge of previous work, it is highly desirable for these endeavours to be supplemented by fieldwork. The two main methods employed are individual depth interviews and group discussions. See the appropriate sections in chapter 9. Morton-Williams in Hoinville et al. (1985, ch. 2) gives details of the use of these methods in the early stages of survey design.

Box 5.3   Establishing the purpose and information requirements of a survey – an example

1 *Translation of general purpose into a more specific aim.* (*note*: this can be expressed in terms either of statements or of questions; translation from one to the other is not difficult).

general purpose: measurement of people's travel plans

This is too vague to help in designing the survey.

more specific: what is the likely impact of changes in travel policy on people's travel plans?

or: a detailed description of local transport usage;

or: the link between travel behaviour and recreational patterns;

or: examination of attitudes and preferences in relation to local transport.

2 *Itemizing of subsidiary topics relating to the central aim or question.* If we take the question on the likely impact of changes in travel policy on people's travel plans, then subsidiary topics/questions might be:

- what are the current roles of public and private transport?
- likely growth in car ownership;
- factors influencing or inhibiting public transport usage;
- safety considerations;
- environmental considerations;
- public attitudes to pedestrian precincts, parking restraints, road building, etc.;
- the extent and nature of travelling difficulties;
- viability of alternative forms of transport services: dial-a-ride, mini-buses, etc.

3 *Formulation of specific information requirements in connection with each of these topics.* In connection with the current roles of public and private transport, there is a need for:

- record of journeys made by various types of transport for different purposes by each member of the family;
- respondents' perceptions of the suitability of public and private transport for different kinds of journeys.

4 *Consideration of the appropriate data collection methods for different items of information.* Note that while a face-to-face interview (or possibly postal questionnaire) would be appropriate for the perceptions of suitability, there would be likely to be memory problems with the journey record information. This might better be obtained by means of a self-completion diary.

(Adapted from Hoinville and Jowell, 1977, pp. 2–3.)

2   *Construct the questionnaire*   This involves deciding on the questions that are to be asked, and on their precise wording; also on their sequence and the layout of the questionnaire. Details are given in chapter 9, in the section on structured questionnaires.

3   *Determine the population and the sample to be selected*   The appropriate poulation is usually relatively straightforward to determine. The research question gives strong pointers (e.g. that you are dealing with car drivers, or with 16–19-year-old pupils with severe learning difficulties). Resource considerations, perhaps interacting with the need to draw a sample which is representative of the population, will often dictate the issue. If you are restricted to, say, a 30-mile radius from your base, then you are going to be in trouble if you are after a random sample from a national population.

Sampling, to be able to convince yourself and others that your chosen sample is representative of the population, is more difficult. The following section considers these issues.

4   *After the Planning Stage*   All that now remains is to carry out the survey. With large surveys, this is a complex management task involving recruiting and training interviewers. Small surveys are obviously easier to manage, particularly when the person planning the survey also carries it out. However, there are important skills to be mastered if the task is to be carried out professionally. Part III covers the methods, chapter 9 dealing with those you are most likely to use with the survey strategy. Further details on important nitty-gritty issues are presented in 'Arranging the Practicalities' (p. 294).

Sampling in Surveys – and Elsewhere

Sampling is an important aspect of life in general and enquiry in particular. We make judgements about people, places and things on the basis of fragmentary evidence. It is what Smith (1975), in an excellent discussion of the place of sampling in social research, refers to as 'the search for typicality' (p. 105). A different way of saying the same thing is that sampling is closely linked to the *external validity* or *generalizability* (chapter 3, p. 70) of the findings in an enquiry; the extent to which what we have found in a particular situation at a particular time applies more generally.

This discussion focuses on survey sampling. Sampling considerations, however, pervade all aspects of research and crop up in various forms no matter what research strategy or investigatory technique we use.

The idea of 'sample' is linked to that of 'population'. *Population refers to all the cases.* It might be, for example, all adults living in the United Kingdom; or all children attending schools in Sunderland; or all privately run homes for the elderly in Kent. The last example illustrates that 'population' is being used in a general sense – it isn't limited to people. The concept can be further stretched to include units that are not 'people-related' at all: for example, populations of situations (e.g. all possible locations in which some-one might be interviewed), or of events or times. It is unusual to be able to deal with the whole of a population in a survey, which is where sampling comes in. *A sample is a selection from the population.*

Non- 'people-related' sampling is in practice very important (e.g. sampling places and times – deciding, for example, where, when and how interviews take place), and is discussed further in the context of case studies (see chapter 6, p. 153). However, particular attention needs to be given to the selection of the 'people sample' in planning a survey. This is because the dependability of a survey is crucially affected by the principles or system used to select respondents – usually referred to as the 'sampling plan'.

There are some circumstances where it is feasible to survey the whole of a population. A national census attempts to do just that, of course, and while it hardly qualifies as the small-scale study targeted in this book, there are occasions when the population of interest is manageably small – say, the line managers in an organization; or the pupils in a particular school; or patients in a hospital; or clients of a particular local social service. It should not be assumed, however, that a full census is necessarily superior to a well thought-out sample survey. There are trade-offs requiring careful thought. Will you actually be able to carry out the full set of interviews, or would it be preferable to do a smaller number of longer, more detailed ones? Can you in fact reach (virtually) everybody? The 'hard-to-get' may differ from the rest in important ways that you should know about. If you are sampling, you might be able to devote more time and resources to chasing them up.

The various types of sampling plan are usually divided into ones based on PROBABILITY SAMPLES (where the probability of the selection of each respondent is known), and on NON-PROBABILITY SAMPLES (where it isn't known). In probability sampling, statistical inferences about the popula-tion can be made from the responses of the sample. For this reason, prob-ability sampling is sometimes referred to as REPRESENTATIVE SAMPLING. The sample is taken as representative of the population. In non-probability samples, you can not make such statistical inferences (Smith, 1983, discusses what kind of inferences can be made in this situation). It may still be poss-ible to say something sensible about the population from non-probability samples – but not on statistical grounds.

What Size of Sample?

While probability samples allow you to generalize from sample to popula-tion, such generalizations are themselves probabilistic. The larger the sample the lower the likely error in generalizing. Formulae have been developed to assist in the choice of an efficient sample size when it is important to limit estimation errors to a particular level. Henry (1990, ch. seven) gives an introduction. Lipsey (1989) provides a more detailed account and a useful general treatment of power analysis, which covers the factors that affect the sensitivity of a design in detecting relationships. Power analysis is applicable in experiments as well as in surveys (Kraemer, 1981; Still, 1982). Cohen (1977) provides 'power tables' to help in choosing sample sizes. They should be treated with care as you need to be clear about the assumptions on which they are based. This is a matter on which it is advisable to seek assistance if it is of importance in your study.

There are some simple general principles worth bearing in mind:-

* There is a tendency for 'diminishing returns' in accuracy from increasing sample size. For example, the same gain in precision obtained from increasing a sample from 90 to 100, might in some circumstances require the doubling in size of a sample of 300.
* The more variability there is in the population, the larger the sample size needed. If people don't vary much on the measures you are taking, you can get away with a smaller sample.
* The type of analysis you are going to do has repercussions on sample size, as does the number of categories into which you will be subdividing the data. Common techniques such as chi-square require certain minimum cell frequencies. *This reinforces the need to consider what you are going to do with the data in terms of analysis at the design stage.*

Probability Samples

Simple Random Sampling

This involves selection at random from a list of the population (known in survey parlance as the 'sampling frame') of the required number of persons for the sample. A lottery method, random number tables (as found in many statistics books), or a computer (e.g. Boyle, 1986) can be used. If properly conducted, this gives each person an equal chance of being included in the sample, and also makes all possible combinations of persons for a particular sample size equally likely. Note that *each* person is chosen at random, as compared with systematic sampling where only the first one is (see below). You can't produce a simple random sample without a full list of the population.

Detailed examples of procedures for this, and the other forms of probability sampling, are given in Baker (1988, pp. 146–56).

Systematic Sampling

This involves choosing a starting point in the sampling frame at random, and then choosing every *n*th person. Thus if a sample of fifty is required from a population of 2,000 then every fortieth person is chosen. There would have to be a random selection of a number between one and forty to start off the sequence. For the sample to be representative, this method relies on the list being organized in a way unrelated to the subject of the survey. Although this may seem to be a simple and straightforward way of drawing a probability sample, it has certain statistical peculiarities. Whereas the initial chance of selection of any person is the same, once the first person has been chosen most persons will have no chance of inclusion and a few will be automatically selected. Similarly, most combinations of persons are excluded from the possible samples that might be chosen. This might be important if the ordering in the list is organized in some way (possibly unknown to yourself).

Both random and systematic sampling require a full list of the population. Getting this list is often difficult. Hence, if there is any possibility of ordering in the list messing up your systematic sample, you may as well go for a random sample as the extra effort is minimal.

Stratified Random Sampling

This involves dividing the population into a number of groups or STRATA, where members of a group share a particular characteristic or characteristics (e.g. stratum A may be females; stratum B males). There is then random sampling within the strata. It is usual to have PROPORTIONATE SAMPLING: that is, where the numbers of the groups selected for the sample reflects the relative numbers in the population as a whole (e.g. if there are equal numbers of males and females in the population, there should be equal numbers in the samples; if 80 per cent of the population are from one ethnic group and 20 per cent from another group, then one sample should be four times the other in size). It may sometimes be helpful to have DISPROPORTIONATE SAMPLING, where there is an unequal weighting. This would allow you to 'oversample' a small but important stratum, or to ensure that there is at least some representation of certain 'rare species' even to the extent of including all examples of them. Also, if it is known (perhaps from pilot work) that there is greater variation in response from one particular stratum, then this is an indication to include a disproportionately large number from that stratum in the overall sample.

Sampling theory shows that in some circumstances stratified random sampling can be more efficient than simple random sampling, in the sense that for a given sample size, the means of stratified samples are likely to be closer to the population mean. This occurs when there is a relatively small amount of variability in whatever characteristic is being measured in the survey *within* the stratum, compared to variability across strata. The improvement in efficiency does not occur if there is considerable variability in the characteristic within the stratum. So, for example, if females tend to give similar measures, ratings or whatever in a particular survey, and males also tend to give similar ratings to other males, but show overall differences from females, there would be advantage in stratifying the sample by sex.

A note on stratified systematic samples   It is of course possible to combine stratification with systematic sampling procedures. However, the same criticisms apply to systematic sampling and there seems little or no reason to prefer them to stratified random samples.

Cluster Sampling

This involves dividing the population into a number of units, or CLUSTERS, each of which contains individuals having a range of characteristics. The clusters themselves are chosen on a random basis. The sub-population within the cluster is then chosen. This tactic is particularly useful when a population is widely dispersed and large, requiring a great deal of effort and travel to get the survey information. Random sampling might well generate a perversely scattered sample, and Murphy's Law (otherwise known as the Law of Maximum Perversity) is likely to ensure that the most distant and difficult to reach are not there when you call, necessitating a second difficult visit. It may also be that permission has to be negotiated to interview repondents, and doing this on what is effectively a one-to-one basis for all respondents will be particularly time-consuming.

An example might involve schoolchildren, where there is initially random sampling of a number of *schools*, and then testing of all the pupils in each school. There are problems in generalizing to the population of children. Strictly, statistical generalization should be limited to the population of *schools* (i.e. the clustering variable). This method has the valuable feature that it can be used when the sampling frame is not known (e.g. when we do not have a full list of children in the population, in the above example).

Multi-stage Sampling

This is an extension of cluster sampling. It involves selecting the sample in stages; i.e. taking samples from samples. Thus one might take a random sample of schools; then a random sample of the classes within each of the schools; then from within the selected classes choose a sample of children. As with cluster sampling, this provides a means of generating a geographically concentrated sampling. The generalizability issue is the same as for cluster sampling, but judicious use of sampling at appropriate stages enables one to tailor the scale of the project to the resources available.

It is possible to incorporate stratification into both cluster and multi-stage sampling. Judgment about the relative efficiencies of these more complicated forms of sampling, and their relationship to the efficiency of simple random sampling, is difficult, and if you are expending considerable resources on a survey it is worth seeking expert advice.

Non-probability Samples

In probability sampling, it is possible to specify the probability that any person (or other unit on which the survey is based) will be included in the sample. Any sampling plan where it is not possible to do this is called 'non-probability sampling'.

Small-scale surveys commonly employ non-probability samples. They are usually less complicated to set up and are acceptable when there is no intention or need to make a statistical generalization to any population beyond the sample surveyed. They can also be used to pilot a survey prior to a probability sample approach for the main survey. They typically involve the researcher using her or his judgment to achieve a particular purpose, and for this reason are sometimes referred to as PURPOSIVE SAMPLES, although it is perhaps more useful to restrict the use of the term as indicated below. A wide range of approaches has been used.

The first two, quota and dimensional sampling, are basically trying to do the same job as a probability sample, in the sense of aspiring to carry out a sample survey which is statistically representative. They tend to be used in situations where carrying out a probability sample would not be feasible, where for example there is no sampling frame, or the resources required are not available. Their accuracy relies greatly on the skill and experience of those involved.

Quota Sampling

Here the strategy is to obtain representatives of the various elements of a population, usually in the relative proportions in which they occur in the population. Hence, if socio-economic status were considered of importance in a particular survey then the categories 'professional/managers & employers/ intermediate & junior non-manual/skilled manual/semi-skilled manual/ unskilled manual' might be used. Interviewers would be given a quota of each category (with examples to assist them in categorization). Within the category, convenience sampling (see below) is normally used. The interviewer will, for example, seek to interview a given number of unskilled manual workers, a given number of semi-skilled manual workers, etc. by, say, stopping passers-by, and will continue until her quota for the day is complete. The common use of the term 'representatives' in quota sampling has to be looked at with some care. They are representative only in number, not in terms of the type of persons actually selected.

All such means of gathering quota samples are subject to biases. Careful planning, experience and persistence can go some way to addressing obvious biases. If, for example, home visits are involved, avoiding houses where there is a Rottweiler or other large dog, or sounds of a ghetto-blaster, or there are no curtains, or the lift is out of order, etc. may be understandable behaviour on the part of the sensitive interviewer, but mitigates against representativeness in householders in the sense of all householders having an equal chance of appearing in the sample.

Dimensional Sampling

This is an extension of quota sampling. The various dimensions thought to be of importance in a survey (perhaps established by pilot work) are incorporated into the sampling procedure in such a way that at least one representative of every possible combination of these factors or dimensions is included. Thus a study of race relations might identify ethnic group and length of stay in this country as important dimensions. Hence the sampling plan could consist of a table or matrix with 'ethnic group' and 'length of stay' constituting the rows and columns. Refinements of this approach involve selection of particular combinations of the dimensions (e.g. 'Kenyan Asians' with '10–15 years residence') either because of their particular importance, or because of an inability through lack of time and resources to cover all combinations.

The critical comments made about quota sampling apply equally to dimensional sampling.

Convenience Sampling

Convenience sampling is sometimes used as a cheap and dirty way of doing a sample survey. It does not produce representative findings.

It involves choosing the nearest and most convenient persons to act as respondents. The process is continued until the required sample size has been reached. This is probably one of the most widely used and least satisfactory methods of sampling. The term 'accidental sample' is sometimes used but is misleading as it carries some suggestion of randomness, whereas all kinds of largely unspecifiable biases and influences are likely to influence who gets sampled. There are sensible uses of convenience sampling, but they are more to do with getting a feeling for the issues involved, or piloting a proper sample survey.

Sampling is used in many contexts other than a sample survey. The following approaches tend to be used in other types of fieldwork, particularly in case studies and where participant observation is involved.

Purposive Sampling

The principle of selection in purposive sampling is the researcher's judgement as to typicality or interest. A sample is built up which enables the researcher to satisfy her specific needs in a project. For example, researchers following the 'grounded theory' approach (Glaser and Strauss, 1967; Strauss, 1987) carry out initial sampling, and from analysis of the results extend the sample in ways guided by their emerging theory (this is sometimes referred to as 'theoretical sampling'). The rationale of such an approach is very different from statistical generalization from sample to population. It is an approach commonly used within case studies.

Snowball Sampling

Here the researcher identifies one or more individuals from the population of interest. After they have been interviewed, they are used as informants to identify other members of the population, who are themselves used as informants, and so on. This is a useful approach when there is difficulty in identifying members of the population, e.g. when this is a clandestine group. It can be seen as a particular type of purposive sample.

Other Types of Sample

Other types of sample may be used for special purposes. They include: –

- *Time samples*, i.e. sampling across time, for example in a study of the characteristics of the persons who use a particular space at different times of the day or week (can be probabilistic or non-probabilistic, depending on how it is organized). Commonly used in observational studies.
- *Homogenous samples*, covering a narrow range or single value of a particular variable or variables.
- *Heterogenous samples*, where there is a deliberate strategy to select individuals varying widely on the characteristic(s) of interest.
- *Extreme case samples*, i.e. concentration on extreme values when sampling, perhaps where it is considered that they will throw a particularly strong light on the phenomenon of interest.
- *Rare element samples*, where values with low frequencies in the population are overrepresented in the sample; similar rationale to the previous approach.

Representative Sampling and the Real World

The exigencies of carrying out real world studies can mean that the requirements for representative sampling are very difficult, if not impossible, to fulfil. Sampling frames may be impossible to obtain. A doctor may not be prepared to provide you with a list of patients, or a firm a list of employees. Or what you get hold of may be out-of-date, or otherwise incorrect. This leads to 'ineligibles' – persons on the sampling frame who are not part of your target population. Conversely, 'eligibles' may not get into the frame. This slippage between what you have and what you want causes problems with representativeness and lowers your sample size.

Non-response can be a very serious problem and it is worth giving considerable time and effort to reducing it (see the suggestions in chapter 11, page 314). The basic issue is that those who do not participate may well differ from those who do, but it is extremely difficult to allow for this. It is worth stressing that even if you get everything else right (perfect random sample from perfect sampling frame), anything other than a very high response rate casts serious doubts on the representativeness of the sample you actually achieve. And once below that rate, it is not so much a question of the rate you get but the (unknown) degree of difference between responders and non-responders that matters. It would be entirely feasible for a response rate of 30 per cent to lead to a more representative sample than one of 60 per cent!

There are things that you can do. In a postal survey it is possible to compare late returners of questionnaires with earlier ones, or those responding after one, or two, reminders with those responding without prompting. If you know some characteristics of the population you can check to see whether the sample you obtained is reasonably typical of the population on these variables (cf Oliver, 1990, who attempts to excuse a 36 per cent response rate on these grounds). In any survey where there is differential responding between categories (say a particularly low rate from Asian females or top executives) you can compare their responses with those from other categories. Or you can make a real effort with a random sub-set of the non-respondents and try to turn them into respondents, then compare these with previous respondents. However, these are only palliatives, and the real answer is that if representativeness is crucial for you, then you so set up your study that virtually everyone responds.

But probability sampling and statistical inference are not all. Bryman (1989, pp. 113–17) shows that in practice few instances of survey research in organization studies are based on random samples. He quotes from Schwab:

> Of course we all know that almost all of the empirical studies published in our journals [organizational studies] use *convenience*, not probability samples. . . . Thus if one took generalization to a population using statistical inference seriously, one would recommend rejecting nearly all manuscripts submitted. (Schwab, 1985, p. 173)

It may be that they should try harder. There will continue to be fields where probability samples are feasible. The theoretical basis for their use is clear and well developed. What is clearly inappropriate is to play one game (convenience or other purposive sampling) according to the rules of another (probability sampling). If one is seeking representativeness or generalizability, and it is not feasible to work with probability samples, or if it is not possible to achieve adequate response rates, then the argument has to follow different lines. There are solutions. Formally, the problem is essentially the same as that encountered in case study research when seeking to generalize from the case. This will occupy us in the next chapter.

Sampling and the Other Research Strategies

Sampling considerations enter into all forms of enquiry. The stress in experimentation is on internal validity, the demonstration of causal relationships. Though lip-service is paid to the need to have representative samples of experimental subjects from known populations, the real effort in experimental work is on randomized allocation of subjects to different experimental conditions so that the logic of statistical inference can be employed. In practice, the volunteers, more often than not 'captive' students in laboratory experiments, are rarely if ever obtained by probability sampling procedures. This does mean that experimental findings are subject to attack concerning their external validity or generalizability.

Case study is explicitly and avowedly not concerned with samples as far as the case is concerned. It is studied in its own right and no attempt is made to seek statistical generalizability. As has already been suggested, external validity is sought by other means. However, other aspects of sampling remain. Important decisions have to be made in case study about things like how, where, when and from who information is to be gathered. Each of these requires sampling decisions. Burgess (1982, section 3) includes several useful papers.

Further Reading

de Vaus, D. A. (1990) *Surveys in Social Research*, 3rd edn. London: UCL Press/Allen & Unwin. Short text covering design and practicalities. Very clear.

Hakim, C. (1987) *Research Design: strategies and choices in the design of social research*. London: Allen & Unwin. See chapter on 'Ad Hoc Sample Surveys' for discussion of design of small surveys.

Hoinville, G., Jowell, R. and Associates (1985) *Survey Research Practice*. London: Gower. Excellent text on the practical aspects of survey design and execution.

Marsh, C. (1982) *The Survey Method: the contribution of surveys to sociological explanation*. London: Allen & Unwin. Though primarily methodological, its interest is wider than the subtitle suggests. Very extensive annotated bibliography.

Moser, C. A. and Kalton, G. (1971) *Survey Methods in Social Investigation*. Aldershot: Gower. Classic exhaustive text on survey design, administration and analysis.

Turner, C. F. and Martin, E. (eds) (1986) *Surveying Subjective Phenomena*, 2 vols. New York: Russell Sage. Detailed reference on central methodological concerns of survey research.

6

Designing Case Studies

The chapter stresses the variety of subjects for, and types of case study.

It advocates a systematic approach to design and emphasizes the need to develop a conceptual framework, research questions and a sampling strategy.

Finally, there is discussion of the skills and preparation required of a case study investigator.

Introduction

We are taking case study to be 'a strategy for doing research which involves an empirical investigation of a particular contemporary phenomenon within its real life context using multiple sources of evidence'. The 'contemporary phenomenon', in other words, the 'case', can be virtually anything. The individual person as the case is probably what springs first to mind. A simple, single case study would just focus on that person, perhaps say in a clinical or medical context where the use of the term case is routine. More complex, multiple case studies might involve several such individual cases.

Case studies are not necessarily studies of individuals, though. They can be done on a group, on an institution, on a neighbourhood, on an innovation, on a decision, on a service, on a programme and on many other things. (There may be difficulties in defining and delimiting exactly what one means by the 'case' when the focus moves from the individual person.) Just to forewarn you, I will also be suggesting that an experiment or a survey is not only an experiment or a survey but also, necessarily, a 'case' of an investigation which might profitably be considered as such.

Case studies are then very various. Box 6.1 gives some indication of different types and of the range of purposes they fulfil.

Box 6.1 Some types of case study

1 *Individual case study* Detailed account of one person. Tends to focus on antecedents, contextual factors, perceptions and attitudes preceding a known outcome (e.g. drug user; immigrant). Used to explore possible causes, determinants, factors, processes, experiences, etc., contributing to the outcome.

Examples: The Jack-Roller and Snodgrass (1982); Hyde-Wright and Cheesman (1990).

2 *Set of individual case studies* As above, but a small number of individuals with some features in common are studied.

Example: Kets de Vries (1990).

2 *Community studies* Studies of one or more local communities. Describes and analyses the pattern of, and relations between, main aspects of community life (politics; work; leisure; family life; etc.). Commonly descriptive, but may explore specific issues or be used in theory testing.

Examples: Stacey (1960); Stacey et al. (1975).

3 *Social group studies* Studies of both small direct contact groups (e.g. families) and larger, more diffuse ones (e.g. occupational group). Describes and analyses relationships and activities.

Example: Whyte (1981).

4 *Studies of organizations and institutions* Studies of firms, workplaces, schools, trades unions, etc. Many possible foci, e.g. best practice; policy implementation and evaluation; industrial relations; management and organizational issues; organizational cultures; processes of change and adaptation; etc.

Examples: Lightfoot (1963); Heclo and Wildavsky (1981); Redmond et al. (1988).

5 *Studies of events, roles and relationships* Focus on a specific event (overlaps with (3) and (4)). Very varied; includes studies of police – citizen encounters; doctor–patient interactions; specific crimes or 'incidents' (e.g. disasters); studies of role conflicts, stereotypes, adaptations.

Examples: Strong and Davis (1977); Levi (1981).

(After Hakim, 1987, pp. 65–72; Whyte 1984, and Yin, 1983, provide a range of other examples.)

Ethnographic Studies

One approach to the study of a group is termed *ethnographic*, and is differentiated by some from the case study approach (e.g. Brause, 1991). This approach seeks to provide a written description of the implicit rules and traditions of a group. An ethnographer, through involvement with the group, tries to work out these rules. The intention is to provide a rich, or 'thick' description which interprets the experiences of people in the group from their own perspective. Fetterman (1989) provides a very readable introduction. In the terms used here, ethnography is exploratory – aiming to develop a theory about how participants accomplish the various actions taking place in the group. The definition of case study adopted here is sufficiently broad to encompass ethnographic studies.

Whatever kind of case study is involved (and the list in Box 6.1 only scratches the surface), there is always the need, as in any kind of research, to have some kind of plan or *research design*. As with other research strategies, the design provides the link between

- the questions that the study is asking,
- the data that are collected, and
- the conclusions drawn.

Case study design has until recently been an undeveloped field. This is partly because, traditionally, case study has been viewed as 'soft' research, by some almost as a 'soft option'. Its practitioners have tended to be averse to pre-structuring, to 'tight' prespecified designs. They would advocate a much looser approach where the questions to be asked, the data to be collected and the appropriate conceptual and theoretical framework emerge (if at all) only after a prolonged involvement in the field with the phenomenon being studied. Researchers following this traditional approach may deny the need for a research design. In fact they have a design, but it is implicit rather than explicit.

Case study need not be of this loose, emergent type. It is true that one of the great strengths of case study is its flexibility. Generally speaking, in experimental designs, any failure to carry out the pre-specified design has serious implications. These are often lethal as far as interpretation is concerned. It is sometimes possible to regard the effect as causing the experimental design to degenerate into a quasi- experimental design – if, for example, the institution in which you are working refuses to allow you to select experimental groups randomly and insists that you work with groups that they have formed for administrative, educational or clinical purposes. As pointed out in chapter 3, there is a more opportunistic flavour to design, analysis and interpretation in quasi-experiments. Surveys call for considerable and detailed pre-planning before you start the survey proper. Basically, in all experimental and survey work, you need to know exactly what you are doing before you start doing it.

Case study, however, is defined solely in terms of its concentration on the specific case, in its context. In principle it can be as pre-structured or 'emergent' as you wish – or, more accurately, as is appropriate for the purposes of your case study. If, for example, the main purpose is *exploratory*, trying to get some feeling as to what is going on in a novel situation where there is little to guide what one should be looking for, then tight pre-structuring is just not possible. If, however, the purpose is *confirmatory*, where previous work, perhaps laboratory experimentation, has suggested relationships between variables or an explanation of some phenomenon, then there is a place for a detailed pre-structured case study out in the field. The case study need not limit itself to confirmation of suggested relationships, of course. It could be embedded in a wider study which might throw further light on the relationships, or even suggest alternative views of the phenomena.

While the extremes of tight pre-structured case study designs and loose emergent ones can be justified in different circumstances, in practice most case study work is likely to fall somewhere between these extremes. Even the least structured researchers will unavoidably come to the study with certain general orienting ideas and interests, and some facility in the use of particular research tools, which mean that they do not start the study as 'tabula rasa'. At the other extreme, it seems foolish to throw away the inherent flexibility of case study research by slavish adherence to what was decided before the study.

Practicalities also tend to rule out the full-blown traditional case study approach as originally practised by anthropologists and some sociologists. The assumptions that there is plenty of time for the study (two to three years is a typical period), and that the focus is some exotic culture or tribe unknown to Western civilization, are patently incorrect for the small-scale research into some aspect of our own culture (often the very part of the culture where the researcher works) which we are targeting in this book. As Miles and Huberman (1984) put it, in these circumstances, 'a loose highly inductive design, is a waste of time. Months of field-work and voluminous case studies will yield a few banalities' (p. 27).

There is an obvious trade-off between *looseness* and *selectivity*. The looser the original design, the less selective you can afford to be in data selection. Anything might be important. On the other hand, the danger is that if you *start* with a strong conceptual framework, this will blind you to important features of the case, or cause you to misinterpret evidence. There is no obvious way out of this dilemma. Practicalities may dictate the pre-structured approach, for example, if the project is on a very tight time-scale, as in much small-scale contract research.

Box 6.2 suggests four main aspects to case study design. This analysis, and the approach developed in the following sections, leans heavily on the work of Miles and Huberman (1984) which I have found of great value in systematizing the approach to case study. They are concerned solely with studies using qualitative data, but the principles that they put forward appear helpful for case studies of all kinds. The point made in Box 6.2 about case study design being a continuing process during the study is important. It is a feature that workers used to other research strategies can find difficult to come to terms with. In experiments and surveys you get the design sorted out at the beginning and then put it into practice. Deviation from the design can be a disaster, possibly entailing you starting again. In case study the design process is in one sense more forgiving; there is the opportunity to modify and change focus. In other senses it is more arduous as the design is a continuing issue during the course of the study.

Box 6.2   Designing a case study

You need:

- a conceptual framework;
- a set of research questions;
- a sampling strategy;
- to decide on methods and instruments for data collection.

Note: It is not necessary to have all, or indeed any, of these in a fully developed form at the start of the study. Work on design can, and should, continue after the start of the study.

Developing a Conceptual Framework

What is a Conceptual Framework?

A conceptual framework covers the main features (aspects, dimensions, factors, variables) of a case study and their presumed relationships.

The term 'feature' is chosen as being relatively neutral. 'Variables' and 'factors' have been captured by experimental and survey researchers, and would be objected to by some case study workers as indicating adherence to a narrowly scientific positivistic paradigm.

Why Do You Need One?

Developing a conceptual framework forces you to be explicit about what you think you are doing. It also helps you to be selective; to decide which are the important features; which relationships are likely to be of importance or meaning; and hence, what data you are going to collect and analyse.

When Do You Do This?

Unless you have a lot of time *and* are looking into a strange or novel situation, the recommendation is that you have an *initial* attempt to do this before starting the study. In all cases this will, at the least, help you to get your initial orientations and prejudices out in the open.

Conversely, unless you are under extreme time pressure, you should not regard this initial framework as definitive. Some time into the study (as a very rough rule of thumb, when a third of the time available for collecting data has passed) you should review the framework in the light of your experience. In the period up to this review you should deliberately attempt to remain open to alternative formulations, or possible features or relationships not captured in your initial framework.

After the review, you weight your efforts heavily towards the features or relationships included in the conceptual framework to get the most, and the best, evidence about it that you can. Even so, try to avoid total blinkering. There may be some important happening or changes late in the study which require a further review of the framework.

How Do You Do It?

While some prefer a narrative or descriptive account of their framework, most seem to find a diagrammatic version more compelling. In crude terms, this is a set of labelled boxes or bins, with links between them. Box 6.3 gives some practical advice for a straightforward single case study. It is not uncommon to link together individual case studies. The issues arising when this is done are considered later in the chapter. Figure 6.1 gives an example.

Box 6.3   Advice on developing a conceptual structure for a single case study

1   Get all of the diagram on to one page. This helps you to grasp the totality of the picture and to map relationships between the boxes.

2   Inputs to the framework come from theoretical formulations and previous related research, together with your personal orientation and what is already known about the case. Try to map all the different

inputs and ways of looking at the issues, so that you can see possible overlaps, inconsistencies, etc. The resulting framework can take on many forms (e.g. descriptive; theory-based) but should aim for internal consistency.

3   You won't get it right first time. Don't worry too much about getting *the* definitive structure. It is unlikely that there is just one way in which you can represent the conceptual framework in the study. Go through two or three attempts or iterations. Successive attempts should aim for greater simplicity.

4   However, if you are unsure whether or not to include a feature or possible relationship it is advisable to include rather than exclude at this initial stage. You can prune at the review stage, when you will probably have a stronger appreciation of how little time is left for data collection and analysis.

5   If more than one researcher is involved in a study, it is a valuable exercise for each to draw up a framework independently. Consensus and agreement over areas of difference is necessary.

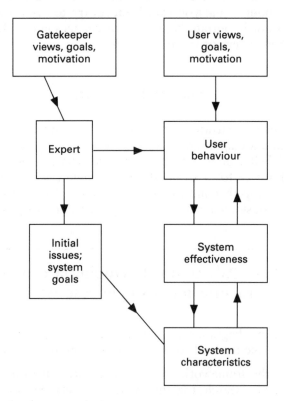

Figure 6.1   Example of conceptual structure

Developing a Set of Research Questions in a Case Study

It is possible to see the link between conceptual structure and research questions in a variety of ways. One view is that the conceptual structure enables us to frame research questions. (This approach may also be helpful for framing research questions when designing experiments and surveys.) If we have a box labelled 'user characteristics' linked by two-way arrows to a second box labelled 'system characteristics' then that suggests questions such as:

> How do the types of users expected affect the kind of system that is developed?

and

> How does the type of system provided affect the way in which people use it?

Some may find it easier to develop research questions initially and work back from that to the conceptual structure. It is, of course, possible to have a mixed strategy. You might start with a conceptual structure and then develop a set of questions, some but not all derived from the structure; then refer the list back to the structure to see whether there are inconsistencies or omissions. At the end of the day you need to have consistency between the questions and the conceptual structure. As it is effectively the set of questions that drives the data collection process, it is important to ensure that all parts of the conceptual structure diagram are covered by the set of questions.

The questions of why you need a set of research questions, and when they should be developed, are answered in the same way as with the conceptual structure. Box 6.4 gives some suggestions on how you might do this.

Box 6.4   Advice on developing a set of research questions

1   It should be possible to formulate some research questions at the initial stages of *all* case studies. These will tend to be general if you are taking a loose, unstructured approach (think of it as getting your assumptions out into the open); more specific if you adopt a more structured approach.

2   Don't worry if questions seem diffuse or 'foggy' initially. You may be able to refine them through successive attempts or iterations, as with

the conceptual structure. Alternatively, it may be a genuine lack of clarity, where you require involvement with the case before you can clear the fog.

3   At the end of the case study you are going to have made headway on only a fairly small number of questions (say up to ten, or twenty at the outside). You may want to have more than this on your initial list so as not to close down options. It helps to group your list of questions under about half a dozen major question headings. Alternatively you can divide the list into 'key' questions central to the study, and 'possible' on which you want to keep an initial eye. Spend the bulk of your time on getting the 'major' or 'key' questions right.

4   Simply because you can ask a question doesn't mean that it is answerable. Look at each one to ensure that it is researchable; that is, that you will be in a position to obtain empirical data relating to the question.

5   Carry your research questions with you (literally and metaphorically) throughout the case study. This is important from the point of view both of revising the questions at the review stage (which may be appropriate when or if the questions do not seem to be capturing important aspects of what is going on), and of reminding you that your task is to collect data relevant to the questions.

Developing a Sampling Strategy

Having taken on board the assertion made in chapter 3 that a major distinction between 'experiments' and 'surveys' on the one hand, and 'case study' on the other is the latter's lack of reliance on sampling methodology, the acute reader may query this return to a discussion of sampling!

Sampling in survey and experimental design is primarily in the service of generalizing from the sample selected to the population from which it comes. While there are some aspects of sampling in *multiple* case studies which have a not dissimilar function (see p. 139), the main use of sampling in single case studies is rather different. It starts, however, from the same point. *It is just not possible to study everything.*

Take a simple small study of the introduction of a different form of organization into a hospital ward or school classroom. It is not feasible to gather detailed information about all the persons involved for all of the time that they are involved. So there has to be some kind of selection or sampling. In general this means that you have to come to some principled decision about:

Who	Which persons are observed, interviewed, etc.?
Where	In (or about) which settings are data collected?
When	At what times?
What	Which events, activities or processes are to be observed, etc.?

In relatively large-scale studies, for example a case study of the closure of a psychiatric hospital, where a major question relates to the quality of life of several hundred former patients when in 'community care', some questions such as the 'who' question may be best addressed by probability sampling procedures; possibly taking random samples or samples stratified according to personal characteristics such as their psychiatric problem or length of institutional stay.

More commonly, and almost always in smaller studies, for example a case study looking at the support given in a particular district to 'carers' of psycho-geriatric relatives, it is likely that *purposive sampling* will give better purchase on the research question. The various types of sampling were discussed in the previous chapter (p. 135).

Miles and Huberman (1984) illustrate the issues involved in this kind of sampling by considering a case study on the arrest and booking of suspects by police officers. Starting from the question 'How do police officers interpret laws when arresting and booking suspects?' they indicate some *initial* sampling choices which are given in box 6.5.

The study then proceeds by taking appropriate combinations of these parameters. For example, if we start with the setting, say the police station, alternative options might be:

a   At the police station, take one kind of police officer, all bookings during the working day, and all instances of the social processes that occur.
b   At the police station, take all types of officers, bookings and justifications for the booking.
c   At the police station, take one police officer and follow that officer through several episodes of arrests, pursuits, bookings and justification.
d   At the police station, start with a booking and reconstitute the prior events.

Whichever way this is done, the choice is determined by the research questions and the conceptual framework which governs the questions that are asked.

'Real life' is also likely to take a hand, in that within constraints of 'real time' and limited access and availability of the persons involved, logistic considerations are usually formidable. Generally you can rely on it that whatever sampling plan is decided upon, it will be impossible to complete it in full! Fortunately the case study approach is sufficiently flexible for this not to be a mortal blow. Box 6.6 gives general advice on sampling in a case study.

Box 6.5   Initial sampling options in a study of police work

sampling parameter	*Possible choices*
settings	police station, squad car, scene of the crime, suspect's residence or hangout
actors	police officers with different characteristics (e.g. rank, seniority, experience, race, beliefs, education) and suspects (age, race, beliefs, education, type of offence)
events	arrests, booking, possibly pursuits of suspects and post hoc justifications of booking to other actors
processes	making the arrest, doing the booking, relating to suspects, interpreting laws, justifying laws, generally 'negotiating' law enforcement in an area

(Adapted from Miles and Huberman, 1984, p. 38.)

Box 6.6   Advice on sampling in a single case study

1   The act of *thinking* in terms of sampling is good for you methodologically. If you choose one kind of person to interview or observe: why chose this kind of person? What are the implications for other choices of person?

2   You are sampling *people, settings, events* and *processes*. It is important to link these with your research questions and consider how you can sample to get unbiased answers making efficient use of your (and others') time. Your initial selections may not prove to fulfil these conditions and you should be prepared to review this, and if necessary change.

3   A good basic rule is that you will never be able to get through all that you wish to do, nor as much as you think you will be able to get through (even when you have taken this rule into account!). One strategy is to start with a 'fall-back' sample; those things which you simply

must cover if you are to have a chance of answering your basic or key questions.

4   There is always a risk that for the above and other reasons you may not sample widely enough. It is worth devoting some part of your effort to 'work a bit at the peripheries': e.g. 'talk with people who are not central to the phenomenon but are neighbours to it, to people no longer actively involved, to dissidents and renegades and eccentrics. Spending a day in the adjoining village or school is also worth the time' (Miles and Huberman, 1984, p. 42.)

Selection of Data Collection Techniques

Having made some initial decisions about *what* you need to know and *why* you need to know it (from the conceptual framework and set of research questions), and similar decisions about *where* and from *whom* you are going to get the information (the sampling issue), the remaining major question is *how* one gets the information.

As with the other questions, case study permits you to approach this in a variety of ways, ranging from loose and unstructured to tight and heavily pre-structured. There are no absolute answers. Though individual researchers will have their personal preferences and prejudices, the basic rule is that the nature of the data collection should depend on the kind of study that you are doing. The conceptual framework, research questions and sampling criteria you have adopted largely determine the approach to data collection.

Looked at in this light, the extremes are as follows. If you are carrying out an *exploratory* case study with little on which to base your conceptual framework, very general research questions and a weakly defined emergent sampling strategy, it is inappropriate to have much, if anything, in the way of prior, standardized data collection devices. If it is a *confirmatory* study, where previous work gives you confidence to adopt a well defined conceptual structure, and specific well focused research questions with a tight and known sampling strategy, then you can use similarly focused, pre-structured data collection techniques. Crudely, if you know what you are after, then you can plan ahead on how best to collect the required information.

Box 6.7 gives details of the mix of data collection techniques and instruments used in Project Impact (Robson et al., 1988). This was used in case studies of the effectiveness of a number of short in-service courses for teachers of pupils with special educational needs. Box 6.8 summarizes the main data collection techniques commonly used in case studies. Remember that the expectation is that a *range* of techniques is used in a case study. Practicalities in the use of the different techniques are covered in the chapters of part III. Box 6.9 gives advice on the selection of data collection techniques.

Box 6.7   Data collection techniques and instruments used in project impact case studies

Evaluation plan for the 'micros' pilot course

It was made clear to all participants, both in writing and verbally, that while it was hoped that they would participate fully in the evaluation to assist in developing the course, such participation was entirely voluntary, The evaluation for this course followed what has now been established as a standard pattern by the project team. This comprised:

a *Pre-course interviews* of a subset of intending course participants.
b *Participants' perceptions and current practice sheet.* All participants were asked to complete a sheet on registration for the course at the beginning of the week. This covered their reasons for attending the course, their views of the course objectives and aspects of their current practice, particularly in connection with microelectronics.
c *Content evaluation sheets.* At the first session of the course all participants were given a content evaluation sheet and were asked to complete this after each session during the week. This covered their ratings of the usefulness and interest of the sessions, their expectations about whether or not the session would change their approach in school and gave an invitation to comment more generally.*
d *During-course interviews.* A subset of course participants including those interviewed prior to the course were also interviewed towards the end of the course to obtain their views on how the course was progressing. They were also invited to comment on the evaluation itself.
e *Information sheets.* Halfway through, the course participants were asked to complete the standard Project Impact information sheet giving details of their background and experience.
f *Participants' perceptions and future plans sheet.* At the end of the course participants were invited to give their views on the contribution of the microcomputer to their work, their present view of the course objectives, what they would do differently in school as a result of the course and also to comment on various general aspects of the course.
g *Follow-up sheet.* All participants were asked to complete a follow-up sheet approximately three months after completion of the course concentrating on ways in which the course has affected their practice.
h *Follow-up interviews.* On receipt of completed follow-up sheets a subset of participants were interviewed and/or observed in school.

*Later evaluations also asked for ratings of previous knowledge of the topic covered in the session.

General note: Project Impact staff were present at virtually all sessions (including a discussion session) of the course throughout the week on a semi-participant basis. Informal discussions with both tutors and participants were held throughout the week.

(*Source*: Robson et al., 1988, p. 87.)

Box 6.8   Data collection in case study – a summary of commonly used techniques

1   Observation

a   *Participant observation*   The investigator takes on a role other than that of passive observer and participates in the events being studied.
b   *Systematic observation*   Use of standardized observation instrument.
c   *Simple observation*   Passive unobtrusive observation (e.g. of facial expression and language use).

2   Interview

a   *Open-ended interview*   No pre-specified set or order of questions; little or no direction from interviewer; goal typically to gain insight into a person's perceptions in a situation.
b   *Focused interview*   Use of interview guide specifying key topics; order of questions not fixed.
c   *Structured interview*   Standardized set of questions.

3   Use of documents and records

Includes a wide range of written or recorded materials, e.g. minutes of meetings, pupil and patient records, diaries.

A wide range of other techniques can be used in case studies, including: questionnaires; standardized tests (e.g. of intelligence, personality or attainment); scales (e.g. of attitude); repertory grids; projective methods (e.g. association and apperception tests); life histories; role play, simulation and gaming; etc.

Box 6.9 Advice on the selection of instruments for data collection in a single case study

1 Even if you are doing a study with pre-structured instruments (e.g. use of structured interview schedules), you should be prepared to modify, if experience suggests that the topic or the approach is wrong. Pre-structured instruments can (and usually should) be revised. This can be a one-off or a continual process. Generally in case studies there is nothing in principle to stop you interviewing (or observing) people and situations more than once – although there may be practical or logistical difficulties.

2 A case study is not a survey, where reliability relies crucially on the characteristics of the data collection instruments. The case study relies on the trustworthiness of the *human* instrument (the researcher) rather than on the data collection techniques per se. Hence the characteristics and skills of the investigator are of crucial importance. Miles and Huberman (1984) consider that you need 'some familiarity with the phenomenon and the setting under study; strong conceptual interests; a multidisciplinary approach . . . ; good investigative skills, including doggedness, the ability to draw people out, and the ability to ward off premature closure' (p. 46).*

3 Thinking about data collection from the start gives useful feedback on the research questions (you may find that a question as originally phrased is unanswerable), sampling (helps in deciding who you are going to see, when and where), clarifies concepts, and sets priorities for data collection.

*While my own prejudices fall very much along these lines, it should be noted that this is a controversial stance. Lack of familiarity with the setting and the importance of a strong disciplinary stance are more commonly advocated.

Types of Case Study

Holistic Case Studies

Yin (1989) differentiates between two versions of the single case study on the basis of the level of the unit of analysis. A study where the concern remains at a single, global level is referred to as HOLISTIC. This would typically (though not necessarily) be how a case study of an individual would be viewed, but would also apply to, say, the study of an institution which remained global rather than seeking to look at and analyse the different functioning of separate sub-units within the institution.

Holistic case studies are appropriate in several situations. The *critical case* is a clear, though unfortunately rare, example. This occurs when your theoretical understanding is such that there is a clear, unambiguous and non-trivial set of circumstances where predicted outcomes will be found. Finding a case which fits, and demonstrating what has been predicted, can give a powerful boost to knowledge and understanding. This is of course the way in which experiment is used classically – the 'crucial experiment'. It is interesting to note that some of the most illustrious of this genre, for example, the verification of Einstein's theory of relativity by measuring the 'bending' of light from a distant star at a rare eclipse, are effectively case studies (being the study of a particular instance in its context) rather than experiments (in that no experimental manipulation of variables is possible).

The *extreme case* also provides a rationale for a simple, holistic case study. A colleague of mine now features as a case in an orthopaedic textbook because of the virtually complete recovery he made from horrific arm and leg injuries in a cycle crash, after skilled surgical and physiotherapy support, together with his own determination, confounded initial gloomy predictions. More generally, the extreme and the unique can provide a valuable 'test bed' for which this type of case study is appropriate. Extremes include the 'if it can work here it will work anywhere' scenario, to the 'super-realization' where, say, a new approach is tried under ideal circumstances, perhaps to obtain understanding of how it works before its wider implementation.

Multiple Case Studies

In many studies it is appropriate to study more than a single case. A very common misconception is that this is for the purpose of gathering a 'sample' of cases so that generalization to some population might be made. Yin (1989) makes the useful analogy that carrying out multiple case studies is more like doing multiple experiments. These may be attempts at replication of an initial experiment: or they may build upon the first experiment, perhaps carrying the investigation into an area suggested by the first study; or they may seek to complement the first study by focusing on an area not originally covered. This activity, whether for multiple case studies or for multiple experiments (or for multiple surveys for that matter; or even for multiple studies involving a range of different research strategies), is not concerned with statistical generalization but with *analytic generalization* (discussed in chapter 12). The first case study will provide evidence which supports some 'theory' about what is going on. This theory, and its possible support or disconfirmation, guides the choice of subsequent cases in a multiple case study. Findings, patterns of data, etc from these case studies which provide this kind of support, particularly if they simultaneously provide evidence which does not fit in with alternative theories, are the basis for generalization.

Put simply, cases are selected where *either* the theory would suggest that the same result is obtained, *or* that predictably different results will be obtained. Given, say, three of each which fall out in the predicted manner, this provides pretty compelling evidence for the theory. This is an over-simplification because case studies and their outcomes are likely to be multi-faceted and difficult to capture adequately within a simple theory. Support for the theory may be qualified or partial in any particular case, leading to revision and further development of the theory, and then probably the need for further case studies.

Requirements from the Investigator

The quality of a case study depends to a great extent on the quality of the investigator. It is not a 'soft' option in the sense that anyone can do it without preparation, knowledge of procedures or analytical skills. Case study *is* soft, however, in the sense that there are no 'hard and fast' routinized procedures, where all you have to do is to follow the formulae. This makes life harder rather than easier – though also more interesting.

Ideally case study calls for well trained and experienced investigators, but other aspects are also important. Personal qualities such as having an *open and enquiring mind*, being a *'good listener'*, general *sensitivity* and *re-sponsiveness to contradictory evidence* are needed. These are commonly regarded as skills central to the professional working with people in what-ever capacity. Relevant professional experience of this kind is also likely to provide you with a firm grasp of the issues being studied in a particular case study.

The professional or practitioner working with people as their job has much to contribute both *as* an investigator or *to* an investigator. As an investigator, probably carrying out 'insider' research, she will need a firm grasp of the material in this book, and experience (this can lead to 'Catch-22' problems – how do you get the experience without carrying out a case study, and vice versa). Working in collaboration with someone who has the methodological skills and the experience is obviously one way forward. Box 6.10 lists skills desirable in case study investigators.

Preparing for a Specific Case Study

An important difference between case study and other approaches is that *if more than one investigator is involved, all should take on essentially similar roles*. The tasks cannot be reduced to rigid formulae with division

---

Box 6.10   General skills needed by case study investigators

1 *Question asking* Need for an 'enquiring mind'. Your task in fieldwork is to enquire why events appear to have happened or to be happening. This is something you ask yourself as well as others, and is mentally and emotionally exhausting.

2 *Good listening* Used in a general sense to include all observation and sensing, not simply via the ears. Also 'listening' to what documents say. *Good* means taking in a lot of new information without bias; noting the exact words said; capturing mood and affective components; appreciating context. You need an open mind and a good memory. (Taping may help but is not a panacea.)

3 *Adaptiveness and flexibility* Case studies rarely end up exactly as planned. You have to be willing to change procedures or plans if the unanticipated occurs. The full implications of any changes have to be taken on board: e.g. you may need to change the design. Need to balance *adaptiveness* and *rigour*.

4 *Grasp of the issues* Investigator needs to *interpret* information during the study, not simply record it. Without a firm grasp of the issues (theoretical, policy etc.) you may miss clues, not see contradictions, requirement for further evidence, etc.

5 *Lack of bias* The preceding skills are negated if they are simply used to substantiate a preconceived position. Investigator should be open to contrary findings. During data collection, preliminary findings should be submitted to critical colleagues who are asked to offer alternative explanations and suggestions for data collection.

---

of function, as in survey research. All the investigators need an intelligent appreciation of what they are doing, and why. Hence it is highly desirable that all are involved in the first stages of conceptualization and definition of the research questions. Similarly, they should all be involved in the development of the case study plan.

The plan contains details of the data collection procedures to be used, and the general rules to be followed. Where there is a single investigator the main purpose of the plan is to enhance the dependability or trustworthiness of the study, but it also acts as an aide-memoire to the investigator. When a team is involved it also serves to increase reliability, in the sense of assisting all investigators to follow the same set of procedures and rules. Box 6.11 gives suggestions for the organisation of the plan.

Box 6.11   The case study plan

It is highly desirable that an explicit plan is prepared and agreed by those involved.
   The following sections may be helpful:

1   *Overview* Covers the background information about the project, that is the context and perspective, and why it is taking place; the issues being investigated and relevant readings about the issues.

2   *Procedures* Covers the major tasks in collecting data, including:
a   access arrangements (see also p. 295);
b   resources available;
c   schedule of the data collection activities and specification of the periods of time involved.

3   *Questions* The set of research questions (see p. 25) with accompanying list of probable sources of evidence and data matrices (see p. 390).

4   *Reporting* Covers the following:
a   outline of the case study report(s);*
b   treatment of the full 'data base' (i.e. totality of the documentary evidence obtained);
c   audience(s).*

*There may be several audiences, for which different reports (in style and length) are needed. Consideration of reports and audiences at this stage, and during the study, helps to guide the study.

Note: The plan should communicate to a general intelligent reader what is proposed. It forms part of establishing the trustworthiness of the study (see p. 66).

Pilot Studies

There is a great deal in favour of *piloting* any empirical research. Advance planning and preparation is all very well but there is no complete substitute for involvement with the 'real' situation, when the feasibility of what is proposed in terms of time, effort and resources can be assessed.
   However, whereas a strong case can be made for every experiment or survey being thoroughly piloted, there are aspects of case study research which can make piloting both more difficult to set up and, fortunately, less crucially important. It may be that there is only one case to be considered,

or that there are particular features of the case selected (such as geographical or temporal accessibility, or your own knowledge of the case), such that there is no sensible equivalent which could act as the pilot.

In circumstances like these the flexibility of case study gives you at least some opportunity to, as it were, 'learn on the job'. Or it may be that the initial formulation leans more toward the 'exploratory' pole of case study design, and later stages with the benefit of experience can have a more 'explanatory' or 'confirmatory' focus.

Yin (1989) distinguishes between 'pilot tests' and 'pre-tests'. He views the former as helping 'investigators to refine their data collection plans with respect to both the content of the data and the procedures to be followed'. For him, the pilot is, as it were, a 'laboratory for the investigators, allowing them to observe different phenomena from many different angles or to try different approaches on a trial basis' (p. 74). I prefer to regard these as case studies in their own right with an essentially exploratory function, where some of the research questions are methodological. What he calls the 'pre-test' is a formal 'dress rehearsal' in which the intended data collection plan is used as faithfully as possible, and is perhaps closer to the usual meaning of a pilot study.

Research Strategies and Real Life

Partly for purposes of exposition, and partly as a reflection of the way that research traditions have developed, the discussion about research strategies has split them into experiments, surveys and case studies. It needs to be stressed, however, that the real life enquirer not only needs to have a good familiarity with the particular solutions that have been put forward to, say, points of experimental design, or ways of developing a conceptual schema for a case study, but also an appreciation that a specific research problem may call out for an approach which does not fall neatly into one of the three categories.

In an important sense each enquiry is a case study. It takes place at particular times in particular places with particular people. Stressing this signals that the design flexibility inherent in the case study is there in all studies until we, as it were, design it out. If we are primarily concerned with causal relationships and have the potential for random sampling and tight control, then the delights of the experiment beckon. But even then augmentation with additional observation or unstructured interaction with participants might be very illuminating. A situation where the amount of data which can be collected from any one individual is pretty minimal precludes the use of case study methodology as commonly understood unless the case is conceptualized at a group or organizational level rather than at an individual one. And if this is done, it may make a lot of sense to follow the canons of survey methodology in selecting the particular individuals to be interviewed, and to adhere closely to what is known about the design of surveys.

The general advice remains the same – let your research questions be your guide. This has to be tempered by such real world qualifications as the time and resources that you have at your disposal. If you can't set up two or more groups and arrange for random allocation to them, then classical experimentation is beyond you even though this might be the preferred strategy.

Viewing any prospective study initially in case study terms has the advantage of bringing the research questions to the fore and of emphasizing and making explicit the relationship between these questions and the conceptual structure of your study. The very fluidity and flexibility of case study design has forced a codification of these aspects which need not necessarily be restricted to case study. When this has been worked through, you will be in a clearer position to see just what shape of study best fits.

Further Reading

Atkinson, P. and Delamont, S. (1985) Bread and Dreams or Bread and Circuses? a critique of 'case study' research in education. In M. Shipman (ed.), *Educational Research, Principles, Policies and Practices*. London: Falmer. Swingeing critique of Simons (1981) (see below).

Bromley, D. B. (1986) *The Case-study Method in Psychology and Related Disciplines*. Chichester Wiley. Main text giving serious attention to case study method in psychology. Repays careful reading.

Kazdin, A. E. (1982) *Single-Case Research Designs: methods for clinical and applied settings*. Oxford: Oxford University Press. Covers single-subject experimental designs. Not multiple method but could be usefully combined with Yin-type approach.

Miles, M. B. and Huberman, A. M. (1984) *Qualitative Data Analysis: a sourcebook of new methods*. Newbury Park and London: Sage. Many useful ideas on design and analysis of case studies (refers to 'cases' as 'sites').

Nisbet, J. D. and Watt, J. (1980) *Case Study*. Rediguide no. 26. Oxford: TRC Rediguides. Short, clear explanation of how to carry out traditional case studies.

Simons, H. (1981) *Towards a Science of the Singular: essays about case study in educational research and evaluation*. CARE Occasional Paper no. 10. Centre for Applied Research in Education, University of East Anglia. Influential set of papers on 'new-wave' approach to educational research. Anti-quantitative.

Yin, R. K. (1983) *The Case Study Method: an annotated bibliography*. Washington, DC: Cosmos. Wide-ranging bibliography covering studies in many disciplines.

Yin, R. K. (1989) *Case Study Research: design and methods*, 2nd end. Newbury Park and London: Sage. Key text on design and analysis of rigorous case studies. First edition (1984) hasn't been changed much.

Choosing a Research Strategy – Summary

Chapters 4–6 have covered the three traditional research strategies of *experiment*, *survey* and *case study*. They represent different styles of enquiry. You have to decide whether to adopt one of these strategies, or to devise some type of *hybrid* or *combined strategy* (a style which in some way puts together features of the traditional strategies).

A Return to the 'Choosing a Research Strategy' Overview on p. 39 and Reread

Recall that while each strategy can in principle be used for any of the research purposes (exploratory, descriptive and explanatory), the most typical linkage is

- experiments for explanatory studies;
- surveys for descriptive studies;
- case studies for exploratory purposes.

The type of research questions to which you seek answers will push you more firmly towards the choice of strategy.

Experiments can study virtually any kind of behaviour (both verbal and non-verbal) but are limited by both practical and ethical considerations to 'low impact' variables and research questions (no experimental studies on murder, please).

Surveys are usually limited to topics on which participants are both willing and able to report verbally (but you could, in principle, have a purely 'observational' survey). They can give you access to large contemporary populations through representative sampling, and your focus can be on past events.

Case studies give you the entrée to variables and research questions concerning individual, naturally occurring entities, whether these be individual people, groups, organizations or whatever. They would normally focus on current events and concerns, and while they can provide theoretical generalizations, e.g. about processes, they do not permit statistical generalizations. Case studies differ from the other two strategies in that they are inherently *multi-method* (typically involving observation, interviewing and analysis of documents and records).

B Remember that each Strategy has its Strengths and Weaknesses

Getting at causal inferences is easier in experiments (although not impossible with the other strategies). Experiments have to satisfy strict design requirements (e.g. on the assignment of subjects to different conditions, and the phasing of interventions). You need to know what you are looking for with high specificity because you are putting your bets on a very small number of variables. Realism and generalizability (to different groups and situations) tend to be sacrificed in experiments.

Good surveys rate highly on generalizability from the sample surveyed to the population from which it is drawn. This is purchased at the expense of a reliance on highly structured verbal reports with categories imposed on respondents. Surveys are only appropriate for topics where respondents are willing and able to report accurately. They are prone to reactive effects.

Case studies, because of their intensive nature, can usually only focus on a small number of cases. This leads to questions about the representativeness of the findings, and whether they provide an adequate base for both the development and the answering of research questions. The researcher's typically close involvement raises questions about her influence on events and persons involved.

C Some Choices of Strategy are Virtually Self-evident

If your prime interest is in causal relationships; *if* your understanding of the field is sufficiently good (from some theoretical framework, previous work, etc.) that you are confident about likely relevant variables; *and if* it is practically and ethically feasible for you to manipulate these variables, and hold others constant – *then* an experiment is indicated.

If you are focusing on a topic where people are likely to be able and willing to respond accurately to your questions; *if* you can obtain a sample representative of the population in which you are interested; *and if* your main concern is to describe the situation in the population relating to your topic – *then* a survey is indicated.

If your main concern is in understanding what is happening in a specific context, *and if* you can get access to, and co-operation from, the people involved – *then* do a case study.

D For Many Studies, Alternative Strategies would be Possible

Many tasks are not so clear-cut and could be approached in different ways. However, although real world studies come in all sorts of shapes, and sizes, two features are very common (it is also fair to say that there is a common call for a straightforward descriptive survey, as covered above):

- relatively little is known about the problem area, in terms of either relevant previous work or what theoretical formulation would be appropriate;
- some form of intervention or change is proposed.

The first feature effectively precludes the use of an experimental strategy. The second might be seen to call for one. A solution is to carry the project out as a case study (or a linked set of case studies). The inherent flexibility of the case study, and its use of multiple methods of investigation, make it feasible to introduce 'experiment-like' features to develop an understanding of the effects of the intervention. Such studies often constitute a form of evaluation, and form the focus of the following chapter.

E A Hybrid Strategy Might Be Called For

The above suggests possible inbreeding between strategies. Particular circumstances may call for styles other than the traditional. Experiments based on before and after surveys have already been mentioned, as have surveys based on experiment-like direct observation. It might be appropriate to develop a form of case study reliant solely on survey-type instruments.

F Consider Combined Strategies Where Resources Permit

Most small-scale studies will be necessarily limited to a single research strategy (which may itself be a hybrid) – the one which appears best to fit the research questions and general circumstances. However, there may be advantage in combining straegies in various ways. Case studies may give sufficient confidence that you know what is going on to permit the design of an experiment properly to establish causal relationships. Or a survey might be complemented by a small number of case studies to throw further light on the associations found in the survey.

7

Designing Evaluations

This chapter covers the distinctive features of evaluations.

It emphasizes the wide range of possible models and purposes of evaluation.

It also stresses the sensitive nature of evaluation and gives warnings to the potential evaluator.

Evaluation – a Purpose, not a Strategy

An evaluation is a study which has a distinctive purpose; it is not a new or different research strategy. The purpose of an evaluation is to assess the effects and effectiveness of something, typically some innovation or intervention: policy, practice or service. This can be done using experimental, survey or case study research strategies – or some appropriate hybrid or combined strategy.

A separate chapter is devoted here to the design of evaluations because of the increasingly high profile being given to the need for evaluation in many different settings. Hence there is an increasing expectation that real world enquirers will be able to carry them out. A second reason is that while an evaluation using, say, a case study approach requires an understanding of the same issues as those covered in the previous chapter, it undoubtedly highlights and brings to the fore the 'real worldness' of the enterprise. Issues concerning clearances and permissions, negotiations with 'gatekeepers', the political nature of the study, ethics, the type of report, etc, are not in themselves design issues but they set an important context for the choice of design. Evaluation is intrinsically a very sensitive activity where there may be a risk (duty?) of revealing inadequacy or worse, and where your intentions may be misconstrued and your findings misused or ignored. The design implication is that you think through very carefully what you are doing and why.

The Importance of Evaluation

Accountability is now a watchword in the whole range of public services involving people, such as education and health and social services. This concern in the United Kingdom arises in part from political and ideological considerations, where it forms part of a drive to place public services within a framework simlar to that governing private profit-making businesses. Similar moves in other parts of Europe, and particularly within the United States, suggest a more general phenomenon. There are, or should be, more 'social' spurs to evaluation. For example, in the field of AIDS education, Freudenberg (1990) claims that

> from the start of the epidemic it has been clear that AIDS education was our most powerful tool for preventing the spread of HIV infection. Unfortunately 10 years later, we know more about the biochemistry of HIV and T cell ratios at various stages of illness than we do about what makes AIDS education programs effective and how to successfully implement such programs. (p. 295)

Similar concerns have been expressed in connection with energy conservation programmes (Kushler, 1989, provides a review and a case study).

Irrespective of its origins, the notion that we should seek to understand and assess critically the functioning of services and programmes has much to commend it. The contentious issues are more to do with who does this, in what way, and for what purposes. This places us in the rapidly growing field of evaluation research.

In fact, much of the enquiry that psychologists and other social scientists get involved with in the real world can be thought of as some kind of evaluation: *an attempt to assess the worth or value of some innovation or intervention, some service or approach*. This is patently obvious in fields such as education, clinical practice and market research, but a high proportion of all applied non-laboratory work has an evaluative dimension to it.

Evaluation is one type of applied research. Applied research in general is seen as being concerned with defining real world problems, or exploring alternative approaches, policies or programmes that might be implemented in order to seek solutions to such problems. Evaluation is primarily concerned with describing and finding the effects of a particular approach, policy or programme. It is a field which has grown rapidly since the 1960s, helped by the US government setting aside a proportion of the budget of the many social programmes initiated at that time for evaluation. Evaluations of such large-scale programmes have not been very conclusive but have tended to show that they did not achieve their aims (e.g. Mullen et al., 1972). There has been widespread criticism of the quality of many evaluations (e.g. Weiss, 1977). Nevertheless, discussion of the problems and issues in carrying out large-scale evaluations (e.g. Cronbach, 1982) has thrown up much of value for use in more manageable small-scale studies.

The characteristics of real world enquiry discussed in the first chapter are present in evaluations in a very clear-cut way. For example, they are commonly commissioned by a client or sponsor, who will often have a direct interest in the thing evaluated. Hence, rather than deciding on the topic that interests them, evaluators have this determined by others; although the approach taken is likely to be the subject of negotiation between evaluator and client. The positive side of this is that evaluation findings are more likely to influence the real world (or at least that bit of it represented by the programme or innovation being evaluated) than traditional research. Ethical issues abound. Whose interests are being served by an intervention? Who is the real client (is it the person funding the study, or those whom the service is intended to benefit)? How are vested interests taken into account? The evaluation, its results and how they are presented may affect people's jobs, education, health and sanity. Political issues are similarly inescapable. The type and style of evaluation chosen, as well as the criteria used, may mean a choice of the perspectives, values and goals of some parties or participants rather than others.

Evaluations also highlight issues to do with change. The service, programme or other subject may well seek to produce or encourage change in those involved. The evaluation may indicate that changes are needed in the programme if it is to be effective. However, evaluation findings are likely to be just one of a complex set of influences on the future development of the programme. Evaluators need to communicate the results and their implications not so much to their peers in the scientific and evaluation community, who are likely to be both knowledgable about and sympathetic to empirical enquiry, but to clients and decision-makers who are not. This means that considerable thought has to be given to the communication process, and to the style and nature of evaluation reports. These topics are picked up again in the final part of the book.

The practical problems of doing real world research also loom large. Evaluation tends to work to short time-spans and tight deadlines. Participants may be difficult to contact, perhaps because they are busy, perhaps because they are keeping out of your way. 'Gatekeepers', such as middle management in a firm or a deputy headteacher in a school, may be obstructive. Administrators may decide to alter the system or context in important ways during the study. External events ranging from national strikes to heavy snowstorms may intervene.

A Note on Possible Subjects for an Evaluation

The list is endless. Box 7.1 gives an example from school education. An evaluation might focus on a new restaurant, an experimental traffic scheme, an advertising campaign, one or more word-processing software packages, or on student seminars in a degree course – to take a pretty random selection. Once one gets involved with evaluation you appreciate the force of Kaplan's 'Law of the Hammer' (give someone a hammer and it transforms their environment into a set of things to be hammered).

Box 7.1   Example of a small-scale evaluation

Saunders (1990) evaluated a residential weekend for the students of an academic A-level class on two successive years. The residential course was run by Saunders himself (a tutor in a sixth form college), assisted by a colleague. It arose from suggestions in the literature that the important aspects of induction courses for such students lie more in areas such as examining identity and motivation than in the transmission of study skills.

Hence, the weekend's residential course did not raise academic issues but sought to establish some of the social and personal preconditions for successful study.

The investigation is a case study and makes use of multiple sources of data collection, with explicit attention to the the strengths and weaknesses of the different methods used. These included:

a   *A skills inventory*   Students were asked to respond to a simple checklist of eighteen items on the theme of personal and social skills, immediately before and after the weekend. Both residential groups showed a significant pre–post increase on the checklist, while a comparison (stay at home) group showed a smaller non-significant increase.

Note: This aspect of the study effectively constitutes a quasi-experiment with two non-randomly assigned experimental treatment groups and a non-equivalent comparison group. The outcome is that of 'A' in box 4.16. In itself this is subject to several threats to validity, although substantially strengthened by the very similar results obtained for the two different years.

b   *Student profiles*   Students were asked to write an account of their experiences on a 'profile' – three sides with a number of headings, and reminders of activities from the weekend. This was to be used in the term following the course, where issues would be discussed on an individual basis, as a form of self-conscious reflection or self-evaluation.

For course evaluation purposes Saunders carried out a formal content analysis (see chapter 10, p. 272). This involved identifying the full set of statements made, categorizing them under different headings – e.g. personal (inner), personal (behaviour), relations in group. Each statement was then assigned as 'positive' or 'negative' with respect to a number of concepts falling within the broad categories (e.g. 'personal change', 'objectives met').

A large majority of positive statements was made, and overall Saunders argues that, with very few exceptions, the profiles demonstrate that real learning had taken place over the weekend.

c *Participant observation* The tutors's observations and impressions over the weekend are used to throw further light on the effects of the residential experience.

d *Non-participant observation* This was supplemented by the observations of a colleague with extensive experience of personal and social education, who sat in on classes before and after the weekend.

The overall evaluation is positive. Saunders concludes that '. . . a fairly level-headed, practical approach to the measurement of outcomes can produce sensible data which, whatever other value they may have, can help in deciding whether or not to devote scarce resources to such an enterprise' (p. 26).

Source: Saunders, 1990.)

The discussion in the rest of this chapter is couched mainly in terms of the evaluation of a 'programme'. This is for simplicity of presentation. Feel free to translate this into terms appropriate to whatever it is that you are called upon to evaluate. The concentration in this text is of course on human enquiry, on the 'people' aspects of the evaluation. In specific cases it may be necessary to supplement this in various ways; for example, software evaluation will have a substantial additional technical agenda.

Defining Evaluation

The position taken here is that *evaluations are essentially indistinguishable from other research in terms of design, data collection techniques and methods of analysis*. This view of continuity between research and evaluation (sometimes highlighted by the use of the term 'evaluation research') is, however, not accepted by some workers (e.g. Worthern and Sanders, 1973; McDonald, 1974). Norris (1990, ch. 7) analyses the various positions.

Evaluations can and do make use of each of the research strategies; sometimes in combination. It is sometimes claimed that the strongest evaluation studies follow an experimental strategy in making comparisons between at least two groups (one of which has received the new programme, service or whatever, while another has not). Unfortunately, there are often severe problems in finding an appropriate control group, or in achieving random allocation to the different groups, or in securing effective isolation between them to avoid cross-contamination.

Moreover, the flexibility in design and execution of the case study, together with the fact that most evaluations are concerned with the effectiveness and appropriateness of an innovation or programme in a specific setting (i.e. that it is a 'case' rather than a sample), make the case study strategy appropriate for many evaluations.

Evaluation is often concerned not only with assessing worth or value but also with seeking to assist in the improvement of whatever is being evaluated. Michael Quinn Patton, a prolific American evaluator, who writes more entertainingly than most in a field littered with turgid texts, considers that

> the practice of evaluation involves the systematic collection of information about the activities, characteristics and outcomes of programs, personnel and products for use by specific people to reduce uncertainties, improve effectiveness, and make decisions with regard to what those programs, personnel, or products are doing and affecting. (Patton, 1982, p. 15)

This definition would not be universally accepted, but is helpful in drawing attention to

- the need for *systematic* information collection;
- the *wide range of topics* to which evaluation has been applied;
- the point that, to be effective, the evaluation has to be *used* by someone;
- the *wide variety of purposes* of evaluations.

It also helps in broadening out the view of evaluation from an exclusive concern for the extent to which someone's objectives have been met. Suchman's (1967) definition of evaluation as 'a method for determining the degree to which a planned programme achieves its desired objective' is typical of this approach, and reflects a view still commonly found. While this is likely to continue to be an important aspect of the evaluation of many planned programmes with explicit objectives, it is clearly, at best, only a part of what an evaluation might concern itself with. Unplanned or unanticipated outcomes or processes may be very important, and would not be looked for. For example, Ross (1973), in surveying a number of evaluations of the effects of legal 'crackdowns', has shown a plethora of unsuspected results. Increasing penalties for speeding, instead of leading to the desired effects, resulted in substantially fewer arrests and a considerably greater proportion of those arrested being found 'not guilty'.

Differing Approaches

There are many *evaluation models* – that is, different conceptualizations as to what evaluation is all about, and prescriptions about how you should

---

Box 7.2 Models of evaluation

A wide range of models has been used. They include:

1 *Systems analysis* Quantitative measurement of inputs and outputs, looking at effectiveness and efficiency.

2 *Behavioural objectives* Focuses on the extent to which clear, specific and measurable goals are achieved.

3 *Needs-based evaluation* Examines the extent to which actual client needs are being met. Sometimes referred to as 'goal-free' evaluation.

4 *Connoisseurship* Considers the extent to which the programme (or whatever is the focus) meets the evaluator's own, expertise-derived, standards of excellence.

5 *Accreditation* External accreditors determine the extent to which the programme meets agreed professional standards.

6 *Adversary* Two teams of evaluators do battle over the pros and cons, and the issue of whether the programme should be continued.

7 *Transaction* Involves a concentration on the programme processes.

8 *Decision-making* The evaluation is structured by the decisions to be made.

9 *Discrepancy* Compares implementation, and outcome ideals, to actual achievements.

10 *Illuminative* Focuses on qualitative methods, inductive analysis and naturalistic inquiry.

11 *Responsive evaluation* Emphasizes responsiveness to all of the 'stake-holders' in evaluation.

(House, 1978, gives further details and references.)

---

carry them out. Box 7.2 gives an indication of some of them. Each model has characteristic strengths and weaknesses. For example, the systems approach, while designed to provide easily usable information about the operation of the programme, tends to emphasize smooth programme operation rather than questions of basic values. The decision-making approach, in equating evaluation with making choices between alternatives, does not come to terms with the fact that decision-makers may unfortunately ignore evaluation findings, and that evaluations have other uses over and above determining policy decisions. The adversary model can bring out facts about

the working of the programme which other models might not, but is vulnerable to any debating weaknesses of the adversaries and ignores the fact that
many value issues should not be resolved in an either–or manner. Corresponding plus and minus points could be made about the other models.

The serious student of evaluation is recommended to spend some time
getting a feel for the different models. House (1978) provides a detailed
discussion. The labels by which the models are usually referred to are not
always very helpful. Responsive evaluation, for example, implies a whole
series of steps not fully captured by 'responsiveness', including:

a   identification of issues from the people directly involved in the pro-
    gramme;
b   use of programme documents to identify further issues;
c   direct observation of working of programme (before designing the
    evaluation);
d   designing an evaluation based on information from (a), (b) and (c).
e   reporting findings directly to all involved through approaches matched
    to each different audience.

(Stake, 1976)

Similarly, Tyler's 'behavioural objectives' approach has been narrowed by
later behaviourist interpretations which virtually call for a specification of
test stimuli and desired responses in advance. As Cronbach (1982, p. 222)
points out, Tyler was much more concerned with providing clear meanings
for vaguely expressed intentions, so that if an educator claimed that a programme would, say, 'build character', he would probe for examples of what
pupils might do that would indicate that this had happened.

Further complication arises from protagonists themselves as well as followers of particular models, modifying details of the approaches. So, while
some knowledge of the different models is useful, if only to remind one of
the wide range of possibilities, there is much to be said for an eclectic
approach. The need is more for flexibility and adaptability, to suit the needs
and purposes of a specific evaluation.

Models of evaluation attempt to be prescriptive. It is also possible to look
at evaluations in a descriptive manner, for which an analysis in terms of
purpose is helpful.

Purposes of Evaluation

Different types of evaluation look at different questions and tend to focus
on different aspects of evaluation. The American Evaluation Research Society has produced a categorization of types of evaluation which covers both
purpose and the kind of activity stressed in the evaluation:

a   *Front-end analysis* (pre-installation, context, feasibility analysis). Takes place before programme starts, to provide guidance in its planning and implementation.
b   *Evaluability assessment.* Assesses feasibility of evaluation approaches and methods.
c   *Formative evaluation* (developmental, process). Provides information for programme improvement, modification and management.
d   *Impact evaluation* (summative, outcome, effectiveness). Determines programme results and effectiveness, especially for deciding about programme continuation, expansion, reduction, funding.
e   *Programme monitoring.* Checks for compliance with policy, tracking of services delivered, counting of clients.
f   *Evaluation of evaluation* (secondary evaluation, meta-evaluation, evaluation audit). Critiques of evaluation reports, re-analysis of data, external reviews of internal evaluations.
                              (Evaluation Research Society, 1980, pp. 3–4)

As with models of evaluation, the intention of including this list here is not to suggest that an evaluation should be a pure type but more to indicate the range of possibilities. In practice an evaluation is likely to concern itself with several if not all of these purposes and activities. Within each of the six general categories there are many more specific evaluative activities which might be listed. These include:

a   *Awareness evaluation.* Who knows about the programme? What do they know?
b   *Cost–benefit evaluation.* Relation between programme costs and benefits (expressed in monetary terms).
c   *Cost-effectiveness evaluation.* Relation between programme costs and benefits (benefits expressed in non-monetary terms).
d   *Criterion-referenced evaluation.* Extent to which specific objectives have been achieved at the desired level of attainment (i.e. at the criterion).
e   *Quality assurance.* Are minimum and accepted standards being routinely and systematically provided? How can quality be monitored and demonstrated?

Patton (1981) lists over a hundred such types of evaluation. He has also pointed out that evaluators may indulge in less than reputable types of activity, such as *quick-and-dirty evaluation* (doing it as fast as possible at the lowest cost); *weighty evaluation* (a thick report); *guesstimate evaluation* (what do we think is happening without collecting proper data); and *personality-focused evaluation* (are the programme staff nice, friendly, helpful, etc.).

Suchman (1967) produces a similar list of 'pseudo-evaluations' incorporating some possible covert motives of those funding evaluations. These include *eyewash* (emphasis on surface appearances); *whitewash* (attempts to cover up programme limitations or failures that have been discovered); *submarine* (the political use of evaluation to destroy a programme); *posture* (the ritualistic use of evaluation research without interest in, or intention to use, its findings – occurs when evaluation was a requirement for funding the programme); and *postponement* (using the need for evaluation as an excuse for postponing or avoiding action). While expressed in jocular fashion, these latter possibilities illustrate the care that one should take before getting into the political situation which virtually all evaluations represent – see the later section on 'Carrying Out an Evaluation'.

Formative and Summative Evaluation

The ERS categorization covered above incorporates FORMATIVE and SUMMATIVE (or IMPACT) approaches to evaluation. This is a distinction which is emphasized in several texts, and is covered here in some detail as experience suggests that clients with some knowledge of the jargon may tend to express their preferences in these terms. To reiterate, the distinction is primarily one of purpose. *Formative evaluation is intended to help in the development of the programme*, innovation or whatever is the focus of the evaluation. *Summative evaluation concentrates on assessing the effects and effectiveness of the programme.* This is likely to cover the total impact of the programme; not simply the extent to which stated goals are achieved, but all the consequences that can be detected. The distinction is not absolute. In particular, summative evaluation could well have a formative effect on future developments, even if it is presented after a particular 'run' of a programme or intervention. Most evaluations are neither totally negative nor totally positive, and typically carry within them strong implications for change. Birney (1988) provides a useful example in the context of the design of a 'flying walk' at a zoo.

It is obvious that formative evaluation needs to be carried out and re-ported on in time for modifications to be made as a result of the evaluation. There is a tension between doing something 'cheap and nasty' (and quick), of likely low reliability and validity, and better-quality work where findings are too late to meet important decision points in the development of the project. This is one aspect of 'real world' working; you are also in 'real time', where the pace tends to be out of the control of the enquirer and in the hands of someone else. In all aspects of carrying out an evaluation, great attention has to be paid to feasibility. The design must take note of constraints of time and resources; of how information is to be collected; of the permissions and co-operation necessary to put this into practice; of what records and other information is available; and so on.

Outcome and Process Evaluation

Similar aspects to those highlighted by the formative/summative distinction are sometimes expressed in terms of PROCESS and OUTCOME respectively.

The traditional view of evaluation restricted the questions asked to those concerning outcome. The task was seen as measuring how far a programme, practice, innovation, intervention or policy met its stated objectives or goals. This approach, while still considered a central feature by many, is more commonly seen as only covering a part of what is needed.

Process evaluation is concerned with answering a how, or 'what is going on?', question. It concerns the systematic observation and study of what actually occurs in the programme, intervention, or whatever is being evaluated. This may well be a crucial part of an evaluation as, without this kind of examination, the nature of what is being evaluated may be obscure or misunderstood. The discrepancy between the 'official' view of what should be going on, and what is actually taking place, may be substantial. A new programme for, say, teaching reading, may have timetabled daily individual sessions. Exigencies of the school's working, and a possible low priority accorded to the programme by a head or deputy, might mean that the majority of such sessions never take place. Generally, relying on an official account or label is dangerous.

Process evaluation provides a useful complement to outcome evaluation of either the *systems analysis* or *behavioural objectives* variety. The latter are essentially 'black box' approaches, concentrating on what goes into the box (i.e. the programme), and in particular what comes out. A study of the intervening processes may help to shed light on this, and assist in determining the causal links involved. Such study of the processes involved may well be valuable in its own right, as well as in giving a better basis for the evaluation of outcomes. In some circumstances the experiences and interactions provided by the programme may legitimately be the focus of interest, and prime criteria for judging its value.

Carrying Out an Evaluation

Evaluations are things to avoid unless you have a good chance of doing them properly. Box 7.3 lists four criteria that should be satisfied before you commit yourself. The *utility* criterion emphasizes that usefulness is at the heart of an evaluation. Otherwise it becomes an essentially pointless activity. The aphorism that 'the purpose of evaluation is not to prove but to improve' expresses this view in strong terms.

Similarly, you have better things to do with your life than to get locked into a study where the results would be suppressed and not acted upon because of political sensitivity; or to accepting a commission where the time and resources available preclude a serious and responsible study. You should similarly beware the 'submarine' – the study set up to to legitimate the closure of a programme or service, or otherwise provide support to some already decided course of action. Obviously anything which prejudices your position in this way is to be avoided.

Box 7.3   Features of evaluation

Any evaluation should meet the following criteria:

1 *Utility* There is no point in doing an evaluation if there is no prospect of its being useful to some audience.

2 *Feasibility* An evaluation should only be done if it is feasible to conduct it in political, practical and cost-effectiveness terms.

3 *Propriety* An evaluation should only be done if you can demonstrate that it will be carried out *fairly* and *ethically*.

4 *Technical adequacy* Given reassurance about utility, feasibility and proper conduct, the evaluation must then be carried out with technical skill and sensitivity.

And finally, also tied up with ethics, you have no business in getting involved in studies unless you can deliver as a technically adequate evaluator. Box 7.4 presents a checklist of some of the things that need to be thought about in planning an evaluation. Box 7.5 lists some of the relevant skills, and it will be clear that they mirror closely many of the topics covered in the text. Hence although this chapter is itself quite short, it is fair to say that virtually all of the book is concerned with what to do when carrying out evaluations. The last skill, 'sensitivity to political concerns', looms particularly large in evaluations and is expanded upon in the following section.

Box 7.4   Checklist for planning an evaluation

1 *Reasons, purposes and motivations*
   - Is the evaluation for yourself or someone else?
   - Why is it being done?
   - Who should have the information obtained?
2 *Value*
   - Can actions or decisions be taken as a result?
   - Is somebody or something going to stop it being carried out?
3 *Interpretation*
   - Is the nature of the evaluation agreed between those involved?
4 *Subject*
   - What kinds of information do you need?

5 *Evaluator(s)*
   - Who gathers the information?
   - Who writes any report?

6 *Methods*
   - What methods are appropriate to the information required?
   - Can they be developed and applied in the time available?
   - Are the methods acceptable to those involved?

7 *Time*
   - What time can be set aside for the evaluation?
   - Is this adequate to gather and analyse the information?

8 *Permissions and control*
   - Have any necessary permissions to carry out the evaluation been sought and received?
   - Is participation voluntary?
   - Who decides what goes in any report?

9 *Use*
   - Who decides how the evaluation will be used?
   - Will those involved see it in a modifiable draft version?
   - Is the form of the report appropriate for the designated audience (style/length)?

And remember:

- *Keep it as simple as possible* – avoid complex designs and data analyses;
- *Think defensively* – if it can go wrong it will, so try to anticipate potential problems.

(Adapted from Harlen and Elliott, 1982; see also Robson et al., 1988, p. 85.)

Box 7.5 Skills needed to carry out evaluations

There are many different kinds of evaluation which call for different mixes of skills. The following seem fundamental to most evaluations:

- writing a proposal;
- clarifying purposes of the evaluation;
- identifying, organizing and working with an evaluation team;
- choice of design and data collection techniques;
- interviewing;
- questionnaire construction and use;
- observation;
- management of complex information systems;

- data analysis;
- report writing, including making of recommendations;
- fostering utilization of findings,
- sensitivity to political concerns.

The Politics of Evaluation

It is almost inevitable that an evaluation has a political dimension to it. Innovations, policies and practices will have their sponsors and advocates. Most will have critics and sceptics. Staff running programmes may have much to gain or lose from particular outcomes of an evaluation. Jobs may be on the line. A positive evaluation may lead to the expansion of a programme; to inflows of money and resources which can make major differences to the lives of clients involved.

Evaluations tend to focus on programmes or initiatives which are in the political arena, whether at national or local level, or simply of concern in an individual business, school or other unit. As Berk and Rossi (1990, p. 2) point out, 'evaluations are almost entirely contained within the current "policy space"'; in other words, with making judgments about policies or programmes on the current agenda of those responsible for making such policies. So, a few years ago, the Department of Education and Science responded to political pressure for provision of 'conductive education' as developed at the Peto Institute in Budapest for children suffering from cerebral palsy by funding a major evaluation into its effectiveness. Currently much evaluation funding is going into topics pushed to centre stage by the introduction of a National Curriculum and associated Standard Attainment Testing. The two most recent evaluations with which I have been involved concern, first, the use to which my institution of higher education has put the one million pounds funding under an 'Enterprise in Higher Education Initiative' and, second, my own department's response to pressure to increase student numbers through moving to more 'student-centred' approaches to course delivery.

Because of these policy implications, the existence and outcomes of an evaluation are likely to be of interest and concern for a whole range of 'stake-holders' – national and local government, both politicians themselves and bureaucrats; the agencies and their officials responsible for administering the programme or policy; persons responsible for direct delivery; the clients or targets of the programme, and groups such as unions responsible for looking after their interests; possibly taxpayers and citizens generally. It would be highly unlikely for the interests of all of these groups to be identical, and one can usually guarantee that, whatever the results and findings of an evaluation, some will be pleased and others not.

This means, among other things, that carrying out an evaluation is not an

activity for those particularly sensitive to criticism, or disturbed by controversy! Criticism may be both methodological (of the way the study has been
carried out) or political (of the findings); or the latter masquerading as the
former (Berk and Rossi, 1990). The main implication is that it pays to give
meticulous attention to the design and conduct of the study, and to ensuring
that the legitimate concerns of gatekeepers have been taken into account.

Needs Assessment

An innovatory programme or new service is usually set up because of a
perceived need which is not being met by current provision. Logically, the
assessment of such needs should take place before the programme is set up
and organized, and it would appear reasonable for it to be the responsibility
of the programme planners. However, it is quite common for evaluators to
be asked to advise on, or even carry out the needs assessment themselves.
Similarly there are situations where those involved both run and evaluate the
programme. Hence a note on the topic might be useful.

Needs assessment is the process whereby needs are identified and priorities among them established. It is fairly clear what is meant by 'needs' at
a common-sense level, but it may help to regard them as arising when there
is a discrepancy between the observed state of affairs and a desirable or
acceptable state of affairs. Several approaches to needs assessment have been
proposed (McKillip, 1987). Box 7.6 outlines one of these. Satcher et al.
(1980) describe the use of a similar strategy in the development of health
service programmes in an inner-city community (see also Kosecoff and Fink,
1982, ch. 2).

Box 7.6   Steps in carrying out a needs assessment

1   *Identify possible objectives*. The first step involves collecting as
comprehensive a set of potential objectives as is possible. These can be
gleaned from a variety of sources, including the literature (if any),
experts in the field, and those likely to be involved in the programme
in any capacity.

2   *Decide on important objectives*. Select groups of participants representing important 'constituencies', e.g. likely consumers of the service
or users of the programme, providers and managers or administrators.
Get them to rate the importance of each of the potential objectives.

3   *Assess what is currently available to meet the important objectives*.
In some cases this can be combined with the previous step by having
respondents rate current availability, and if possible give information

---

about how needs are currently being met. Alternatively, information can be sought from records or through a small-scale survey.

4 *Select final set of objectives.* Judgement must now be exercised in selecting a set of objectives which rate high on importance and low on current availability. Other criteria such as feasibility may also be incorporated. Different needs and objectives may be best addressed by different kinds of programme or service (e.g. it may be that the providers wished to develop a self-instructional training programme, but the needs assessment throws up objectives which can be best addressed by individual consultancy.

The danger of concentrating on 'accessible' needs must be acknowledged. As Judd et al. (1991, p. 408) point out, such technical decisions have ideological consequences. They cite crime prevention programmes. Considering the events leading to crime as a long causal chain, intervention at any point along that chain might reduce crime. This could range from intervening in the childhood experiences of potential delinquents, through providing job skills for the unemployed, to promoting better home security measures. Programmes focusing on the installation of door locks, security lighting and burglar alarms are much more accessible, with clear outcome measures, but they carry the ideological implication that reducing crime is about protecting potential victims.

Evaluation and Enquiry

Virtually the whole of this book is relevant to the potential evaluator. You need to have an understanding of the issues involved in the initial development of a proposal, in the selection of a general research strategy, and of specific methods and techniques of collecting data. There has been a tendency in small-scale studies to equate evaluations with the use of questionnaires (as the sole method) but evaluation is a complex field where the benefits of multiple methods are particularly clear. Many evaluations collect both qualitative and quantitative data and you need to know appropriate analysis and interpretation techniques. Reporting in a way that is understandable and helpful for those who have to act on the findings is crucial.

This chapter has sought to give some indication of where the very young science of evaluation research is at, and in particular to encourage an appreciation of the complexity and sensitivity of the evaluator's task. Your job is to select a research strategy and a method of data collection and analysis (probably, in most evaluations, several methods). A thorough knowledge of the programme being evaluated is an essential precursor to your selection and subsequent sensitive use of the methods.

What is advocated is an open-minded exploration of the most suitable strategy and best methods for the task in hand. Rigour and systematic data collection are important. *But what is particularly important is the usefulness of the data for the purposes of the evaluation, and not the method by which it is obtained.* As Jones (1985) puts it:

> If you can find out something useful about a program by talking to a few disgruntled employees, then talk to them. If the only way you can get the data you need is by participant observation, then participate and observe (and do not forget to take good notes). If you need a time series design with switching replications, then set it up and switch when the time comes. If you need archival data, then locate the necessary records and extract whatever you require. Use whatever you have in your toolbox that will get the job done. (p. 258)

Further Reading

Berk, R. A. and Rossi, P. H. (1990) *Thinking About Program Evaluation.* Newbury Park and London: Sage. Short text covering central ideas of evaluation.

Cronbach, L. J. (1982) *Designing Evaluations of Educational and Social Programs.* San Francisco: Jossey-Bass. Not an easy read, and focused on large-scale evaluations, but well worth the effort if you want a grasp of the complexities of evaluation.

Eisner, E. W. (1985) *The Art of Educational Evaluation.* London: Falmer. Humanistic approach by main advocate of connoisseurship model.

Guba, E. G. and Lincoln, Y. S. (1982) *Effective Evaluation.* San Francisco: Jossey-Bass. Advocates 'naturalistic' evaluation. Makes a good case for qualitative approaches.

Hamilton, D. et al. (eds) (1977) *Beyond the Numbers Game.* London: Macmillan. Influential polemic in favour of 'illuminative' evaluation.

Murphy, R. and Torrance, H. (eds) (1987) *Evaluating Education: issues and methods.* New York: Harper and Row. Useful collection of wide-ranging papers. Stronach on 'Practical Evaluation' gives good flavour of practicalities.

Norris, N. (1990) *Understanding Educational Evaluation.* London: Kogan Page. Includes historical/political analysis of development of educational evaluation.

Patton, M. Q. (1982) *Practical Evaluation.* Newbury Park and London: Sage. Readable approach to programme evaluation. See also *Creative Evaluation* (1981) and *Utilisation-Focused Evaluation* (1978) by the same author.

Rossi, P. H. and Freeman, H. (1985) *Evaluation: a systematic approach,* 4th edn. Newbury Park and London: Sage.
Good, standard introductory text.

Note: Sage also publish a wide range of other evaluation texts (including a 'Program Evaluator's Kit' and a multi-volume *Handbook of Evaluation Research*) and journals (e.g. *Evaluation and the Health Professions*).

Part III

Tactics – the Methods of Data Collection

Following the metaphor, developed in chapter 2, of 'real world enquiry' as akin to 'detective work', we can now proceed to the practicalities of making our enquiries. In carrying out real world enquiry, our options are essentially the same as those available to the detective and to ourselves in day-to-day living. We can *watch* people and try to work out what is going on; we can *ask* them about it; and we can look out for fingerprints (as well as any other evidence they leave behind them).

Put in the more usual research language, watching becomes OBSERVATION, asking becomes INTERVIEWING and using QUESTIONNAIRES. Interviewing is usually taken as implying personal, face-to-face (or in the case of telephone interviewing, increasingly common in the United States, voice-to-voice) interaction. Questionnaires may be administered in an interview, face-to-face situation; or the researcher's questions can be presented without direct, personal, interaction – as in a postal survey.

Observation provides the focus for the first of these chapters concerned with data collection. Interviews, questionnaires and other related methods are covered in chapter nine. Chapter ten gathers together some other methods that you might use. There is an emphasis on the study of documents and other artefacts produced by people. Letters and notices, school curricula and timetables, office memos, graffiti, litter and other ephemera may sometimes speak louder than a response to an interview question, or tell us about something we were not in a position to observe. The problem for enquiry purposes lies in finding and selecting such artefacts; then in analysing and interpreting them.

Selecting the Method(s) – Overview

Selecting a method or methods is based on what kind of information is sought, from whom and under what circumstances. It is usually decided early in a project, and once made, it may be very difficult to change, although it may be feasible to add supplementary methods during the project. As in aspects of design and analysis, there is greater flexibility in selection of methods in case studies than within the other strategies.

A A Rational Choice?

The rational approach is to ask – given the chosen research problem and questions, and a decision on research strategy, what methods are most suitable? However, in practice, the choice of particular methods may well precede the choice of a research problem. As Walker (1985) puts it:

> Just as an instrumentalist will not change from playing the clarinet to playing the trumpet because a particular piece demands it, but will usually turn to another piece of music, searching for pieces that suit both the instrument and the player, so researchers generally give a lot of time and thought to the formulation of possible and potential research problems, looking for those that appear to fit their interests and preferred methods. (p. 47)

This phenomenon of 'methods in search of problems' rather than the reverse is a genuine one. In one sense it does not matter providing that the methods fit the problem chosen. However, it can cause difficulties in real world research where the problem is presented to you, and the choice might be between using an inappropriate method or turning the work away. The moral is to seek to get a broad grounding in all strategies and a broad range of methods, so that you are in a position to make a rational choice.

B What Methods are Available?

Many. Interviews and questionnaires, and direct observation of different kinds, tend to be the most popular. Experiments also use some form of controlled observation but the actual technique is often specific to the particular field of study.

Simple rules of thumb for selecting methods include:

- To find out what people do in public use *direct observation*.
- To find out what they do in private, use *interviews, questionnaires* or *diary techniques*.
- To find out what they think, feel, believe, use *interviews, questionnaires* or *attitude scales*.
- To determine their abilities, or measure their intelligence or personality, use *standardized tests*.

C Consider Practicalities

Anything you propose to do must be within the constraints of available time and resources. You may wish to carry out a participant observation study, but if it would take three months for you to be accepted and fully involved, then it is impracticable for a one-month maximum study period. A second-best alternative involving interviews may be called for.

Business confidentiality or other high sensitivity or stress might rule out direct observation. It might be that you can at least get some purchase on the topic through a simulation study. Ethical consideration will similarly rule out some methods in some situations.

8

Observational Methods

The chapter discusses the advantages and disadvantages of direct observation.

It analyses the stance of participant observer and considers its implications.

The chapter concludes with a discussion of structured observation and the development of coding schemes.

Introduction

As the actions and behaviour of people are a central aspect in virtually any enquiry, a natural and obvious technique is to watch what they do, to record this in some way and then to describe, analyse and interpret that we have observed. Much research with people involves observation in a general sense. The typical experiment, whether in the laboratory or in the field, is simply a form of controlled observation. However, we use a rather more restricted definition here, sticking primarily to DIRECT OBSERVATION as carried out by the human, observer.

Fundamentally different approaches to the use of observational methods in enquiry have been employed. The two polar extreme types are PARTICIPANT OBSERVATION – an essentially qualitative style originally rooted in the work of anthropologists and particularly associated with the Chicago school of sociology; and STRUCTURED OBSERVATION – a quantitative style which has been used in a variety of disciplines. Each of the styles has a distinctive contribution to make and I will try to set out the stall for each of them in turn. However, in common with the basic stance taken in this book, I will also try to encourage at least the consideration of a more 'pick and mix' approach where you look at the particular needs and possibilities in the situation you are enquiring into, and perhaps use elements of both approaches – or even some hybrid which is both structured and participatory.

Advantages and Disadvantages of Observation

Advantages

A major advantage of observation as a technique is its directness. You do not ask people about their views, feelings or attitudes; you watch what they do and listen to what they say. Note in passing, by the way, that the language of people, and other behaviours associated with language, are often of crucial interest and importance in any enquiry. Perhaps because, historically, much observational work has focused on non-human animals (for example the work of ethologists – see Tinbergen, 1963; McFarland, 1985) there is some tendency for observation studies to concentrate on non-linguistic aspects. There are practical problems in recording language adequately, but these are by no means insuperable.

This directness contrasts with, and can often usefully complement, information obtained by virtually any other technique. Interview and questionnaire responses are notorious for discrepancies between what people say that they have done, or will do, and what they actually did or will do (Oskamp, 1977; Hanson, 1980). As Agnew and Pyke (1982) put it, 'on a questionnaire we only have to move the pencil a few inches to shift our scores from being a bigot to being a humanitarian. We don't have to move our heavyweight behavior at all' (p. 129). Or as Montaigne, over four hundred years ago, put it succinctly, 'saying is one thing; doing is another'. These inherent difficulties in the reliability and validity of such data, arising from deficiencies in memory and the wish to present oneself in a favorable light (the 'social desirability response bias') among many other factors, are discussed in the following chapter (p. 232).

Observation also seems to be pre-eminently the appropriate technique for getting at 'real life' in the 'real world'. It is, of course, possible to observe through one-way glass in a laboratory, or set up some other contrived situation and observe that (see, for example the section on 'simulation' techniques, p. 286); but direct observation in the field permits a lack of artificiality which is all too rare with other techniques.

Disadvantages

This appropriateness does not imply that observation is an easy or trouble-free option. There is a major issue concerning the extent to which an observer affects the situation under observation. It is commonly claimed that this can be overcome – for example, by seeking to ensure that the observed are unaware of being observed, at one extreme; or by them being so accustomed to the presence of the observer that they carry on as if she were not there, at the other extreme.

However, there is a lingering logical problem here. How do we know what the behaviour would have been like if it hadn't been observed? And, moreover, whether one takes on a very detached or very involved role as an observer, or something in between, there are related methodological and ethical problems.

There is also the very practical problem with observation that it tends to be time-consuming. The classic 'participant observation' study deriving from social anthropology, and in particular the work of Malinowski in the 1920s and 1930s (e.g. Malinowski, 1922; 1935a; 1935b) demands an immersion into the 'tribe' for two or three years. While there is a trend toward a more 'condensed field experience' based on observation (cf Stenhouse, 1982) which has become popular in applied fields such as education, this still requires a substantial time commitment. More structured approaches, normally requiring the use of some kind of observation schedule, can reduce the actual observation time substantially, but there is a correspondingly increased time investment required in developing such an instrument from scratch. Even on those rare occasions when an existing observation schedule developed by a previous worker is suited to your task, acquiring proficiency in its use can take much time and effort.

Observation in Enquiry

Observation, in part because it can take on a variety of forms, can be used for several purposes in a study. It is commonly used in an *exploratory phase*, typically in an unstructured form, to seek to find out what is going on in a situation as a precursor to subsequent testing out of these insights as hypotheses.

Observation can also be used as a *supportive* or *supplementary* technique to collect data that may complement or set in perspective data obtained by other means. Suppose that the main effort in a particular study is devoted to a series of interviews; observation might then be used to validate or corroborate the messages obtained in the interviews. It is not unusual, however, for observation to be the *primary* method in a particular study, especially though not exclusively when the main intention is descriptive. Or it could be used in a multi-method case study where other methods, such as documentary analysis, supplement the observational data.

Observation also has a potential role in *experimental research*. Apart from experiment itself being a form of controlled observation, direct observation in the narrower sense considered here is a technique not uncommonly used within the context of an experiment. Observation within the laboratory experiment is outside the remit of this book, but its employment in the type of field experiment discussed in chapter 4 is extremely common. This use almost invariably concentrates on structured observation, but there is no difference in principle between its use in field experiments and in case studies.

The use of observation as a technique in *survey research* is fairly unusual.

Simple structured observational techniques could be used to substitute for, or complement, the ubiquitous interview or questionnaire to determine, for example, frequency of use of hats or other kind of headwear by different groups in different locations – or the gender of users of open access computer terminals in libraries.

Approaches to Observation

In prospect it may seem very straightforward, but the experience of being put in a situation with the instruction 'observe!' is daunting even to the experienced enquirer. There seems to be either so much, or so little, going on. And how does one characterize and capture it?

As with all enquiry, the driving force behind the use of observation for enquiry purposes is the research question or questions, even though these may be very broad, general and loosely phrased in an exploratory study. Leading on from this is the type of information which will be most appropriate in answering these research question(s). There is a major divide here between NARRATIVE ACCOUNTS and CODED SCHEDULES. The former, typified by the reports arising from classic participant observation by social anthropologists and some sociologists, are regarded by some psychologists as 'humanistic' rather than 'scientific' (see, e.g. Bakeman and Gottman, 1986). However, as discussed in earlier chapters (pp. 19 and 57) the intention in this text is to welcome such endeavours within a broad notion of science, providing adequate attention is given to rigour in such those matters as reliability, validity and believability (Shipman, 1988). Whether or not such those working within these traditions welcome this welcome into science is another matter!

It may also be worth stressing at this point that narrative accounts, though traditionally almost exclusively dependent on single-method qualitative approaches, need not be so. A narrative account can be constructed from quantitative, structured schedule data, and it is encouraging to note multi-method case studies incorporating participant observation being advocated by anthropologists (e.g. Fetterman, 1989).

Structured observation through the use of observational schedules has tended to be the method used most by psychologists, although it is not uncommon to see something akin to a narrative account used in the pilot stage of developing a coding scheme. A distinction is also sometimes made between the use of RATING SCALES in connection with observation, and the coded schedule type of structured observation (Cairns and Green, 1979).

Classifying Observational Methods

The preceding discussion highlights one important dimension of difference in approaches to observation; the degree of *pre-structure* in the observation exercise. This can be dichotomized as FORMAL or INFORMAL INFORMATION GATHERING. Informal approaches are less structured and allow the observer considerable freedom in what information is gathered and how it is recorded. They would include note-taking, diary-keeping and generally gathering information from informants. This kind of information is relatively unstructured and complex, and requires the observer to perform difficult tasks of synthesis, abstraction and organization of the data. Formal approaches impose a large amount of structure and direction on what is to be observed. The observer has only to attend to these pre-specified aspects; everything else is considered irrelevant for the purposes of the study. High reliability and validity are easier to achieve with these latter formal approaches, but at the cost of a loss of complexity and completeness by comparison with the informal approach.

A second dimension, in practice by no means independent of the formality/structure dimension, concerns the *role* adopted by the observer in the situation observed. Specifically, this relates to the extent of her PARTICIPATION in that situation. We will concentrate here on the two extreme positions on this dimension, where the intention is either to participate fully, effectively to become a part of the group or whatever is being studied, or to be a 'pure' observer, seeking to be an unnoticed part of the wallpaper. These two 'ideal types' carry with them very different methodological and philosophical views about the nature and purposes of observation, echoing the general discussion in part IV about qualitative and quantitative approaches. The participant observer will tend to use qualitative, unstructured approaches. The pure observer might use qualitative approaches but has tended towards the quantitative and structured. While the pure observer typically *uses* an observation instrument of some kind, the participant observer *is* the instrument.

Participant Observation

A key feature of participant observation is that the observer seeks to become some kind of member of the observed group. This involves not only a physical presence and a sharing of life experiences, but also entry into their social and 'symbolic' world through learning their social conventions and habits, their use of language and non-verbal communication, and so on. The observer also has to establish some role within the group.

This may sound warning bells of subjectivity and general 'bad science' to those trained in traditional views of experimental design and quantitative analysis. However, it can be argued persuasively that when working with people scientific aims can be followed by explaining the meaning of the experiences of the observed through the experiences of the observer. This arises from a perspective that the social world involves subjective meanings and experiences constructed by participants in social situations. The task of

interpreting this can only be achieved through participation with those involved (cf Schutz, 1954; 1967; Manis and Meltzer, 1967).

Whether or not one is prepared to accept this view as recognizably
science, it is still possible to follow the touchstones established in chapter 2
as canons of scientific method. In particular the necessary bases of reliability
and validity can be achieved. Similarly, objectivity can be approached through
a heightened sensitivity to the problem of subjectivity, and the need for
justification of one's claims. The approach needed to demonstrate causal
inference remains unchanged. Admittedly, by no means all of the studies
published which use participant observation pay serious attention to these
canons. Several are more appropriately judged in terms of journalism or
literature. This is not intended as a dismissive statement. If the intention is
polemical, or to throw light on the human condition, then it would be crass
scientific hegemony to claim that science is the only, or the best, means of
persuasion or illumination.

There are, however, particular benefits from playing the science game, as
already rehearsed. The claim made here is that by giving particular attention
to reliability, validity and objectivity, participant observation, along with
other essentially qualitative techniques, can be 'good science'.

Participant observation, even in an abbreviated version where the involvement is measured in weeks or even days rather than the years of the classical
anthropological model, places a considerable burden on the shoulders of the
observer. The primary data are the interpretations by the observer of what
is going on around her. The observer *is* the research instrument, and hence
great sensitivity and personal skills are necessary for worthwhile data.
Lincoln and Guba (1985) warn that 'one would not expect individuals to
function adequately as human instruments without an extensive background
of training and exposure' (p. 195). With participant observation it is difficult
to separate out the data collection and analysis phases of an enquiry. Analysis takes place in the middle of data collection and is used to help shape its
development. If this rings a bell for you it is because this kind of approach
is a revisiting at the level of method or technique of the issues raised at the
level of research strategy when case study was discussed in chapter 6. This
flexibility helps to explain why many case studies have some form of participant observation as the primary method of data collection; and why
many participant observers use the case study strategy.

For some people, what is referred to in this book as case study would be
termed participant observation (or even field studies, or qualitative research).
My quarrel with these usages is that their 'participant observation' is likely
to include other methods in addition to observation, such as interviews and
the use of documents and other artefacts; that 'field study' appears to refer
to where the study takes place rather than to the kind of study it is; and
similarly that 'qualitative' appears to refer to the kind of data collected
rather than the methods or strategies used in their collection. However,
tradition may well be stronger than logic.

Participant observers can either seek to hide the fact that they are carrying out some kind of enquiry, or make it clear from the start what their purpose is in participating. Both roles have their problems, as discussed below.

The Complete Participant

The COMPLETE PARTICIPANT ROLE involves the observer concealing that she is an observer, acting as naturally as possible and seeking to become a full member of the group. Festinger et al. (1956), in a widely known study, infiltrated a group of persons who believed a prediction of the imminent destruction of the world on a known day. Similar studies have been carried out of criminal fraternities, homosexual groups and military training units. In each case a justification for keeping the group in ignorance of the researchers' real purposes was made in terms of the group's likely refusal to co-operate if these purposes were revealed. A subsidiary consideration was that the behaviour under observation would change if it were known that someone was prying into it.

There are obvious and strong ethical objections to this stance. Entering into a situation with the deliberate and planned intention to deceive is regarded as indefensible by many researchers and it is becoming increasingly rare. There are enough problems in carrying out real world enquiry without being saddled with that particular guilt. There are also methodological problems with the complete participant role. The tendency to 'go native' (a problem shared by anthropologists and colonial administrators) is probably greatest when observation and recording have to be covert activities. This refers to the situation where the role you have adopted in the group takes over to the extent that the research perspective is lost. Great care has to be taken that your activities are appropriate to the role; or suspicions and consequent distortions may be produced. Postponing recording until one is safely alone heightens the danger of seriously incomplete and selectively biased accounts; and there is always the risk that your true purpose will be discovered.

Increasingly, the position taken by Kirby and McKenna (1989) is being adopted:

> It is essential that as a participant who is also a data gatherer, the researcher recognise the obligation to inform those in the setting about the research (i.e. what sort of research it is, for what purposes, and who is involved). Research from a *covert* or *manipulative* perspective is not generally acceptable. (p. 78)

> *These considerations suggest that you should avoid taking on the 'complete participant' role. If it appears impossible to carry out the enquiry if your research purpose were to be revealed, you are strongly recommended to seek the advice of experienced participant observers, and to ensure that your study falls within the appropriate code of conduct (see page 29).*

The Participant as Observer

A feasible alternative is the PARTICIPANT-AS-OBSERVER ROLE. The fact that the observer *is* an observer is made clear to the group from the start. The observer then tries to establish close relationships with members of the group. This stance means that as well as observing through participating in activities, the observer can ask members to explain various aspects of what is going on. It is important to get the trust of key members of the group (key either because of their position or because of personal qualities such as openness or interest in the ways of the group). Maintaining the dual role of observer and participator is not easy, and acceptance will be heavily dependent on the nature of the group and the interaction of particular features of the observer with the group. Variables such as age, class, gender and ethnic background can be important in particular circumstances.

Intuitively it would appear that this role would have more of a disturbing effect on the phenomena observed than that of the complete participant, and several experienced participant observers have documented this (e.g. Whyte, 1981; 1984). However, one such effect is that members of the group, particularly key informants, are led to a more analytic reflection about processes and other aspects of the group's functioning. There are situations, for example in the evaluation of an innovatory programme, where this can be of positive benefit.

One possible strategy for the participant as observer is to *evoke* a particular situation or behaviour from members of the group. Essentially this involves setting up a situation which has meaning for the group and then observing what happens. There are potential ethical problems here and also the danger of artificiality. The group may perhaps do something, or do something in a different way, to please or placate the 'important' observer. This kind of active involvement borders on carrying out an informal field experiment, or if viewed in a different light can be seen as a kind of simulation or role play exercise.

It may also be possible to take advantage of the roles ascribed to one in a situation to gather information in a more active fashion. For example, working as a participant observer in some schools, particularly those for younger children or for children with special educational needs, the children commonly view you as something akin to a teacher. They then are not surprized to be quizzed by you on any and every aspect of their school life. Similarly, the researcher in hospitals is likely to be classified as some subspecies of the 'helping and caring' staff, providing potential insights into patient relationships with such staff.

The special case of observing a group of which you are already a member carries obvious advantages and disadvantages. Your knowledge of the group's ways may well be extensive but there is a corresponding problem in achieving objectivity if you are already a native. Similarly, existing relationships with individuals can short-circuit a lengthy process of development of trust, but it may prove difficult for others to see you in your new role as observer and there may be an artificiality and hesitancy in seeking to get shared understandings explicit and out into the open. In settings where there is a strong hierarchical structure, such as a school or hospital, a high-status member may look askance at being observed or questioned by a low-status member. (See chapter 15 for a discussion of general issues in researching in one's own organization).

The Marginal Participant

In some situations it may be feasible and advantageous to have a lower degree of participation than that envisaged in the preceding sections. This can be done by adopting the role of a largely passive, though completely accepted, participant – a passenger in a train or bus, or a member of the audience at a concert or sports meeting. Your likely familiarity with such roles helps, but it can also get in the way of the observer role. Conscious attention to active and open-minded observation is needed. Roles permitting note-taking are advantageous (e.g. student in a library, lecture theater or seminar). Zeisel (1981) warns against assuming that while *you* know what role you are playing, others automatically come to the same conclusion: 'the marginal observer assumes when watching an informal football game in the park that he is taken to be a casual spectator. Meanwhile the football players think he is a park attendant about to tell them to stop playing on the grass' (p. 119).

Careful attention to dress and behaviour can help with such problems. 'Props' can be useful, such as bringing along a child if you are observing in a children's playground. Zeisel also suggests that you can test assumptions about how you are perceived by others by slightly changing your normal behaviour to see how people in the situation respond.

Some marginal roles are effectively indistinguishable from that of the 'complete observer' – someone who does not take part in the activity, and whose status as a researcher is unknown to the participants.

The Observer-as-Participant

This is someone who takes no part in the activity, but whose status as research is known to the participants (Gold, 1958). Such a state is aspired to by many researchers using systematic observation. However, it is questionable whether anyone who is known to be a researcher can be said not to take part in the activity – in the sense that their role is now one of the roles within the larger group that includes the researcher.

Getting Started

Actually getting into, and getting to be a part of, the group that you are interested in can loom large as a problem. There is a real worry that you might 'blow it' by unintentional insensitivity or crassness. Anthropology abounds with horror stories of choosing as one's sponsor someone disliked or mistrusted by the rest of the group – see Barley (1989) for an engaging account of these issues. If, as may well be the case, you already have links with the group, these may provide what Lofland (1971) refers to as 'pre-existing relations of trust'.

There are differing views as to how much work you should have done before starting observation. The classic view, of many researchers using participant observation, typified by Whyte (1951) is that the theory should emerge from the observation and that hence you need a minimum of initial theoretical orientation. Jones (1985) makes a useful distinction between the 'how' and the 'what and why' questions in this respect. In participant observation, our central research questions are likely to be 'hows': How does the teacher control the class? How does a committee come to decisions? Clues about these things should be gathered during and as a result of the observation. The 'whats' and the 'whys', primarily factual things like the context, details of the setting and its history can profitably be found out ahead of time.

The immersion process of actually getting 'into' the group can be both confusing and stressful. Have faith – what may initially seem to be total chaos will, with time, reveal pattern, structure and regularity. 'Getting started' issues are picked up again in general terms in marked pages on 'Arranging the Practicalities' (p. 294).

Collecting Data

The basic task of the participant observer is to observe the people in the group, unit, organization or whatever is the focus of the enquiry, while being involved with them. Accounts are collected from informants. However, to give form and precision to the data, the observer often has to *ask questions* about the situation and the accounts that are given. These are both questions to oneself, and, more sparingly, explicit questions to group members.

This may seem to go against the notion of direct observation, and be more akin to interviewing. The distinction is blurred, but in participant observation you are less likely to have 'set piece' interviews and much more likely to have opportunistic 'on the wing' discussions with individuals. None the less, interviewing skills are very useful to the participant observer (see chapter 9).

It is common practice to start with DESCRIPTIVE OBSERVATION. The basic aim here is to describe the setting, the people and the events that have taken place. Spradley (1980) distinguishes nine dimensions on which this descriptive data may be collected, explained below in box 8.1.

Box 8.1   Dimensions of descriptive observation

1	Space	layout of the physical setting; rooms, outdoor spaces, etc.
2	Actors	the names and relevant details of the people involved
3	Activities	the various activities of the actors
4	Objects	physical elements: furniture etc.
5	Acts	specific individual actions
6	Events	particular occasions, e.g. meetings
7	Time	the sequence of events
8	Goals	what actors are attempting to accomplish
9	Feelings	emotions in particular contexts

An early task is to develop a detailed portrait using this descriptive approach. This is the initial STORY or NARRATIVE ACCOUNT based on the events with which you have been involved. There is a similarity here to the approach of the investigative journalist who is after the 'story'. The Chicago school which pioneered the serious use of participant observation within sociology (see Hammersley, 1989, for a detailed and interesting account) had direct roots in journalism. The big difference between the researcher and the journalist (assuming that the latter is wanting to do a responsible job and wanting to get to the bottom of the story) is that the researcher has to go beyoud the story. This next stage involves developing a set of concepts, a theoretical framework, properly grounded in the detail of the story, which helps you to understand, and explain to others, what is going on.

Particular dimensions may loom large in some studies. Considering these dimensions, in the light of the research questions which led you to choose this group or setting in the first instance, is likely to lead to a greater focusing of the questions. This FOCUSED OBSERVATION might be on a specific dimension or dimensions, or on themes which cross the dimensions.

For example, Burgess (1983), in a study of a comprehensive school, used his descriptive observations, within a general theoretical framework derived from symbolic interactionism, to focus his questions on such topics as: –

> How do teachers define the Newsom course? How do pupils define and re-define the course? What strategies, negotiations and bargains are used by the teachers and pupils? To what extent do activities in the Newsom department influence work within the core courses which Newsom pupils attend? (p. 209)

The concepts, such as 'negotiation', 'strategy' and 'bargain' led him to an understanding of the concepts which were used by the participants to come to terms with the situations in which they were located (see Burgess, 1983, pp. 115–35 for an extended discussion).

Stated in somewhat more formal terms, the process involved in partici-pant observation has been regarded as an example of ANALYTIC INDUCTION (Denzin, 1970; Robinson, 1951). This is summarized in box 8.2.

Box 8.2   The process of analytic induction

1   Formulate a rough definition of the phenomenon of interest.

2   Put forward an initial hypothetical explanation of this phenomenon.

3   Study a situation in the light of this hypothesis, to determine whether or not the hypothesis fits.

4   If the hypothesis does not fit the evidence, then *either* the hy-pothesis must be reformulated, *or* the phenomenon to be explained must be redefined so that the phenomenon is excluded.

5   Repeat with a second situation. Confidence in your hypothesis in-creases with the number of situations fitting the evidence. Each nega-tive one requires either a redefinition or a reformulation.

Notes   Situations should be selected to maximize the chances of discov-ering a decisive one. In this way weaknesses are more quickly exposed.

'Situation' is used as a general term to indicate an instance, phenomenon, case, aspect (or whatever) that is observed.

Note that observation and analysis are intertwined here. This is char-acteristic of the case study strategy (which is highly likely to be fol-lowed by participant observers) as discussed in chapter 6. There is more detailed coverage of the analysis of the qualitative data produced through participant observation in chapter 12.

Recording in Participant Observation

In principle, the fact that one is a participant does not preclude or prescribe any approach to recording, providing that the group knows and accepts that you have this role and task of observer. However, in practice, the continued use of certain types of structured observation schedule could inhibit your participation in the group. This need not be the case. It is, for example, feasible that a group *for its own purposes* wishes to have its activities observed and analysed (possibly stimulated in this desire by your presence in their midst as a researcher – a beneficial 'Hawthorne'-like effect). In this case your role in participating is that of observer. Issues in recording of structured observation are covered in the following section.

By the nature of the activity, it is not possible to be prescriptive about the recording of unstructured observation, even if this were desirable. Issues to do with the use of recording devices (audio cassette recorders and, possibly, video cameras and recorders) are the same as those discussed in the context of interviews (see chapter 9, p. 232).

Observational Biases

The human instrument as used in participant observation has a lot going for it. It is very flexible and can deal with complex and 'fuzzy' situations which give even powerful computers a headache. It does have deficiencies as an instrument, though. Knowing what distortions and biases we are likely to introduce in our observation should help in counteracting them.

Such effects are the stock-in-trade of many psychologists in the fields of memory, perception and social interaction, although the extent to which there is transfer of this knowledge to colleagues engaging in observational tasks is questionable! The following is very much a lay person's guide to a complex area.

Selective Attention

All perceptual processes involving the taking in of information by observation and its subsequent internal processing are subject to bias. Attention – the concentration on some aspects of our surroundings rather than others – is an essential feature of coping with the overwhelming complexity of those surroundings. Our *interests*, *experience* and *expectations* all affect what we attend to. Features of the situation we are observing will also have differential salience – in the sense that some are likely to stand out and be more likely to be attended to. At a simple level, if you can see a person's face, then you are more likely to attend to what she or he says than to someone with

Box 8.3 Recording of participant observation

1   Even with the most unstructured observation it is crucial to have a system which allows you to capture information unambiguously and as faithfully and fully as possible.

2   Where possible a record is made of observation *on the spot, during the event.* This may be very condensed, using abbreviations, etc. Their main purpose is to remind you of what happened when you are writing up detailed notes. Baker (1988, p. 24) refers to these as 'memory sparkers': who was there; any unusual details of the physical scene; important/interesting verbatim comments; incongruencies (it may help to ask yourself questions – why did he do that? etc.).

3   The record must as a matter of routine be gone through shortly afterwards to add detail and substance and to ensure that the record is understandable and says what you intended it to say.

4   Getting this full record right may take as long as the original observation did. Lofland and Lofland (1984) suggest five types of materials to be included in the record:

- *Running descriptions*: specific, concrete, descriptions of events who is involved, conversations. Keep any inferences out (e.g. A was trying to get B to . . .).
- *Recalls of forgotten material*: things that come back to you later.
- *Interpretive ideas*: notes offering an analysis of the situation. You need both notes addressing the research question, and ones which will add supportive or elaborative material.
- *Personal impressions and feelings*: your subjective reactions.
- *Reminder to look for additional information*: reminder to check with A about B, take a look at C, etc.

You will need a system to to mark and separate out these different types of material (e.g. round brackets, square brackets, double brackets, etc.).

5   'Lap-top' microcomputers, if available, can be very effective in producing these records actually in the field. In any case there is considerable advantage in getting the record on to a computer using word-processing or specialist text analysis software. This enables multiple copies of typescripts to be generated easily, for record and analysis purposes; or the computer file can be analysed directly. The organization and analysis of this kind of qualitative data is covered in chapter 12.

6   If you feel that this on-the-spot recording interferes with your observation, or alternatively when your participating role gets in the way,

then notes should be made as soon as feasible afterwards. It may be worthwhile developing facility in the use of a mnemonic system (see, for example, Yates, 1966) which can have a dramatic effect on the number of items recallable. Inevitably, however, notes made after the event are subject to greater distortion, particularly when there are intervening events.

7 A good basic rule is that you should always prepare the detailed notes of the full report within twenty-four hours of the field session, and certainly never embark on a second observation session until you are sure that you have sorted out your notes for the first one.

---

their back to you. The basic message is to *make a conscious effort to distribute your attention widely and evenly*. There are sampling techniques, commonly used in systematic observation, which can assist you to do this and which could be used in some participant observation situations without doing violence to the approach.

Selective Encoding

Expectations inevitably colour what you see, and in turn affect the encoding and interpretation of this. This is a rapid, usually unconscious, set of processes and hence difficult to guard against. Related to this is the 'rush to judgment' where something is categorized on the basis of initial and very partial information. Later information, which might have been used to modify the judgment, is as a result not taken into account. Hence, *try to start with an open mind – and keep it open*.

Selective Memory

The longer you wait after the event in constructing a narrative account, the poorer such an account will be in terms of its accuracy and completeness; and the more it will be in line with your pre-existing schemas and expectations. The moral is clear. *Write up field notes into a narrative account promptly*.

Interpersonal Factors

In the early stages of a participant observation, because of your own insecurity and other factors, you may focus on, and interact with, only a few of the group members; probably those who seem welcoming and easy to get

---

**Box 8.4 When participant observation might be
useful in a small project**

1 *With small groups* You need to be able to get to know virtually
all the people involved in a way that would not be feasible in a large
group.

2 *For events/processes that take a reasonably short time* That is,
unless you can afford to give up a major slice of your life to the study.
Even then the 'information overload' would be horrendous.

3 *For frequent events* Participant observation is in general more easily
handled in situations where there is repetition of the central activities
fairly frequently (e.g. it's easier to study an office with a daily routine
than a merger between two businesses – though the latter could well
incorporate some participant observation within a multi-method case
study).

4 *For activities that are accessible to observers* This is an obvious
point, but don't forget that direct observation can supplemented by
discussions with group members.

5 *When your prime motivation is find out what is going on* The
wealth of information available in a participant observation study is
such that you can probably find supporting evidence for virtually any
initial hypothesis. Hence it is a dangerous (though seductive) technique
for those simply wishing to confirm their prejudgements.

6 *When you are not short of time* Even a small participant observation study takes up a lot of time, both day-to-day (writing up adequate field notes) and in terms of the 'immersion' you need to get
anywhere. It is difficult to budget this time in advance.

---

on with. This is probably inevitable, but carries with it the potential for bias.
Those who welcome you may do so because they don't get on with other
members of the group. Perhaps they are marginal or disaffected members.
As you get to know more about the group, you should be able to avoid this,
but there is still the danger of your developing relationship with the more
friendly and helpful members affecting your picture of the whole. There are
still the likely biasing effects of your own presence. The general strategy is
to *seek to recognize and discount all biases.*

Structured Observation

Readers who worry about such things will appreciate that making the divide in this chapter between 'participant' and 'structured' observation lacks a little in logic. The former covers one extreme on the dimension of the observer's participation in the situation; the latter an extreme in the degree of structure that is used in observation. As discussed previously, participant observers have primarily used qualitative techniques, and in some senses their work could be labelled unstructured or unsystematic. However, to my ears at least, this carries a somewhat pejorative tone which I consider to be unwarranted. In fact, good participant observation *is* systematic, but more in terms of the logical inference system used than the degree of pre-structure of observational categories.

It is, of course, possible to have non-participant observation which is unstructured. The *ethological approach* (Tinbergen, 1963), for example, starts with careful, exploratory, observation seeking a detailed and comprehensive description of the animal's (or human's) behaviour. As with many participant observers, their observation is concerned with hypothesis generation, rather than the confirmation of pre-formed hypotheses (Blurton Jones, 1972). ECOLOGICAL PSYCHOLOGISTS also make central use of observation and eschew hypothesis testing (Wicker, 1979). Their specific concern is the *setting* in which the behaviour takes place; and the dependency of the behaviour on that setting. They are also similar to participant observers in attempting to develop narrative accounts rather than coded schedules, though their accounts share with much mainstream systematic observation a concern for providing an objective record of specific observable behaviours.

Structured observers tend to take a detached, 'pure observer', stance. For them, structured observation is a way of quantifying behaviour. There have been important recent developments in the use of quantitative systematic observation which deserve wider recognition (e.g. Sackett, 1978; Bakeman and Gottman, 1986).

Coding Schemes

Coding schemes contain predetermined categories for recording what is observed. They range from simply noting whether or not a particular behaviour has occurred, to complex multi-category systems. Other forms of structured observation are possible – you can, for example, ask observers for global ratings of what they have seen over the whole of a session (or even based on an extended period). Barlow et al. (1984, pp. 134–8) give examples. Such global ratings are effectively *rating scales*, and are dealt with in chapter 9 (p. 255).

> *The key features of much structured observation are the development of a coding scheme, and its use by trained observers.*

The start is, as always, from some research question. Researchers then need to define important concepts and devise ways in which they can be measured. And of course they need to concern themselves with reliability and validity. An essential feature is that the reliability of the measuring instrument used, the coding scheme, depends crucially on the skills of the observer. Hence a major, and often very time-consuming, task is to train observers so that they produce essentially the same set of codes when confronted with a particular instance or sequence of behaviour.

Achieving adequate inter-observer reliability is primarily a technical matter, calling for a knowledge of the characteristics of a usable coding scheme and adequate time spent in training observers. It may be worth stressing the likely congeniality of structured observational work to the frustrated experimentalist, yearning for the relative certainties and simplified complexities of laboratory-based experimental work, and thwarted by the exigencies of the real world. The 'instrument makers' have now developed this type of observational methodology to a fine art, particularly in connection with sequential interaction.

Checklists and Category Systems

A distinction is sometimes made between observation systems based on checklists, and those based on category systems. Rob Walker (1985) uses the term CATEGORY SYSTEM for 'systems that, unlike checklists, use a relatively small number of items, each of which is more general than a typical checklist item, but which attempts to use the system to maintain some sort of more-or-less continuous record' (p. 136). Checklists are seen as providing a long series of items which can be recorded as present or absent. The distinction is blurred in many cases and the general term 'coding scheme' will be used here.

Experimentation and Coding Schemes

Structured observation is commonly used in field experiments, particularly in obtaining measures on the dependent variable(s). Simple coding schemes are likely to be used. It is not unusual for the 'observation' to be carried out by an automatic device (e.g. a microswitch which detects whether or not a child is sitting at a desk).

Possible Bases for a Coding Scheme

We have to decide what type of activity is going to be observed. A widely used system, which seems to be adaptable to a range of research questions, is derived from Weick (1968). It is summarized in box 8.5.

Box 8.5 Possible bases for the development of codes

There is a wide range of possibilities, including:

1 *Non-verbal behaviours* Bodily movements not associated with language.

2 *Spatial behaviours* The extent to which individuals move towards or away from others.

3 *Extra-linguistic behaviours* Covers aspects of verbal behaviour other than the words themselves. This includes speaking rates, loudness and tendency to interrupt or be interrupted.

4 *Linguistic behaviours* Covers the actual content of talking and its structural characteristics.

(Smith, 1975, pp. 203ff, provides examples of the use of these dimensions.)

Observer Effects

Moving away from the laboratory, with its comforting screens and one-way mirrors, tends to leave the observer exposed to the observed. The extent of this exposure depends on the setting, the group involved and the research task. It is probably not too difficult to carry out unobserved systematic observation on the terrace of a soccer ground, if one can select a good vantage point, even without access to the high-definition police video camera carrying out its own observation task. It is well nigh impossible to achieve the same degree of invisibility in a secondary school classroom.

However, even when it is possible to carry out a study without the knowledge of the observed, ethical issues could well be involved once more. These are largely a matter of common sense, and of consideration of the principles underlying 'codes of practice' (see chapter 2, p. 29). If a multi-method approach is used, where structured observation is supplemented by the use of other methods, then, given that the other available methods tend almost always to depend on the knowledge and co-operation of the persons involved, we have a practical reason for disclosure to support the ethical one.

Once the observed persons know that this is happening, then the observer is, willy nilly, to some extent a participant in the situation, and the observation becomes potentially reactive (i.e. potentially changing the thing observed). The two main strategies used to minimize such 'observer effects' are MINIMAL INTERACTION with the group, and HABITUATION of the group to the observer's presence. Minimal interaction is achieved through such obvious strategies as avoiding eye contact, the use of simple behavioural techniques such as not reinforcing attempts at interaction from the group, and planning one's position in the environment to be 'out of they way'. Habituation involves one's repeated presence in the setting so that, particularly when you are an unrewarding, minimal interactor, it is no longer noticed.

It is never logically possible to be completely sure that your presence has not in some way changed what you are seeking to observe, but there are several indicants which provide some reassurance:

- The pattern of interaction stabilizes over sessions.
- Different observers code essentially identical patterns for different sessions.
- Members of the group appear to accept your presence to the extent that they do not seek interaction.
- Group members say that your presence doesn't affect what is going on. (It is helpful here to check this with different 'constituencies' present. A teacher may say that nothing has changed, whereas pupils may claim that lessons are better prepared!)

It is worth noting that in some circumstances an essentially non-interacting observer may be of more continuing interest and disturbance than one who gives a friendly smile or nod from time to time. It may also be more 'natural' and less disturbing to take up an explicit role in the situation. In work in special school classrooms, for example, we have found it profitable sometimes to take the role of 'teaching assistant', thus providing a natural entrée to interaction with the child about events in the classroom, while not precluding periods of busy, non-interacting, systematic observation.

Deciding on a Coding Scheme

As with participant observation, it is likely that the first phase of a study which ends up using structured observation study will be exploratory, and that this exploration will occur prior to the choice of a coding scheme. The need for a coding scheme arises when it has been decided (at least tentatively) that structured observation, probably alongside other techniques, is to be used. The research question(s) and, in appropriate situations, the related literature, will after a period of unstructured observation and, probably, gathering supporting information from other sources such as interviews and questionnaires, suggest how the processes you wish to study might be captured by various observational categories.

In certain circumstances it may be appropriate to start, as it were, even further back than this: that is, to regard the initial exploratory observation sessions as essentially fulfilling a *hypothesis generation* function. The style advocated for this phase is essentially the 'analytic induction' approach (see p. 201).

The Use of Existing Coding Schemes

Given that the development of a coding scheme is a difficult and time-consuming task, and given also that there are already in existence a multiplicity of such schemes, one solution seems obvious. Take one off the shelf! Furthermore, the concern sometimes expressed that researchers in psychology and the social sciences often seem more interested in paddling their own canoes rather than doing their bit by adding another brick to the grand collective scientific enterprise indicates that more replication of studies would not come amiss.

However, the position advocated here, which is the mainstream methodological view, is that the research question comes first. Sort that out, refine it and operationalize your concepts though pilot work; that then leads you to the specification of the coding scheme. The Law of Maximum Perversity will be likely to guarantee that no existing coding scheme does the job that you want it to.

This should not, however, stop you from seeking one. Several collections are available, including Simon and Boyer (1970a; 1970b; 1974), which are mainly American, and Galton (1978), a British counterpart. Even if the instrument is not directly usable, you are likely to get valuable ideas about different possible approaches. Box 8.6 shows the widely used system devised by Flanders (1970) for analysing teacher and pupil behaviour in the classroom. Of the ten categories, seven refer to aspects of teacher talk, and two to student or pupils talk, with the tenth being a 'residual' category. An interval coding system is used where coders are expected to code every three seconds. Figure 8.1 shows a typical recording sheet. Each row represents one minute of time (twenty three-second intervals) and hence the sample would allow for ten minutes coding. The first five minutes have been completed, illustrating the fact that the appropriate category has to be inserted in the matrix for each coding interval. This obviously requires the coder to have fully memorized and internalized the coding system.

This system has been used in a very large number of studies (see examples in Croll, 1986) and attempts have been made to categorize classrooms through a variety of indices which can be derived from the analysis. These include proportions of teacher talk to student talk; the extent to which pupils initiate interactions (category 9 as a proportion of all pupil talk), etc. The very short time internal makes this what is termed a 'quasi-continuous' schedule; three seconds is seen as short compared with the processes that go on in classrooms. A particular use has been the study of 'interaction matrices' looking at pairs of observations, where the matrix shows how many times a particular type of utterance is followed by other types (Croll, 1986, ch. 5 gives an example).

Box 8.6   Flanders interaction analysis (IA) system

Categories:

1 *Teacher accepts student feeling* Accepts and clarifies an attitude or the feeling tone of a pupil in a non-threatening manner. Feelings may be positive or negative. Predicting and recalling feelings are included.

2 *Teacher praises student* Praises or encourages pupil action or behaviour. Jokes that release tension, but not at the expense of another individual; nodding head, or saying 'mm hm?' or 'Go on' are included.

3 *Teacher use of student ideas* Clarifying, building or developing ideas suggested by a pupil. Teacher extensions of pupil ideas are included but as the teacher brings more of his ideas into play, switch to category 5.

4 *Teacher questions* Asking a question about content or procedure, based on teacher ideas, with the intention that a pupil will answer.

5 *Teacher lectures* Giving facts or opinions about content or procedures; expressing *his* own ideas, giving *his* own explanation, or citing an authority other than a pupil.

6 *Teacher gives directions* Directions, commands or orders to which a pupil is expected to comply.

7 *Teacher criticizes student* Statements intended to change pupil behaviour from non-acceptable to acceptable pattern; bawling someone out; stating why the teacher is doing what he is doing; extreme self-reference.

8 *Student response* Talk by pupils in response to teacher. Teacher initiates the contact or solicits pupil statement or structures the situation. Freedom to express own ideas is limited.

9 *Student-initiated response* Talk by pupils which they initiate. Expressing own ideas; initiating a new topic; freedom to develop opinions and a line of thought, like asking thoughtful questions; going beyond the existing structure.

10 *Silence or confusion* Pauses, short periods of silence and periods of confusion in which communication cannot be understood by the observer.

(From Flanders, 1970, p. 34.)

Minute

1	5 5 5 5 5 5 5 5 4 4 4 4 8 8 2 3 3 3 3 5
2	5 5 5 6 6 6 6 8 8 1 1 6 6 0 0 7 7 7 7 7
3	5 5 5 5 5 5 5 5 5 5 5 5 5 5 5 5 5 5 5 5
4	5 5 0 0 0 0 7 7 0 0 7 7 4 4 4 4 8 8 3 3
5	4 4 4 8 8 2 2 2 3 3 3 5 5 5 5 9 9 7 7 7

6

7

8

9

10

Figure 8.1 Sample recording sheet for Flanders interaction analysis
Note: category '10' is coded as '0' for ease of coding.

Developing Your Own Scheme

The use of an initial exploratory observational stage in helping to clarify and focus your research questions has been described above. The first version of the coding scheme which emerges from this process should incorporate those behaviours and distinctions which you think are important in providing answers to these questions.

It is not possible to give a 'cook book' set of procedure for this process. However box 8.7 suggests a number of things which may be of help. Box 8.8 gives details of an example.

It may be useful to have more than one coding scheme in a study. Bryman (1989, pp. 207–9) describes an influential study of managerial work by Mintzberg (1973) which used three: A *chronological record*, categorizing the types of activities in the manager's working day, and their beginning and end times; a *mail record*, covering the nature of mail received, how it is dealt with, and the mail generated (this is largely a documentary analysis but involves observational coding of the kind of attention given to each item of

Box 8.7 Considerations in developing a coding scheme

Note: If there is an existing scheme which appears appropriate, consider using or adapting it.

The categories should be devised to provide information relevant to the research questions in which you are interested (your preliminary exploratory observation should help in clarifying the question). To be straightforward and reliable in use it will help if they are:

a *Focused* Only looking at carefully selected aspects of what is going on. Simply because you can observe it doesn't mean that you have to code it; ask yourself 'what use will the data be?'

b *Objective* Requiring little inference from the observer.

c *Non context-dependent* The observer's task is more difficult if the category to be used in coding an event depends on the context in which it occurs (however, if such contextual information is essential to answer the research question, then the observer will have to live with it).

d *Explicitly defined* Through a detailed definition of each category, with examples (both of what falls within the category and what doesn't).

e *Exhaustive* Covering all possibilities so that it is always possible to make a coding (to be compatible with (a) above it may be necessary to have a large 'residual' or 'dump' category)

f *Mutually exclusive* A single category for each thing coded (if the system has both (e) and (f) characteristics it is commonly referred to as an MEE system – a Mutually Exclusive and Exhaustive System). Note, however, that in some situations it may be simpler to have an event multiply categorized.

g *Easy to record* Just ticking in a box rather than requiring recall of which of a large number of categories to use. Observers will, though, need to be completely familiar with the category system if they are to use it properly.

Box 8.8   Example of use of observational schedule

Barton et al. (1980) studied naturally occurring interactions between staff and residents in a home for the elderly. They developed an observational schedule with five categories:

Independent behaviour   A resident's carrying out of bathing, dressing, eating, grooming or toileting tasks (or parts of such tasks) without assistance. Can be self-initiated or initiated by others.

Dependent behaviour   A resident's request for, or acceptance of, assistance in bathing, dressing, eating, grooming or toileting.

Independence-supportive behaviour   Staff verbal encouragement of, or praise for, a resident's execution of personal maintenance tasks without help; *and* staff discouragement of, or scolding for, a resident's request for assistance or non-attempts of execution of self-maintenance tasks.

Dependence-supportive behaviour   Staff assistance in a resident's personal maintenance, praise for a resident's acceptance; *and* discouragement of a resident's attempts to execute personal maintenance tasks without help.

Other behaviour   Staff or resident behaviour that is not related to personal maintenance tasks.

(*Source*: Barton et al., 1980.)

mail – read, skimmed etc.); and a *contact record*, detailing the meetings, calls and tours of the chronology record, categorizing their purposes and initiators.

Coding Sequences of Behaviour

Your use of the scheme depends on the type of data you wish to collect. This in turn depends on the research questions you are seeking to answer.

It may be that simple frequency measures will suffice. This is adequate if all that is necessary is to compare frequencies; say the relative frequencies of staff's 'dependence-supportive' and 'independence-supportive' behaviours when using Barton et al.'s (1980) schedule. However, in many studies the concern is when, and under what circumstances, different behaviours occur. Is residents' independence behaviour followed by staff independence-supportive behaviour? Is staff reliance on dependence-supportive behaviour associated with trends in residents' behaviour? Because of this common need for sequence information, the rest of this section focuses on the use of coding schemes for observing behaviour sequences.

A central issue concerns the 'unit' which is to be coded. The two main alternatives are to base this either on *time* or on an *event*. In the former, a particular time interval is coded (e.g. as 'child talking to mother'). In the latter, observers wait for a particular event to occur and note what type of event it was. One can also distinguish between 'momentary events' and 'behavioural states'. Momentary events are relatively brief and separate events (such as a child's smile) and the likely interest is in when they occur, and how frequently. Behavioural states are events of appreciable duration (such as a baby sleeping) and in addition to 'when', and 'how often', the likely concern is with 'for how long'. Obviously there is not a strict dichotomy between the two – all events take some time to complete. Technically it is now straightforward, using event recorders, or computers effectively functioning as event recorders, to store the times of occurrence of momentary events, and the start and end times of behavioural states.

Event Coding

Events can be recorded in a variety of ways. Essentially the observer responds whenever the event occurs, using either pencil and paper, or some more complex recording instrument. Alternatives are shown in figure 8.2.

Tallying events with a simple checklist will often be sufficient. It provides frequency data, both in absolute terms (i.e. how many times each event has occurred) and relatively (i.e. the relative frequency of different events). The sequence record adds the order in which different events occur, hence providing informations about transitions (i.e. which events follow which). Adding a time line gives information about the time interval between similar events and times for the various transitions. It obviously contains within it the simple sequence information, and the frequency information can be computed from both the last two records, so it could be argued that there is virtue in always recording both sequence and time. However, this does give the observer a more complex task, and the general principle is still that the type of recording should be determined by what information is needed to answer the research questions.

State Coding

While simple checklists and sequence records (usually indicating 'change of state' – e.g. from 'asleep' to 'awake') may sometimes be useful, it is usual to include time information giving the duration of particular states. Electronic recording devices make it straightforward to record start (onset) and finish (offset) times for the states being coded. This information produces a record equivalent to that shown in figure 8.3. In practice, the onset of

1 Simple checklist

event   1   2   3

2 Sequence record

event   2 1 2 2 2 1 3 1 2 2

3 Sequence record on time-scale

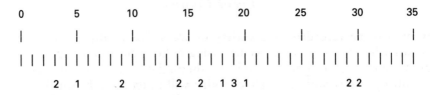

Figure 8.2   Alternative ways of coding events

a particular state will probably be coded by pressing a key or button on a keyboard, and its offset in a similar way.

Many coding schemes have codes which are MUTUALLY EXCLUS-IVE AND EXHAUSTIVE ('MEE' schemes). This means that the definitions of states are such that if one state occurs, it is not logically possible for this to be so at the same time as any other state occurs (mutual exclusion); and that the total set of possible states covers all eventualities (exhaustiveness). Such MEE schemes have considerable advantages when it comes to analysis. Box 8.9 gives a simple example.

For recording, there is also the practical advantage that only 'onset' times need be recorded – as each 'onset' necessarily means the 'offset' of some other state (illustrated in figure 8.4).

Interval Coding

Interval coding is triggered by time rather than by events. The observation period is divided into a number of intervals, say of ten or fifteen seconds in duration. The job of the observer is to note down information about what

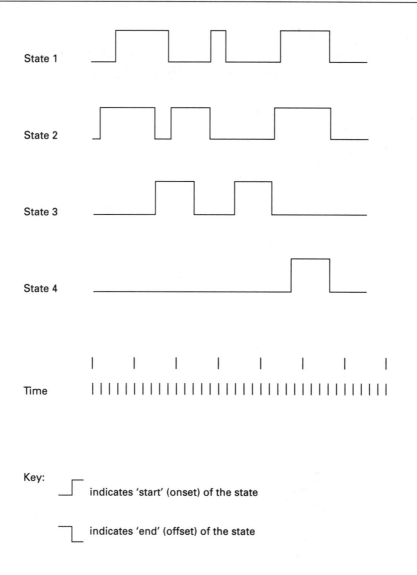

State 1

State 2

State 3

State 4

Time

Key:

indicates 'start' (onset) of the state

indicates 'end' (offset) of the state

Figure 8.3 Record of 'onset' and 'offset' of states

happened during the interval. This can be done in various ways, but a common strategy is to code with the category which best represents what occurred during that interval (e.g. the most frequent event, or the dominant state – the state present during the greater part of the interval).

This can be coded with pencil and paper using a simple sequence record (as in figure 8.2 above) or a specially designed sheet incorporating the time intervals can be used (as in figure 8.5 below).

More complicated schemes may be called for. A commonly used variation

---

Box 8.9   Example of a simple mutually exclusive and exhaustive coding scheme

State 1:   child 1 talks; child 2 silent

State 2:   child 1 silent; child 2 talks

State 3:   both child 1 and child 2 talk

State 4:   both child 1 and child 2 silent

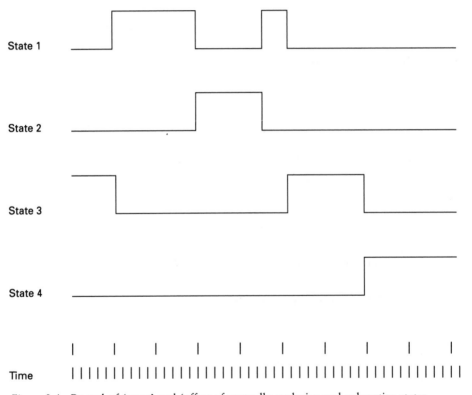

Figure 8.4   Record of 'onset' and 'offset of mutually exclusive and exhaustive states

Time interval

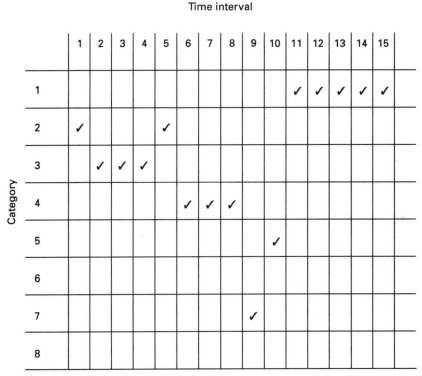

Figure 8.5 Coding sheet for interval coding (pencil and paper)
Note that a mutually exclusive and exhaustive scheme is in use.

is to have different types of coding for different time intervals. For example, general coding is carried out for five successive ten-second intervals, and the next ten seconds is used is a different way (say, counting the number of children in the group who are 'on task').

This type of interval coding can be made easier to carry out by means of a 'bug in the ear'. That is, a simple device which gives a click audible only to the observer at the end of each interval. Special pieces of equipment are available for this purpose, but it is a simple matter to use a cassette recorder on which the time intervals have been recorded, together with an earpiece. It is also possible to record additional 'aide-memoire' information on the tape to help the observer.

Interval coding, though widely used, is not without its critics. Distortion can be introduced into the data if the interval chosen is not shorter than the shortest duration typically encountered for a codable state. Bakeman and Gottman's advice is that

> when simplicity and low cost of instrumentation matter more than accuracy, or when the interval is shorter than most codable events and observes prefer checking or categorizing intervals to recording onset times, then an interval

coding strategy probably makes sense. For all other cases, some variant of event coding should probably be used. (Bakeman and Gottman, 1986, p. 61)

Time Sampling

It time sampling, some principle is used to select the time intervals during which coding takes place. These are interspersed with intervals where there is no coding (or a different form of coding, as in the example given in the preceding section). The principle may be random – random number tables can be used to select the time intervals in seconds, minutes or whatever, from, say, the end of one coding interval to the start of the next. Or some regular sequence may be used – say five minutes 'on' followed by fifteen minutes 'off'. This approach is sometimes used when the 'off' non-observing intervals are used actually to make the recording.

Careful thought must be given to assessing whether the type of sampling used leads to a representative picture of the phenomenon under observation. General sampling principles, as discussed in chapter 5, p. 135, apply. Time sampling can be a useful and efficient way of measuring how much time is spent within the various categories of the coding scheme. It is likely to be a poor way of collecting sequential information, however, because of the gaps between observation periods.

Cross-classifying Events

In situations where you have acquired a substantial appreciation of what is going on and hence are in a position to focus your observation sharply on certain kinds of events, an alternative approach to classification may be valuable.

Suppose you are interested in what happens when a child misbehaves in the classroom – say when she or he takes something from another child. Observers might be asked to note not only the occurrence of this behaviour, but specific aspects of what the two children were doing immediately before the incident; what kind of a disturbance occurred; and how it was settled. If mutually exclusive and exhaustive sets of codes can be devised for each of these phases, it becomes possible to CROSS-CLASSIFY this event. Analysis can then subsequently show what is likely to lead to what and hence aid in its understanding (see chapter 11, p. 333 for possible ways of analysing these kinds of data).

Reliability and Structured Observation

When using structured observation the observation schedule *as used by the observer* is the instrument, and an important question is: how good an instrument? Reliability and validity raise their heads once more. Validity concerns are essentially similar to those raised by any method of investigation (as discussed in chapter 3, page 66), but an assessment of the reliability of data obtained from structured observational schedules has attracted particular specialist approaches.

Problems occur if the observer-instrument shows variation at different times, or if different observer-instruments vary from each others. Hence there are two kinds of reliability; *intra-observer reliability* (sometimes called *observer consistency*) and *inter-observer reliability* (or *inter-observer agreement*).

OBSERVER CONSISTENCY is the extent to which an observer obtains the same results when measuring the same behaviour on different occasions (e.g. when coding the same audio- or video-tape at an interval of a week). INTER-OBSERVER AGREEMENT is the extent to which two or more observers obtain the same results when measuring the same behaviour (e.g. when independently coding the same tape).

It is highly desirable to have more than one observer in any study involving structured observation. With a single observer, even if she shows high consistency, it may be that she is using the observation schedule in a totally idiosyncratic fashion. Demonstrating good inter-observer agreement defends against this, and indeed goes some way towards showing validity. Even if a study is predominantly single-observer it is often possible to enlist the help of a colleague who will devote the time necessary to learn to use the schedule and observe a proportion of the sessions to be coded.

Both observer consistency and inter-observer agreement are measured by the same means. Several indices have been developed. They involve the calculation either of the degree of correlation between the two sets of measurements, or of the agreement (sometimes called concordance) between them. There is some disagreement as to the relative merits of these two approaches. Martin and Bateson (1986) consider that 'an index of concordance need only be used if there is some reason why agreement over each occurrence of the behaviour is an important issue, or if the behaviour is measured on a nominal scale' (p. 92). However, Bakeman and Gottman (1986) feel that this kind of agreement is generally valuable, particularly in sequential analyses involving coding over time. They advocate the use of concordance measures, such as Cohen's Kappa, which correct for chance agreement. There would be advantages in comparing results obtained in different studies and with different instruments if there were some standardization in this area. Box 8.10 illustrates the computation of an index of concordance and of Cohen's Kappa with simple data. Bakeman and Gottman (1986, pp. 70–99) give an extended discussion with examples and further references.

Construction of the 'confusion matrix' has the advantage that it shows very clearly where the two observers are differing in their judgment. This can be valuable at the training stage to highlight these confusions. It may be that further training is needed, or that some attention has to be given to the definitions of the categories.

With some coding schedules the 'units' being coded are non-problematic

Box 8.10 Measuring inter-observer agreement

1 *Draw up the 'confusion matrix'.* Suppose that the coding schedule has five different categories (A, B, C, D and E) and that there are 100 occasions when coding has taken place. With two observers, an *agreement* takes place when they both use the same code for the occasion. If they use different codes then that is a *disagreement*. The pattern of agreements and disagreements can be shown on a two-dimensional matrix (often referred to as a 'confusion' matrix).

| | Observer two | | | | | |
Observer one	A	B	C	D	E	Total
A	8	0	0	0	0	8
B	2	21	1	0	0	24
C	1	0	18	2	1	22
D	0	0	0	24	6	30
E	1	0	0	1	14	16
Total	12	21	19	27	21	100

Note that scores on the diagonal from top left to bottom right indicate agreement between the two observers; scores off this diagonal indicate their disagreement.

2 *Calculate the proportion of agreement* (P_0). This is given by

$$\frac{(\text{number of agreements})}{(\text{number of agreements} + \text{number of disagreements})}$$

which in this case is

$$\frac{(8 + 21 + 18 + 24 + 14)}{(100)} \text{ or } 0.85.$$

NB *The index of agreement (or concordance) is simply this proportion expressed as a percentage* (i.e. in this case, 85 per cent).

3 *Calculate the proportion expected by chance* (P_c). Probability theory shows that if the probability of the first observer using, say, code A is P_{1A}; and the probability of the second observer using the same code is P_{2A}, then the probability of them both using the same code by chance is simply the product of these two separate probabilities (i.e. $P_{1A} \times P_{2A}$ or 0.08×0.12). Hence the total chance proportion for all five codes is

$$P_c = (0.08 \times 0.12) + (0.24 \times 0.21) + (0.22 \times 0.19)$$
$$+ (0.30 \times 0.27) + (0.16 \times 0.21)$$
$$= 0.262.$$

4   *Calculate Cohen's Kappa* (K). This is given by the formula

$$K = \frac{P_0 - P_c}{1 - P_c}$$

In the example,

$$K = \frac{0.850 - 0.262}{1 - 0.262} = 0.797.$$

Note that the value of Kappa, while still quite high, is noticeably smaller than the uncorrected proportion of agreement.

There are ways of assessing the significance of Kappa (see Bakeman and Gottman, 1986, p. 80). However, as with other statistics, statistical significance is not everything and, particularly with large samples, it is possible to achieve statistical significance with proportions which show little agreement between the observers. Fliess (1981) has suggested the following 'rules of thumb':

Kappa of 0.40 to 0.60: 'fair';
Kappa of 0.60 to 0.75: 'good';
Kappa of above 0.75: 'excellent'.

and different observers will have no problems in recognizing them. Suppose you simply have to categorize each complete contribution that a child and an adult make to a conversation; it is easy to determine whether it is the child or the adult speaking – the difficulty comes when you have to decide how to code that utterance. However, if you have a scheme where each of the contributions they make has to be split up into different sequential units ('gives instruction', 'provides model', 'gives praise', etc.), the transition points between the units may well be a source of disagreement between observers. In this situation it is necessary first to establish to satisfactory inter-observer agreement on the unit boundaries (which can be done in a similar way to that for the coding schedule itself – Bakeman and Gottman, 1986, pp. 84–7 give details) before going on to the main task of assessing agreement on the categories.

Reactivity of Assessing Inter-observer Agreement

Just as there is the problem that the observer may change the thing observed, so the observer's observing may be affected by testing for inter-observer agreement. Taplin and Reid (1973) looked at the effects of different ways of monitoring the reliability of observation. They monitored observers continuously but told different groups different things. The poorest performance in terms of reliability was from observers who did not think that they were being monitored. Intermediate performance came from those who knew that they were being monitored on specific occasions. The best performance came from those under the impression that they were being monitored covertly on randomly selected occasions. The implications are clear. It is desirable not only to have inter-observer agreement checks, but also for observers to know this but not know which sessions will be checked. This is, of course, easier to organize when analysis takes place via a video or other tape than when sessions are coded live.

'Observer Drift'

The kinds of threats to validity discussed in chapter 3 in the context of experimental, and particularly quasi-experimental, design (see p. 71) rear their head again when structured observation is used. 'Instrumentation' is a particular problem. This is caused by possible changes in the measuring instrument and refers here to changes in the way that the observer uses the schedule, and is usually termed 'observer drift'. Increased familiarity with its use may well make it easier to 'see' examples of particular categories, or there may be subtle differences in the ways in which category definitions are interpreted over time. Inter-observer agreement checks go some way to minimizing these effects as the drift is likely to be individual and idiosyncratic. Intra-observer checks, perhaps by returning periodically to the rating of training examples, can also be used.

Expectancy Effects

Observers coding behaviour after some intervention may well expect to see 'positive' changes compared to the pre-intervention situation. This is a classic Rosenthal-type expectancy situation (cf Rosenthal, 1976; Rosenthal and Rubin, 1978), particularly so when the observer is also the person with a stake in the outcome of the study. Again, inter-observer agreement tests will give some safeguard, although (unconscious?) collusion can occur. 'Blind' coding of various kinds should be considered. If there are comparison groups, observers may not be told to which group the individual observed belongs. It might be feasible for observers to be 'blind' as to whether they are watching a pre or post session. A system where one observer is closely involved in that particular trial and knows exactly what is going on, but a second trained observer (who may be closely involved in another trial) is 'blind' to these features, can sometimes be set up.

The use of video-tape provides other solutions. Pre and post sessions can be coded in a random sequence after all the data have been collected. However, even if considerable care is taken, it is virtually impossible to eliminate all clues (clothing, decorations, leaves on trees, etc.). Taped material has other advantages, particularly in giving the opportunity of multiple viewing, but its use should be carefully thought through, piloted and time-budgeted. The tape necessarily captures only one perspective of the events and it is very seductive to accumulate large quantities of to-be-coded tapes.

Further Reading

There is little, if any, overlap between the participant observation and structured observation literatures, and hence this further reading is presented in two sections.

Participant Observation

Adler, P. A. and Adler, P. (1987) *Membership Roles in Field Research*. Newbury Park and London: Sage. Insightful analysis of the difficulties encountered in different roles (peripheral, active and complete membership).

Burgess, R. G. (1984) *In the Field: an introduction to field research*. London: Allen & Unwin. Chapter 4 provides good short review of main issues.

Jorgenson, D. (1989) *Participant Observation: a methodology for human studies*. Newbury Park and London: Sage. Useful short text concentrating on participant observation.

Lofland, J. and Lofland, L. (1984) *Analyzing Social Settings: A guide to qualitative observation and analysis*, 2nd edn. Belmont, Ca: Wadsworth. Very readable book with good discussion of both methodological issues and practicalities.

McCall, G. J. and Simmons, J. L. (eds) (1969) *Issues in Participant Observation: A text and reader*. Reading, Mass.: Addison-Wesley. Wide-ranging set of readings covering all aspects of participant observation. Includes useful section comparing it to other methods.

Patton, M. Q. (1980) *Qualitative Evaluation Methods*. Newbury Park and London: Sage. Extensive discussion of participant observation issues in context of evaluation.

Whyte, W. F. (1984) *Learning from the Field: a guide from experience*. Newbury Park and London: Sage. A sociologist using anthropological methods relevant for psychologists. Discussion and dissection of issues in field work with focus on participant observation.

Structured Observation

Bakeman, R. and Gottman, J. M. (1986) *Observing interaction: an introduction to sequential analysis.* Cambridge: Cambridge University Press. Straightforward, clear and detailed. Essential reading for anyone doing a structured observational study involving process-oriented aspects of behaviour. Very practical. Sections on recording, assessing agreement, representing and analysing the data.

Croll, P. (1986) *Systematic Classroom Observation.* London: Sussex: Falmer. Provides general introduction to systematic observation in the context of classroom studies. Final chapter analyses critiques of the approach.

Fassnacht, G. (1982) *Theory and Practice of Observing Behaviour.* London: Academic Press. Emphasis on theoretical issues (e.g. nature of objectivity, recognizing units of behaviour, relation between observation and experimentation).

Hutt, S. J. and Hutt, C. (1970) *Direct Observation and Measurement of Behaviour.* Springfield, Ill.: Thomas. Detailed and clear account of ethological methods. Many examples.

Martin, P. and Bateson, P. (1986) *Measuring Behaviour: an introductory guide.* Cambridge: Cambridge University Press. Comes from biology/animal behaviour but of general relevance. Covers wider range than Bakeman and Gottman in less detail. Excellent annotated reference section.

Sackett, G. P. (ed.) (1978) *Observing Behavior*, vol. 2: *data collection and analysis methods.* Baltimore: University Park Press. Slim volume covering wide range of methodological aspects of using structured observation (e.g. category definition, sampling, analysis, recording and reliability).

Weick, K. E. (1968) Systematic Observational Methods. In G. Lindzey and E. Aronson (eds), *Handbook of Social Psychology*, vol. 2, 2nd edn. Reading, Mass.: Addison-Wesley. Very thorough coverage of a wide range of approaches. Useful source of ideas. Later edition of the *Handbook* (1985) has very different, complementary, chapter by Weick.

9

Interviews and Questionnaires

The chapter discusses general issues in interviewing together with the practicalities of carrying out various types of interview.

It stresses the special features of self-completed questionnaires.

The chapter concludes with a discussion of diaries, and of the development of scales and tests.

Introduction

When carrying out an enquiry involving humans, why not take advantage of the fact that they can tell you things about themselves? One important category of enquiry method is based on asking people questions, or otherwise getting them to respond, and then getting a record of their responses. Major self-report techniques include *interviews*, *questionnaires*, and a variety of *scales and tests* which respondents fill in for you.

These methods can be used as the primary or only approach in a study, as in a conventional survey which often relies solely on a self-administered questionnaire. However, they lend themselves well to be used in combination with other methods, in a multi-method approach. A case study might employ some kind of formal interview or questionnaire to complement participant observation. A field experiment using structured direct observation could often usefully incorporate a post-intervention questionnaire or less formal interview to help incorporate the subject's perspective into the findings.

As in the subject of the preceding chapter, there are devotees of two extreme approaches: the self-completion questionnaire, based on a fixed sequence of largely closed questions, and the 'free-range' interview with a fluid agenda and open-ended questions. However, there is also a commonly used middle ground, based on semi-structured interviews, where the interviewer has clearly defined purposes, but seeks to achieve them through some flexibility in wording and in the order of presentation of questions.

This book is mainly concerned with small-scale enquiry. The typical scenario is where you, working as a student, professional psychologist, teacher, social worker or whatever, are wanting to carry out a study with limited resources and time; perhaps alone, perhaps with a colleague or some part-time assistance, possibly concerned with some situation in which you are already an actor. In such situations, the face-to-face interview can be a powerful tool, though not without its problems – practical, theoretical and analytical, among others. Group, as well as individual one-to-one interviews may have a place. Postal and other questionnaires administered outside the interview situation, raise different problems and can provide a different, possibly complementary, data source.

Question content

A distinction is commonly made between seeking to find out what people know, what they do, and what they think or feel. This leads, respectively, to questions concerned with *facts*, with *behaviour*, and with *beliefs* or *attitudes*.

Facts are relatively easy to get at, although errors can occur due to lapses in memory or to response biases of various kinds (age may be claimed to be less than it is by the middle-aged; inflated by the really aged). The best responses are obtained to specific (as against general) questions about important things, in the present or recent past.

The same rules apply to questions about behaviour, and of course the respondent is often in a uniquely favourable position to tell you about what they are doing or have done. Beliefs and attitudes form a very important target for self-report techniques, and are relatively difficult to get at. They are often complex and multi-dimensional and appear particularly prone to the effects of question wording and sequence. These problems point to the use of multiple questions related to the belief or attitude and can be best attacked by the construction of appropriate scales.

Interviews

The interview is a kind of conversation; a conversation with a purpose. Interviews carried out for research or enquiry purposes are a very commonly used approach, possibly in part because the interview appears to be a quite straightforward and non-problematic way of finding things out. A situation where one person talks and another listens: what could be easier? We do it all the time. However, as Powney and Watts (1987) point out in a recent text devoted solely to interviewing, such apparent simplicity is deceptive. They argue that it is 'as easy as writing a book – most of us have basic literacy skills but few attain literary art'.

What kind of conversation is an interview then? According to Cannel and Kahn, as cited by Cohen and Manion, it is one 'initiated by the interviewer for the specific purpose of obtaining research-relevant information and focused by him on content specified by research objectives of systematic description, prediction or explanation' (Cohen and Manion, 1989, p. 307). This is a useful definition as it can encompass a wide range of type of interview, ranging along one dimension, from totally structured to completely unstructured examples. What matters are the intentions and actions of the enquirer, which, as we will see, can be very various.

Advantages and Disadvantages of Interviews

The interview is a flexible and adaptable way of finding things out. The human use of language is fascinating both as a behaviour in its own right, and for the virtually unique window that it opens on what lies behind our actions. Observing behaviour is clearly a useful enquiry technique, but asking people directly about what is going on is an obvious short cut in seeking answers to our research questions.

Face-to-face interviews offer the possibility of modifying one's line of enquiry, following up interesting responses and investigating underlying motives in a way that postal and other self-administered questionnaires cannot. Non-verbal cues may give messages which help in understanding the verbal response, possibly changing or even, in extreme cases, reversing its meaning.

To make profitable use of this flexibility calls for considerable skill and experience in the interviewer. The lack of standardization that it implies inevitably raises concerns about reliability. Biases are difficult to rule out. There are ways of dealing with these problems but they call for a degree of professionalism which does not come easily. Nevertheless, although the interview is in no sense a soft option as a data-gathering technique (illustrating once more that apparently 'soft' techniques emphasizing qualitative data, are deceptively hard to use well), it has the potential of providing rich and highly illuminating material.

Interviewing is time-consuming. The actual interview session itself will obviously vary in length. Anything under half an hour is unlikely to be valuable; anything going much over an hour may be making unreasonable demands on busy interviewees, and could have the effect of reducing the number of persons willing to participate, which may in turn lead to biases in the sample that you achieve. Above all, don't say that it will take half an hour and then keep going for an hour and a half. It is up to you to terminate the interview on schedule, and you have the professional responsibility of keeping this, as well as all other, undertakings that you make. The reverse phenomenon is not unknown: that of the interviewee so glad to have a willing ear to bend that you can't escape. How you deal with this depends very much on your own skills of control and closure. Remember that, just as you are hoping to get something out of the interview, it is not unreasonable for the interviewee to get something from you.

In some fields it appears to be increasingly difficult to obtain co-operation from potential interviewees. Wilson et al. (1989), studying communication between pharmacists and their customers, observed a number of exchanges and then approached thirty-eight of the customers involved and asked if they would be prepared to be interviewed at home in one to two days' time. Twenty-six said no; four were interviewed; three weren't available; and five were inaccessible through living out of the area. They contrasted this response with that in a similar study involving GP's where fewer than one in ten refused to be interviewed. This high acceptance rate was achieved even though the ethical committee vetting the research had insisted that the approach was made by a receptionist (making it easier to refuse?).

As discussed below, all interviews require careful preparation, which takes time. Arrangements to visit; securing necessary permissions; confirming arrangements; rescheduling appointments to cover absences and crises; these need more time. Notes need to be written up; tapes if used require whole or partial transcription (allow something like a factor of ten between tape time and transcription time unless you are highly skilled; i.e. a one hour tape takes ten hours to transcribe fully). Subsequent analyses are not the least of your time-eaters. As with all other techniques, time planning and time budgeting is a crucial skill of successful enquiry in the real world.

Backett's (1990) study of 'health-enhancing' behaviours in middle-class families illustrates the value of interviews in getting at information difficult to reach by other approaches. It involved three rounds of interviews spread over an eighteen-month period with twenty-eight married couples each with two children aged between three and ten years at the start of the study. Each session focused on their daily lives and lifestyles and was one hour and a half to two hours in length, and was transcribed verbatim. In the first round, men and women were interviewed separately, in the second round jointly, and in the third round both separately and jointly. An ancillary study involved interviewing the children and having them draw and write, and post pictures of food into 'healthy' and 'unhealthy' boxes. The various modes of interviewing elicited different, and often contradictory, kinds of responses about health-related activities, with major distinctions between 'public' and 'private' accounts.

Types and Styles of Interviews

A commonly made distinction is based on the degree of structure or formality of the interview. This highlights a dimension of difference, where at one extreme we have the *fully structured interview*, with predetermined set questions asked, and the responses recorded on a standardized schedule (effectively a questionnaire where the interviewer fills in the responses), through *semi-structured interview*, where the interviewer has worked out a set of questions in advance, but is free to modify their order based upon her perception of what seems most appropriate in the context of the 'conversation', can change the way they are worded, give explanations, leave out particular questions which seem inappropriate with a particular interviewee or include additional ones, to the *unstructured (completely informal) interview*, where the interviewer has a general area of interest and concern, but lets the conversation develop within this area.

Powney and Watts (1987, ch. 2) prefer a different typology, making the basic distinction between *respondent interviews* and *informant interviews*. In respondent interviews, the interviewer remains in control (or at least that is the interviewer's intention!) throughout the whole process. All such interviews are necessarily structured to some extent by the interviewer. In this type, or style, of interview the central point is that the intention is that 'interviewers rule'; their agenda is what matters. Both fully and semi-structured interviews are typically, in this sense, respondent.

In informant interviews (sometimes referred to as *non-directive*, in reference to the interviewer's role), the prime concern is for the interviewee's perceptions within a particular situation or context. From the point of view of the interviewer such a session will almost inevitably appear unstructured, as she is unlikely to be privy to the interviewee's agenda. However, it could be much more structured as far as the interviewee is concerned.

This distinction appears to derive, in a historical sense, from the tradition of *survey research* on the one hand, and that of *clinical interviews* on the other. Structured interviews and questionnaires have played a central part in survey research, which has represented an important methodological strand within social science, and has had (at least at some times, and with certain sympathetic administrations) a determining influence on social policy. Such researchers have tended to have a great and understandable concern for the selection of the samples that they interview, seeking to ensure representativeness through randomization and other devices. They have also developed considerable technical expertise in the design of interview schedules, primarily in the service of objectivity and the standardization of the interview situation to ensure comparability of reponse from different interviewees. However, this kind of archetypal 'respondent' interview tends to be associated with a myopic certainty that there is nothing at all problematic about the data that is collected. See, for example, Brenner (1978) for an incisive analysis of the sins of survey researchers in this regard.

General Advice for Interviewers

While the interview *is* a kind of conversation, it does demand rather different emphases in the social interaction that takes place from those in ordinary conversation. Your job as interviewer is to try to get interviewees to talk freely and openly. Your own behaviour has a major influence on their willingness to do this.

To this end you should:

a   *Listen more than you speak*. Most interviewers talk too much. The interview is not a platform for the interviewer's personal experiences and opinions.

b   *Put questions in a straightforward, clear and non-threatening way*. If people are confused or defensive, you will not get the information you seek.

c   *Eliminate cues which lead interviewees to respond in a particular way*. Many interviewees will seek to please the interviewer by giving 'correct' responses ('Are you against sin?').

d   *Enjoy it (or at least look as though you do)*. Don't give the message that you are bored or scared. Vary your voice and facial expression.

It is also essential that you take *a full record of the interview*. This can be from notes made at the time and/or from a recording of the interview. Experienced interviewers tend to have strong preferences for one or other of these approaches. McDonald and Sanger have given a detailed account of their relative advantages and disadvantages (Walker, 1985, pp. 109–16 provides a summary). The literature (discussed in Hoinville and Jowell, 1977) suggests that various kinds of questions should be avoided, and these are summarized in box 9.1.

Box 9.1   Questions to avoid in interviews

Long questions   The interviewee may remember only part of the question, and respond to that part.

Double-barrelled (or multiple-barrelled questions   e.g. 'what do you feel about current pop music compared with that of five years ago?' The solution here is to break it down into simpler questions (e.g. 'what do you feel about current pop music?'; 'Can you recall any pop music from five years ago?'; 'How do you feel they compare?').

Questions involving jargon   Generally you should avoid questions containing words likely to be unfamiliar to the target audience. Keep things simple to avoid disturbing interviewees; it is in your own interest as well.

Leading questions   e.g. 'Why do you like Huddersfield?' It is usually straightforward to modify such questions, providing you realize that they are leading in a particular direction.

Biased questions   Provided you are alert to the possibility of bias it is not difficult to *write* unbiased questions. What is more difficult however is not (perhaps unwittingly) to lead the interviewee by the manner in which the question is asked, or the way in which you receive the response. Neutrality is called for, and in seeking to be welcoming and reinforcing to the interviewee you should try to avoid appearing to share or welcome her or his views.

Content of the Interview

In interviews which are to a greater or lesser extent pre-structured by the interviewer, the content, which can be prepared in advance, consists of a *set of items (usually questions)*, often with alternative subsequent items depending on the responses obtained; suggestions for so-called *probes* and *prompts*; and a proposed *sequence for the questions* which, in a semi-structured interview, may be subject to change during the course of the interview.

The Items or Questions

Three types are used in research interviews: *closed (or 'fixed-alternative')*, *open*, and *scale* items. Closed questions, as the fixed alternative label suggests, force the interviewee to choose from two or more fixed alternatives. Open questions provide no restrictions on the content or manner of the reply other than on the subject area (e.g. 'What kind of way do you most prefer to spend a free evening?'). Scale items, which may well not be in question form, ask for a response in the form of degree of agreement or disagreement (e.g. strongly agree/agree/neutral/disagree/strongly disagree). Logically they are the closed or fixed-alternative type, but are sometimes regarded as a separate type. Additional discussion on the issues raised by closed and scale items is presented on pp. 243 and 253 respectively. As open-ended questions are probably more commonly used in interviews than in other settings, it is appropriate to discuss them here.

Cohen and Manion (1989) list the advantages of open-ended questions:

> they are flexible; they allow the interviewer to probe so that he may go into more depth if he chooses, or clear up any misunderstandings; they enable the interviewer to test the limits of a repondent's knowledge; they encourage cooperation and rapport; and they allow the interviewer to make a truer assessment of what the respondent really believes. Open-ended situations can also result in unexpected or unanticipated answers which may suggest hitherto unthought-of relationships or hypotheses. (p. 313)

The disadvantages lie in the possibilities for loss of control by the interviewer, and in particular in being more difficult to analyse than closed ones.

Probes

A probe is a device to get the interviewee to expand on a response when you intuit that she or he has more to give. The use of probes is something of an art-form and difficult to transmit to the novice interviewer. Sometimes the interviewer may be given instructions to probe on specific questions. There are obvious tactics, such as asking 'Anything more?' or 'Could you go over that again?' Sometimes when an answer has been given in general terms, a useful probe is to seek a personal response, e.g. 'What is your own personal view on this?' There are also very general tactics, such as the use of

- a period of silence;
- an enquiring glance;
- 'mmhmm . . .';
- repeating back all or part of what the interviewee has just said.

Zeisel (1981, pp. 140–54) gives an extended analysis of different types of probe. Probes are particularly useful in focused interviews (see p. 238).

Prompts

Prompts suggest to the interviewee the range or set of possible answers that the interviewer expects. The list of possibilities may be read out by the interviewer, or a 'prompt card' with them on can be shown. (e.g. a list of names of alcoholic drinks for a question on drinking habits). All prompts must be used in a consistent manner by different interviewers and with different interviewees, and form part of the interview record.

The Sequence of Questions

The conventional sequence is as follows.

1 *Introduction*: interviewer introduces herself, explains purpose of the interview, assures of confidentiality, asks permission to tape and/or make notes.
2 *'Warm-up'*: easy, non-threatening questions at the beginning to settle down both of you.
3 *Main body of interview*: covering the main purpose of the interview in what the interviewer considers to be a logical progression. In semi-structured interviewing, this order can be varied, capitalizing on the

responses made (ensure 'missed' topics are returned to unless this seems inappropriate or unnecessary. Any 'risky' questions should be relatively late in the sequence so that, if the interviewee refuses to continue, less information is lost.

4 *'Cool-off'*: usually a few straightforward questions at the end to defuse any tension that might have built up.

5 *Closure*: thank you and goodbye. The 'hand on the door' phenomenon, sometimes found at the end of counselling sessions, is also common in interviewing. Interviewees may, when the recorder is switched off or the notebook put away, come out with a lot of interesting material. There are various possible ways of dealing with this (switch on again, reopen the book, forget about it) but in any case you should be consistent, *and* note how you dealt with it.

Carrying out Structured Interviews

Much of the responsibility for the structured interview achieving its purpose falls on the preparatory work which precedes the interviews themselves. This may include observation and informal interviews, with likely pre-pilot (to develop areas for questions) and pilot (to develop the questions themselves) work. This culminates in the preparation of a detailed *Interview Schedule* which covers:

• what the interviewer says by way of introduction;
• introductions to particular questions, or groups of questions;
• the questions (word for word);
• prompts (and how they are to be used);
• response codes;
• possible 'skips' in sequence (e.g. where a 'yes' answer is followed by a particular question; a 'no' answer by a 'skip' to a different question);
• closing comments;
• reminders to the interviewer about procedure.

It is helpful to distinguish those parts of the schedule which are an 'aide-memoire' to the interviewer from those which are to be said to the interviewee (e.g. by having them in different colours, or by having one group in lower case and the other in CAPITALS).

The codes for different responses are usually circled directly, during the interview, by the interviewer to assist in subsequent analysis. Any apparently open-ended questions are often provided with a set of pre-categorized responses, and it is the interviewer's responsibility to decide in which of these categories the response lies. Either this is done during the interview, or a verbatim response is recorded during the interview and the coding carried out as soon as possible afterwards. The set of pre-categorized responses is developed during pilot work, using a procedure which is in essence the same as that used to categorize open-ended responses during analysis (see p. 253). The sample interview schedule given in box 9.3 on p. 238 includes this, and other, types of question.

When specialist interviewers are used in a project it is helpful to have a separate *interview guide*. This gives detailed instructions on procedure, to try to ensure that this is standardized across different interviewers. Often there will also be training sessions with the same aim. For the relatively small-scale project on which this text focuses, and in particular where the researcher(s) are also doing the interviewing, a separate interview guide may not be necessary. Sufficient procedural instructions can be incorporated in the interview schedule. However, it is crucial that these details of procedure are not lost, and are incorporated in the report eventually arising from the interviews. Box 9.2 gives general advice appropriate for all structured interviews.

Box 9.2   General advice for interviewers carrying out structured interviews

1   *Appearance*   Dress in a similar way to those you will be interviewing. If in doubt err on the side of neatness and neutrality.

2   *Approach*   Be pleasant. Try to make the respondent comfortable.

3   *Familiarity with questionnaire*   View yourself as an actor, with the interview schedule as your script. Know it thoroughly.

4   *Question wording* Use the exact wording of questions and keep to their sequence.

5   *Answers*   Record the answers exactly. Don't make cosmetic adjustments, correct or fabricate.

6   *Probes*   Use the standard probes only.

Comparisons Between the Structured Interview and the Self-Completion Questionnaire

The structured interview schedule is very similar to a questionnaire, and the terms are often used interchangeably. The crucial procedural difference is of course that while the respondent fills in the questionnaire, the interviewer completes the interview schedule. This may seem a straightforward difference but it has complex ramifications. The presence of the interviewer opens the door for factors to do with the interviewer: her skills, experience, personality, and degree of involvement in or alienation from the research, to name but a few. When several interviewers are employed in a project, it is easy to show that factors, such as these can have major effects on the responses of interviewees. With single interviewers, such effects are still present but their effects are virtually impossible to gauge. Interactions between interviewer and interviewee can also be influential; differences or similarities in class, ethnic origin, gender, age and status can affect rapport and the extent to which the interviewee seeks to please, or reacts against, the interviewer. Ways of dealing with these problems are discussed in the section on *interviewer effects* on p. 232.

Lest these complexities be taken as an incitement always to prefer the questionnaire, it should be pointed out that this latter technique has its own problems. Essentially, the researcher is ignorant of many of the factors influencing the choice of response to a question. While there are ways of assessing a subject's consistency, for example by including different forms of the same question at different points in the questionnaire, these are themselves problematic as it is well documented that small and seemingly innocuous changes in wording can sometimes have substantial effects on response. It is virtually impossible to determine whether or not the respondent is giving serious attention to the questions, or regarding the exercise as a tedious chore to be completed in a perfunctory manner. An interview permits the assessment of this type of factor, and gives the possibility of differentiating respondents on this basis. Also, because of the fact of person-to-person interaction in the interview, involvement, and hence the quality of data, is likely to be enhanced *vis-à-vis* the impersonal questionnaire.

Related to this feature, and of considerable importance, is the fact that the refusal rate for personal interviews is typically very much smaller than the non-response rate for postal questionnaires. While, as pointed out in the section on questionnaires (see p. 250), good planning can increase the response rate for questionnaires, this remains a major problem. The basic point is that we have little or no knowledge about the views and characteristics of those who do not respond, which can seriously vitiate any claims to generalizability.

Carrying Out Semi-structured Interviews

With semi-structured interviews we are dealing with a dimension of greater or less structure, rather than suggesting that there is a qualitative difference between this and the previous type. In Powney and Watts's (1987) terminology, this is still a respondent interview. Interviewers have their shopping list of topics and want to get responses to them, but as a matter of tactics they have greater freedom in the sequencing of questions, in their exact wording, and in the amount of time and attention given to different topics.

The *interview schedule* can be simpler than the one for the structured interview. It will be likely to include the following:

- introductory comments (probably a verbatim script);
- list of topic headings and possibly key questions to ask under these headings;
- set of associated prompts;
- closing comments.

It would be common to incorporate some more highly structured sequences (e.g. to obtain standard factual biographical and other material). One strategy is to have the different topics and associated questions and prompts on a series of cards. The interviewer will have an initial topic but will then be to some extent guided by the interviewee's responses as to the succeeding sequence of topics. Cards can be put on one side when they have been covered. If notes are being made during the interview, it is helpful to allow a substantial amount of space for each topic as you won't know in advance how much material you will obtain in any particular area. The prompts may of course not be necessary but they provide a useful structure for organizing your notes. Box 9.3 gives an example of an interview schedule for semi-structured interviews.

Box 9.3   Example of interview schedule for semi-structured interview

Appendix B: Interview Schedule

Thank you for being willing to take part in a follow up interview to the previous survey. Can I first of all assure you that you will remain completely anonymous and no records of the interview will be kept with your name on them.

1   Can I first ask you if you are now in employment?

If yes take details of –
    a   job
    b   How person came to hear of job
    c   Application procedure
    d   Selection procedure
    e   Why this one was successful in contrast to previous attempts?
    f   What problems did the person experience in previous attempts? (Probe until topic exhausted)
    g   Advance to 2)

If no take details of
    a Last job applied for
    b How person came to hear about job
    c Application procedure
    d Selection procedure
    e Why was this one unsuccessful?
    f If person not interviewed ask above questions about the last job that got as far as interview. If none ask above questions about the one they felt they got nearest to.
    g What problems does the person in general experience in relation to finding work. Probe until topic exhausted.
    h Advance to 2)

2 What careers advice have you received –
    a At school?
    b From local careers service?
    c From any other source including informal sources?

3 How would you evaluate that advice? (Ask in relation to all sources identified in 2.)

4 Have you taken part in any of the services for the unemployed provided locally? – Probe this and explain but do not prompt with examples at this stage.

5 How would you evaluate these services? (Ask in relation to all sources identified in 4.)

6 Take respondents through the following list and ask them if they are aware of the service, what is provided, if they have had direct experience, and if they had, how they would rate that experience. Omit from the list any services already covered in 4 and 5 above)
    a Adult Training
    b Youth Training
    c Training Access Points
    d Worklink
    e Kirklees Community Enterprise Training Agency (KCETA)
    f Start-up Business Units
    g Business access Scheme
    h Workers Co-operatives
    i Careers and Education Advice Service for Adults (CEASA)
    j Careers Service
    k Redundancy Counselling

7 What kinds of services could be provided that would help you personally to get a job (or would have made it easier if in employment)? Probe and direct to less obvious areas such as child minding and transport – pick up on factors mentioned in 1 and 2 above – but do not neglect more obvious direct services.

8   Have you been helped by any informal organizations? Probe on community-based initiatives, job clubs, local support networks etc. Do not neglect simply the help and advice of relatives, friends and neighbours.

9   How do the factors identified in 8 compare to help received through formal services? Probe in what ways better, similar, worse or different.

10 Do you have a regular routine to organize your time for the week? Probe the extent to which this includes finding employment or perhaps precludes it. NB if now employed ask in relation to time when unemployed.

11 Do you find your present income adequate and fair? If in employment contrast with time when out of employment.

12 Some people see the society we live in as a ladder to climb to greater rewards: others see it as divided between the haves and haves not. How do you see society? Probe on social imagery.

13 Thank you very much for helping us and giving up your time. Can I finally ask you if you think there is any aspect of your experience of looking for work that has not been covered in this interview?

(*Source*: Cliff et al., n.d.)

Focused Interviews

Informant interviews are not simply casual conversations. In one version, known as the *non-directive interview*, the direction of the interview and the areas covered are totally in the control of the informant (the interviewee). Carl Rogers (1945) has used this approach widely in therapeutic settings, and it has had a considerable influence on interviewing style. However, there are important differences between clinical and research purposes. In Rogerian therapy, the interview is initiated by the client, not the therapist; the motivation, and hence the purpose of the interview, is to seek help with a problem; and the extent to which it is helpful is the index of success. Because of this, Whyte (1984) has claimed that a genuine non-directive interviewing approach is not appropriate for research. Powney and Watts (1987, p. 20) suggest that Piaget's type of clinical interviewing, as used in his studies of cognitive development (e.g. Piaget, 1929; 1930), where he is insistent that the child must determine the content and direction of the conversation, fits better into research purposes. There is a certain irony here, as experimental psychologists, while recognizing Piaget's theoretical contributions, have been very dismissive of his methodology.

An approach which allows people's views and feelings to emerge, but which gives the interviewer some control, is known as the *focused interview*

(Merton et al., 1956). It can be used where we want to investigate a particular situation, phenomenon or event (e.g. a youth training progamme, an X-ray unit, or a TV programme). Individuals are sought who have been involved in that situation (e.g. they are all in an open prison and have been subjected to a 'short, sharp, shock' treatment).

The first task is to carry out a *situational analysis*, by means of observation, documentary analysis or whatever. Typically this covers

* the important aspects of the situation to those involved;
* the meaning these aspects have for those involved and;
* the effects they have on those involved.

An interview guide is then developed covering the major areas of enquiry and the research questions. The interviews concentrate on the subjective experiences of those involved.

Newson and Newson (1976), discussed in Cohen and Manion (1989, pp. 328–9), provide a good example of this approach. It demands considerable experience and skill on the part of the interviewer and great flexibility. In particular, the probe is a crucial aspect. Zeisel (1981, ch. 9) provides detailed and useful suggestions.

Other Approaches to Interviewing

There are many other approaches. *Group interviews* are widely used in market research for testing reactions to new products (e.g. Stewart and Shamdasani, 1990). They are attractive in some research contexts (Watts and Ebbutt, 1987), for example when the research involves studying an established group. There are clear disadvantages in that it is difficult or impossible to follow up the views of individuals; and group dynamics or power hierarchies effect who speaks and what they say. A particular problem is when one or two persons dominate. They may not only take over from you but not let others contribute. An overt appeal for other contributions can help. There may be indications from others' body language that they wish to contribute, and you can capitalize on these.

Telephone interviews, given the high proportion of phones in many populations of interest, are increasingly used. They share many of the advantages of face-to-face interviewing: a high response rate; correction of obvious misunderstandings; possible use of probes, etc. Rapport may be more difficult to achieve but this is compensated for by evidence of smaller interviewer effects and a lower tendency towards socially desirable responses (Bradburn and Sudman, 1979). The lack of visual cues may cause problems in interpretation. The major advantage, particularly if the sample to be reached is geographically dispersed, is the lower cost in terms of time, effort and money. They can be safer as well; you won't get physically attacked over the phone.

The technique of *random digit dialling* involves the 'local' part of a telephone number (i.e. the '786543' of a number such as '0345 786543') being generated randomly, using tables or a computer. It avoids some of the biases in sampling from telephone directories (no new subscribers or ex-directory numbers) at the expense of needing to screen out non-allocated and non-household numbers. Baker (1988, pp. 189–96) gives further details.

Finally, McCracken (1988) advocates the use of what he calls the *'long interview'*. By this he means not simply an interview which takes a long time, but an ethnographic style which might be substituted for participant observation in situations where the latter is impossible because of time or other constraints.

Analysis of Interview Data

The ways in which interviews have been reported in the social sciences (or anywhere else, for that matter) have not in general been noteworthy for their standards of rigour or detail. Typically, accounts are strong on content and its interpretation, much weaker on providing sufficient information to judge the trustworthiness (including reliability and validity) of those accounts. Carlisle (1990) provides an extreme example. This consists solely of a verbatim interview with an animal rights activist. While it could be argued to be illuminative, bearing similarities to the *objet trouvé* approach to art, the lack of system or analysis puts it outside the range of a scientific study. Recent work is seeking to remedy these deficiencies (see, for example, Powney and Watts, 1987). Chapters 11 and 12 provide a discussion of the issues involved, covering quantitative and qualitative aspects respectively.

Skills in Interviewing

You don't become a good interviewer just by reading about it. Skills are involved which require practice, preferably under 'low risk' conditions where it is possible to receive feedback on your performance.

The skills involved in structured interviews are relatively low-level. Is the script being kept to? Are standard questions being asked in the same way to all interviewees? Are the 'skips' depending on particular answers carried out correctly? Are all interviewees responded to in the same way? And so on. The less the degree of structure in the interview, the more complex the performance required from the interviewer.

It is highly desirable that the pilot (or a pre-pilot) stage includes explicit interviewer assessment and training. Clearly if you are totally alone as a researcher, this causes problems, but it is obviously possible to ask the interviewees in the pilot to comment on the interviewer's performance as well as on the interview schedule. A recording (audio or video) will facilitate the interviewer's evaluation of her performance.

If you are working with colleagues, then mutual (constructive) assessment of each other's interview performance is feasible. This type of feedback information is not only helpful for training purposes but also helps in the general task of viewing the interview situation as a complex social interaction whose characteristics have to some extent to be captured when analysing the interview method.

Self-completed Questionnaires

Self-completed questionnaires, which respondents fill in for themselves, are very efficient in terms of researcher time and effort. Copies of a questionnaire could be distributed to, say, all 1,000 pupils in a school, or to a similar number of workers in a firm, be completed by them and returned to you in about the same amount of time that it takes to complete a single interview. If the questionnaire has been well constructed, the time needed to code and analyse responses can also be short, particularly if computer coding or analysis is available. With such efficiency, no wonder that this type of questionnaire is a widely used tool.

There are problems, though. The data are, necessarily, superficial. There is little or no check on the honesty or seriousness of responses. Responses have to be squeezed into predetermined boxes which may or may not be appropriate. Recall your frustration when you have been filling in such a questionnaire and the questions are not the ones you would have asked; or none of the permitted responses seems right. There are hidden costs as well. For the results to have any hope of meaningfulness, the questionnaire must be painstakingly constructed, with very clear and unambiguous instructions, and careful wording of questions. And while analysis may be easy, interpretation can be problematic.

Figure 9.1 gives a simple example and box 9.4 provides suggestions, based on empirical studies, for the design of self-administered questionnaires.

It is worth stressing the need to cut down open-ended questions to a minimum with this type of questionnaire, unless you can afford to spend a lot of time on analysis or only have a small number of responses to deal with. The desire to use open-ended questions appears to be almost universal in novice researchers, but is usually rapidly extinguished with experience. Pilot work using interviews and open-ended questions can provide suggestions for closed alternatives. Another possibility is to have some open-ended questions in the self-administered questionnaire, and to have respondents classify their own open-ended response using provided categories (e.g. as 'very positive', 'positive', etc.).

There is much that one can do to increase the likelihood of getting a high response rate, as set out in box 9.5.

Consumer behaviour and green attitudes.

FIRST SOME FACTS ABOUT YOU

1.   Sex   Male ☐   Female ☐

2.   Age Group

      16-24 ☐   25-34 ☐   35-49 ☐   50-64 ☐   65+ ☐

NOW SOME QUESTIONS ABOUT THE THINGS YOU BUY

3.   Of the following household items, which brands do you normally buy?:

Toilet roll

Washing powder

Washing-up liquid

Household cleaners/polishes

Nappies

4.   With regard to the goods just mentioned, which of the following things would you say influenced you when choosing what you buy?

Quality	☐	Reliability	☐
Reputation	☐	Advertising	☐
Presentation/Packaging	☐	Brand name	☐
Cost	☐	'Environmental friendliness'	☐
Ethics (e.g. S. Africa, Animal testing)	☐		

Figure 9.1   Example of a self-completed questionnaire

5. Do you have any insulation in your home?

    None ☐   Loft ☐   Cavity ☐

6. Does anyone in your household run a car?

    Yes ☐   No ☐

    If Yes, do any of them run on unleaded petrol?

    Yes ☐   No ☐

7. How often do you use the following:-

	Always	Sometimes	Never
Bottle banks			
Recycled paper			

8. Does the use of artificial additives and preservatives affect what foods you buy?

    Yes ☐   No ☐

9. With reference to any issues have you, during the past 5 years, done any of the following?:-

    Signed a petition ☐   Been a member of a political party ☐
    Written to an M.P. ☐   Been part of a demonstration ☐
    Been a member of a pressure group ☐

NOW SOME OPINIONS ABOUT THE FOLLOWING STATEMENTS

10. The following is a set of statements about attitudes to green issues.
For each statement please say whether you agree strongly, agree, are neutral, disagree or disagree strongly with it. Tick the appropriate box.

P.T.O.

(Figure 9.1 cont.)

	Strongly Agree	Agree	Neutral	Disagree	Strongly disagree
Britain should not allow its air pollution to cause acid rain in Scandinavia.					
There is too much panic about running out of resources.					
Manufacturers shouldn't make things that are harmful to the environment.					
Recycling is just a fad.					
Countries with rain forests are entitled to chop them down to sell their timber.					
Live for today. Don't worry about tomorrow.					
Industries should stop damaging the countryside, even if prices must rise to pay for it.					
Being 'Green' is just another youth craze.					
The government should invest more money into looking at alternatives to nuclear power.					

JUST A FEW MORE FACTS ABOUT YOU

11.   What is your occupation. Please give details

....

....

12.   What is the income level of your household?

£5,000-9,999 ☐   £10,000-14,999 ☐   £15,000-19,999 ☐   £20,000 and over ☐

13.   Educational qualifications

None ☐   O-levels ☐   A-levels ☐   Degree ☐   Other (please give details) ☐

....

....

14.   What point in this scale best indicates your political views?
       Circle the appropriate number.

       Left   1   2   3   4   5   6   7   **Right**

THANK YOU VERY MUCH FOR YOUR COOPERATION

(Figure 9.1 cont.)   Source Gibbs, n.d.

Box 9.4   Designing self-completed questionnaires

The design of self-completed questionnaires for surveys and other purposes has tended to be an art form, depending on informal knowledge and personal experience. However, there is now a reasonable body of experimental evidence which has implications for this task. The following suggestions arise from the research literature.

1   *Specific questions are better than general ones*

The goal of standardized measurement is central to survey research; specific questions provide more standardization. With more general questions there is (a) wider range of interpretations by respondents; (b) greater susceptibility to order effects; and (c) poorer prediction of behaviour.

Examples:

general   List the newspapers and magazines you looked at yesterday.

specific   Which of these newspapers and magazines did you look at yesterday? (show list)

general   How would you say you are these days: very happy, pretty happy, or not too happy?

specific   How would you describe your marriage: very happy, pretty happy, or not too happy?

2   *Closed questions are usually preferable to open questions*

The advantage is again in potential differences in interpretation with the open form. They are also more difficult to code and analyse. However, in some circumstances the open form is preferable (e.g. when not enough is known to write appropriate response categories; and in the measurement of sensitive or disapproved behaviour).

Examples:

open   People look for different things in a job; what would you most prefer in job?

closed People look for different things in a job; which one of the following five things would you most prefer in a job: work that pays well; work that gives a feeling of accomplishment; work where there is not too much supervision and you make most of the decisions yourself; work that is pleasant and the other people are nice to work with; or work that is steady with little chance of being laid off?

3 Offer a 'no-opinion' option

Polls often assume that because a problem is of importance everyone will have an opinion about it. There is evidence that if no option is given substantial numbers of people manufacture an opinion for the survey. Many people (one-third to one-eighth) will choose this option if it is explicitly presented. The size of the effect depends on how the option is offered.

Examples:

separated 'no opinion' filter	The Russian leaders are basically trying to get along with the West. Do you have an opinion on that? (*If Yes*) Do you agree or disagree?
'no opinion' response option	The Russian leaders are basically trying to get along with the west. Do you agree, disagree, or not have an opinion on that?

Note: the former produces a larger effect.

4 Omit the middle alternative and measure intensity

There is disagreement on the wisdom of including a 'middle alternative'. On the one hand it may encourage a non-committal response; on the other it allows for an additional gradation of opinion. Typically, 20 per cent of respondents may use the middle category, but it appears that its inclusion or exclusion does not affect the relative proportions of those actually expressing opinions. The respondents using the middle category are those without strong feelings on the issue and a suggested strategy is not explicitly to provide the middle category (and hence lose information about the direction in which some people lean) but follow the question with an intensity item, thus being able to separate those with strong feelings from those with 'leanings'.

Example:

no middle category	Should divorce in this country be easier or more difficult to obtain than it is now?
middle category	Should divorce in the country be easier to obtain, more difficult to obtain, or stay as it is now?

The most commonly used measures are:

Note on measurement of intensity	How strongly do you feel about this? Extremely, strongly, very strongly, somewhat strongly, or not at all strongly.

or How strongly do you feel about this? Where would you place yourself on this scale?

Extremely   1 2 3 4 5 6 7   Not at all
strongly   strongly

5 Use of forced choice rather than 'agree/disagree' statements

Agree/disagree statements (as commonly used in attitude measurement) suffer from 'acquiescence response set' i.e. the tendency of respondents to agree irrespective of item content. Generally forced choice items appear more apt to encourage a considered response than agree/disagree statements.

Example:

forced-choice   Would you say that most men are better suited emotionally for politics; that men and women are equally suited; or that women are better suited than men in this area?

agree/disagree   Do you agree or disagree with this statement?: Most men are better suited emotionally for politics than are most women.

6 Question order

The meaning of almost any question can be altered by a preceding question. However, research has not to date suggested any general rules to order questions, beyond the suggestion that general questions should precede specific questions.

7 Wording effects

While small changes in wording can have large effects on the answers of many respondents, it is difficult to predict in advance whether or not a particular wording change will have an effect. This indicates the importance of not basing conclusions on results from a single question. Strategies for doing this include:

creation of split-sample comparisons   different forms of words can be incorporated into the surveys administered to different people. This can be handled by multiple questionnaires, or different skip patterns in a single questionnaire.

asking multiple questions on a topic   This is essentially the solution adopted when attitude or other scales are used.

(Detailed justification for the assertions made above is provided in Converse and Presser, 1986.)

Box 9.5 Factors in securing a good response rate to a postal questionnaire

1 The appearance of the questionnaire is vital. It should look easy to fill in, with plenty of space for questions and answers.

2 Clarity of wording and simplicity of design are essential. Give clear instructions (e.g. 'put a tick').

3 Arrange the contents to maximize co-operation, e.g. ensure that early questions don't suggest to respondents that the enquiry is not for them. Interpose any attitude questions throughout the questionnaire to vary the response required.

Design and layout

4 Coloured pages (e.g. different colour for instructions) can clarify the structure.

5 Answering by putting ticks in boxes is familiar to most respondents. Circling pre-coded answers can confuse.

6 Sub-lettering questions (e.g. 5a, 5b, etc.) can help in grouping questions on a specific issue.

7 Repeat instructions if confusion is possible.

8 Initial questions should be easy and interesting. Middle questions cover the more difficult areas. Make the last questions interesting to encourage return of the questionnaire.

9 *Wording of questions is of crucial importance. Pretesting is essential.*

10 A brief note at the end can:
a ask respondents to check that they have not accidently omitted to answer any questions;
b solicit an early return of the questionnaire;
c thank them for their help; and
d offer to send an abstract of the findings.

Initial mailing

11 Use good-quality envelopes, typed and if possible addressed to a named person.

12   Use first class postage, stamped not franked if possible.

13   Enclose a stamped addressed envelope for return of the questionnaire.

14   For 'home' surveys, Thursday is the best day for sending out; for organizations, Monday or Tuesday.

15   Avoid a December mailing.

Covering letter

16   This should indicate the aim of the survey and convey its importance; assure confidentiality; and encourage reply. If serial numbers or other codings are used, say why.

17   Tailor it to the audience (e.g. a parent survey might stress its value for child-care).

18   Give the name of the sponsor or organization carrying out the survey on the letterhead and in the body of the letter.

19   Pre-survey letters, advising respondents of the forthcoming questionnaire, can increase response rate.

Follow-up letter

20   This is the most productive factor in increasing response rates. All the above suggestions apply.

21   Emphasize the importance of the study and the value of the respondents participation.

22   Conveying disappointment and surprise at non-response can be effective.

23   Don't suggest that non-response is common.

24   Send a further copy of the questionnaire and another stamped addressed envelope.

Further follow-ups

25   These are subject to the law of diminishing returns but are worthwhile. Three reminders are commonly recommended. They can increase response rates by a further third.

Use of incentives

26 Incentives accompanying the initial mailing appear to be more effective than rewarding the return of completed questionnaires (e.g. through a prize draw). They should be a token rather than a payment: e.g. a ball-point pen.

(Hoinville and Jowell, 1977 give further details and suggestions.)

The Coding of Responses

Codes are symbols, usually numbers, which are used to identify particular responses, or types of response, in questionnaires or similar instruments. They are used to assist in the organization, quantification and analysis of data. For example, the responses to a question about the respondent's sex might be coded as '1' for female, and '2' for male. The numbers here are arbitrary; they could be reversed or different numbers used, provided there is consistency in the treatment of responses to a particular question in a questionnaire.

Closed Questions

With closed questions, and other items such as attitude and other scales, there should be little difficulty in coding. The range of possible responses will have been checked and, if necessary, modified during piloting. Numerical symbols are assigned to the various answer categories, and analysis can proceed directly. From the point of view of analysis it is preferable to include the codes on the questionnaire. For example:

At which of the following ages did your *father* finish his full-time education?

Please tick the appropriate box.   official
                                          use only

14 or younger __1
15 __2
16 __3
17 or 18 __4
19 or 20 __5
21 __6
22 or over __7

(The code is included in the box to help the analyst; the code of the box ticked is written by the analyst in the right-hand column.)

You are free to assign any meaning that you wish to a coding digit (or digits) – *providing that the meaning is consistent within a particular coding scheme.* The code can be arbitrary (e.g. yes = 1; no = 2) or can be the actual number (e.g. age in years = 27 or whatever). It is preferable to have a code for non-reponse (e.g. '0' or '–1') rather than leaving a blank. Whether or not this needs to be discriminated from (and hence separate codes used for) 'don't know', 'not sure', etc., will depend on the particular survey.

Open Questions

Coding of responses here involves combining the detailed information contained in the response into a limited number of categories that enable simple description of the data and allow for statistical analysis. The main purpose is to simplify many individual responses by classifying them into a smaller number of groups, each including responses that are similar in content. *This process inevitably involves some loss of information.*

Coding of open questions should be based on a substantial, representative sample (say fifty cases) selected from the total set of responses. It should not be based solely on early responses, as these may well be unrepresentative, and it may prove necessary subsequently to develop a revised set of coding categories, which leads to wasteful recoding of those already analysed.

The standard procedure has been to copy all the responses to a particular question on a (large) sheet of paper, headed by the text of the question, and with each reponse preceded by the case number (i.e. the code given to that person's questionnaire). The object is then to try to develop a smallish set of categories (say eight to ten) into which these responses can be sorted. This is not an easy exercise; it is, obviously, largely driven by the nature of the responses and the themes and dimensions they suggest. However, one should also bear in mind the purposes of the survey in general and of that question in particular, and try to ensure that the coding categories are such that a minimum of relevant information is lost. The number of categories that it is sensible to use is in part dependent on the overall number of cases in the sample and on the detail of the statistical analysis you wish to carry out.

This process has the effect of turning the answers to open questions to a defined set of standard responses. It is sometimes used at the pilot stage of a questionnaire study to produce a set of categories for closed questions.

Chapter 11 refers to the quantitative analysis of questionnaire data (p. 365). Computer software is now available to assist in the task of categorization, and more generally in the treatment of questionnaire data.

Diaries

A diary, considered as a research tool, is a kind of self-administered questionnaire. As such, it can range from being totally unstructured to a set of responses to specific questions. Diaries are tantalizingly attractive because they appear, on the surface, to provide the means of generating very substantial amounts of data with minimal amount of effort on the part of the enquirer. They can also serve as a proxy for observation in situations where it would be difficult or impossible for direct observation to take place (as with Coxon's (1988) use of sexual diaries for mapping detailed sexual behaviour).

The diary, however, places a great deal of responsibility on the respondent. Unstructured diaries leave the interpretation of the task very much with the pen of the respondent. There is evidence (e.g. Bourgue and Back, 1982) in favour of using a specific set of questions, which ask about the respondent's activities at given times. But even simplifying and structuring the task in this way produces data which is prone to bias. A recent diary study of university lecturers produced striking evidence of the large number of hours per week that they work. The respondents' knowledge that this information would be used in support of a pay claim casts doubt on its objectivity.

Even when the situation provides no obvious distorting factors of this kind, there are worries. The kind of enthusiastic involvement that one would seek carries with it dangers of mis-reporting (perhaps to please the enquirer), or even of changing the to-be-reported-on behaviour (perhaps to show the diarist in a good light). These are phenomena potentially present in any enquiry where the respondents know they are involved in an enquiry, but they are sufficiently bothersome here to cast doubt on the use of the diary as the *sole* method in an investigation. Bourque and Back (1982), for example, combined a structured diary approach with direct observation, and cross-checks against formal timetabled activity in a way that gave confidence about the reliability and validity of the diary method in the situation in which they were using it.

Burgess (1981) has argued for the use of diaries as precursor to interviewing, especially as a means of generating the list of questions to be covered in the interview. This approach was used by Zimmerman and Wieder (1977), who go so far as to suggest that this dual tactic of diary followed by interview can fulfil many of the purposes of participant observation when the latter is precluded by resource considerations.

The type of question asked will, as with other techniques, be dictated by the purpose of your study. Box 9.6 gives suggestions for the development of a diary form (see Gullan et al., 1990 for an example).

Variants of the diary method have been used. One attempts to combine the keeping of a diary with the 'critical incident' approach (e.g. Bryman, 1989). This attempts to separate out, and to get people to notice, specific happenings that they consider to be important. Thus, in a managerial context,

---

Box 9.6   Notes for guidance in developing a diary form

1   Think of it as a questionnaire. You need to devote the same amount of care and preparation (and piloting) as you would for other questionnaires (see box 9.3).

2   Because the diary involves self-completion of a series of forms, co-operation is vital. You need to ensure that respondents know *what* they have to do; *why*; and *when*.

3   As with other questionnaires, include an item only if you know what you are going to do with it. You should be clear, before you start the study proper, how the items relate to your research questions, and how you will analyse it subsequently.

4   In a study extending over time, do not assume that 'things are going on all right'. Check, preferably by a personal contact.

5   General considerations about confidentiality, anonymity, feedback of results, permissions, etc. apply.

---

these might be whatever is crucial or critical in achieving a satisfactory outcome in a particular task. Respondents are then asked to rate these incidents according to their difficulty and importance to the job.

Scales and Tests

Psychologists and other social scientists have developed a substantial range of self-report measuring instruments to assess people's abilities, propensities, views, opinions and attitudes – to name but a few. Most widely known by the lay public is the IQ or intelligence test, but there are also tests of attainment, of creativity and of personality. They are, in effect, versions of structured interviews or of self-completion questionnaires, though not usually referred to as such.

Technically, such tests provide a *scale* on which we can assess, usually quantitatively, the individuals' performance or standing on the attribute in question. There are other measurement scales where the function is not to test, but to gain some insight into what people feel or believe about something. Most common is ATTITUDE MEASUREMENT. This is singled out here partly because it is common – many psychologists want to measure people's attitudes, to the environment, to abortion, to Europe, to single-parent families, etc. – and also because the same principles apply to the development of many other scales.

Attitude Measurement

The term 'attitude' is somewhat slippery. It falls in the same kind of sphere as opinion, belief or value, but opinions vary as to how these different terms are interrelated. Lemon (1973) provides a clear analysis for those who wish to take this further, but also suggests that the term's widespread usage derives in part from this very fuzziness; each worker has been able to tailor it to suit her own purposes. So, in this area, your own common-sense notion is unlikely to get you into trouble.

There is a substantial technology and associated mystique about attitude measurement. Central to this is the belief that it is not possible to assess something like attitude by means of a single question or statement. For example, suppose someone strongly disagreed with the statement: 'Economic aid should be given to countries in Eastern Europe.' By itself this could not be taken as indicating an unsympathetic attitude to those countries plight. The respondent might feel that such assistance would act against their interests, perhaps by inhibiting necessary changes in their economy. Answers to a range of statements can help in teasing out such issues. Having a set of ten or twenty items is another form of TRIANGULATION; the response to each gives something of a 'marker' on the respondent's attitude. Putting the responses together enables us to build up a much fuller picture. The problems arise in selecting the items or statements and in working out how to put together the responses.

Arbitrary Scales   It is still distressingly common to see attitude scales cobbled together by assembling an arbitrary group of statements which sound as if they would be relevant, with similar 'off the top of the head' ratings assigned to different answers, and a simple addition of these ratings to obtain some mystical 'attitude score'. Put like this, the deficiencies are obvious. We need some form of systematic procedure so that we can demonstrate that the different items are related to the same attitude. Similar justification is needed for the assignment of numbers of some kind to particular answers.

The summated rating (or Likert) scale   While there are several types of systematic scaling techniques which have been used in attitude measurement, the summated rating approach is very widely used – and has the added advantage of being relatively easy to develop. It was originally devised by Likert in the 1930s (Likert, 1932) and scales developed by this method are commonly termed *Likert scales*. Box 9.7 gives procedural details and box 9.8 an example of such a scale.

Items in a Likert scale can look interesting to respondents, and people often enjoy completing a scale of this kind. This can be of importance, not

Box 9.7 Developing a summated rating (Likert) scale

1 *Gather together a pool of items that appear to be related to or important to the issue.* This can be done by reading round the issue, borrowing from existing scales and 'brainstorming'. Items should reflect both a positive and a negative stance to the issue. Extreme positive and extreme negative statements should be avoided as they may be insensitive to individual differences in attitude (we want to discriminate between individuals – extreme statements may get everyone giving the same response). There should be about the same number of positive and negative statements.

2 *Decide on a response categorization system.* The most common is to have five fixed alternative expressions, labelled 'strongly agree', 'agree', 'undecided', 'disagree' and 'strongly disagree'.* Weights of 1, 2, 3, 4 and 5 are assigned to these alternatives, with the direction of weighting depending on whether the statement is positive or negative (e.g. 5 for a 'strongly agree' with a positive statement, and 'strongly disagree' with a negative statement).

3 *Ask a large number of respondents to check their attitudes to the list of statements.* The list should be in random order with positive and negative statements intermingled. The respondents should be a representative sample from the population whose attitude you wish to measure.

4 *Obtain a total score for each respondent.* This is done by summing the value of each of the responses given (e.g. 'agree' to positive item scores 4; 'strongly disagree' with negative item scores 5; 'neutral' to either scores 3; 'agree' to negative item scores 2; etc.). Rank the respondents according to total score obtained.

5 *Select items for final scale using 'item analysis'.* Each item (i.e. statement) is subjected to a measurement of its *discriminative power* (DP) That is, its ability to discriminate between the responses of the upper quartile (25 per cent) of respondents, and the responses of the lower quartile (25 per cent) – see worked example below. Items with the highest DP indices are chosen for the final scale. A typical scale would consist of 20–30 items.

Notes
a There are alternative techniques for selecting the items for the final scale (e.g. each statement can be correlated with the overall score – those items with the highest correlations are retained).

b Scales can be tested for validity and reliability using the methods covered in Rust and Golombok (1989), pp. 164–8.

*alternatives are possible (e.g. 3, 4, 6 or 7 alternatives – odd numbers permit a neutral mid-point which is usually considered desirable); different labels for the alternatives may be used where appropriate (e.g. 'almost always', 'frequently', 'occasionally', 'rarely', and 'almost never').

Calculating the discriminative power (DP) of items

1 Suppose the scale is tested on a sample of sixty respondents. The upper quartile will thus consist of the fifteen respondents (25 per cent of sixty) with the highest total scores; the lower quartile the fifteen respondents with the lowest total scores.

2 The distribution of scores (i.e. number of 1s, 2s, 3s, 4s and 5s) for the upper quartile group is tabled for each item.

3 The distribution of scores (i.e. number of 1s, 2s, 3s, 4s, and 5s) for the lower quartile group is tabled for each item.

4 Weighted totals and means are calculated separately for the upper and lower quartile groups, for each item:

Example for one item

Weighted group	Number in group	Item scores 1 2 3 4 5	Weighted total	Weighted mean
Upper	15	0 1 2 7 5	(1.2) + (2.3) + (7.4) + (5.5) = 61	61/15 = 4.07
Lower	15	3 8 3 1 0	(3.1) + (8.2) + (3.3) + (1.4) = 32	32/15 = 2.13

5 The index of discriminative power (DP) for an item is the difference between the weighted means.

For the example above, DP = 4.07 − 2.13 = 1.94.

Box 9.8 Example of Likert scale – generalized expectancy for success scale

Highly improbable   1   2   3   4   5   Highly probable

In the future I expect that I will:

 1. find that people don't seem to understand what I am trying to say.
 2. be discouraged about my ability to gain the respect of others.
 3. be a good parent.
 4. be unable to accomplish my goals.
 5. have a successful marital relationship.
 6. deal poorly with emergency situations.
 7. find my efforts to change situations I don't like to be ineffective.
 8. not be very good at learning new skills.
 9. carry through my responsibilities successfully.
10. discover that the good in life outweighs the bad.
11. handle unexpected problems successfully.
12. get the promotions I deserve.
13. succeed in the projects I undertake.
14. not make any significant contributions to society.
15. discover that my life is not getting much better.
16. be listened to when I speak.
17. discover that my plans don't work out too well.
18. find that no matter how I try, things just don't turn out the way I would like.
19. handle myself well in whatever situation I'm in.
20. be able to solve my own problems.
21. succeed at most things I try.
22. be successful in my endeavours in the long run.
23. be very successful in working out my personal life.
24. experience many failures in my life.
25. make a good impression on people I meet for the first time.
26. attain the career goals I have set for myself.
27. have difficulty dealing with my superiors.
28. have problems working with others.
29. be a good judge of what it takes to get ahead.
30. achieve recognition in my profession.

(*Source*: Fibel and Hale, 1978.)

only because if they are interested they are likely to give considered rather than perfunctory answers, but also because in many situations people may, not unreasonably, just not be prepared to co-operate in something that appears boring. However, even though the items may look arbitrary and similar to those in magazine self-rating exercises, the systematic procedures used do help to ensure that the scale has internal consistency and/or the ability to differentiate among individuals.

The equal appearing interval (or Thurstone) scale   In this approach, which was systematized by Thurstone and Chave (1929), a small number of items form the final scale with each of them representing a particular scale value with respect to the attitude, ranging from highly favourable through neutral to highly unfavourable.

The development of a Thurstone scale is considerably more cumbersome and difficult than the development of a Likert scale. Perhaps for this reason it is less frequently used and summary details only are given in box 9.9. If, having read the summary given, you think that you are in a position to follow the Thurstone approach, you will find further details in Lemon (1973).

Box 9.9   Development of an equal-appearing interval (Thurstone) scale – summary only

1   *Collect a large number of statements relating to the attitude in question.* Similar sources can be used to those suggested in Likert scaling (reading around the topic, consulting published scales, brainstorming, etc.). However, it is important to have several very extreme positive and very extreme negative statements in the set.

2   *Give the statements to 50–100 'judges'.* Judges are asked to work independently, and to rate each of the statements on an 11-point scale according to the degree of favourableness it shows towards the attitude (11 most favourable, 6 neutral and 1 most unfavourable). Judges are asked *not* to rate in terms of their own attitude, simply to try to rate in terms of favourableness.

3   *Find the scale value of each statement.* The median rating for each statement is computed. The amount of variability in rating for each is also calculated.

4   *Select a number of statements spread evenly along the scale.* Statements are selected from those with low variability in rating across judges. A second standardization is sometimes introduced at this stage by getting a sample from the population on which the scale is to be used to respond to each item on a yes/no basis (usually agree/disagree).

Items which show good *discriminating power* (as with the Likert scale) between those having favourable and unfavourable attitudes are selected for the final scale. The items selected should cover the full range of scale values, and should evenly spread along the scale. A typical scale includes 10–30 items.

Note: The items are presented in randomized order when the scale is used. Respondents are asked if they agree or disagree with the various items. The attitude measure is the median of the scale values that the respondent agrees to.

The practical problem with this approach, in addition to the considerable amount of labour involved if it is done thoroughly, is in getting hold of the requisite number of 'judges'. There is nothing magic about the suggested number of 50 to 100 judges and a somewhat smaller number is unlikely seriously to affect the liability and validity of the scale. However, getting this kind of number of individuals who can and will make a conscientious assessment of the favourableness of a set of a hundred or more items to a particular attitude is no easy undertaking. It is also important to ensure that these judges themselves have a wide range of attitudes as, although they are asked to discount their own attitude when rating items, there is evidence that judges' attitudes have a substantial effect on the ratings (e.g. Hovland and Sherif, 1952).

Although, in their traditional format, Likert and Thurstone scales differ in the type of response asked for, hybrids are possible. For example, Eysenck and Crown (1949) constructed a scale along Thurstone principles and then administered it in the Likert fashion ('strongly agree', 'agree' etc.). The advantage of this approach is that it enables one to find out not only those statements which the respondent endorses, but also the strength or emphasis with which they hold the opinion.

The cumulated (or Guttman) scale   Critics of both Thurstone and Likert scales have pointed out that they may contain statements which concern a variety of dimensions relating to the attitude. For example, a scale on attitudes to nuclear power stations could include ethical and moral statements, concerning the economic consequences of developing nuclear power, a health dimension, an environmental aspect, etc., etc. Combining statements relating to several dimensions on the one scale may well reflect the underlying structure of the attitude, but will make it difficult to interpret cumulative scores.

Approaches to determining the structure of attitudes fall into two broad categories (Lemon, 1973): *phenomenological* – such as repertory grid technique (see below p. 287); and *mathematical* – as in factor and cluster analysis (see chapter 11). The Guttman approach (Guttman, 1944) overcomes this complexity by seeking to develop a unidimensional scale.

In this type of scale, items have a cumulative property. They are chosen and ordered so that a person who accepts (agrees with) a particular item will also accept all previous items. An analogy is sometimes made with high-jumping. If someone has cleared the bar at 2 metres, we can be confident that she would also do so at 1.8 metres, 1.60, 1.40, 1.20 etc. Box 9.10 summarizes the steps needed to develop a Guttman scale and box 9.11 shows how the analysis is carried out. Additional details can be found in Lemon (1973); Scott (1968); and Dawes and Smith (1985).

Box 9.10   Developing a cumulated (Guttman) scale

1   *Collect a large number of apparently relevant and usable state-ments*. The approach is the same as with the Thurstone scale.

2   *Administer the statements to a standardization group*. Members of the group have to answer in a yes/no (agree/disagree) fashion.

3   *Carry out a scalogram analysis of the standardization group's re-sponses*. This involves attempting to arrange the responses into the 'best' triangular shape – as demonstrated in box 9.11.

4   *Apply the scale to respondents*. The attitude measure is usually the total number of items accepted or agreed to.

Box 9.11   Guttman's scalogram analysis – example

In practice, the analysis will be based on a substantially greater number of items and subjects in the standardization group than those included here. The principles are the same.

1   *List items and subjects in order of the total number of 'agrees'* (x = agrees; o = disagrees).

Subject	3	6	7	1	9	8	10	2	5	4	Total for item
Item 5	x	x	x	x	x	x	x	x	x	x	10
Item 7	o	x	x	x	x	x	x	x	x	x	9
Item 8	o	o	x	o	x	x	x	x	x	x	7
Item 9	o	x	o	x	x	x	x	x	x	x	7
Item 12	o	o	x	x	o	x	x	x	x	x	7
Item 1	o	o	o	o	x	x	x	x	x	x	6

Item 15	o	o	o	x	o	x	x	o	x	x	5
Item 2	o	o	o	o	x	o	x	x	x	x	5
Item 11	o	o	o	o	x	o	o	x	x	x	5
Item 6	o	x	o	o	o	o	o	x	o	x	3
Item 14	o	o	o	o	o	o	o	x	x	x	3
Item 10	o	o	o	x	o	o	o	o	o	x	2
Item 3	o	o	o	o	o	o	o	o	x	x	2
Item 4	o	o	o	o	o	x	o	o	o	o	1
Item 13	o	o	o	o	o	o	o	o	o	x	1
Total for subject	1	4	4	6	7	8	8	10	11	13	

2 Select those items which give the closest approximation to a triangular shape, i.e. to this pattern:

```
x  x  x  x  x
o  x  x  x  x
o  o  x  x  x
o  o  o  x  x
o  o  o  o  x
o  o  o  o  o
```

This will involve some trial and error, and possible reorderings of the columns (i.e. the subjects) when rows are removed.

Subject	3	6	7	1	8	10	9	2	5	4	Total
Item 5	x	x	x	x	x	x	x	x	x	x	10
Item 7	o	x	x	x	x	x	x	x	x	x	9
Item 8	o	x	o	x	x	x	x	x	x	x	8
Item 9	o	o	x	o	x	x	x	x	x	x	7
Item 1	o	o	o	o	x	x	x	x	x	x	6
Item 2	o	o	o	o	o	x	x	x	x	x	5
Item 11	o	o	o	o	o	o	x	x	x	x	4
Item 14	o	o	o	o	o	o	o	x	x	x	3
Item 3	o	o	o	o	o	o	o	o	x	x	2
Item 13	o	o	o	o	o	o	o	o	o	x	1
Total for subject	1	3	3	3	5	6	7	7	9	10	

3 Assess the reproducibility of the responses (i.e. the extent to which the subjects' pattern of responses is predictable from their total score.

This amounts to the same thing as the divergence from the perfect triangular shape. Guttman proposes a 'coefficient of reproducibility' which he suggests should be at least 0.9 if the scale is to be used. The coefficient $R = 1 - e/nk$, where

e = number of errors,
n = number of respondents, and
k = number of items.

In the example, there are 2 errors (both with subject 7; with a score of 3 the subject would have been expected to agree with item 8 and disagree with item 9). Hence $R = 1 - 2/100 = 0.98$.

4 *Administer the test to a fresh set of respondents and replicate the results to an acceptable degree of reproducibility.* This step is important (and unfortunately often omitted) as the initial selection of a relatively small set of items from a long list will inevitably capitalize on chance to some extent. It may be necessary to incorporate substitute items at this stage,which then necessitates further replication.

There are obvious attractions in the simplicity of a scale which gives a unidimensional assessment of attitude, so that one feels that the score obtained gives much firmer ground for subsequent interpretation and analysis than the multidimensional complexity of the other approaches we have discussed. The other side of this is that it is best adapted to measuring a well defined and clear-cut dimension, so that items reflecting unidimensionality can be generated without undue difficulty.

Semantic Differential Scales

A widely used type of scale, the *semantic differential scale* (Osgood et al., 1957) takes a very different approach. It is concerned with assessing the subjective meaning of a concept to the respondent, instead of assessing how much they believe in a particular concept. The scale is designed to explore the ratings given along a series of bipolar rating scales (e.g. bad/good; boring/exciting). Factor analyses have shown that such ratings typically group together into three underlying dimensions – activity, evaluation, and potency. In this sense it provides a kind of attitude scale.

ACTIVITY refers to the extent to which the concept is associated with action (dimensions might be 'fast', 'active', 'exciting', etc.). EVALUATION refers to the overall positive meaning associated with it ('positive', 'honest', 'dependable', etc.). POTENCY refers to its overall strength or importance ('strong', 'valuable', 'useful', etc.). A list of appropriate adjective pairs is generated for the particular concept you are trying to measure. However, broadly similar lists can be used in many contexts. Sources of lists include

Osgood et al. (1957) and Valois and Godin (1991). Box 9.12 gives an example of a semantic differential scale.

Box 9.12   Example of a semantic differential scale

Instructions: for each pair of adjectives place a cross at the point between them which reflects the extent to which you believe the adjectives describe policemen.

clean :	:	:	:	:	:	:	: dirty
honest :	:	:	:	:	:	:	: dishonest
kind :	:	:	:	:	:	:	: cruel
helpful :	:	:	:	:	:	:	: unhelpful
fair :	:	:	:	:	:	:	: biassed
delicate :	:	:	:	:	:	:	: rugged
strong :	:	:	:	:	:	:	: weak
stupid :	:	:	:	:	:	:	: intelligent
unreliable :	:	:	:	:	:	:	: reliable
heavy :	:	:	:	:	:	:	: light
foolish :	:	:	:	:	:	:	: wise
passive :	:	:	:	:	:	:	: active
energetic :	:	:	:	:	:	:	: lazy
boring :	:	:	:	:	:	:	: exciting
valuable :	:	:	:	:	:	:	: useless
impulsive :	:	:	:	:	:	:	: deliberate

Using the scale   The scale is administered to the chosen sample of respondents in a standard fashion. It is scored simply by summing the ratings given to each adjective pair on a 1–7 scale (or whatever the number of alternatives have been given). Average ratings can be computed, and comparisons between sub-groups in the sample are feasible. To take it further, it is necessary to carry out a factor analysis (see p. 349) to assess the relationship of the different adjective pairs, and link them to the evaluative dimensions.

Other Scaling Techniques

There are several other possibilities, including the following.

Q-sorts   A technique used to measure the relative position or ranking of an individual on a range of concepts. Stephenson (1980) describes an example where a four-year-old girl was asked to sort a number of postcard pictures of other little girls. The sorting is done successively on different criteria, e.g. 'most like me'; 'like me according to my mother'; 'like me according to my teacher', etc. The technique has been most often used with individuals or with small numbers, as the analysis becomes extremely complex with large numbers (see also Stephenson, 1953).

Sociometric scales   A technique used to describe relationships between individuals in a group. In its simplest form, it requires members of a group to make choices among other members of a group (e.g. whom they like). It is a versatile technique and has been used with groups ranging from pre-school children to prisoners. The technique is straightforward and results can be displayed in the form of 'sociograms' which give a diagrammatic representation of the choices made. Dane (1990, pp. 282–5) gives a simple introduction.

A Note on Psychometric Testing and Assessment

The development of tests for assessing some aspect or other of human functioning is a complex and burgeoning enterprise. It could well be that a useful measure in a study is provided by scores on an attainment test (e.g. in relation to reading) or that other indices (such as scores on a test of intelligence) provide valuable supplementary evidence. Considerable use is also made of tests seeking to assess aspects of personality, such as the Eysenck Personality Questionnaire (EPQ), Minnesota Multiphasic Personality Inventory (MMPI), and Sixteen Personality Factor test (16PF).

It is crucial that any such tests are professionally competent. One way to achieve this is by picking an existing test 'off the shelf'. The prime source of information on existing British and American tests is the series known as the *Buros Mental Measurement Yearbooks* (see for example Buros, 1978). These are five-yearly publications detailing available tests, with information extracted from their manuals, reviews and references to papers and theses in which they have been used. If a test appears to be suitable you can then send off for the test and its associated manual. This will give details on the reliability and validity of the test, and the test norms (i.e. the results of standardizing the test by using it with a given sample, so that you have a comparative base-line to assist in interpeting the scores you obtain).

Kline (1990) provides a useful set of suggestions for 'selecting the best test'. Many tests are now available in a computer-based version (French, 1990) which can cover both the administration of the test and its analysis. Beaumont and French (1987) discuss a range of these, including verbal and non-verbal IQ, personality and aptitude tests. It is unlikely to be cost-effective for you to tool up to use a computer-assisted test for a small one-off enquiry, but there may be opportunities for making use of facilities developed for other purposes. It should also be borne in mind that tests with a cumbersome or complex scoring procedure which has previously inhibited their use (such as the MMPI) become much more feasible with computer analysis.

An alternative is, of course, to develop your own test. My advice is – don't; unless you already possess skills and expertise in this area, and are prepared to devote considerable time and resources to the exercise. Rust and

Golombok (1989, ch. 10) provide an excellent guide to the main stages of test construction, and show how to tailor it for specific purposes.

The middle way is to change an existing instrument so that it better fits your needs. This is preferable to starting from scratch, but you should remember that the existing reliability, validity and norms will not then apply, and will have to be re-established. If the material is copyright, modification will require the permission of the copyright holder. The easiest and most common modification is to shorten the test by omitting items. If data are available from the original development of the test, it may be possible to use them to re-establish validity and reliability. You may alternatively wish to change the response options (e.g. from seven to five alternatives, perhaps to fit in with other questionnaire items). Changes of question wording are tricky, because of major effects apparently minor changes can have on responding, but there may be justification in moving from general questions to more specific ones or in modifying a test targeted for one professional group to be appropriate for a different one. In this connection, the use of a sample very different from the one on which the test was standardized will call for new validation of the test.

Tests and Scales Based on Observation rather than Self-Report

It may have occurred to you that we have dealt here with a very similar agenda of issues to those faced in the development of a structured direct observation instrument (p. 212). There are very considerable overlaps. In a self-report situation, the respondent is effectively acting as an observer of her own behaviour. Direct observation reduces potential biases and distortions arising from this process, but it is obviously limited to those things that can be directly observed. Thoughts and feelings, beliefs and attitudes need self-report. Low-frequency and private behaviours are best approached in this way as they would be expensive and obtrusive to observe directly. The next chapter discusses an alternative, complementary tactic, focusing on so-called 'unobtrusive measures' which provide *indirect* evidence about what has occurred.

Further Reading

Interviews and Questionnaires

Burgess, R. G. (1984) *In The Field: an introduction to field research*. London: Allen & Unwin. Chapter on 'Interviews as Conversations' (unstructured interviews).
Hoinville, G., Jowell, R. et al. (1977) *Survey Research Practice*. London: Heinemann. (Later reprints, Aldershot: Gower). Wealth of practical information on design and construction of structured instruments. Sections on sampling, interviewing, organizing fieldwork, postal surveys, and data preparation.

Moser, C. A. and Kalton, G. (1971) *Survey Methods in Social Investigation*. Aldershot: Gower. Enduring text with detailed sections on interviewing and questionnaires.

Payne, S. L. (1951) *The Art of Asking Questions*. Princeton, NJ: Princeton University Press (paperback 1980). Engaging and witty classic which will sensitize you to the problems in wording questions.

Powney, J. and Watts, M. (1987) *Interviewing in Educational Research*. London: Routledge & Kegan Paul. Covers both practical and theoretical issues on interviewing. Relevant to social science generally. Six detailed case studies included ranging from large- to small-scale. Useful guidelines. Strong on transcription, logging, analysis and reporting of interview data.

Walker, R. (ed.) (1985). *Applied Qualitative Research*. Aldershot: Gower. Useful chapters by Jones on 'Depth Interviewing' and 'The Analysis of Depth Interviews'; and by Hedges on 'Group Interviewing'.

Scales and Tests

Beech, J. R. and Harding, L. (eds) (1990) *Testing People: a practical guide to psychometrics*. Windsor: NFER-Nelson. Straightforward introduction to the statistical basis for tests, with guide to the production of your own test.

Hersen, M. and Bellack, M. S. (eds) (1981) *Behavioral Assessment: a practical handbook*, 2nd edn. Oxford: Pergamon. Wide-ranging compendium of assessment techniques.

Lemon, N. (1973) *Attitudes and their Measurement*. London: Batsford. Detailed exposition of the issues and practicalities in measuring attitudes.

Moser, C. A. and Kalton, G. (1971) *Survey Methods in Social Investigation*. Aldershot: Gower. Succinct and lucid exposition of the different types of scale.

Mueller, D. J. (1986) *Measuring Social Attitudes*. New York: Teachers College Press. Straightforward introduction to the use of different scaling methods with useful examples.

Oppenheim, A. N. (1966) *Questionnaire Design and Attitude Measurement*. New York: Basic. Very clear presentation of the logic and skills of scale construction.

Powell, G. E. (1989) Selecting and Developing Measures. In G. Parry and F. N. Watts (eds) *Behavioural and Mental Health Research: a handbook of skills and methods*. Hillsdale, NJ: Laurence Erlbaum Associates. Good concise introduction to measurement and scales, with clear discussion of their reliability, validity and generalizability.

Rust, J. and Golombok, S. (1989) *Modern Psychometrics: the science of psychological assessment*. London: Routledge. Up-to-date introduction. Includes practical step-by-step guide to the development of a test.

10

Unobtrusive Measures and Other Approaches

The chapter focuses on unobtrusive measures, including documentary analysis and the use of data archives.

There is a brief review of other approaches including role-play, language studies, repertory grids, meta-analysis and feminist research methods.

The chapter concludes by reasserting the value of multiple methods in an enquiry.

Introduction

Apart from direct observation and self-report methods, there is one major group of methods known variously as *unobtrusive measures* or *indirect observation*; this also includes *documentary*, *content* and *archival analyses*. Although extensively used in specific fields, they are relatively neglected approaches in many areas of investigation. This may be due to ignorance or, more charitably, to an appreciation of their serious drawbacks when they are used as the sole method of investigation. They do appear, though, to have considerable general usefulness when conceptualized as a complement to the use of other methods.

The opportunity is taken, later in the chapter, to give a brief introduction to a range of other methods and techniques which might merit consideration in some studies. No attempt is made to give sufficient detail for a practical use of the techniques, but appropriate references are provided for each of them. The chapter, and hence part III covering methods, concludes with a discussion of some of the practicalities, advantages and problems in carrying out multi-method studies.

Trace Measures

We are becoming increasingly conscious of the effects that humans have on their environment, particularly in relation to pollution: 'ozone holes', radioactive waste and so on. One particular class of such effects covers the artefacts that people make and leave behind them; things created 'on purpose', ranging in time from prehistoric cave paintings, through medieval cathedrals to styrofoam containers for take-away pizzas. There is a general case to be made that humans reveal something of themselves through such productions; that such things contain clues about the nature of society's lifestyles.

Whether unintended outcome or intentional creation, the 'things' that people produce provide opportunities for the real world enquirer. Eugene Webb and his colleagues (Webb et al., 1966; 1981) have sensitized social scientists to a wide range of what they term 'unobtrusive measures': that is, of things which might, through ingenuity and inference, be considered as indices of some aspect of human behaviour. Their most often-quoted example is of the floor tiles around the hatching-chick exhibit at Chicago's Museum of Science and Industry which needed replacing at six-weekly intervals, while tiles in other parts of the museum did not need to be replaced for years. This 'selective erosion' provided an index of the relative popularity of exhibits.

Webb and colleagues distinguished between such 'erosion' measures and 'accretion' measures. The latter, for example, might be counting empty spirit bottles in rubbish bins as a measure of the level of home consumption of alcohol in a town that was officially 'dry'. Both types are TRACE MEASURES – the physical effects of interaction which remain after that interaction. They are sometimes referred to as 'behavioural by-products' (Barlow et al., 1984). For example, weight as a by-product of eating has been used as a measure in studies of obesity (Mahoney et al., 1973).

Accretion Measures

Accretion is something extra or added; the build-up of a product or residue. Apart from analyses of different types of garbage – particularly popular with archaeologists but less so with social scientists (could it be to do with the stench dissipating over time?) – examples include litter and graffiti. Litter has been used as an index of usage patterns in public places. Graffiti have been related to territoriality; for example in areas of Belfast. Usage is a popular focus for accretion measures – the number of date stamps in a library book; or mileage logged by a car or van; or persons through a turnstile. However, some evidence on virtually any phenomenon is there for the taking. Looking at the 'internal mail' envelopes that have just landed on my desk, with their sequentially completed and crossed out addressees in

---

Box 10.1 Advantages and disadvantages of 'trace' measures

Advantages

1 They are unobtrusive and non-reactive. That is, the enquirer does not need to be in direct contact with the person(s) producing the trace, and hence there is no reason why the behaviour should be influenced by the enquiry.

2 They can provide valuable cross-validation of other measures, either in support or disconfirmation of them.

3 They encourage ingenuity and creativity on the part of the enquirer.

Disadvantages

1 The person(s) responsible for the trace and/or the population from which they come may be difficult or impossible to specify.

2 Similarly, it may not be reasonable to assume that all persons involved make equivalent contributions to the trace (a single person may make a substantial contribution through repetitive involvement).

3 Apparent link between cause and effect (e.g. usage and trace) may be mediated by other factors (e.g. softness of ground).

4 Ethical difficulties of researching without people's knowledge or consent (likely to depend on the case – a study of whisky bottles or letters in rubbish bins is more dubious than footpath wear patterns).

---

their little boxes on the envelopes, suggests a potential tool for getting at communication patterns within my institution.

Erosion Measures

Erosion refers to deterioration or wear; something being worn down or removed totally. Again usage is the most obvious focus, with wear giving measures of interaction patterns, relative popularities, etc.

Box 10.1 lists some advantages and disadvantages of 'trace' measures. It is probably a fair assessment that physical trace measures have only a small part to play in research involving humans; certainly few psychologists or other social scientists have made serious use of them to date. They do have, though, a strong potential contribution to a multiple method approach. Looked at in this light many of their disadvantages dissolve, and their non-reactivity can provide useful validation for other, more central methods.

Using Documents

Although the use of physical trace measures has never achieved much more than curiosity value in the social sciences, there has been particular interest in the use of a particular kind of artefact: the *document*. By this is meant, primarily, the written document, whether this be a book, newspaper or magazine, notice, letter or whatever, although the term is sometimes extended to include non-written documents such as films and television programmes, pictures, drawings and photographs.

This *documentary analysis* is commonly referred to as CONTENT ANALYSIS. It differs from the techniques that we have considered so far in that it is *indirect rather than direct*. Instead of directly observing, or interviewing, or asking someone to fill in a questionnaire for the purposes of our enquiry, we are dealing with something produced for some other purpose.

This is an example of an *unobtrusive measure* (see following section); that is, the nature of the document is not affected by the fact that you are using it for the enquiry. Another way of saying the same thing is to refer to it as *non-reactive*. There are exceptions. You may be asking respondents to fill in diaries or some other account for your project, and these may well be amenable to content analysis. In this case it is not an unobtrusive technique. The fact that a person is filling in a diary for the project may in some way alter their behaviour; in other words, there is a possible reactive effect.

Content analysis has been defined in various ways. Krippendorff's (1980) definition, that 'content analysis is a research technique for making replicable and valid inferences from data to their context' (p. 21), while perhaps over-inclusive in not making clear that we are dealing with certain kinds of data (those coming from documents of various kinds), does have the virtue of stressing the relationship between content and context. This context includes the *purpose* of the document as well as institutional, social and cultural aspects. It also emphasizes that reliability and validity are central concerns in content analysis.

It is possible to do other things with documents over and above analysing their contents. Such approaches, for example focusing on the authenticity of the document, or the intentions of the writer, are derived from the methods of historians. They are essentially concerned with the problems of selection and evaluation of evidence (see Barzun and Graff, 1977; Marwick, 1970). Barzun and Graff provide a view of research from the perspective of the historian which constitutes a very valuable extension to the methodological education of any psychologist.

The checklist of criteria suggested by Gottschalk et al. (1945), in relation to the use of personal documents in history, anthropology and sociology, covers important concerns relevant to the accuracy of all documents:

1. Was the ultimate source of the detail (the primary witness) *able* to tell the truth?
2. Was the primary witness *willing* to tell the truth?
3. Is the primary witness *accurately reported* with regard to the detail under examination?
4. Is there any *external corroboration* of the detail under examination? (p. 35)

Content analysis is in several senses akin to structured observation. This similarity is particularly evident when structured observation is carried out on a recording of the situation observed. A video-recording of such a session appears to be a very similar kind of artefact to, say, a video-recording of a television programme. The main difference is that in the former case the intention is to obtain a closely equivalent picture to that which the 'live' observer would have seen in the situation. Selectivity of focus and direction will be made with the needs of the observer in mind. The edited picture making up the TV programme appears under the direction of the pro-gramme maker who has her own agenda, which is unlikely to include the needs of the content analyst.

This illustrates a general problem in content analysis. The material to be analysed is not only unstructured, or at least not structured with the needs of the observer in mind; it will in general be a document with a purpose. And that purpose is important in understanding and interpreting the results of the analysis. A distinction is sometimes made in documentary analysis between *witting* and *unwitting* evidence. Witting evidence is that which the author intended to impart. Unwitting evidence is everything else that can be gleaned from the document.

Uses of Content Analysis

Content analysis came to prominence in the social sciences at the start of the twentieth century, in a series of quantitative analyses of newspapers, prim-arily in the United States. In a debate prefiguring current concerns in this country about the tabloid press, campaigns against 'cheap yellow journal-ism' were bolstered by statistical studies showing how 'worthwhile' news items were being increasingly dropped in favour of gossip, sports and scan-dals (Krippendorff, 1980, pp. 13–15 provides details). This type of content analysis was subsequently extended to radio, and then to television, and continues unabated in, for example, studies of advertising, and of porno-graphy and violence in the media.

Similar studies have attempted to assess bias in school textbooks, and the depiction of favourable or unfavourable attitudes to blacks, females and homosexuals both in texts and other publications. While the main interest has probably continued to be in the field of mass communications, content analysis has more recently been used in a wide variety of psychological and sociological areas. In particular, the approach discussed here can be readily adapted for use in the analysis of qualitative interview and questionnaire data (e.g. in the coding of open-ended questions in surveys) and of direct observation (typically through coding of tapes and transcripts).

Documents themselves cover a very wide range, including for example:

minutes of meetings;
letters, memoranda, etc.;
diaries;
speeches;
newspapers and magazine articles.

Particular contexts generate specific types of document. Studies involving schools or other educational establishments might include:

written curricula;
course outlines and other course documents;
timetables;
notices;
letters and other communications to parents.

Remember also that 'document' is taken to include such non-written forms as:

films;
television programmes;
comic strips and cartoons;
photographs.

These require somewhat different approaches to analysis from those discussed below, although the basic principles remain the same (see Fetterman, 1989; and Walker and Adelman, 1975, specifically on using photographs).

The main focus here is on the use of content analysis as a secondary or supplementary method in a multi-method study. This does not preclude carrying out a study based solely on content analysis, but there are substantial difficulties and deficiencies (see box 10.3 below on 'Advantages and Disadvantages of Content Analysis'). On the other hand, it is often possible to 'acquire' copies of documents of a variety of types in conjunction with interviews and observations which may be used for triangulation purposes, or to provide something of a longitudinal dimension to a study when a sequence of documents is available extending back in time.

How to Carry Out a Content Analysis

As with virtually all the techniques covered in this text, content analysis is 'codified common sense': a refinement of ways that might be used by lay persons to describe and explain aspects of the world about them.

1 *Start with a research question* Once again, the effective starting point for the process is the research question. Perhaps 'Is there a greater emphasis on sex and violence in the mass media now that there was ten years ago?' A different research question might derive from the comment, commonly heard in listeners' responses to radio programmes, that there is political bias in radio programmes. For example, the BBC Radio 4 *Today* programme seems particularly adept at generating near apoplexy in right-wing listeners. Note here that, while the communication here is initially 'on the air', in practice any study of the programme's content will be likely to be based on a transcript of what is heard. It may be, however, that an audio-tape will also be helpful, enabling you to judge from intonation whether a particular comment is to be taken in a sarcastic or ironic sense.

There may be occasions when you have documents but no properly formulated notion of what you are looking for. In many methodology texts, this so-called 'fishing trip' is severely frowned on, e.g. for example: 'content analysis cannot be used to probe around a mass of documents in the hope that a bright idea will be suggested by probing. Content analysis gets the answers to the question to which it is applied' (Carney, 1973, p. 284). However, in the general spirit of 'exploratory data analysis' which is advocated in this text (Tukey, 1977; Marsh, 1988), this prohibition on 'fishing' appears unnecessarily limiting. Obviously, the choice of data is justified by what you want to know: but to suggest that there is a difference in value between the research of one enquirer who starts out with the question, and that of another who gets the idea for the question from peeking at the data, verges on the metaphysical. Either we have good evidence about the question from the data, or we haven't.

2 *Decide on a sampling strategy* It is usually necessary to reduce your task to manageable dimensions by *sampling* from the population of interest. General principles of sampling apply, as discussed in chapter 5. Thus, in the case of the *Today* programme, it might be considered appropriate to take a random sample of, say, twenty programmes from those transmitted over a three-month period. Or, possibly, some form of stratification might be considered – perhaps ensuring that all presenters of the programme are equally represented in the sample. A different approach would be to have as one's sample all the programmes transmitted over an extended period, but to focus, from the point of view of the analysis, on a small part of the content, say, on references to a particular incident or type of incident.

There may be situations where the relevant documents are so rare or difficult to get hold of that sampling in this sense is inappropriate.

3 *Define the recording unit* In addition to deciding on categories, it is necessary to select a *recording unit*. The unit most commonly used is probably the *individual word*. In the simplest version, all occurrences of the word would be treated as equal, and counts of them made and compared. A somewhat more sophisticated approach would differentiate between the different senses of words that have multiple meanings (e.g. 'right' as 'correct'; or as 'non-left') and code phrases constituting a semantic unit (e.g. 'ice cream' or 'Houses of Parliament'). It is also common to use *themes, characters* (i.e. the actors or individuals mentioned in the document, as in the analysis of the fiction example in box 10.2 below), *paragraphs* or *whole items* as the recording unit.

Other possibilities suggest themselves for particular tasks. For example, when analysing newspaper or magazine content these might be:

number of stories on a topic;
column inches;
size of headline;
number of stories on a page;
position of stories within the page or paper as a whole;
number and/or type of pictures;

and so on. For some purposes, it may be necessary to examine the *context* in which a recording unit is set in order to categorize it. Although you may have fixed on the word as recording unit, if you are interested in coding whether a treatment is positive or negative, favourable or unfavourable, it is likely that you will have to take into account the sentence in which the word appears.

There is some argument in content analysis circles about the degree of inference which coders should be called upon to make when categorizing items. This is sometimes expressed in terms of *manifest* and *latent* content, corresponding essentially to low- and high-inference items respectively. Manifest items are those which are physically present (e.g. a particular word); latent content is a matter of inference or interpretation on the part of the coder. At its simplest this may just require a judgment of warmth, favourableness etc., but some might require use of a complex personality typology. As with other techniques of data collection, it is obviously likely to be more straightforward to achieve reliable results with low-inference systems. However the research question should determine the type of system you are using, and it may well be that a high-inference system is appropriate. This then puts greater stress on ensuring that you can demonstrate reliability through the use of independent coders, or by some other means such as triangulating with data obtained through other sources.

4 *Construct categories for analysis* It is difficult to give helpful general comments here, as there is such a wide range of possible types of research question for which content analysis might be used. Holsti (1969) lists several types of categories. Thus, in looking at what is said in the document, categories might be concerned with: –

subject matter	what is it about?
direction	how is it treated, e.g. favourably or not?
values	what values are revealed?
goals	what goals or intentions are revealed?
methods	what methods are used to achieve these intentions?
traits	what are the characteristics used in describing people?
actors	who is represented as carrying out the actions referred to?
authority	in whose name are statements made?
location	where does the action take place?
conflict	what are the sources and levels of conflict?
endings	in what way are conflicts resolved (e.g. happily)?

As with structured observation systems, it is highly desirable that these categories are *exhaustive* and *mutually exclusive*. The former ensures that everything relevant to the study can be categorized (even if you have to resort to a 'dump' category for things that you don't know how to deal with). The latter means that anything to be analysed can only be categorized in one way; if it is categorized in one particular way it can't also be categorized as something else.

The categories also have to be *operationalized*: that is, an explicit specification has to be made of what indicators one is looking for when making each and any of the categorizations. *Sorting Out The Categories is the Most Crucial Aspect of The Content Analysis.* As Berelson (1952) points out, 'since the categories contain the substance of the investigation, a content analysis can be no better than its system of categories'. Box 10.2 gives examples of category systems.

Box 10.2   Examples of category systems

1   To answer questions about characteristics of heroines in fiction targeted at adolescents

physical characteristics
   height
   weight
   'vital statistics'
   age

    hair colour
    eye colour (etc.)
social characteristics
    ethnic background
    socio-economic class
    occupation
    housing
    income
    religion (etc.)
emotional characteristics
    warm
    aloof
    stable
    anxious
    hostile (etc.)

2   To answer questions on trends in contents of newspapers

domestic news
    political
    ecological
    crime
    transport (etc.)
foreign news
    European
    American
    Russian
    Chinese
    Third World (etc.)
cultural
    music
    theatre
    art
    opera (etc.)

sport
business and financial
television and radio
children's and young people's items
women's items
cartoons
advertisements (etc.)

(All of the above could be sub-categorized.)

5   *Test the coding on samples of text and assess reliability*   This is the best test of the clarity and lack of ambiguity of your category definitions. It is highly likely that this process will lead to the revision of your scheme. With human (as against computer) coding, at least two persons should be involved at this stage. When the scheme appears workable, tests of reliability should be made (these are formally equivalent to the tests carried out when assessing the inter-observer agreement of structured observation schedules – see chapter eight, page 221). If the reliability is low, further practice is necessary and it may also be necessary to revise the coding rules. The process should be repeated until the reliability is acceptable. If computer coding has been used, it is necessary to check for errors in computer procedures (see p. 311).

6   *Carry out the analysis*   In formal terms, the analysis is equivalent to the set of activities you carry out when using and analysing a structured observation schedule. The statistical analysis of the data obtained can follow exploratory data analysis procedures or more conventional hypothesis testing approaches (see chapter 11). The most common approach is to relate variables from the content analysis to other 'outside' variables (e.g. gender of the persons producing the documents; or type of school from which they come). More complex procedures involve the use of factor analysis, as either an exploratory or a confirmatory tool, to identify themes in texts; and the subsequent use of techniques such as analysis of variance to outside variables.

Box 10.3 lists advantages and disadvantages of content analysis.

Computers and content analysis

Content analysis can be extremely laborious and time-consuming. It is a field where computerization has led to substantial benefits. Analyses which would have been beyond the resources of small-scale research can now be completed routinely given access to a reasonably powerful microcomputer and specialized software. The text can be easily manipulated and displayed in various ways (e.g. showing all sentences, or other units, containing a particular word or phrase). The availability of optical character recognition (OCR) devices can transform a document directly into a computer file without the necessity for typing.

A major methodological advantage of computer-aided content analysis is that the rules for coding the text have to be made completely explicit, or the computer will not be able to carry out the task. Once these rules have been established and written into the software (itself no mean task) then it is possible to work through a range of documents and achieve results which are formally compatible with each other. At the same time, once the development stage has been completed, and any 'bugs' removed from the

---

Box 10.3   Advantages and disadvantages of content analysis

Advantages

a It is an 'unobtrusive' measure (Webb et al., 1966). You can 'observe' without being observed.

b The data are in permanent form and hence can be subject to re-analysis, allowing reliability checks and replication studies.

c It may provide a 'low cost' form of longitudinal analysis when a 'run' or series of documents of a particular type is available.

Disadvantages

a The documents available may be limited or partial.

b The documents have been written for some purpose other than for the research, and it is difficult or impossible to allow for the biases or distortions that this introduces (note need for triangulation with other accounts, data sources to address this problem).

c As with other non-experimental approaches, it is very difficult to assess causal relationships. Are the documents causes of the social phenomena you are interested in, or reflections of them (e.g. in relation to pornography and/or violence in the mass media)?

---

system, the computer provides perfect coder reliability in applying the rules built in to the program.

This does not mean that all problems have been solved. Little matters of validity, interpetation and explanation remain. You also still face the inescapable fact that content analysis is concerned with *data reduction*. You throw away much of the information in a document to see the wood for the trees. Weber (1985) provides a good review of ways in which the computer can help in carrying out content analysis and these related ground clearing tasks. Box 10.4 highlights some of these approaches.

More complex multivariate data analysis techniques are also facilitated by using computers. Weber (1985, pp. 58–64) presents an extended analysis and interpretation of an example using factor analysis. However, he stresses the need to return to the document to validate the interpretation of themes derived from such statistical results.

Box 10.4   Computer aids to content analysis

1   *Key-word-in-context (KWIC) list*   Provides a list of contexts in which any selected 'key word' appears. This would give the location of each use of the key word and, say, the ten preceding and ten following words. KWIC lists are equivalent to *concordances*, which are much used in literary analysis and biblical study. They sensitize the analyst to variations in use and meaning of particular words, possibly suggesting the need to separate out different uses in the content analysis. They similarly draw attention to phrases or idioms which might be dealt with as separate units.

2   *Word frequency list*   Provides lists of words in the document, or-dered according to the number of times that they appear; together with the frequencies themselves. Usually the (say) twenty highest-frequency words are listed. Specific words such as 'a', 'an', 'the', 'is', 'are', etc. can be omitted. Can be used for comparative purposes with different documents, but needs treating with care. For example, use of pronouns and synonyms can decrease apparent frequencies; lumping together the different meanings of a word increases them. More sophisticated pro-grams can 'disambiguate' such meanings through syntactical and other cues.

3   *Category counts*   Providing the rules can be fully and explicitly specified, there is no problem in the computer moving from word counts to category counts, which is the central activity in content analysis. Although more complex approaches can be used, comparison of simple percentages of use is often all that is needed.

4   *Combined criteria list*   It is feasible not only to search documents for the occurrence of particular words or content analysis categories, but also to have more complex criteria for searching (e.g. for joint occurrences of two words or phrases in a sentence or passage). These are sometimes termed *collocations*. Such co-occurrences can be selected on the basis of research questions or hypotheses.

Note that these techniques can be used for any data in the form of written text. The computer doesn't mind if this comes from a docu-ment or the transcript of an interview.

Using Data Archives

An archive is simply a record, or set of records. Some records are in the form of documents containing text, as covered in the preceding section. Others may contain quantitative statistical information. Such archives share an important feature with the documents just discussed in that they have been produced for some other purpose than for your use as a researcher. They will have been collected and paid for by someone else (though there is also the possibility of revisiting a study you carried out previously, with a view to carrying out a different or extended analysis). The ten-yearly National Census is an archetypal example, but there are many recurrent and one-off surveys (e.g. the Current Population Survey, General Household Survey, British Social Attitude Survey, American General Social Survey, British Workplace Industrial Relations Survey, British Crime Survey, and others; Hakim, 1987, ch. 7, provides details).

Such data have clear advantages and disadvantages. It is possible to tap into extensive data sets, often drawn from large representative samples, well beyond the resources of the individual researcher. Recent data sets should have good documentation including full code-books describing the variables and codes that have been used, and easily accessible recording methods. National collections exist (e.g. the ESRC Data Archive maintained at the University of Essex). The ESRC (Economic and Social Research Council) has also, since 1984, been developing a Survey Link Scheme which enables researchers to participate in the formulation and execution of major British surveys carried out by central government and commercial agencies. The disadvantages flow from the fact that even those surveys carried out for research purposes are unlikely to be directly addressing the research question you are interested in.

It is, of course, perfectly possible to focus one's research solely on the *secondary analysis* of such data. This is defined by Hakim (1982) as 'any further analysis of an existing data set which presents interpretations, conclusions or knowledge additional to, or different from those presented in the first report' (p. 1). This can be an attractive strategy as it permits you to capitalize on the efforts of others in collecting the data. It has the advantage of allowing you to concentrate on analysis and interpretation. Baker (1988, pp. 254–60) discusses the issues involved and presents examples.

Archival research is not limited to the re-analysis of survey data. Bryman (1989, ch. 7) gives varied examples from the field of organization studies. A frequently quoted study is by Grusky (1963) who analysed the performance of sports teams in relation to turnover of personnel such as team coaches and managers. Later studies have followed related themes – in part, one suspects, because sports performance is an area where there is a surfeit of published statistical information.

Using Administrative Records and
Management Information Systems

Many small-scale real life studies involve in some way relating to an organization, such as an office, school or hospital. A feature they all have in common is the collection of records and other information relating to their function. Such records can form a valuable supplementary resource, and it is often possible to obtain access to them. (The usual ethical principles apply in relation to confidentiality, and there may be particular problems associated with information collected for one purpose being used for a different one.)

The records are, however, unlikely to provide direct answers to the questions we are interested in when carrying out research. Indeed, they may form a tempting distraction, with pages of descriptive statistics on individual measures, and cross-tabulations between measures, amassed to little or no purpose. Simply to know that there are 73 per cent of males on an innovatory programme, or that 23 per cent of the males and 48 per cent of the females are from low-income families, carries little meaning in its own right. The issue is, *what light can this information throw on our research questions?* We may be interested in answering questions on recently introduced crèche facilities, or different access arrangements, and this kind of routine data may in such circumstances be of direct value. Nevertheless, a thorough exploratory study of existing data may suggest questions, or act as a starting point for unforeseen lines of enquiry. It is well worth while spending a fair amount of time looking at and playing with data from record systems. Patterns may suggest themselves and trends emerge which had not previously occurred to you.

Typically it will be necessary to rearrange the data in various ways, so that, for example, you can compare data over different time periods. Your research questions assist in selecting from what can easily be a data mountain. If, as is increasingly the case, these routine systems have been computerized, your task *may* be simplified. It is, for example, usually relatively easy to provide suitably anonymized extracts from computer records. Previously it would have been necessary to go through filing cabinets and record cards to obtain the information you need. This has the possibility of introducing transcription errors, and may also require that the researchers have access to confidential or private records. Access to computer records should be subject to strict controls and any necessary clearances must be obtained. Remember, however, that there is no guarantee at all that the computer system designed to cope with routine data collection has the flexibility to deliver the comparisons or selections that you need.

Hakim (1987, ch. 4) discusses the design of studies based exclusively on administrative records. She makes the point that they have to be designed 'back to front'. That is, instead of designing the study and then collecting the data, the researcher starts by finding out what data are available in the set of records and then identifies a possible research model. The situation is rather different in a multi-method case study. If administrative records are available, they are examined to see what additional corroboration other light they can throw on the case. If they don't help with your research questions, then either don't use the administrative records, or consider whether it makes sense to modify what you are after in the light of what they can tell you.

Box 10.5 lists some issues to be taken into account when using administrative records from management information systems; box 10.6 gives an example of their use.

Box 10.5   Issues in using administrative records for research purposes

1 *The quality of the data must be assessed*   Generally, information central to the activities of an organization will be of better quality than more peripheral items. Check on what actually happens (e.g. are large batches of forms filled in cursorily long after the event?). Find the views of the persons entering the data. If they think that 'the yellow form always goes into the dustbin' (actual quotation from a social worker) then they are unlikely to fill them in conscientiously.

2 *Careful study of existing record systems may allow you to avoid unnecessary duplication in data collection*   Informants in studies are often busy people and it is highly desirable to minimize the extra load you put on them for the purposes of research. Even though an existing question may not be asking for exactly what you had in mind, it may provide you with a close enough approximation of the information you need. It is sometimes feasible to add temporary 'research' questions to standard administrative forms.

3 *Sampling from administrative records may well be needed*   A variety of approaches may be possible (e.g. time samples, sampling of individuals, sampling of items).

Note: As administrative records often give information on a rigidly defined set of topics over considerable periods of time, they lend themselves to some form of time series analysis (see chapter 11, p. 366).

Caputo (1988) and Bronson et al. (1988) provide useful background on the use of management information systems, covering theoretical and practical (including computer) aspects respectively.

Box 10.6 Example of the use of administrative records in an evaluation

The evaluation focused on the effects and effectiveness of a widely used training package on the use of behavioural techniques in the education of persons with severe learning difficulties (the EDY package; see Foxen and McBrien, 1981).

A main aspect of the evaluation involved a substantial postal survey of persons who had completed the course, and their instructors. The second main aspect involved a series of case studies of the use of the package in a range of different settings.

The instructors of persons who had successfully completed the course had been, since its inception, invited to send in a request form to the sponsoring institution. Providing their performance reached certain criteria they were then sent an official certificate. The request form incorporated useful information which was analysed as part of the evaluation. This included biographical and career information which established the representativeness of this sample in relation to the survey sample.

There were also indices of the trainees' performance at an early stage and on completion of the course. It was appreciated that the 'demand characteristics' of this situation on the instructors might lead to an under-reporting of the latter. Nevertheless, useful corroborative information was gained. For example, early high scores, in connection with some skills covered in the course, supported evidence from the case studies and assisted in framing recommendations for the revision of the course.

(*Source*: Robson et al., 1988.)

Brief Review of Additional Approaches

This section briefly covers some specialized techniques which may be worth considering for particular tasks. They could be fitted into the categories of direct observation, report and indirect observation covered previously but, for convenience, are brought together here.

Some of the approaches (e.g. repertory grids) are embedded within a theoretical view of the person and the world they live in, to the extent that it could be dangerous to view them as 'off-the-peg' techniques usable without buying into the theory. Others, while regarded by some commentators as methods of investigation, might be better thought of as different research strategies (e.g. action research or simulation/role-playing) or as analytic techniques (e.g. meta-analysis). In short, they are a mixed bag. They by no means exhaust the possibilities. Smith (cited in Rob Walker, 1985, pp. 60–6) presents a catalogue of thirty-eight distinct and different methods, with pen-picture and basic references.

Simulation and Role-playing

Simulations attempt to carry over the essential structural elements of some real world phenomenon into a relatively well controlled environment. They imitate the processes of a system to try to see how it works. Although some experiments in which a few variables are manipulated are sometimes thought of as simulations, the more common usage, following the work of Kurt Lewin in the 1930s (Lewin, 1952), tries to capture the whole of the pattern which is likely to involve a myriad of variables. The focus is on what happens when the phenomenon, one hopes with all its essential characteristics, is transposed to a controlled setting.

Suppose one is interested in the working of juries in legal cases. This is very difficult to examine in a real 'real life' setting which is not open to the investigator. Simulation of the jury room, and the task, is feasible – though much work in this field has been criticized because of its artificiality in following the experimental approach of manipulating single variables such as the attractiveness of the defendant.

Simulations commonly call for participants to play an explicit role. This calls attention to our expectations about how someone fulfilling a particular role will behave. As Harré and Secord (1972) put it, humans in social situations are 'rule-following agents'. A notorious example is the simulated prison cell block investigated by Zimbardo and his colleagues (Haney et al., 1973). Students were paid to role-play 'prisoners' and 'guards' under very realistic conditions. Prisoners, for example, were actually arrested by local police; handcuffed, searched, cautioned, etc. The study was terminated less than halfway through its planned duration because of the strong effects that it had on both prisoners (including extreme depression and anxiety) and guards (enjoyment of the power in their roles). Ethical criticisms are obvious, as well as the concern about the adequacy of the simulation in representing the reality of prison life. Note that this is a different issue from whether or not the participants take the situation seriously and are fully involved, which is a common problem in simulations. This feature can be employed with advantage when the simulation is used as a teaching tool, and in intervention studies where the intention is to modify behaviour.

Simulation can be viewed as an alternative research strategy (e.g. Kern, 1991), or as a means of implementing a case study, as it can involve different methods of investigation. The Zimbardo study, for example, used various checklists and personality tests, diaries, questionnaires and direct observation.

Suggested reading is provided at the end of the chapter.

Language Studies

A great deal of research based on humans, particularly approaches which generate qualitative data, focuses on language. There are, however, researchers interested in language as such – how it is used and with what consequences. To the outsider this might appear as a topic area rather than a method in itself, but it is claimed that it has such a central role in social life, that the study of language provides the key to understanding our social functioning. In these approaches it is not only the substance of what is said (which forms the basis for conventional analyses) that is important, but the styles and strategies of the language users – how they say things.

The term DISCOURSE ANALYSIS (sometimes CONVERSATIONAL ANALYSIS) is used, but unfortunately there is little agreement as to its usage. For some, it covers all research concerned with language in its social and cognitive context (van Dijk, 1985). Others focus on the variations in the use of language of different social groups (e.g. Milroy, 1980). The variants likely to be of greatest value in the type of enquiry covered in this text are not primarily linguistic but more social-psychological (e.g. Potter and Weatherell, 1987). Typically, they call for a very detailed analysis of small fragments of discourse and require a good understanding of the theoretical framework for the analysis.

Suggested reading is provided at the end of the chapter.

Repertory Grid Techniques

George Kelly proposed a theory of personality based on the notion of PERSONAL CONSTRUCTS (Kelly, 1970). Personal constructs are the dimensions we use to make sense of, and extend, our experience of the world. He views humans as effectively acting as scientists in their day-to-day activities, seeking to understand the course of events in which they are involved. We evaluate the phenomena making up our world through a limited number of constructs which we have found helpful in creating our personal view.

Kelly suggests that these personal constructs are bipolar (e.g. on a dimension from 'good' to 'bad'; or from 'makes me feel angry' to 'makes me feel pleased'). Repertory grid techniques are ways of eliciting these constructs and have been widely used, both by followers of Kelly and by others who simply find them useful. Kelly's use of the technique required a subject to complete a set of cards showing the names of a number of significant persons in their life (e.g. 'mother', 'best friend'). They were then asked to provide an important way in which two of the persons differed from the third – perhaps that two were 'kind' and one was 'cruel'. This was repeated several times to elicit a range of such constructs, which then constituted how that subject interpreted the behaviour of people important in her life.

A grid could then be constructed, displaying the matrix of constructs against 'elements' (persons).

Such grids have been used in clinical and counselling sessions and are finding their way into research studies. A current debate concerns how far it is necessary to stay with 'elicited' constructs which are necessarily idiosyncratic to the individual, and often difficult to deal with in research, or whether it is possible to work with 'provided' constructs. Although this seems to go against the basic tenet of the Kellian approach, it has been advocated by some of his followers (e.g. Bannister and Mair, 1968 – who do however point out the dangers of provided constructs).

A range of different types of grid has been developed. Approaches such as 'laddering', which look at the location of individual constructs within the overall construct system, have also been used. A tension can increasingly be detected between the technology of 'gridding' (for which several computer packages are now available) and the philosophical roots of Kelly's view of personality.

Suggested reading is provided at the end of the chapter.

Meta-analysis

Meta-analysis is a process used in summarizing the results of a number of different studies. It is an analysis of the analysis (hence a meta-analysis). It can be viewed as a method of doing research although it is more usually regarded as an analytic technique. It may be a sensible use of the time and resources of even a small-scale enquirer to put together findings from previous work in a heavily researched area, rather than carry out one more empirical study.

Meta-analysis should be distinguished from the *research review* (which has the more synoptic aim of putting together and evaluating different kinds of findings in a particular field of interest) and *secondary analysis* (concerned with extending the analysis of, or carrying out a different analysis on, existing data).

Most work has been carried out on the meta-analysis of quantitative studies, particularly of experiments. The aim here is to provide an integrated study of research results on a specific question, giving particular attention to the size of effects and to statistical significance. Rosenthal and Rubin's study, summarizing the first 345 studies on experimenter expectancy, provides a good example (Rosenthal and Rubin, 1978; 1980). Mullen et al. (1990) provide a smaller-scale example, analysing studies on the effects of obedient and disobedient models on jay-walking. Considering the large numbers of studies on such topics as the effects of psychotherapy on patients, or of class size on student learning, we should surely be reaching some overall conclusions – or perhaps the lack of any such conclusion will begin to throw serious doubt on the type of social research which has been carried out! Statistical methods have been developed which go beyond a simple summing of significant and non-significant results, although they do have quite restrictive assumptions. The technique is also reliant on material from all relevant studies being published and available. The bias in favour of positive results in the publication policies of some journals also causes problems. Finally, the quality of the studies included is obviously of importance – garbage in, garbage out!

Meta-analysis can also be used in conjunction with a literature review in order to assess the influence of different research designs and other methodological factors on results obtained by different studies in the same area (e.g. Crain and Mahard, 1983, on the effect of school desegregation on the educational achievements of black children).

Some attempts have been made to extend meta-analysis to studies incorporating qualitative data (e.g. Yin, 1989, pp. 123–4).

Suggested reading is provided at the end of the chapter.

Feminist Research Methods

Chapter 3 covered the contribution of feminist approaches to methodology (p. 000). There is a corresponding contribution at the level of methods. It has been argued that there are, or should be, specific feminist research methods (e.g. Roberts, 1981; see Clegg, 1985, for a dissenting voice). The view is that accepted ways of carrying out research (particularly positivistic, quantitative approaches) are dominated by males and miss many of the issues specific to women. Structured interviews are regarded as a form of exploitation arising from the differential relationship between the researcher and respondent, particularly when the former is male and the latter female (Oakley, 1981). Theories, which influence the way in which questions are framed, and data are collected and analysed, even if not inherently male, distort the experiences of women in the accounts that are collected. This is also taken as support for feminist research methods that are qualitative and non-positivist.

The stance taken in this book (p. 63), while not accepting the full feminist critique, is that there is considerable virtue for 'real world' research in taking on board feminist proposals – particularly in acknowledging the emotional aspects of such research and the value in emphasizing commitment as against detachment. Certainly qualitative approaches must not be eschewed. Whether such methods are best labelled as feminist is left to the reader.

Suggested reading is provided at the end of the chapter.

Using Multiple Methods

Even when the overall research strategy has been decided, a research question can, in almost all cases, be attacked by more than one method. As emphasized earlier, it is often the personal preferences of investigators, influenced by their past experiences, which dictate to them that they should use a particular strategy such as an experimental approach, or a survey. Similarly, specific methods may be selected simply because they are familiar. However, while there are questions for which, say, the structured interview seems the obvious tool to choose, it does not usually take much ingenuity to come up with a totally different approach which might be used.

There is no rule that says that only one method must be used in an investigation. Using more than one method in an investigation can have substantial advantages, even though it almost inevitably adds to the time investment required. One important benefit of multiple methods is in the *reduction of inappropriate certainty*. Using a single method and finding a pretty clear-cut result may delude investigators into believing that they have found the 'right' answer. Using other, additional, methods may point to differing answers which remove specious certainty. Unfortunately, such conflicting results across methods do add to confusion and uncertainty. Partisans of particular methods, or particular findings, may be convinced of the rightness of their opposing positions. There is also the general problem that, in so far as such conflicting findings get publicized and disseminated, they tend to reinforce lay views about the unreliability of social science research. Brewer and Hunter (1989) discuss strategies for minimizing these potential problems.

The main advantage of employing multiple methods is commonly cited as permitting *triangulation*. Triangulation, in surveying, is a method of finding out where something is by getting a 'fix' on it from two or more places. Analogously, Denzin (1988) suggested that this might be done in social research by using multiple and different *sources* (e.g. informants), *methods*, *investigators* or *theories*.

It is impossible to avoid the confounding effects of methods on our measurements. With a single method, some unknown part or aspect of the results obtained is attributable to the method used in obtaining the result. Because we can never obtain results for which *some* method has not been used to collect them, the only feasible strategy is to use a variety of methods. (Blaikie, 1991, is one of several critics of this approach, arguing that it is inappropriate to combine methods based on different theoretical positions.) On this model, we should choose methods which are very different from each other to get a better estimate of 'the' answer. Using a logic equivalent to that of classical test theory, the error due to methods is regarded as averaging out when multiple methods are used.

Multiple methods can help in other ways. Rather than focusing on a single, specific research question, they may be used to address different but complementary questions within a study; the COMPLEMENTARY PURPOSES model. This focuses on the use of different methods for alternative tasks. It is in effect what is happening when initial exploratory work is done by means of unstructured interviews, and subsequent descriptive and explanatory work employs a sample survey.

Multiple methods can also be used in complementary fashion to ENHANCE INTERPRETABILITY. For example, in a primarily quantitative study, the interpretation of statistical analyses may be enhanced by a qualitative narrative account. Conversely, a qualitative account may be the major outcome of a study, but it can be enhanced by supportive quantitative evidence used to buttress and perhaps clarify the account. Two or more quantitative, or two or more qualitative methods could also be combined (cf Bradford, 1990, who rated the behaviour of children during X-ray procedures on a systematic observation schedule, and followed the families up, assessing them on a number of psycho-social variables).

Finally, the complementary purposes notion can be used to *assess the plausibility of threats to validity* of the primary research technique used. This is a tactic used particularly in the context of quasi-experimental approaches (see chapter 4, p. 71). The basic notion is that the particular pattern of findings and context of a specific quasi-experimental design may leave its interpretation open to particular 'threats'. So, for example, in a time series design some persons may drop out of a treatment group during the course of a study (the 'mortality' effect). Interviews might be undertaken, both from this group and from those continuing, to assess whether there are differences between those who drop out and those who continue.

The basic message is that you need not be the prisoner of a particular method or technique when carrying out an enquiry. There is much to be said for multi-method enquiry.

Further Reading

Brewer, J. and Hunter, A. (1989) *Multimethod Research: a synthesis of styles.* Newbury Park and London: Sage. Covers advantages of, and issues in, using multiple methods.

Hakim, C. (1982) *Secondary Analysis in Social Research: a guide to data sources and methods with examples.* London: Allen & Unwin. Very useful introduction to, and appraisal of, the uses of secondary analysis.

Holsti, O. (1969) *Content Analysis for the Social Sciences and Humanities.* Reading, Mass.: Addison-Wesley. Classic text; wide-ranging and clear.

Krippendorff, K. (1980) *Content Analysis: an introduction to its methodology.* Newbury Park and London: Sage. Comprehensive introduction with detailed suggestions for carrying out an analysis. Covers computer analysis.

Scott, J. (1990) *A Matter of Record.* Cambridge: Polity. Issues in documentary research. Useful appraisal grid for analysis of documentary evidence.

Webb, E. J., Campbell, D. T., Schwartz, R. D., Sechrest, L. and Grove, J. B. (1981) *Nonreactive Measures in the Social Sciences,* 2nd edn. Boston: Houghton Mifflin. Compendium of possible unobtrusive measures. Ingenious and wide-ranging. Covers ethics, and limitations of the measures. First edition (1966) seems to be more readily available and is almost equally valuable.

Zeisel, J. (1981) *Inquiry by Design: tools for environment – behaviour research.* Cambridge: Cambridge University Press. Good chapter on archives and their use.

Further Reading for 'Additional Approaches'

In addition to the suggested reading for specific methods given below, two collections include introductions to several 'new paradigm' and other methods:

Morgan, G. (ed.) (1983) *Beyond Method: strategies for social research*. Newbury Park and London: Sage.
Reason, P. and Rowan, J. (eds) (1981) *Human Inquiry: a sourcebook of new paradigm research*. New York: Wiley.

Simulation and role-playing
Bryman, A. (1989) *Research Methods and Organisation Studies*. London: Unwin Hyman. Pages 214–20 cover uses of simulation in organizational research (including in-basket tests, simulating organizations, and computer simulation).
Cohen, L. and Manion, L. (1989) *Research Methods in Education*, 3rd edn. London: Routledge. Chapter on role-playing, setting it in the context of role-play as a substitute for deception in social psychological studies. Concentrates on role-play in educational settings, with examples.
van Ments, M. (1983) *The Effective Use of Role Play: a handbook for teachers and trainers*. London: Kogan Page. Good on the practical details of setting up and running effective simulations.

Language studies
Coulthard, M. (1977) *An Introduction to Discourse Analysis*. London: Longman. General introduction covering both social and cognitive aspects.
Harre, R. and Second, P. F. (1972) *The Explanation of Social Behaviour*. Oxford: Blackwell. Not concerned with discourse analysis per se, but gives influential 'ethogenic' approach to the analysis of social accounts.
Potter, J. and Wetherell, M. (1987) *Discourse and Social Psychology: beyond attitudes and behaviour*. Newbury Park and London: Sage. Accessible introduction to the theory and application of discourse analysis within social psychology. Wide range of examples.

Repertory grid techniques
Bannister, D. (ed.) (1970) *Perspectives in Personal Construct Theory*. London: Academic Press. Review by leading British exponent.
Burr, V. and Butt, T. (1992) *Invitation to Personal Construct Psychology*. London: Whurr. Very readable short introduction.
Cohen, L. and Manion, L. (1989) *Research Methods in Education*, 3rd. edn. London: Routledge. Chapter 14 covers up-to-date review, mainly of educational applications.
Fransella, F. and Bannister, D. (1977) *A Manual for Repertory Grid Technique*. London: Academic Press. Straightforward introduction to using grids.

Meta-analysis
Hunter, J. E., Schmidt, F. L. and Jackson, G. B. (1982) *Meta-analysis: Cumulating Research Findings Across Studies*. Newbury Park and London: Sage. Thorough review of quantitative meta-analysis in the context of organizational research.

Noblitt, G. W. and Hare, R. D. (1988) *Meta-ethnography: synthesizing qualitative studies*. Newbury Park and London: Sage. Interesting attempt to apply meta-analysis to studies with qualitative data.

Rosenthal, R. (1984) *Meta-analytic Procedures for Social Research*. Newbury Park and London: Accessible general coverage of quantitative meta-analysis.

Feminist research methods

Eichler, M. (1988) *Nonsexist Research Methods: a practical guide*. London: Hyman. Provides a systematic approach to identifying, eliminating and preventing sexist bias in social science research.

Harding, S. (ed.) (1987) *Feminism and Methodology*. Milton Keynes: Open University Press. Useful book of readings.

Hollway, W. (1989) *Subjectivity and Method in Psychology: gender, meaning and science*. Newbury Park and London: Sage. Attempts to show how 'psychology can be done differently'. Uses her work on subjectivity and gender difference to illustrate her feminist methodology.

Kirby, S. and McKenna, K. (1989) *Experience, Research, Social Change: methods from the margins*. Toronto: Garamond. Feminist methods text based on the thesis that 'research, which has so far been largely the instrument of dominance and legitimation of power elites, must be brought to serve the interests of dominated, exploited and oppressed groups'. Lively and readable.

Arranging the Practicalities

A *You Need to Know What you are Doing before Starting the Data Collection*

Persevering to this stage should have got you fully equipped with a focus for your enquiry and some related research questions, which may be quite specific and concrete but are more likely to be relatively tentative. You will have given thought to the most appropriate research strategy and have sorted out the methods and techniques you need to implement this strategy.

Perhaps. This is the rational, sequential version of the enquiry process. However, there is a 'reconstructed logic' to the process, mirroring that of the scientific paper (Silverman, 1985, p. 4). Buchanan, et al. (1988), in a paper which should be required reading for anyone contemplating real world research, emphasize the necessarily opportunistic flavour to much field research. For example,

> a friend made a casual enquiry about our research. . . . he suggested that we study his own company . . . We then discussed what the company would be prepared to let us do, and the research design was settled over a mixed grill and two pints of beer . . . the following week, after a couple of telephone calls and an exchange of letters, we met the manager responsible . . . It became clear that we should interview the head of the new word-processing section . . . our first interview with him started there and then . . . the manager suggested that as the computer system was to be shut down on Wednesday . . . we could come back tomorrow . . . and interview our first batch of video typists. He also asked if we would like to see the minutes of the working party that had decided to install the system, and he produced from the drawer figures charting the performance of the company's typists since 1975. (pp. 54–5)

They stress that the published account (Buchanan and Boddy, 1982) implies that the research questions were based on a prior assessment of the literature, with the research strategy and methods being selected as most appropriate in this context. In fact there was no opportunity to carry out a formal literature review, explore other possible methods, or design and pilot interview schedules. In other words, enquiry in the real world is very much the 'art of the possible'. *They were able to carry out the study successfully because of a prior familiarity with the literature and the field, which helped frame the research questions, and their experience in carrying out similar studies.*

There has in recent years been something of a spate of 'insider accounts' of research projects which make very valuable reading for anyone seeking to carry out a project. These include Burgess (1984b), Shipman (1976), Bell and Newby (1977) as well as Bryman (1988b) which provides many other examples. Watson (1968) provides a gripping account of the research leading to the discovery of the structure of DNA.

Such accounts reveal the fact that *experienced researchers can and do make a variety of mistakes*, including false starts and initial overambitiousness requiring substantial refocusing of the study. Novice researchers should take considerable heart from this. Such mistakes do not indicate that you are no good as a researcher; more that you are human. The accounts also highlight the 'luck' or 'serendipity' factor (the 'happy knack of making fortunate discoveries').

This injection of reality into the discussion does not indicate that consideration of the earlier sections of this text is a waste of time. The matters covered need to be internalized before you are in a position to follow this free-form approach. There are similarities to what Martin (1981) calls the 'garbage can' model of research. Here the four elements of research – theory, methods, resources and solutions – swirl about in the garbage can or decision space of the research project. Each influences the others, and the assumption of a sequence of steps in the research process is discarded.

B Negotiating Access

Much real world research takes place in settings where you require *formal* agreement from someone to gain access. Issues about access vary to a considerable extent with the kind of task you are carrying out. For more or less pure researchers, the agenda is set by their perceptions of what is important in the academic discipline, say, in the development of a theoretical position, or in response to recent research. Thus it is the researcher's agenda that is important, and the access issue is essentially persuading people to let you in. If you are clear about your intentions, perhaps with a pretty tight, pre-structured, design then the task is probably easier initially, in that you can give them a good indication of what they are letting themselves in for. With a looser, more emergent design, there may be more difficulties as you are to some extent asking them to sign a 'blank cheque' as it is impossible to specify in advance exactly what you will do.

Studies with a more applied focus simplify some access problems and make others more complex, and more sensitive. If the study looks at 'practice' in some professional, industrial or business situation, there is the considerable advantage that you can legitimately present the study as relating to, and probably arising from, the concerns of practitioners.

Box 10.7   Checklist on negotiating access

1 Establish points of contact, and individuals from whom it is necessary to get permission.

2 Prepare on outline of the study.

3 Clear any necessary official channels by formally requesting permission to carry out the study. Permission may be needed at various 'levels'.

4 Discuss the study with 'gatekeepers' (e.g. manager, headteacher). Go through study outline (purposes, conditions – including consent and participation). Attempt to anticipate potentially sensitive issues and areas.

5 Discuss the study with likely participants. Go through outline as above. May be with a group or with individuals, depending on circumstances.

Be prepared to modify the study in the light of these discussions (e.g. in respect of timing, treatment of sensitive issues).

When you have been asked to do the study by persons from the institution or organization concerned, then at first sight this seems to solve problems of access. However, the investigator might, legitimately or not, be seen as a 'tool of management' supporting the squeezing of more blood out of the workers; or, conversely, as a dangerous agitator upsetting labour relations. In particular, studies with an overt 'change' approach are, almost by definition, disturbing. Even in a 'commissioned' study, you are very likely to want to observe and collect information from persons who were not party to the request for you to be involved.

Several researchers stress the need to be flexible and opportunistic. Buchanan et al. (1988) recommend using friends, relatives and contacts wherever possible. This is, of course, not always feasible, and for some styles of research may lead to sampling problems. However, they stress that in real world enquiry, the contest between what is theoretically desirable and practically possible must be won by the practical.

It is helpful to regard the negotiation of access as a continuing process rather than a single event. The checklist in box 10.7 gives an indication of the things you might consider. Much of this is common sense and simply requires you to be sensitively alert to requirements of the situation. Given that you are inevitably going to trespass upon other people's time, and are probably giving them extra work to do, for you to be there in good faith you must believe, and do all you can to ensure, that they get something out of it. This can be at many levels. People often derive considerable satisfaction from talking about what they are doing to a disinterested but sympathetic ear. Taking part in a study can often lead to respondents reflecting on their experience in a way they find helpful. Stebbins (1987) makes helpful suggestions about 'fitting in', agreeing with Lofland and Lofland (1984) that you need to 'have enough knowledge about the setting or persons you wish to study *to appear competent to do so*'.

In working through the checklist, bear in mind the distinction between what is *formally* necessary to gain access, and what may be necessary over and above this to gain support and acceptance. The 'system' may not require you to get formal approval from a deputy head in a school, but if she is hostile to the study, it is not difficult for her to subvert it by, say, changing the timetabling arrangements. Formalities are necessary, not only to get you in, but also to refer back to if something goes wrong. People forget what they have agreed to, particularly if they had not thought through some of its implications. It can help to remind them of their agreed conditions, although they should be able to withdraw from the study if they wish.

Box 10.8 gives a specification for a 'fully informed consent' form and box 10.9 an example. This is common in North American practice (cf Lincoln and Guba, 1985, p. 254), which has tended to be more formalized than that in this country, and from which we could learn. The option of withdrawing from the study at a later time, without prejudice, is particularly necessary when relatively loose, emergent, designs are used. In these circumstances it may not be possible to foretell all that is involved when the respondent is first approached for consent.

A note on access and the 'insider'

It is increasingly common for researchers to carry out a study directly concerned with the setting in which they work. Teachers look at their own local authority, school or even classroom, social workers or 'health' personnel seek to evaluate or otherwise study some aspect of the service they are providing. The personnel department of a firm investigates its own interviewing procedures.

There are clear practical advantages to this kind of 'insider' research. You won't have to travel far. Generally you will have an intimate knowledge of the context of the study, not only as it is at

---

Box 10.8   Specification for 'fully informed consent' form

You should prepare this form in advance of any contact with respondents, containing at a minimum:

1   The name, address and telephone number of the person and/or agency seeking the consent.

2   A statement of the purpose of the enquiry, sufficient to convey to the respondents what their role will be, and how information collected will be used.

3   Specific information on consent and participation, as follows:
a   intention to maintain confidentiality and anonymity;
b   measures to be taken to prevent data being linked with a specific informant and to limit access to data;
c   note that the respondent has the right to withdraw from the study at any time;
d   note that participation is entirely voluntary unless the respondent has already agreed, as a part of a prior contract, to participate in legitimate studies.

4   A sign-off space for the participant in which she or he acknowledges having read and agreed to the previous stipulations as a condition of signing, with a space for the date.

5   If the investigator intends to quote respondents, the consent form should also provide a second sign-off space in which that consent is specifically given.

6   A copy of the signed consent form should be provided to the respondent.

---

present, but in a historical or developmental perspective. You should know the politics of the institution, not only of the formal hierarchy but also how it 'really works' (or, at least, an unexamined common-sense view of this). You will know how best to approach people. You should have 'street credibility' as someone who will understand what the job entails, and what its stresses and strains are. In general, you will already have in your head a great deal of information which it takes an outsider a long time to acquire.

The disadvantages are, however, pretty substantial. Your addition of the role of researcher to that of colleague is difficult both for

Box 10.9 Example of 'informed consent' form

*(To be read out by researcher before the beginning of the session –
interview, experiment, etc. One copy of the form to be lift with the
respondent; one copy to be signed by the respondent and kept by the
researcher.)*

My name is_____. I am doing research on a project entitled
_____. The project is sponsored by _____.
I am [X is] directing the project and can be contacted at

_____

_____

(address and telephone number) should you have any questions.

Thank you for agreeing to take part in the project. Before we start I
would like to emphasize that:

– your participation is entirely voluntary;
– you are free to refuse to answer any question;
– you are free to withdraw at any time.

The interview [or whatever] will be kept strictly confidential and will
be available only to members of the research team. Excerpts from the
interview/individual results may be made part of the final research
report, but under no circumstances will your name or any identifying
characteristics be included in the report.

Please sign this form to show that I have read the contents to you.

_____ (signed)

_____ (printed)

_____ date

Please send a report on the results of the project:

      YES   NO   (circle one)

Address for those requesting a research report

_____

_____

_____

*(Interviewer to keep signed copy and leave unsigned copy with
respondent.)*

yourself and for your colleagues. Interviewing colleagues can be an uncomfortable business; particularly so in hierarchical organizations when they are higher in status to yourself. Supposing that you obtain confidential information, appropriately enough within the conditions of confidentiality of the case study; is this going to affect your working relationship with colleagues? If you make mistakes during the study, you are going to have to live with them afterwards. More fundamentally, how are you going to maintain objectivity, given your previous and present close contact with the institution and your colleagues?

Grady and Wallston (1988, pp. 29–31) discuss these issues in the context of health care settings, but their principles are general:

- *Try to foresee likely conflicts* – e.g. collecting data about drug and alcohol abuse by pregnant teenagers called for a non-reactive researcher; the same person as 'helping professional' appreciated the consequences of the abuse.
- *Make a plan to deal with them* – in the abuse example, non-reaction might be construed as acknowledgement that the behaviour was not harmful, or that no help was available, and so a procedure was developed to provide appropriate referrals at the end of the interview session when base-line data had been collected.
- *Record your responses* – it helps to have a full log with notes made after each session so that they can be subsequently scrutinized for possible contaminating effects on the research.
- *Where possible get the collaboration of researcher colleagues from outside the situation* – they will help you to maintain the researcher stance.

C Get Yourself Organized

As soon as is feasible, you need to work out schedules for the arrangement and timing of sessions for observation, interviewing, etc. The extent to which this is pre-plannable depends very much on the style of your enquiry, but even with a flexible case study you are likely to be pressed for time and need (flexible) plans. Use calendars or wall charts to draw up timed and sequenced activity lists or flow charts. Howard and Sharp (1983) suggest techniques useful for complex projects, including network analysis and control charts.

D Pilot if at all Possible

The first stage of any data gathering should, if at all possible, be a 'dummy run' – a pilot study. This helps you to throw up some of the inevitable problems of converting your design into reality. Some methods and techniques necessarily involve piloting in their use (e.g. in the development of a structured questionnaire or a direct observation instrument). An experiment or survey can and should be piloted on a smallscale in virtually all circumstances. Case studies have sufficient flexibility to incorporate piloting within the study of the case itself. The effort needed in gaining access and building up acceptance and trust is often such that one would be reluctant to regard any case study simply as a pilot. Of course, if things go seriously wrong for whatever reason, or it appears that the case is not going to deliver in relation to your research questions, then it is better to abort and transfer your efforts elsewhere.

E Work on Your Relationships

Formal approval from the boss may get you in but you then need informal agreement and acceptance from informants, respondents or subjects in order actually to gather worthwhile data. This is largely a matter of relationships. You have to establish that you can be relied on to keep promises about confidentiality, etc. It is assumed that you are not proposing to deceive them and so you can share with them the general aims of your study and genuinely get over the message that you are there because you feel they can contribute.

F Don't just Disappear at the End

It helps you, and everybody concerned, if your initial negotiations set a period for your involvement and a date for your departure. It can be difficult to leave, particularly when things have gone well and you are an accepted part of the scene. There will almost always be more data that it would be desirable to collect. However, in real world enquiry, cutting your coat to fit a fixed length of cloth is often part of the reality, and it helps to concentrate your efforts.

Make sure that people know that you are going. Honour your commitments. Keep your bridges in good order so that you can return if necessary – and so that you haven't queered the pitch for others.

G Don't Expect it to Work Out as You Planned

'Trouble awaits those unwary souls who believe that research flows smoothly and naturally from questions to answers via a well organised data collection system' (Hodgson and Rollnick, 1989, p. 3). It is as well to appreciate this from the start in real world research or you will be in for a dispiriting shock. Measles may play havoc with your carefully planned school sessions, or unseasonal snow cut you off. Strikes close the plant or, even more frustrating, a 'work to rule' or 'withdrawal of goodwill' closes it to you. Communication channels do not function. The hospital you phoned yesterday to confirm an appointment denies your very existence. Hodgson and Rollnick provide a serious set of suggestions on 'how to survive in research' in a jocular manner. This includes a list of aphorisms well worth taking on board ('*Getting started will take at least as long as the data collection*'; a *Research project will change twice in the middle*'; etc.) and a set of maxims for keeping going, based on the practices of Alcoholics Anonymous (e.g. 'one day at a time'; don't be overwhelmed by the size of the task; focus on smaller goals).

Having some flexibility built in and a 'forgiving' design (where it is possible to substitute one case or activity for another) helps. Experimental designs, sabotaged by breakdowns in sampling procedures or some other reason, can be sometimes patched up as quasi-experimental equivalents. Hakim (1987, ch. 10) provides a very useful section on 'trading down to a cheaper design' to cope with reductions in resources or time available.

Part IV

Dealing with the Data

The central, totally indispensable, part of an enquiry is the collection of data. No data – no project. The specifics of data collection are bound up with the different methods of investigation, and have been dealt with in the chapters of part III. Whatever methods are used, there is a need for a systematic approach to the task – a need probably, paradoxically, at its greatest in the 'soft' methods of participant observation and unstructured interviewing. This is 'system' in the sense of being fully prepared for the task. If you are using a tape- recorder, you are an expert in its use, have fully charged batteries and a spare set if not a backup system. If you are writing up accounts after the session, you schedule time to do this, and use consistent conventions when producing the account to standard formats. It is not a question of asking for inappropriate rigour in, say, aping the structured questionnaire by asking the same questions in standard wording and a fixed sequence.

The Qualitative/Quantitative Debate

Some see quality and quantity as the fundamental dichotomy in social science research – the flags waved by the warring factions of interpretive ethnographers and positivistic scientists respectively. This book has followed Bryman (1988a) in playing down these differences, and in regarding the distinction as being primarily technical. There are qualitative and quantitative data – and one has to deal with them in rather different ways, which are covered in the two following chapters.

There are, admittedly, major differences in style between many of those who do studies producing qualitative data, and those whose studies produce quantitative data, which are not simply a function of the type of data. An extensive literature on qualitative/quantitative distinctions exists, including Glassner and Moreno (1989), Hammersley (1989) and Fielding and Fielding

(1986). Attempts have been made to build bridges and seek a rapprochement (cf Cook and Reichardt, 1979; Ragin, 1987).

In simple terms, *chapter 11, dealing with quantitative data analysis, covers what you do with data when following the experimental or survey strategies. Chapter 12, on qualitative data analysis, covers much of the data analysis requirements in case studies*, and, probably, most hybrid studies. Case studies, however, are likely to lead to at least some quantitative data, and the techniques used in chapter 11 to summarize and scale data, and to produce descriptive statistics, will be helpful.

Collecting the Data

Collecting the data is about using the selected methods of investigation. Doing it properly means using these methods in a systematic, professional fashion. The chapters in part III cover the issues raised in the use of specific methods. At this stage you need to ask yourself the following questions:

A   Have You Explored Thoroughly the Choice of Methods Techniques?

The position adopted in this text is that there is no general 'best method'. The selection of methods should be driven by the kind of research questions you are seeking to answer. This has to be moderated by what is feasible in terms of time and other resources; by your skills and expertise; and possibly, in commissioned research, by the predilections of the sponsor.

B   What Mix of Methods Do You Propose to Use?

The virtues of multi-methods enquiry have been emphasized (p. 69). All methods have strengths and weaknesses and you are seeking to match the strength of one to the weakness of another, and vice versa. If it is impracticable to use more than one method, don't worry – many studies are still mono-method. Don't give up too easily though – it is often possible to devote a small fraction of your effort to a complementary method. This might be an unstructured interview session at the end of an experiment. Or, perhaps, two or three mini case studies based on observation, interview and document analysis – linked to a questionnaire survey.

C Have You Thought Through Potential Problems in Using the Different Methods?

You don't choose methods unless you have the skills and personality characteristics they call for (I would pay a fairly substantial amount not to have to do a telephone survey involving 'cold' calling). Nor if they would be unacceptable in the setting involved. Nor if they raise ethical concerns. Pilot work almost always brings out problems; better then than in the middle of a rigidly designed study.

D Do the Methods Have the Flexibility that you Need?

Broadly speaking, if you need flexibility in the design of the study (e.g. when exploring a new or little-known field) then you are pushed strongly to case studies. The methods, at least in the early stages of the study, must have a corresponding flexibility (e.g. relatively unstructured observation and interview). You might wish to move on to a confirmatory phase at a later stage of the study where more structured instruments would be called for.

E Whatever Methods You Use, Data Collection Calls for Commitment

You have to care. Both about the substantive area, and about your responsibilities as a researcher (to science, if that doesn't put you off). This dual commitment is crucial. Care solely about getting answers to the research questions, and particularly about 'helping' and you are in danger of losing objectivity and the ability to appraise the evidence fairly. Caring only about doing a good piece of research may lead to the degree of detachment rightly castigated by feminist methodologists (see p. 65). And you need high commitment not only to do a quality job, but also to get you through the inevitable bad times.

Analysing and Interpreting the Data

After data has been collected in an enquiry, it has at some stage to be analysed and interpreted. The traditional model is for this to take place after all the data are safely gathered in. Sometimes, however, particularly with a case study, it makes sense to start this analysis and interpretation when you are in the middle of the enquiry. Analysis is necessary because, generally speaking, data in their raw form do not speak for themselves. The messages stay hidden and need careful teasing out. The process and products of analysis provide the bases for interpretation. It is often the case that, while in the middle of analysing data, ideas for interpretation arise (which is a disadvantage of relying on the now virtually ubiqitous, and immensely useful, computer packages for analysis).

Analysis, then, is not an empty ritual, carried out for form's sake between doing the study and interpreting it. Nor is it a bolt-on feature which can be safely not thought about until the data is safely gathered in. Once more, Murphy's Law raises its head to make it highly likely that if you do this, you end up with an unanalysable mish-mash of data which no known test or procedure can redeem.

Hence, as emphasized in part II, thinking about how the analysis *might* be carried out forms an integral part of the design process for any investigation. A particular disposition of your resources which, say, gets more data from a smaller number of respondents, or fewer data from a greater number of respondents, might make all the difference between there being a straightforward path of analysis and a highly dubious one. If you have thought through such an analysis, that is then available as a 'banker'. You can then, with confidence, explore the data when they are in, and see if there are alternative or additional messages you can get from them.

The intention here is to sensitize you to analysis issues and to cover a range of ways of dealing with both quantitative and qualitative data. *The aims are primarily to set out guidelines and principles to use in selecting appropriate procedures, and to discuss how the results obtained from these procedures might be interpreted.*

Little attempt is made to cover computational aspects. The advent of powerful computers and wide-ranging program packages on statistical and other procedures obviate the need for factual knowledge about formulae or for craft skills in performing complex calculations. No doubt, inertia in the presentation of courses, and remnants of the puritan ethic, will force further generations of students through these satisfyingly labour intensive hoops. However, there are more profitable ways of spending your time than doing something which a computer can do better, and more quickly. This does not gainsay, as mentioned above, the value to interpretation of really getting to know your data by playing about with them. And this is also something with which the computer can help.

Preparing for Analysis

You have collected some, or all, of your data. You now need to understand them. Data come in all sorts of shapes and sizes – audio- and video-tapes, sets of instrument readings or test results, responses to questionnaires, diary entries, reports of meetings, documents, etc., etc.

Many of them fall effectively into two categories – words or numbers. Or they can, without too much difficulty, be turned into words or numbers. And some features of the words can be captured in numbers.

A Be Prepared to Carry Out both Qualitative and Quantitative Analyses

So we have *qualitative analysis* (for words, and other data which come in a non-numerical form) and *quantitative analysis* (for numbers, and other data that can be transformed into numbers). Most real world study produces data which call for both qualitative and quantitative analysis and it is important that you are able to deal competently with both aspects.

B Seek Advice about Quantitative Analysis

A vast technology of quantitative (or statistical) analysis exists and it would be foolish to expect everyone carrying out an enquiry to have all of it at their finger-tips. There is a tendency to gain some familiarity with a narrow range of approaches and then use them willy-nilly. This means either inappropriate analyses or severe restrictions on the type of research questions you can tackle (the analytic equivalent of the one-track methods person who tackles everything with a questionnaire). The technique of 'analysis of variance' as used by some experimental psychologists, provides a case in point.

A more extreme, though not uncommon, response is to eschew all things quantitative and stick solely to qualitative analyses. Although this may be presented in terms of ideological objection to positivistic quantitative approaches, suspicion remains that there may be other blocks to the use of statistics.

One solution is to get advice from a consultant or other person familiar with a wide range of approaches to the quantitative analysis of social research data; and to get that advice at the design stage of your project, *not after you have collected the data*. The advice should also, in many cases, home you in on a computer package which will do the analytical work for you. All this does not mean that you come naked to the consultant's table. It is important that you have at least an intuitive grasp of the kinds of approaches that might be taken, so that you know what is being talked about. Chapter 11 seeks to do that job. Even if you are on your own with no consultant available, it will sensitize you to a range of possibilities which, with further reading, you should be able to implement.

C *You Are Going to Have to Do Much of the Qualitative Analysis for Yourself*

Qualitative analysis has now, like horticulture, moved out of the 'muck and magic' phase. It was commonly held that there was some ineffable mystique whereby the methods could only be used by experienced researchers admitted to the magic circle only after a lengthy apprenticeship. Following Merton et al.'s insistence (1956, p. 17) that this is no 'private and incommunicable art', serious attempts have been made to show that qualitative analysis can be systematized and made widely accessible. These approaches are discussed in chapter 12.

However, while there are helpful routines and procedures, they are less technical and differentiated than much statistical analysis – closer to codified common sense. It will undoubtedly be helpful to get external help and support to carry out qualitative analysis from someone with experience in this field. This, however, is more concerned with getting feedback on the processes you are using, and checking the warrant for the interpretations you are making. There are computer packages to facilitate the process, but they in no sense do the job of analysis for you in the way that a statistical package does.

11

The Analysis of Quantitative Data

This chapter covers techniques for displaying and summarizing quantitative data.

It emphasizes the need to explore the data and recommends the use of software packages to do this.

It discusses ways of analysing relationships and differences with various types of data.

Introduction

You would have to work quite hard in an enquiry not to generate at least some data in the form of numbers; or which could not be sensibly turned into numbers of some kind. Techniques for dealing with such quantitative data are hence an essential feature of your professional tool-kit. Their analysis covers a wide range of things, from simple organization of the data to complex statistical analysis. This chapter does not attempt a comprehensive treatment of all aspects of quantitative data analysis. Its main aim is to help you appreciate some of the issues involved so that you have a feeling for the questions you need to ask when deciding on an appropriate kind of analysis.

Three Assumptions

1 *It is assumed that you are likely to be using one or more of the excellent software packages now available for microcomputers* If you only have a very small amount of quantitative data, it may be appropriate for you to carry out analyses by 'hand' (or with the help of an electronic calculator). However, the drudgery and potential for error in such calculation, and the ease with which the computer can perform such mundane chores for you, suggest strongly that you make use of the new technology if at all possible. Large-ish data sets may call for the use of 'mainframe' computers, but for

the relatively small-scale projects targeted in this book microcomputer software is now available for most likely tasks.

Two recent books have been produced which concentrate on quantitative data analysis using a specific software package. These are Bryman and Cramer (1990) which is keyed in to 'SPSS' (the Statistical Package for the Social Sciences) and Monk (1991), which is linked to 'Minitab'. Each of these texts provides an accessible, well thought through introduction to the sensible use of a wide range of statistical techniques.

If you have Access to 'SPSS' or 'Minitab' (both of which, while initially developed for use with large computer systems, are now available in personal computer versions) *it may be sensible for you to switch to Bryman and Cramer, or to Monk, at this stage to help in carrying out the quantitative analysis.*

This chapter provides examples of the ways in which a third package, 'Statview', deals with analysis and shows how the results of the main analyses are presented. 'Statview' runs on Macintosh computers. While not currently as widely used or as comprehensive as SPSS or Minitab, it is a particularly simple and straightforward package to use. In the jargon, it is 'user- friendly'. Because of this, it is possible to illustrate general principles of value whichever package (or none) is used. To use Statview itself, you will need to refer to the accompanying manual (Feldman et al., 1991). Gibbs (1990) provides an invaluable introduction for the novice computer user.

2 *It is assumed that you have some prior acquaintance with the basic concepts and language of statistical analysis* If not, you are recommended to spend some time with one of the many texts covering this at an introductory level (e.g. Robson, 1983).

3 *It is assumed that you will seek help and advice in carrying out quantitative data analysis* The field of quantitative data analysis is complex and specialized and it is unreasonable to expect everyone carrying out real world enquiry to be a statistical specialist. It is, unfortunately, a field where it is not at all difficult to carry out an analysis which is simply wrong, or inappropriate, for your data or your purposes. And the negative side of readily available analytic software is that it becomes that much easier to generate elegantly presented rubbish (remember GIGO – Garbage In, Garbage Out).

Preferably, such advice should come from an experienced statistician sympathetic to the particular difficulties involved in 'human' enquiry. It should be sought at the earliest possible stage in the *design* of your project. Inexperienced non-numerate researchers often have a touching faith that enquiry is a linear process in which they first collect the data and then the statistician shows them the analysis to carry out. It is, however, all too easy to end up with unanalysable data, which, if they had been collected in a somehat different way, would have been readily analysable. In the absence of personal statistical support, you should be able to use this chapter to get an introduction to the kind of approach you might take. The references provided should then help with more detailed coverage.

Organization of the Chapter

The chapter first covers the creation of a 'data set' as a necessary precursor to using microcomputer software for data analysis. Various ways of exploring the data set are then suggested, followed by advice on the selection and use of formal statistical tests.

Creating a Data Set

The point has already been made that you should be thinking about how your data are to be analysed at the design stage of your project. This is important not only to ensure that what you collect is analysable, but also to simplify as much as possible the actual process of analysis.

If you are to make use of a software package for analysis, then the data must be entered into the computer in the form required by the software. This may be done in different ways:

1   *Direct automatic entry.* It may be feasible for the data to be generated in such a way that entry is automatic. For example, you may be using a structured observation schedule with some data collection device (either a specialized instrument or a lap-top computer) so that the data as collected can be directly usable by the analysis software.

2   *Creation of a computer file which is then 'imported' to the analysis software.* It may be easier for your data to be entered into a computer after collection. For example, a survey might use questionnaires which are 'optically readable'. Respondents or the person carrying out the survey fill in boxes on the form corresponding to particular answers. The computer can directly transform this response into data which it can use. Such data form a computer 'file' which is then 'imported' into the particular analysis software being used. This is feasible with Statview although you may need assistance to ensure that the transfer takes place satisfactorily.

3   *Direct 'keying' of data into analysis software.* For much small-scale enquiry, automatic reading or conversion of the data into a computer file will either not be possible or not be economically justifiable. There is then the requirement for manual entry of data into the analysis software. The discussion below assumes that you will be entering the data in this way.

Whichever approach is used the same principle applies – try at the design stage to capture your data in a form which is going to simplify this entry process. Avoid intermediate systems where the original response has to be further categorized. The more times that data are transferred between coding systems, the greater the chance of error. SINGLE-TRANSFER CODING (i.e. where the response is already in the form which has to be entered into the computer) is often possible with attitude and other scales, multiple-choice tests, inventories, checklists, and many questionnaires. In a postal or similar survey questionnaire, you will have to weigh up whether it is more important to simplify the task of the respondent or the task of the person transferring the code to the computer. Box 11.1 shows possible alternatives.

Box 11.1   Question formats requiring (a) single-transfer coding and (b) double-transfer coding

a   How many children are there in your school?

under 40	40–49	50–59	60–69	70–79	80–89	90–100	over 100
code 1	2	3	4	5	6	7	8

enter code ( )

b   How many children are there in your school?
                                 (please circle)

under 40   40–49 50–59 60–69 70–79 80–89 90–100   over 100

(response has then to be translated into appropriate code)

The conventions on coding are essentially common sense. Suggestions were made in chapter 9 (p. 252) about how this might be dealt with in relation to questionnaires. Note that it is helpful to include the coding boxes on the questionnaire itself, conventionally in a column on the right-hand side of each page.

The data sets obtained from other types of enquiry will be very various. However, it is almost always possible to have some sensible arrangement of the data into *rows* and *columns*. Typically each row corresponds to a *record*. This might be all of the data obtained from a particular respondent. A record consists of *cells* which contain data. The cells in a column contain the data for a particular *variable*. Box 11.2 presents a simple example derived from a survey-type study. A similar matrix would be obtained from a simple experiment where, say, the columns represent scores obtained under different experimental conditions.

Box 11.2   Faculty, A level points, and degree classification of a sample of students

Student	Faculty	Sex	A level points	Degree class
1	A	F	7	2.1
2	EN	M	3	2.2
3	EN	M	2	Fail
4	ED	F	5	2.2
5	S	M	2	2.1
6	B	F	6	2.1
7	A	F	8	2.1
8	EN	M	3	3
9	EN	M	3	3
10	ED	M	*	2.2

Key: A = Arts; B = Business; ED = Education; EN = Engineering;
S = Sciences; M = Male; F = Female; * = missing data.

Note: data are fictitious, but modelled on those in Linsell and Robson, 1987.

Entering the Data into the Analysis Software

The details of the procedure for entering this data set into the computer vary according to the particular software you are using. Older software commonly uses a system originally based on standard computer cards. These have eighty columns, and each of your data variables would occupy one or more of the columns on the card. Each computer card represents a row (if you can't fit all the data for a respondent into the eighty columns of a single card then two or more cards would be used for each respondent). SPSS works in this way (Bryman and Cramer, 1990, ch. 2, esp. pp. 18–22). Youngman (1979, ch. 2) gives a very clear account of this way of entering the data set.

Statview's approach is rather different, and is straightforward to use, particularly if you are familiar with the operation of spreadsheets.

Columns   Each column represents a variable in your data. You have to define what each column will look like and what kind of data will be entered in the cells of a column. Various types of data can be dealt with, including INTEGERS (whole numbers), REAL NUMBERS (numbers with fractional parts) and CATEGORIES (e.g. 'gender' which has the ELEMENTS 'male' and 'female').

Creating a data set with Statview simply involves defining the characteristics for each column in the data set. This is done in a dialogue where you
respond to prompts on the screen.

Rows Each row represents a record. In the example these are the data for
an individual student. When the columns have been defined, all you have to
do is to open the file containing the specification of the data set and enter
the data, one record at a time. Box 11.3 shows the result of doing this: a
simple recreation of the data table from Box 11.2.

Box 11.3 Data table in format generated by Statview (part only)

	faculty	gender	A level points	degree class
1	arts	female	7	upper second
2	engineer	male	3	lower second
3	engineer	male	2	fail
4	education	female	5	lower second
5	sciences	male	2	upper second
6	business	female	6	upper second
7	arts	female	8	upper second
8	engineer	male	3	third
9	engineer	male	3	third
10	education	male	•	lower second
11	sciences	male	6	upper second
12	business	female	6	lower second
13	education	female	4	lower second
14	sciences	male	4	first
15	business	female	3	lower second
16	arts	female	6	upper second
17	arts	male	3	third
18	sciences	male	9	lower second
19	education	male	7	upper second
20	business	male	4	upper second
21	business	male	4	lower second
22	sciences	female	4	lower second
23	sciences	female	5	lower second

24	business	female	5	lower second
25	business	female	9	upper second
26	arts	male	7	lower second
27	education	female	7	lower second
28	sciences	male	5	upper second
29	engineer	male	9	upper second
30	arts	male	8	upper second
31	arts	female	12	lower second
32	business	male	6	lower second
33	business	male	4	pass
34	business	female	5	pass
35	engineer	male	5	upper second
36	scineces	female	10	upper second
37	sciences	female	6	lower second
38	arts	female	6	first
39	business	female	6	lower second
40	engineer	male	5	lower second
41	business	female	8	upper second
42	sciences	male	8	pass
43	sciences	female	•	upper second
44	arts	male	7	lower second

Missing Data 'The most acceptable solution to the problem of missing information is not to have any' (Youngman, 1979, p. 21). While this is obviously a counsel of perfection, it highlights the problem that there is no really satisfactory way of dealing with missing data. In social research, it may well be that the reason why data are missing is in some way related to the question being investigated. Those who avoid filling in the evaluation questionnaire, or who are not present at a session, may well have different views from those who responded. So it is well worth spending considerable time, effort and ingenuity in seeking to ensure a full response. Software normally has one or more ways of dealing with missing data when performing analyses and it may be necessary to investigate this further as different approaches can have substantially different effects on the results obtained.

Technically there is no particular problem in coding data as missing. There simply needs to be a signal code which is used for missing data, and only for missing data. Often 0 (zero) is used but this can cause confusion if the variable in question could have a zero value, or if any analytic procedure treats it as a value of zero. Statview uses the 'period' or 'full stop' symbol (.) to signify missing data and deals with it intelligently (e.g. by computing averages based only on the data present). It appears in the display as a large dot (as shown in Box 11.3 for students 10 and 43).

It is worth noting that a distinction may need to be made between missing data where there is no response from someone, and a 'don't know' or 'not applicable' response, particularly if you have catered for possible responses of this type by including them as one of the alternatives.

Cleaning the Data Set after Entry

Just as one needs to proof-read text for errors, so a computer data set needs to be checked for errors made while 'keying in' the data. One of the best ways of doing this is for the data to be entered twice, independently, by two people. Any discrepancies can then be resolved. This can be very time-consuming but may well be worthwhile, particularly if substantial data analysis is likely.

A valuable tip is to make use of 'categorical' variables whenever feasible. So, in the data set of box 11.2 'degree class' has the categories 'first, 'upper second', etc. The advantage is that the software will only accept the specific categories that you have declared (with Statview you only need to enter sufficient letters to specify uniquely each of the categories – e.g. 'fi' or 'fa' for 'first' or 'fail' respectively). While this eliminates several potential mistakes, it is, of course, still possible to enter the wrong class for an individual.

The direct equivalent of proof-reading can be carried out by checking the computer data set carefully against the original set. Simple FRE-QUENCY ANALYSES (see below, p. 318) on each of the columns (variables) are helpful. This will throw up whether 'illegal', or highly unlikely, codes have been entered. For continuous variables BOX PLOTS can be drawn, and potential 'outliers' highlighted (see p. 325).

CROSS-TABULATION (see below, p. 333) can show up more subtle errors. This involves counting the codes from one variable that occur for each code in a second variable. Suppose that the two variables are 'withdrew before completing degree' and 'class of final degree'. Cross-tabulation might throw up one or two students who appeared to have withdrawn before completion, but were nevertheless awarded a classified degree. These should then be checked as while this might be legitimate (perhaps they returned) it could well be a miscoding. Cross-tabulation is easy when the variables have only a few values, as is the case with most categorical variables. However, it becomes very tedious when continuous variables such as age or income, which can take on many values, are involved. In this circumstance, SCATTERPLOTS (see below, p. 336) provide a useful tool. These are graphs in which corresponding codes from two variables give the horizontal and vertical scale values of points representing each record. 'Deviant' points which stand out from the general pattern can be followed up to see whether they are genuine or miscoded.

The 'cleaned' data set is an important resource for your subsequent analyses. It is prudent to keep a couple of copies, with one of the copies being at a separate physical location from the others. You will be likely to modify the set in various ways during analysis (e.g. by combining codes); however, you should always retain copies of the original data set.

Exploring the Data Set

With a cleaned data set available in the analysis software, you are now in the position to find out just what your enquiry has thrown up quantitatively. The beauty of such software is that it enables and encourages you to play with the data so that you really get to know it through exploring the patterns and relationships presented to you.

The Exploratory Data Analysis (EDA) Movement

Exploratory approaches of various kinds have been advocated at several points during this book. They chime in very well with an influential modern approach to quantitative analysis known as exploratory data analysis (EDA) advocated by Tukey (1977) – see also Velleman and Hoaglin (1981) and Lovie and Lovie (1991). Tukey's approach and influence come in at two levels. First, he has proposed several ingenious ways of displaying data diagramatically. These devices, such as 'box plots', are non-controversial, deserve wider recognition, and are discussed below.

The more revolutionary aspect of the EDA movement is the centrality it places on an informal, pictorial approach to data. As Lovie A.D. (1986) puts it, the pictures do not merely represent the data in an alternative form, they

> serve both *descriptive* and *inferential* purposes in that hypothesis seeking (one of the major characteristics of EDA) consists of drawing pictures that emphasize both surprising and important aspects of the data. In other words, they do not merely present the data in a different, more compact form but the form positively *aids* subsequent hypothesis detection/confirmation'. (p. 165)

Thus there is a breakdown of the distinction, commonly found in statistics texts, between descriptive and inferential statistics. EDA is criticized for implying that the pictures are all that you need; that the usual formal statistical procedures involving tests, significance levels, etc. are unnecessary. However, Tukey (1977) does acknowledge the need for a confirmatory data analysis (CDA), using the more formal processes of statistical hypothesis testing. This complements EDA and provides a way of formally testing the relatively risky inductions made through EDA.

To a large extent EDA is simply regularizing the very common process whereby researchers make inferences about relationships between variables after an enquiry which their study was not designed to test formally – or which they had not expected prior to the enquiry – and providing helpful tools for that task.

> *The treatment in this chapter is influenced by EDA and seeks to follow its spirit. However, there are overlaps between the 'exploring' and 'confirming' aspects as developed here. In particular, formal statistical tests have been incorporated at various points in this 'exploring' section where the analyst is likely to need them.*

The Minitab program is based on EDA principles. Statview also encourages this approach, particularly through the ease with which graphical presentations of the data can be generated and manipulated. SPSS is less oriented to EDA approaches, although it is possible to use it to generate box plots and other displays. Display techniques have, of course, been around before 1977 and EDA. Several of these are presented in the following sections.

Frequency Distributions and Graphical Displays

A simple means of exploring many data sets is to recast them in a way which counts the frequency (i.e. the number of times) that certain things happen, or to find ways of displaying that information. For example, we could look at the number of students achieving different degree classifications. Some progress can be made by drawing up a FREQUENCY DISTRIBUTION as shown in figure 11.1. This simply gives the number of students (referred to in Statview as the 'count' and otherwise known as their 'frequency') with each class of degree. Adding the percentage column in figure 11.1 helps to produce a standard format, so that groups of different sizes can be more easily compared. Figure 11.1 can, alternatively, be presented as a HISTOGRAM (figure 11.2).

		X_1: degree class	
Bar:	Element:	Count:	Percent:
1	first	4	4%
2	upper second	36	36%
3	lower second	48	48%
4	third	5	5%
5	pass	6	6%
6	fail	1	1%

Figure 11.1 Example of frequency distribution (distribution of students across 'class of degree')

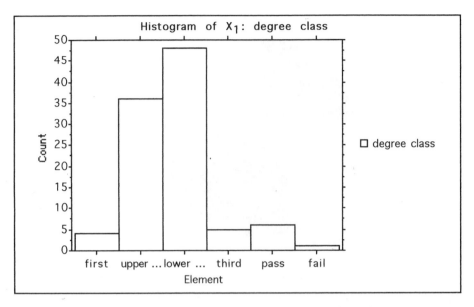

Figure 11.2 Histogram showing distribution of students across 'class of degree'

The chart can be shown with either counts (frequencies) or percentages on the vertical axis; be sure to indicate which you have used. The ordering of classes of degree is from first 'downward' going from left to right. For other variables (e.g. for faculties) this ordering might be arbitrary.

A distinction is sometimes made between HISTOGRAMS and BAR CHARTS. A bar chart is a histogram where the bars are separated from each other, rather than being joined together. The convention has been that histograms are only used for continuous variables (i.e. where the bar can take on any numerical value and is not, for example, limited to whole number values). However, Statview does not make this distinction and there seems little value in maintaining it.

PIE CHARTS provide an alternative way of displaying this kind of information (see figure 11.3). Histograms and pie charts are probably preferable ways of summarizing data to the corresponding tables of frequency distributions. They are more quickly and easily understood by a variety of audiences (see Spence and Lewandowsky (1990) for a review of relevant empirical studies). Note, however, that with continuous variables (i.e. ones which can take on any numerical value, not simply whole numbers) both frequency tables and histograms may lose considerable detailed information. This is because of the need to group together a range of values for a particular row of the frequency table or bar of the histogram. In all cases there will be a trade-off between decreasing the complexity of the display and losing information.

There are EDA display techniques, such as the STEM AND LEAF DISPLAY (see Marsh, 1988 for a particularly clear account), which do not involve this

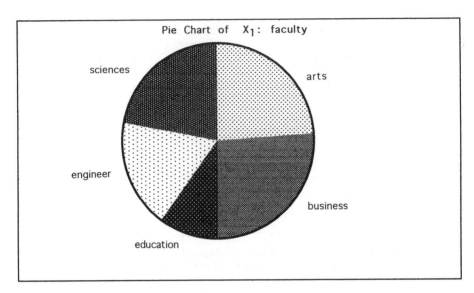

Figure 11.3 Pie chart showing relative numbers of students in different faculties

loss of information. However, they suffer from the difficulty that their meaning is not intuitively obvious, and requires explaining to a lay audience. An alternative summarizing display is the BOX PLOT. This, and some further techniques of graphical display, are returned to later in the chapter, following the discussion on summary statistics below (see p. 325).

Graphs (line charts) are well known ways of displaying data. Statview provides a wide range of ways of generating and displaying them. Specialized graphics packages commonly have a range of such displays available. Increasingly, professional standard displays are expected in presenting the results of projects, and apart from assisting communication, can help in getting over messages about the quality of the work. It is a matter of judgement whether or not any package to which you have access provides output of a quality adequate for presentation to a particular audience.

Marsh (1988) gives detailed, helpful and down-to-earth suggestions for hand-produced material in appendices on 'Good Table Manners' (pp. 139–42) and 'Guide to Effective Plotting' (pp. 196–8). Tufte (1983) provides a fascinating compendium for anyone who needs to take graphical display seriously.

Summary Statistics

Summary statistics (also commonly known as 'descriptive statistics) are ways of representing some important aspect of a set of data by a single number. The two aspects most commonly dealt with in this way are the LEVEL of the distribution and its SPREAD. Statistics summarizing the level are known as 'measures of central tendency'. Those summarizing the spread are called 'measures of variability'. The 'skewness' (asymmetricality), and other aspects of the shape of the distribution which are also sometimes summarized, are considered below in the context of the 'Normal distribution' (see p. 330).

Measures of central tendency   The notion here is to get a single figure which best represents the level of the distribution. The most common such measure to the lay person is the 'average', calculated by adding all of the scores together and then dividing by the number of scores. In statistical parlance, the figure obtained by carrying out this procedure is referred to as the ARITHMETIC MEAN. This is because 'average' as a term in common use suffers from being imprecise – some other more-or-less mid-value might also be referred to as average. There are, however several other measures of central tendency in use, some appropriate for special purposes. Box 11.4 covers some of them.

Box 11.4   Measures of 'central tendency'

The most commonly used are:

a   *Mean* (strictly speaking this should be referred to as the *arithmetic mean*) – this is the average, obtained by adding all the scores together and dividing by the number of scores.

b   *Median* – this is the central value when all the scores are arranged in order of size (i.e. for eleven scores it is the sixth). It is also referred to as the '50th percentile' (i.e. it has 50 per cent of the scores below it, and 50 per cent above it).

c   *Mode* – the most frequently occurring value.

Statistics texts give formulae and further explanation.

Measures of variability   The extent to which the data values in a set of scores are tightly clustered or relatively widely spread out is a second important feature of a distribution for which several indices are in use. Box 11.5 gives details of the most commonly used measures.

   In common with many statistics packages, Statview provides a very wide range of summary statistics (listed with brief descriptions in box 11.6). Essentially, what is provided is an optional menu of ways of summarizing any column within your data table.

Box 11.5   Measures of variability

Some commonly used measures are:

a   *Range* – difference between the highest and the lowest score.

b   *Inter-quartile range* – difference between the score which has one quarter of the scores below it (known as the 'first quartile', or '25th percentile') and that which has three-quarters of the scores below it (known as the 'third quartile', or '75th percentile').

c   *Variance* – a measure of the average of the squared deviations of *individual* scores from the mean.

d   *Standard deviation* – square root of the variance.

e   *Standard error* – a measure of the standard deviation of the *mean* score.

Statistics texts give formulae and further explanation.

Further Graphical Displays for Single Variables

It is possible to incorporate summary statistics into graphical displays in various ways. Statview provides various ways of doing this.

Standard deviation error bars   For example, Statview will generate a display showing the mean value as a dot, which has extending above and below it an 'error bar'. This represents one standard deviation unit above and below the mean. Typically, about two-thirds of the observed values will fall between these two limits (see the discussion of the Normal distribution below, p. 330).

This is often a useful way of displaying the relative performance of sub-groups, and more generally of making comparisons. See, for example, figure 11.4. The display makes clear both the similar variability in male and female scores, and the relatively small difference in means compared with variability.

A similar-looking display can be used to show the CONFIDENCE INTERVALS for the mean. These are limits within which we can be (probabilistically) sure that the *mean* value of the population from which our sample is drawn lies: 95 per cent limits (i.e. limits within which we can be 95 per cent sure) are commonly used, but others can be obtained. Figure 11.5 illustrates this.

Univariate scattergrams   Scattergrams are discussed below (p. 336) as a very useful way of displaying the relationship between two variables. They

Box 11.6   Summary statistics produced by Statview

All the measures of central tendency given in box 11.4, and the measures of variability in box 11.5 can be given by Statview (you have to work out the 'inter-quartile range' as the difference between '25th %' and '75th %'). Additionally you can get:

Coefficient of variation – standard deviation divided by mean and expressed as a percentage (i.e. multiplied by 100). It is effectively a standardized version of the standard deviation.

Sum of squares – what it says, i.e. simply adding together all the squared scores.

Percentiles – The 10th, 25th, 50th, 75th and 90th percentiles are given (i.e. the score that has 10 per cent of the scores below it; 25 per cent; etc.). The number of scores below the 10th percentile and above the 90th are also available.

Confidence intervals – various confidence intervals can be provided. They are linked to the *t*-test (see below, p. 352) and give the probability that the population mean is within a certain interval. In the output shown in the table below we are told that there is a 95 per cent chance it lies between 5.533 and 6.302; a 90 per cent chance it lies between 5.596 and 6.329.

The *geometric mean* and *harmonic mean* are unlikely to be of interest. For *kurtosis* and *skewness* see figure 11.11. The other information given should be self-evident.

X1: A level points					
Mean:	Std. Dev.:	Std. Error:	Variance:	Coef. Var.:	Count:
5.918	1.908	.194	3.639	32.237	97
Minimum:	Maximum:	Range:	Sum:	Sum of Sqr.:	# Missing:
2	12	10	574	3746	3
t 95%:	95% Lower:	95% Upper:	t 90%:	90% Lower:	90% Upper:
.384	5.533	6.302	.322	5.596	6.239
# < 10th %:	10th %:	25th %:	50th %:	75th %:	90th %:
9	4	5	6	7	9
# > 90th %:	Mode:	Geo. Mean:	Har. Mean:	Kurtosis:	Skewness:
3	•	5.602	5.263	.156	.435

Note: The *mode* is shown as •, indicating that there is no single score with the highest frequency.

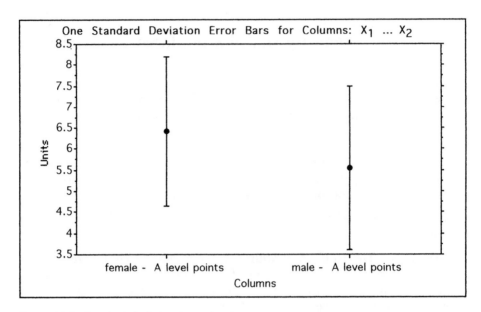

Figure 11.4 Standard deviation 'error bars'

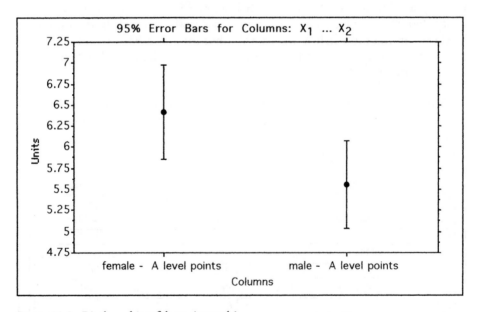

Figure 11.5 Display of 'confidence intervals'

can be used with a single variable where each of the observations is displayed separately along the horizontal (X) axis and the value of the observation determines its position on the vertical (Y) axis. Statview shows the mean value as a horizontal line, and also gives dotted lines above and below corresponding to one standard deviation above the mean, and one standard deviation below the mean, respectively. Figure 11.6 gives an example. It is also possible to set these lines as other numbers of standard deviations (say two, or three) above and below the mean.

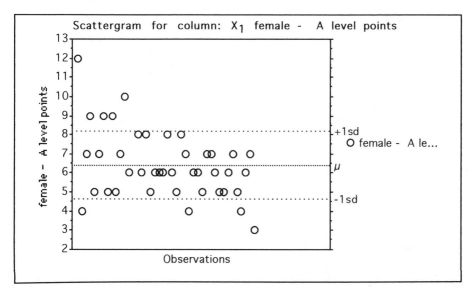

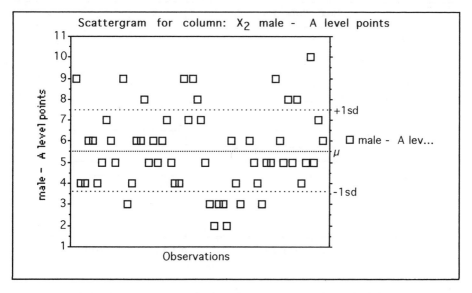

Figure 11.6 Univariate scattergram display (showing mean and standard deviation lines)

Box plots and whiskers The BOX PLOT was developed by Tukey (1977). Statview provides a variant developed by Cleveland (1985). Figure 11.7 shows the general meaning of the box and its upper and lower 'whiskers'; figure 11.8 provides an example.

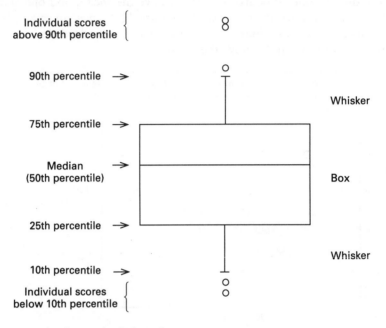

Figure 11.7 The 'box and whisker' plot

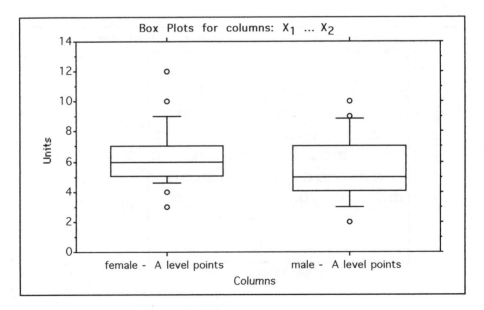

Figure 11.8 Example of 'box and whisker' output

A variant is the 'notched' box, as exemplified in figure 11.9. The notches represent 95 per cent confidence bands about the median value.

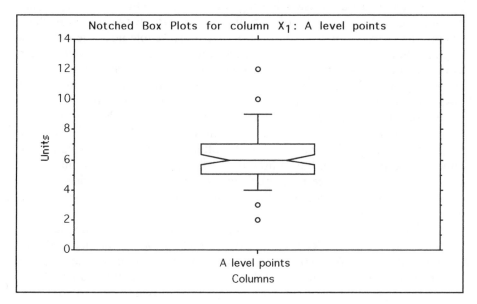

Figure 11.9 The 'notched' box
The 'notches' represent a 95 per cent confidence band around the median.

Note that the plot is based on medians and other percentiles, rather than on means and standard deviations. The circles shown in the figures, above and below the 'whiskers' extending from the box, are individual extreme values (the top and bottom 10 per cent). Emphasizing them in this way helps in deciding whether there is justification in omitting them, or otherwise treating them differently from the rest of the data. The term OUTLIER is commonly used for a value which is inconsistent from the others on objective grounds. For example, an error might be made in entering the data set where separate entries of '2' and '7' get entered together as '27'. If no objective reason of this kind can be unearthed then its treatment is problematic. Criteria for rejection of extreme values based solely on their degree of extremeness have been proposed (e.g. Marsh, 1988, p. 108). Lovie, (1986) provides a very helpful summary of the issues. Barnett and Lewis (1984) give a comprehensive review.

Many statistical procedures are very sensitive to the presence of outliers. For example, one advantage of the median over the mean as a measure of central tendency is its lack of such sensitivity. EDA has been much interested in outliers, both in their own right, and in the study of measures which are robust (i.e. relatively unaffected) in their presence.

Manipulating the Data

Marsh (1988, p. 42) points out that '... data ... is produced, not given'. This stance rejects our classical heritage in two ways. The derivation of data is 'things given', and the word is plural – one datum; two or more data. Taking the latter point first, it appears that most people now use data as a singular noun. However, in a field where the term is used frequently, such as the reports of enquiry, you may be perceived as ignorant of the 'correct' usage if you follow the popular trend. Not wanting to put you in that position, I propose to play the pedant and stick to the plural use.

The 'produced not given' point is important. Many of the data that we collect are actually produced during the enquiry itself. They tend not to be things lying around that we pick up. We often have a very active hand, not only in what is collected, but in how it is collected. The actual numbers that we subject to analysis are very much formed by a process of selection and choice – at a very simple level, for example, do we use grams, kilograms, ounces, pounds, tons, ...?

This basic choice will have been made at the time that the data are collected. In the example, this would probably now be metric, with the specific unit chosen to avoid very large, or very small, numbers (e.g. 5 grams rather than 0.005 kilograms; 2.3 kilograms rather than 2,300 grams). There is still the possibility of manipulating the data subsequently, so that it is easier to analyse; or so that attention can be focused on features of interest, or so that it is easier to compare two or more sets of data. As in so many aspects of enquiry, this process is driven by your research questions. Are there things that you can do with your data that can help give clearer answers to these questions?

It perhaps needs saying that this is nothing to do with 'How to Lie with Statistics' (Huff, 1973). 'Massaging' the data to give a biased or downright untruthful message should have no place in the kind of enquiry covered in this book. The prime safeguard is your own honesty and integrity, but this should be supported by detailed reporting. Sufficient detail should be included to enable the sceptical reader to follow the trail from the collected data, through whatever you do to it, to the interpretation and conclusion.

Scaling data   The earlier section on descriptive statistics emphasized two aspects of a set of data: its *level* and its *spread*. The two simplest ways of scaling data involve these aspects directly.

1   *Adding or subtracting a constant.* A straightforward way of focusing attention on a particular aspect of the data is to add or subtract a particular constant amount from each of the measurements. The most common tactic is to subtract the arithmetic mean from each score. Scores transformed in this way are referred to as DEVIATIONS, i.e.

$$\text{deviation} = (\text{individual score}) - (\text{mean score})$$

This has the advantage of making clear how far each score is from the mean, though with the possible disadvantage that about half the deviation scores will have minus signs associated with them. A similar tactic can be used when the median, or some other measure of central tendency has been employed.

2   *Multiplying by a constant.* This is sometimes referred to as SCALING or RESCALING the variable. It is what you do when changing from weight in imperial measure (pounds, ounces, etc.) to metric (kilograms, grams). This tactic is particularly useful in comparing different sets of data which have initially been measured on different scales. For example, the prices of goods or services in different European countries could be better compared by transforming them all into the standard 'ecu', or into one particular currency.

3   *Other transformations.* There are many other things that you can do. *Taking logarithms, or taking a power (e.g. square, square root, reciprocal)* are tactics commonly used when the distribution of the scores is asymmetrical or in some other way inappropriate for the type of statistical analysis proposed. Details are given in Marsh (1988, ch. 11). Statview includes these transformations in a list of thirty-five possible ways in which the data can be transformed (it is also worth noting that the list includes transforming into ranks and to percentages).

Standardizing data   One way of manipulating data is very commonly used. It involves combining the two approaches covered above, i.e. subtracting the mean (or other measure of central tendency) and dividing by the standard deviation (or other measure of spread).

$$\text{standardized score} = \frac{(\text{individual score}) - (\text{mean score})}{(\text{standard deviation})}$$

expressed in terms of symbols, this becomes

$$\text{standardized score} = \frac{X - \overline{X}}{SD}$$

or

$$\text{standardized score} = \frac{(\text{individual score}) - (\text{median score})}{(\text{semi-inter-quartile range})}$$

$$= \frac{X - M(X)}{dQ}$$

This standardization means that the mean (or median) of the standardized distribution is 0, and its standard deviation (or semi-inter-quartile range) is 1. Distributions that have been standardized in this way are much easier to compare, and in some circumstances combine, than unstandardized ones. Again, this transformation is available from the 'transformations' menu in Statview. It is also possible to display a standard score frequency distribution, which again aids comparisons between distributions.

The Normal Distribution

There are theoretical distributions for which the shape is completely determined once the mean and standard deviation are known. The so-called NORMAL (or GAUSSIAN) DISTRIBUTION is the best known of these. An example is shown as figure 11.10. Many distributions of scores obtained in practice are reasonable approximations to the normal distribution. To find if this is the case for a particular set of scores, they are first standardized as shown above and then scrutinized to see whether the proportion of cases falling at different distances from the mean are as predicted from tables showing the theoretical distribution.

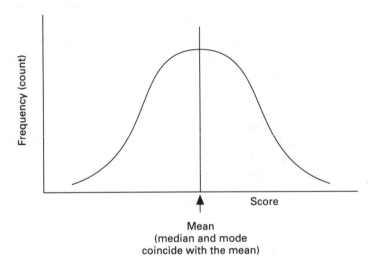

Figure 11.10   The theoretical 'normal' distribution

For example, the expectation is that:

68 per cent of cases are within one SD of the mean,
95 per cent of cases are within two SDs of the mean, and
99.7 per cent are within three SDs of the mean.

Further details, and appropriate tables are in many statistics texts (Robson, 1983, provides a simple account). It is possible to test the 'goodness of fit' of your data to the normal distribution by using a version of the chi-square test (see below, p. 336).

Whether or not a distribution of scores can reasonably be represented as normal is then of value in describing, summarizing and comparing data. However, don't fall into the trap of thinking that 'only "normal" is normal'. Data won't necessarily fall into this pattern. This is no major disaster; your job is to seek to understand what you have got, playing about with the scale if this seems to help. Such transformations may bring the distribution closer to normal, but in itself that may not further your understanding.

The normal distribution also has a part to play if one wants to go on to carry out formal statistical tests on the data. Many of the more commonly used tests are based on the assumption that a normal distribution is involved. Often these tests are *robust* in the sense that deviations from normality do not appear to have much effect on the outcome of the test. However there are 'distribution free' tests (commonly called 'non-parametric' tests) available (Siegel and Castellan, 1988; Meddis, 1984) which do not make assumptions about the shape of the distributions involved.

Skewness As can be seen from figure 11.10, the normal distribution is symmetrical about its centre (which is where the mean, median and mode coincide). In practice, a distribution may be 'skewed' as shown in figure 11.11. 'Negative' skew suggests that the majority of extreme observed values are less than the mean; 'positive' skew that the majority of extreme observed values are above the mean. A simple indication of this can be obtained by comparing the mean and median values. If the median is less than the mean this suggests that over 50 per cent of the values are below the mean, and hence to compensate the right hand or upper tail of the distribution must extend further – indicating positive skew. Statview will also generate an '*Index of Skewness*'. This is the average of the cubed standard scores (z-values) for the distribution. Cubing gives greater weight to the extreme values and hence a positive value for the index indicates a positive skew to the distribution (and vice versa).

Exploring Relationships between Two Variables

Having considered how one might deal with individual variables, let us switch the focus to one of the main concerns in carrying out social research – looking for relationships between variables. Here we will limit ourselves to relations between two variables.

To say that there is a relationship between two variables means that the distribution of scores or values on one of the variables is in some way linked to the distribution of values on the second variable – that, say, higher scores on one variable for that case (person, perhaps) tend to occur when there are higher scores on the second variable for that case. An example would be the relationship between smoking and lung cancer; those who smoke are more likely to develop lung cancer.

Cross-tabulation

Cross-tabulation is a simple and frequently used way of showing whether or not there is a relationship between two variables. It is an extension of the

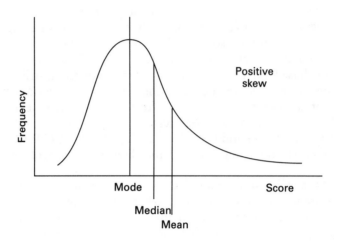

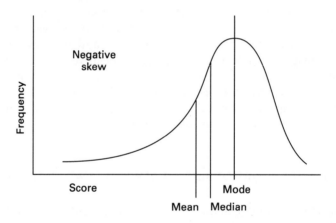

Figure 11.11 Positively and negatively skewed distributions
Note: Statview provides an index of *skewness*. For symmetrical distributions this is 0; it takes on positive values for positive skew and vice versa. A *kurtosis* measure is also provided. This an index of the 'peakiness' of the distribution. See statistics texts for details.

use of frequency tables as discussed in connection with the analysis of single variables. Take once more the data on student intake presented in box 11.2. Let us say that we are interested in the relationship between faculty and the relative number of male and female students, i.e. between the variables 'faculty' and 'gender'. Figure 11.12 presents these data in what is usually called a 'contingency table' in the form produced by Statview. There are six faculties (six levels of the variable 'faculty') and two sexes (two values of the variable 'gender') and hence twelve (six times two) possible combinations of levels of the variables. The boxes in the table, corresponding to each of these

Observed Frequency Table

	arts	business	education	engineer	sciences	Totals:
female	12	15	6	1	8	42
male	12	11	4	17	14	58
Totals:	24	26	10	18	22	100

Figure 11.12   Contingency table showing the relationship between 'faculty' and 'gender'

combinations, are referred to as CELLS. The total for each row and each column is given at the end of the row or column. These totals are called the ROW MARGINALS and COLUMN MARGINALS respectively.

Statview also provides tables of 'Percentages of Row Totals' and 'Percentages of Column Totals' as shown in figure 11.13. The row total presentation shows the way in which females (and males) are distributed across the faculties. The column total presentation shows the relative percentages (or

(a)

Percents of Row Totals

	arts	business	education	engineer	sciences	Totals:
female	28.571%	35.714%	14.286%	2.381%	19.048%	100%
male	20.69%	18.966%	6.897%	29.31%	24.138%	100%
Totals:	24%	26%	10%	18%	22%	100%

(b)

Percents of Column Totals

	arts	business	education	engineer	sciences	Totals:
female	50%	57.692%	60%	5.556%	36.364%	42%
male	50%	42.308%	40%	94.444%	63.636%	58%
Totals:	100%	100%	100%	100%	100%	100%

Figure 11.13   Contingency tables presented in terms of (a) row and (b) column percentages

proportions) of males and females in different faculties (e.g. the proportion of males in the science faculty). The contingency table, presented in terms of percentages, helps to highlight any relationships between the two variables. Here the low percentage of females in the engineering faculty is a striking, though unsurprising, feature.

The 'Significance' of Relationships in Contingency Tables

It is possible to assess the statistical significance of relationships in contingency tables. This amounts to an assessment of the probability of obtaining the observed relationship if only chance factors are in operation. If this probability is sufficiently small (conventionally taken as 1 in 20, i.e. $p = 0.05$) there is taken to be a 'real', as against a chance, relationship. The chi-square (χ^2) test is commonly used to assess the statistical significance of such relationships in contingency tables.

Figure 11.14 shows the 'expected values' of frequencies for the data in figure 11.12 as produced by Statview. These are the values which would be expected or predicted if there were *no relationship* between the variables. The chi-square statistic is an index of the discrepancy between the observed and expected frequencies, and is also given in figure 11.14, together with an associated probability. If this probability is 0.05 *or less*, then the chi-square is conventionally referred to as statistically significant. Some workers refer to a probability of 0.01, or less (as achieved in this analysis), as 'highly statistically significant'. An alternative is to note that statistical significance has been achieved, and quote the exact probability (here 0.0054).

Statisticians warn against the use of chi-square when one or more *expected* frequencies fall below a particular value, usually taken as 5 in small tables. The present example is border-line in this respect (one expected frequency is 4.2) and it would probably be acceptable to include the analysis but add a caveat about this relatively low expected frequency. Fisher's Exact Test is a substitute which can be used in circumstances where the expected frequencies are too low for chi-square (see Siegel and Castellan, 1988).

A chi-square analysis, if statistically significant as in the present case, indicates that *overall* there is a relationship between the two variables (here 'faculty' and 'gender'). Statview, however, also provides a means of identifying the *particular cells* in a contingency table which are responsible for the significant chi-square. These are known as the 'post hoc cell contributions' which are also shown in figure 11.14. This is an approximately normally distributed statistic with mean of zero and standard deviation of one. Hence it is significant at the 5 per cent level ($p = 0.05$) if it exceeds 1.96 (see tables of the normal distribution). So, in the example given, the significant contributions to the overall chi-square come from the engineering faculty. This is as inspection of the data had already suggested. Don't worry that the conclusions of common sense and statistical analysis coincide. The formal

Expected Values

	arts	business	education	engineer	sciences	Totals:
female	10.08	10.92	4.2	7.56	9.24	42
male	13.92	15.08	5.8	10.44	12.76	58
Totals:	24	26	10	18	22	100

Coded Chi-Square X_1: faculty Y_1: gender

Summary Statistics

DF:	4	
Total Chi-Square:	14.69	p = .0054
G Statistic:	17.336	
Contingency Coefficient:	.358	
Cramer's V:	.383	

Post-Hoc Cell Contributions

	arts	business	education	engineer	sciences
female	.911	1.885	1.216	-3.46	-.606
male	-.911	-1.885	-1.216	3.46	.606

Figure 11.14 'Expected frequencies' and results of a chi-square analysis

analysis is after all only a type of 'codified common sense'; i.e. commonsense applied according to consistent rules.

In two-by-two contingency tables (where both variables only have two values) statisticians use a somewhat different formula incorporating a 'correction for continuity' (sometimes referred to as 'Yates' correction') for computing chi-square. Statview will do this automatically for two-by-two tables producing an appropriately adjusted chi-square and associated probability.

Using chi-square to test for 'goodness of fit'   Chi-square can also be used to compare frequencies on a single variable to see how closely they 'fit' to those expected or predicted on some theoretical basis. A common theoretical expectation is for all frequencies to be the same; or perhaps it may be desired to test the goodness of fit to the frequencies expected if the data were normally distributed. The difference in terms of computation is that these expected frequencies have to be supplied, rather than being generated automatically from the observed frequencies.

Scattergrams

A SCATTERGRAM (also known as a scatterplot or scatter diagram) is a graphical representation of the relationship between two variables. It only makes sense when it is possible to order the values for each of the variables in some non-arbitrary manner. Hence in the data set of box 11.2 it would be reasonable to draw a scattergram for, say 'degree class' against 'A level points'; but not for 'faculty' against 'A level points'. This is because any particular ordering of the faculties along an axis is arbitrary, and the apparent graphical relationship between the variables will vary with the ordering.

Figure 11.15 presents a scattergram showing, with hypothetical data, the relationship between age and income for a sample of graduates. It shows the position of each person on the two variables. For example, the top right point on the scattergram corresponds to someone who is 39 years old and has an income of about £32,000. Various techniques are available to deal with overlap of points; figure 11.16 shows an example.

Scattergrams are a powerful pictorial device, giving a clear picture of the nature and strength of the relationship between the variables. They have their limitations, however. Many types of data are not readily amenable to display in this way, particularly when there are very few values on one or both of the variables. Nevertheless, unless you have data where the ordering of values is arbitrary, you should always consider the feasibility of drawing a scattergram for two-variable data. It is possible to produce contingency tables from the same data, summarizing by taking appropriate intervals along the variables when they take on many values.

Multiple groups (strata) are often shown together on scattergrams to facilitate comparisons between sub-groups. Figure 11.17 shows one of several ways of doing this available with Statview.

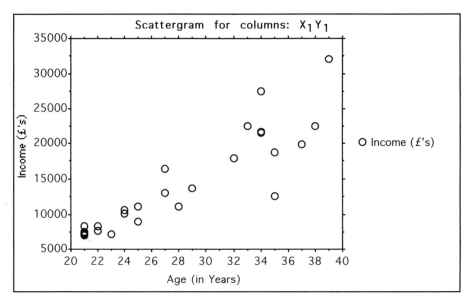

Figure 11.15 Scattergram showing relationship between age and income for a sample of graduates

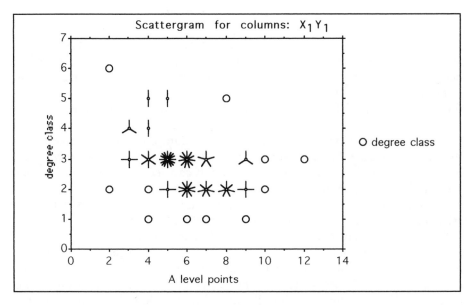

Figure 11.16 Scattergram with 'sunflower' display to deal with overlap of points ('Sunflowers' are points with 'petals'. A single data point is shown, as usual, as a circle. For two or more data points there is a corresponding number of petals.)

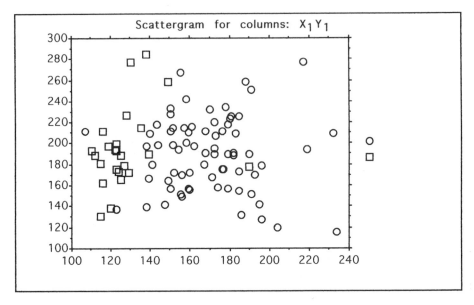

Figure 11.17 Differentiation of sub-groups in a scattergram
(Circles are males; squares are females.)

Correlation Coefficients

Measures of correlation, referred to as CORRELATION COEFFICIENTS, give an indication of both the strength and the direction of the relationship between the variables. The commonly used coefficients assume that there is a *linear relationship* between the two variables. Figure 11.18 demonstrates this in the idealized form of the 'perfect' linear correlation. However, perfection is not of this world. Certainly, you are very unlikely to get that degree of 'tightness' in the relationship, with data concerning humans and their doings. Figure 11.19 illustrates the kind of picture you are likely to see if there is a strong linear correlation. As you can see, the points fall within a cigar-shaped 'envelope'. The thinner the cigar, the stronger the relationship. With weaker correlations, the cigar is fatter; an essentially zero correlation shows no discernable pattern in the scattergram.

Statview routinely computes a Pearson's correlation coefficient (r). The output also provides the square of the correlation coefficient (r^2). This is a useful index as it corresponds to the proportion of the variation in values of one of the variables which can be predicted from the variation in the other variable. Broadly speaking, if this is low (say less than 0.3 – but this will depend on circumstances) then it is unlikely to be profitable to exert much further time and effort in investigating the relationship. High values might suggest carrying out a subsequent regression analysis (see below).

Other coefficients are available. Statview can calculate the Spearman rank correlation coefficient and Kendall's rank correlation coefficient (known as

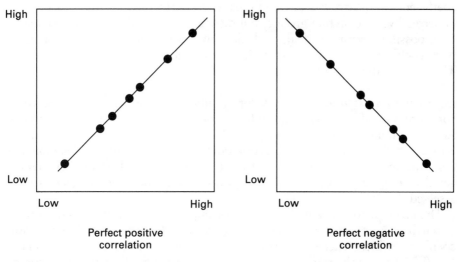

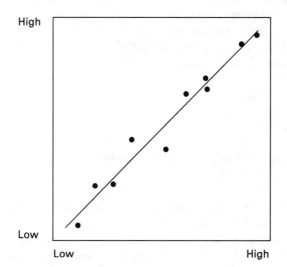

Figure 11.18   A 'perfect' linear correlation

Figure 11.19   Example of a high positive correlation

Kendall's Tau). As their labels suggest, they are both used with data in the form of ranks, or orderings of data (what is first, second, etc.). The data may have been collected in this form, perhaps through participants expressing their preferences for different objects or situations, or may have been collected in other forms and subsequently converted into ranks. They do not assume normal distribution of the data and hence may be used when that assumption, on which the Pearson's coefficient is based, is dubious. They are, however measures of linear correlation (see below). The Spearman coefficient is effectively a Pearson coefficient performed on the ranks and is preferred by some on that ground, but most analysts appear to prefer Kendall's Tau, possibly because it deals with ties more consistently. Statview presents these coefficients both with and without correction for ties, if any are present. The former, lower, value should be used.

Measuring the 'significance' of a correlation   The statistical significance of correlation coefficients is commonly computed and is generated by Statview as a probability statement (e.g. $p = 0.01$) for the Spearman and Kendall's Tau coefficients. Note that Statview does not do this for the Pearson coefficient, apparently assuming that large coefficients will be further investigated through a regression analysis (see below), where significance is then assessed.

The given probability is that a relationship of at least this size could have arisen by chance. It is important to appreciate that the size of correlation coefficient which reaches a particular statistical significance (conventionally $p = 0.05$ being taken as the largest acceptable probability for this type of significance) is very strongly affected by the size of the sample of data involved. Thus for twenty pairs of scores the value of the Pearson correlation coefficient is 0.44 (two-tailed test – see below, page 352); for fifty it is 0.28; for 100 less than 0.2; and for 500 less than 0.1. This illustrates the point that *statistical* significance has little to do with *significance* as commonly understood. Certainly, with a large sample such as 500, you can achieve statistical significance when less than 1 per cent of the variability in one variable is predictable from variation in the other – 99 per cent comes from other sources!

The message is that if the statistical significance of a correlation is to be quoted, make sure that the size of the correlation and of the sample also get quoted.

Non-linear relationships between variables   It is perfectly possible to have some form of non-linear relationship between two variables. One value of the scattergram is in highlighting such non-linearities, in part because they are likely to call for discussion and explanation. They should also give a warning against using statistical techniques which assume linearity. *Curvi-linear relationships* might be found. The envelope, instead of being cigarshaped might be better represented by a banana or boomerang, as in figure 11.20.

This is one situation where the data transformations discussed earlier in the chapter (p. 329) may be of value, as the appropriate transformation might convert the relationship in figure 11.20 to something closely approaching linearity – and hence more amenable to statistical analysis. Even if this transformation does 'work' in that sense, there may be consequent problems of interpretation. To know that there is a strong linear correlation between one variable and, say, the square of another variable may be of descriptive and even predictive value, but defy your attempts at understand-

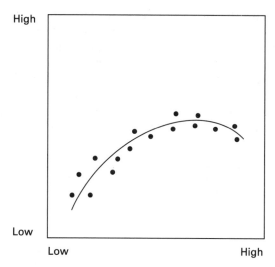

Figure 11.20   Example of a curvilinear relationship

ing. However, finding that a reciprocal transformation works, such that a non-linear relationship involving 'time elapsed' as one variable, becomes linear when a 'rate' measure (i.e. reciprocal of time) is used, may well be readily interpretable.

Lines of 'best fit'   It is possible to draw a LINE OF BEST FIT on a scattergram. This can be estimated by drawing a line having roughly equal numbers of points above and below it, and making each point as near to the line as possible (using the minimum, i.e. perpendicular, distance from the line in each case).

There are systematic means of drawing such a line, which should be employed if it is to be used in any formal way. One approach which is commonly used is LINEAR REGRESSION. This involves finding the line for which the squared deviation of individual points from the line (in the vertical, i.e. the Y dimension) is a minimum. This can be routinely performed by many computer packages, including Statview. There are alternative ways of deriving these lines (see, for example, Marsh, 1988, pp. 188–92, who advocates 'resistant lines'). When data are 'well behaved' (reasonably normal distributions with no problematic 'outliers'), linear regression is probably preferable, if only because of the ease with which the task can be completed.

The 'line of best fit', when obtained by one of the above means, is a powerful and useful way of summarizing the linear relationship between two variables. All straight lines can be expressed by a simple algebraic formula, one form of which is

$$Y = bX + a,$$

Where Y and X are the two variables (conventionally, when there are dependent and independent variables, Y is the dependent variable and X the independent variable); and a and b are constants which typify the particular line of best fit. The constant a is known as the INTERCEPT and is the point where the line cuts the vertical or Y axis; b is known as the SLOPE. This is shown diagramatically in figure 11.21. In this example the slope in 1030.175 and the intercept −14633.589 (the intercept looks as if it is positive on the graph simply because there is not a true zero at the left of the X axis).

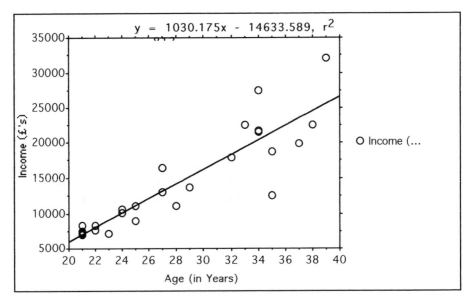

Figure 11.21   Fitting a 'line of best fit' for relationship between age and income

In addition to providing an elegant way of summarizing the data, the line of best fit (or the coefficients a and b, which amount to the same thing) can be used for predictive purposes – for example to give an estimate of the likely increase in income over a specified number of years. As b represents the increase per year (£1,030 per annum), the predicted increase over, say, five years would be £5,150.

There is a difficulty with the data in that the amount of variability of the points around the regression line is not constant. It appears to increase with higher values of age and income. This not uncommon feature goes by the somewhat fearsome name of HETEROSCEDASTICITY and, strictly, violates one of the assumptions on which Pearson's correlation coefficient is based. Again, this is a situation where possible transformations of the data might be attempted. Figure 11.22 illustrates the effect of taking the reciprocal of income. It appears to reduce the unwanted effect considerably – but then leaves an interpretation problem!

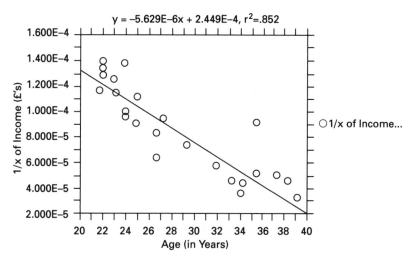

$y = -5.629E{-}6x + 2.449E{-}4, r^2 = .852$

Figure 11.22 Effect of transformation of data in figure 11.21

Analysis of Covariance

It may be appropriate to mention here a technique which combines regression with analysis of variance methods (discussed later in the chapter; see p. 355). It is a technique introduced by Ronald Fisher in the 1930s for the statistical, as against experimental, control of the effects of one or more uncontrolled variables. Suppose we are concerned with comparing three methods of teaching some part of the curriculum. Each method is used with a different randomly assigned group and tests of achievement administered. The groups may differ in intelligence, and it appears likely that their performance on the test correlates with intelligence. If measures of intelligence are available they can be used as a COVARIATE in the analysis to adjust for the effect of intelligence and produce a corrected measure of the effects of the three methods. Standard statistical texts provide computational details (see, for example Winer, 1971).

There are major interpretational problems with this approach; basically, any statistical adjustment is based on assumptions that are quite difficult to justify. The approach is certainly no substitute for seeking control of extraneous variables directly in the enquiry. Nevertheless it is used, and there are specialist applications where it is of value. It is not directly available using Statview but is covered in SPSS and Minitab.

Exploring Relationships among Three or More Variables

Establishing a relationship between two variables is important but not necessarily the end of the matter as far as analysis is concerned. If an experimental design has been used, this may be adequate in demonstrating a causal link between the two variables, although often experimental designs are more sophisticated, involving multiple variables which call for different approaches to analysis. Multivariate analyses which are concerned with the *joint* effects of multiple variables are covered later in the section. We will, however, first consider approaches which look at the effects of taking into account a third variable on the relationship between two variables.

Three-variable Contingency Tables: the 'Elaboration' Approach

With non-experimental strategies, it is often essential to explore the effects of other variables when seeking to understand the basis of a two-variable relationship. One set of techniques, sometimes referred to as 'elaboration analysis', is commonly used with contingency tables. The basic approach is straightforward and involves the following steps: –

a   establish a relationship between two variables;
b   subdivide the data on the basis of the values of a third variable;
c   review the original two-variable relationship for each of the sub-groups.
d   compare the relationship found in each sub-group with the original relationship.

The third variable is referred to as the TEST VARIABLE (or CONTROL VARIABLE). The original relationship between the two variables, where the third variable is not being held constant at a particular value, is called the ZERO-ORDER RELATIONSHIP. The relationship that is found for a particular value of the test variable is known as a PARTIAL RELATIONSHIP.

The pattern of effects of the test variable on the zero-order relationship can help in interpreting and understanding what is going on. Possibilities include the following:

1 *Partial relationships essentially the same as zero-order relationship.* This is a *replication* of the original relationship showing the lack of effect of the control variable.

2 *Partial relationships reduced essentially to zero.* The interpretation depends on your view of the logical link between the test variable and the original variables. It can be *either* (a) an ANTECEDENT VARIABLE, that is, a logically prior variable affecting both the original variables directly, *or* (b) an INTERVENING VARIABLE – affect*ed* by the original indepependent variable, and affect*ing* the original dependent variable.

If the test variable is antecedent then this suggests that the original zero-order 'relationship' was *spurious*. There is no causal relationship between the two original variables, the apparent link being the effect of the test variable.

If the test variable is intervening then we have made progress in *interpreting* the way in which the initial independent variable is affecting the dependent variable. We are strengthened in the view that the original relationship was causal and have some understanding as to how the causal process is working.

Clearly it is crucial that one can differentiate between antecedent and intervening variables. For example, suppose that a study of Russia suggests that the economic collapse in the early 1990s was a causative factor in the revival of religious observance. Here a likely third variable is the breakdown of the Communist system. Considering the time sequence, and intuitively, it seems more plausible that the Communist breakdown was an antecedent variable affecting both the economy and religious observance, than that the economic collapse led to the Communist breakdown which then acted as an intervening variable. Hence the conclusion is that the apparent link between economic collapse and religious revival is spurious.

3 *Differential effects on different partial relationships* (e.g. one reduced essentially to zero, another virtually unchanged). This indicates a MODERATED RELATIONSHIP. In the example given it means that we have specified the conditions under which the original relationship occurs. This pattern is commonly referred to as an INTERACTION between the two original variables (particularly in the context of analysis of variance; see p. 360).

4 *Partial relationships substantially stronger than zero-order relationship.* Test variables are normally only used when there is a sizeable original relationship. However, it is feasible in some circumstances that a weak original relationship is strengthened when a test variable is introduced. Rosenberg (1968) referred to control variables having this effect as SUPPRESSOR variables. It is even possible for the direction of the original relationship to be changed through use of a test variable. Rosenberg (1968, pp. 94–5) cites the hypothetical example of an original relationship between social class and attitudes toward civil rights – with the working classes being somewhat stronger civil rights supporters than the middle classes. Using the test variable of race, he found the opposite in the partial relationships, with slightly stronger middle-class support among whites, and very substantially greater middle-class support among blacks. Race is then a distorter variable (the reversal being possible because of the widely differing proportions of middle and working class in the black and white groups).

The approach to data analysis is simply a somewhat more complex version of the use of contingency tables, which were covered earlier.

The real world is complex and analysis may well not generate patterns as clear-cut as those discussed above. Thus the original relationship may, with an antecedent test variable, drop to a fraction of its original value without approaching zero. This would tend to suggest a more complex situation where the original relation is partially spurious and the test variable is having some causative influence. In practice it is likely that multiple causation is the norm for many of the phenomena which interest us and that

models which allow for multiple independent variables are to be preferred
(see below).

It is possible to extend this type of analysis to four or even more variables
(i.e. to two or more test variables) but it rapidly becomes unwieldy, particularly when there are several categories on each variable. Unless large amounts
of data have been collected, the data base for each sub-group becomes very
small. The choice of test variables for elaboration analysis is obviously of
central importance as it is only possible to include very few of them. They
have to be pre-specified at least to the extent that you have collected the
necessary data (some of the variables on which data have been collected can,
of course, be omitted at the analysis stage).

Using Partial Correlations

Essentially the same type of logical analysis can be carried out using partial
correlation coefficients, rather than proportions in contingency tables. This
amounts to examining the correlation between two variables and then seeing
how, if at all, it changes when one or more other variables are held constant.

In the three-variable case, the correlation matrix is first calculated, which
gives each of the three possible correlations between the variables. A partial
correlation matrix is then calculated (note that in Statview this can be obtained as part of the computations carried out for factor analysis). Interpretation of the relationship between the variables is based on the pattern of
correlations and the logical potential link between the test variable and the
two original variables (e.g. antecedent or intervening).

The partial correlation approach cannot be used when testing for a 'moderated' relationship (see above, p. 345) because this depends on comparing
the relationship for different categories of the test variable and the partial
correlation effectively gives you a single averaged figure. There are also
problems in computing the correlation coefficients if one of the variables has
a small number of categories or values.

Multivariate Analyses

It is also possible to explore relationships when there are two or more
independent variables as well as a dependent variable. The section focuses
on the use of MULTIPLE REGRESSION as it is a flexible, widely used approach
which has been made readily accessible through computer packages.

Other possibilities include PARTIAL CORRELATION, as discussed above,
although this is difficult to interpret when more than three or four variables
are involved. There is much current interest in CLUSTER ANALYSIS (otherwise known as NUMERICAL TAXONOMY), which concerns itself with ways of
classifying, or clustering, entities on the basis of a large number of measures
(Everitt, 1980). MULTIPLE DISCRIMINANT FUNCTION ANALYSIS provides a
method for investigating multiple differences between groups in a set

(Lachenbruch, 1975). Youngman (1979, ch. 9) provides a useful introduction to these and related approaches to dealing with ways of classifying and discriminating within complex data sets.

Taking the simplest possible case, for multiple regression, of one dependent variable and two independent variables, the regression equation (refer back to page 341) is

$$y = a + b_1x_1 + b_2x_2$$

where y is the dependent variable, x_1 and x_2 are the two independent variables, a is the intercept, and b_1 and b_2 the regression coefficients for the two independent variables. The regression coefficient gives you the change in the dependent variable for each unit change in that independent variable, *with the effect of any of the independent variables controlled* ('partialled out').

While multiple regression can be used in the same way as linear regression, to give a line of best fit and to provide predictions through substitutions of different values of x_1 and x_2, its main use is to provide an estimate of the relative importance of the different independent variables in producing changes in the dependent variable. To do this, it is necessary to convert the regression coefficients to allow for the different scales on which they have been measured. When this is done, they are referred to as STANDARDIZED REGRESSION COEFFICIENTS or BETA WEIGHTS. They then tell you how many standard deviation units the dependent variable will change for a unit change in that independent variable. Figure 11.23 provides an example. The printout incorporates several useful statistics. These include: –

R-squared This is the MULTIPLE COEFFICIENT OF DETERMINATION: a measure of the proportion of the variance in the dependent variable which is explained by the independent variables in the equation. In the example, as R^2 is 0.52, the proportion of variance explained is 52 per cent. An 'adjusted R^2' is also produced. This will be smaller than R^2 and is adjusted in the sense that it takes into account the number of independent variables involved and would normally be preferred to the unadjusted value.

t-value of coefficients This presents a test of whether or not the associated beta coefficient is significantly different from zero. The probability value is given in each case.

Standard error of coefficients This is a measure of the accuracy of the individual regression coefficients (see p. 347). *90 per cent and 95 per cent confidence limits*, both upper and lower, are also given. This information is useful in assessing the likely accuracy of predictions based on the regression equation.

This discussion merely scratches the surface of multiple regression and its possibilities as an analytic tool. If a major concern is in developing a model,

Multiple Regression Y₁:Chol-3yrs   3 X variables

Count:	R:	R-squared:	Adj. R-squared:	RMS Residual:
43	.721	.52	.483	26.171

Analysis of Variance Table

Source	DF:	Sum Squares:	Mean Square:	F-test:
REGRESSION	3	28916.585	9638.862	14.073
RESIDUAL	39	26712.159	684.927	p = .0001
TOTAL	42	55628.744		

Residual Information Table

SS[e(i)-e(i-1)]:	e ≥ 0:	e < 0:	DW test:
42643.56	21	22	1.596

Note: 52 cases deleted with missing values.

Multiple Regression Y₁:Chol-3yrs   3 X variables

Beta Coefficient Table

Variable:	Coefficient:	Std. Err.:	Std. Coeff.:	t-Value:	Probability:
INTERCEPT	50.252				
Variable 1	.028	.065	.062	.427	.6715
Variable 2	.618	.42	.184	1.473	.1487
Variable 3	.694	.146	.654	4.751	.0001

Residual : Column 29 Std. Residual : Column 30 Fitted : Column 31

Multiple Regression Y₁:Chol-3yrs   3 X variables

Confidence Intervals and Partial F Table

Variable:	95% Lower:	95% Upper:	90% Lower:	90% Upper:	Partial F:
INTERCEPT					
Variable 1	-.103	.159	-.081	.137	.183
Variable 2	-.231	1.467	-.089	1.325	2.171
Variable 3	.398	.989	.448	.94	22.574

Figure 11.23   Results of a multiple regression analysis

effectively in deciding on an appropriate regression equation, then an option known as STEPWISE REGRESSION is worth considering. This starts with the simplest possible model and then step-by-step examines the implications of adding further independent variables to the equation.

You are strongly recommended to seek advice when considering using multiple regression, as not only is it complicated but it is particularly easy to do something silly and inappropriate with the packages available. It is worth noting, however, that multiple regression can be used with a wide variety of types of data. In particular, it can be used with categorical variables such as 'gender' and 'faculty' in the example we have been using. The apparent difficulty here is that the ordering of categories is essentially arbitrary for such variables, and particularly when there are more than two categories for a variable, the ordering chosen would affect the result obtained. This can be handled by the use of so-called 'dummy variables'. It involves coding particular categories as 'present' (say coded '1') or absent (say coded '0'). Bryman and Cramer (1990, pp. 240–1) give details.

Factor Analysis

Factor analysis is another approach to making sense of a large number of correlations between variables. It has similarities with regression analysis but differs in that the variables all have equal status; no single variable is designated as the dependent or criterion variable. Factor analysis starts with a matrix of correlations.

Matrices of this type, particularly when they contain up to a hundred or so variables, are very difficult to interpret. Factor analysis aids in this process by pointing to clusters of variables which are highly intercorrelated. The 'factors' referred to are hypothetical constructs developed to account for the intercorrelations between the variables. Factor analysis seeks to replace a large and unwieldy set of variables with a small and easily understood number of factors. Suppose that your correlation matrix arises from a fifty-item questionnaire on aggression and aggressiveness. You find, say, that there are strong intercorrelations between twelve items concerning aggression towards family and friends, and similar intercorrelations between nine items concerning aggressiveness towards people in authority, but no other strong clusters. This then provides good evidence that two factors are important in understanding your results.

The technique is widely used in the development of tests and scales (see, for example, Rust and Golombok, 1989, ch. 8). It allows you to assess the extent to which different test items are measuring the same concept (strong intercorrelations), or whether their answers to one set of questions are unrelated to their answers on a second set. Hence we get an assessment of whether the questions are measuring the same concepts or variables.

Factor analysis is typically used as an exploratory tool. An alternative version referred to as 'confirmatory factor analysis' (Long, 1983) assesses the extent to which the solution obtained matches a hypothesized pattern. Exploratory factor analysis starts with the correlation matrix. For it to be worthwhile to carry out the analysis, the matrix should show a substantial number of significant correlations (either positive or negative).

The number of respondents or subjects should exceed the number of variables. When the interest is not simply to describe the factors summarizing the relations between variables, but to try to get a reliable estimate of these underlying factors, then minima of five times the number of subjects to the number of variables have been suggested. There are many versions of factor analysis including canonical, alpha, image and maximum likelihood factoring, but the most commonly used are PRINCIPAL-COMPONENTS ANALYSIS and PRINCIPAL-AXIS FACTORING (sometimes simply referred to as 'factor analysis'). Accounts of the process are found in Wright and Fowler (1986), and in specialized texts such as Child (1990) and Gorsuch (1983).

Statview provides several factor analysis options. Bryman and Cramer (1990, pp. 256–65) provide details of the procedures to be followed and the kinds of output obtained when the SPSS is used to carry out principal-components and principal-axis analyses.

Exploring Differences

This chapter has, so far, focused on displaying, describing and summarizing quantitative data; and on exploring relationships among data. We now turn to what has, traditionally, been viewed as the major task when analysing quantitative data. Are there *differences* between the scores, values or observations obtained under one condition and those obtained under another condition (or conditions)?

It is to answer questions of this type that many of the *tests of statistical inference* have been developed. The basic logic behind such tests is not difficult, although its working out in specific tests can be complex. The test is commonly used to make decisions about the state of affairs in some 'population' as compared with the actual sample of scores or observations that we have obtained. For example, suppose we want to find out whether the ratio of men to women in a particular sample is such that we can consider it representative of a specific population where the ratio of men to women is known. If there is a fifty–fifty split in the population but there are no women in a sample of twenty, then common sense might be unwilling to regard this as a representative sample, and perhaps cast doubts upon the randomness of the procedure used to select the sample. However, even if we decide that the sample was not drawn from the fifty–fifty population, we could be wrong. A sample of twenty consisting of twenty women is in fact just as likely to occur as any other specific sample (the analogy often drawn is with tossing coins – it is possible to have a sequence of twenty heads in a row; and that sequence is just as likely as any other specific sequence such as HTTHTTTHHTHHTHTTTTHH). There are, however, many possible ways in which one could end up with, say, eleven males and nine females, but in fact only one sequence which gives all twenty females. It is then possible to come to the decision (based on probabilities) that the sample didn't come from the population when it in fact did, an error known as a TYPE ONE ERROR.

Statistical tests provide ways of assessing this type of error. In fact the term STATISTICAL SIGNIFICANCE, already used in connection with tests mentioned earlier in the chapter, simply refers to the probability of making a type one error. The convention has also been mentioned of setting this at a probability of 0.05 (i.e. 1 in 20), referred to as *significant*; or sometimes at 0.01 (i.e. 1 in 100), referred to as *highly significant*. However, the fact that many computer programmes now generate exact probability figures for the chance of making a type one error, rather than saying that it is 'less than 0.05' or 'less than 0.01', means that there is an increasing tendency for such exact probabilities to be quoted.

There is also a TYPE TWO ERROR: that is, the probability of deciding that the sample came from the population when in fact it did not. There is an inverse relationship between the two types of error, in the sense that we can reduce our chances of making a type one error by setting the significance level at a very low probability (say 0.001, or 1 in 1,000). However, setting the decision line at this point produces a corresponding increase in the chances of making a type two error. A simple account of the meaning of statistical significance is given in Robson (1983). Hays (1981) gives a more adequate account.

The Significance of Statistical Significance

Statistical significance testing is a deeply entrenched part of the research process for most empirically oriented psychologists, and not a few other social scientists. However, many serious questions have been asked about the value of using tests of significance (Barlow et al., 1984, pp. 27–9). Meehl (1978) goes so far as to conclude that reliance on statistical significance was one of the 'worst things that ever happened in the history of psychology' (p. 817).

A major problem is that statistical significance is not related to the size or importance of the effect. It is *statistically* significant only in the sense of being unlikely to be attributable to chance factors. It does not refer to 'significance' in anything like the normal meaning of the word – the *statistically* significant result could well be trivial. The chance of obtaining a statistically significant result increases as the sample size increases, because you then get a more sensitive test of any difference between the conditions tested. But there is always likely to be *some* difference between the conditions. Hence the common injunction to 'use a larger number of subjects' may buy statistical significance at the expense of real life triviality.

Paradoxically, if one is using statistical significance, there is much to be said for keeping the sample small so that only robust effects are going to be picked up.

Attempts have been made to shift the criterion to CLINICAL, as against statistical, significance (Hersen and Barlow, 1976). Alternatively, statistical measures such as *proportion of variance accounted for* (e.g. Hays, 1981) attempt to estimate the size and importance of effects. However, the use of statistical significance is still so deeply entrenched that you omit it at your peril.

Single-group Tests

In most situations we are concerned with comparing the scores or values obtained under one condition with those obtained under another condition during the enquiry. However, you might want to compare what you have obtained with some expectation arising outside the study to see whether there is a difference. Statview incorporates two tests of this kind.

Chi-square as a test of 'goodness of fit'   This test has already been mentioned (p. 336). It is described in Statview as a One-Group Chi-Square. Figure 11.24 gives an example.

One-group t-test   The *t*-test is a very widely used test used to compare two means. In this version, the comparison is between a mean obtained from the particular sample of scores that you have obtained under some condition, and a hypothesized population mean. For example, we might wish to test whether the mean of the A level grades given in the data set of box 11.2 (sample mean = 5.9) differs significantly from the overall mean of A level grades for the corresponding national intake (population mean = 5.5). Figure 11.25 presents the results of this analysis.

The probability value given here is referred to as '2-tail'. It is possible to opt for either '1-tail' or '2-tail' probabilities. '2-tail' means that one is simply concerned with establishing the probability of a difference between the two means. With '1-tail' the hypothesis is that the difference will be in a particular direction (hence referred to as a 'directional' hypothesis). '2-tail' probabilities should be selected unless there is a strong a priori reason for expecting the difference to be in a particular direction. Statistics texts give detailed explanations.

Two-group tests

Many of the questions we are interested in when carrying out a study producing quantitative data boil down to whether there are differences between the scores obtained under two conditions, or by two groups. Do mature students admitted without standard entry qualifications get poorer

	Observed Alcohol Use	Expected Alcohol Use
1	32	23.750
2	33	23.750
3	28	23.750
4	2	23.750

One Group Chi-Square X$_1$: Observed Alcohol Use   Y$_1$: Expected Alcoh...

DF:	Chi-Square:	Probability:
3	27.147	.0001

Figure 11.24   Chi-square as a test of 'goodness of fit'
Observed alcohol use under conditions 1 to 4 is compared with the expectation of an even distribution (32 + 33 + 28 + 2) /4 = 23.75.

One Sample t-Test   X$_1$: A level points

DF:	Sample Mean:	Pop. Mean:	t Value:	Prob. (2-tail):
96	5.918	5.5	2.156	.0336

Note: 3 cases deleted with missing values.

Figure 11.25   One-group *t*-test

degrees than 18-year-old 'A level' entrants? Do patients suffering from low back pain get better more quickly when treated by chiropractic than by drugs? And so on.

Two-group t-tests   The *t*-test is very commonly used to compare the means of two groups. It comes in two versions. The *paired two-group t-test* (sometimes called the *dependent samples t-test*) should be used when there are pairs of scores. This would be, for example, if the same person provided a score in each of the conditions. The *unpaired two-group t-test* (otherwise known as the *independent samples t-test*) is where there is no such basis for putting together pairs of scores. Figure 11.26 gives an example of the Statview output from the tests. It is good practice, when recording the results of such tests, to include not only the *t*-value and its statistical significance (the probability value, which must be lower than 0.05 for conventional significance) but also the means and standard deviations of the two sets of scores.

Incidentally, a minus sign for the value of t is not of importance, and does not affect its significance; it simply indicates that the mean of whatever has been taken as the first set of scores is less than that for the second group of scores. The 'DF' which occurs in this and many other printouts, refers to 'degrees of freedom'. It is a statistical concept of some importance but is in many cases, including this, simply related to the size of the sample.

(a)

Unpaired t-Test			
DF:		Unpaired t Value:	Prob. (2-tail):
93		-.537	.5926

Group:	Count:	Mean:	Std. Dev.:	Std. Error:
male	71	190.085	35.299	4.189
female	24	194.625	37.322	7.618

(b)

Paired t-Test	X_1: Weight	Y_1: Weight-3yr	
DF:	Mean X - Y:	Paired t value:	Prob. (1-tail):
42	-1.907	-1.558	.0634

Note: 52 cases deleted with missing values.

Figure 11.26 Results of two-group t-tests
(a) unpaired version; (b) paired version.

Nonparametric equivalents to the t-test Statview, in common with many statistical packages, provides a range of 'nonparametric' tests. Parametric tests (of which the t-test is an example) are ones that have been based in their derivation on certain assumptions as to the nature of the distributions from which the data come (usually that they are normal). Nonparametric tests are based on other principles and do not make this kind of assumption. Proponents of parametric tests argue that they are more *efficient* (in the sense that they will detect a significant difference with a smaller sample size than the corresponding non-parametric test); that it is possible to carry out a greater range and variety of tests with them; and that they are *robust* (meaning that violations of the assumptions on which they are based, e.g. about the normality of the distribution from which the data samples are drawn, have little or no effect on the results they produce).

Nonparametric advocates counter with the arguments that their tests tend to be easier to use and understand and hence less prone to mindless regurgitation; that because of the fewer assumptions on which they are based they are usable in a wider variety of contexts; that the best of such tests are virtually identical efficiency-wise to parametric ones in situations where the latter can legitimately be used – and obviously preferable in other situations; and that there is now an adequate range of tests to deal with virtually any situation (Meddis, 1984).

I would suggest a pragmatic approach, driven mainly by the kind of data you are likely to have to deal with, and the range of tests to which you have access through computer packages. Unless your data are obviously non-normal, or are in the form of ranks (i.e. first, second, etc. – nonparametric test typically work on ranks, and scores are first transformed into ranks when they are computed), then use a parametric test if one is available. With computer packages, we do not need to worry about the amount of computation required.

The *Mann–Whitney U test* is a nonparametric equivalent of the unpaired two-group *t*-test. The *Wilcoxon signed-rank test* is a nonparametric equivalent of the paired two-group *t*-test. Computation is straightfoward and the Statview output in both cases provides 'z'-scores (see p. 310) and associated probabilities. If there are ties in the scores, a corrected z-score is also provided and should be used. Strictly, the tests should not be used if there is a substantial proportion of ties.

Statview can also carry out two further nonparametric test which, in the version used in Statview, are appropriate for use for the same type of situation as a Mann–Whitney U test. These are the *Kolmogorov–Smirnov test* and the *Wald–Wolfowitz Runs test*. They are not widely used.

Three- (or more) group tests

It is not uncommon, in experiments, to have three or more conditions. You may wish, for example, to compare the effects of 'high', 'medium' and 'low' stress levels on performance in some situation. It would be possible to take these conditions in pairs and carry out three separate *t*-tests. However there are techniques which allow this to be done in a single, overall, test. It is necessary to separate out the 'independent samples' and 'paired samples' designs in the same kind of way as was done with the *t*-test.

Analysis of variance (single factor-independent samples) This situation requires the simplest version of a very widely used, and extremely versatile, technique known as ANALYSIS OF VARIANCE. Figure 11.27 shows the format of data referred to. In Statview terminology this is called a 'Single Factor Factorial, Non-Repeated Measure Design'. This is somewhat confusing as a factorial design is usually thought of as one with two or more independent variables and this only has a single independent variable (see chapter 4, p. 90 for a discussion), but is used because the analysis can be readily generalized to incorporate more independent variables. Figure 11.28 illustrates the type of output generated by Statview for this design; very similar output is produced by other packages.

Experimental conditions (two or more)
i.e. 'levels' or the independent variable (X)

One	Two	Three	Four

Scores are the
values of the
dependent variable (Y)

Figure 11.27　Format of single-factor independent samples analysis of variance

The key finding here is that *there is no overall difference between the means under the different conditions*. This is shown by the F-test result and its associated probability, which exceeds the 0.05 level. This would be reported as:

> The difference between groups is not significant (F = 0.125, p = 0.945; with 3 and 91 df).

If there is a significant overall difference between the groups, the various additional statistics given help one to pinpoint which of the differences between particular pairs of means are contributing to this overall difference. These are the *Fisher PLSD test*, the *Scheffé F-test* and the *Dunnett t-test*. They are alternative ways of dealing with the problem of assessing significance level when a sequence of similar tests are carried out on a data set. Effectively what 'significant at the 5 per cent level' means is that if you carry out, say, twenty tests you would expect one of the twenty (5 per cent) to be significant even if there is no real effect and only random factors are at work.

Any of the three tests could be used, but the Scheffé test is probably the most 'conservative' (i.e. giving the most stringent criteria for significance) and hence is the safest bet. Any significant difference between two conditions is indicated by an asterisk – but only report it as such if the overall F-test is significant.

As with *t*-tests, it is helpful to report not only the results of the statistical test but also to give the summary statistics, such as the means and standard deviations under the different conditions. This applies when reporting any

One Factor ANOVA X_1: IV Y_1: DV

Analysis of Variance Table

Source:	DF:	Sum Squares:	Mean Square:	F-test:
Between groups	3	6.688	2.229	.125
Within groups	91	1620.006	17.802	p = .945
Total	94	1626.693		

Model II estimate of between component variance = -.877

One Factor ANOVA X_1: IV Y_1: DV

Group:	Count:	Mean:	Std. Dev.:	Std. Error:
one	59	69.316	3.824	.498
two	12	68.917	6.207	1.792
three	7	70.143	3.409	1.289
four	17	69.324	4.172	1.012

One Factor ANOVA X_1: IV Y_1: DV

Comparison:	Mean Diff.:	Fisher PLSD:	Scheffe F-test:	Dunnett t:
one vs. two	.399	2.654	.03	.299
one vs. three	-.827	3.35	.08	.49
one vs. four	-.008	2.307	1.523E-5	.007
two vs. three	-1.226	3.986	.124	.611
two vs. four	-.407	3.16	.022	.256

One Factor ANOVA X_1: IV Y_1: DV

Comparison:	Mean Diff.:	Fisher PLSD:	Scheffe F-test:	Dunnett t:
three vs. four	.819	3.764	.062	.432

Figure 11.28 Results of single-factor independent samples analysis of variance

analysis of variance findings and helps you, and the reader, to appreciate what the analysis means.

Kruskal–Wallis test   This is a nonparametric equivalent to the above analysis of variance. It is simpler to compute manually but with computer assistance there seems little reason to prefer it when the data are in a form for which a parametric test is suitable.

Analysis of variance (single factor – repeated measures)   The only difference between this design and the previous analysis of variance is that there is a basis for pairing individual scores across the conditions (usually because the same person produces a score under each condition, i.e. there are 'repeated measures'). Figure 11.29 gives an example and Figure 11.30 shows the type of output generated by Statview. The result would be reported as:

> The difference between groups (treatments) is significant ($F = 24.759$, $p = 0.001$; with 3 and 12 df).

Note that the analysis also tells you whether there are significant differences between subjects. In other respects, the output follows the same format as the previous analysis of variance.

Friedman test   This is a nonparametric equivalent to the above paired samples analysis of variance. Again, it is simpler to compute manually but with computer assistance there seems little reason to prefer it when the data are in a form for which a parametric test is suitable.

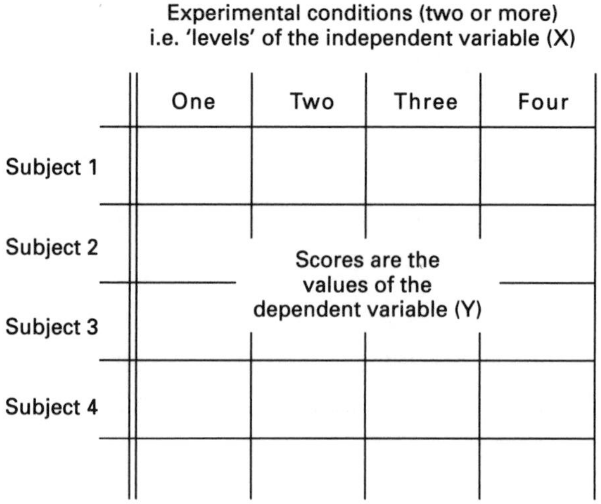

Figure 11.29   Format of single-factor repeated measures analysis of variance

One Factor ANOVA-Repeated Measures for $X_1 \ldots X_4$

Source:	df:	Sum of Squares:	Mean Square:	F-test:	P value:
Between subjects	4	680.8	170.2	3.148	.0458
Within subjects	15	811	54.067		
treatments	3	698.2	232.733	24.759	.0001
residual	12	112.8	9.4		
Total	19	1491.8			

Reliability Estimates for- All treatments: .682   Single Treatment: .349

One Factor ANOVA-Repeated Measures for $X_1 \ldots X_4$

Group:	Count:	Mean:	Std. Dev.:	Std. Error:
one	5	26.4	8.764	3.919
two	5	25.6	6.542	2.926
three	5	15.6	3.847	1.72
four	5	32	8	3.578

One Factor ANOVA-Repeated Measures for $X_1 \ldots X_4$

Comparison:	Mean Diff.:	Fisher PLSD:	Scheffe F-test:	Dunnett t:
one vs. two	.8	5.923	.057	.413
one vs. three	10.8	5.923*	10.34*	5.57
one vs. four	-5.6	5.923	2.78	2.888
two vs. three	10	5.923*	8.865*	5.157
two vs. four	-6.4	5.923*	3.631	3.301

* Significant at 99%

One Factor ANOVA-Repeated Measures for $X_1 \ldots X_4$

Comparison:	Mean Diff.:	Fisher PLSD:	Scheffe F-test:	Dunnett t:
three vs. four	-16.4	5.923*	23.844*	8.458

* Significant at 99%

Figure 11.30 Results of single-factor repeated measures analysis of variance

Testing Differences when Two (or More) Independent Variables are Involved

As discussed in chapter 4, it is feasible to have two or more independent variables in an experiment, commonly in what are called factorial designs (p. 90). This is the area where analysis of variance is most widely used, and there is a plethora of different analyses for the many different designs. The following account simply tries to introduce some main issues.

Simple two-variable (or factor) analysis of variance   Figure 11.31 illustrates the form of the data with this design, and Figure 11.32 gives corresponding output from Statview. The analysis permits an assessment of the effect of each variable separately (the 'main effect' of variables A and B) and also the 'interaction' (or 'AB effect') between the two variables (refer back to chapter 4, p. 92). If the interaction is significant, any main effects are dubious and the pattern of results should be further examined. The 'AB incidence table' allows one to do this, giving the count and mean in each 'cell' (i.e. each combination of the levels of the two variables). It often helps to display any significant interaction graphically, as shown in Figure 11.33. This emphasizes the different relative effects of the two drugs on the two types of patient.

The above analysis assumes that there are the same number of scores in each of the cells (called a 'balanced' model). Statview can also cope with differing numbers in the cells under some circumstances (an 'unbalanced' model).

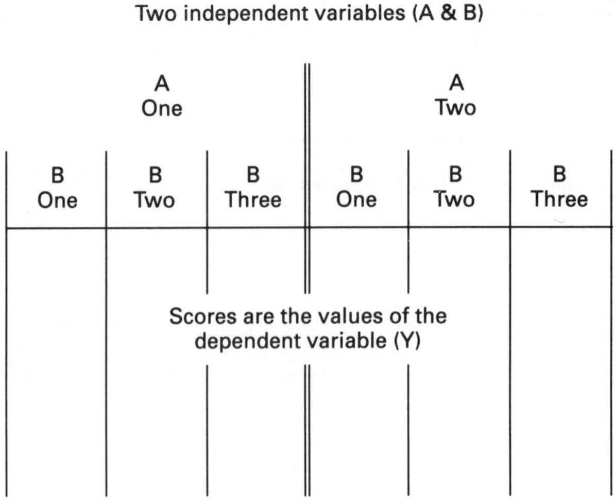

Two independent variables (A & B)

A One			A Two		
B One	B Two	B Three	B One	B Two	B Three

Scores are the values of the dependent variable (Y)

Figure 11.31   Format for simple two-variable analysis of variance

Anova table for a 2-factor Analysis of Variance on Y_1: Rating

Source:	df:	Sum of Squares:	Mean Square:	F-test:	P value:
Category of Patient (...	1	18	18	2.038	.1789
Drug (B)	2	48	24	2.717	.1063
AB	2	144	72	8.151	.0058
Error	12	106	8.833		

There were no missing cells found.

The AB Incidence table on Y_1: Rating

	Drug:	drug a	drug b	drug c	Totals:
Category	schizophre...	3	3	3	9
		4	8	6	6
	depressives	3	3	3	9
		10	2	12	8
	Totals:	6	6	6	18
		7	5	9	7

Figure 11.32 Results of simple two-variable analysis of variance

Two-variable (or factor) analysis of variance with repeated measures A frequently used complication of the above design is to add repeated measures. Thus, subjects may not be simply tested once under a particular combination of levels of the two variables, but may be given a series of trials. Figure 11.34 gives an example and Figure 11.35 provides the corresponding Statview output. Although more complicated in appearance, no new principles are introduced. Various incidence tables are also provided which are not reproduced here. Again, any significant interaction (here the 'AB' interaction) should be thoroughly investigated.

Testing Differences when Two (or More) Dependent Variables are Involved

The above analyses are all limited to dealing with a single dependent variable. In studies with more than one, it is possible simply to repeat the analysis for

12
10
8
6
4
2
Rating
Depressives
Schizophrenics
Drug A
Drug B
Drug C

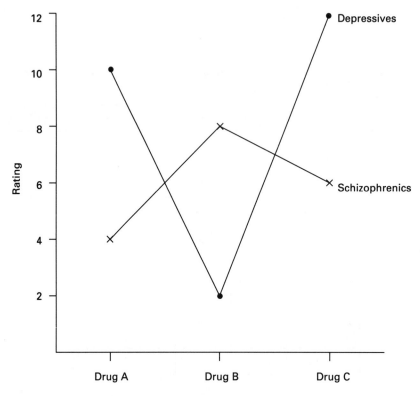

Figure 11.33 Illustration of interaction between two variables

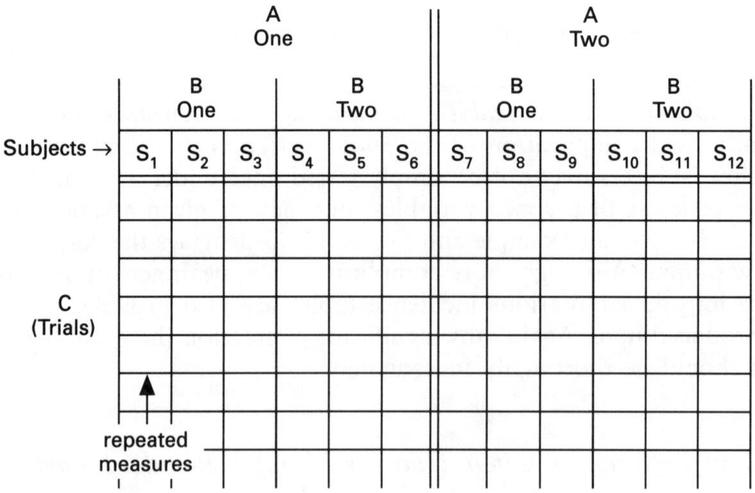

A
One
A
Two
B
One
B
Two
B
One
B
Two
Subjects →
S_1 S_2 S_3 S_4 S_5 S_6 S_7 S_8 S_9 S_{10} S_{11} S_{12}
C
(Trials)
repeated
measures

Figure 11.34 Format for two-variable analysis of variance with repeated measures A and B are 'between-subjects' variables; C is 'within-subjects'.

The BC Incidence table

Repeated Mea...		Trial 1	Trial 2	Trial 3	Trial 4	Totals:
Tension	none	6	6	6	6	24
		16.833	11	7.333	3.167	9.583
	high	6	6	6	6	24
		16.167	12	8.167	5.333	10.417
Totals:		12	12	12	12	48
		16.5	11.5	7.75	4.25	10

Page 1 of the ABC Incidence table

Tension:		none				high	
Repeated Mea...		Trial 1	Trial 2	Trial 3	Trial 4	Trial 1	Trial 2
Anxiety	low	3	3	3	3	3	3
		17	12	8.667	4	15.333	10
	high	3	3	3	3	3	3
		16.667	10	6	2.333	17	14
Totals:		6	6	6	6	6	6
		16.833	11	7.333	3.167	16.167	12

Page 2 of the ABC Incidence table

Tension:		high		Totals:
Repeated Mea...		Trial 3	Trial 4	
Anxiety	low	3	3	24
		7	2.333	9.542
	high	3	3	24
		9.333	8.333	10.458
Totals:		6	6	48
		8.167	5.333	10

Figure 11.35 Results for two-variable analysis of variance with repeated measures

Anova table for a 3-factor repeated measures Anova.

Source:	df:	Sum of Squares:	Mean Square:	F-test:	P value:
Anxiety (A)	1	10.083	10.083	.978	.3517
Tension (B)	1	8.333	8.333	.808	.3949
AB	1	80.083	80.083	7.766	.0237
subjects w. groups	8	82.5	10.312		
Repeated Measure (C)	3	991.5	330.5	152.051	.0001
AC	3	8.417	2.806	1.291	.3003
BC	3	12.167	4.056	1.866	.1624
ABC	3	12.75	4.25	1.955	.1477
C x subjects w. groups	24	52.167	2.174		

There were no missing cells found.

The AB Incidence table

	Tension:	none	high	Totals:
Anxiety	low	12	12	24
		10.417	8.667	9.542
	high	12	12	24
		8.75	12.167	10.458
	Totals:	24	24	48
		9.583	10.417	10

The AC Incidence table

	Repeated Mea...	Trial 1	Trial 2	Trial 3	Trial 4	Totals:
Anxiety	low	6	6	6	6	24
		16.167	11	7.833	3.167	9.542
	high	6	6	6	6	24
		16.833	12	7.667	5.333	10.458
	Totals:	12	12	12	12	48
		16.5	11.5	7.75	4.25	10

(Figure 11.35 cont.)

each dependent variable in turn. However, there are advantages in carrying out a single, global, analysis. One version of this is called *multivariate analysis of variance (MANOVA)*. The analysis and its interpretation are complex and should not be undertaken without advice. MANOVA is not available on Statview but is included on some versions of SPSS. Bryman and Cramer (1990) provide a basic introduction.

Quantitative Analysis and the Research Strategies (Experiment, Survey and Case Study)

This chapter has not attempted to make one-to-one correspondences between the research strategies and particular techniques of quantitative analysis. Ways of displaying, summarizing and manipulating data are essentially common to all strategies. Many of the ways of exploring relationships among the data are applicable to each of them. There are, admittedly, problems when tests of significance are used in the absence of random sampling (discussed on p. 137) but they do not so much preclude their use in case studies, or quasi-experiments, or surveys with, say, quota samples, as require the analyst to think very carefully about interpretation.

There are, of course, strong links between some analytical approaches and particular research strategies, which have been referred to at various points in the chapter. Analysis of variance was developed to deal with the analysis of the true experiment. Correlation matrices and associated techniques such as factor analysis are commonly used in surveys and similar non-experimental settings. However, labelling each test as appropriate only for a specific strategy would be as unnecessarily restrictive as insisting that a particular method of data collection, such as direct observation, should only be used in an experiment – when it could well play a part in a case study, or even in a survey.

It may be helpful, nevertheless, to highlight issues in the analysis of data from two types of experimental study likely to be of real world interest; quasi-experiments and single-subject experiments.

The Analysis of Quasi-Experiments

Three possible quasi-experimental designs were recommended for serious consideration in chapter 4: the pre-test post-test non-equivalent groups design, the interrupted time series design, and the regression discontinuity design (pp. 102–8). The three designs require differing approaches to their analysis.

Pre-test post-test non-equivalent groups design   This is a very common design and it is not unusual for researchers to ignore the fact that it is not a true experiment and not to acknowledge this in both their description and analysis. The non-equivalence of the groups means that there are possible selection effects that may bias the results. Several techniques are available which attempt to separate out the treatment effect (i.e. the effect of the independent variable on the dependent variable) from the effect of selection differences. The most frequently used approaches are:

a   simple analysis of variance;
b   analysis of variance with blocking or matching of subjects;
c   analysis of variance based on 'gain' scores (e.g. difference between pre and post scores)
d   analysis of covariance (with either single or multiple covariates).

Reichardt (1979) provides details of each of these approaches, and of the difficulties they raise. He concludes that 'any one of these statistical methods could be biased enough so that a useful treatment might look harmful and a harmful treatment could look benign or even beneficial' (p. 197). His recommendation is not that we give up and regard the statistical procedures as worthless, but that we give them a relatively minor role – by seeking to eliminate, or at least trying to reduce, the effect of selection and other threats through the *design* of the study rather than relying on the statistical analysis removing their effects. One interesting approach is to try to 'bracket' the effect of a treatment by using a variety of different but reasonable techniques of analysis (see Cook et al.'s (1975) evaluation of the *Sesame Street* TV series for an example).

Interrupted time series design   The approaches to the analysis of this design which are generally regarded as satisfactory (e.g. the use of autoregressive integrated moving average models – ARIMA models – as developed by Box and Jenkins, 1976) require a minimum sequence of about fifty data points, and preferably over 100 of them. Series of this length tend to be very rare in small-scale studies, although if anyone manages to generate this amount of data, the discussion by Glass et al. (1975), provides useful suggestions.

For smaller amounts of data, the use of repeated measures analysis of variance has been advocated. This assumes that the data are independent, that is that with events occurring in time, those close together in time are no more closely correlated with each other than those further apart in time, which is a very dubious assumption. Another form of 'bracketing' technique has been proposed by Greenhouse and Geisser (1959) to deal with this issue.

Similar data patterns to those found in interrupted time series designs occur with single-subject designs, and hence the forms of analysis suggested for single-subject designs may be appropriate in some cases (see below).

Regression discontinuity design   In contrast to the two previous designs, there is a satisfactory and readily accessible means of analysing data from this design. The recommended approach is to use the analysis of covariance, with the pretest as the single covariate. Reichardt (1979, pp. 202–5) gives details.

The Analysis of Single-subject Experiments

The simple form of single-subject experiment involves a single independent variable and a single dependent variable (traditionally the *rate* of some response, although this is not a necessary feature). Hence it might have been dealt with earlier together with other two-variable situations. However, there are major differences of ideology about purposes and procedures of analysis between single-subject experimenters and others, that warrant their separate consideration.

Researchers using single-subject designs have avoided statistical analysis and relied upon 'eyeballing' the data – looking at a comparison, in graphical form, of the subject's performance (sometimes called 'charting') in the different phases of the study. They tend to claim that if statistical techniques were needed to tease out any effects, then the effects were not worth bothering about (see Sidman, 1960 for a clear exposition of the ideas underlying this methodology). This argument has undeniable force, though we will see that, as usual, things are more complicated. It arose in part because of the applied focus of many single-subject studies (see the *Journal of Applied Behavior Analysis* for examples), where the distinction is commonly made between *clinical significance* and *statistical significance*. As discussed previously (p. 351) the latter refers to the unlikeliness that a result is due to chance factors; clinical significance means that a treatment has produced a substantial effect such that, for example, a person with problems can now function adequately in society.

However, while Skinner and his fellow experimenters working with rats or pigeons in the laboratory were able to exert sufficient control so that stable base-lines could be obtained from which the performance in subsequent phases could be differentiated, this has not surprisingly proved more difficult in applied 'field' studies with humans. Other researchers with 'applied' interests have questioned the wisdom of ignoring non-dramatic changes, particularly in exploratory work (e.g. Hersen and Barlow, 1976). They argue that we should determine whether changes are reliable, and then subsequently follow them up. It has also been demonstrated that the reliability of 'eyeballing' as a technique can leave a lot to be desired, with different individuals reaching different conclusions as to what the data were telling them (e.g. DeProspero and Cohen, 1979).

These factors have led to an increasing interest in, and use of, statistical tests of significance in single-subject studies, although this is still a controversial area. Kazdin (1982, ch. 10) provides a balanced account. The techniques advocated are themselves the subject of controversy, largely for the same reason encountered in considering time series quasi-experimental designs: the lack of independence of successive data points obtained from the same individual. Again, the sequence of data points obtained in most real world single subject-experiments is insufficient to use standard time series approaches, but they provide a good solution if extensive data are available. Additional possibilities include the following:

Use of t-tests and analysis of variance   Used to assess whether there is a significant change between two phases (*t*), or amongst a number of phases (ANOVA). Assumes that there is independence in the observations.

Randomization tests   Can only be used if the different experimental conditions can be randomly assigned over time, e.g. on a weekly basis.

R_A *test of rank*   Used in multiple base-line designs, with the intervention being applied to the different base-lines in randomized order. Minimum of four base-lines needed to give possibility of a significant result.

Split-middle test   Basically a descriptive technique that can be used with most single-subject designs, but can incorporate statistical significance through use of the binomial test. Needs several equally spaced observations over a number of phases.

Further details on these tests and their application, together with references, are provided in Kazdin (1982, appendix B).

Further Reading

Bryman, A. and Cramer, D. (1990) *Quantitative Data Analysis for Social Scientists*. London: Routledge. Non-technical introduction to quantitative analyses. Extensive use of the widely available 'Statistical Package for the Social Sciences' (SPSS). Good range of tests covered and exercises (with answers).

Marsh, C. (1988) *Exploring Data: an introduction to data analysis for social scientists*. Cambridge: Polity. Very clear and detailed exposition of exploratory data analysis (EDA) approaches. Concentrates more on analysis of large-scale studies but much of value here.

Meddis, R. (1984) *Statistics Using Ranks: a unified approach*. Oxford: Blackwell. Comprehensive coverage of nonparametric statistics. Includes computer program for microcomputer.

Monk, A. (1991) *Exploring Statistics with Minitab: a workbook for the behavioural sciences*. Chichester: Wiley. Does what it promises (Minitab is a widely used computer package).

Myers, J. L. (1979) *Fundamentals of Experimental Design*, 2nd edn. Boston: Allyn and Bacon. Essentially an analysis of variance book. Clear and adopts an approach usable for virtually all ANOVAs.

Pilcher, D. M. (1990) *Data Analysis for the Helping Professions: a practical guide*. Newbury and London: Sage. Part I gives guidelines on selection of statistical procedures. Part II gives illustrations of how the analysis can be done, covering an unusually wide range of tests.

Siegel, S. and Castellan, N. J. (1988) *Nonparametric Statistics for the Behavioral Sciences*, 2nd edn. New York: McGraw-Hill. Second edition of widely used book on nonparametric statistics. Deservedly popular.

Winer, B. J. (1971) *Statistical Principles in Experimental Design*, 2nd edn. New York: McGraw-Hill. Compendium of analysis of variance designs. Less of a cookbook than Myers. Statview manual keyed into this text for ANOVA.

Youngman, M. B. (1979) *Analysing Social and Educational Research Data*. London: McGraw-Hill. Good coverage of standard analyses, both univariate and multivariate. Also covers cluster analysis, questionnaire analysis, analyses needed in connection with scales and tests (item analysis; assessment of reliability and validity; and change measurement). Oriented to computer analysis.

12

The Analysis of Qualitative Data

This chapter considers approaches to the systematic analysis of qualitative data.

It emphasizes that there are no prescriptive formulae for this task.

It looks on analysis during data collection as mainly concerned with data reduction ...

... and focuses on ways of displaying data to assist in drawing conclusions.

Introduction

Qualitative data have been described as an 'attractive nuisance' (Miles, 1979). Their attractiveness is undeniable. Words, which are by far the most common form of qualitative data, are a speciality of humans and their organizations. Narratives, accounts and other collections of words are variously described as 'rich', 'full' and 'real', and contrasted with the thin abstractions of number. Their collection is often straightforward. They have a quality of 'undeniability' (Smith, 1975) which lends versimilitude to reports.

The 'nuisance' refers to the legal doctrine that if you leave an attractive object, such as an unlocked car, where children can play with it, you may be liable for any injuries they sustain. Naïve researchers may be injured by unforeseen problems with qualitative data. This can occur at the collection stage, where overload is a constant danger. But the main difficulty is in their analysis.

There is no clear and accepted set of conventions for analysis corresponding to those observed with quantitative data. Indeed, many 'qualitative' workers would resist their development, viewing this enterprise as more of an art than a science. But for those who do wish to work within the kind of scientific framework advocated in this book, and who wish to persuade scientific or policy-making audiences, there are ways in which qualitative

;ystematically. This chapter seeks to provide an intro-

nulti-method approach, it may well be that one or
;enerates qualitative data. Some such data, say from
', open responses in questionnaires, may be best dealt
echniques discussed in chapter 10 under the heading
)ther verbal data are likely to be very various and to
In the typology of research strategies that has been
ase studies are the prime generators of large amounts
itative data.
,y, however, be useful in supplementing and illustrat-
Jata obtained from an experiment or survey. Small
: data used as an adjunct within a largely quantitative
letailed and complex analysis. Often the need is simply
ve' and communicate to the reader through the telling
nple. However, when methods generating qualitative
)r a substantial, aspect of the study, then serious and
:ds to be given to the principles of their analysis.

Two Assumptions

1 *It is assumed that if you have a substantial amount of qualitative data you will use a microcomputer to deal with it.* Standard software, even a simple word-processing package, can do much to reduce the sheer tedium of qualitative data analysis. There are now specialist qualitative data analysis packages which aid the process even more. For anything other than a small amount of data, the amount of drudgery you can avoid, and the ease with which you can relate to the data, make the microcomputer near to essential.

2 *It is assumed that you will be helped or advised by someone with experience in this type of analysis.* The dominant model for carrying it out has been that of apprenticeship. Without accepting all the implications of such a model (which tends, for example, to include a principled inarticulacy about process) there is undoubted value in expert advice. The help provided by software is very different from that in quantitative analysis. There the 'expert's' role is largely to point you towards an appropriate test and to ensure that you understand the outcome. In qualitative data analysis, both the experienced person and the computer help you through a not very well specified process.

Types of Qualitative Analysis

Tesch (1990) has produced a useful, if complex, typology of qualitative analyses. She distinguishes a total of twenty-six different kinds of approach to qualitative research, which she reduces to four basic groupings, where the interest is in:

a   the characteristics of language;
b   the discovery of regularities;
c   the comprehension of the meaning of text or action; and
d   reflection.

This constitutes a progression from more to less structured and formal, the final grouping 'reflection' being one whose proponents are particularly resistant to any systemization of their analytical process. The rest of this chapter concentrates to a large extent on the discovery of regularities, although some of the approaches suggested are adaptable to other purposes.

Approaches to Analysis

Irrespective of whether your study generates qualitative or quantitative data, the major task is to find answers to your research questions. This has a a major influence on the kinds of analysis needed. To come up with trustworthy answers, the analysis has to treat the evidence fairly and without bias, and the conclusions must be compelling, not least in ruling out alternative interpretations.

There have, in recent years, been several workers who have given serious attention to these issues. Most notable are Robert Yin (1989) and Miles and Huberman (1984), who have sought to achieve a corresponding degree of rigour in the analysis of qualitative data to that traditionally expected in the analysis of quantitative data. They advocate what Campbell (1989) has referred to as a *'quasi-experimental case study approach'* (p. 8). That is, the kind of logic adopted in the design and analysis of quasi-experimental designs is carried over into the analysis of qualitative data. For example, considerable use is made of the 'threats to validity' approach involving a logical analysis of the specifics of the study in relation to the particular pattern of findings obtained. In general the stance is scientific in a fairly conventional sense.

Dennis Bromley's important text on the case study method (Bromley, 1986) similarly seeks to locate case study within science (see, in particular, pp. 286–96), but advocates a more radical reappraisal of the kind of analytic approach which is appropriate, when the concern is for the singular case and the data are predominantly qualitative. He is eclectic, incorporating, for example, decision analysis (Wright, 1984) and Toulmin's approach to the analysis of arguments, sometimes referred to as 'practical' or 'informal' logic (Toulmin, 1958; Toulmin et al., 1979). However, his central notion is that a *'quasi-judicial case study method'* is needed. By this is meant an approach that combines features of judicial procedure and scientific method ... a way of solving scientific and professional problems raised by the occurrence of actions and circumstances. It attempts to apply rigorous reasoning in the interpretation of empirical evidence systematically collected. (p. 9)

It is interesting to note that workers coming to case study from a very different background, taking what might be termed an *ethnographic case study approach*, are beginning to look for a corresponding degree of rigour in analysis – see, for example, the analytic strategies described by Goetz and LeCompte (1981) and Fetterman (1989). There are also considerable overlaps with suggestions made by Lincoln and Guba (1985) for the processing of 'naturalistically obtained' data, and by Bell (1985) in calling for rigour in 'action inquiry' (his term for an approach combining elements from action research and case study).

This commonality of concern by methodologists of very different ideological persuasions is encouraging. It would be wrong, though, to overemphasize the degree of consensus, even in connection with what Kaplan (1964) calls 'research-in-use' rather than the 'research-in-theory' likely to be found in texts on research methodology. Atkinson and Delamont (1985) have castigated the anti-intellectualism and lack of methodological rigour of much of the case study work which is currently fashionable in English educational research. There remain those who view the analysis of qualitative data as more 'art' than science, and consider that intuitive approaches will suffice. This tends to go along with the view that an apprenticeship with an experienced practitioner is essential before you can do it ('it' being both the collection and the analysis of qualitative data). There are also principled objections from phenomenologically oriented researchers who do not see a social reality 'out there' to be accounted for, and find a concern for things like validity and reliability alien.

The attempt here is not to convert those of such persuasions, but rather to provide tools for those who appreciate that qualitative data are important and attractive, but don't know how to handle them in a rigorous and disciplined way. The 'quasi-experimental' approach to analysis is emphasized in the presentation in this chapter. Similarities with the kinds of processes used in quantitative data analysis are stressed. It is hoped that this form of continuity with what is for many the mainstream approach will be helpful. However, a number of approaches to analysis deriving from 'ethnographic' views of case study have also been incorporated. Be warned, though, that this in no way exhausts the range of brands of research producing qualitative data. Tesch (1990, p. 58) lists twenty-six terms covering different perspectives (interpretive, experiential, etc.), traditions (phenomenology, ethnomethodology, etc.), and research approaches (discourse analysis, action research, etc.) likely to require the analysis of qualitative verbal data. She demonstrates that, while they cover an immense range of views as to how such analyses should be conceptualized, there is in practice much similarity in the procedures used.

The Importance of the Quality of the Analyst

The central requirement in qualitative analysis is clear thinking on the part of the analyst. As Fetterman (1989) puts it, in the context of an ethnographic stance, the analysis is as much a test of the enquirer as it is a test of the data: 'First and foremost, analysis is a test of the . . . ability to think – to process information in a meaningful and useful manner.' As emphasized at the beginning of part Four, qualitative analysis remains much closer to codified common-sense than the complexities of statistical analysis of quantitative data. However, humans as 'natural analysts' have deficiencies and biases corresponding to the problems that they have as observers (see chapter 8, p. 202). Some of these are listed in box 12.1. This chapter suggests ways of adopting a more systematic approach which will help to minimize these human deficiencies. However, there is an emphasis on *interpretation* in dealing with much qualitative data which precludes reducing the task to a defined formula. Hence, the suggestions made in this chapter are more in the nature of guides to possible approaches than tight prescriptions.

Box 12.1 Deficiencies of the human as analyst

1 *Data overload* Limitations on the amount of data that can be dealt with (too much to receive, process and remember).

2 *First impressions* Early input makes a large impression so that subsequent revision is resisted.

3 *Information availability* Information which is difficult to get hold of gets less attention than that which is easier to obtain.

4 *Positive instances* There is a tendency to ignore information conflicting with hypotheses already held, and to emphasize information that confirms them.

5 *Internal consistency* There is a tendency to discount the novel and unusual.

6 *Uneven reliability* The fact that some sources are more reliable than others tends to be ignored.

7 *Missing information* Something for which information is incomplete tends to be devalued.

8 *Revision of hypotheses* There is a tendency either to over- or to under-react to new information.

9 *Fictional base* The tendency to compare with a base or average when no base data is available.

> **10** *Confidence in judgement* Excessive confidence is rested in one's judgement when once it is made.
>
> **11** *Co-occurrence* Co-occurrence tends to be interpreted as strong evidence for correlation.
>
> **12** *Inconsistency* Repeated evaluations of the same data tend to differ.
>
> (Adapted and abridged from Sadler, 1981, pp. 27–30.)

The Quasi-judicial Approach

The quasi-judicial approach, as elaborated by Bromley (1986), covers a set of basic rules and procedural steps for how a case study should be carried out from start to finish. However, it appears to have particular value in structuring and conceptualizing the analysis of qualitative data. The approach is summarized in box 12.2. Much of Bromley (1986) is devoted to an elaboration of this approach, and repays careful reading (see also Bromley, 1977, pp. 173–202).

He terms it 'quasi-judicial' because it is modelled on jurisprudence (the 'science' of law). It should not be confused with the adversarial procedure central to both British and North American courts of law, and is closer to the French 'inquisitorial' system, or the procedure adopted in England by a judge when in charge of an enquiry into a disaster, or scandal, or some other public matter. It is an exercise in problem-solving, rather than in interpreting the law. At its core is the notion of a systematic procedure which uses rational argument to interpret empirical evidence.

The list of ten procedural steps emphasizes that analysis is not left to the end of the process but is a continuing concern, dealt with by iteration. Bromley (1986) recommends that throughout this process, one should keep in mind four important questions:

  1 What is at issue?
  2 What other relevant evidence might there be?
  3 How else might one make sense of the data?
and 4 How were the data obtained? (p. 100).

The quasi-judicial approach does not produce tight prescriptions for analysis of the kind generated by statistical tests when dealing with quantitative data. As with the 'real' judicial approach it is, to a large extent, concerned with *evidence* and *argument*. Issues to do with how the evidence or data were obtained, what reliance we can place on them, etc. are not specific to case study and have already been rehearsed in connection with the analysis of documents in chapter 10 (where there is the likelihood that what you are using as evidence was produced for other purposes).

Box 12.2   Procedural steps in the quasi-judicial method

1   State the initial problems and issues as clearly as possible.

2   Collect background information to provide a context in terms of which the problems and issues are to be understood.

3   Put forward prima facie explanations and solutions to the problems and issues.

4   Use these explanations to guide the search for additional evidence. If they do not fit the available evidence, work out alternative explanations.

5   Continue the search for sufficient evidence to eliminate as many of the suggested explanations as possible, in the hope that one will account for all the available evidence and be contradicted by none of it. Evidence may be direct or indirect, but must be admissible, relevant and obtained from competent and credible sources.

6   Closely examine the sources of evidence, as well as the evidence itself. All items should be checked for consistency and accuracy. This is analogous to legal cross-examination in the case of personal testimony.

7   Enquire critically into the internal coherence, logic and external validity of the network of argument claiming to settle the issues and solve the problems.

8   Select the most likely interpretation compatible with the evidence.

9   Formulating an acceptable explanation usually carries an implication for action, which has to be worked out.

10   Prepare an account in the form of a report. It should contribute to 'case law' by virtue of the general principles employed in explaining the specific case.

(Adapted from Bromley, 1986, p. 26.)

While the quasi-judicial approach provides a useful reorientation, and a new framework, for dealing with qualitative case study data, it is admittedly less helpful in suggesting what one does with the data collected. Various recent texts (including Miles and Huberman, 1984; Lofland and Lofland, 1984; Tesch, 1990; and Delamont, 1992) have attempted to formulate some basic rules for this task. Box 12.3 provides a summary.

Box 12.3   Basic rules for dealing with qualitative data

1   Analysis of some form should start as soon as data is collected. Don't allow data to accumulate without preliminary analysis.

2   Make sure you keep tabs on what you have collected (literally – get it indexed).

3   Generate themes, categories, codes, etc. as you go along. Start by including rather than excluding; you can combine and modify as you go on.

4   Dealing with the data should not be a routine or mechanical task; think, reflect! Use analytical notes (memos) to help to get from the data to a conceptual level.

5   Use some form of filing system to sort your data. Be prepared to re-sort. Play with the data.

6   There is no one 'right' way of analysing this kind of data – which places even more emphasis on your being systematic, organized and persevering.

7   You are seeking to take apart your data in various ways and then trying to put them together again to form some consolidated picture. Your main tool is comparison.

The rest of the chapter tries to suggest how you might go about this task.

General Strategies for Analysis

Yin (1989, p. 106) describes two possible strategies, to which a third, rejected by Yin, might be added. They link in to the approach to the design of case studies discussed in chapter 6.

Basing the Analysis on Theoretical Propositions

In many cases a study is based on a particular set of theoretical propositions. The theoretical stance, in some sense 'given' to you (perhaps through reviewing previous work, or more literally by you being asked to do work in these terms) will have helped frame the research questions to be asked, and through them the design of the study. This strategy can be a powerful aid in guiding the analysis, indicating where, and on what, attention should be focused.

Basing the Analysis on a Descriptive Framework

In exploratory and descriptive case studies you may, quite possibly, not start within a particular theoretical framework. An alternative, considered inferior by Yin, is to develop a case description. You are looking for a set of themes or areas, linked to the research questions once again, which appear to give an adequate coverage of the case. One version, common in applied, real world studies, is to work towards an *issues analysis*, where the issues can be used as a means of organizing and selecting material.

Exploring the Data

Yin is dubious about this as a strategy, one problem being that it does not provide guidance in selecting which aspects of the data to concentrate on, or how to go about dealing with them. Certainly it would be foolhardy (a not unknown foolhardiness!) to amass filing cabinets stuffed with transcripts and records, and turn to these at the end of the study for a quick exploratory trawl. However, just as case study design is flexible, with the final version evolving through interaction with the case, so case study analysis should be started at a relatively early stage while the enquiry is still in progress. In the absence of a theoretical framework, 'playing with the data' at this intermediate stage may well assist in identifying themes which can form the basis for a workable descriptive framework. Even with a theoretical frame, initial exploration of this kind may give an early warning of its inadequacy, and perhaps lead to a beneficial recasting.

The idea, within the quasi-judicial method, of analysis being iterative, or cyclical, is also central to ethnographic approaches (see, for example, Hammersley and Atkinson, 1983; Taylor and Bogdan, 1984). Versions of action research, much used in recent studies focusing on educational topics (e.g. Elliott, 1982; Winter, 1989), have a similar view as to the place of analysis in enquiry. A distinction is sometimes made between *informal* and *formal* analysis, the former being what is done while you are still directly involved with the case, the latter taking place afterwards.

This would permit a greater range of patterns of results to be interpreted. The general principle in quasi-experimentation is that, whenever feasible, threats to validity should be made explicit before data collection begins, so that you have all the measurements required for matching obtained data with a pattern of relationships. In this way, threats to valid causal inference can ruled out.

Quasi-experimentation presents a more flexible, ad hoc and opportunistic stance than classical experimental design. Case study can be thought of as a further progression along these dimensions, where much less is predetermined. The 'threats to validity' approach remains a potent weapon, but, to continue the analogy, it is rarely feasible to have a precisely formulated battle plan for coping with these threats before you go into action. Which is why, when carrying out a case study, you should not only carry with you (literally and metaphorically) your research questions but also be alerted to the implications of emerging patterns of results in respect of these threats. Ongoing analysis of this kind should help you to appreciate what other kinds of data need collecting to meet the threats. All of this places a very high premium on the sensitivity of the case study enquirer. There are however useful formats for interim data analysis (e.g. page 385) which can be of considerable help.

A second approach to pattern-matching focuses on independent variables rather than on dependent variables. For this you require a set of theoretical propositions which seek to provide an explanation of what is taking place. The different explanations should involve mutually exclusive patterns of independent variables, so that if one explanation is valid then the others cannot be. This is in effect an extension of the 'threats to validity' approach as the usual set of threats can themselves be seen as alternative explanations.

Pattern-matching techniques are applicable in both single and multiple case studies. Multiple case studies can be used to provide either *literal replication* or *theoretical replication* across cases. In the former, you look for two or more cases where the pattern of dependent or independent variables predicts the same outcome, and if that is achieved, then your conclusions are strengthened. The latter is where you find a predicted different outcome due to different circumstances.

In the real world of a complex case study, or series of case studies, clear-cut confirmatory or differential patterns are difficult to come by. Yin's advice is to stick to postulating simple patterns, such that by 'eyeballing' the data you are more likely to see, at a gross level, whether or not you have got a match.

Explanation-building

This is an iterative version of pattern-matching. It is, self-evidently, primarily concerned with explanatory case studies, where the goal is to provide an explanation of what is happening in the case. Yin (1989) suggests that the final explanation is the result of the following series of iterations:

- making an initial theoretical statement or an initial proposition . . . ;
- comparing the findings of an *initial case* against such a statement or proposition;
- revising the statement or proposition;
- comparing other details of the case against the statement or proposition;
- again revising the statement or proposition;
- comparing the revision to the facts of *a second, third, or more cases*; and
- repeating the process as many times as it is needed. (pp. 114–15)

Notice the similarity, although the terminology is different, with the proce
dural steps in the quasi-judicial method. The difference from pattern-matching
is that the final explanation changes from that with which you start. However,
it is similar in that a range of alternative or rival explanations has to be
developed and the objective is to show how they do not fit with the actual
pattern of results obtained in the case study or studies.

The process is also very similar to one which has been widely used in
sociology, known as ANALYTIC INDUCTION (Lindesmith, 1968; Denzin,
1988), which was discussed earlier (chapter 8, p. 201). The latter differs in
that it stresses the importance of maximizing the chances of discovering a
decisive *negative* case ('case' here can be taken here as a detail – aspect,
facet, phenomenon or whatever – within a single case study, or in the usual
sense within a multiple case study). Thus, when in the revising process, the
suggestion is that one should go out of one's way to look for negating
evidence.

Kidder (1981) has produced a systematized version, known as NEGATIVE
CASE ANALYSIS. This involves continuously revising and refining a hypothesis until it accounts for all known cases without exception. She cites as an
example a study by Cressey (1953), summarized in box 12.4.

Box 12.4   Example of negative case analysis

1 The initial version of the hypothesis is:

*Embezzlement occurs when someone has learned in connection with
the business or profession in which he is employed that some forms of
violation of trust are merely technical and are not really illegal or
wrong. Conversely, that if this definition has not been learned then
violations do not occur.*

2 Interviews with imprisoned embezzlers made it clear they knew it
was illegal. Hypothesis changed to:

*Embezzlement occurs when the holder of a position of trust defines a
need for extra funds or extended use of property as an emergency
which cannot be met by legal means.*

3 Some interviewees said they had taken money without an emergency; others said they had at times been confronted by an emergency
but had not taken money. Hypothesis changed to:

*Embezzlement occurs when persons in positions of trust conceive of
themselves as having incurred financial obligations which are not socially sanctionable and which must be satisfied by private means.*

4 Checking against previous and subsequent interviews revealed instances in which nothing existed that could be considered a financial obligation; and others in which non-sanctionable obligations had existed without embezzlement. Hypothesis changed to:

Embezzlement occurs not only for the reason cited in the previous hypothesis, but also because of present discordance between the embezzler's income and expenditure.

5 Further study of the interview records revealed instances where the conditions existed but embezzlement had not occurred. Hypothesis changed to its final version:

Trusted persons violate that trust when they see themselves as having a financial problem which is non-shareable; are aware that this problem can be secretly resolved by violation of the position of trust; and are able to apply to their own conduct in that situation verbalizations which enable them to adjust their conception of themselves as users of the entrusted funds or property.

This hypothesis was tested against all the data gathered previously and new data, no negative cases being found.

(Adapted from Kidder, 1981, p. 243.)

Kidder suggests that negative case analysis replaces statistical analysis in qualitative research. This kind of inductive analysis violates the canons of conventional hypothesis-testing approaches by forming hypotheses to fit the data rather than finding data to test the hypotheses. However, her argument is that with abundant data, resulting from having made many observations and recorded many instances, the conclusions can be convincing.

Her version insists on *zero* exceptions. Lincoln and Guba (1985, p. 312) consider that this is too rigid a criterion, equivalent to the perfect statistical finding, significant at the 0.000 level! They suggest that in practice, even if the final hypothesis were true, there would be likely to be apparent exceptions (e.g. due to people lying, or practising unconscious deception, or forgetting) which one may be unable to uncover). Hence, that a hypothesis which fits a good proportion of the cases gives substantial evidence of its acceptability.

For any version of these explanation-building approaches to be rigorous, substantial safeguards have to be built into the process. You need to be punctilious in documenting the initial statement and its changing versions, together with the rival explanations, and the chain of evidence which leads you to your conclusions. The use of standardized data display and summary devices (discussed later in this chapter, p. 390) is recommended.

Chronologies

A chronological analysis is a way of organizing data from a case study over time. As a strategy, case study can be longitudinal; that is, it allows the enquirer to trace events over time, although this would be precluded in small-scale studies for anything apart from situations where the time spans are relatively short. It is possible to extend the time dimension beyond your direct involvement by seeking retrospective information through interviews and documentary evidence.

An attraction of chronological organization is the help that it gives in determining causal relationships. Causes must precede effects in time. As with pattern-matching, the chronology is compared with that predicted by some explanatory theory. Plausible rival sequences predicted by other explanatory theories should be constructed, and if they are disconfirmed, confidence in the 'fitting' theory is enhanced.

A particular form of chronology is the LIFE HISTORY approach, which has been used in many earlier case studies (e.g. Mandelbaum, 1973; Frank and VanderBurgh, 1986). It is usually taken as a full-length account of a single person's life, in that person's own words (see, for example, Hitchcock and Hughes, 1989, pp. 113–22). There are alternatives to a chronological presentation, for instance, using dimensions or aspects of the person's life; the principal 'turnings' in their life, and their life conditions between them; and their characteristic means of adaptation (Mandelbaum, 1973). They are typically expressed in narrative form, and are often of compelling interest.

An analysis couched solely in life history terms is unlikely to be of central interest for the more applied concerns covered in this text. However, 'mini life histories', restricted in length and range (e.g. simply covering in some detail one or more individuals' involvement with, say, an intervention which forms the basis of the case study) can be a useful component of an analysis.

Time Series Analysis

Time series designs, although usually associated with the experimental strategy, and in particular with quasi-experimental designs, can be used with case study data. Analysis of time series designs is primarily an analysis of the patterning of data over time – asking questions about, for example, whether there is a discontinuity in the pattern which coincides with a change in treatment. The same is true about single-subject designs, which although developed separately, overlap substantially with time series approaches. The analysis of these designs when quantitative data have been generated has already been discussed in the previous chapter (see p. 366).

Kidder (1981) has provided a fascinating and convincing interpretation showing examples of researchers using qualitative techniques who are, in their analysis, carrying out an analogous process to that involved in time series designs. This is because the multiple observations and nonsimultaneous 'treatments' which they use permit them to rule out threats to external validity. She makes it clear that while this has not been done explicitly they, in effect, rule out rival explanations in arriving at their conclusions about the necessary steps, stages or conditions for the process that they are interested in to have taken place.

Triangulation

As already made clear, triangulation in its various guises (for example using multiple methods, or obtaining information relevant to a topic or issue from several informants), is an indispensable tool in real world enquiry. It is particularly valuable in the analysis of qualitative data where the trustworthiness of the data is always a worry. It provides a means of testing one source of information against other sources. Both correspondences and discrepancies are of value. If two sources give the same messages then, to some extent, they cross-validate each other. If there is a discrepancy, its investigation may help in explaining the phenomenon of interest.

A case study of the effects of introducing national testing into primary schools might incorporate, as well as the test results, interview data from the children involved, in relation to their own views and feelings, and further interview data from their teachers. Triangulation of information about progress might, for example, indicate that for some children the test data and teachers' views suggest good progress, whereas the children consider their own progress to have been unsatisfactory. This discrepancy might be hypothesized as related to increased stress and could help in suggesting comparisons with pupils who have realistic views about their progress; in suggesting additional topics to explore in discussion; or suggest including the parents' views in the study.

Here, and in many cases, the by-products of triangulation are as useful as its primary purpose in validating information. It improves the quality of data and in consequence the accuracy of findings. An alertness for possible triangulation opportunities is a valuable quality in the enquirer.

Key Events

Key or focal events are also used in ethnographic-style case studies where they are widely used to form a focus for analysis. They are a feature of classical anthropological studies, for example in the portrayal of Balinese life through the key event of the cock fight (Geertz, 1973). Their use is not only in helping to understand the group or situation, but also in helping to share that understanding with others.

Observation during our involvement in a number of small special schools for pupils with severe learning difficulties revealed that there were big differences, sometimes within the same school, in the way in which the staff's morning coffee break took place. In some, the teacher and her assistant would both take coffee at the same time in the staffroom while the children had an outside 'play time'. In others, teacher and assistant would do this at different times, and possibly places. Yet others would have their coffee in the classroom while the children were still present. These differences were clearly related to the general climate and approach in the school and became a useful metaphor for what was going on, which appears to 'speak' to teacher audiences.

Fetterman (1989, p. 94) considers the introduction of computerization to be a classic key event in the study of modern offices. It can be used to reveal tensions that otherwise remain buried in daily interaction; to study how staff members accept or reject the innovation; to see how its use changes the social dynamics of the group; etc.

Carrying out Analysis during Data Collection

The suggested general approaches to qualitative data analysis emphasize the importance of ongoing analysis during data collection. Analysis in 'real time' where additional data are continually being collected calls for considerable organization on your part. This section provides practical suggestions for systematization so that this becomes a feasible task.

The techniques suggested are influenced greatly by Miles and Huberman (1984), which is strongly recommended as a source of examples, further details and additional approaches. They consist of a set of 'formats' for data reduction and display. It should be stressed that while these techniques provide useful tools which help considerably with the task of data management, they need to be used flexibly or they may undermine the strengths of qualitative research by overly mechanistic data analysis.

The raw data will be primarily in the form of words: notes made during observation or interview (either in handwritten or portable computer file format), tapes of events, documents and so on. Visual representations in the form of maps and charts are also considered. Other forms are possible, but will not be covered here. These include photographs (see Collier and Collier, 1986; Becker, 1979; Bogdan and Biklen, 1982) and videotapes (see McPhail and Wohlstein, 1982).

Initial Processing of Raw Data

(This part of the analysis is also covered in chapter 8 in connection with participant observation – see p. 199.)

Notes made 'in the field' should first be converted into what is usually called a *write-up*. This is a version of the raw notes which is intelligible to another reader (and to yourself in six months time!). Your raw notes are likely to contain private abbreviations, to be partly illegible, and to be sketchy. The write-up should be made shortly after the experience so that missing elements stimulated by reading the notes, amplifications and corrections can be made. Additions made at this stage should be differentiated from material directly derived from the raw data. Reflections which occur to you while doing the processing (for example, a hypothesis as to what is happening) can usefully be incorporated, providing that they are properly differentiated.

Tape recordings also need to be processed shortly after they have been made. The alternatives are a full transcription, which is a very lengthy business, or making of notes and selection of excerpts (both keyed into tape counter numbers).

Aids to Analysis

The following suggestions are arranged in rough sequence from those which should be started early in your involvement with the case to ones appropriate for later, and from simple to more complex. They are described here in fairly general and flexible terms. Miles and Huberman (1984, ch. III) give more prescriptive versions which are invaluable for larger projects involving several workers and a substantial amount of pre-planning, but may well be over-formalized for a small-scale study.

1 *Session summary sheet* Shortly after a data collection session (e.g. an interview or observation session) has taken place and the data have been processed, a single sheet should be prepared which summarizes what has been obtained. It is helpful if this sheet is in the form of answers to summarizing and focusing questions (e.g. who was involved; what issues were covered; relevance to research questions; new hypotheses suggested; implications for subsequent data collection).

2 *Document sheet* A similar sheet should be prepared for each document collected. This clarifies its context and significance, as well as summarizing the content of lengthy documents. Specific techniques for the analysis of the content of documents are discussed in chapter 10 (p. 275).

3 *Development of coding categories* Qualitative data rapidly cumulate, and even with regular processing and summarizing it is easy to get overwhelmed. The material is unstructured and difficult to deal with. CODING provides a solution. *A code is a symbol applied to a group of words to classify or categorize them.* They are typically related to research questions, concepts and themes. Codes are retrieval and organizing devices that allow you to find and then collect together all instances of a particular kind. Formally, this is essentially the same task as that of developing a category system in content analysis, also discussed in chapter 10.

Miles and Huberman (1984) distinguish between first- and second-level coding. First-level coding is concerned with attaching labels to groups of words. Second-level or PATTERN CODING groups the initial codes into a smaller number of themes or patterns. They regard it as the qualitative data analysis technique equivalent to factor or cluster analysis of quantitative data.

The development of pattern codes is an integral part of first-level coding, where you need to be continually asking yourself 'what seems to go with what?' and elaborating on and checking these hunches. You will probably start with a very small number of potential patterns, modify and add to them during the course of analysis, and finally be left with a small number once more as various 'runners' are disconfirmed by the data. The work that you do in creating these codes is central to developing an understanding of your data. It lays the foundation for your subsequent analysis. Guidelines for coding are presented as box 12.5.

Box 12.5 Guidelines for coding of qualitative data

1 Coding is of *categories* in the data. Try to discover genuine categories and give them a (provisional) name – don't simply precis phrases in the document or other material.

2 Relate these categories as specifically and variably as possible to the contexts in which they occur (e.g. conditions, consequences).

3 Relate categories to each other; construct sub-categories where appropriate.

4 Always do this on the basis of specific data, underlining or highlighting each occurrence; reference frequently, giving page, line, etc.

5 Develop core categories, relating all categories and sub-categories to the core.

6 Discard totally or largely unrelated categories, unless you can find some way of linking them to the core.

(Adapted from Strauss, 1987, p. 81.)

---

4 *Memoing* A memo is 'the theorizing write-up of ideas about codes and their relationships as they strike the analyst while coding' (Glaser, 1978). The length is not important; they are simply attempts either to link data together, or suggest that a particular piece of data falls within a more general category. They should be adequately labelled so that they can be sorted and retrieved. Memoing is a useful means of capturing ideas, views and intuitions at all stages of the data analysis process.

A wide range of types of memo have been suggested, including:

a   initial, orienting memo;
b   preliminary memo;
c   memo 'sparks';
d   memo that opens an attack on new phenomena;

e   memo on a new category;
f   initial discovery memo;
g   memo distinguishing between two or more categories;
h   memo extending the implications of a borrowed concept;
i   additional thoughts memo;
j   integrative memo;
k   organizing, summary memo.

Box 12.6 provides suggested guidelines for writing memos.

Box 12.6 Guidelines for writing memos

1 Keep memos and data separate (apart from possibly including clearly demarcated data as illustrations in a memo). Reference memos to documents or field notes from which they emerged.

2 Any memos simply based on a hunch, for which you have no grounding in the data, must be indicated as such.

3 If necessary, interrupt data gathering or coding to write a memo when an idea occurs. If you can't stop jot down a brief memo to do a later memo! If you have two ideas for memos at the same time, finish one before doing the other (perhaps a brief memo initially on the second so you don't lose the idea).

4 Modify memos as the enquiry develops. They are not the data; they are what you are using to help you understand the data.

5 Keep the list of current codes to hand when memoing, to help pick up relationships.

6 If memos on different codes seem very similar, look at the codes to see if there are differences in them that you are not picking up – if not, consider combining the codes.

7 Continue with memos which open up new field as long as resources allow.

8 Memos are primarily about codes and the conceptual relationships between them; keep people out of them apart from as indicators/illustrations.

9 When you are satisfied with a category and your understanding of it (i.e. you have reached 'saturation'), indicate this in a memo.

10 Be flexible when memoing. You have to find what works for you.

(Adapted from Glaser, 1978, pp. 81–91.)

5   *The interim summary*   This is an attempt to summarize what you have found out so far, and highlight what still needs to be found out. It should be done before you are halfway through the time you have available for data collection. The summary should cover not only what is known but also the confidence you have in that knowledge, so that gaps and deficiencies can be spotted and remedied. *The flexibility of case study design enables you to do this in a way which would not be feasible in an experiment or a survey, but to capitalize on this flexibility you must force yourself to find the time to do this interim summary while you can still take advantage of its findings to direct and focus the later phases of data collection.* The summary can also usefully incorporate a DATA ACCOUNTING SHEET which lists the different research questions and shows, for different informants, materials, settings, etc. whether adequate data concerning each of the questions have been collected.

When there are several persons involved in data analysis and collection, it is important that they are all involved in the preceding exercises. While it may be possible in surveys to get much of the routine work carried out by 'hired hands' who follow fully standardized procedures, the importance of the sensitivity and judgement of the 'human instrument' precludes this tactic in case study. All workers on a case study have essentially similar roles. It is crucial that there are shared understandings about the process of analysis, that, for example, the codings are carried out in the same way. Cross-checking should be carried out in as many ways as possible. Formal meetings will be needed (see Miles and Huberman, 1984, pp. 72–5).

Filing and Storage Systems

For relatively small amounts of data, the traditional approach has been to store your coded data, and the various analysis and summary sheets, in note books and folders, and on filing cards (sizes larger than the standard 5 by 3 inches card are preferable). Several specific systems have been suggested. Lofland and Lofland (1984), for example, recommend three types of file:

1   *Mundane files* consist of a set of folders where the processed data are organized by categories such as people, settings, events, etc.
2   *Analytic files* consist of cut-up photocopies of coded data segments. Each folder contains the copies of data relevant to particular codes or patterns of codes. The organization of the analytic files will change as analysis proceeds, and new patterns are tried or old ones discarded. If the system suggested here is followed, a separate file or files could be maintained for the analysis and summary sheets. All files are cross-referenced.

3   *Fieldwork file* is a folder in which material on the process of the research itself is accumulated. Most types of report are expected to include a section which gives an account of how the research was conducted, and it helps to build this up from day one.

Software Tools for Qualitative Analysis

The preceding sections make it clear that qualitative data analysis calls for multiple copies of different segments of the written material which have to be played about with in various ways. This task requires a typescript. *The one indispensable technical skill for anyone contemplating qualitative data analysis is typing.* Anyone familiar with word-processors will appreciate that their 'cut' and 'paste' routines make them very much more suitable for these kinds of tasks than typewriters. However, standard word-processors are not ideal for the kinds of manipulation of text called for in qualitative data analysis and more specialized software tools are now available for this task.

Given their existence and the amount of sheer drudgery that they can help you avoid, together with the decreasing cost and increasing availability of ever more powerful microcomputers, you are strongly advised to make use of them for everything apart from the analysis of very small-scale data sets.

Tesch (1990), who provides a detailed description of the capabilities of several of the most widely used packages, distinguishes between TEXT RETRIEVERS and TEXT DATA BASE MANAGERS. Text retrievers are designed to operate on individual words or phrases. They do things like making lists of all the words in a document, or of specified words. They count how often words appear, create indices consisting of alphabetical lists with information where each word is in the document, and concordances (lists of words with a specified number of words surrounding them in the document).

While these functions can be very helpful in analysis, text data base managers are probably of greater use. They consist of 'records' which can be defined to suit the convenience of the analyst (say the account of an interview, or of a period of observation). The record can be split into 'fields', perhaps the natural units of your data (e.g. individual utterances) which can be coded with 'key words'. The data base can consist of a large number of records. It is possible to search within this data base in a wide variety of ways – perhaps pulling out any term in the data base and displaying any record which contains that term, highlighting the term itself. Data base managers are superior to word-processors at this type of task as they are designed for rapid searching both across and within records.

Tesch (1990) gives details of a range of software available at the time she was writing. These include TAP (Text Analysis Package), ETHNO, QUALPRO, The Ethnograph, TEXTBASE ALPHA and HyperQual. This is an area of rapid change and additional software is already available for

microcomputer use (e.g. NUDIST – Non-numerical unstructured data index-
ing, searching and theory-building – Richards, 1987).

If you are going to use computer analysis of your data, there is much to
be said for using lap-top microcomputers or similar devices actually to
capture the data from interview or observation in the first instance (Fetterman,
1989, pp. 74–7).

Analysis on Completion of Data Collection

The drawing of conclusions and their verification is the major remaining
analytic task. Some of this may be done while data collection is still in progress, and verifying a particular conclusion may call for an unanticipated
additional wave of data collection, but generally this is a task which follows
the data collection phase.

The major thrust of the analytic techniques recommended for use during
data collection was data reduction; seeking to make the data mountain
manageable through summary and coding. The corresponding thrust here is
on *display*: finding methods which present the data in such a form that valid
conclusions can be drawn. Traditionally, researchers using qualitative data
have gone fairly directly from their written-up notes with associated codes
to a case study report in the form of a narrative text. In a general sense, such
a report is one way of displaying your conclusions, but if it is solely narrative has serious drawbacks as a means of display. In particular, it is
essentially sequential – one thing is dealt with at a time – with information
being spread over many pages.

There are standardized means of displaying quantitative data which were
dealt with in the preceding chapter. No self-respecting experimentalist or
survey researcher would dream of producing quantitative analysis devoid of
display in the form of graphs, histograms, scattergrams and the like. Miles
and Huberman (1984) have sought to give corresponding tools to qualitative researchers which 'encourage the creation and display of innovative and
reliable data displays for qualitative data' (p. 79).

Their approach is not difficult to follow. The basic principle is to consider
what forms of display are most likely to bring relevant data together in a
way that will encourage the drawing of conclusions. They focus on matrices,
but other types of display may be of value.

Matrices

The simplest, and probably most used and most useful, matrices are two-
dimensional, i.e. you have a dual categorization where the rows represent
one dimension and the columns the second dimension. Figure 12.1 gives an
example which seeks to summarize the components of 'preparedness' along

Conditions	Early Users (n=2) 1977–8	Later Users (n=6) 1978–80	Administrators 1977–8	Administrators 1978–80
Commitment	*Adequate-Ideal* Bayeis: 'I was committed.' Quint: 'I don't know why I stayed with it.'	*Inadequate-Adequate:* 'I had no choice.' (3) 'I was excited about it.' (1) Why not? (2)	*Bldg. Level Inadequated* 'I wasn't that sold on it.' *Central office Adequate*	*Bldg. Level: Adequate* 'pushing it hard' *Central office: Adequate*
Understanding	*Absent:* Didn't know what was going on.' 'All very confusing.'	*Absent-Inadequate:* 'Didn't know what it was all about?' 'Understandable.' 'Not bad, but not how it all fit together.'	*Bldg. Level: Absent* 'little jumbled.' *Central office:* *Absent-Inadequate* 'I don't know anything about reading.'	*Bldg. Level: Adequate* Trained and experienced *Central office: Adequate* Delegated to trainers
Materials	*Absent:* 'Nothing was ready.' 'Had to do it all myself.'	*Ideal:* 'Emily Boud just marveled at that.' 'Everything was ready.'	N.A.	N.A.
Front-end Training	*Inadequate:* 'I should have had more training.' 'They really only know what they had done themselves.'	*Inadequate:* 'Short and strenuous.' 'I was overwhelmed— too much thrown at me.' 'Better than I had thought before starting in. It worked.'	*Absent*	*Adequate:* short, intensive training at D/D site
Skills	*Inadequate:* 'Can't think of anything I was prepared in.' 'Just had the very basics.'	*Minimally adequate:* 'Enough to get started with.'	N.A.	N.A.

N.A. = not applicable

Figure 12.1 Excerpt from a checklist matrix
Source: Miles and Huberman, 1984, p. 84.

the rows, and to compare the preparedness of those holding different roles through different columns. There is substantial data reduction in the matrix, which is derived from 8–10 pages of interview notes (although the matrix shown is only part of the summary table produced). Because you are displaying only a small proportion of the available data, it is crucial that there are explicit decision rules for what is included, and that these rules are fully documented. Suggestions for doing this, and other practical tips on building and using matrix displays, are given in Miles and Huberman (1984, pp. 211–14). The data have also been *scaled*: 'preparedness' is categorized along this dimension as absent/inadequate/adequate/ideal. Again, rules for this would have to be specified and documented. Note that this transforms the qualitative data into a form which is capable of quantification. Given this scaling, it would be feasible to determine, say, the number of users for whom preparedness was absent, etc. The general issue of quantification of data originally collected in qualitative form is discussed below, on p. 400.

Many forms of matrix are possible. A very simple version would just list illustrative excerpts from interviews with no attempt to categorize by standardizing or scaling. Instead of quotations, more abstract data based on the analyst's inferences might be entered into the matrix. The functions in all cases, however, are the same – to collect data in one place so that you can see more readily what they are telling you; to suggest other displays and analyses; and to facilitate comparison with other displays. The matrices, together with an appropriate analysis, are also likely to be useful for inclusion in the report. In all cases, the approach selected will be driven by your research questions, and in order for it to do its job, you are likely to have to go through several versions. Box 12.7 lists some of the different types of matrix that are discussed by Miles and Huberman (1984).

Matrices can be developed by hand on paper, or on a black- or whiteboard. There is advantage in having a large display area on which substantial amounts of data can be entered, and from which selection can be made for the final matrix. If computers are being used, versions of spreadsheets or database programs are likely to be most useful.

It is possible to deal with more than two dimensions on a matrix. Three dimensions can be coped with by subdividing each of the columns into the categories of the third dimension; four dimensions by also doing the same thing with the rows. Alternatively you can use sub-matrices, e.g. by having a separate matrix for each of the categories on the third dimension. Playing about with different ways of doing this should reveal the most useful display.

Maps and Charts

Layouts, plans, maps and diagrams are visual representations which can form useful display tools in qualitative analysis. As with the matrix, making some form of map forces you to abstract and select from a large amount of

---

Box 12.7   Different types of matrix

1   *Checklist matrix*   Uses data which can be combined into an index or scale (e.g. the 'preparedness' scale of figure 12.1).

2   *Time-ordered matrix*   Columns are arranged in time sequence. A specific version of this is known as an *event listing*, where concrete events, sorted into categories, are arranged into time sequence.

3   *Role-ordered matrix*   Rows represent data from sets of individuals occupying different roles (e.g. doctor/nurse/administrator/patient).

4   *Conceptually clustered matrix*   Columns arranged to being together items 'belonging together' (e.g. relating to same theme).

5   *Effects matrix*   Displays data on outcomes (i.e. on dependent variable(s)).

6   *Case dynamics matrix*   Columns concern issues, what happens in connection with them (e.g. who does what), and outcomes.

Note: There are also several variants, including hybrids.

(*Source*: Miles and Huberman, 1984.)

---

information so that a representation can be made on a single sheet of paper. Studies in school classrooms, hospital wards and other units, etc. may benefit from a labelled plan showing the layout of furnishings, seating arrangements, lines of travel, 'action zones' and so on. Figure 12.2 provides an example. The change in physical organization of the two classrooms was associated with a substantial increase in educational activities in classroom 2. Hitchcock and Hughes (1989, pp. 170–91) give other examples in educational contexts, and several references; Zeisel (1981, pp. 212–25) gives varied examples from environment-behaviour research.

Flow-charts   The flow-chart is a well known device which is useful in the study of processes. The formal set of procedures leading to the decision being made that a child should be 'statemented' as being in need of special educational provision, can be represented in a complex flow-chart (Evans et al., 1989, p. 131), which is reproduced in figure 12.3. Comparison with the actuality of the process in specific cases is not only of descriptive value but is of direct assistance in understanding the working of that system. Similar approaches are of value in understanding, for example, the underlying processes leading to the decision that an old person should be admitted to

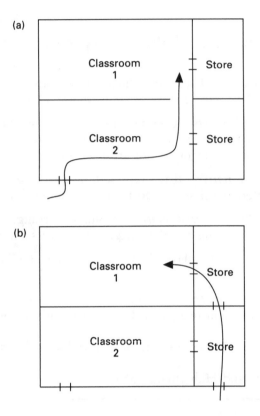

Figure 12.2 Plans showing a change of layout between two classrooms
(a) route to classroom 1 causes maximal disruption in classroom 2; (b) new route to classroom
1 causes minimal disruption in classroom 2

specialist psycho-geriatric provision, and generally in evaluating the working of health and social welfare programmes. Fetterman (1989, p. 95) refers to the value of flow-charts in studies of production line operations, citing the example of the mapping of what happens to a book from its arrival in a research library to appearing on the shelf as providing a base-line of under-standing about the system.

Organizational charts The standard, formal, organizational chart of a business, service, programme is a representation of certain kinds of relation-ship and obviously assists in understanding its functioning. It may exist as a document, or may have to be pieced together by the enquirer. Compari-sons between formal and informal hierarchies are instructive in the same kind of way as those between formal and informal flow-charts.

Miles and Huberman (1984, pp. 91–5) recommend the use of a particular kind of informal chart, which they term a CONTEXT CHART. Case study is, of course, the study of a phenomenon in its context, and this device helps to emphasize important contextual factors. A context chart differs from an organizational chart in that it is selective. It will be based on any available organizational charts and other documents, supplemented by your notes based on interview and observation. As ever, it is driven by your research questions in the sense that it concentrates on information relevant to them. The chart shows relationships and influences, usually, but not necessarily, between individuals, to help put their behaviour in context and understand its meaning. Figure 12.4 provides an example. Forcing yourself to draw a context chart at an early stage of data collection is a valuable discipline. It highlights what you do not know, and where your evidence for the nature of relations is sketchy, and so helps guide the development of the study.

Causal networks   A causal network is a diagram which includes the most important independent and dependent variables in a case study, and the relationships between them. In simple terms, it consists of a number of labelled boxes with arrowed links between them, and some associated text. We have already had an initial attempt at this in the conceptual framework, which was discussed in chapter 6 (see p. 150) and advocated as a means of getting out into the open one's theoretical, and other, presuppositions about the case study. It is worth stressing that the causal network *is* about cause and effect relationships and not simply correlational ones. The type of causality focused on initially is what has been termed LOCAL CAUSALITY – the actual events and processes that lead to specific outcomes in this particular case.

The conceptual framework and research questions with which you started the study may well have been modified along the way. To develop a causal network, you need to look at them in conjunction with the set of codes, including the pattern codes, that you have developed from the data analysis, together with the memos and other summary sheets you have produced. Miles and Huberman's advice is to go for 'causal fragments' initially, by:

a   translating the pattern codes into variables;
b   drawing lines between variables which are related;
c   drawing a directional arrow on the lines from cause to effect; and
d   reviewing other codes to see if there is a candidate for a possible intervening variable between the two you have linked (see earlier discussion on intervening variables on p. 345).

Figure 12.5 presents an example, concerned with the adoption of a school-based training programme in behavioural techniques. This illustrates an innovation for which there were high resource needs and low official support from outside the school. However, there was a compensating high level of self-help in implementing the project, which both increased the efforts of those involved and assisted in the development of mastery in the practice of the innovation. There was also an indirect effect on mastery through the high efforts made by participants.

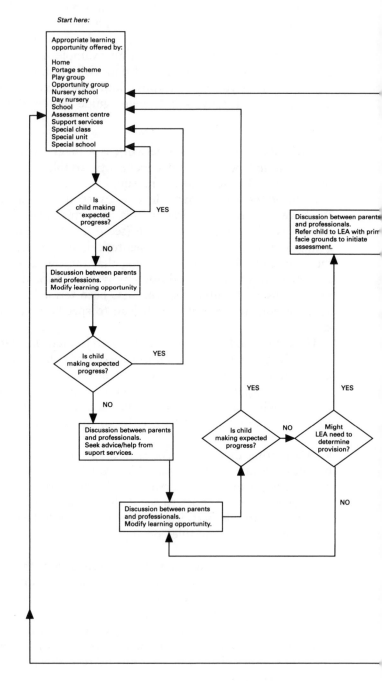

Figure 12.3 Decision-making for special needs: a flow-chart
Source: Evans et al., 1989.

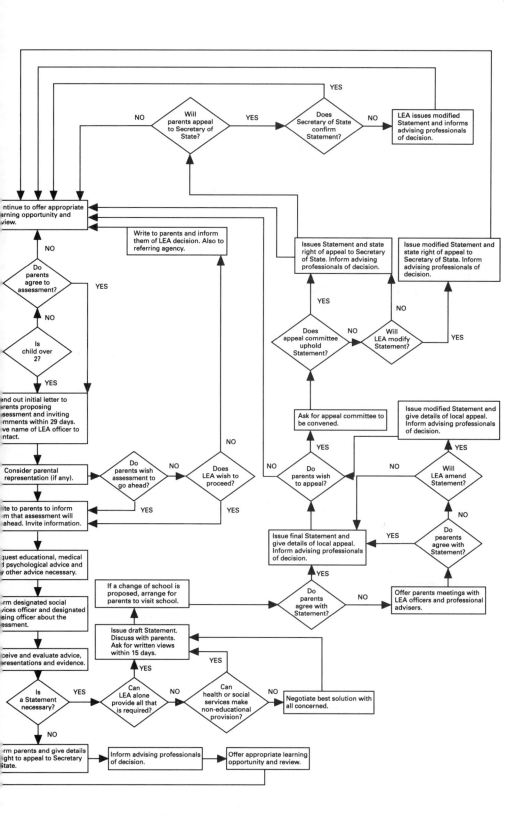

Will parents appeal to Secretary of State? — NO → Continue to offer appropriate learning opportunity and review.

YES → **Does Secretary of State confirm Statement?** — NO → LEA issues modified Statement and informs advising professionals of decision.

YES (loops back)

Write to parents and inform them of LEA decision. Also to referring agency.

Issues Statement and state right of appeal to Secretary of State. Inform advising professionals of decision.

Issue modified Statement and state right of appeal to Secretary of State. Inform advising professionals of decision.

Do parents agree to assessment? — YES

NO → **Is child over 2?** — YES

Does appeal committee uphold Statement? — NO → **Will LEA modify Statement?** — YES / NO → (loops)

YES

Ask for appeal committee to be convened.

Issue modified Statement and give details of local appeal. Inform advising professionals of decision.

Send out initial letter to parents proposing assessment and inviting comments within 29 days. Give name of LEA officer to contact.

Consider parental representation (if any).

Do parents wish assessment to go ahead? — NO → **Does LEA wish to proceed?** — NO

Do parents wish to appeal? — NO / YES

Will LEA amend Statement? — YES / NO

YES / YES

Write to parents to inform them that assessment will go ahead. Invite information.

Request educational, medical and psychological advice and any other advice necessary.

Issue final Statement and give details of local appeal. Inform advising professionals of decision.

Do parents agree with Statement? — YES / NO

Inform designated social services officer and designated housing officer about the assessment.

If a change of school is proposed, arrange for parents to visit school.

Do parents agree with Statement? — NO → Offer parents meetings with LEA officers and professional advisers.

YES

Receive and evaluate advice, representations and evidence.

Issue draft Statement. Discuss with parents. Ask for written views within 15 days.

Is a Statement necessary? — YES → **Can LEA alone provide all that is required?** — NO → **Can health or social services make non-educational provision?** — NO → Negotiate best solution with all concerned.

YES / YES

NO

Inform parents and give details of right to appeal to Secretary of State.

Inform advising professionals of decision.

Offer appropriate learning opportunity and review.

Twin Pines School

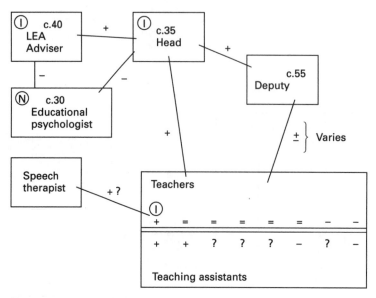

Key:
Ⓘ Innovation advocate
Ⓝ Innovation opposer
+ = ? – In boxes: attitude to innovation; between boxes: character of relationship

Figure 12.4   Example of a 'context chart'

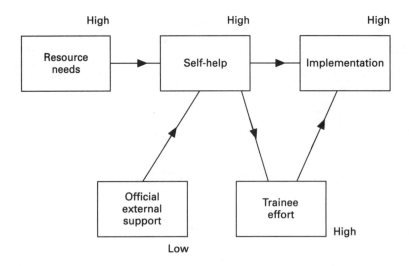

Figure 12.5   Example of a 'causal fragment'

This process can obviously be repeated for other parts of the causal network. It may also help if, towards the end of data collection, you have a go at brainstorming a full list of variables which seem to enter into the case, say, between about fifteen and forty. The earlier analyses, particularly the different matrices, assist in putting the network together. For example, the 'conceptually clustered' matrix helps in getting at relationships in a particular group of variables; the 'effects' matrices and 'event listing' help to give cause–effect relations; the 'case dynamics' matrices help with both.

It should not be thought that this is an automatic process for getting at 'the truth' about the case. It is an attempt to provide an integrated summary of what you know about it, but is necessarily more suggestive than definitive. You can also, at this final stage, go back to informants and get their feedback on the network you have produced. Such 'member checking' (Lincoln and Guba, 1985, p. 314), is discussed later in connection with procedures for establishing trustworthiness (p. 404).

One form of seeing whether what you have produced has value, which is appropriate for explanatory case studies, is to use it to generate predictions about what is likely to happen in the short to medium term, say within a year. Again, informants can be asked, at that time, about the accuracy of the predictions.

The Analysis of Multiple Case Studies

Many, probably most, small-scale studies are likely to be single rather than multiple case studies. There may be some occasions where it makes sense to conceptualize what you are doing as half a dozen small linked studies, rather than to devote the same total effort to a single case.

Use of the various suggestions for reporting, summary and display outlined in the previous sections does much to provide the degree of standardization which makes cross-case comparisons a relatively straightforward task. The most obvious tactic is to bring all corresponding single-case summarizing charts together in one large matrix. Ways have then to be found of displaying and highlighting important similarities and differences between the cases. Again, Miles and Huberman (1984, ch. V) present a range of matrices and other displays, which are primarily concerned with detecting and matching patterns across the cases. A summary is provided in box 12.8.

Drawing Conclusions from Qualitative Data

Displays, summary tables and the like are useful strategies for making sense of qualitative data. However, there are some specific tactics used in the process which help in coming to conclusions. They have been mentioned at

---

Box 12.8   Examples of matrix displays for multiple case studies

1   *Meta-matrix ordered by cases*   Matrix type as for single case, but includes separate data from all cases, categorized and ordered on main variable being displayed. It is usually possible to generate several summary tables from such meta-matrices, e.g. showing number of cases of particular type.

2   *Case-ordered predictor–outcome matrix*   Cases ordered on a main outcome (criterion) variable, with data from each case on what are considered the main predictor (antecedent) variables.

3   *Time-ordered meta-matrix*   Columns arranged in time sequence, rows give cases.

4   *Scatterplots*   Data displayed on two or more dimensions of interest; 'points' on the plot are cases. Data need to be scaled to do this.

5   *Case-ordered meta-matrix*   Cases are sorted by degrees of probable cause (e.g. high/medium/low). Different effects (outcomes) shown for each case.

6   *Causal models*   As with single cases. There are also techniques for combining separate single-case causal networks.

Note also the technique of *substructing* (Lazarsfeld et al., 1972), also known as *typology construction* (Lofland, 1971). It is useful when you are seeking to clarify an outcome variable used to sort cases, and suspect that more than one dimension is involved.

(*Source*: Miles and Huberman, 1984.)

---

earlier points, but it may be of value to isolate them at this stage. They are summarized in box 12.9.

Counting and the Use of Statistical Analysis

Counting and statistical analysis are viewed as anathema by many advocates of qualitative research. However, a surprising amount of counting goes on when judgments based on qualitative data are concerned. It is worth remembering that although the qualitative and quantitative camps are prone to mutual sniping if not all-out war, 'mainstream' qualitative researchers use

---

Box 12.9   Drawing conclusions from qualitative data – tactics

1   *Counting*   Categorizing data and measuring the frequency of occurrence of the categories.

2   *Patterning*   Noting of recurring patterns or themes.

3   *Clustering*   Grouping of objects, persons, activities, settings, etc. with similar characteristics.

4   *Factoring*   Grouping of variables into a small number of hypothetical factors.

5   *Relating variables*   Discovery of the type of relationship (if any) between two or more variables.

6   *Building of causal networks*   Development of chains or webs of linkages between variables.

7   *Relating findings to general theoretical frameworks*   Attempt to find general propositions that account for the particular findings in this study.

---

frequency counts to verify hypotheses. In symbolic interactionist approaches, this is termed 'behavioural validity' (cf Denzin, 1988, p. 95).

A distinction can be made between covert and overt counting. The former provides the base for many of the statements made in qualitative analysis, particularly in generalizations about trends or patterns in the data. The 'many' in the previous sentence is an example, others are terms like 'frequently', 'common', 'rare', etc. Such terms indicate categorization and counting. However they are not necessarily precisely defined (although they can be in particular circumstances – say, 'rare means not more than two occurrences of —— per day'). The main thing here is that the data and the conclusions are reported in sufficient detail for the reasonableness of the use of the term to be checked by the reader.

A strong case can be made, however, for the overt and self-conscious use of frequencies, so that actual numbers are generated. It is a powerful data reduction device, assisting in making sense of large and intractable mounds of data, and because of the necessary explicitness of definition gives greater protection against bias. Remember the deficiencies of the human when carrying out 'intuitive data analysis' (box 12.1, p. 375). The argument is not that all qualitative data should be converted into quantitative data, but that if you are wanting to make statements about frequencies, it is better to use numbers – which you can subsequently label as 'frequent' etc., on the basis of overt definitions. These data can be subjected to statistical analysis, using one or more of the techniques covered in the previous chapter.

It is common to have data which, while in principle numerical, cannot be precisely quantified. These have been termed 'quasi-statistics' (Lazarsfeld and Barton, 1955, pp. 346–348). Becker and Geer (1960) give the example of frequency or distribution information about where different student groups sit in lectures. Without actually counting, an observer comes to the conclusion that, say, members of freshman fraternities sit together while other students sit in less stable smaller groupings. The observer may get confirmation of this finding from observing other lectures (taking note of their likely biases towards this hypothesis), or by asking others in a position to know. The observer can then decide how likely it is that the conclusion about the frequency or distribution of the quasi-statistic is correct – in a similar way to that in which judgments are made about statistics using significance levels and the like. Such methods are limited to clear and definite differences.

Establishing the Trustworthiness of Enquiry Based on Qualitative Data

Anyone moving away from studies based on quantitative data is likely to have to face criticisms that the work is unreliable, invalid and generally unworthy of admission into the magic circle of science. Many funding agencies and other likely sponsors expect 'hard' (i.e. quantitative) data for their money. The stance taken here is that there is virtue in multi-method approaches which generate both quantitative and qualitative data; but that the qualitative data need not have a secondary or subservient role. And, hence, that the approach to qualitative data and its analysis needs to be rigorous and systematic.

Researchers collecting and analysing qualitative data have to take serious note of the potential for bias in these processes. The problem, which is a central strength at the same time, is the reliance on the 'human instrument'. As Miles and Huberman (1984) put it: 'Each [qualitative researcher] is a one-person research machine: defining the problem, doing the sampling, designing the instruments, collecting the information, reducing the information, analyzing it, interpreting it, writing it up' (p. 230). The substantial body of research evidence on the fallibility of the human in making the judgments involved in these kinds of activities (reviewed in Nisbett and Ross, 1980), provides conclusions which correspond closely with those identified in anthropological field work (Wax et al., 1971). These are 'representativeness', 'availability' and 'weighting'. Many pitfalls centre on representativeness being assumed when it is suspect. There are tendencies for over-reliance on accessible informants (informants may therefore be nonrepresentative); on accessible events (which may well be nonrepresentative); and on plausible explanations (inferences may be drawn from nonrepresentative processes). Anthropologists refer to the latter as the 'holistic bias' – where everything seems to fit into the picture; achieved by ignoring, or giving little weight to, the things that don't.

Lincoln and Guba (1985, p. 290) suggest that there are four questions which must be addressed in any systematic enquiry into humans and their ways:

1 *Truth value.* How can one establish confidence in the 'truth' of the findings of a particular enquiry for the persons with which, and the context in which, the enquiry was carried out?
2 *Applicability.* How applicable are these findings to another setting or group of people?
3 *Consistency.* How can one have confidence that the findings would be replicated if the study were repeated with the same (or similar) persons, in the same (or similar) situation?
4 *Neutrality.* How can we be sure that the findings are determined by the respondents and the situation and context, and not by the biases, motivations, interests or perspectives of the enquirer?

The concepts of 'internal validity', 'external validity' (or 'generalizability'), 'reliability' and 'objectivity', discussed in the previous chapter in connection with quantitative data, represent the criteria which have been developed in response to these questions within the experimental and survey traditions. Lincoln and Guba (1985, pp. 294–301) make out a strong case that these conventional criteria are inappropriate when dealing with qualitative case study data. They propose four alternatives which appear to reflect more faithfully the assumptions behind this strategy – *credibility, transferability, dependability* and *confirmability.*

Credibility

Here the goal is to demonstrate that the enquiry was carried out in a way which ensures that the subject of the enquiry was accurately identified and described. This is the parallel construct to 'internal validity', considered to be inappropriate here by Lincoln and Guba because it depends ultimately on a 'naïve realist' philosophy of science stance. It is interesting to note, however, that, even in terms of the Campbell and Stanley (1963) 'threats to internal validity' approach, discussed at length in chapter 3, p. 71), case study designs stand up well in comparison with quasi-experimental approaches. Case study is admittedly more prone to the 'instrumentation' threat – but 'statistical regression' does not apply, and 'maturation' and 'maturation/selection interaction' essentially depend on the relative duration of the two types of study. The other threats seem to apply equally in case study and quasi-experimental contexts.

Several techniques have been suggested to enhance credibility. These include the following:

Prolonged involvement   This is the investment of sufficient time to learn the 'culture', test for misinformation, build trust, and generally go through the iterative procedures central to case study design. Margaret Mead's classic study of Samoa (Mead, 1971) has had its credibility subsequently severely questioned (Freeman, 1984), a major criticism being levelled at her for not spending the time needed to 'learn the culture'. This aspect is most crucial to anthropological case studies in exotic and unfamiliar settings, but the general point that case studies demand substantial involvement remains.

Persistent observation   Specific situations within the case study need to be observed over a sufficient period for you to identify those aspects of a situation that are most relevant to the issues involved, and focus on them. Persistent observation brings depth to the study. In a recent project, our first two or three observations of a particular teaching assistant in a classroom were simply noted as being concerned with making a mobile, tidying the stock room and preparing masks for Hallowe'en. Persistent observation and subsequent interviews revealed a tacit agreement, never verbalized, that the assistant did not interact with the children concerned; and a confirmed prediction of problems when the teacher attempted to initiate individual work.

Triangulation   The use of evidence from different sources, of different methods of collecting data and of different investigators, where feasible, are all triangulation techniques which enhance credibility.

Peer debriefing   Exposing one's analysis and conclusions to a colleague or other peer on a continuous basis can assist in the development of both the design and the analysis of the study. The exercise of being explicit in formulating something for presentation to a peer fosters subsequent credibility.

NEGATIVE CASE ANALYSIS (p. 380) and MEMBER CHECKS are also suggested by Lincoln and Guba as ways of improving credibility. In one sense the latter, checking with those from whom the data are derived, gets to the heart of credibility; if they believe the findings from their several perspectives, it is, tautologically, credible! However, care needs to be taken as all the members may have an interest in presenting a misleading or biased case – especially if the study is perceived as having relevance to some possible change in their circumstances (e.g. a study of a unit where members feel that the study might be used as ammunition in its closure). Guba and Lincoln (1981, pp. 110–11) provide a useful review of factors involved.

Transferability

This is the construct corresponding to external validity or generalizability in conventional quantitative research. When a sampling methodology is not used, it is clearly inappropriate to seek to make the same kind of statistical generalization to a population which is a fundamental part of statistical inference. Kennedy (1976) refers to this as the 'first decision span' in generalization. He also distinguishes a 'second decision span' which is concerned with applying the findings about one situation or case to a second one which is considered to be sufficiently similar to the first to warrant that generalization.

The onus thus shifts to the person interested in making such a generalization or transfer to make that decision. The job of the person carrying out and reporting on the first case study is to provide the information needed to do this. That is, as Lincoln and Guba (1985) put it, 'it is . . . *not* the task to provide an *index* of transferability; it *is* his or her responsibility to provide the *data base* that makes transferability judgments possible on the part of potential appliers' (p. 316). In their view this is done by providing a 'thick description' (Geertz, 1973; see Denzin, 1989 for a detailed account). Broadly speaking, this is a description which specifies everything that a reader may need to know to understand the findings, which appears suspiciously circular as a definition. The findings themselves are not part of the thick description, though it must be interpreted in their light.

Marshall and Rossman (1989) stress the need for a full specification of the theoretical framework on which the study is based. This then helps those designing studies or making policy within that framework to determine whether or not the case(s) described can be transferred to other settings. The reader or user of specific research can see how that research ties into a body of theory. They cite the example of a case study of the implementation of a new staff development in a school, which can be linked to the theory of implementation of innovations in organizations, leadership, adult career socialization theory, etc. The study could then be used in the development of further studies in a variety of settings; not limited to the type of school in which the original study took place, or to schools at all; and not limited to staff development. It could, for example, be used in research about organizations, building a link with organization theory.

Dependability

Dependability is analogous to reliability. Just as reliability is a necessary, though not sufficient, condition for validity, so that a study that is valid must needs be reliable, then dependability is necessary, though not sufficient, for credibility. Hence a study that is shown to be credible is also dependable. Guba (1981) has used this as an argument in favour of concentrating on credibility, and leaving dependability to follow from that, but there would seem to be virtue in assessing dependability directly. Triangulation, discussed above in connection with credibility, could be argued as being more obviously a means of assessing dependability.

The ENQUIRY AUDIT, also suggested by Guba, is based upon the auditing approach familiar in connection with business and finance. An auditor has two basic tasks: to examine the processes used in keeping the accounts of the company, and to examine the product, the 'books' and the financial statement. If the processes, when checked, are acceptable and in line with accepted standards, then the auditor can attest to their dependability. The academic or enquiry auditor has the same two functions, and again if the processes followed are clear, systematic, well documented, providing safeguards against bias, and so on, this constitutes a dependability test.

Confirmability

This is the corresponding concept to objectivity. The change signals a move away from some attribute of the enquirer (is she or he objective?) to the case study itself. Have we been told enough about the study not only to judge the adequacy of the process, but also to assess whether the findings flow from the data?

The second aspect of the enquiry audit provides a technique for attesting confirmability. Halpern (1983; see also Lincoln and Guba, 1985, appendices A and B) has provided a detailed operationalization of the enquiry audit concept. This includes techniques for following the 'audit trail' and an algorithm for the audit process. The notion is that a person is appointed as auditor. In order for her to be able to do the job, various categories of information will be required, e.g.:

a   raw data – field notes, documents, tapes, etc.;
b   processed data and analysis products – write-ups, summaries, etc.;
c   data reconstruction and synthesis products – codes, patterns, matrices, etc. and final report
d   process notes – procedures, designs, strategies, etc.;
e   materials relating to intentions and dispositions – original proposal, personal notes, intentions, expectations, etc.;
f   instrument development information – pilot forms, schedules, observation formats, etc.

The material here constitutes the audit trail, and after perusing it, the auditor has to determine the project's auditability: is the trail comprehensible, useful and linked to the purposes of the study? If the answer to this is positive, she is then in a position actually to follow the trail and come to a judgment about the trustworthiness of the study.

Carried out conscientiously, according to Halpern's algorithm, this is a formidable task for both auditor and audited. This is, again, an area where the use of microcomputers has much to offer in the recording and display of the various steps (Conrad and Reinharz, 1985). There is little doubt, however, that, whether carried out by computer or otherwise, the approach would do much to ensure high quality of enquiry. It is over-optimistic, and probably over-formalistic, to expect all small-scale researchers to follow this route at this time. Nevertheless, it provides a useful example, even if only used on an 'as-if' basis. Conducting an enquiry in such a way that you collect and maintain the materials which would make up an audit trail, where you are asking yourself whether an outside person could follow what had gone on, and also whether you could justify your findings and conclusions to them in relation to the material in the audit trail, is a valuable exercise in its own right.

Further Reading

Burgess, R. G. (1984) *In the Field: an introduction to field research*. London: Allen & Unwin. Chapter 8 provides a short and clear treatment of the analysis of qualitative data. Annotated references.

Burgess, R. G. (ed.) (1982) *Field Research: a sourcebook and field manual*. London: Allen & Unwin. Section 9 contains a selection of papers on analysing and reporting qualitative field data.

Fetterman, D. (1989) *Ethnography Step by Step*. Newbury Park and London: Sage. Good chapter on analysis.

Miles, M. B. and Huberman, A. M. (1984) *Qualitative Data Analysis: a sourcebook of new methods*. Newbury Park and London: Sage. Invaluable collection of techniques to assist in the systematic analysis of qualitative data. Oriented to large-scale studies but much of relevance.

Patton, M. Q. (1990) *Qualitative Evaluation and Research Methods*. Newbury Park and London: Sage. Clear exposition of approaches to qualitative analysis.

Strauss, A. L. (1987) *Qualitative Analysis for Social Scientists*. Cambridge: Cambridge University Press. Provides a systematic approach to the analysis and interpretation of qualitative data along 'grounded theory' lines.

Strauss, A. L. and Corbin, J. (1990) *Basics of Qualitative Research: grounded theory procedures and techniques*. Newbury Park and London: Sage. Good, clear, practical introduction to using the 'grounded theory' approach.

Tesch, R. (1990) *Qualitative Research: analysis types and software tools*. London: Falmer. Makes a useful distinction between structural and interpretational analysis types, and shows how the computer can be used with each of them.

Werner, O. and Schoepfle, G. M. (1987) *Systematic Fieldwork*, vol. 2: *Ethnographic Analysis and Data Management*. Newbury Park and London: Sage. Weighty handbook with wealth of suggestions for analysing qualitative data.

Yin, R. K. (1989) *Case Study Research: Design and Methods*, 2nd edn. Newbury Park and London: Sage. Short but useful chapter on analysis.

Part V

Making an Impact

The first chapter stressed some of the special features of real world enquiry. Not least of these are your responsibilities when all the data has been collected in and its analysis completed. In the real world, it may well be that a major part of the effort comes after this. For many such studies, the same person who carried out the research is expected to find ways of putting the findings into practice. Even if this is not the case, you may be expected to make suggestions and proposals that others can take on board. This extension of the researcher's role is by no means universally accepted and it poses a substantial challenge.

The following chapter covers an area common to all scientific enquiry: the responsibility and need to make one's findings public. It is argued that the way in which reports are presented must take serious note of the audience to whom one seeks to communicate. Real world enquiry commonly has to reach out to several different audiences and hence there is a requirement to master a range of styles of report.

The final chapters concern themselves with implementation and change and with the kinds of roles that researchers and practitioners need to take on if they are to play a part in these processes. 'Action research', a name for a family of approaches which accept this kind of agenda, is discussed and an attempt made to present a balanced view about the important but limited role of systematic enquiry in real world concerns.

13

Reporting on the Enquiry

The chapter discusses the traditional scientific journal format in relation to real world enquiry.

It covers several approaches to reporting case studies and stresses the special nature of evaluation reports.

There is discussion of issues in writing for clients, and of alternative presentations for different purposes.

The chapter concludes with advice on writing.

Introduction

Consideration of the form that a report of your enquiry might take brings to the fore, once again, the implications of a 'real world' focus. This highlights the notion of *audience*; who is the report for? And what are you seeking to achieve by reporting to them?

It may be useful to distinguish between reports produced for the 'invisible college' of fellow researchers, and other types of report. Let us start with the former, as it is easier to specify the requirements. There is, as you are no doubt aware if you are a student of psychology or a related discipline, a strong and highly conventionalized model for the format of articles in scientific journals. There are other ways of disseminating findings to fellow researchers, most notably through conference papers (and other conference activities such as 'poster sessions' where you display a summary of your research and stand by the posters to answer questions and discuss the work with interested conference members) and seminar papers. There is sometimes an unexamined assumption that these latter types of activities should mimic the journal paper in style. As with many unexamined assumptions this is very questionable, and you may well communicate more effectively face-to-face by adopting one of the more relaxed formats covered later in the chapter.

The student on a degree or other course is also commonly required to follow the scientific paper format for all reports. There is a strong case for students being required to gain skills in other kinds of presentation. Report writing for scientific journals is likely to be a high-frequency activity for only a small minority of students in their subsequent careers. Many more will have to produce reports for other audiences.

Ethics and Reporting

Several parties are likely to be concerned with what is reported, and with how it is reported. You have both an interest in, and a responsibility for, ensuring that the results of your study get into the 'public domain' (to publish is, literally, to make public). Publish or perish may be over-dramatic, but it is inescapable that if your role permits you to carry out enquiry, then a likely index of your work and worth will be the quantity and quality of the reports that you produce.

Participants in the research may well be concerned with how they appear in the report, and whether their interests, individually or collectively, are affected by publication. Can you keep to the assurances of anonymity and confidentiality that you gave them? Surveys and experiments are usually straightforward in this respect. But case studies, and similar small-scale research projects where the context is important, pose problems. Obviously it is possible to use pseudonyms for persons and settings, but this may not guarantee anonymity (particularly internally) and further changes that you make to seek disguise may distance your report from the reality it is seeking to describe or understand. The basic stance usually adopted is to take reasonable precautions to ensure anonymity, and then publish.

When the study has been carried out for sponsors, they also have concerns. How are they, and/or whoever they represent, being portrayed? Will the report be used by others to criticize, compete with or undermine them? Can they stop you (discussed below)? 'Gatekeepers' will be interested in the outcomes of any approval they gave for the study to take place. Are they going to get hassle from others as a result?

Reporting What You Have Found

The needs in this respect can be expressed simply. The difficulty lies in actually doing it.

A   Reporting is an Essential Part of the Enquiry Process

For an enquiry to count in research terms it must be made public. The report is the way you do this.

B The Appropriate Format for the Report Depends on the Nature and Purpose of the Enquiry

If you have academic intent, it may well be that the conventional scientific journal format is appropriate. For other purposes, other formats may well communicate better.

C You Need not be Limited to a Single Type of Report

Real world research often seeks to inform and influence several different audiences. It is unlikely that the same style of report will be best suited to all of them. There is nothing (apart from the effort involved) to stop you producing several different reports. They don't (all) have to be written reports.

D Real World Enquiry Calls for Professional Standards of Reporting and Presentation

This applies if you are simply seeking to inform. It is probably even more important if you want the report and findings to be acted on in some way.

The Scientific Journal Format

Almost all journals require contributors to follow a specific format and to keep within certain areas of subject content and limits of length. Instructions are given, usually on one of the inside covers, and may include reference to a 'style manual' of which probably the most common in the psychological field is that published by the American Psychological Association (APA). Many educational and clinical journals follow similar formats, but other social science disciplines may differ considerably. In any of these cases, a good strategy is to peruse recent journal issues and seek a suitable model.

The traditional writing style expected has been impersonal, past tense, and in the passive voice (as in 'subjects were asked to complete all questions'). This is understandable as an attempt to demonstrate the scientific credentials of the activity, but can lead to a dryness and lack of impact in the writing. Several journals do not now require the passive impersonal style (e.g. 'We found that . . .' is accepted in the stead of the traditional 'It was found that . . .'). Conversely, too much authorial intrusion, with 'I did this and then I . . .' sounds naïve, at least to my ear.

Continued use of the past tense for things that have already happened (for previous studies referred to, and also what *was* done in the one you are reporting on), does however seem justified. The term 'subject' for those who have taken part in the study has also been criticized, in part as suggesting an inappropriate role – that they are 'subjected' to various things. Although still common, it is in many contexts possible to replace it with 'respondent', 'informant', 'participant', or just 'person'. Sexist language should be avoided, as discussed earlier in chapter 3 (pages 63–4). Several texts give detailed discussions of the process of writing a journal article (e.g. Sternberg, 1987; Day, 1983). Box 13.1 presents a checklist of areas commonly covered in a report produced in journal format.

Box 13.1 Checklist of areas covered in report for scientific journal

1 *Title page*
   (title summarizes main topic of paper):
   a   name and institution(s) of author(s);
   b   running head (shortened title for top of pages);
   c   acknowledgements (help and research funds).

2 *Abstract*
   (concise summary in *c.*150 words).

3 *Introduction*:
   a   explain nature of study;
   b   describe background and previous work;
   c   give design and research questions (or hypotheses) with rationale for choice.

4 *Method*
   (detailed account of procedures used which would enable the reader to repeat the study):
   a   participants
       i   number
       ii   selection process
       iii   characteristics
       iv   means of handling refusals/nonreturns;
   b   apparatus/materials
       i   description of tests/scales/observation schedules, etc.
       ii   development procedures for new instruments
       iii   scoring/coding procedures;
   c   procedure
       i   observers/interviewers etc; characteristics and training
       ii   reliability and validity of instruments/procedures
       iii   description of setting

>   iv   verbatim instructions to participants
>   v   duration, number, and timing of sessions.
>
> 5   *Results*
>   a   methodological checks (e.g. showing matching of two groups);
>   b   quantitative data analysis
>   i   descriptive statistics
>   ii   exploratory data analysis
>   iii confirmatory data analysis;
>   c   qualitative data analysis;
>   d   tables and figures (appropriately interspersed);
>   e   summary statement.
>
> 6   *Discussion*
>   a   answers to research questions (support or otherwise for hypotheses);
>   b   relationship to earlier findings;
>   c   implications;
>   d   suggested improvements; questions raised; suggestions for further research.
>
> 7   *Notes and references*
>   a   text of notes (indicated by superscript numbers in the article itself);
>   b   list of references cited in the article, in standard format.
>
> NB: check the *specific* requirements of the journal to which you propose to send your paper.

If you wish to make progress as a professional enquirer or researcher then writing accounts in this type of format is, in an important sense, a 'real world' activity for you. Reputation, progress and research money are strongly related to the number and quality of articles accepted for publication in reputable, refereed journals. And rightly so. The conventions of this style of publication, with detailed and explicit concern for descriptions of procedure and analysis, together with the system of anonymous review by peers, provide important safeguards of the quality of the collective scientific endeavour. Scandals where the system breaks down, due to fraud, delusion or collusion, are not unknown. Broad and Wade (1985) discuss a range of examples. The alleged fraud within psychology, perpetrated by Sir Cyril Burt (Hearnshaw, 1979) has been the subject of much controversy and the British Psychological Society has recently delivered an 'open verdict' (British Psychological Society, 1992; see also Joynson, 1989 and Fletner, 1991). The system within science, in principle though not always in practice, should be self-correcting because of the replicability of findings (maverick findings are highly likely to be checked by others, and faked results will not replicate).

There are potential difficulties and tensions in reporting applied studies. Many concentrate on specific settings, persons or organizations, selected because of practical concerns rather than through some representative sampling procedure. Such case studies may appear difficult to fit into the traditional format, but their flexibility extends to the possible ways in which they can be presented.

The suggestion, then, is that where you are seeking journal publication or presenting a thesis, you should follow, in broad terms, the above sequence of introducing the issue or problem being studied, the methods used, the findings from the data that you have collected and analysed, and the conclusions and implications from the study. This can be used for exploratory, descriptive and explanatory studies. Further details on the 'scientific journal' format for reporting case studies are presented in the following section.

More fundamental problems occur when other audiences are considered. It could be argued that to make good its claim to be 'real world' enquiry, the prime focus in reporting should be on the clients or sponsors who have funded the research. Or on professional, or practitioner, or lay, audiences who have legitimate rights and vested interests in the area of the enquiry and its findings (Rob Walker, 1985, ch. 5). However, as Walker goes on to point out, this switch of audience, and consequently of style of presentation, challenges values basic to the scientific enterprise: 'While there might seem good reasons for closing the gap from the professional viewpoint, such values serve to maintain independence, objectivity and credibility in research and should not be transgressed lightly' (p. 181).

One way out comes from realizing that this is not necessarily an either/ or situation. Many applied studies can legitimately seek to reach multiple audiences through multiple publication. The sponsor, the wider practitioner and lay audiences can receive appropriate treatment(s). The scientific audience can be reached through thesis and journal article. Possible formats to consider when communicating to these different audiences are also included in the next section on case study reports, and taken up in a more general sense afterwards.

The Case Study Report

There are numerous examples of experimental reports and survey reports, and clear models. Reports of multi-method case studies, while common in some fields, are difficult to come across in others. Case studies can be written up in many different ways – in fact they need not necessarily be presented in written format. Video–tapes, tape–slide sequences and oral presentations are all possibilities.

Before suggesting some alternatives it is worth emphasizing that, as with case study design and analysis, reporting is not a once-only event tagged on to the end of the process. Yin (1989, p. 127), from extensive experience, advocates composing parts of the report (e.g. the bibliography) at an early stage, and that you keep drafting and re-drafting other parts of the report (e.g. the methodological section) rather than waiting for the end of the data analysis process.

The 'Scientific Journal' Case Study Format

Use of this standard approach for structuring research reports is feasible with case studies, and has the advantage that it is familiar to the person steeped in the traditions of laboratory-based enquiry. It is similarly the style of presentation least likely to raise hackles in academic circles. Conversely, it is unlikely to be the most appropriate format in communicating to other audiences.

The 'issue/methods/findings/conclusions' structure provides the broad framework. Lincoln and Guba (1985, p. 362), advocate the use of case study reporting as a way of getting some order into qualitative field research reports (which have previously been characterized variously by Lofland, 1971, p. 109, as showing 'democratic pluralism', 'chaos' or 'anarchy'). They suggest the following structure a main report consisting of:

a   an explanation of the focus of the case study (e.g. problem, issue, policy option, topic of evaluation);
b   a description of the context or setting in which the enquiry took place, and with which it was concerned;
c   a description and analysis of the data obtained; and
d   a discussion of the outcomes of the enquiry;

followed by a methodological appendix containing a description of:

e   the credentials of the investigator(s), to include training and experience, together with a statement about the methodological predispositions and any biases towards the problem or setting;
f   the methods employed and the nature of the design as finally implemented; and
g   the methods used to enhance and assess trustworthiness.

Lincoln and Guba also stress the need for assessing each of these considerations at several different times in the study so that the report incorporates what was *intended* in respect of each of them and what was actually *implemented*.

Other Formats for Case Study Reports

These formats are based on Yin (1989, pp. 132–41), who cites examples of published case studies following the different formats.

The suspense structure   Here there is an inversion of the normal sequence as presented above. The main findings are presented in the initial chapter. The rest of the report is devoted to building up to this conclusion, showing what was done in the study, the picture that emerged; and how alternative explanations had to be discarded, so that that particular outcome was reached. It has considerable merit in explanatory studies (probably most people read the main findings first anyway!) as a presentational device.

The narrative report   A classic case study report format is the straight-forward account of the case. This might be bolstered by tables, figures and photographs, but the story is essentially told in continuous prose without the kind of analytic sub-divisions found in the previous format. Multiple case studies are handled by having a section for each of these cases, with a separate section for consideration of cross-case considerations.

A variant replaces the narrative by a series of questions and answers bringing out the findings from the study, which can be supplemented by an abbreviated narrative. Repetition of the same questions across cases permits easy comparisons in a multiple case study. Alternatively, multiple case studies can be presented in a narrative form where the organization is issue-based rather than case-based. This type of account can be supplemented by abbreviated summaries of individual cases.

The comparative structure   Here the same case is examined two or more times sequentially, each time in terms of a different explanatory or descriptive framework. The purpose is to demonstrate, or to give the reader sufficient information to judge, which of the explanations or descriptions best fits the data. This is a global version of the pattern-matching technique already referred to in chapter 12 in the context of qualitative analysis (p. 378).

The chronological structure   Evidence is presented in the report in chronological sequence. Its chief virtue is in explanatory studies where the emphasis on temporal order assists in the teasing out of cause–effect relationships. Insistence on strict chronology as being the only organizational principle, in anything but very simple case studies, can however provide a confusing and unnecessarily muddled account.

Theory-generating structures   Here the structure serves to support a theoretical case that is being made. Each succeeding section establishes a further part of, or link in, the argument, so that the totality provides a convincing case for a particular theoretical formulation. It can be used for either explanatory or exploratory case studies. This approach demands considerable powers of exposition and analytic grasp if it is not only to be theoretically convincing but also demonstrate a rigorous approach to data analysis and interpretation.

Unsequenced structures A structure where sequence of the different sections is of little or no importance. May be appropriate for descriptive case studies. Several important and frequently quoted descriptive case studies – e.g. the Lynd and Lynd (1929) 'Middletown' study – are unsequenced. A problem is that with this type of very open structure it may be difficult to know, or establish, whether important areas have been omitted.

These structures may suggest ideas for presentation of particular kinds of case study to different audiences. The 'suspense structure' is simply a re-ordering of the kind of material presented in the 'scientific journal' style of report. The other structures do not lend themselves readily to the production of a report demonstrating the degree of rigour which will have characterized a study which has taken serious note of the suggestions for design, procedure and analysis detailed in earlier chapters. This is not necessarily a disadvantage. Such pernicketiness, if it has not already put you off (and it shouldn't – it is there for the very good and worthwhile purpose of enhancing the quality of the case study), will almost certainly put off many audiences. A well written narrative account, totally bereft of tables of data, possibly presented in question and answer form, may communicate best to the manager, or social worker, or lay audience. And more technical details can be included as appendices.

Writing for Clients – the Technical Report

Many real world projects involve carrying out an enquiry for someone, whom we will refer to as the client. Evaluations, for example, often come into this category. The client may be an outside agency of some kind which has given you financial and other assistance to do a project, probably on a contractual basis. Or this might be a normal part of your job where you have been asked to do it by your boss, section head or manager, where she is the client. Or, again within your job, it might be a part of your professional responsibility to carry out projects, largely on your own initiative. In this latter case, and to some extent in the previous ones, the clients may be thought of as the persons forming the focus of the study; for example, staff and children in schools, or nurses, doctors and patients in hospitals.

The nature of report for a sponsor or superior, which we will refer to as a *technical report*, is very much conditioned by their requirements and expectations. For a body such as the Economic and Social Research Council (ESRC) in the United Kingdom, or equivalent bodies in other countries, the required report is very much along the lines of the 'scientific journal article' model. For other clients, this may be totally inappropriate. In case studies, the alternative formats considered in the previous section deserve serious consideration.

The Rowntree Trust (n.d.), a major British funder of social research, has a strong position on dissemination. It requires projects to be of value to policy-makers, decision-takers and practitioners and is hence concerned to ensure that research findings

> are presented in a form which can be grasped quickly by influential people who are normally too busy to read long reports or books. The Trust attaches importance to reports which are short, to the point and written in plain English. Compact summaries of research findings are likely to provide the basis of the Trust's Dissemination activities.... it seriously doubts whether scholarly publications ever represent an effective means of communication with policy makers and practitioners, certainly in the short term. (p. 10)

In contract research, the type, length and date of presentation of the final report is usually specified in the terms of the contract itself. The issue here is whether you can live with these terms. They may be negotiable but are frequently standard. Major concerns with a contract are more likely to relate to methodological issues (are they insisting that the project must be based on a sample survey when you think that this won't answer the questions to which they want answers?), duration and funding (it can't be done in the time, and with the resources they are prepared to fund), rather than the report itself.

What does need clarification about reports in the initial contract is the degree of control that the sponsors have over content and publication. Some may expect a power of veto, and modification or exclusion of things they object to (e.g. Jenkins, 1984). Others simply expect consultation at a draft stage. The issue may be not so much about your report to them, but whether they seek restrictions on further reports to other audiences. This is a particularly contested area with evaluation studies, largely because of the likely sensitivity of the findings for both sponsors and other parties (McDonald, 1974; see also chapter 7). There are no general answers here apart from making sure that you know where you stand before you get into the project, and feeling that you can live with the constraints both practically and ethically. The sponsors should appreciate, however, that they are paying for your expertise and that your concern is to 'tell it as it is'. If they seek to muffle or distort that message, then to an extent they are wasting their money.

Practicalities of Technical Report Writing

Find out what is expected   Ask. Some clients will want everything included, perhaps an adaptation of the 'scientific journal' format but with minimal use of jargon, particularly of statistical terminology. Others may simply want major findings. Implications and suggested courses of action may either be specifically required, or excluded. It often helps to check the form, style and length of any similar reports for the same sponsor – ask to see any they thought to be particularly helpful, good models, etc. Be ruthless on length; do not exceed what they have asked for.

Provide an 'executive summary' This is a short (usually one page), punchy summary, usually covering the problem, methods used, results and conclusion.

Put as much material as possible into appendices Any supplementary materials which you feel should be included, but which are not crucial to understanding what has been done, should be put in appendices. Put them in a separate volume if they are likely to make the report appear off-puttingly large. Or you may want them in the same volume to emphasize how much work you have done with the client's money. Their main function is to provide additional detail for readers with specialized interests. Typical appendix items would be

- detailed tables, charts and statistical analyses (summary charts would usually be in the main report);
- copies of instruments and documents used (e.g. questionnaires, coding and other instructions, observation schedules, form letters);
- glossary of terms, including acronyms, used (also explained on first use in the main body of the report).

Make sure that the presentation of the report is to a professional standard The sponsor has the right to expect professionalism in presentation of the report, just as much as in your carrying out and analysing the study. Anyhow, good presentation aids communication. See the general comments on writing and presentation below (p. 424).

Special Features of Evaluation Reports

A distinctive feature of many evaluation reports is the emphasis on *recommendations*. Box 13.2 provides suggestions on the writing of effective recommendations (i.e. ones likely to be acted on).

Alternative Forms of Presentation

Applied research may be most effectively communicated to some audiences through forms different from a written report – whether in scientific paper, case study or technical report format. Alternatives include oral presentations, audio-visual ones of various kinds, and literary forms other than the report. They are thought of here mainly as supplementary ways of communicating what you have done. They are adding to some kind of report in which you can demonstrate, both to your own and to others' satisfaction,

---

Box 13.2 Recommendations in evaluation reports

1 *The most important aspects are that recommendations should*:
   a *be clearly derived from the data*; and
   b *be practical (i.e. capable of implementation).*

2 It is helpful to distinguish among:
   a *findings* – information about the situation;
   b *interpretations* – explanations offered about the findings;
   c *judgements* – values brought to bear on the data; and
   d *recommendations* – suggested courses of action.

Patton (1982) describes exercises designed to develop skills in making these distinctions. He suggests taking a set of data and writing a final section of the report in which the findings, interpretations, judgements and subsequent recommendations are summarized *in one place*. The reasonableness of a recommendation depends on its being logically backed up by a set of findings, a reasonable interpretation of the findings and a judgement applied to them. Criteria for the making of judgements should be made explicit. Interpretations are necessarily speculative, and may be the subject of dispute. Resolution should be sought through discussion, and returning to the findings, to ensure that interpretations are grounded in these findings.

3 The process of generating recommendations takes time. A carefully carried out evaluation can be ruined by seeking to produce recommendations under severe time pressure. There should be the opportunity to discuss provisional recommendations with those holding a stake in the evaluation.

4 Consider presenting recommendations as a *set of options*. Given a list of findings, there may be several reasonable interpretations and different value positions which will generate a whole range of options. Each should be fully documented, showing fairly how the findings, interpretations and judgements support the option.

5 The nature of recommendations should be negotiated with decision-makers, or whomever form the audience for the report, at an early stage. This will have implications for the kind of evaluation carried out and the questions addressed. Note that it is possible that decision-makers may not want the evaluator to present recommendations but simply deliver findings, with or without analysis and interpretation.

> 6   The people who will make use of the evaluation information should be closely involved in generating the recommendations. They are more likely to act on things that they have thought out for themselves than on ideas foisted on them by an outside evaluator. From your point of view as an evaluator, they are a valuable resource enabling you to escape being over-influenced by your own prejudices. This does mean that they will have to be prepared to invest time and effort in making the progression from facts to recommendations. Getting them in the way of doing this may have spin-offs way beyond the particular evaluation.
>
> (Patton, 1982 provides a full discussion on the writing of evaluation reports.)

the rigour and quality of your study – although there may be circumstances in which, say, a video-tape by itself provides the best means of communication to your main audience.

It is increasingly common for the culmination of a piece of funded research with an applied focus to involve not simply a technical report and journal publication, but also oral presentations both to the funding body and other audiences. For some studies, there may be the need for workshop sessions with practitioner groups where the implications of the study for action form the bases of practical sessions. This begins to take us into wider dissemination issues, which are developed in the following chapter.

Practical constraints will often have a major influence on these alternative forms of presentation. You may have fifteen minutes with the board of directors, or the team of community workers in a particular area. Or a one-day in-service training course for teachers. Or a four-page A5 supplement to a newsletter sent out to proprietors of private residential homes for the elderly. Each of those would present a substantial, and different, presentational challenge.

Comments are made below on a few possibilities. The suggestions are all obvious and owe more to common sense than systematic analysis, but the abysmal quality of many presentations indicates they may be helpful.

Oral Presentations

Possibilities include the use of overhead projectors, slides and flip-charts to get over information via different media. Professional standards here are just as important as with the report. Particular attention should be given to the quality and legibility of lettering, its size being such that it is easily read by all those present. A handout which complements the oral presentation is helpful. Mere repetition in the handout of what is said is a waste of time and opportunity.

Alternative Literary Presentations

A greater degree of creativity in this respect seems to have been shown by evaluators than those doing other types of study, although there seems to be no reason against them being used more widely. Approaches include the following:

Portrayal Advocated by Stake (1976), who considers that a broad and accurate reflection of the programme's complex 'transactions' is both more important than, and antithetical to, a focus on analysis. Walker (1985, pp. 165–6) gives extracts from such a 'portrayal' in an evaluation of a summer school programme. This consists of a short pamphlet with descriptive information about the 'who', 'what' and 'where' of the programme, together with judgments made by students who followed different parts of it.

Adversarial presentation Consists of two statements: one by an advocate arguing in favour of the innovation, or whatever is evaluated; the other taking a hostile stance. No attempt is made to reconcile the two positions or to achieve a consensus. That task is left to the reader. It has been used by Stake (1976) to complement the lack of an overview when portrayal is used, but is also a quite well developed approach in its own right (e.g. Owens, 1973; Popham, 1982). In some versions, the similarity to the legal adversary model is enhanced by having two teams of investigators. One is for the 'defence' (looking for evidence favourable to the subject of the evaluation), and one for the 'prosecution' (looking for unfavourable evidence). While this approach might seem likely to be prone to be more concerned with 'winning the case' than 'finding the truth', it does have the virtue of ensuring that alternative evidence and explanations are given serious consideration. Similar strategies have been suggested as a way of counteracting 'group-think' in organizations (Anderson, 1980, p. 67).

Dialogue presentation MacDonald and Stake (1974) used a variant of the adversarial approach where the presentation was in the form of a dialogue between the two 'sides'. Walker (1985) claims that

> The very form of the dialogue makes a point not made in other ways. It invites participation; in itself it rejects (at one level) an authoritative judgment; it demonstrates 'open-endedness', divergence of view, unresolved conflict and discrepancy in a manner that statements cannot. (p. 171)

However, Walker also makes the point that the research sponsors were unhappy with this format, and that much time was spent discussing it rather than the substantive issues concerned.

Dialogic presentation is not necessarily linked to the adversarial approach. Pick and Walker (1976) used interview transcripts from an evaluation of a curriculum project as a basis for producing a radio play. Quotations from some twenty teachers were selected and put into the mouths of four characters.

Pamphlet production The task of compressing an account of a project into a short pamphlet for a general audience is daunting. Emphasis should be on the findings and on implications for action. Jargon should be ruthlessly excised. An attractive uncluttered layout with strong headings, and use of photographs, drawings and simple tables is needed. Resist the temptation to get in as many words as you can. Give an indication of what the interested reader can do to follow up, by providing references to other publications and an address.

This kind of short document is one way in which you can fulfil promises made to participants to let them know about the outcome of the project. The full report is not usually suitable for this purpose, although it should normally be available on request. 'Member checking' and the production of 'negotiated accounts' represent a very different kind of activity and reponsibility to participants, and must be completed prior to publication of any final reports (see chapter 12, p. 404).

News releases One way of reaching a wider audience is through newspapers, and radio and television stations. For a small-scale study, the local and possibly regional media are the likely targets. A short news release, usually on one side of A4, written in a lively style with an eye-catching heading, is required. Regard it as a further boiling down of the pamphlet described in the previous section. Give a telephone contact number and try to prepare for questions, so that you can avoid injudicious quotations.

A problem is that you do not have control over what is written. Busy journalists are likely to use at least parts of the release verbatim – a likelihood enhanced by your lively writing – but they will be prone to inserting their own distortions and (mis)interpretations. While it may be wisest not to seek publicity for studies carried out in some sensitive areas, there is a general onus to help promote a better informed general public that all who carry out research involving humans should recognize. These topics are returned to in the final chapter.

Writing Skills

The actual activity of writing receives scant attention in most books on the doing of research. It is similarly rarely dealt with explicitly on research methods courses – apart from that form of summative evaluation of reports of investigations, otherwise known as marking or assessment. There is research relevant to this kind of writing (e.g. Hayes and Flower, 1986), and a substantial literature on factors affecting readability of text (e.g. Armbruster and Anderson, 1985) and other facets of text production and presentation.

Hartley (1985) provides a practical guide, which, although oriented toward instructional text such as textbooks, contains much of relevance to anyone seeking to communicate through writing. It is, incidentally, very readable! As with other skills, writing benefits from practice, particularly if detailed and early feedback can be provided by a constructive colleague.

The First Draft

The importance of having a clear sense of audience has already been stressed in relation to style, length and general approach. If you have followed the suggestions for a structured approach to design, data collection and analysis made in earlier chapters, this should have provided you with a substantial base of material for the report. The advice, stressed in connection with case studies, of starting to write parts of the report while still involved with data collection, could usefully be generalized to other research strategies. Even so, there has to be a period toward the end of a study where the major task is writing – putting it all together, and getting the 'first draft'.

There are major individual differences in preferred approach to this task (see Hartley and Branthwaite, 1989 for a review of how a number of 'productive' British psychologists go about it). The word-processor has much to commend it, particularly in the ease with which amendments to drafts can be made, both in content and in sequence. Many users report a liberating effect with proficiency in word-processing, where a more 'playful' writing style emerges, with lower barriers both to starting (the 'blank page' phenomenon) and continuation. (Kren, 1988, provides an interesting analysis of the social impact of computers on the process of academic writing.) However, it is important that you possess a good working knowledge of the system and its features; and absolutely crucial that you stick to 'good housekeeping' principles including regular 'saving' of what you have typed, 'backing up' of copies of computer files, and the equally regular printing out of drafts of what you have produced.

Notwithstanding its advantages, there is no rule which says that you must use a word-processor if you are to produce a good report. If you can best deliver when writing longhand, or speaking into a dictating machine, then go ahead. *What is essential is that you allow yourself sufficient uninterrupted time for the activity.* And go for 'prime time'. Writing is difficult and you should devote the time of the day when you are most effective to it. For many people this is the first two or three working hours in the day, but it could well be in the evening or some other time. A regular schedule helps.

Interruptions reduce efficiency. Try to organize a period when you are 'incommunicado'. An answering machine or colleague (possibly on a reciprocal basis) can deal with the phone. Get it known and respected that you are not available for discussion, or whatever, at that time. Obviously, details depend on your individual circumstances but the principle is that this is an important activity which has to take precedence if you are to do your job properly.

For many people, starting is difficult, both right at the beginning and at each writing session. This argues for putting your available time into substantial-sized blocks. One tactic is to finish a session in mid-paragraph so that you know exactly where to pick things up next time. Outlines and structures, as discussed earlier in the chapter, are helpful, but don't feel that you must go through them in a linear manner. In particular, with the scientific journal format, early parts such as the title, abstract, and the final version of the introduction are best left until you see what the rest of the report is going to look like.

Revising the Draft

There are, again, individual differences in preferred approach. It is often recommended (e.g. Parry, 1989, p. 116) that in producing the first draft, you should concern yourself primarily with content, and leave style of writing as a task that you concentrate on when revising the draft.

The aim is to communicate. Go for clear, simple and lively English. There are several useful general guides to writing style, of which the best known are Fowler (1983) and Gowers (1986). More specific texts include Day (1983). Barzun and Graff (1977), although oriented towards research in the humanities, has much that is generally valuable on writing. Box 13.3 suggest some guidelines for revising text.

Hartley (1985) used a multiple-method study in evaluating the effectiveness of this procedure, comparing 'before' and 'after' versions of an existing three-page document, and showed that the revised version was easier to read, that the rate of extracting information from it was increased and that judges were more likely to prefer the revised version.

Computers can assist in revising drafts. Many word-processors incorporate a spelling checker, and there is also 'thesaurus' software useful for suggesting alternatives to words that you may tend to over-use. Various 'writer's aids' programs are available which provide facilities such as checking on punctuation as well as on spelling errors, repeated words, split infinitives, long sentences, sexist language, readability indices, etc.

The Final Typescript

This should be a polished jewel. Spelling, punctuation and typing should be perfect. There should be a simple and consistent system of headings and subheadings, and of spacings between sections. If the report is intended for publication in some form, the publishers will have requirements or preferences about format as well as style. Blackwell's *Guide for Authors* (1991) is a good example and includes a wide range of information on the preparation of typescripts and illustrations. Double spacing and wide margins are required. References often cause problems. These include inconsistency in

Box 13.3   Guidelines for revising the first draft

Whether you can work on the paper as a whole, or sections of it at a time, obviously depends on its length.

1 Read the text through.

2 Read the text again and ask yourself:
   - what am I trying to say?
   - who is the text for?

3 Read the text again and ask yourself:
   - What changes will make the text clearer and easier to follow?

4 To make these changes, you may need:
   - to make *global* or big changes (e.g. rewriting sections); or
   - to make minor *text* changes.

You need to decide whether you are going to focus first on global changes, or first on text changes.

5 *Global* changes you might like to consider in turn are:
   - reordering parts of the text;
   - rewriting sections;
   - adding examples;
   - changing the examples for better ones;
   - deleting parts that seem confusing.

6 *Text* changes you might like to consider in turn are:
   - using simpler wording;
   - using shorter sentences;
   - using shorter paragraphs;
   - using active rather than passive tenses;
   - substituting positive constructions for negatives;
   - writing sequences in order;
   - spacing numbered sequences or lists down the page (as here).

7 Read the revised text through to see if you want to make any further global changes.

8 Finally, repeat this whole procedure some time (say twenty-four hours) after making your original revisions, and do it without looking back at the original text.

(Adapted from Hartley, 1989, p. 90.)

format, parts missing, references mentioned in the text but not present in the reference list (and vice versa), and inconsistencies between the name(s) or dates in the text and those in the list.

If you are using a word-processor, it is at this stage that your expertise and attention to detail will be tested. If you can't reach a high standard, give the job to someone who can. Tables and figures for work sent for publication go at the end of the text with their position indicated in the text. Computer packages are available for graphics. Some systems can produce very high-quality work (e.g. packages with the Apple Macintosh and a laser printer) but again require facility in their use, and you may have to use the services of a professional graphic illustrator.

There is no substitute for painstaking proof-reading, preferably by someone else. This is not simply because this is a very boring job, but mainly because your familiarity with the text is likely to impede your effectiveness at the task. Parry (1989, pp. 105–22) provides a more detailed account angled towards the scientific journal paper, taking the process beyond this stage to the independent review system and possible outcomes.

Further Reading

Barzun, J. and Graff, H. F. (1977) *The Modern Researcher*. New York: Harcourt Brace Jovanovich. Focuses on the humanities but contains much of value for reporting social research (esp. chs 11–13).

Becker, H. S. (1986) *Writing for Social Scientists: how to start and finish your thesis, book or article*. Chicago: University of Chicago Press. Excellent on the practicalities. From an experienced writer, researcher and editor.

Day, R. A. (1983) *How to Write and Publish a Scientific Paper*, 2nd edn. Philadelphia: ISI Press. Clear and detailed account on traditional scientific reporting.

Fowler, H. W. (1983) *A Dictionary of Modern English Usage*, 2nd edn (revised). Oxford: Oxford University Press. Classic text. Balanced non-dogmatic guide to usage. Have at your side to cut through confusion (infer or imply?; decimate? etc.).

Gowers, E. (1987) *The Complete Plain Words*, 3rd edn. London: Penguin. How to say things clearly and simply.

Parry, G. (1989) Writing a Research Report. In G. Parry and F. N. Watts (eds) *Behavioural and Mental Health Research: a handbook of skills and methods*. London: Laurence Erlbaum Associates. Clear introduction dealing with issues up to and including how to get a paper published.

Sternberg, R. J. (1988) *The Psychologist's Companion: a guide to scientific writing for students and researchers* Cambridge: Cambridge University Press/British Psychological Society. Detailed and thorough account of most aspects of reporting in scientific paper style.

Walker, R. (1985) *Doing Research: a handbook for teachers*. London: Methuen. Chapter 5 gives useful coverage of alternative approaches to the traditional.

Acting on the Findings

A *You Should Have Clarified any Responsibilities in this Area when Developing the Project*

As with many aspects of enquiry, you need to have sorted this one out in general terms at an early stage. If the only action required is to produce a report for an academic journal or its equivalent (say a thesis or dissertation), then you needn't read on.

If, however, either for your own purposes or for those of a client of some kind, there is a hope or intention that the findings will be used for some real world purpose, you may have much to do and think about.

The need for early clarification is partly because the kind of potential action may have implications for the way in which the enquiry is carried out. For example, a collaborative approach with direct involvement in the research by those you are working with may help in subsequent implementation of an innovatory programme. It may also have implications for data collection, analysis and reporting (what kinds of evidence will 'speak' to those involved?).

B *You Need to Know Something about the Change Process*

The process of change and the implementation of innovation is complex. If you are seeking to help bring about change you need a good working understanding of what is involved.

C *Know Your Limitations – and the Limitations of Systematic Enquiry*

If you get yourself in the situation where you do have responsibilities for fostering some change or development (either personally or through providing advice for others), it is important to have a realistic appreciation of what is possible. Try not to bite off more than you can chew. A set of small gains is greatly preferable to a heroic failure. And remember that, though we may be addicted to it, systematic enquiry is only a minor bit player in the great game of life.

14

Intervention and Change

This chapter worries about the lack of impact that research has and analyses why this is so.

It seeks an understanding of the change process, and investigates the claims of action research in promoting change.

Introduction

I suspect that very little small-scale research carried out outside laboratories is pure in the sense of being part of a disinterested search for knowledge and understanding for its own sake. More studies might qualify as pure if we include exercises conducted by students as a requirement of courses in 'methods of investigation' or something similar. In practice, the 'real world' often only permits or encourages enquiry if it 'helps' in some way, usually to assist in deciding on some kind of change. In the case of an existing system or practice, how might it be improved or made more effective? In the case of an innovation, is it a good thing? In what way is it better or worse than the present or a previous situation? For an individual, how might they deal with some problem?

In terms of a 'pure' vs. 'applied' distinction, the argument is that real life studies commonly have an applied dimension. It has been argued, however, that the distinction between pure and applied is in fact of little value (see, for example, Skinner, 1963). Every practical problem can be seen as a problem in research which might lead to the advancement of pure learning as well as to an increase in efficiency. Popkewitz (1984) considers that 'the question of "how do things work" is also a question of how to change those things ... The study of "what is" has reformist as well as descriptive qualities' (p. 185).

When the game changes from being solely a concern for understanding, to also admitting an interest in social and personal change, then a whole gamut of thorny issues come to the fore. Should scientists be involved in this way? Does a concern for change inevitably lead to bad science? Can, and should, scientific objectivity be maintained? Do the enquirer's values influence the enquiry? Is a political commitment inescapable, perhaps even desirable? Let us assume that the enquirer is an honourable person, seeking to remain faithful to what Kaplan (1964) calls the Scientist's Oath: 'As long as my breath is in me and the spirit of God is in my nostrils, my lips will not speak falsehood and my tongue will not utter deceit' (Job). How do we in practice maintain an ethical stance in real world enquiries? Note, however, that issues to do with objectivity, values and ethics must, as pointed out in part I, be addressed in any scientific undertaking; the point made here is that they are more prominent in real world studies.

Any move away from the traditional 'pure scientist' stance is 'looked down on in some quarters as invariably representing the corruption of the scientific impulse by the taste for power' (Kaplan, 1964, p. 165). Karl Marx's famous dictum that 'philosophers have only interpreted the world in various ways, ... the point is to change it' (see Marx, 1941) will be regarded by some as exemplifying this corruption, by others as identifying *the* proper role for scientists. Shipman (1988) sees the dangers particularly strongly:

> Evaluators of social programmes are often so appalled by the conditions they observe that they act to improve the situation not to study it. This is the real rejection of scientism. The objective of social research becomes the exposure of injustice and the overthrow of the arrangements that secure it. (p. 165)

Rather than agonize unduly about whether or not 'real life' researchers could or should keep their hands clean and their science respectable, I prefer to approach the problem from a different angle.

By common consensus, we do not yet appear to have achieved perfection, either on the large scale in the way that society is organized, or in the smaller-scale units with which we are centrally concerned in our professional and personal lives. I suggest, ultimately as an article of faith, but not perhaps as an unreasonable proposition, that systematic enquiry is a useful potential tool for those seeking improvement. The alternatives in current use, such as political dogma or personal whim; managerial fiat or majority vote; committee deliberation, bandwagon spotting or even common sense, while undoubtedly satisfying a variety of needs, have manifest inadequacies. The argument is not for some psychologist's Utopia along the lines of Skinner's Walden Two (Skinner, 1948) where enquiry is king, the sole arbiter of how we organize our lives and society; it is more that enquiry can be a help, enabling both the democratically organized unit to achieve its ends more effectively, and the autocratic manager to increase productivity and profit. This type of 'neutrality of use' itself raises major ethical issues for the persons involved in enquiry, equivalent to those which were faced by physicists involved in atomic energy research. There may, however, be at least a partial 'out' to this dilemma for those involved in intervention research with humans in that 'real' change in individuals and organizations appears to take place most readily under particular conditions which may be loosely characterized as 'democratic'. These arguments are developed in the following section.

Change in itself is not of course the same thing as improvement or progress. Those in education and the helping and caring professions have been so deluged with changes in recent years that many echo the views of the eighteenth-century French philosopher de Maistre that 'When it is not necessary to change, it is necessary not to change.' Enquiry should not be seen as necessarily supporting change. It can provide evidence that a particular change is not worthwhile; that its effects, whether anticipated or not, are such that the status quo is preferable. In such circumstances, rejecting a proposed 'reform' is more progressive than accepting it.

The (Lack of) Impact of Research

Psychology and the social sciences have undoubtedly made an impact on present-day life and thought. New ideas, terms, concepts and techniques derived from the social sciences are picked up avidly. As Levy-Leboyer (1986) puts it:

> T-groups, sensitivity training, programmed learning, quality circles, job enrichment, autonomous groups, uncoercive education, behavioural therapy – all were more easily accepted than power looms in the textile industry and robotization in automative plants. (p. 25)

There is a serious danger, however, that such users will not have 'read the small print'. There is typically little concern for the generalizability of techniques. They are accepted as efficient because others are using them. In this way fads and fashions bloom and decay (Young, 1965). Education is particularly prone to them, ranging from 'discovery learning' to the use of the Makaton signing system for pupils with special needs. Once techniques are adopted, they are peculiarly resistant to refutation.

Theories and concepts, if they strike the right chord, seem almost to be accepted simply because they have been stated (contrast the popular acceptance and use of Oedipus complex, id, ego, super-ego, etc., and the highly contested view of the value of Freudian approaches within psychology). Managers are attracted to 'packaged' social science approaches to leadership, organizational change and problem-solving (e.g. Peters and Waterman, 1982; Goldsmith and Clutterbuck, 1984) typically regarded by professional social scientists as methodologically naïve and theoretically unsound (e.g. Heller, 1986).

Levy-Leboyer (1986) goes on to develop the thesis that the social sciences are too easily and too loosely applied. Her concern is with the misuse of theories and techniques which arises from a lack of appreciation of the complexity and specificity of real life situations. These features go some way towards helping to understand the apparent paradox that while theories, concepts and techniques have high apparent acceptability, evidence for the impact of research on practice is striking in its paucity.

For example, Barlow et al.'s (1984) discussion of research in clinical and educational settings reached the bald and depressing conclusion that 're-search has little influence on practice' (p. 31). They consider this attributable in large part to the inappropriateness of traditional experimental research methodology for the concerns of practitioners, arguing in very similar terms to those advanced here in favour of the use of case study methodology in real world settings. They note that practitioners do not consume research findings. Bergin and Strupp (1972) have surveyed the views of leading cli-nicians and provide strong support for this view. For example, Matarazzo, who is both a clinician and a researcher, asserts that 'even after 15 years, few of my research findings affect my practice. Psychological science doesn't guide me one bit . . . My clinical experience is the only thing that has helped me in my practice to date' (cited in Barlow et al., 1984, p. 32). Studies by Cohen (1976; 1979) on research utilization include surveys suggesting that educational and mental health professionals consider that fewer than 20 per cent of research articles have any applicability in professional settings. This state of affairs is mirrored in other fields. Schindele (1981), in a review of the field of rehabilitation medicine, describes how the same limitations in experimental research methodology limit the usefulness and applicability of research to practice.

In a different field, Stenhouse's analyses of research into school curric-ulum and teaching points to the severe limitations of what he terms the 'psycho-statistical paradigm' (Stenhouse, 1978; 1979). Nisbet and Broadfoot (1980) provide detailed documentation of the lack of impact of research and development on policy and practice in education in both North America and Europe, concluding that 'Educational research lacks impact because its relatively underdeveloped state leads to fragmentary and contradictory con-clusions. . . . But this lack of development in the subject is itself attributable to the fact that the enterprise is so closely constrained and so little believed in by potential customers and sponsors of research' (p. 45). Argyris (1970) and Argyris and Schon (1974) provide corresponding critiques of much organizational research.

A range of models for looking at the impact of research have been pro-posed, summarized in box 14.1 (see also Weiss, 1979; 1982).

Shipman (1988) analyses the strengths and weaknesses of these models, concluding that the enlightenment model best exemplifies the way in which research evidence affects the way in which practitioners think about social issues. Any impact is typically through an indirect permeation process. How-ever, he also notes that it is 'not only tailor-made but second-hand inter-pretations of evidence that will be influential'. Hence, striking, well publicized, 'findings' are likely to be influential even when their scientific standing is dubious. Rosenthal and Jacobson's (1968) *Pygmalion in the Classroom*, which

Box 14.1   Models of the impact of research

1 *Classical*   Pure research leads to applied research, leads to development followed by dissemination.

2 *Problem-solving*   Problem identified then research carried out to solve it.

3 *Interactive*   Continuing dialogue between researchers and policy-makers.

4 *Political*   Research sponsored to support political decision or policy.

5 *Procrastination*   Research contracted to delay having to make a decision.

6 *Enlightenment*   Indirect permeation of policy-making by research.

7 *Multiple influence*   Research seen as one of many influences on policy.

(Adapted from Weiss, 1979.)

purported to show that teachers' expectations of children's performance bring that performance up to the expectations, is a striking example of this phenomenon. As Shipman himself documents (Shipman, 1988, ch. 7), the study has been severely criticized on grounds of reliability and has proved virtually impossible to replicate (Elashoff and Snow, 1971). But it is still commonly cited as describing an established finding, and arguably has had more impact on educational practice than virtually any other research, with the possible exception of Piagetian studies.

Weiss's analysis presupposes a three-way split not only in role, but in personnel, between researchers, policy-makers and practitioners. If practitioners can be assisted to 'own' the research by whatever means, most obviously in participating directly in the enquiry process, then the 'problem-solving' model comes into the frame. Policy-makers at national, regional or local level are still going to set the agenda by legislating for a national curriculum, or 'privatized' arrangements for a school or hospital, or a new computer system for the branches of a building society. However, it is the local implementation of such initiatives which will ultimately decide the success of these grand schemes. What is now known about the factors which affect implementation of change suggests strongly that impact will be increased if the practitioners directly involved, the teachers in a school or the nurses on a ward or whoever, play a part in carrying out these studies.

Models of the Change Process

'How to get new educational programs to work in practice has increasingly frustrated and mystified those involved in education over the past two decades' (Fullan, 1982, p. ix). Education has been one area where major efforts have been made, both in Europe and North America, to improve provision. Reading and mathematics, languages, humanities and science have all seen major programmes, as have special educational needs and multi-cultural education.

The effectiveness of this educational innovation has been questioned in many studies, of which Gross et al. (1971) and Smith and Keith (1971) are commonly quoted examples. They also make the point that successful implementation does not necessarily take place even when the people involved give every appearance of being in favour of the innovation. This apparent lack of effectiveness of many planned interventions is by no means restricted to the educational sphere (Karapin, 1986).

However, there is at least one useful outcome from this rather depressing story. As a result of these efforts – which, to be fair, do include some (at least partial) successes – there is now a much better understanding of why attempts at change fail or succeed (Berk and Rossi, 1990, pp. 113–17, provide a useful list of well designed and influential programme evaluations). Before getting down to an analysis of what appears to be involved, it may be worth stressing that there is nothing world-shatteringly novel about what is proposed; what Fullan (1982) calls 'organized common sense' is the central theme. Bennis et al. (1985) provide a useful general introduction to the voluminous literature on planned change.

Change through Adoption of Research

The classical model of the impact of research has provided an influential model of the change process. It is known variously as the CHANGE AS MANAGEMENT, CENTRE TO PERIPHERY or RESEARCH, DEVELOPMENT, DISSEMINATION AND ADOPTION (RDDA) approach (e.g. Wronski, 1969; Hahn, 1975). Box 14.2 summarizes the model.

Various efforts have been made to assess the effectiveness of this approach, typically involving surveys of users to assess their knowledge of, and commitment to, the innovation or studies of the way that the approach is actually implemented. Attempts to find out how far the general aims of the innovation have been achieved, or the extent to which there have been unanticipated effects, have been rarer.

Hall (1975) has developed a 'levels of use' instrument which focuses on the degree of implementation of the innovation. Six levels are identified, ranging from 'non-use' through 'integration' (where the innovation is combined with existing approaches) to 'renewal' (where users have evaluated for themselves the usefulness of the innovation, and have sought modifications

---

Box 14.2   The 'RDDA' model of the change process

1 Initial 'pure' *research* identifies, conceptualizes and tests ideas.

2 *Development* translates research findings into an approach, possibly involving materials or a programme, which can be used in a 'field' setting.

3 *Dissemination* (or diffusion) follows when the approach, programme etc. is publicized and made available to a wider audience.

4 *Adoption* completes the process when the new approach becomes an accepted part of practice.

---

to suit their own circumstances). This suggests the possibility of *adaptation* as well as *adoption* of the innovation, and thus helps to counter one criticism of the RDDA model – that it makes the unreasonable claim to be 'user-proof'. In other words, both the procedures and the product of the model are assumed to be appropriate for any group and for any purpose. Many applications of the model make this assumption, either explicitly or implicitly, in the sense that they do not consider how adaptation might take place to meet the needs of different situations.

Within the field of special needs education, training courses in behavioural techniques based upon learning theory research (e.g. the 'Education of the Developmentally Young' course – Foxen and McBrien, 1981 and McBrien and Foxen, 1981) provide clear examples. Both 'user' surveys and case studies of actual practice in schools with which I have been involved (Robson et al., 1988) show a wide degree of adaptation of what was designed and developed as a highly prescriptive set of materials. Users, for example, leave out substantial parts of the training course, change the sequence of units and commonly introduce unscheduled activities.

Popkewitz (1984) makes a more fundamental set of criticisms of the model. For him, it

> takes for granted the structure of the institution by declaring itself neutral to a system's goals and purposes. There is no conception of social structure by which one is to relate the possibilities and effects of change. In its place, the procedures of reform/change are considered as change itself. One does a survey of perceptions or use of the technologies. Observations are made to assess levels of use. Change becomes the implementation of procedures to make established procedures more efficient. Motion and activity become a substitute for change. (p. 139)

Popkewitz gives a fully documented example in support, but it is difficult to judge how far these outcomes arise from specific pressures and procedures within a particular project, or are a necessary feature of the RDDA model.

Change through Democratic Problem-solving

Disillusionment with the RDDA model has grown. There is evidence that research-derived top-down projects do not have the effect envisaged at the periphery, nor is the process adequately represented by the proposed linear sequence (Weiss and Bucuvalas, 1980b). At the same time there is evidence of a developing rhetoric favouring local participation and control; a swing towards the view that the identification and development of innovation should lie with the persons taking part in the local concrete situation.

The resulting approach is concerned not so much with the content of an innovation, nor even its outcome, but mainly with the *process* of change. It favours a concentration on problem-solving. Local personnel identify their own needs and seek solutions to them. The rationale is that those who are closest to the problem and the process are in the best position to come up with solutions, and then to implement them.

As with the previous model, a sequence of stages is usually seen to be involved. Paul and Lipham (1976), for example, identify a seven-stage model and assume that the process is guided by a change-agent.

Box 14.3   The problem-solving model of the change process

1   Developing a need for change, including an awareness of problems and desire for help.

2   Establishing relations with external consultant, development of collaborative arrangement.

3   Diagnosis of problem.

4   Examination of alternative goals and formulation of plans for action.

5   Development of innovations based on plans for action.

6   Generalizing and stabilizing the change.

7   Achieving a 'terminal' relationship, leading to going it alone without consultant.

(Adapted from Paul and Lipham, 1976, p. 234.)

Goodlad (1975) presents a similar though simpler scheme, again involving an outside expert who helps the organization to be sensitive to its own needs and capable of using its resources to meet them. His stages are:

1   Dialogue about issues and problems.
2   Decisions to concentrate on specific problems and what might be done about them.
3   Actions to address the selected problems.
4   Evaluation of the effectiveness of the action.

Action Research

The problem-solving approach is similar to variants of 'action research' which have gained popularity in some research circles in Britain. (It is sometimes referred to in educational research as 'case study' – a much more restricted use of the term than that adopted in chapter 6.)

Conventional laboratory-derived research styles seek to minimize the degree of involvement between the researcher and the researched in the interests of objectivity. This falls foul of much that is known about the change process, and of conditions facilitating change. The discrepancy is not surprising as the task of conventional pure scientific research is to describe, understand and explain – not to promote change. Coming to terms with the dual 'understanding' and 'promoting change' roles calls for a different view of research which has been touched on at several points during the book.

This perspective owes much to the work of Kurt Lewin, who coined the term ACTION RESEARCH for it (Lewin, 1946). In his formulation this involves a spiral of cycles of *planning, acting, observing* and *reflecting.*

Planning is seen as starting with a general idea. For one reason or another it is thought desirable to reach a certain objective. More fact-finding about the situation is likely to be required. If this period of planning is successful, two items emerge: an 'overall plan' of how to reach the objective and a decision about the first step of action. The next period is concerned with carrying out the first step of the overall plan. The next step again is composed of a circle of planning, executing and fact-finding to evaluate the results of the second step. This assists in preparing the basis for planning the third step, and, perhaps, for modifying the overall plan once more.

The term 'action research' has been used in somewhat different senses by later workers (see Kemmis and McTaggart, 1981). Rapoport (1970) stressed the dual nature of its concerns. For him, action research 'aims to contribute both to the practical concerns of people in an immediate problematic situation and to the goals of social science by joint collaboration within a mutually acceptable framework' (p. 1). Stenhouse (1985), in considering the applicability of action research to teaching, takes exception to the 'goals of social science' aspect, and wants this contribution to be towards a theory of education and teaching which is accessible to teachers; for the audience for action research to be teachers and not social scientists. *Improvement* and *involvement* seem central to all uses of the term. There is,

> firstly, the improvement of a *practice* of some kind; secondly, the improvement of the *understanding* of a practice by its practitioners; and thirdly, the improvement of the *situation* in which the practice takes place ... Those involved in the practice being considered are to be involved in the action research process in all its aspects of planning, acting, observing and reflecting. (Carr and Kemmis, 1986, p. 165)

The emphasis on a specific situation, of looking at practice in a particular context and trying to produce change in that context, puts action research firmly within the case study strategy as developed in chapter 6. (Bell, 1985, has proposed a hybrid called 'action inquiry' which explicitly links features of action research and case study approaches.) The requirements for collaboration between researchers and practitioners, and for practitioner participation in the process, are typically seen as central to action research (Whyte, 1984).

This democratic aspiration is important. Lewin, writing and working just after the Second World War, saw action research as a tool for bringing about democracy. Later action researchers see it more as an embodiment of democratic principles in research. They have called for a direct involvement of practitioners in the design, direction, development and use of research, so that the conditions under which they work could be changed.

Action research developments in education were initially largely stimulated by professional researchers (particularly John Elliott and colleagues at the Centre for Applied Research in Education at the University of East Anglia; cf Norris, 1990). There has subsequently been a tendency to de-emphasize the role of the external expert and to stress the value of groups of practitioners carrying out their own enquiries into their own situation, though linked for mutual support in a loose network. Elliott (1989) describes his development in this direction; examples include the collections in Nixon (1981) and Webb (1990).

The action research cycle, as interpreted by Elliott, is shown in Figure 14.1.

Action research has come in for strong criticism from various quarters. Travers, for example, in reviewing a number of action research projects, claims:

> The writer's evaluation of the last fifty studies which have been undertaken which compare the outcomes of one teaching methodology with another is that they have contributed almost nothing to our knowledge of the factors that influence the learning process in the classroom. (Quoted by Cohen and Manion, 1989, p. 215)

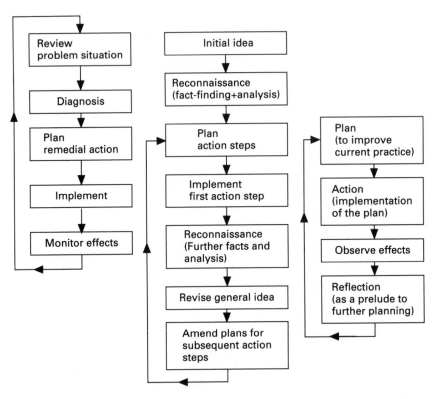

Figure 14.1   The action research cycle (as interpreted by Elliott)
Source: adapted from Elliott, 1982.

This is a criticism from the point of view of traditional scientific research. Adelman (1989) considers much of educational action research to be 'inward looking and ahistorical' and of poor quality. In his view, the claims for action research as an 'alternative research paradigm, as a democratizing force and means of achieving informed, practical change arising from issues at the grass roots' are 'overbearing' (p. 179). Atkinson and Delamont (1985) have been severely critical of the way that this approach has developed in educational research, castigating its atheoretical posture and denial of the need for systematic methods.

Popkewitz (1984), previously cited as critical of the RDDA model, is also concerned about these democratic versions of the problem-solving approach:

> The belief that school staffs can identify and plan to alter their own assumptions and power arrangements through a focus on process seems to belie experience. Schools are complex social contexts. There is little time for critical reflection. Their social and political values are often anti-intellectual, anti-democratic and anti-educational. These values are built into the way curriculum is defined, the social organization of classrooms, and administrative theories of

---

Box 14.4 Simplified action research model

1 *Data collection* and the generation of hypotheses.

2 *Validation* of hypotheses through use of analytic techniques.

3 *Interpretation* by reference to theory, established practice and practitioner judgement.

4 *Action* for improvement that is also monitored by the same research techniques.

(Adapted from Hopkins, 1985, p. 114.)

---

schooling. Because of the implicit quality of these values, they are psychologically compelling to participants and the publics of schooling. To consider change as process without form is to lose sight of the substance that underlies reform and to conserve what is to be changed. (p. 146)

These critical comments appear to apply with equal force to settings other than schools. The units and organizations in industry and commerce and in the helping and caring professions are not self-evidently less complex, nor less over-stretched, nor more favourable to intellectual analysis and democratic processes.

Are there ways in which the clear advantages of the action research approach could be retained while taking note of these criticisms? Hopkins (1985), who like Adelman (1989) wishes to see high-quality action research, considers that the kinds of sequences of activities given by Elliott and others are too complex and prescriptive. His simplified model is presented as box 14.4.

Winter (1989) makes the point that this conceptualization of the action research process is incomplete in that:

a   data gathering cannot begin without a perceived problem to give it relevance and direction;
b   validation of hypotheses and ·the adequacy of interpretations will be further tested by the action phase;
c   the action decided upon as a result of the enquiry will inevitably generate further issues which could well be the topic of further enquiry;
d   the process will inevitably be cyclical; any phase of data gathering and interpretation can only be one tentative step forward, not a final answer.

Unfortunately, incorporation of these features into the simplified model virtually returns us to the complexity of Elliott's model. What is different is that Hopkins explicitly advocates the link to more conventional social science methodology, which emphasizes the need for related enquiry skills. This safeguard goes a considerable way to meeting criticisms of action research. In fact, the approach is then very much along the lines covered in earlier chapters – with the exception that the 'action' stage is seen as an integral part of the research itself.

A Way Forward

Notwithstanding the failings and shortcomings of the approaches to implementing change, and accepting the force of the critical comments made, it appears that something of value can be gleaned from the substantial efforts of the past two decades. As Fullan (1982, 1991) points out, from this experience we now know, admittedly at a pragmatic and common-sense level, a considerable amount about what we should and should not do when seeking to implement change. Heller (1986) approaches this from a consideration of users' needs. They need to be given *access* to the research findings, proposals, programme or whatever. They need to *seriously consider* them; there may well be 'deep-seated non-intellectual obstacles that prevent serious consideration of new findings or ideas'. They then need to *make a decision* which may not be simple acceptance or adoption but could involve postponement until further work is done. If it has been decided to go ahead, then *implementation* is necessary. Heller stresses that things can go wrong at each of these stages.

Fullan's work, though focusing on change in educational settings, provides a useful general framework for both understanding and effecting change. He stresses that *change is a process, not an event* (see also Hall and Loucks, 1977). His simplified model of that process is shown in figure 14.2.

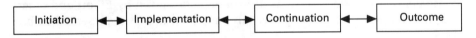

Figure 14.2 Simplified model of the change process

There are of course many more factors operating at each of the four phases. The two-way arrows emphasize that this is not a simple linear process; events at one phase can feed back to alter earlier decisions made at previous phases, which then work through in a continuous interactive manner. The distinction between the RDDA and problem-solving models is seen by Fullan as simply a matter of emphasis. Is the concern mainly to do with the programme and the fidelity with which it is implemented (which brings it closer to the RDDA approach)? Or is it more to do with mutual adaptation and evolution (closer to problem-solving)?

He provides useful checklists of factors associated with the various phases which are well worth consulting when involved with a 'change' project, and a set of general maxims which are presented, in abridged form, as box 14.5.

Box 14.5   Assumptions for those wishing to initiate change

1   Don't assume that your version of what the change should be is the one that could or should be implemented. You have to exchange your reality of what should be through interaction with others concerned.

2   Change involves ambiguity, ambivalence and uncertainty about the meaning of the change. Effective implementation is a process of clarification.

3   Some conflict and disagreement are not only inevitable but fundamental to change.

4   People need pressure to change (even in directions they desire) but it is only effective under conditions that allow them to react and interact. Resocialization is at the heart of change (otherwise you need to replace the people involved!).

5   Effective change takes time. It is a developmental process that takes at least two years.

6   Lack of implementation isn't necessarily because of rejection or resistance. There are many other reasons, including insufficient resources or time elapsed.

7   Don't expect all, or even most, people or groups to change. Progress occurs by increasing the number of people affected.

8   You need a plan based on these assumptions and underpinned by a knowledge of the change process.

9   Change is a frustration, discouraging business. If you are not in a position to make the above assumptions, which may well be the case, don't expect significant change, *as far as implementation is concerned.*

(Adapted and abridged from Fullan, 1982, p. 91.)

Further Reading

Argyris, C., Putnam, R. and Smith, D. M. (1985) *Action Science.* San Francisco: Jossey-Bass. Comprehensive account of an influential approach to social enquiry designed to generate knowledge that is both theoretically valid and practically useful.

Brunning, H., Cole, C. and Huffington, C. (1990) *The Change Directory: the key issues in organisational development and the management of change.* Leicester:

British Psychological Society. Booklet outlining key 'change' issues. Written for clinical psychologists, but of general relevance.

Fullan, M. (1991) *The New Meaning of Educational Change*, 2nd edn. London: Cassell. Wide-ranging analysis of attempts at educational change. Scholarly but with practical guidelines. First edition (1982) has been very influential.

Hakel, M. D., Sorcher, M., Beer, M. and Moses, J. L. (1982) *Making it Happen: designing research with implementation in mind*. Newbury Park and London: Sage. Provocative analyses of what is involved in doing 'real world' research. Detailed case study on research and implementation, with suggestions for related workshop activities.

Heller, F. (ed.) (1986) *The Use and Abuse of Social Science*. Newbury Park and London: Sage. Analyses successful and unsuccessful applications of social science research, and some abuses. Covers wide range of disciplines. Includes thorough literature review on the use of social science (Karapin).

Lomax, P. (ed.) (1989) *The Management of Change*. Clevedon, Philadelphia: Multilingual Matters Ltd. Set of papers on how change can be managed through use of action research.

Winter, R. (1989) *Learning from Experience: principles and practice in action-research*. London: Falmer. Advice for practitioners in 'people' professions on the process of action research as a means of professional learning.

15

Researchers and Practitioners

This final chapter reviews the relative roles of researchers and practitioners in real world enquiry.

It discusses the advantages and disadvantages of the practitioner-researcher.

It then considers the role of the research consultant and the 'giving away' of skills.

The book concludes with modest proposals about the place of systematic enquiry in society.

Introduction

Developments since the early 1980s have placed increasing emphasis on accountability in the 'human' professions. The climate in education at all levels from first schools to higher education, and throughout the health and social services, has become closer to that experienced by workers in industrial and commercial organizations. There is an emphasis on priorities within fixed budgets, appraisal and evaluation, and generally on 'value for money'.

Rationally, an important element in this situation would be the collection and analysis of relevant information about these issues as an aid to decision-making. Systematic enquiry techniques could do this. The strategies and methods advocated in this text, and elsewhere, permit the carrying out of rigorous enquiries, including evaluations, in such real world, non-laboratory situations. It would, though, be unrealistic to view the results of such studies as the only, or even a major, input to the decision-making processes which determine practices in these different settings.

The dogged reader who has reached this final chapter by consuming the earlier ones in a linear fashion will have appreciated that this kind of enquiry in the real world has its problems. Methodologists consider that it raises issues about the nature of research and of science. The professional researcher can be expected to know about and understand these issues, and have expertise in the strategies, methods and analytic techniques available. Notwithstanding these difficulties and the obvious benefits that skills and experience bring, the underlying common-sense core, as highlighted in previous chapters, is not difficult to grasp. Such a grasp enables the interested practitioner to be directly involved in carrying out worthwhile studies – to become a 'practitioner–researcher' (Barlow et al., 1984, refer to this same hybrid as a 'scientist practitioner').

The main task of this chapter is to tease out the relative roles of researchers, practitioners and practitioner–researchers.

The Practitioner–Researcher

The practitioner–researcher is some one who holds down a job in some particular area and at the same time carries out systematic enquiry which is of relevance to the job. In education, this might be the teacher carrying out a study of a way of helping an *individual child* with a learning difficulty; or a project on delivering some aspect of curriculum to a *school class*; or (possibly working with colleagues from the same or other schools) a systematic enquiry into a proposed local authority initiative to improve communication *between first and secondary schools*. Corresponding foci of enquiry, from *individual* through *group* to *organization*, are not difficult to envisage for practitioners in other professions. In all these cases, the carrying out of the enquiry is likely to be in addition to their normal full-time responsibilities. Another version of the practitioner–researcher is the true hybrid: someone whose job is officially part-practitioner, part-researcher. This might be a short-term arrangement to enable the enquiry to take place, or a continuing joint appointment. Or there could be less formal arrangements, with some remission of normal responsibilities.

Increasingly, post-graduate and post-experience study is moving away from the notion that the practitioner–student determines the focus of her studies, and in particular that of any project or thesis work, solely on the basis of her own individual interests. The move is towards study relevant to the professional setting, in part at least determined by the agenda and concerns of that setting. Reduction in individual freedom is balanced by an increasing likelihood of implementation, and of additional resources and time for the practitioner–researcher. As Zeisel (1981) puts it, 'research seen as problem- and situation-specifc becomes a tool to achieve someone's purposes rather than an end in itself' (p. 226).

Practitioner–researchers are often at a considerable disadvantage *vis-à-vis* outside professional researchers, but they have complementing advantages. Box 15.1 lists some of them. Anyone carrying out a sequence of studies in a particular setting can build up a specialized expertise about that type of setting which may well be unrivalled (cf Sommer and Wicker, 1991, who make the case for 'gas station' psychology).

Box 15.1 Practitioner–researchers compared with 'outside' researchers

Disadvantages of the practitioner–researcher role

1 *Time* Probably the main disadvantage. Trying to do a systematic enquiry on top of normal commitments is very difficult.

2 *Lack of expertise* This obviously depends on the individual. There is a need for some background in designing, carrying out and analysing studies. A major problem can be 'not knowing what it is that you don't know'.

3 *Lack of confidence* Lack of experience in carrying out studies leads to lack of confidence.

4 *'Insider' problems* The insider may have preconceptions about issues, solutions. There can also be hierarchy difficulties (both ways, i.e. with high-status and low-status practitioner–researchers); and possibly the 'prophet in own country' phenomenon (i.e. outside advice may be more highly valued).

Advantages of the practitioner–researcher role

1 *'Insider' opportunities* You will have a pre-existing knowledge and experience base about the situation and the people involve.

2 *'Practitioner' opportunities* There is likely to be a substantial reduction of implementation problems.

3 *'Practitioner–researcher' synergy* Practitioner insights and role help in the design, carrying out and analysis of useful and appropriate studies.

Most professional workers in the 'human services' professions, whether in the public or the private sector, are busy people. While there appears to be an increasing acceptance that investigation, enquiry, evaluation and innovation are all part of the professional role, in concepts such as 'extended professionality' and the 'reflective professional' (Schon, 1983), the time or energy to carry them out on top of one's normal load is often missing. However, Allen-Meares and Lane (1990) have argued, in the context of social work practice, that there is a potential synergy between research and practice, such that their integration is of benefit to both. The traditional solution of creating a division of labour in professional work between practitioners and researchers has its own problems when the intention is to influence practice. Neither does it help in developing the extended professional.

What other solutions are possible? Logically, one could increase the amount of time available for these activities by reducing the weight of other commitments. If the extended professional is a better professional, then find the time for this extension to take place. Or the time commitment needed to carry out worthwhile studies could be decreased, that is, we look for an *economical* approach to enquiry, feasible at the same time as a substantial practitioner workload. Or the practitioner–researcher gets support; perhaps in terms of research assistance or at a consultancy level. Ex-practitioners have their uses. The former nurse or salesman will retain considerable knowledge and experience and should have high credibility.

These suggestions are not mutually exclusive. The other disadvantages of lack of expertise and confidence, and those arising from the fact that the person is working inside her own organization, could all be mitigated by access to a research consultant. An experienced consultant could, in a short span of time, suggest what is feasible in a given situation, giving the practitioner–researcher confidence as to its feasibility and appropriateness. Similarly it is, paradoxically, easy for an outsider to spell out the generality of the likely problems to arise from insider status.

Winter (1989, pp. 34–7) presents an insightful analysis of the problems of the practitioner–researcher. He asks the question how a small-scale investigation by a practitioner can lead to genuinely new insights:

> Experienced practitioners approach their work with a vast and complex array of concepts, theoretical models, provisional explanations, typical scenarios, anticipation of likely outcomes, etc. ... A 'research' process must demonstrably offer something over and above this pre-existing level of understanding' (p. 34)

This leads to a need to establish a clear *difference* of procedure between the research and the procedures of professional practice itself, to guard against the 'we knew that already' or 'we do that every day of our professional lives'.

He also considers that the methods used must be *accessible*, in the sense that they must be readily available to anyone who seeks to adopt them, and *rigorous* – that is, that they are 'systematically grounded in justifiable and coherent principles' (p. 36). Winter considers that practitioner action research cannot simply use the research methods of conventional social science and advocates a reflexive, dialectical approach (see also Winter, 1987, to which the interested reader is referred).

However, it is possible to accept his analysis of the problems without necessarily adopting his solutions. The need for a differentiated, rigorous and systematic approach to real life issues as faced by any enquirer is fully accepted and is probably the major theme within this book. Accessibility is an interesting problem. It was argued in the first chapter (see p. 9) that the methods of systematic real world enquiry are not a private garden to which only the graduate of psychology or a related discipline has access. Some time and effort will certainly be needed by the professional without this background if she is to enter, but again this is a process facilitated by the sympathetic and experienced adviser or consultant.

Advice to the Practitioner–Researcher

Part of your time will be devoted to carrying out research. The preceding chapters of the book are intended as a general resource in aid of this task. There are some features specific to the joint nature of your role:

Negotiate a time allowance to carry out the enquiry If this dual practitioner–researcher role has been agreed, your firm, institution or whatever presumably sees the advantages of an 'insider' carrying out the enquiry (see p. 297). Make it clear that to capitalize on these advantages you need adequate time to carry out the enquiry properly. In particular, don't forget the time needed to write up the report(s) and disseminate the findings and their implications. If the dual role is a long-term arrangement, it is better to have an agreed proportion of your time allocated to the research work on a continuing basis rather than to negotiate separately for each enquiry.

Work in a team whenever possible Working on an enquiry, particularly if it involves evaluation or has change implications, can be very stressful and it helps for this to be a collective endeavour. There are practical advantages in assessing reliability of observational and other data, and more generally in sharing perceptions about issues, developing conceptual structures, analytical frameworks, etc.

Seek support There is much 'legwork' and drudgery in carrying out even a small-scale enquiry. It is likely to be more cost-effective for your organization to provide clerical and similar support to help with surveys, code questionnaires, transcribe tapes etc., rather than have you do it all yourself.

Seek advice Unless you have a strong and up-to-date research methodology background, and considerable experience in carrying out real world enquiries it is again likely to be cost-effective for your organization to buy in consultancy support. This need not be extensive. Working through this book will not substitute completely for such advice, but should substantially reduce the consultancy time requirement as you will have an appreciation of what it is you need to know, and will be able to return to the book for details about specific methods and techniques of analysis.

There is an increasing number of research consultancy firms, and individuals offering consultancy services can be contacted through the Register of Chartered Psychologists, available in reference libraries (but make sure you get someone experienced in real world enquiry). Another tactic is to contact a local university. Their departments in relevant areas (e.g. psychology, social sciences, human sciences, health sciences, social work, education, management) are increasingly involved in short-term consultancy work of this kind.

A possibility, which may be helpful in career terms, is to register for a research degree or other postgraduate award and carry out the enquiry as a part of it, receiving supervisory support to do this. Formal training in research methods is increasingly an important part of such programmes. Credit accumulation and transfer schemes, now running in many higher education institutions, permit the kind of prior experience and learning acquired as a part of professional work to count as substantial credit toward qualifications.

The Researcher Role

Persons with research or enquiry expertise can take on a variety of roles in real world research. The main distinction between such roles is in your actually carrying out the enquiry (with or without colleagues or other support), or your advising other persons who then carry it out for themselves. We will consider the latter separately, under the heading of the 'consultancy role'.

An underlying assumption in this book is that if you are going to carry out an enquiry it is, in virtually all cases, because someone has asked you to do so. The basic notion is of a client, sponsor or boss who wishes you to do this. This includes the situation where you made the first move – perhaps persuaded your head of unit, or the manager of the firm down the road that it would be a good thing if . . . and they took the suggestion on board. It also covers the situation on a course in 'Methods of Enquiry' or the like, where it is the course tutor who has asked you to carry out the study, in part as a training for carrying out subsequent real world enquiries. As a researcher rather than a practitioner–researcher, you are most likely to be external to the setting or organization forming the focus of the enquiry, if only because relatively few 'human service' organizations have so far appreciated the wisdom of having a researcher per se on the payroll.

The assumption that the study is carried out for this kind of instrumental purpose does not preclude the possibility that it might make some contribution to our understanding in general terms of what goes on in the primary classroom, or of the selection process for sales trainees, or of personality disorders, or whatever. But such a contribution is a spin-off from a welldesigned, executed and analysed study rooted in previous work and/or conducted within a particular theoretical framework. The main concern of the study is practical, and to provide answers relevant to that specific context. Does the study help to solve the problem or throw light on the issue presented?

Figure 15.1 presents a model for the real world enquiry process involved and, as a contrast, the traditional type of model given in most research methodology texts.

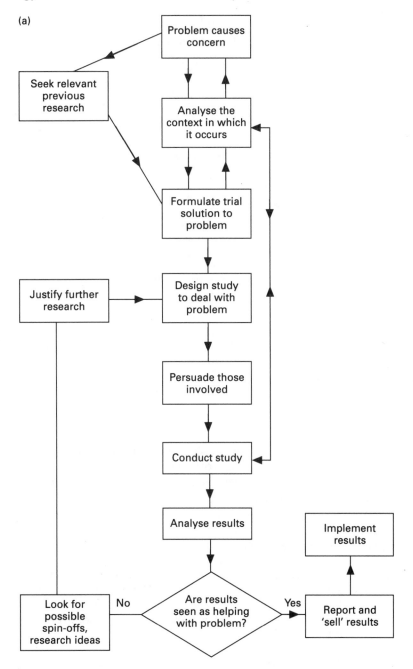

(a)

Figure 15.1 (a) 'real world' and (b) traditional models of the research process contrasted
Source: adapted from Boehm, in Hakel et al., 1982, pp. 29, 31.

(b)

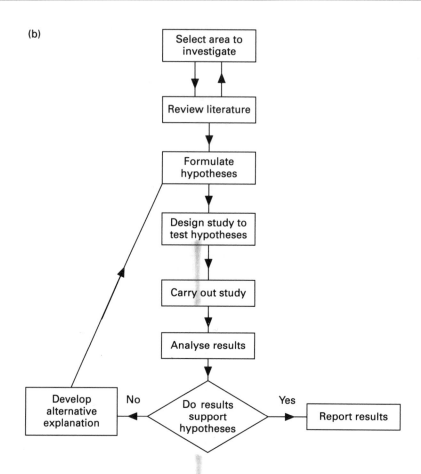

Cursory comparison of the models indicates several differences. As already stressed, the focus in real world enquiry shifts from the usual scientific task to the solution of a problem or resolution of an issue. The model is also substantially more complex, with a greater number of processes involved and more, and more complex, interactions between the various stages.

Real world research has tended to be viewed as a methodologically flawed version of 'proper' research.

> In terms of the traditional model this is perfectly true – much 'real world' research is messy – uncontrolled variables abound, predictor and criterion measures interact, alternative hypotheses cannot be ruled out; standard statistical measures cannot be applied without massive violation of assumptions. (Boehm, 1980, p. 498)

This book has tried to indicate how you might go about things in this difficult situation for traditional research, urging, in particular, the virtues of the systematic multi-method case study. What it implies for the researcher or enquirer is the willingness to acquire and develop a rather different set of research skills; and, just as importantly, to have a more flexible, interactive, view of the task.

It should be recalled that, as discussed in the previous chapter, the real world investigator's responsibilities often extend further than is expected in the traditional model. It may not be their responsibility actually to implement the results in the sense of overseeing a change in practice or whatever, but what might somewhat clumsily be termed their 'implementability' has got to be very much in the mind of the enquirer, both in conducting the enquiry and in the form in which the results are presented. Utopian solutions involving impossible staff ratios or physical resources that are way outside budget are of no great help. As the teacher said when one-to-one teaching sessions were advocated to solve her problems in teaching slow learners to read – 'what do I do when the other twenty-nine are swinging from the lampbulbs?' If one-to-one sessions really do provide a solution, then the task of the investigator is widened – either come up with some solution for the other twenty-nine, or give convincing arguments to 'management' for the necessary resources.

Advice to the Real World Researcher

The intention behind the book is to provide a resource for those carrying out this task; from conceptualizing it, through design, selecting a research strategy and choosing the method(s), to procedure, analysis, interpretation and reporting; I hope it helps. Some specific issues arise from your likely position as an 'outsider'.

Know the environment of the study As a likely outsider, you will need to find out a substantial amount about the 'client's' needs and expectations, and to be aware of the setting and context in which the study will take place. An awareness and recognition of these matters will enhance your credibility and be likely to obtain more interest from participants in the study. You will need to be able to show the link between 'internal' issues and the research questions.

Be prepared to 'sell' the idea of the research Persuasion is one of the many skills you need to carry out this kind of applied work. There seems to be an idea about that it is morally wrong to seek to 'sell' your research project to the client and other likely participants. I don't see this; always provided, of course, that you are acting in good faith, and that you are selling rather than over-selling. Even when the commission to carry out a study comes directly from the client, you are likely to have to persuade them that, for example, while they saw the problem as X, your view is that it is really about Y; or that while they wanted a sample survey, the question would be better addressed by a case study (or vice versa). It is important to try to give your best estimate of the likely costs and benefits, both of the project itself and of any changes that seem likely to arise if its findings were implemented. In an organization, persuasion may well be needed at several levels in the hierarchy, with the message appropriately tailored to the audience.

Be prepared to 'sell' the findings of the research   The same case for 'selling' can be made in connection with outcomes from the research. For the client, the findings and their usefulness are the most important part of the process. Persuasion is particularly important when, as is often the case, implementation of some new approach or way of working is indicated. You need a sophisticated understanding of the change process and the likely barriers that will be erected (see p. 443).

Remember that you are likely to be judged on your communication and interaction skills   There will be little interest in your knowledge of the literature or of research methodology. Much more important is how you 'present' when interacting with the client and participants, initially during the project and when disseminating the findings.

Hakel et al. (1982) provide a useful analysis of the communication skills required by the applied researcher, summarized in box 15.2. They focus on organizational studies but the points that they make have general relevance. Suggestions are provided for role-play (behaviour modelling) exercises designed to develop these skills.

Box 15.2   Communication skills needed by the real world researcher

1 *Explaining the rationale for a project* (showing the client and others what is in it for them):

- describe objectives in non-technical terms and advantages of conducting the project with suggested methodology;
- ask for and listen to reactions;
- explain how findings will benefit client and organization, and contrast this with consequences or implications of not being involved.

2 *Listening and reacting* (showing understanding and generating confidence in the researcher):

- convince client of your personal interest in the project;
- ask client how their personal or organizational effectiveness might be influenced by the project – listen openly;

- ask client to elaborate on points where you disagree and discuss your own views;
- thank client for views and promise they will be considered before proceeding;
- (if appropriate) set follow-up date to redefine project or get agreement.

3 *Defending or presenting an idea, opinion or project* (showing professional competence and ability to contribute to management/ organizational objectives):

- express your opinion and explain why you hold it (versus alternatives);
- explain relationship between what you propose and their objectives;
- ask for and listen to reaction;
- ask for elaboration on points where you disagree;
- discuss and compare your opinion and theirs in reference to the best criteria you can identify for measuring their objectives.

4 *Redirecting or redefining their expressed interest or objectives* (ensuring that research results will be useful and making sure that the research answers the questions they *should* be asking);

- express your understanding of their interests and objectives and suggest a more fundamental perspective, together with your reasons for offering it;
- explain the relationship between your more fundamental perspective and their need;
- ask for and discuss their reactions to your recommendation;
- (if necessary) outline how their interest or objectives will be met by following a more fundamental recommendation.

5 *Getting agreement and commitment* (making sure that they understand what must be done to provide support and follow-up):

- review with client/management the rationale of the project;
- indicate and discuss specific responsibilities, tasks, milestones and deadlines;
- ask for and discuss reactions;
- agree to summarize the schedule and actions in writing, and submit these for record;
- set specific follow-up dates to review progress at each milestone.

(Adapted and abridged from Hakel et al., 1982, pp. 105–8.)

The Research Consultant (Project Adviser) Role

Organizations make use of many kinds of consultants, such as legal experts, financial advisers and advertising agents. There are also consultants who provide expertise based to a greater or less extent on the theories, findings and methods of the social sciences, such as communications, job training, management, marketing, organizational development (OD), personnel selection and public relations consultants. Consultancy as a role is not limited to formal organizations. Varela (1975), for example, discusses consultancy in the context of individuals with emotional problems and youth gangs, as well as the staffs of community agencies and the sales forces of manufacturing companies.

Hornstein (1975) has provided a classificatory scheme to distinguish among types of consultants based upon the kind of service that the consultant provides, the level of the organization in which she works, and the kinds of target with which the consultant is concerned (e.g. personal functioning of individuals, internal processes or external relationships). Lippitt and Lippitt's (1978) classification emphasizes multiple consultancy roles, and is shown in box 15.3.

Research consultancy as envisaged here is closer to the non-directive pole of the Lippitts' classification. It amounts to a personal advisory service to the individual or group charged with mounting some form of enquiry. Indeed, because of these other connotations of the term 'consultant', it may be wiser to refer to the role as 'research adviser' (or even, because of the antipathy to 'research' in some contexts, as 'project adviser'). The aim is to provide advice, information and support so that internal practitioner–researchers can overcome their relative lack of expertise and experience in designing, running, analysing and reporting on the enquiry.

Within this general framework, several variants are possible – mainly reflecting the extent to which the project remains internal; or is a partnership between consultant and internal researchers; or becomes the consultant's project with the internal researchers carrying out most of it. There are advantages and disadvantages of each, although in the latter two the role is not so much consultant as researcher: they provide one way of minimizing the disadvantage of being an outsider by involving internal colleagues. In action research and other approaches focusing on change, the distinction between researcher and consultant becomes blurred. In any case it is important to establish at a very early stage which role you are expected to play.

The following discussion assumes that you are simply advising rather than taking over the project. A common approach is for the consultant to have a substantial voice in the design, choice of research strategy and methods to be used; but after that simply a watching brief where further advice is proffered if problems crop up, and when important milestones are achieved.

Box 15.3 Multiple roles of the consultant

non-directive							directive
Objective observer/reflecter	Process counsellor	Fact finder	Alternative identifier and linker	Joint problem-solver	Trainer educator	Informational expert	Advocate
raises questions for reflection	observes problem-solving process and raises issues mirroring feedback	gathers data and stimulates thinking	identifies alternatives and resources for client and helps assess consequences	offers alternatives and participates in decisions	trains client	regards, links, and provides policy or practice decisions	proposes guidelines, persuades or directs in the problem-solving process

(Adapted from Lippitt and Lippitt, 1978, p. 31.)

The 'Giving Away' of Skills

Your task as consultant is in part to 'give away' skills and experience. This is increasingly seen as a necessary task for psychologists and other social scientists if what these disciplines have to offer, both in terms of theories and findings, and methodologically, is to make an impact on society. However, dangers of misuse and misapplication, have to be guarded against.

In the applied field with which I have mainly been concerned, the education of children with severe learning difficulties, psychologists have devised approaches to in-service training whereby the research skills involved in using behavioural techniques, originally the province of psychologists, have been made accessible to teachers and other 'hands-on' workers (see e.g. Foxen and McBrien, 1981; McBrien and Foxen, 1981). Similar approaches have successfully disseminated skills associated with assessing and fostering language development (Robson, 1987b). Other examples, discussed in Robson et al. (1988), include a variety of research-based examples – the development of counselling skills (Mallon, 1987), skills in the use of alternative modes of communication (Kiernan et al., 1988), and a range of skills appropriate for the education of profoundly and multiply handicapped people (e.g. in relation to the assessment and management of auditory, visual and motor development – Sebba, 1988).

Work of this kind is open to the criticism that the skills are necessarily esoteric and should only be open to the select few who have completed a full academic and professional training in psychology or other relevant discipline. The answer to this is in part through such attempts to give away skills being fully evaluated to determine their success or otherwise empirically (e.g. Robson et al., 1988).

In relation to enquiry and the skills needed to carry this out effectively, the pragmatic point is that much of what goes on in the practice of the 'human' professions at individual, group or organization level is not currently subject to systematic enquiry and evaluation. Pressures in that direction may lead to researchers being asked to carry out such studies, which is to be welcomed. However, the trend in many services seems to be to seek to do this 'in-house'. There are clear advantages to this trend, both in extending the professionalism of the practitioners concerned, and in increasing the likelihood of findings being implemented. But the work may be of poor quality. Which is where the consultant comes in; not only to provide advice on specifics but to reinforce the notion that the only worthwhile studies are rigorous, systematic and unbiased.

Advice to the Research Consultant (Project Adviser)

Seek an early clarification of your role Is the role purely advisory? Is it one-off advice in setting up the project, or is there a continuing involvement (e.g. to comment on instruments used or developed; to give advice on development of fieldwork and possible modification of design; to make suggestions about analysis, need for further data, form and content of report, dissemination strategy and tactics)?

Assess capability of the practitioner–researcher(s)   Have they sufficient knowledge/experience/skills to carry out the intended project? Can you assist them so that they can cope? Or can the project be reformulated so they can handle it? Are they sufficiently committed to the ideals of enquiry to produce a full and unbiased study (or would they just do a 'cosmetic' job)? *If you are not happy with these answers, withdraw* (let them, and the organization, know why – tactfully).

Seek answers to these questions

a   Where does the project come from? (Who wants it done? Why?)
b   What is the problem/issue?
c   What do they see as the research questions?
d   What resources are available (mainly time availability of practitioner/ researcher(s))?
e   What is the time-scale of the project?
f   What methodology (strategy; research methods), if any, is proposed?
g   What problems do they envisage? (Opposition? suspicion?)
h   How will the study be reported?
i   How will the findings be used?
j   What is the position on confidentiality/anonymity?

The extent to which you get answers on these issues gives an indication of their research sophistication, and of the extent to which things have been thought through. This helps you to assess the feasibility of their task within the constraints of time and resources, and to give realistic advice.

An Enquiring Society?

The opening of a submission that I made a few years ago to a British Psychological Society conference on 'The Future of the Psychological Sciences' asserted:

> It verges on the embarrassingly trite to note that the problems and concerns in our society are largely to do with people, how they behave and interact, their attitudes and expectations. Unemployment is a problem not in the sense that a lack of paid employment equates to starvation, but rather that generally people do not wish to be unemployed, only in part for economic reasons. Stockpiles of nuclear weapons may be inherently dangerous things to have

around but the threat is most likely to become actual by one or more persons engaging in button-pushing behaviour. The simplest solution to murder, rape, mugging, football hooliganism and the dropping of litter is for the individual or group concerned not to do it. (Robson, 1987, p. 141)

I am happy to reiterate that claim, while admitting that the expression is somewhat tricksy. My feeling was, and is, that psychology and psychologists, and other social scientists, could and should have a greater part in helping to provide solutions for 'people' problems, but that any such potential or actual contribution goes largely unacknowledged by the populace at large, and decision-makers and persons in power in particular. This may simply be part of a general lack of public recognition that it is possible to make a serious study of behaviour, but a likely factor is that the nature and emphases of training in psychology do not develop the skills, inclination or confidence to address directly 'real world' problems – and in particular to carry out enquiry outside the cosy confines of the laboratory. Which takes us full circle to the intentions expressed in the opening chapter.

In the initial plan for this book, the idea was to conclude with a rousing plea for a move towards a society in which enquiry was king (or queen): a society where systematic enquiry provides an engine for the development and improvement of human enterprises such as education and social and health services, and was able to do much the same thing for the important and neglected 'people' aspects of industry and commerce. However, wider reading, reflecting on my own experience and that of others, and the writing itself, have left me somewhat less sanguine (= 'ardent, confident and inclined to hopefulness') about such a manifesto.

Things are undoubtedly more complex. Lindblom and Cohen (1979) make a powerful case for 'professional social inquiry' being:

only one among several analytical methods, because other forms of information and analysis – ordinary knowledge and causal analysis foremost among them – are often sufficient or better than [professional social inquiry] for social problem solving. (p. 10)

Donald Schon (1987) makes the same kind of point when considering what is involved in 'educating the reflective practitioner':

In the terrain of professional practice, applied science and research-based technique occupy a critically important though limited territory, bounded on several sides by artistry. (p. 13)

For him, 'artistry' is 'an exercise of intelligence, a kind of knowing', central to the practice of the high-quality professional person, and recognizable through studying their performance.

Carol Weiss (1986), in discussing what she terms the 'limited partnership' between research and policy-making, concludes:

Researchers need to be aware that the work that they do, no matter how applied in intent and how practical in orientation, is not likely to have major influence on the policy decision at which it is purportedly directed. . . . Adherence to all the traditional strictures – acceptance of decision-makers' constraints, focus on manipulative variables, timeliness, jargon-free communication and the like – seems only to increase the application of research results marginally. . . . When competing with other powerful factors, such as officials' concern with political or bureaucratic advantage, one limited study (and all studies are limited in some way) is likely to have limited impact. (p. 232)

These sombre warnings argue for a much greater degree of humility among proponents of systematic enquiry. However, advantage can be gained from this initially depressing realization. What is called for is a rapprochement between artistry and research-based technique in professional practice; between ordinary knowledge and professional social enquiry in social problem-solving. And, above, all a realistic appreciation of limits to likely impact.

It has long been acknowledged that in carrying out an experiment, one can only proceed by trusting and using a vast amount of 'ordinary knowledge'. Perhaps we overemphasize the specialness of the information gained by the use of systematic enquiry. There may well be good pragmatic reasons for this. Insistence on the 'mystery' (variously defined as 'rites known only to the initiated' and 'anything artfully made difficult') of our activities as psychologists and social scientists when carrying out experiments and other studies has political advantages as it helps to enhance our power. The corresponding disadvantages when carrying out real world enquiry are in distancing ourselves from the participants and potential collaborators in such studies; in exclusion of practitioner–researchers unless they too are members of our magic circle; and hence in severely reducing the applicability and chance of implementation of findings from the studies.

There may be advantage in regarding the whole edifice of systematic enquiry strategies, methods and techniques of analysis as simply aids to ordinary knowledge – as means of organizing common sense and intuitive problem-solving so as to guard against some of their shortcomings. I found the following experience illuminating.

When working with teachers on the development of the skills of 'structured teaching' (akin to behavioural techniques) we found that immediately after the training course virtually all of them showed substantial use of the techniques in their classrooms in clearly defined special sessions with individual pupils. This persisted through regular visits over the next few weeks. Returning several months later, we discovered that several of them appeared to have dropped these sessions. However, careful systematic observation in the classroom showed a high use of the techniques in a larger number of shorter one-to-one interactions, and discussion with the teachers drew comments like 'once I got the confidence that I could do it, I preferred to do it flexibly when the occasion demanded and the child seemed ready', or 'it's more of an attitude to teaching really; being careful about your interaction and clear as to the goal', or 'I still use the formal sessions with some children but only when it's particularly tricky'.

The key messages seem to be that while there is a place for the differentiated special session, there is considerable flexibility in the use of the specialized techniques, and a percolation of their use into the general approach to teaching, amounting in some cases to a change in attitude about the nature of the task. Viewing this as an analogy for the place of enquiry in real world settings is dangerously seductive, but it encourages me to conclude by putting forward the speculative vision of box 15.4.

Box 15.4   The place of systematic enquiry in the practice of the 'human' profession – some modest proposals

1   That systematic enquiry is accepted and routinized as a tool to assist human-focused services in dealing with issues and problems at individual, group and institutional level.

2   That formal enquiry of this type is pursued on a highly selective basis, restricted to topics of particular complexity, interest or importance.

3   That the enquiry is carried out either by internal practitioner-researchers, calling where necessary on external consultants; or by researchers who (whether internal or external) work in a close and collaborative manner with internal colleagues.

4   That every effort is made to demystify the enquiry process – consonant with not compromising its rigour! We are building on and systematizing common sense and ordinary knowledge, not replacing them.

5   Given an involvement in such enquiries either as participants or practitioners – researcher, and an appreciation of the benefits that have flowed from them, an attitude may be fostered where the aims and practices of enquiry increasingly permeate individuals' approach to their work. Nothing grandiose: simply the recognition that you get better-quality information to deal with issues if you approach them as mini-enquiries.

This is not the same as 'Do-It-Yourself Social Science' (Heller, 1986). Such DYSS is an extension of the DIYE (Do-It-Yourself Economics) which Henderson (1986) found in the Treasury, the UK government department responsible for formulating economic policy. Senior civil servants held doctrines that were 'intuitive and self-generated: those who held them thought that what they were saying was plain common sense which needed no prompting or authority' (p. 15). Such attitudes range across all fields covered by the social sciences, and are prevalent in management and decision-makers in general. A major educational task is called for, demonstrating through involvement the virtues and pay-offs of systematic enquiry. Small successes, through small-scale enquiry carried out in propitious circumstances, should be well within your grasp.

Further Reading

Barlow, D. H., Hayes, S. C. and Nelson, R. O. (1984) *The Scientist Practitioner: research and accountability in clinical and educational settings.* Oxford: Pergamon. Attempts to bridge the gap between researchers and practitioners by providing practical research strategies that can be incorporated into daily practice. Concentrates on single-case design. First chapter provides useful review of the scientist–practitioner role.

Bennett, N. and Desforges, C. (1985) Ensuring Practical Outcomes from Educational Research. In M. Shipman (ed.) *Educational Research: principles, policies and practices.* London: Falmer. Analyses different approaches. Balanced review of collaborative research involving practitioners.

Campbell, D. T. (1973) The Social Scientist as Methodological Servant of the Experimenting Society. *Policy Studies Journal,* 2, 72–5. Examines the role of the social scientist in the 'enquiring' society.

Jayaratne, S. and Levy, R. L. (1979) *Empirical Clinical Practice.* New York: Columbia University Press. Describes how an empirical approach and research orientation can be integrated into practice.

Schon, D. (1983) *The Reflective Practitioner.* London: Temple Smith.

Schon, D. (1988) *Educating the Reflective Practitioner.* San Francisco: Jossey-Bass. Thought-provoking analysis of how enquiring reflective practitioners might function and be educated.

Walker, R. (1985) *Doing Research: a handbook for teachers.* London: Methuen. Examines the role of research by practitioners in 'developing a community of knowledgeable users' (chapter 6).

Webb, R. (ed.) (1990) *Practitioner Research in the Primary School.* London: Falmer. Set of accounts of research carried out by class teachers and other practitioners in primary schools. Useful example of the 'teacher-as-researcher' movement.

Appendix A

Writing a Project Proposal

These suggestions are targeted at relatively small-scale research or enquiry, such as that carried out as a project on a taught post-graduate course or for a research degree. They may also be of value in connection with small grant applications to funding organizations.

Research is an activity which is essentially in the public domain. Carrying it out is rarely a totally solo exercise. All research seeks to make links to what other researchers have done previously. It usually involves access to and the use of public resources. Much research, particularly in the arts and social sciences, is in some sense based on other people and their responses and productions. On completion, there is an onus on the researcher to make her findings available through some form of publication (= 'making public').

It is, therefore, appropriate that any proposed research should be laid out for inspection and comment by others; and, in many cases, that it should be approved by others. Any student certainly requires her proposal to be formally approved. Those seeking funding require the approval of the funding agency to which they apply, or they will not receive support. In these cases there will almost always be some required format to the proposal. It is an obvious part of the professional approach advocated here that any specific rubric should be strictly adhered to. If a maximum of two thousand words is required for the first of May, you do not send in three thousand on the eighth.

The concern here is for general issues appropriate to all small-scale research proposals. A useful analogy has been made by several writers between researchers and architects (e.g. Hakim, 1987; Leedy, 1989). Planning is the main link. The architect plans buildings. The researcher draws up plans to investigate issues and solve problems. In each case these plans must say something about structure, about how the task is conceptualized, and about the methods to be used in carrying out the plans.

For both the researcher and the architect, it is insufficient simply to present the concept of the problem and its suggested mode of solution (tower block or ranch house; survey or experiment). Factors like the resources needed to carry out the work; the qualifications and experience of those involved; previous work that has already been carried out by the applicant and others; computer facilities; obtaining of any necessary permissions and clearances; all these and many other matters are important.

> *The research proposal is your opportunity to persuade the 'client' that you know what you are talking about. That you have thought through the issues involved and are going to deliver. That it is worthwhile to take the risk and give you licence to get on with it.*

There is a temptation to think of writing the research proposal as merely an irksome formality, a hurdle that has to be jumped before you can get on with the real work of research. Viewed in this light it is, literally, a waste of time. Approached like this, it is not unlikely that you will produce a skimped and unconvincing proposal which, quite rightly, gets vetoed. It is much more helpful to see it as an important and integral part of the research process. The work that you do at this stage may not produce the definitive proposal which gives an accurate account of what you are going to do in the research, and what will come out of it. Little research has that degree of certitude. But if you can persuade experienced and disinterested judges that what you are proposing looks interesting and do-able within the constraints of resources and time that you have available, you should take heart. Remember that you are the one who has most to lose if you get into a situation where the research is a failure, and that you want the best insurance policy that you can get. Viewed in that light, it is well worth investing in a good research proposal.

How to Recognize a Good Proposal

• *A good proposal is direct and straightforward* It tells what you are proposing to do; and why you are proposing to do it. The former is concerned with aims which should be clear and explicit. For the latter, you will have to show why it is interesting and timely, which will involve a demonstration of your awareness of the empirical and theoretical context.

Good research demands clarity of thought and expression in the doing and the reporting. The proposal provides good evidence on your clarity of thought and expression. Make it pro rather than con.

• *A good proposal communicates well* The basic purpose is to communicate your intentions. Anything that gets in the way of this should be cut out. Complex mega-sentences illustrating the complexity and subtlety of your thought processes should be avoided. Fine writing with arcane vocabulary (such as 'arcane') does not help. Unless it is specifically asked for, you do not seek to impress by gargantuan book lists illustrating what you have read, or hope to read. The few key works central to your proposal are more appropriate.

As with any research-related writing, the question of audience is important. Appropriate assumptions may vary for different kinds of proposals, but it is often helpful to regard the reader not as an expert in the exact sub-field of your research, but more as a cross between an intelligent lay person and a generalist in the discipline.

• *A good proposal is well organized* The structure of your proposal should be simple and self-evident. It helps to have a consistent system for indicating and, if you need to, lettering or numbering, headings and sub-headings. The expected style is usually standard paragraphing and continuous prose. Don't produce a minutely sectionalized, note-form proposal.

Remember that research demands organization above virtually everything else. A poorly organized proposal does little for your cause.

The Content of a Research Proposal

If you have to work to a standard format on a proposal form or grant application, this obviously determines how you set things out. However there is substantial overlap between many of these, and it is likely that you will have to provide the following.

• *Abstract or summary*   Should be brief, clear, and informative, giving a flavour of what is intended and why. This will be the first thing read so you want to give a good impression. Don't exceed any word limit which is specified.

• *Background and purpose*   A major section where you impress by your commitment and professionalism. Will include a short review of relevant work done by others. It is crucial that you unearth and include any very recent work. Its presence will be reassuring to a specialist reviewer and its absence potentially damning. You want to show that there is a gap to be filled, or a next step to be taken, or a concern arising – and that you have a good idea how this should be addressed.

Relevance is very important. Don't show off by displaying ideas or knowledge which do not contribute directly. It helps to get a sympathetic critic to read your draft. If you have been preparing this for some time, you will be so close to it that you find it difficult to put yourself into the position of someone reading it for the first time. Complex constructions may need unpacking; the implicit made explicit.

Your aim is to lead the reader inexorably towards the conclusion you have reached: that this is the work that must be done, now, with these aims, and in this way.

• *The plan of work*   Here you go into some detail about the methods and procedures to be used. The detail which is necessary or possible will vary according to the nature of the enquiry. A traditional experiment will require close specification of the design to be used, how variables are to be operationalized, and details of chosen tests or measures (justifying the specific choice if alternatives are possible). If more flexible strategies are used, you still have to demonstrate that you know what is involved (see following section on 'The Problem of Pre-specifying an Emergent Design').

It is often helpful, and reassuring to the reader, if you have carried out some previous work to prepare the ground for the study. This may have been part of an earlier study or project which inspired you to develop it further. Or you might have carried out specific pilot work, perhaps to demonstrate the feasibility of what you are now proposing. This can get you out of a common 'Catch-22' situation. If you are, say, simply repeating a procedure that others have used, this does not constitute novel research; if you go for a novel procedure, how do you know that it is going to work?

You need to be clear where the research will take place and who will be involved. Will you be doing all the work or is it in some sense a group exercise? If the latter, how is your contribution to be demarcated from the larger enterprise? If it is at all feasible, the scale of the enterprise should be stated (e.g. size of any samples). Any necessary permissions for access, co-operation or involvement will have to be negotiated prior to presenting the proposal and statements about this made here (possibly with documentation, such as confirmatory letters, as well).

The plan will also need to specify how data will be analysed. You should, once again, convince the reader that you have thought through the issues. Above all, you have to guard against the impression that you are going to gather the data and then think about analysis afterwards. Or that you will simply subject the data to an unspecified barrage of computer-generated analyses. You should indicate the nature and extent of any computer support needed, and how the need will be met.

- *Financial aspects* Any proposal which involves financial implications should spell these out and indicate who is going to pay. For a student, this may involve equipment, computer time, photocopying, printing, telephone, etc. A member of staff or a practitioner or professional doing work for her own organization may also have to include a sum to cover for the time she is involved, and for any additional staff time (whether secretarial, technical or research assistance). Bids for external funding would include all these headings and substantial amounts for overheads. Different institutions and different funding bodies each have their own interpretations of what is admissible, and you obviously have to play the game according to their rules.

There is a general tendency to underestimate the financial implications of any research, particularly when times are hard and money scarce. The best advice is to be as realistic as you can. Research is, by definition, problematic and unforeseen circumstances inevitably tend to increase costs. Cutting corners and skimping financially is a false economy. It may slightly increase your chances of getting approval (though not necessarily; experienced assessors might regard it as an indication of a lack of professionalism) but it will almost certainly decrease your chances of delivering satisfactorily on time. If you find that you do not have the time or resources to complete the project as envisaged, the situation can be sometimes rescued by 'trading down' to a different design (see Hakim, 1987, pp. 120–3).

- *Ethical implications* For many forms of research, certainly for much research involving humans or other animals, proposals will require ethical vetting. This will seek to ensure that it falls within an appropriate 'code of practice' (see p. 29 and appendix B for further details). It will usually be sensible to seek clearance at an early stage of the preparation of the proposal, when its main features have been settled. The formal proposal would then simply certify that approval had been granted.

There may also be legal implications of certain kinds of research. One which potentially affects much research arises from the UK Data Protection Act. This is designed to protect individuals from having personal data stored on computer and other files without their knowledge, agreement and access. If any such data are stored in your research, you need to seek advice on your responsibilities.

The Problem of Pre-specifying an Emergent Design

There are styles of research, variously labelled as ethnographic, interpretive, qualitative or naturalistic (labelled 'case study' in this text), in which there is a principled resistance to pre-specifying details of the research project. The design and, with some of these perspectives, the theoretical and conceptual framework, is viewed as *emerging* during the project.

Box A.1   Ten ways to get your proposal turned down

1   Don't follow the directions or guidelines given for your kind of proposal. Omit information that is asked for. Ignore word limits.

2   Ensure that the title has little relationship to the stated objectives; and that neither title nor objectives link to the proposed methods or techniques.

3   Produce woolly, ill-defined objectives.

4   Have the statement of the central problem or research focus vague, or obscure it by other discussion.

5   Leave the design and methodology implicit; let them guess.

6   Have some mundane task, routine consultancy or poorly conceptualized data trawl masquerade as a research project.

7   Be unrealistic in what can be achieved with the time and resources you have available.

8   Be either very brief, or, preferably, long-winded and repetitive in your proposal. Rely on weight rather than quality.

9   Make it clear what the findings of your research are going to be, and demonstrate how your ideological stance makes this inevitable.

10   Don't worry about a theoretical or conceptual framework for your research. You want to do a down-to-earth study so you can forget all that fancy stuff.

Proposals for this type of research must convince that the researcher has both the need for, and the right to, this kind of flexibility. The proposal must justify why the research questions are best dealt with in this way. It must also convince, through its argument and referencing, that you are competent to carry out this style of research and capable of using the proposed methods. Marshall and Rossman (1989) provide helpful suggestions for the development and description of this kind of proposal.

Shortcomings of Unsuccessful Proposals

There are, of course, an almost unlimited number of ways in which to present an unsatisfactory research proposal which would justifiably be unsuccessful. Leedy (1989, ch. 6) examines the matter thoroughly. He cites a range of analyses of American grant applications which, although they relate to applications for external funding, have considerable relevance to all research proposals. Four major factors come out as shortcomings of poor applications:

1 The problem being of insufficient importance, or unlikely to produce any new or useful information.
2 The proposed tests, methods or procedures being unsuited to the stated objective.
3 The description of the research being nebulous, diffuse or lacking in clarity, so that it could not be adequately evaluated.
4 The investigator not having adequate training, or experience, or both, for the research.

Box A.1 gives a list of things you might like to think about when appraising your own research proposal. It is not exhaustive.

Further Reading

Krathwohl, D. R. (1988) *How to Prepare a Research Project: guidelines for funding and dissertations in the social and behavioral sciences*; 3rd edn. Syracuse, NY: Syracuse University Press. Detailed and authoritative account. Keyed to the American context, but many of the issues are of general validity.

Leedy, P. D. (1989) *Practical Research: planning and design*, 4th edn. New York: Macmillan. Chapter 6 is devoted to 'Writing the Research Proposal'. Based on a review of relevant literature on successful and unsuccessful proposals.

Brooks, N. (1989) Writing a Grant Application. In G. Perry and F. N. Watts (eds), *Behavioral and Mental Health Research: a handbook of skills and methods*. Hove, Sussex: Laurence Erlbaum Associates. Angled towards clinical research, but the advice is helpful in connection with making any grant application in social research.

Appendix B

Ethical Principles for Conducting Research with Human Participants (British Psychological Society)

1 Introduction

1.1 The principles given below are intended to apply to research with human participants. Principles of conduct in professional practice are to be found in the Society's Code of Conduct and in the advisory documents prepared by the Divisions, Sections and Special Groups of the Society.

1.2 Participants in psychological research should have confidence in the investigators. Good psychological research is possible only if there is mutual respect and confidence between investigators and participants. Psychological investigators are potentially interested in all aspects of human behaviour and conscious experience. However, for ethical reasons, some areas of human experience and behaviour may be beyond the reach of experiment, observation or other form of psychological investigation. Ethical guidelines are necessary to clarify the conditions under which psychological research is acceptable.

1.3 The principles given below supplement for researchers with human participants the general ethical principles of members of the Society as stated in The British Psychological Society's Code of Conduct (q.v.). Members of The British Psychological Society are expected to abide by both the Code of Conduct and the fuller principles expressed here. Members should also draw the principles to the attention of research colleagues who are not members of the Society. Members should encourage colleagues to adopt them and ensure that they are followed by all researchers whom they supervise (e.g. research assistants, postgraduate, undergraduate, A-Level and GCSE students).

1.4   In recent years, there has been an increase in legal actions by members of the general public against professionals for alleged misconduct. Researchers must recognize the possibility of such legal action if they infringe the rights and dignity of participants in their research.

2   General

2.1   In all circumstances, investigators must consider the ethical implications and psychological consequences for the participants in their research. The essential principle is that the investigation should be considered from the standpoint of all participants; foreseeable threats to their psychological well-being, health, values or dignity should be eliminated. Investigators should recognize that, in our multi-cultural and multi-ethnic society and where investigations involve individuals of different ages, gender and social background, the investigators may not have sufficient knowledge of the implications of any investigation for the participants. It should be borne in mind that the best judge of whether an investigation will cause offence may be members of the population from which the participants in the research are to be drawn.

3   Consent

3.1   Whenever possible, the investigator should inform all participants of the objectives of the investigation. The investigator should inform the participants of all aspects of the research or intervention that might reasonably be expected to influence willingness to participate. The investigator should, normally, explain all other aspects of the research or intervention about which the participants enquire. Failure to make full disclosure prior to obtaining informed consent requires additional safeguards to protect the welfare and dignity of the participants (see Section 4).

3.2   Research with children or with participants who have impairments that will limit understanding and/or communication such that they are unable to give their real consent requires special safe-guarding procedures.

3.3   Where possible, the real consent of children and of adults with impairments in understanding or communication should be obtained. In addition, where research involves all persons under sixteen years of age, consent should be obtained from parents or from those 'in loco parentis'.

3.4   Where real consent cannot be obtained from adults with impairments in understanding or communication, wherever possible the investigator should consult a person well-placed to appreciate the participant's reaction, such as a member of the person's family, and must obtain the disinterested approval of the research from independent advisors.

3.5   When research is being conducted with detained persons, particular care should be taken over informed consent, paying attention to the special circumstances which may affect the person's ability to give free informed consent.

3.6 Investigators should realize that they are often in a position of authority or influence over participants who may be their students, employees or clients. This relationship must not be allowed to pressurize the participants to take part in, or remain in, an investigation.

3.7 The payment of participants must not be used to induce them to risk harm beyond that which they risk without payment in their normal lifestyle.

3.8 If harm, unusual discomfort, or other negative consequences for the individual's future life might occur, the investigator must obtain the disinterested approval of independent advisers, inform the participants, and obtain informed, real consent from each of them.

3.9 In longitudinal research, consent may need to be obtained on more than one occasion.

4 Deception

4.1 The withholding of information or the misleading of participants is unacceptable if the participants are typically likely to object or show unease once debriefed. Where this is in any doubt, appropriate consultation must precede the investigation. Consultation is best carried out with individuals who share the social and cultural background of the participants in the research, but the advice of ethics committees or experienced and disinterested colleagues may be sufficient.

4.2 Intentional deception of the participants over the purpose and general nature of the investigation should be avoided whenever possible. Participants should never be deliberately misled without extremely strong scientific or medical justification. Even then there should be strict controls and the disinterested approval of independent advisers.

4.3 It may be impossible to study some psychological processes without withholding information about the true object of the study or deliberately misleading the participants. Before conducting such a study, the investigator has a special responsibility to (a) determine that alterative procedures avoiding concealment or deception are not available; (b) ensure that the participants are provided with sufficient information at the earliest stage; and (c) consult appropriately upon the way that the withholding of information or deliberate deception will be received.

5 Debriefing

5.1 In studies where the participants are aware that they have taken part in an investigation, when the data have been collected, the investigator should provide the participants with any necessary information to complete their understanding of the nature of the research. The investigator should discuss with the participants their experience of the research in order to monitor any unforeseen negative effects or misconceptions.

5.2 Debriefing does not provide a justification for unethical aspects of any investigation.

5.3 Some effects which may be produced by an experiment will not be negated by a verbal description following the research. Investigators have a responsibility to ensure that participants receive any necessary debriefing in the form of active intervention before they leave the research setting.

6 Withdrawal from the Investigation

6.1 At the onset of the investigation investigators should make plain to participants their right to withdraw from the research at any time, irrespective of whether or not payment or other inducement has been offered. It is recognized that this may be difficult in certain observational or organizational settings, but nevertheless the investigator must attempt to ensure that participants (including children) know of their right to withdraw. When testing children, avoidance of the testing situation may be taken as evidence of failure to consent to the procedure and should be acknowledged.

6.2 In the light of experience of the investigation, or as a result of debriefing, the participant has the right to withdraw retrospectively any consent given, and to require that their own data, including recordings, be destroyed.

7 Confidentiality

7.1 Subject to the requirements of legislation, including the Data Protection Act, information obtained about a participant during an investigation is confidential unless otherwise agreed in advance. Investigators who are put under pressure to disclose confidential information should draw this point to the attention of those exerting such pressure. Participants in psychological research have a right to expect that information they provide will be treated confidentially and, if published, will not be identifiable as theirs. In the event that confidentiality and/or anonymity cannot be guaranteed, the participant must be warned of this in advance of agreeing to participate.

8 Protection of Participants

8.1 Investigators have a primary responsibility to protect participants from physical and mental harm during the investigation. Normally, the risk of harm must be no greater than in ordinary life, i.e. participants should not exposed to risks greater than or additional to those encountered in their normal lifestyles. Where the risk of harm is greater than in ordinary life the provisions of 3.8 should apply. Participants must be asked about any factors in the procedure that might create a risk, such as pre-existing medical conditions, and must be advised of any special action they should take to avoid risk.

8.2   Participants should be informed of procedures for contacting the investigator within a reasonable time period following participation should stress, potential harm, or related questions or concern arise despite the precautions required by the Principles. Where research procedures might result in undesirable consequences for participants, the investigator has the responsibility to detect and remove or correct these consequences.

8.3   Where research may involve behaviour or experiences that participants may regard as personal and private the participants must be protected from stress by all appropriate measures, including the assurance that answers to personal questions need not be given. There should be no concealment or deception when seeking information that might encroach on privacy.

8.4   In research involving children, great caution should be exercised when discussing the results with parents, teachers or others in loco parentis, since evaluative statements may carry unintended weight.

9   Observational Research

9.1   Studies based upon observation must respect the privacy and psychological well-being of the individuals studied. Unless those observed give their consent to being observed, observational research is only acceptable in situations where those observed would expect to be observed by strangers. Additionally, particular account should be taken of local cultural values and of the possibility of intruding upon the privacy of individuals who, even while in a normally public space, may believe they are unobserved.

10   Giving Advice

10.1   During research, an investigator may obtain evidence of psychological or physical problems of which a participant is, apparently, unaware. In such a case, the investigator has a responsibility to inform the participant if the investigator believes that by not doing so the participant's future well being may be endangered.

10.2   If, in the normal course of psychological research, or as a result of problems detected as in 10.1, a participant solicits advice concerning educational, personality, behavioural or health issues, caution should be exercised. If the issue is serious and the investigator is not qualified to offer assistance, the appropriate source of professional advice should be recommended. Further details on the giving of advice will be found in the Society's Code of Conduct.

10.3   In some kinds of investigation the giving of advice is appropriate if this forms an intrinsic part of the research and has been agreed in advance.

11 Colleagues

11.1 Investigators share responsibility for the ethical treatment of research participants with their collaborators, assistants, students and employees. A psychologist who believes that another psychologist or investigator may be conducting research that is not in accordance with the principles above should encourage that investigator to re-evaluate the research.

Appendix C

Guidelines on Anti-sexist Language (British Sociological Association)

It is BSA policy that anti-sexist language should be used in its journals, in conference papers and in the delivery of such papers at conferences and so on. These guidelines are intended to assist BSA members in avoiding sexist language by sensitizing people to some of the forms it takes and by suggesting anti-sexist alternatives. They will help readers to consider the extent to which and the ways in which we either challenge or reproduce inaccurate, sexist and heterosexist assumptions in our work. Teachers and students of sociology, as well as authors, may find the guidelines useful.

'He/Man' Language

Do not use 'man' to mean humanity in general. There are plenty of alternatives:

sexist	anti-sexist
man/mankind	person, people, human beings
mankind	men and women, humanity, humankind

When reference to both sexes is intended, a large number of phrases use the word man or other masculine equivalents (e.g. 'father') and a large number of nouns use the suffix 'man', thereby excluding women from the picture we present of the world. These should be replaced by more precise non-sex-referent alternatives as listed below:

sexist	anti-sexist
the man in the street	people in general
layman	lay person
man-made	synthetic, artificial, manufactured
the rights of man	peoples'/citizens' rights; the rights of the individual
Chairman	Chairperson, Chair
foreman	supervisor
manpower	workforce, staff, labour power

craftsman/men	craftsperson/people
manning	staffing, working, running
to a man	everyone, unanimously, without exception
manhours	workhours
the working man	workers, working people
models of man	models of the person
one man show	one person show
policeman/fireman	police officer/firefighter
forefathers	ancestors
founding fathers	founders
old masters	classic art/artists
masterful	domineering; very skilful
master copy	top copy/original
Dear Sirs	Dear Sir/Madam
yours fraternally	best wishes

The generic 'man' is often accompanied by the generic 'he'. The generic 'he' should be avoided. *Both* feminine and masculine pronouns can be used where appropriate: he/she, s/he, his/her etc. Alternative strategies included (a) the use of the plural and (b) the omission of third person pronouns entirely:

a *sexist*: Each respondent was asked whether *he* wished to participate in the survey.
  anti-sexist: Respondents were asked whether *they* wished to participate in the survey.
b *sexist*: The child should be given ample time to familiarize *himself* with the test material.
  anti-sexist: Ample time should be allowed for the child to become familiar with the test material.

Sexist language, apart from being offensive, may also mislead the reader since it is frequently ambiguous. For example, the use of 'he/man language' in a discussion about people, be they workers, the elderly or 'untouchables' may suggest that the circumstances of the whole group are under consideration until statements like the following make it clear that the group or the people are in fact men only: 'hardly a week goes by without an "untouchable" being murdered or his house burned or his wife raped'.

When by 'he' 'men' etc. you do actually mean *only* men it is advisable to make this explicit. 'Male managers' or 'men executives' is less ambiguous than 'business-men' which is either used 'generically' or with the implicit assumption that all busi-ness personnel are male. Such careful, anti-sexist use of language helps in avoiding the mistake of referring to, e.g. 'managers and their wives'. Women managers do not have wives!

'Ladies', 'Girls' and Women

The words 'boys' and 'gentlemen' are rarely used to refer to men in written work or speech. Nevertheless, women continue to be referred to or spoken to as if they were a 'breed apart' from 'mere women' ('ladies') and/or as if they had not yet reached adulthood. The use of such terms is often patronising and offensive and should be avoided. In written work it is inaccurate to write 'young girls' when one is referring to teenage young women. In speech, terms like 'love' and 'dear' also frequently cause offence and should similarly be avoided.

Heterosexism

The above guidelines are intended to help 'make women visible' in our work. In the face of growing homophobia, members of the Association are asked to consider the extent to which their work is heterosexist. For example, in discussions about 'two-earner households' do phrases like 'the man and his partner' appear? Men do not occur in lesbian households. In discussions about young women and sexuality, is it assumed that becoming 'sexually active' means becoming sexually active with men? Our subject is one which has a concern with social realities in the world. We have a responsibility therefore to reflect on and change our heterosexist assumptions.

References and
Author Index

The references incorporate an author index. The numbers in bold at the end of each entry indicate where the publication is referred to in this book.

Acredolo, L. P. (1978) Development of Spatial Orientation in infancy. *Developmental Psychology*, 14, 224–34. **13**

Adams, K. L. and Ware, N. C. (1989) Sexism and the English Language: the linguistic implications of being a woman. In J. Freeman (ed.), *Women: A Feminist Perspective*. Mountain View, Cal.: Mayfield. **64**

Adelman, C. (1989) The Practical Ethic Takes Priority over Methodology. In W. Carr (ed.), *Quality in Teaching: arguments for a reflective profession*. London: Falmer. **440, 441**

Agnew, N. M. and Pyke, S. W. (1982) *The Science Game: an introduction to research in the behavioral sciences*, 3rd edn. Englewood Cliffs, NJ: Prentice-Hall. **80, 191**

Allen-Meares, P. and Lane, B. A. (1990) Social Work Practice: integrating qualitative and quantitative data collection techniques. *Social Work*, 35, 452–6. **447**

American Psychological Association (1987) *Casebook on Ethical Principles of Psychologists*, revised edn. Hyattsville, Md: APA. **29**

Anderson, B. F. (1980) *The Complete Thinker*. Englewood Cliffs, NJ: Prentice-Hall. **423**

Anderson, N. (1965) Averaging versus Adding as a Stimulus-combination Rule in Impression Formation. *Journal of Experimental Psychology*, 70, 394–400. **13**

Anderson, R. A., Baron, R. S. and Logan, N. H. (1991) Distraction, Control and Dental Stress. *Journal of Applied Social Psychology*, 21, 156–71. **11**

Argyris, C. (1970) *Intervention Theory and Method: a behavioral science view*. Reading, Mass.: Addison-Wesley. **433**

Argyris, C. and Schon, D. A. (1974) *Theory in Practice*. San Francisco: Jossey-Bass. **433**

Armbruster, B. B. and Anderson, T. H. (1985) Producing 'Considerate' Expository Text: or easy reading is damned hard writing. *Journal of Curriculum Studies*, 17, 247–74. **424**

Aronson, E. and Carlsmith, J. M. (1986) Experimentation in Social Psychology. In G. Lindzey and E. Aronson (eds), *Handbook of Social Psychology*, 2nd edn. Reading, Mass.: Addison-Wesley. **81**

Asch, S. E. (1956) Studies of Independence and Conformity, I: a minority of one against a unanimous majority. *Psychological Monographs*, 70, 9, no. 416. **81**

Atkinson, P. and Delamont, S. (1985) Bread and Dreams or Bread and Circuses: a critique of 'case study' research in education. In M. Shipman (ed.), *Educational Research, Principles, Policies and Practices*. London: Falmer. **373, 440**

Backett, K. (1990) Image and reality: health-enhancing behaviours in middle-class families. *Health Education Journal*, 49, 61–3. **230**

Bakeman, R. and Gottman, J. M. (1986) *Observing Interaction: an introduction to sequential analysis*. Cambridge: Cambridge University Press. **193, 206, 220, 221, 223**

Baker, T. L. (1988) *Doing Social Research*. New York: McGraw-Hill. **137, 203, 242, 282**

Bannister, D. and Mair, J. M. M. (1968) *The Evaluation of Personal Constructs*. New York: Academic. **288**

Barber, T. X. (1976) *Pitfalls in Human Research: ten pivotal points*. Oxford: Pergamon. **81**

Bargar, R. R. and Duncan, J. K. (1982) Cultivating Creative Endeavour in Doctoral Research. *Journal of Higher Education*, 53, 1–31. **62**

Barley, N. (1989) *Not a Hazardous Sport*. London: Penguin. **199**

Barlow, D. H., Hayes, S. C. and Nelson, R. O. (1984) *The Scientist Practitioner: research and accountability in clinical and educational settings*. Oxford: Pergamon. **7, 109, 114, 206, 270, 351, 433, 446**

Barnett, V. and Lewis, T. (1984) *Outliers in Statistical Data*, 2nd edn. Chichester: Wiley. **325**

Barrett, F. J. and Cooperrider, D. L. (1990) Generative Metaphor Intervention: a new approach for working with systems divided by conflict and caught in defensive perceptions. *Journal of Applied Behavioural Science*, 26, 219–39. **53**

Barton, E. M., Baltes, M. M. and Orzech, M. J. (1980) Etiology of Dependence in Older Nursing Home Residents during Morning Care: the role of staff behaviors. *Journal of Personality and Social Psychology*, 38, 423–31. **214**

Barzun, J. and Graff, H. F. (1977) *The Modern Researcher*. New York: Harcourt Brace Jovanovich. **272, 426**

Beaumont, J. G. and French, C. C. (1987) A Clinical Field Study of Eight Automated Psychometric Procedures: the Leicester/DHSS project. *International Journal of Man-Machine Studies*, 26, 661–82. **266**

Becher, T. (1990) Physicists on Physics. *Studies in Higher Education*, 15, 3–20. **58**

Becker, H. S. (1979) Do Photographs Tell the Truth? In T. D. Cook and C. S. Reichardt (eds), *Qualitative and Quantitative Methods in Evaluation Research*. Newbury Park and London: Sage. **384**

Becker, H. S. and Geer, B. (1960) Participant Observation: the analysis of qualitative field data. In R. N. Adams and J. J. Preiss (eds), *Human Organisation Research: field relations and techniques*. Homewood, Ill.: Dorsey Press. **402**

Bell, C. and Newby, H. (1977) *Doing Sociological Research*. London: Allen & Unwin. **295**

Bell, G. H. (1985) Can Schools Develop Knowledge of their Practice? *School Organisation*, 5, 175–84. **373, 439**

Bennett, H. L. (1983) Remembering Drink Orders: the memory skills of cocktail waitresses. *Human Learning*, 2, 157–69. **14**

Bennis, W. G., Benne, K. P. and Chin, R. (1985) *The Planning of Change*, 4th edn. New York: Holt, Rinehart and Winston. **435**

Berelson, B. (1952) *Content Analysis in Communications Research*. New York: Free Press. **277**

Bergin, A. and Strupp, H. (1972) *Changing Frontiers in the Science of Psychotherapy*. Chicago: Aldine. **433**

Berk, R. A. and Rossi, P. H. (1990) *Thinking about Program Evaluation*. Newbury Park and London: Sage. **183, 184, 435**

Bhaskar, R. (1978) *A Realist Theory of Science*, 2nd edn. Brighton: Harvester. **80**

Bickman, L. (ed.) (1980) *Applied Social Psychology Annual*, vol. 1. Newbury Park and London: Sage. **11**

Birney, B. A. (1988) Brookfield Zoo's 'Flying Walk' Exhibit: formative evaluation aids in the development of an interactive exhibit in an informal learning setting. *Environment and Behavior*, 20, 416–34. **179**

Blackwell (1991) *Guide for Authors*, 2nd edn. Oxford: Blackwell. **426**

Blaikie, N. W. H. (1991) A Critique of the Use of Triangulation in Social Research. *Quality and Quantity*, 25, 115–36. **290**

Blalock, H. M. (1964) *Causal Inferences in Nonexperimental Research*. Chapel Hill: University of North Carolina Press. **79**

Blurton Jones, N. (ed.) (1972) *Ethological Studies of Child Behaviour*. Cambridge: Cambridge University Press. **206**

Boehm, V. R. (1980) 'Research in the Real World' – a conceptual model. *Personnel Psychology*, 33, 495–503. **452**

Bogdan, R. C. and Biklen, S. K. (1982) *Qualitative Research for Education: an introduction to theory and methods*, 2nd edn. Boston: Allyn and Bacon. **384**

Bourgue, L. B. and Back, K. W. (1982) Time Sampling as a Field Technique. In R. G. Burgess (ed.), *Field Research: a sourcebook and field manual*. London: Allen & Unwin. **254**

Box, G. E. P. and Jenkins, G. M. (1976) *Time-Series Analysis: forecasting and control*. San Francisco: Holden-Day. **366**

Boyle, C. (1986) *Statistics with your Microcomputer*. London: Macmillan. **137**

Bradburn, N. and Sudman, S. (1979) *Improving Interview Method and Questionnaire Design*. San Francisco: Jossey-Bass. **241**

Bradford, R. (1990) The Importance of Psychosocial Factors in Understanding Child Distress during Routine X-ray Procedures. *Journal of Child Psychology and Psychiatry*, 31, 973–82. **291**

Brause, R. S. (1991) Hypothesis Generating Studies in Your Classroom. In R. Brause and J. S. Mayher (eds), *Search and Research: what the inquiring teacher needs to know*. London: Falmer. **148**

Brenner, M. (1978) Interviewing: the social phenomenology of a research instrument. In M. Brenner, P. Marsh and M. Brenner (eds), *The Social Contexts of Method*. London: Croom Helm. **231**

Brewer, J. and Hunter, A. (1989) *Multimethod Research: a synthesis of styles*. Newbury Park and London: Sage. **290**

British Psychological Society (1991) *Code of Conduct, Ethical Principles and Guidelines*. Leicester: BPS (mimeo). **29**

British Psychological Society (1992) The Late Sir Cyril Burt: Statement. *The Psychologist*, 15, 147. **414**

British Sociological Association (1989a) *BSA Guidelines on Anti-Sexist Language*. London: BSA (mimeo). **63**

British Sociological Association (1989b) *Anti-Racist Language: guidance for good practice*. London: BSA (mimeo). **64**

Broad, W. and Wade, N. (1985) *Betrayers of the Truth: fraud and deceit in science.* Oxford: Oxford University Press. 414

Bromley, D. B. (1977) *Personality Description in Ordinary Language.* Chichester: Wiley. 375

Bromley, D. B. (1986) *The Case-study Method in Psychology and Related Disciplines.* Chichester: Wiley. 51, 56, 372, 375, 376

Bronfenbrenner, U. (1977) Toward an Experimental Ecology of Human Development. *American Psychologist*, 32, 513–31. 8

Bronson, D. E., Pelz, D. C. and Trzinski, E. (1988) *Computerizing Your Agency's Information System.* Newbury Park and London: Sage. 284

Brown, I., Berg, I., Hullin, R. and McGuire, R. (1990) Are Interim Care Orders Necessary to Improve School Attendance in Truants Taken to Juvenile Court? *Educational Review*, 42, 231–45. 86

Bryman, A. (1988a) *Quality and Quantity in Social Research.* London: Unwin Hyman. 6, 20, 303

Bryman, A. (ed.) (1988b) *Doing Research in Organisations.* London: Routledge. 295

Bryman, A. (1989) *Research Methods and Organisation Studies.* London: Unwin Hyman. 80, 124, 143, 212, 254, 282

Bryman, A. and Cramer, D. (1990) *Quantitative Data Analysis for Social Scientists.* London: Routledge. 310, 313, 349, 350, 365

Buchanan, D. A. and Boddy, D. (1982) Advanced Technology and the Quality of Working Life: the effects of word processing on video typists. *Journal of Occupational Psychology*, 55, 1–11. 294

Buchanan, D., Boddy, D. and McCalman, J. (1988) Getting In, Getting On, Getting Out and Getting Back. In A. Bryman (ed.), *Doing Research in Organisations.* London: Routledge. 294, 296

Bulmer, M. (1986) *Social Science and Social Policy.* London: Allen & Unwin. 83

Burgess, R. G. (1981) Keeping a Research Diary. *Cambridge Journal of Education*, 11, 75–83. 254

Burgess, R. G. (1982) *Field Research: a sourcebook and field manual.* London: Allen & Unwin. 144

Burgess, R. G. (1983) *Experiencing Comprehensive Education: a study of comprehensive education.* London: Methuen. 200, 201

Burgess, R. G. (1984a) *In the Field: an introduction to field research.* London: Allen & Unwin. 40

Burgess, R. G. (ed.) (1984b) *The Research Process in Educational Settings: ten case studies.* London: Falmer. 295

Buros, O. K. (1978) *The VIIth Mental Measurement Year Book.* Highland Park, NJ: Gryphon Press. 266

Byrne, D. (1961) Anxiety and the Experimental Arousal of Affiliation Need. *Journal of Abnormal Social Psychology*, 63, 660–2. 13

Caetano, R., Suzman, R. M., Rosen, D. H. and Voorhees-Rosen, D. J. (1983) The Shetland Islands: longitudinal changes in alcohol consumption in a changing environment. *British Journal of Addiction*, 78, 21–36. 119

Cairns, R. B. and Green, J. A. (1979) How to Assess Personality and Social Patterns: observations or ratings? In R. B. Cairns (ed.) *The Analysis of Social Interactions: methods, issues and illustrations.* Hillsdale, NJ: Laurence Erlbaum. 193

Campbell, D. T. (1969) Reforms as Experiments. *American Psychologist*, 24, 409–29. 74, 83, 119

Campbell, D. T. (1989) Foreword. In R. K. Yin, *Case Study Research: design and methods*, 2nd edn. Beverly Hills: Sage. 47, 60, 372

Campbell, D. T. and Stanley, J. C. (1963) Experimental and Quasi-Experimental Designs for Research on Teaching. In N. L. Gage (ed.), *Handbook of Research on Teaching*. Chicago: Rand McNally. Also published separately as *Experimental and Quasi-experimental Designs for Research on Teaching*. Chicago: Rand McNally. **3, 46, 56, 69, 70, 403**

Campbell, D. T. and Stanley, J. C. (1966) *Experimental and Quasi-Experimental Designs for Research*. Chicago: Rand McNally. **98**

Campbell, J. T., Daft, R. L. and Hulin, C. L. (1982) *What to Study: generating and developing research questions*. Newbury Park and London: Sage. **25, 26**

Caputo, R. K. (1988) *Management and Information Systems in Human Services*. New York: Haworth. **284**

Carlisle, J. (1990) The Rights of Animals: an interview with Ann S. *Changes*, 8, 190–7. **242**

Carney, T. F. (1973) *Content Analysis*. Winnipeg: University of Manitoba Press. **275**

Carr, W. and Kemmis, S. (1986) *Becoming Critical*. London: Falmer. **7, 59, 439**

Chalmers, A. F. (1982) *What is this Thing Called Science?* 2nd edn. Milton Keynes: Open University Press. **57, 59**

Charmaz, K. C. (1975) The Coroner's Strategies for Announcing Death. *Urban Life*, 4, 296–316. **13**

Child, D. (1990) *The Essentials of Factor Analysis*, 2nd edn. London: Cassell. **350**

Chisholm, L. (1990) Action Research: some methodological and political considerations. *British Educational Research Journal*, 16, 249–57. **65**

Clegg, S. (1985) Feminist Methodology – Fact or Fiction. *Quality and Quantity*, 19, 83–97. **289**

Cleveland, W. S. (1985) *The Elements of Graphing Data*. Monterey, Cal. Wadsworth. **325**

Cliff, D. R., Sparks, G. and Gibbs, G. R. (n.d.) Looking for Work in Kirklees: a study of the experience of unemployment in Kirklees MBC. Huddersfield, W. Yorks: The Polytechnic in collaboration with the Policy and Performance Review Unit, Kirklees MBC. **240**

Cohen, J. (1977) *Statistical Power Analysis for the Behavioral Sciences*. New York: Academic. **137**

Cohen, L. H. (1976) Clinician's Utilisation of Research Findings. *JSAS Catalog of Selected Documents in Psychology*, 6, 116. **433**

Cohen, L. H. (1979) The Research Readership and Information Source Reliance of Clinical Psychologists. *Professional Psychology*, 10, 760–86. **433**

Cohen, L. and Manion, L. (1989) *Research Methods in Education*, 3rd edn. London: Routledge. **229, 233, 241, 439**

Collier, J. and Collier, M. (1986) *Visual Anthropology: photography as a research method*. Albuquesque: University of New Mexico Press. **384**

Conrad, P. and Reinharz, S. (1985) Special Issue on Computers and Qualitative Data. *Qualitative Sociology*, 7, Summer. **406**

Converse, J. M. and Presser, S. (1986) *Survey Questions: handcrafting the standardized questionnaire*. Newbury Park and London: Sage. **249**

Cook, T. D., Appleton, H., Conner, R., Schaffer, A., Tamkin, G. and Weber, S. J. (1975) *'Sesame Street' Revisited: a case study in evaluation research*. New York: Russell Sage Foundation. **366**

Cook, T. D. and Campbell, D. T. (1979) *Quasi-Experimentation: design and analysis issues for field settings*. Chicago: Rand McNally. **46, 56, 70, 71, 77, 96, 97, 98, 119, 120**

Cook, T. D. and Reichardt, C. S. (1979) (eds) *Qualitative and Quantitative Methods in Evaluation Research*. Newbury Park and London: Sage. **304**

Cooper, H. M. (1989) *Integrating Research: a guide for literature reviews*, 2nd edn. Newbury Park and London: Sage. **24**

Cooperrider, D. L. and Srivastva, S. (1987) Appreciative Inquiry into Organizational Life. In W. A. Pasmore and R. W. Woodman (eds), *Research in Organizational Change and Development*, vol. 1. Greenwich, Conn: JAI. **53**

Coxon, T. (1988) 'Something Sensational': the sexual diary as a tool for mapping detailed sexual behavior. *Sociological Review*, 36, 353–67. **254**

Crain, R. L. and Mahard, R. E. (1983) The Effect of Research Methodology on Desegregation-achievement Studies – a meta-analysis. *American Journal of Sociology*, 88, 839–54. **289**

Cressey, D. R. (1953) *Other People's Money: a study in the social psychology of embezzlement*. New York: Free Press. **380**

Croll, P. (1986) *Systematic Classroom Observation*. London: Falmer. **210**

Cronbach, L. J. (1982) *Designing Evaluations of Educational and Social Programs*. San Francisco: Jossey-Bass. **62, 171, 177**

Dane, F. C. (1990) *Research Methods*. Pacific Grove: Brooks/Cole. **266**

Dawes, R. M. and Smith, T. L. (1985) Attitude and Opinion Measurement. In G. Lindzey and E. Aronson (eds), *The Handbook of Social Psychology*, 3rd edn. New York: Random House. **262**

Day, R. A. (1983) *How to Write and Publish a Scientific Paper*, 2nd edn. Philadelphia: ISI Press. **413, 426**

Delamont, S. (1992) *Fieldwork in Educational Settings: methods, pitfalls and perspectives*. London: Falmer. **376**

Delbecq, A. L., Van de Ven, A. H. and Gustafson, D. H. (1975) *Graph Techniques for Program Planning*. Chicago: Scott Foresman. **27**

Denzin, N. K. (ed.) (1970) *Sociological Methods*. Chicago: Aldine. **201**

Denzin, N. K. (1988) *The Research Act: a theoretical introduction to sociological methods*, 3rd edn. Englewood Cliffs, NJ: Prentice-Hall. **290, 380, 401**

Denzin, N. K. (1989) *Interpretive Interactionism*. Newbury Park and London: Sage. **405**

DeProspero, A. and Cohen, S. (1979) Inconsistent Visual Analysis of Intrasubject Data. *Journal of Applied Behavior Analysis*. 12, 573–9. **367**

Dhooper, S. S., Royle, D. D. and Wolfe, L. C. (1990) Does Social Work Education Make a difference? *Social Work*, 35, 57–61. **117**

Diaper, G. (1990) A Comparative Study of Paired-reading Techniques Using Parents as Tutors to Second Year Junior School Children. *Child Language Teaching and Training*, 6, 13–24. **47**

Ehrenfeld, D. (1978) *The Arrogance of Humanism*. Oxford: Oxford University Press. **57**

Eichler, M. (1980) *The Double Standard: a feminist critique of feminist social science*. London: Croom Helm. **63**

Eichler, M. (1988) *Nonsexist Research Methods: a practical guide*. London: Unwin Hyman. **63, 64, 65, 66**

Elashoff, J. D. and Snow, R. E. (1971) *Pygmalion Reconsidered*. Belmont, Ca: C.A. Jones. **434**

Elliott, J. (1982) *Action Research: a framework for self-evaluation in schools*. Working Paper no. 1: Teacher-Pupil Interaction and the Quality of Learning. London: Schools Council. **378, 440**

Elliott, J. (1989) Knowledge, Power and Teacher Appraisal. In Carr, W. (ed.), *Quality in Teaching: arguments for a reflective profession*. London: Falmer. **439**

Evaluation Research Society (1980) *Standards for Evaluation*. Washington, DC: ERS. **178**

Evans, J., Everard, B., Friend, J., Glaser, A., Norwich, B. and Welton, J. (1989) *Developing Services for children with Special Educational Needs*. London: HMSO. **393, 396**

Everitt, B. S. (1980) *Cluster Analysis*, 2nd edn. London: Heinemann. **346**

Eysenck, H. J. and Crown, S. (1949) An Experimental Study in Opinion-Attitude Methodology. *International Journal of Opinion and Attitude Research*, 3, 47–86. **261**

Fee, E. (1983) Women's Nature and Scientific Objectivity. In M. Lowe and R. Hubbard (eds), *Women's Nature in Rationalisations of Inequality*. Oxford: Pergamon. **65**

Feldman, D. S., Gagnon, J., Hofmann, R. and Simpson, J. (1991) *Statview II: Statview SE + Graphics*, 5th edn. Berkeley: Abacus Concepts, Inc. **310**

Festinger, L. Riecken, H. W. and Schachter, S. (1956) *When Prophecy Fails*. New York: Harper and Row. **196**

Fetterman, D. M. (1989) *Ethnography Step by Step*. Newbury Park and London: Sage. **148, 193, 274, 373, 374, 384, 390, 394**

Feyerabend, P. K. (1975) *Against Method: an outline of an anarchistic theory of knowledge*. London: New Left Books. **58**

Fibel, B. and Hale, W. D. (1978) The Generalized Expectancy for Success Scale – a new measure. *Journal of Consulting and Clinical Psychology*, 4, 924–31. **259**

Fielding, N. G. and Fielding, J. L. (eds) (1986) *Linking Data*. Newbury Park and London. **304**

Fienberg, S. E. (1977) Next Steps in Qualitative Data Collection. *Anthropology and Education Quarterly*, 8, 50–7. **45**

Fisher, R. A. (1935) *The Design of Experiments*. Edinburgh: Oliver and Boyd. **46**

Flanders, N. (1970) *Analyzing Teaching Behavior*. New York: Wiley. **210, 211**

Fletner, R. (1991) *Science, Ideology and the Media: the Cyril Burt scandal*. New York: Transaction. **413**

Fliess, J. L. (1981) *Statistical Methods for Rates and Proportions*. New York: Wiley. **223**

Folkins, C. H. (1970) Temporal Factors and the Cognitive Mediators of Stress Reaction. *Journal of Personality and Social Psychology*, 14, 173–84. **13**

Fowler, H. W. (1983) *A Dictionary of Modern English Usage*, 2nd revised edn. Oxford: Oxford University Press. **426**

Foxen, T. and McBrien, J. (1981) *The EDY Course for Mental Handicap Practitioners*. Manchester: Manchester University Press. **436, 458**

Frank, G. and VanderBurgh, R. M. (1986) Cross-cultural Use of Life History Methods in Gerontology. In C. L. Fry and J. Keith (eds), *New Methods for Old Age Research: strategies for studying diversity*. Bergin and Garvey. **382**

Freeman, D. (1984) *Margaret Mead and Samoa*. London: Penguin. **404**

French, C. (1990) Computer-assisted Assessment. In J. R. Beech and L. Harding (eds), *Testing People*. Windsor, Berks: NFER-Nelson. **266**

Freudenberg, N. (1990) Developing a New Agenda for the evaluation of AIDS Education. *Health Education Research*, 5, 295–8. **171**

Fried, M. L. and DeFazio, V. J. (1974) Territoriality and Boundary Conflicts in the Subway. *Psychiatry*, 37, 47–59. **13**

Fullan, M. (1982) *The Meaning of Educational Change.* New York: Columbia University Press. **435, 442, 443**

Fullan, M. (1991) *The New Meaning of Educational Change,* 2nd edn. London: Cassell. **442**

Galton, M. J. (1978) *British Mirrors: a collection of classroom observation systems.* Leicester: University of Leicester School of Education. **210**

Garrison, J. W. (1986) Some Principles of Post-positivistic Philosophy of Science. *Educational Research,* 15, 12–18. **59**

Gash, S. (1989) *Effective Literature Searching for Students.* Aldershot: Gower. **24**

Geertz, C. (1973) *The Interpretation of Cultures.* New York: Basic Books. **383, 405**

Gibbs, G. (1991) *The Statistical Analysis of Data Using Statview: introductory manual.* Huddersfield: Huddersfield Polytechnic (mimeo). **310**

Gibbs, G. (n.d.) *Consumer Behaviour and Green Attitudes.* Questionnaire, Huddersfield, W. Yorks: The Polytechnic (mimeo). **244**

Glaser, B. G. (1978) *Theoretical Sensitivity: advances in the methodology of grounded theory.* Mill Valley, Ca: Sociology Press. **386, 387**

Glaser, B. and Strauss, A. (1967) *The Discovery of Grounded Theory.* Chicago: Aldine. **142**

Glass, G. V., Willson, V. L. and Gottman, J. M. (1975) *The Design and Analysis of Time-Series Experiments.* Boulder, Col.: Colorado Associated University Press. **366**

Glassner, B. and Moreno, J. D. (eds) (1989) *The Qualitative–Quantitative Distinction in the Social Sciences.* Dordrecht: Kluwer. **303**

Glueck, W. F. and Jauch, L. R. (1975) Sources of Research Ideas among Productive Scholars. *Journal of Higher Education,* 46, 103–14. **21**

Goetz, J. P. and LeCompte, M. D. (1981) Ethnographic Research and the Problem of Data Reduction. *Anthropology and Education Quarterly,* 12, 51–70. **373**

Gold, R. L. (1958) Roles in Sociological Field Observations. *Social Forces,* 36, 217–23. Reprinted in G. J. McCall and J. L. Simmons (eds) (1969), *Issues in Participant Observation: a text and reader.* Reading, Mass.: Addison-Wesley. **198**

Goldsmith, W. and Clutterbuck, P. (1984) *The Winning Streak.* London: Penguin. **432**

Goodlad, J. (1975) *The Dynamics of Educational Change: towards responsive schools.* New York: McGraw-Hill. **438**

Gorsuch, J. (1983) *Factor Analysis.* Hillsdale, NJ: Laurence Erlbaum. **350**

Gottschalk, L., Kluckhohn, C. and Angell, R. (1945) *The Use of Personal Documents in History, Anthropology and Sociology.* New York: Social Science Research Council. **273**

Gowers, E. (1986) *The Complete Plain Words,* 3rd edn. London: HMSO. **426**

Grady, K. E. and Wallston, B. S. (1988) *Research in Health Care Settings.* Newbury Park and London: Sage. **300**

Green, B. L. et al. (1990) Buffalo Creek Survivors in the Second Decade: comparison with unexposed and non-litigant groups. *Journal of Applied Social Psychology,* 20, 1033–50. **119**

Greenhouse, S. W. and Geisser, S. (1959) On Methods in the Analysis of Profile Data. *Psychometrika,* 24, 95–112. **366**

Gross, N., Giacquinta, J. and Bernstein, M. (1971) *Implementing Organizational Innovations: a sociological analysis of planned educational change.* New York: Basic Books. **435**

Grusky, O. (1963) Managerial Succession and Organisational effectiveness. *American Journal of Sociology*, 69, 21–31. **282**

Guba, E. G. (1981) Criteria for Assessing the Trustworthiness of Naturalistic Inquiries. *Educational Communication and Technology Journal*, 29, 75–92. **405**

Guba, E. G. and Lincoln, Y. S. (1981) *Effective Evaluation.* San Francisco: Jossey-Bass. **404**

Gullan, E., Glendon, A. I., Matthews, G., Davies, D. R. and Debney, L. M. (1990) The Stress of Driving: a diary study. *Work and Stress*, 4, 7–16. **254**

Guttman, L. (1944) A Basis for Scaling Qualitative Data. *American Sociological Review*, 9, 139–50. **261**

Haas, J. (1977) Learning Real Feelings: a study of high steel ironworkers' reactions to fear and danger. *Sociology of Work Occupations*, 4, 147–70. **13**

Hahn, C. (1975) Eliminating Sexism from the Schools: an application of planned change. *Social Education*, 29, 134. **435**

Hakel, M. D., Sorcher, M., Beek, M. and Moses, J. L. (1982) *Making it Happen: designing research with implementation in mind.* Newbury Park and London: Sage. **451, 454, 455**

Hakim, C. (1982) *Secondary Analysis in Social Research: a guide to data sources and methods with examples.* London: Allen & Unwin. **282**

Hakim, C. (1987) *Research Design: strategies and choices in the design of social research.* London: Allen & Unwin. **10, 38, 126, 131, 147, 282, 283, 302, 464, 467**

Hall, G. (1975) Levels of Use of the Innovation: a framework for analysing innovation and adaptation. *Journal of Teacher Education*, 26, 52–6. **435**

Hall, G. and Loucks, S. (1977) *A Developmental Model for Determining Whether the Treatment is Actually Implemented.* Research and Development Center for Teacher Education, University of Texas. **442**

Halpern, E. S. (1983) *Auditing Naturalistic Inquiries: the development and application of a model.* Unpublished doctoral dissertation, Indiana University. **406**

Hammersley, M. (1989) *The Dilemma of Qualitative Method: Herbert Blumer and the Chicago tradition.* London: Routledge. **200, 303**

Hammersley, M. and Atkinson, P. (1983) *Ethnography: principles in practice.* London: Tavistock. **378**

Haney, C., Banks, C. and Zimbardo, P. (1973) Interpersonal Dynamics in a Simulated Prison. *International Journal of Criminological Penology*, 1, 69–97. **286**

Hannon, P. and Tizard, B. (1987) Parental Involvement – A No-score Draw? *Times Educational Supplement*, 3 April 1987. **48**

Hanson, D. J. (1980) Relationship between Methods and Judges in Attitude Behavior Research. *Psychology*, 17, 11–13. **126, 191**

Harding, S. (ed.) (1987) *Feminism and Methodology.* Milton Keynes: Open University Press. **63**

Harding, S. and Hintikha, M. B. (1983) *Discovering Reality: feminist perspectives on epistemology, metaphysics, methodology and philosophy of science.* Dordrecht: Reidel. **63**

Harlen, W. and Elliott, J. (1982) A Checklist for Planning or Reviewing an Evaluation. In R. McCormick (ed.), *Calling Education to Account.* London: Heinemann. **182**

Harré, R. (1981) The Positivist–Empiricist Approach and its Alternative. In P. Reason and J. Rowan (eds), *Human Inquiry: a sourcebook of new paradigm research.* New York: Wiley. **62**

Harré, R. and Secord, P. F. (1972) *The Explanation of Social Behaviour.* Oxford: Blackwell. **286**

Hartley, J. (1985) *Designing Instructional Text,* 2nd edn. London: Kogan Page. **425, 426**

Hartley, J. (1989) Tools for Evaluating Text. In J. Hartley and A. Branthwaite (eds), *The Applied Psychologist.* Milton Keynes: Open University Press. **427**

Hartley, J. and Branthwaite, A. (1989) The Psychologist as Wordsmith: a questionnaire study of the writing strategies of productive British psychologists. *Higher Education,* 18, 423–52. **425**

Hayano, D. M. (1980) Communicative Competency Among Poker Players. *Journal of Communication,* 30, 113–20. **13**

Hayes, J. R. and Flower, L. S. (1986) Writing Research and the Writer. American *Psychologist,* 41, 1106–13. **424**

Hays, W. L. (1981) *Statistics,* 3rd edn. New York: Holt, Rinehart and Winston. **351, 352**

Hearnshaw, L. S. (1979) *Cyril Burt: Psychologist.* London: Hodder and Stoughton. **414**

Heclo, H. and Wildavsky, A. (1981) *The Private Government of Public Money: community and policy inside British politics,* 2nd edn. London: Macmillan. **147**

Heller, F. (ed.) (1986) *The Use and Abuse of Social Science.* Newbury Park and London: Sage. **14, 16, 432, 442, 462**

Henderson, D. (1986) *Innocence and Design: the influence of economic ideas.* Oxford: Blackwell. **462**

Henry, G. T. (1990) *Practical Sampling.* Newbury Park and London: Sage. **136**

Heron, J. (1981) Philosophical Basis for a New Paradigm. In P. Reason and J. Rowan (eds), *Human Inquiry: a sourcebook of new paradigm research.* New York: Wiley. **60**

Hersen, M. and Barlow, D. H. (1976) *Single Case Experimental Designs: strategies for studying behavior change.* Oxford: Pergamon. **352, 367**

Hesse, M. (1980) *Revolutions and Reconstructions in the History of Science.* Bloomington: Indiana University Press. **59**

Hitchcock, G. and Hughes, D. (1989) *Research and the Teacher: a qualitative introduction to school-based research.* London: Routledge. **382, 393**

Hodgson, A., Clunies-Ross, L. and Hegarty, S. (1984) *Learning Together: teaching children with special educational needs in the ordinary school.* Windsor, Berks: NFER/Nelson. **125**

Hodgson, R. and Rollnick, S. (1989) More Fun, Less Stress: how to survive in research. In G. Parry and F. N. Watts (eds), *Behavioural and Mental Health Research: a handbook of skills and methods.* Hove, East Sussex: Laurence Erlbaum. **302**

Hoinville, G. and Jowell, R. (1977) *Survey Research Practice.* Aldershot: Gower. **122, 134, 232, 252**

Hoinville, G., Jowell, R. and Associates (1985) *Survey Research Practice.* London: Gower. **133**

Hollway, W. (1989) *Subjectivity and Method in Psychology: gender, meaning and science.* Newbury Park and London: Sage. **63**

Holsti, O. R. (1969) *Content Analysis for the Social Sciences and Humanities.* Reading, Mass.: Addison-Wesley. **277**

Hopkins, D. (1985) *A Teacher's Guide to Classroom Research.* Milton Keynes: Open University Press. **441**

Hornstein, H. A. (1975) Social Psychology as Social Intervention. In M. Deutsch and H.A. Hornstein (eds), *Applying Social Psychology: implications for research, practice and training*. Hillsdale, NJ: Erlbaum. **456**

House, E. (1978) Assumptions Underlying Evaluation Models. *Educational Researcher*, 7, 4–12. **176, 177**

Hovland, C. I. and Sherif, M. (1952) Judgmental Phenomena and Scales of Attitude Measurement: item displacement in Thurstone scales. *Journal of Abnormal and Social Psychology*, 47, 822–32. **261**

Howard, K. and Sharp, J. A. (1983) *The Management of a Student Research Project*. Aldershot: Gower. **24, 300**

Huff, D. (1973) *How to Lie with Statistics*. London: Penguin. **328**

Hyde-Wright, S. and Cheesman, P. (1990) Teaching Reading Vocabulary to a Language-delayed Child. *Child Language Teaching and Therapy*, 6, 1–12. **147**

Jack Roller, The and Snodgrass (1982) *The Jack Roller at Seventy: a fifty year followup*. Lexington, Mass.: Lexington Books. **147**

Jenkins, D. (1984) Chocolate Cream Soldiers: sponsorship, ethnography and sectarianism. In R. Burgess (ed.), *The Research Process in educational Settings: ten case studies*. London: Falmer. **419**

Jones, R. A. (1985) *Research Methods in the Social and Behavioral Sciences*. Sunderland, Mass.: Sinauer. **186, 199**

Joynson, R. B. (1989) *The Burt Affair*. London: Routledge. **414**

Judd, C. M., Smith, E. R. and Kidder, L. H. (1991) *Research Methods in Social Relations*, 6th edn. New York: Holt, Rinehart and Winston. **98, 185**

Jung, J. (1990) Global vs Health-specific Social Support. *Journal of Applied Social Psychology*, 20, 1103–11. **119**

Kaplan, A. (1964) *The Conduct of Inquiry: Methodology for Behavioral Science*. San Francisco: Chandler. **373, 431**

Karapin, R. S. (1986) What's the Use of Social Science? A review of the literature. In F. Heller (ed.), *The Use and Abuse of Social Science*. Newbury Park and London: Sage. **435**

Kasl, S. V., Chisholm, R. F. and Eskenazi, B. (1981) The Impact of the Accident at Three Mile Island on the Behaviour and Wellbeing of Nuclear Workers. *American Journal of Public Health*, 71, 472–95. **83**

Kazdin, A. (1982) *Single-Case Research Designs: methods for Clinical and Applied Settings*. Oxford: Oxford University Press. **114, 368**

Keller, E. F. (1985) *Reflections on Gender and Science*. New Haven, Conn.: Yale University Press. **65**

Kelly, G. A. (1970) A Brief Introduction to Personal Construct Theory. In D. Bannister (ed.), *Perspectives in Personal Construct Theory*. London: Academic. **287**

Kemmis, S. and McTaggart, R. (1981) *The Action Research Planner*. Geelong, Victoria: Deakin University Press. **34, 438**

Kennedy, M. M. (1976) Generalizing from Single Case Studies. *Evaluation Quarterly*, 3, 661–78. **405**

Kerlinger, F. (1964) *Foundations of Behavioral Research*, 3rd edn. New York: Holt, Rinehart and Winston. **124**

Kern, J. M. (1991) An Evaluation of a Novel Role Play Methodology: the standardized idiographic approach. *Behaviour Therapy*, 22, 13–29. **286**

Kets de Vries, M. F. R. (1990) The Imposter Syndrome: developmental and societal issues. *Human Relations*, 43, 667–86. **147**

Kidder, L. H. (1981) Qualitative Research and Quasi-Experimental Frameworks. In

M. B. Brewer and B. E. Collins (eds), *Scientific Enquiry and the Social Sciences.* San Francisco: Jossey-Bass. **380, 381, 382**

Kidder, L. H. and Judd, C. M. (1986) *Research Methods in Social Relations,* 5th edn. Tokyo: CBS Publishing Japan. **132**

Kiely, J. and Hodgson, G. (1990) Stress in the Prison Service: the benefits of exercise programmes. *Human Relations,* 43, 551–72. **54**

Kiernan, C. C., Reid, B. and Goldbart, J. (1988) *Foundations of Communication and Language.* Manchester: Manchester University Press. **458**

Kimmel, A. J. (1988) *Ethics and Values in Applied Social Research.* Newbury Park and London: Sage. **33**

Kinsey, A., Pomeroy, W. and Martin, C. (1953) *Sexual Behavior in the Human Female.* Philadelphia: Saunders. **4**

Kirby, S. and McKenna, K. (1989) *Experience, Research, Social Change: methods from the margins.* Toronto: Garamond. **22, 196**

Kline, P. (1990) Selecting the Best Test. In J. R. Beech and L. Harding (eds), *Testing People.* Windsor, Berks: NFER/Nelson. **266**

Kosecoff, J. and Fink, A. (1982) *Evaluation Basics: a practitioner's manual.* Newbury Park and London: Sage. **184**

Kraemer, H. C. (1981) Coping Strategies in Psychiatric Clinical Research. *Journal of Counselling and Clinical Psychology,* 49, 309–19. **137**

Krantz, J. (1990) Commentary on the Barratt and Cooperrider Article. *Journal of Applied Behavioral Science,* 26, 241–3. **53**

Kratochwill, T. R. (ed.) (1978) *Single Subject Research.* New York: Academic. **107**

Kren, G. M. (1988) Scholars and Computers. *History Microcomputer Review,* 4, 33–5. **425**

Krippendorff, K. (1980) *Content Analysis: an introduction to its methodology.* Newbury Park and London: Sage. **272, 273**

Kuhn, T. S. (1970) *The Structure of Scientific Revolutions,* 2nd edn. Chicago: Chicago University Press. **58**

Kushler, M. B. (1989) Use of Evaluation to Improve Energy Conservation Programmes: a review and case study. *Journal of Social Issues,* 45, 153–68. **171**

Lachenbruch, P. A. (1975) *Discriminant Analysis.* New York: Haffner. **347**

Lakatos, T. and Musgrave, A. (eds) (1970) *Criticism and the Growth of Knowledge.* Cambridge: Cambridge University Press. **58**

Lamal, P. A. (1991) Psychology as Common-sense: the case of findings concerning work motivation and satisfaction. *Psychological Science,* 2, 129–30. **9**

Lancioni, G. E. (1982) Normal Children as Tutors to Teach Social Responses to Withdrawn Mentally Retarded Schoolmates: training, maintenance, and generalization. *Journal of Applied Behavior Analysis,* 15, 17–40. **113**

Lazarsfeld, P. F. and Barton, A. (1955) Some Functions of Qualitative Analysis in Sociological Research. *Sociologica,* 1, 324–61. **402**

Lazarsfeld, P. F., Pasanella, A. K. and Rosenberg, M. (1972) *Continuities in the Language of Social Research.* New York: Free Press. **400**

LeCompte, M. D. and Goetz, J. P. (1982) Problems of Reliability and Valdity in Ethnographic Research. *Review of Educational Research,* 52, 31–60. **72, 73**

Leedy, P. D. (1989) *Practical Research: planning and design.* 4th edn. New York: Macmillan. **464, 468**

Lemon, N. (1973) *Attitudes and their Measurement.* London: Batsford. **256, 260, 262**

Levi, M. (1981) *The Phantom Capitalists.* London: Heinemann. **147**

Levy-Leboyer, C. (1986) Applying Psychology or Applied Psychology. In F. Heller (ed.), *The Use and Abuse of Social Science*. Newbury and London: Sage. **432**

Lewin, K. (1946) Action Research and Minority Problems. *Journal of Social Issues*, 2, 34–6. **286, 438**

Lightfoot, S. L. (1963) *The Good High School: portraits of character and culture*. New York: Basic Books. **147**

Likert, R. (1932) A Technique for the Measurement of Attitudes. *Archives of Psychology*, no. 140. **256**

Lincoln, Y. S. and Guba, E. G. (1985) *Naturalistic Inquiry*. Newbury Park and London: Sage. **59, 60, 61, 195, 297, 373, 381, 399, 403, 405, 406, 416**

Lindblom, C. E. and Cohen, D. K. (1979) *Usable Knowledge: social science and social problem-solving*. New Haven, Conn.: Yale University Press. **4, 126, 460**

Lindesmith, A. (1968) *Addiction and Opiates*. Chicago: Aldine. **380**

Linsell, S. and Robson, C. (1987) *Study of One Year's Intake at Huddersfield Polytechnic: their qualifications and progress*. Huddersfield: Huddersfield Polytechnic (mimeo). **313**

Lippitt, G. and Lippitt, R. (1978) *The Consulting Process in Action*. La Jolla, Cal.: University Associates Inc. **456, 457**

Lipsey, M. W. (1989) *Design Sensitivity: statistical power for experimental research*. Newbury Park and London: Sage. **137**

Littlewood, J., Hardiker, P., Pedley, J. and Dilley, D. (1990) Coping with Home Dialysis. *Human Relations*, 43, 103–11. **55**

Locke, E. A. (1986) *Generalizing from Laboratory to Field Settings*. Lexington, Mass.: Lexington Books. **82**

Locke, E. A. and Latham, G. P. (1991) The Fallacies of Commonsense 'Truths'. A Reply to Lamal. *Psychological Science*, 2, 131–2. **9**

Lofland, J. (1971) *Analysing Social Settings*. Belmont, Cal.: Wadsworth. **199, 400, 416**

Lofland, J. and Lofland, L. H. (1984) *Analyzing Social Settings: a guide to qualitative observation and analysis*, 2nd edn. Belmont, Cal.: Wadsworth. **22, 203, 297, 376, 388**

Long, J. S. (1983) *Confirmatory Factor Analysis*. Newbury Park and London: Sage. **349**

Lovie, A. D. (1986) Getting New Statistics into Today's Crowded Syllabuses. In A. D. Lovie (ed.), *New Developments in Statistics for Psychology and the Social Sciences*, vol. 1. London: Methuen. **317**

Lovie, A. D. and Lovie, P. (1991) Graphical Methods for Exploring Data. In P. Lovie and A. D. Lovie (eds), *New Developments in Statistics for Psychology and the Social Sciences*, vol. 2. London: Routledge. **317**

Lovie, P. (1986) Identifying Outliers. In A. D. Lovie (ed.) *New Developments in Statistics for Psychology and the Social Sciences*, vol. 1. London: Methuen. **327**

Luce, R. D., Smelser, N. J. and Gerstein, D. R. (1990) *Leading Edges in Social and Behavioral Science*. New York: Russell Sage. **78**

Lynch, M. (1985) *Art and Artifact in Laboratory Science: a study of shop work and shop talk in a research laboratory*. London: Routledge & Kegan Paul. **2**

Lynd, R. S. and Lynd, H. M. (1929) *Middlestown: a study in modern American Culture*. New York: Harcourt Brace Jovanovich. **418**

McBrien, J. and Foxen, T. (1981) *The EDY Course for Mental Handicap Practitioners: the instructor's handbook*. Manchester: Manchester University Press. **436, 458**

McCracken, G. (1988) *The Long Interview*. Newbury Park and London: Sage. **242**

McDonald, B. (1974) Evaluation and the Control of Education. In R. Murphy and H. Torrance (eds) (1987), *Evaluating Education: issues and methods*. London: Harper and Row. **174, 419**

McDonald, B. and Stake, R. (1974) *The First Year of the National Development Programme in CAL from an Issues Perspective*. Norwich: CARE, University of East Anglia. **423**

McFarland, D. (1985) *Animal Behaviour, Psychobiology, Ethology and Evolution*. London: Pitman. **195**

McKillip, J. (1987) *Need Analysis: tools for the human sciences and education*. Newbury Park and London: Sage. **184**

McPhail, C. and Wohlstein, R. T. (1982) Using Film to Analyze Pedestrian Behavior. *Sociological Methods and Research*, 10, 347–75. **384**

Mahoney, M. J., Moura, N. M. and Wade, T. C. (1973) The Relative Efficiency of Self-reward, Self-punishment and Self-monitoring Techniques for Weight Loss. *Journal of Consulting and Clinical Psychology*, 40, 404–7. **270**

Malinowski, B. (1922) *Argonauts of the Western Pacific*. London: Routledge & Kegan Paul. **192**

Malinowski, B. (1935a) *Coral Gardens and their Magic*, vol. 1. London: Allen & Knwin. **192**

Malinowski, B. (1935b) *Coral Gardens and their Magic*, vol. 2. London: Allen & Knwin. **192**

Mallon, B. (1987) *An Introduction to Counselling Skills for Special Educational Needs*. Manchester: Manchester University Press. **458**

Mandelbaum, D. G. (1973) The Study of Life History. Reprinted in R.G. Burgess (ed.) (1982), *Field Research: a sourcebook and field manual*. London: Allen & Unwin. **382**

Manicas, P. T. (1987) *A History and Philosophy of the Social Sciences*. Oxford: Blackwell. **58**

Manicas, P. T. and Secord, P. J. (1983) Implications for Psychology of the New Philosophy of Science. *American Psychologist*, 38, 399–413. **58**

Manis, J. G. and Meltzer, B. N. (eds) (1967) *Symbolic Interactionism: a reader in social psychology*. Boston: Allyn and Bacon. **195**

Manstead, A. S. R. and Semin, G. R. (1988) Methodology in Social Psychology: turning ideas into action. In M. Hewstone, W. Stoebe, J-P. Codol and G. M. Stephenson (eds), *Introduction to Social Psychology*. Oxford: Blackwell. **38**

Marsh, C. (1982) *The Survey Method: the contribution of surveys to social explanation*. London: Allen & Unwin. **121**

Marsh, C. (1988) *Exploring Data: an introduction to data analysis for social scientists*. Cambridge: Polity. **275, 319, 320, 325, 329, 341**

Marshall, C. and Rossman, G. B. (1989) *Designing Qualitative Research*. Newbury Park and London: Sage. **42, 75, 405, 468**

Martin, J. (1981) A Garbage Can Model of the Psychological Research Process. *American Behavioral Scientist*, 25, 131–51. **295**

Martin, P. and Bateson, P. (1986) *Measuring Behaviour: an introductory guide*. Cambridge: Cambridge University Press. **221**

Marwick, A. (1970) *An Introduction to History*. Oxford: Oxford University Press. **272**

Marx, K. (1941) Theses on Feuerbach. In A. Engels (ed.), *Ludwig Feuerbach*. New York: International Publishers. **431**

Medawar, P. B. (1963) Is the Scientific Paper a Fraud? *The Listener*, 12 September. Reprinted in D. Edge (ed.) (1964), *Experiment*. London: BBC. **62**

Medawar, P. B. (1969) *The Art of the Soluble: creativity and originality in science*. London: Penguin. **19**

Medawar, P. B. (1979) *Advice to a Young Scientist*. New York: Harper and Row. **26**

Meddis, R. (1984) *Statistics Using Ranks: a unified approach*. Oxford: Blackwell. **331, 355**

Meehl, P. E. (1978) Theoretical Risks and Tabular Asterisks: Sir Karl, Sir Ronald, and the slow progress of soft psychology. *Journal of Consulting and Clinical Psychology*, 46, 806–35. **351**

Merton, R. K., Fiske, M. and Kendall, P. L. (1956) *The Focused Interview*. Glencoe, Ill.: Free Press. **241, 308**

Mies, M. (1983) Toward a Methodology for Feminist Research. In G. Bowles and R. D. Klein (eds), *Theories of Women's Studies*. London: Routledge & Kegan Paul. **65**

Miles, M. B. (1979) Qualitative Data as an Attractive Nuisance: the problem of analysis. *Administrative Science Quarterly*, 24, 590–601. **370**

Miles, M. B. and Huberman, A. M. (1984) *Qualitative Data Analysis: a sourcebook of new methods*. Newbury Park and London: Sage. **51, 75, 149, 155, 156, 157, 160, 372, 376, 384, 385, 388, 390, 392, 393, 394, 399, 400, 402**

Miller, E. (1989) Preparing a Research Project. In G. Parry and F. N. Watts (eds), *Behavioural and Mental Health Research: a handbook of skills and methods*. Hove, E. Sussex: Laurence Erlbaum. **77**

Milroy, L. (1980) *Language and Social Networks*. Oxford: Blackwell. **287**

Mintz, N. L. (1956) Effects of Esthetic Surroundings, II: prolonged and repeated experience in a 'beautiful' and an 'ugly' room. *Journal of Psychology*, 41, 459–66. **82**

Mintzberg, H. (1973) *The Nature of Managerial Work*. New York: Harper and Row. **212**

Monk, A. (1991) *Exploring Statistics with Minitab: a workbook for the behavioural sciences*. Chichester: Wiley. **310**

Moser, C. A. and Kalton, G. (1971) *Survey Methods in Social Investigation*. Aldershot: Gower. **41**

Moses, D., Hegarty, S. and Jowett, S. (1988) *Supporting Ordinary Schools: LEA initiatives*. Windsor: NFER Nelson. **125**

Mullen, B., Copper, C. and Driskell, J. E. (1990) Jaywalking as a Function of Model Behavior. *Personality and Social Psychology Bulletin*, 16, 320–30. **288**

Mullen, E., Dumpson, J. and Associates (1972) *Evaluation of Social Interventions*. San Francisco: Jossey-Bass. **171**

Neale, J. M. and Lambert, R. M. (1986) *Science and Behavior: an introduction to methods of research*, 2nd edn. Englewood Cliffs, NJ: Prentice-Hall. **62**

Newcomb, M. D., Rabow, J., Monto, M. and Hernandez, A. C. R. (1991) Informal Drunk Driving Intervention: psychosocial correlates among young adult women and men. *Journal of Applied Psychology*, 21, 1988–2006. **51**

Newson, J. and Newson, E. (1976) Parental Roles and Social Contexts. In M. D. Shipman (ed.), *The Organisation and Impact of Social Research*. London: Routledge & Kegan Paul. **241**

Nisbet, J. and Broadfoot, P. (1980) *The Impact of Research on Policy and Practice in Education*. Aberdeen: Aberdeen University Press. **433**

Nisbet, J. D. and Watt, J. (1980) *Case Study*. Rediguide no. 26. Oxford: TRC Rediguides. **56**

Nisbett, R. and Ross, L. (eds) (1980) *Human Inference: strategies and shortcomings of social judgment*. Englewood Cliffs, NJ: Prentice-Hall. **402**

Nixon, J. (ed.) (1981) *A Teacher's Guide to Action Research: evaluation, enquiry and development in the classroom*. London: Grant McIntyre. **439**

Norris, N. (1990) *Understnding Educational Evaluation*. London: Kogan Page. **174, 439**

Oakley, A. (1981) Interviewing Women: a contradiction in terms. In H. Roberts (ed.), *Doing Feminist Research*. London: Routledge & Kegan Paul. **289**

Oliver, N. (1990) Work Rewards, Work Values and Organisational Commitment in an Employee-owned Firm: evidence from the UK. *Human Relations*, 43, 513–26. **143**

Orne, M. T. (1962) On the Social Psychology of the Psychological Experiment with Particular Reference to Demand Characteristics and their Implications. *American Psychologist*, 17, 776–83. **81**

Osborn, A. (1963) *Applied Imagination*, 3rd edn. New York: Scribners. **27**

Osgood, C. E., Suci, C. J. and Tannenbaum, P. H. (1957) *The Measurement of Meaning*. Urbana, Ill.: University of Illinois Press. **264, 265**

Oskamp, S. (1977) Methods of Studying Social Behavior. In L. S. Wrightsman (ed.), *Social Psychology*, 2nd edn. Monterey, Ca: Brooks/Cole. **191**

Owens, T. (1973) Educational Evaluation in Adversary Proceeding. In E. House (ed.), *School Evaluation: the politics and the process*. Berkeley, Ca: McCutchan. **423**

Parry, G. (1989) Writing a Research Report. In G. Parry and F. N. Watts (eds), *Behavioural and Mental Health Research: a handbook of skills and methods*. London: Laurence Erlbaum. **426, 428**

Patton, M. Q. (1981) *Creative Evaluation*. Newbury Park and London: Sage. **178**

Patton, M. Q. (1982) *Practical Evaluation*. Newbury Park and London: Sage. **175, 421**

Paul, D. and Lipham, J. (1976) Strengthening Facilitative Environments. In J. Lipham and M. Fruth (eds), *The Principal and Individually Guided Education*. Reading, Mass.: Addison-Wesley. **437**

Pearson, J. C. (1985) *Gender and Communication*. Dubuque, Iowa: Wm C Brown. **64**

Peters, T. J. and Waterman, R. H. (1982) *In Search of Excellence: lessons from America's best run companies*. New York: Harper and Row. **432**

Piaget, J. (1929) *The Child's Conception of the World*. New York: Harcourt Brace. **240**

Piaget, J. (1930) *The Child's Conception of Physical Causality*. London: Routledge & Kegan Paul. **240**

Pick, C. and Walker, R. (1976) *Other Rooms, Other Voices* (radio script). Norwich: CARE, University of East Anglia. **423**

Piliavin, I. M., Rodin, J. and Piliavin, J. A. (1969) Good Samaritanism: an underground phenomenon? *Journal of Personality and Social Psychology*, 13, 289–99. **13**

Popham, J. (1982) Melvin Belli, Beware. *Educational Researcher*, 11, 11–15. **423**

Popkewitz, T. S. (1984) *Paradigm and Ideology in Educational Research*: the social functions of the intellectual. London: Falmer. **430, 436, 440**

Potter, J. and Wetherell, M. (1987) *Discourse and Social Psychology: beyond attitudes and behavior*. Newbury Park and London: Sage. **287**

Powney, J. and Watts, M. (1987) *Interviewing in Educational Research*. London: Routledge & Kegan Paul. **228, 231, 237, 240, 242**

Prince, G. M. (1970) *The Practice of Creativity: a manual for dynamic group problem-solving*. New York: Harper and Row. **27**

Ragin, C. C. (1987) *The Comparative Method: moving beyond qualitative and quantitative strategies*. Berkeley, Cal.: University of California Press. **304**

Rapoport, R. N. (1970) Three Dilemmas in Action Research. *Human Relations*, 23, 499–513. **60, 438**

Redmond, P., Evans, P. L. C., Ireson, J. and Wedell, K. (1988) Comparing the Curriculum Development Procedures in Special MLD Schools: a systematic qualitative approach. *European Journal of Special Needs Education*, 3, 147–60. **147**

Reichardt, C. S. (1979) The Statistical Analysis of Data from Nonequivalent Group Designs. In T. D. Cook and D. T. Campbell, *Quasi-Experimentation: design and analysis issues for field settings*. Chicago: Rand McNally. **366, 367**

Reynolds, P. D. (1979) *Ethical Dilemmas and Social Science Research*. San Francisco: Jossey-Bass. **29**

Richards, T. J. (1987) *User Manual for NUDIST: a text analysis program for the social sciences*, Replee P/L, Melbourne, Australia. **390**

Roberts, H. (1981) *Doing Feminist Research*. London: Routledge. **63, 289**

Robinson, W. S. (1951) The Logical Structure of Analytic Induction. *American Sociological Review*, 16, 812–18. **201**

Robson, C. (1983) *Experiment, Design and Statistics in Psychology*, 2nd edn. London: Penguin. **310, 351**

Robson, C. (1985) Small N: Case Studies? In S. Hegarty and P. Evans (eds), *Research and Evaluation Methods in Special Education*. Windsor, Berks: NFER/Nelson. **62, 109**

Robson, C. (1987a) Applying Psychology. In A. Gale (ed.), *Position Papers: conference on the future of the psychological sciences*. Leicester: British Psychological Society. **460**

Robson, C. (1987b) Evaluation of a Self-Instructional Training Package. In J. Hogg and P. Mittler (eds), *Staff Training in Mental Handicap*. London: Croom Helm. **458**

Robson, C., Sebba, J., Mittler, P. and Davies, G. (1988) *Inservice Training and Special Educational Needs: running short school-focused courses*. Manchester: Manchester University Press. **157, 159, 182, 285, 436, 458**

Roethlisberger, F. I. and Dickson, W. T. (1939) *Management and the Worker*. Cambridge, Mass.: Harvard University Press. **84**

Rogers, C. R. (1945) The Non-directive Method as a Technique for Social Research. *American Journal of Sociology*, 50, 279–83. **240**

Rogers, C. R. (1961) *On Becoming a Person*. London: Constable. **31**

Rosenberg, M. (1968) *The Logic of Survey Analysis*. New York: Basic Books. **343**

Rosenthal, R. (1966) *Experimenter Effects in Behavioral Research*. New York: Appleton Century Crofts. **22**

Rosenthal, R. (1976) *Experimenter Effects in Behavioral Research*, revised edn. New York: Irvington. **224**

Rosenthal, R. and Jacobson, L. (1968) *Pygmalion in the Classroom*. New York: Holt, Rinehart and Winston. **433**

Rosenthal, R. and Rosnow, R. (1975) *The Volunteer Subject*. New York: Wiley. **82**

Rosenthal, R. and Rubin, D. B. (1978) Interpersonal Expectancy Effects: the first 345 studies. *Behavioral and Brain Sciences*, 3, 377–86. **82, 224, 288**

Rosenthal, R. and Rubin, D. B. (1980) Summarising 345 Studies of Interpersonal Expectancy Effects. In R. Rosenthal (ed.), *New Directions for Methodology of Social and Behavioral Science*, no. 5. San Francisco: Jossey-Bass. **288**

Ross, H. L. (1973) Law, Science and Accidents: the British Road Safety Act of 1967. *Journal of Legal Issues*, 2, 1–75. **119, 175**

Ross, H. L., Campbell, D. T. and Glass, G. V. (1970) Determining the Social Effects of a Legal Reform. *American Behavioral Scientist*, 13, 492–509. **107**

Rossi, P. H. (1980) The Presidential Address: the challenge and opportunities of applied social research. *American Sociological Review*, 45, 889–904. **11**

Rowntree Trust (n.d.) *Research and Development Programme.* York: Joseph Rowntree Memorial Trust. **418**

Rust, J. and Golombok, S. (1989) *Modern Psychometrics: the science of psychological assessment.* London: Routledge. **266, 349**

Sackett, G. P. (ed.) (1978) *Observing Behavior, vol. 2: data collection and analysis types.* Baltimore: University Park Press. **206**

Sadler, D. R. (1981) Intuitive Data Processing as a Potential Source of Bias in Educational Evaluation. *Educational Evaluation and Policy Analysis*, 3, 25–31. **375**

Sanders, C. R. (1974) Psyching Out the Crowd: folk performers and their audiences. *Urban Life Culture*, 3, 264–82. **13**

Satcher, D., Kosecoff, J. and Fink, A. (1980) Results of a Needs Assessment Strategy in Developing a Family Practice Program in an Inner-city Community. *Journal of Family Practice*, 10, 871–9. **184**

Saunders, S. (1990) An Evaluation of a Residential PSE Course for an Academic A-level Class. *Pastoral Care in Education*, 8, 22–6. **173**

Schaude, R. G. (1979) Methods of Idea Generation. In S. C. Gryskiewicz (ed.), *Creativity Week 1: 1978 proceedings.* Greensboro: Center for the Study of Industrial Innovation. **27**

Schindele, R. (1981) Methodological Problems in Rehabilitation Research. *International Journal of Rehabilitation Research*, 4, 233–48. **433**

Schon, D. A. (1979) *Metaphor and Thought.* Cambridge: Cambridge University Press. **53**

Schon, D. A. (1983) *The Reflective Practitioner.* London: Temple Smith. **447**

Schon, D. A. (1987) *Educating the Reflective Practitioner.* San Francisco: Jossey-Bass. **460**

Schutz, A. (1954) Concept and Theory Formation in the Social Sciences. *Journal of Philosophy*, 51, 257–73. **195**

Schutz, A. (1967) *The Phenomenology of the Social World.* Evanston, Ill.: Northwestern University Press. **195**

Schwab, D. P. (1985) Reviewing Empirically Based Manuscripts: Perspectives on progress. In L. L. Cummings and P. J. Frost (eds), *Publishing in the Organisational Sciences.* Homewood, Ill.: R. D. Irwin. **143**

Schwartz, P. and Lever, J. (1976) Fear and Loathing in a College Mixer. *Urban Life*, 4, 314–431. **13**

Scott, W. A. (1968) Attitude Measurement. In G. Lindzey and E. Aronson (eds), *Handbook of Social Psychology*, vol. 2, 2nd edn. New York: Addison-Wesley. **262**

Sebba, J. (1988) *The Education of People with Profound and Multiple Handicaps: resource materials for staff training.* Manchester: Manchester University Press. **458**

Shipman, M. D. (1976) *The Organisation and Impact of Social Research*. London: Routledge & Kegan Paul. **295**

Shipman, M. D. (1988) *The Limitations of Social Research*, 3rd edn. London: Longman. **62, 74, 193, 431, 433, 434**

Sidman, M. (1960) *The Tactics of Social Research*. New York: Basic Books. **69, 109, 367**

Siegel, S. and Castellan, N. J. (1988) *Nonparametric Statistics for the Behavioral Sciences*, 2nd edn. New York: McGraw-Hill. **331, 334**

Silverman, D. (1985) *Qualitative Methodology and Sociology*. Aldershot: Gower. **294**

Simon, A. and Boyer, G. (1970a) *Mirrors for Behavior*, vol. 1. Philadelphia: Research for Better Schools Inc. **210**

Simon, A. and Boyer, G. (1970b) *Mirrors for Behavior*, vol. 2. Philadelphia: Research for Better Schools Inc. **210**

Simon, A. and Boyer, G. (1974) *Mirrors for Behavior*, vol. 3. Philadelphia: Research for Better Schools Inc. **210**

Skinner, B. F. (1938) *The Behavior of Organisms: an experimental analysis*. New York: Appleton. **109**

Skinner, B. F. (1948) *Walden Two*. New York: Macmillan. **431**

Skinner, B. F. (1953) *Science and Human Behavior*. New York: Macmillan. **109**

Skinner, B. F. (1963) The Flight from the Laboratory. In M. Marx (ed.), *Theories in Contemporary Psychology*. New York: Macmillan. **80, 430**

Skinner, B. F. (1974) *About Behaviourism*. London: Cape. **109**

Skinner, C. J. (1991) Time Series. In P. Lovie and A. D. Lovie (eds), *New Developments in Statistics for Psychology and the Social Sciences*. vol. 2. London: BPS and Routledge. **105**

Smith, D. (1987) *The Everyday World as Problematic*. Toronto: University of Toronto Press. **63**

Smith, H. W. (1975) *Strategies of Social Research: the methodological imagination*. London: Prentice-Hall. **135, 208, 370**

Smith, L. and Keith, P. (1971) *Anatomy of Educational Innovation: an organisational analysis of an elementary school*. New York: Wiley. **435**

Smith, T. M. F. (1983) On the Validity of Inferences from Non-random Samples. *Journal of the Royal Statistical Society*, series A, 146, 394–403. **46, 136**

Sommer, R. and Wicker, A. W. (1991) Gas Station Psychology: the case for specialisation in ecological psychology. *Environment and Behavior*, 23, 131–49. **446**

Spence, I. and Lewandowsky, S. (1990) Graphical Perception. In J. Fox and J. S. Long (eds), *Modern Methods of Data Analysis*. Newbury Park and London: Sage. **319**

Spradley, J. P. (1980) *Participant Observation*. New York: Holt, Rinehart and Winston. **19, 200**

Stacey, M. (1960) *Tradition and Change: a study of Banbury*. Oxford: Oxford University Press. **147**

Stacey, M. et al. (1975) *Power, Persistence and Change: a second study of Banbury*. London: Routledge & Kegan Paul. **147**

Stake, R. E. (1976) *Evaluating Educational Programmes: the need and the response*. Paris: OECD. **423**

Stanley, L. and Wise, S. (1983) *Breaking Out: feminist consciousness and feminist research*. London: Routledge & Kegan Paul. **63, 65**

Stebbins, R. A. (1987) Fitting In: the researcher as learner and participant. *Quality and Quantity*, 21, 103–8. **297**

Stenhouse, L. (1978) Applying Research to Education. Reprinted in J. Rudduck and D. Hopkins (eds) (1985), *Research as a Basis for Teaching*. London: Heinemann. **433**

Stenhouse, L. (1979) Using Research Means Doing Research. In H. Dahl, A. Lysne and P. Rand (eds), *Spotlight on Educational Problems: Festshrift for Johannes Sandven*. Oslo: Oslo University Press. Reprinted in J. Rudduck and D. Hopkins (eds) (1985), *Research as a Basis for Teaching*. London: Heinemann. **433**

Stenhouse, L. (1982) The Conduct, Analysis and Reporting of Case Study in Educational Research and Evaluation. In R. McCormick (ed.), *Calling Education to Account*. London: Heinemann. **192**

Stenhouse, L. (1985) Action Research and the Teacher's Responsibility for the Educational Process. In J. Rudduck and D. Hopkins (eds), *Research as a Basis for Teaching*. London: Heinemann. **438**

Stephenson, W. (1953) *The Study of Behavior*. Chicago: University of Chicago Press. **266**

Stephenson, W. (1980) Newton's Fifth Rule and Q-methodology: applications to educational psychology. *American Psychologist*, 35, 882–9. **265**

Sternberg, R. J. (1988) *The Psychologist's Companion: a guide to scientific writing for students and researchers*. Cambridge: Cambridge University Press/British Psychological Society. **413**

Stewart, D. W. and Shamdasani, P. N. (1990) *Focus Groups*. Newbury Park London: Sage. **241**

Still, A. W. (1982) On the Number of Subjects Used in Animal Behaviour Experiments. *Animal Behaviour*, 30, 873–80. **137**

Strauss, A. L. (1987) *Qualitative Analysis for Social Scientists*. Cambridge: Cambridge University Press. **75, 142, 386**

Strong, P. M. and Davis, A. G. (1977) Roles, Role-formats and Medical Encounters: a cross-cultural analysis of staff-client relationships in children's clinics. *Sociological Review*, 25, 775–800. **147**

Suchman, E. A. (1967) *Evaluative Research: principles in public service and action programs*. New York: Russell Sage. **175, 178**

Susman, C. I. and Evered, R. D. (1978) An Assessment of the Scientific Merits of Action Research. *Administrative Science Quarterly*, 23, 582–603. **60**

Tajfel, H. (1984) *The Social Dimension: European developments in social psychology*. Cambridge: Cambridge Unversity Press. **8**

Taplin, P. S. and Reid, J. B. (1973) Effects of Instructional Set and Experimenter Influence on Observer Reliability. *Child Development*, 44, 547–54. **224**

Taylor, S. J. and Bogdan, R. (1984) *Introduction to Qualitative Research Methods: the search for meanings*. New York: Wiley. **378**

Tesch, R. (1990) *Qualitative Research: analysis types and software tools*. London: Falmer. **371, 373, 376, 389**

Tesser, A. and Rosen, S. (1972) On Understanding the Reluctance to Transmit Negative Information, the MUM Effect: the effects of similarity of objective fate. *Journal of Personality and Social Psychology*, 23, 46–54. **13**

Thurstone, L. L. and Chave, E. J. (1929) *The Measurement of Attitude*. Chicago: University of Chicago Press. **260**

Thyer, B. A. and Geller, E. S. (1987) The Buckle Up Dashboard Sticker: an effective environmental intervention for safety belt promotion. *Environment and Behavior*, 19, 484–94. **111**

Tinbergen, N. (1963) On Aims and Methods of Ethology. *Zeitschrift für Tierpsychologie*, 20, 410–33. **191, 206**

Topping, K. J. (1988) *The Peer-tutoring Handbook: providing cooperative learning.* London: Croom Helm. **47**

Toulmin, S. E. (1958) *The Uses of Argument.* Cambridge: Cambridge University Press. **372**

Toulmin, S. E. (1967) *The Philosophy of Science*, revised edn. London: Hutchinson. **58**

Toulmin, S. E., Rieke, R. and Janik, A. (1979) *An Introduction to Reasoning.* London: Collier Macmillan. **372**

Trist, E. L. (1976) Engaging with Large-scale Systems. In A. W. Clark (ed.), *Experimenting with Organizational Life: the action research approach.* London: Plenum. **11**

Trochim, W. M. K. (1984) *Research Design for Program Evaluation: the regression-discontinuity approach.* Newbury Park and London: Sage. **107**

Tufte, E. R. (1983) *The Visual Display of Quantitative Information.* Cheshire, Conn.: Graphics Press. **320**

Tukey, J. W. (1977) *Exploratory Data Analysis.* Reading, Mass.: Addison-Wesley. **275, 317, 326**

Valois, P. and Godin, G. (1991) The Importance of Selecting Appropriate Adjective Pairs for Measuring Attitudes Based on the Semantic Differential Method. *Quality and Quantity*, 25, 57–68. **265**

Valsiner, J. (ed.) (1986) *The Individual Subject and Scientific Psychology.* New York: Plenum. **56**

van Dijk, T. A. (ed.) (1985) *Handbook of Discourse Analysis*, 4 vols. London: Academic Press. **287**

Varela, J. A. (1975) Can Social Psychology Be Applied? In M. Deutsch and H. A. Hornstein (eds), *Applying Social Psychology: implications for research, practice and training.* Hillsdale, NJ: Erlbaum. **456**

Velleman, P. F. and Hoaglin, D. C. (1981) *Applications, Basics and Computing of Exploratory Data Analysis.* Boston: Duxbury. **317**

Verplanken, B. (1989) Beliefs, Attitudes and Intentions toward Nuclear Energy before and after Chernobyl in a Longitudinal Within-subject Design. *Environment and Behaviour*, 21, 371–92. **119**

Walker, R. (1985) *Doing Research: a handbook for teachers.* London: Methuen. **188, 207, 232, 286, 415, 423**

Walker, R. and Adelman, C. (1975) *A Guide to Classroom Observation.* London: Methuen. **274**

Watson, J. D. (1968) *The Double Helix.* London: Weidenfeld and Nicolson. **295**

Watts, M. and Ebbutt, D. (1987) More than the Sum of the Parts: research methods in group interviewing. *British Educational Research Journal*, 13, 25–34. **241**

Wax, M. L., Diamond, S. and Gearing, F. O. (eds) (1971) *Anthropological Perspectives on Education.* New York: Basic Books. **402**

Webb, E. J., Campbell, D. T., Schwartz, R. L. and Sechrest, L. (1966) *Unobtrusive Measures: nonreactive research in the social sciences.* Chicago: Rand McNally. **270, 280**

Webb, E. J., Campbell, D. T., Schwartz, R. D., Sechrest, L. and Grove, J. B. (1981) *Nonreactive Measures in the Social Sciences*, 2nd edn. Boston: Houghton Mifflin. **270**

Webb, R. (ed.) (1990) *Practitioner Research in the Primary School.* London: Falmer. **439**

Weber, R. P. (1985) *Basic Content Analysis.* Newbury Park and London: Sage. **280**

Weick, K. E. (1968) Systematic Observational Methods. In G. Lindzey and E. Aronson (eds), *The Handbook of Social Psychology*, vol. 2, 2nd edn. Reading, Mass.: Addison-Wesley. 207

Weick, K. E. (1985) Systematic Observational Methods. In G. Lindzey and E. Aronson (eds), *The Handbook of Social Psychology*, 3rd edn. New York: Random House. 13

Weiss, C. H. (ed.) (1977) *Using Social Research in Policy Making*. Lexington, Mass.: D.C. Heath. 171

Weiss, C. H. (1979) The Many Meanings of Research Utilization. *Public Administration Review*, 426–31. 433, 434

Weiss, C. H. (1982) Policy Research in the Context of Diffuse Decision-making. *Journal of Higher Education*, 53, 619–40. 433

Weiss, C. H. (1986) Research and Policy-making: a limited partnership. In F. Heller (ed.), *The Use and Abuse of Social Science*. Newbury Park and London: Sage. 460

Weiss, C. H. and Bucuvalas, M. J. (1980a) *Social Science Research and Decision-making*. New York: Columbia University Press. 14

Weiss, C. H. and Bucuvalas, M. J. (1980b) Truth Test and Utility Test: decision makers' frames of reference for social science research. *American Sociological Review*, 302–13. 437

Wells, G. L. and Luus, C. A. E. (1990) Police Line-ups as Experiments: social methodology as a framework for properly conducted line-ups. *Personality and Social Psychology Bulletin*, 16, 106–17. 82

Whyte, W. F. (1951) Observational Field Work Methods. In G. Jahoda (ed.), *Research Methods in Social Relations*, vol. 2. New York: Dryden. 199

Whyte, W. F. (1981) *Street Corner Society: the social structure of an Italian slum*, 3rd edn. Chicago: University of Chicago Press. 147, 197

Whyte, W. F. (1984) *Learning from the Field: a guide from experience*. Newbury Park and London: Sage. 147, 197, 240, 439

Wicker, A. W. (1979) *An Introduction to Ecological Psychology*. Monterey, Cal.: Brooks-Cole. 206

Wilson, M., Robinson, E. J. and Ellis, A. (1989) Studying Communication between Community Pharmacists and their Customers. *Counselling Psychology Quarterly*, 2, 367–80. 230

Wilson, V. L. and Putman, R. K. (1982) A Meta-analysis of Pre-test Sensitization Effects in Experimental Design. *American Educational Research Journal*, 17, 249–58. 90

Winer, B. J. (1971) *Statistical Principles in Experimental Design*, 2nd edn. New York: McGraw-Hill. 343

Winter, R. (1987) *Action-Research and the Nature of Social Enquiry*. Aldershot: Gower. 448

Winter, R. (1989) *Learning from Experience: principles and practice in action-research*. London: Falmer. 378, 441, 448

Worthen, B. R. and Sanders, J. R. (1973) *Education Evaluation: theory and practice*. Worthington, Ohio: C.A. Jones. 174

Wright, G. (1984) *Behavioural Decision Theory: an introduction*. London: Penguin. 372

Wright, G. and Fowler, C. (1986) *Investigative Design and Statistics*. London: Penguin. 350

Wright, J. C. (1960) *Problem Solving and Search Behavior under Noncontingent Reward*. Unpublished doctoral dissertation, Stanford University. 13

Wronski, S. (1969) Implementing Change in Social Studies Programs. In D. Fraser (ed.), *Social Studies Curriculum Development Prospects and Problems.* Washington, DC: National Council for the Social Sciences. **435**

Yates, F. A. (1966) *The Art of Memory.* London: Penguin. **204**

Yin, R. K. (1981) The Case Study as a Serious Research Strategy. *Knowledge: Creation, Diffusion, Utilisation,* 3, 97–114. **5, 43**

Yin, R. K. (1983) *The Case Study Method: an annotated bibliography.* Washington, DC: Cosmos. **147**

Yin, R. K. (1989) *Case Study Research: design and methods,* 2nd edn. Newbury Park and London: Sage. **5, 44, 160, 161, 165, 289, 372, 377, 379, 415, 416**

Young, M. (1965) *Innovation and Research in Education.* London: Routledge & Kegan Paul. **432**

Youngman, M. B. (1979) *Analysing Social and Educational Research Data.* London: McGraw-Hill. **313, 315, 347**

Zeisel, J. (1984) *Inquiry by Design: tools for environment–behavior research.* Cambridge: Cambridge University Press. **82, 126, 198, 234, 241, 393, 446**

Zimbardo, P. G. (1969) The Human Choice: individuation, reasons and order versus deindividuation, impulse, and chaos. In W. J. Arnold and D. Levine (eds), *Nebraska Symposium on Motivation,* vol. 17. Lincoln: University of Nebraska Press. **13**

Zimmerman, D. H. and Wieder, D. L. (1977) The Diary: diary-interview method. *Urban Life,* 5, 479–98. **254**

Zito, J. M. (1974) Anonymity and neighboring in an urban, high-rise complex. *Urban Life Culture,* 3, 243–63. **13**

Index